PUERTO VALLARTA

BRUCE WHIPPERMAN & ROBIN NOELLE

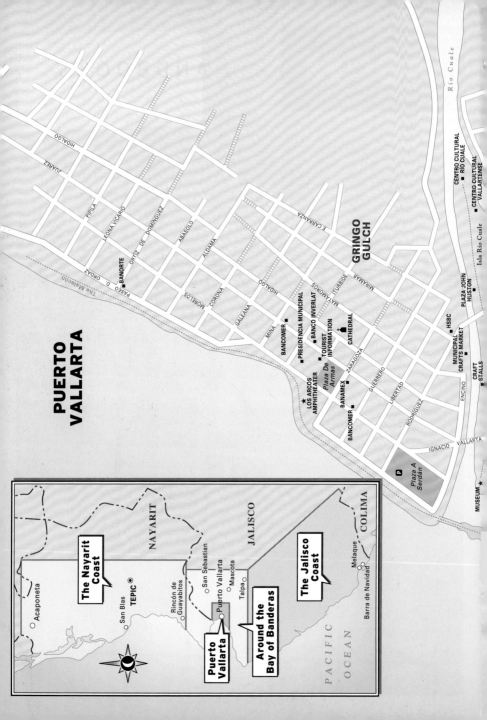

PUERTO VALLARTA

The Malecón

HIDALGO

JUAREZ

PIPILA

LEONA VICARIO

ORTIZ DE DOMINGUEZ

ABASOLO

ALDAMA

PASEO D. ORDAZ

BANORTE

MORELOS

CORONA

GALEANA

HIDALGO

E. CARRANZA

MATAMOROS

ITURBIDE

MIRAMAR

GRINGO GULCH

MINA

BANCOMER

PRESIDENCIA MUNICIPAL

BANCO INVERLAT

TOURIST INFORMATION

Plaza De Armas

ZARAGOZA

CATHEDRAL

LOS ARCOS AMPHITHEATER

BANAMEX

GUERRERO

BANCOMER

LIBERTAD

RODRIGUEZ

IGNACIO VALLARTA

P

Plaza A Serdán

HSBC

MUNICIPAL CRAFTS MARKET

ENCINO

CRAFT STALLS

CENTRO CULTURAL RIO CUALE

CENTRO CULTURAL VALLARTENSE

Isla Río Cuale

PLAZA JOHN HUSTON

Río Cuale

MUSEUM

Inset map

The Nayarit Coast

NAYARIT

JALISCO

COLIMA

PACIFIC OCEAN

Acaponeta

San Blas

TEPIC

Rincón de Guayabitos

San Sebastián

Puerto Vallarta

Mascota

Talpa

Melaque

Barra de Navidad

Puerto Vallarta

Around the Bay of Banderas

The Jalisco Coast

CALLE CAMICHIN

NARANJO

JACARANDAS

AGUACATE

INSURGENTES

SUPERMARKET
GUTIERREZ RIZO

FARMACIA
GUADALAJARA

CARRANZA

VENUSTIANO

BADILLO

M. DIEGUEZ

PULPITO

HOSPITAL
MEDASIST

FRANCISCA

RODRIGUEZ

BASILIO

5 DE FEBRERO

CONSTITUCIÓN

SERDAN

CARDENAS

AQUILES

LAZARO

FCO

MADERO

STREET)

(NOT THROUGH

200

200

OLD
TOWN

P

Plaza Lázaro
Cárdenas

LOCAL
BUSES
NORTH

LONG DISTANCE
TELEPHONE AND FAX

PINO SUÁREZ

OLAS ALTAS

BANK/
ATM

Andador

GOMEZ

PULPITO

PILITAS

AMAPAS

ANDADOR

Playa
Olas
Atlas

WATER TAXIS
TO YELAPA

NEW PIER

Playa Los
Muertos

Bahía de Banderas

© AVALON TRAVEL

0   100 yds

0   100 m

Contents

Discover Puerto Vallarta

Puerto Vallarta and its surrounding areas have long had die-hard fans. Gold beaches embrace the calm waters of the Bay of Banderas, one of the largest, deepest bays in the world. This aquatic haven is home to myriad species, making the bay a provider of abundant seafood for the region and also of diverse recreational activities. It shelters Puerto Vallarta from storms and provides a protected habitat for endangered sea turtles and whales that give birth on its shores and in its warm waters each year. From the wild, undeveloped southern coast to the funky beach towns of the northern shores, it's plain to see why visitors return year after year.

Nestled into a verdant valley, Puerto Vallarta is resource rich. Fertile farmlands, tropical fruit orchards, and Blue Agave fields surround the area, giving rise to craggy, volcanic mountains. In petite coves and along sweeping seashores, small settlements provide a glimpse into what Puerto Vallarta used to be before Hollywood turned its spotlight on it.

While Old Town, or Zona Romántica as it is called, retains its rustic charm, Vallarta has grown into a modern city complete with posh discos, upscale designer boutiques, modern cinemas, and casinos. It may be hard for long-time Vallarta fans to see the contemporary changes to their beloved vacation spot, but the transition has brought new prosperity and opportunity to the residents.

The heart of Puerto Vallarta remains in Old Town and the lively Malecón (seafront walkway) that runs along the shoreline. Along the Malecón you'll find endless entertainment, from sand sculptures and living statues to clowns and musicians. The Malecón comes alive at night as people congregate to watch the sunset and later enjoy the live entertainment, delicious street food, and ever-entertaining people-watching that are always available.

There's something for everyone in the Puerto Vallarta area: from the spunky beach town of Barra de Navidad to the tranquil and timeless San Blas; slumbering fishing hamlets to the exclusive communities of the rich and famous; surf towns, wild beaches, campgrounds, RV parks and towns so removed that you can only reach them by sea. The diversity of the area attracts more people each year, many who return again and again and eventually retire here. Let this book be your guide to discovering your special place in this magical region.

Planning Your Trip

▶ WHERE TO GO

Puerto Vallarta

Puerto Vallarta is divided north and south by the gentle, vine-swathed Río Cuale, which ripples from its foothill canyon. The old town north and south of the river retains much of its original charm, especially south of the river in the Avenida Olas Altas district and the adjacent Playa los Muertos. The appeal continues to the south, along the villa-decorated Conchas Chinas headland, past the bayshore villages of Mismaloya (and the nearby offshore Los Arcos giant rocks snorkeling/scuba sanctuary), and farther south, to petite Boca de Tomatlán shoreline village.

North of the Río Cuale, the old town spreads uphill to the meandering lanes of Gringo Gulch, the bayfront Los Arcos amphitheater, and the airy Malecón shoreline promenade. Farther north, the beach boulevard passes through the Zona Hotelera lineup of world-class hotels along golden-sand Playa de Oro, continuing past the plush Marina condo-home district and golf course to the airport at the town limits.

Around the Bay of Banderas

There's so many wonderful things to do and see around the Bay of Banderas. Bucerías lies along the northern shoreline, followed by Punta Mita and coral-strewn Playa Anclote, all great places for sunbathing, surfing, and snorkeling. Excursions to wildlife-rich offshore Islas Marietas are a popular adventure as well.

Visitors find even more in the cool Sierra Cuale, a trio of invitingly old-world colonial-era towns, not far east of Puerto Vallarta. San Sebastián, curled around a precious little

IF YOU HAVE. . .

A LONG WEEKEND: Stick to Puerto Vallarta proper and enjoy Old Town, the Malecón and the local beaches. Snorkel at Los Arcos, pet a lion cub at the zoo or go bird and butterfly watching at the botanical gardens.

A WEEK: Stay close by but check out the beaches at Mismaloya and Boca de Tomatlán, or grab a water taxi and visit Yelapa. Don't skip the pie.

TWO WEEKS: Head north and explore Bucerías, Punta Mita, Sayulita or San Pancho for an overnight or two without getting too far away. Visit the tianguis (flea market) in La Peñita, beachcomb in Lo de Marco or join the party at Rincón de Guayabitos.

LONGER: The world is your oyster. For funky beach town ambience, hit Barra de Navidad for a few nights and then work your way up the coast through the wild beaches of Costalegre. Love history, farmlands and cool mountain air? Hit San Sebastián, Mascota or Talpa. For a mix of both great beaches and historical significance, head to San Blas for superb surf and great sightseeing.

Get up close and personal at the Puerto Vallarta Zoo.

Snorkel or scuba at the Los Arcos Marine Preserve.

plaza, offers comfy country inns and old gold mines to explore. Mascota adds tasty home-cooked country food and museums. Nearby, picturesque Talpa is a pilgrimage town, home of the miraculous Virgin of Talpa, that affords a fine museum and good restaurants.

The Nayarit Coast

For years, the Nayarit Coast has been one of Puerto Vallarta's best-kept secrets. Visitors come to enjoy the gorgeous beaches, good surfing, snorkeling, wildlife-watching, and charming country-Mexico ambience.

Moving north, the highlights include hot surf-town Sayulita, sleepy Playa San Francisco, and precious Playa Chacala. Finally comes San Blas, famous for bird-watching, wildlife-viewing, and world-class surfing. Beyond San Blas is the idyllic auto-mobile-free Mexcaltitán, an island village where an excellent museum tells the island's fascinating story.

On the way south back toward Puerto Vallarta lies Tepic, the cooler, upland mid-sized Nayarit state capital. Visitors come here for its good museums and excellent shopping for Huichol handicrafts. An hour south of town, you'll find the spectacularly sylvan mountain Crater Lake Santa María.

The Jalisco Coast

For travelers yearning to follow the path less traveled, the Jalisco Coast may be just the ticket. From Puerto Vallarta, it stretches more than 100 miles south, traversing pine-tufted mountains, deserty savannah, lush tropical forest, and seemingly endless pristine golden strands.

On the three broad bays that indent the Jalisco Coast—Bahía Chamela, Bahía Tenacatita, and Bahía Navidad—a few villages, including Pérula, El Super, Tenacatita, and La Manzanilla, provide a modicum of food, lodging, and services for the growing trickle of travelers seeking a Mexican South Seas paradise.

Furthermore, a number of splendidly isolated

boutique hotels sprinkle the Jalisco Coast. If you enjoy being pampered in the wilderness, this is the place to do it.

Many travelers' Jalisco Coast journeys wind down at the drowsy far southern twin resorts of Melaque and Barra de Navidad, where they enjoy lots of sun, golden sand, and sparkling Pacific sunsets.

▶ WHEN TO GO

The most popular time to visit Puerto Vallarta is high season (Christmas–Easter) when the days are warm and dry and the nights cool. With exception of the actual holidays, this is when prices are highest and hotels crowded.

Travelers looking for lower costs and less crowds should visit before Christmas, from about late October. The weather is still lovely and there's no shortage of hotel rooms or deals.

True bargain hunters and surfers looking for big waves should visit in summer. Days are steamy and hot but the evenings are cooled by spectacular thunderstorms, washing away the dust and presenting brilliant evening light shows. Summer is low season and savvy visitors can take advantage of discounts on everything from hotels to massages.

To catch the best cultural events, visit during the first two weeks of December during the celebration of the Virgin of Guadalupe. Streets are closed off and nightly processions of floats, folkloric dancers, and musicians head to the cathedral. If you are a foodie,

Enjoy the sunset from one of the many Malecón restaurants.

don't miss Restaurant Week in mid-May. The best restaurants in Puerto Vallarta offer prix fixe meals under $25.

▶ BEFORE YOU GO

No vaccinations are necessary when heading to Mexico for your vacation. During the rainy summer months there is an abundance of mosquitoes, some of which carry dengue, an unpleasant but rarely fatal tropical virus. Dengue shouldn't be a concern unless you are staying in rural areas, close to standing water.

Keep the tourist visa you receive when traveling into Mexico. You will face fines if you try to leave without it. If you are traveling from or through the United States, you will need a valid passport to return from Mexico.

If you plan on traveling with your pet, make sure you have current health records and a rabies vaccination (given within 30 days of your arrival). Few hotels are pet friendly so it's best to check in advance.

Explore Puerto Vallarta

▶ THE BEST OF PUERTO VALLARTA

For the most intimate view of Puerto Vallarta, stay in a comfortable hotel within close walking distance of the colorful Old Town sights, cafés, restaurants, and shops. If you opt to stay in the north-end Hotel Zone or the Marina, you can easily hail a taxi ($5–8) or hop a local bus to go where the action is. In any case, use the relevant destination sections of this book for the details that will smooth your visit and provide background for your Puerto Vallarta adventures. If it's your thing, be sure to reserve seats ahead for a Fiesta Mexicana show.

Day 1

The majority of flights arrive at the Puerto Vallarta airport in the late afternoon. After customs and transportation to your hotel, that doesn't leave much time for sightseeing and who wants to rush out after a long day of travel anyway?

Change out of your travel clothes into some casual beach attire, grab your camera, your travel companions, and maybe a book and head down to a beach restaurant and dig your toes into the sand. Order a tropical drink and some fresh guacamole, then people watch and decompress until you catch your first brilliant Vallarta sunset. Take a dozen pictures to impress your friends. Ahhhh, isn't that better?

After drinks and chips, you probably won't be very hungry, so stroll along the Malecón and nibble on crepes, tacos, and fresh fruit from the food stands as the mood strikes. Check out the central Plaza de Armas, and watch the concert (or the clowns) at the adjacent shoreline Los Arcos amphitheater.

Things start picking up at the dance clubs around midnight so head over to Hilo or the Puerto Vallarta Zoo to get your groove on and work off those margaritas.

Los Arcos amphitheater

THE BEST THINGS IN LIFE ARE FREE

Budget travel seems to be playing on everyone's lips these days. Fortunately, there are lots of bargains to be had in Puerto Vallarta and beyond. Whether you want to save money on food, lodging, or activities, here are some ways to lighten the load on your wallet:

Things You Can Do for Under $5:

- Visit the Puerto Vallarta Zoo
- Visit the Vallarta Botanical Gardens
- Dine on four tacos and a drink at a taco stand
- Get two slices of pie in Yelapa
- Watch musicians, clowns, and performers on the Malecón
- Visit a fair or flea market in the park
- Do an Art Walk
- Buy a whole roasted chicken with tortillas and rice and go on a picnic
- Have a margarita and watch the sunset on the beach
- Buy a pound of organic Nayarit coffee
- Hike from Boca de Tomatlán to Las Animas and take a water taxi back
- Snorkel in Mismaloya
- Rent a boogie board for the day

Things You Can Do for Under $20:

- Buy a kilo (2.2 lbs) of shrimp and a watermelon
- Get a henna tattoo

Make sure to visit the Puerto Vallarta Zoo.

- Rent a hotel room (single)
- Get a 30-minute massage or a spa pedicure
- Buy a day-use pass at a resort
- Go to Yelapa for the day
- Play with a lion or jaguar cub at the zoo
- Spend the day at a beach club
- Buy a bottle of tequila and two shot glasses
- Buy two movie tickets, a large caramel corn, and two sodas at the theater (many movies are in English)
- Take a ride on a banana boat

Day 2

Who can resist the beach on your first full day? Head out and start beach exploring. Start at the seafront park just north of the Río Cuale and stroll south over the river bridge and continue along the seashore *andador* (walkway) along Playa los Muertos. Walk out on the New Pier to see what's biting or grab a lounge chair at any of the restaurants and beach clubs. There's plenty of people-watching, friends to be made, and margaritas to drink!

Still have the urge to explore? Head south by local Mismaloya or Boca bus (from the corner of Constitución and Basilio Badillo). Visit Mismaloya (or alternatively, nearby Chino's

It's easy to rent a *panga* for fishing or snorkeling from the pier in Punta Mita.

friendly entertainment at either Ándale pub or Garbo in the Olas Altas district). Tired of techno and dance music? Hit Club Roxy for a some raucous rock and roll.

Day 4

After all of the previous activity, it may be best simply to rest for a day. Or if you prefer, head for an out-of-town adventure at Punta Mita or Sayulita village (an hour by bus north of town). There you can stroll, boogie board, and maybe try your hand at surfing.

If you are taking a break from the sun and surf, make a stop at the Puerto Vallarta Zoo to cuddle a lion cub and/or the Vallarta Botanical Gardens to view their amazing collection of orchids and the picturesque grounds. Both are excellent for nature photography and bird watching.

Tonight, head north for either some killer salsa dancing at J&B's or check out the upscale dance club at Christine's in the hotel zone.

Day 5

Part of your last day will be spent picking up mementos of your trip and trinkets for the folks back home. Head down to the Isla Cuale and check out the wares for sale in the many shops and stalls. If you can handle the heat, head into the Municipal Crafts Market just downhill from the bridge. Grab some Mexican vanilla, organic coffee, or colored glassware for affordable and useful gifts.

For the rest of your day, lovers of the great outdoors might schedule a special tour, such as horseback riding or a whale-, dolphin-, and bird-watching excursion to the Islas Marietas. Don't miss your last Puerto Vallarta sunset!

If you've still got one more night of partying left, spend it like a local at the dive bar La Cantina. Just mind your manners because things can get pretty rowdy here.

Paradise or El Edén swimming-hole cascades) and then head back into town to watch the sunset at one of many establishments along the famous Malecón. Or, if you prefer, continue south a few miles past Mismaloya, to the unmissable Le Kliff Restaurant overlooking the ocean, on the right.

If you are fortunate, it will be Friday and ladies' night at ZTai. No cover plus open bar for the ladies, $25 cover for the men with open bar. You are sure to make new friends in this stylish club with thumping techno beats.

Day 3

You've done the beaches and now it's time to hit the water. Take a relaxing day cruise for snorkeling at Los Arcos and a waterfall swim at either Quimixto or idyllic Yelapa on the Bay of Banderas's jungly southern shore. Don't miss the pie ladies of Yelapa.

Head back into town for dinner and then do a little nightclub-hopping along the Malecón (or seek out more conversation-

► SIX WAYS TO FIND ADVENTURE

Some people come to Puerto Vallarta to lounge under a *palapa* and read beach novels or to lie by the pool and sip margaritas, never leaving the hotel grounds. But Puerto Vallarta has lots of exciting outdoor activities for adventurous types. Here are six ways to get the adrenaline pumping on your vacation.

Scuba Diving and Snorkeling

While Puerto Vallarta might not have the aquamarine waters of the Caribbean, it does offer a wide variety of aquatic life that ranges from rainbow colored tropical fish to jaw-dropping giant manta rays that grow as large as 25 feet across. Puerto Vallarta has two marine life preserves, Los Arcos and Las Islas Marietas, both of which offer fantastic diving and snorkeling opportunities. More advanced divers can do the amazing wall dive at Los Arcos where the continental shelf drops more than five miles down or partake in a night dive when the predators like lobsters and octopuses come out to feed.

Surfing

Surfing enthusiasts can find plenty of action in the Puerto Vallarta region. The best surfing conditions customarily occur during the late summer–early fall, when Pacific hurricanes sometimes drive huge swells ashore at many favorite spots along the coast.

The most renowned surfing spot is Playa Matanchén, near San Blas, world famous for very long runs. For surf lessons, check out Stoner's Surf Camp, in San Blas.

Several great local spots, north and south of Puerto Vallarta, include the following: on the Bay of Banderas's north shore, Punta el Burro and El Faro (good intermediate and advanced breaks, at Punta Mita, near the lighthouse); on the Nayarit Coast, Sayulita, Playa el Naranjo (beginning and intermediate), and

the marina landmark of El Faro, the lighthouse

Matanchén. On the Bay of Banderas's south shore, try Boca de Tomatlán and Quimixto for intermediate breaks. On the Jalisco Coast, go to Ipala and Las Peñitas (intermediate to advanced, on the Cabo Corrientes coast south of Tehualmixtle), Playa el Tecuán, Playa la Manzanilla (intermediate to advanced breaks), and Barra de Navidad (beginning and intermediate, at the jetty).

Whale-watching

December 8–March 24th marks the return of the humpback whales to the Bay of Banderas for their annual mating and birthing. Whale-watching trips usually leave early in the morning and get back midday. You'll have an opportunity to get up close and personal with these magnificent beasts, plus, if you are lucky, you'll see all kinds of mating behavior such as tail-slapping, breaching, and maybe even the mating itself! Just be sure to

The oft-gentle surfing breaks at Playa Sayulita are popular with a winter cadre of beginning surfers.

pick a licensed and ethical company when you book your tour.

Horseback Rides into the Jungle

For the equestrian, Puerto Vallarta offers a variety of horseback riding adventures. If you are only looking for a day trip, take a short jungle ride to a waterfall or for a longer adventure, an eight-hour day ride into the Sierra Madres. For true horseback riding lovers, there are trips ranging from an overnight camp in the jungle to weeklong rides to various mountain towns. Lunch is almost always included.

Mountain Biking Tours

Several local providers offer different bike tours for riders ranging from beginner to expert. The tours take you through small Mexican pueblos, along rivers and through some of the most beautiful countryside that Mexico has to offer. Lunch is included in all trips and many of tours include stops for swimming. If you prefer the water to the land, book a kayak tour instead.

Canopy Tours

There are several canopy tours available but the most popular is Los Veranos. Starting with an open-air drive to the Los Veranos ecological preserve, visitors will get to see some of the beautiful coastline south of Puerto Vallarta. Los Veranos has 14 cables with the longest being 400 feet. Daring visitors will zip from tree to tree at up to a whopping 35 miles per hour. Afterward, you can swim, eat, or visit with the monkeys. For safety reasons, there is weight limit of 250 pounds for the zip-lines.

▶ BEST BEACHES

Although a "best" beach for some folks might be horrible for others, many people would agree that a good, all-purpose beach should have convenient bus or car access, somewhere to stay and eat, gentle surf with no more than mild undertow, and also be safe for boogie boarding and swimming.

Best All-Purpose Beaches

Beginning on Puerto Vallarta's south side, Playa los Muertos is the hands-down favorite. It's long enough that you can spread out if you don't wish to join the throngs of beachgoers, but also has all of the amenities you could want including beach clubs, restaurants, and bars.

Out of town, the south-side best beaches are at Mismaloya and Boca de Tomatlán. On the north side of town, the best beach comprises the Hotel Zone strip between the Hotel Sheraton and the Hotel NH Krystal, ending just before the Terminal Maritima

Playa Chacala

(cruise-ship terminal). There's plenty of public access spots, all marked with signs on the main highway. Like most beaches, you are usually welcome to grab a chair in front of any hotel or restaurant as long as you plan on ordering from their bar or restaurant.

the beach at San Francisco

Playa Boca de Iguanas

On the bay's northwest side, Playa Bucerías is a favorite for calm surf and family-friendly conditions. The beach gets more crowded at the southern end near the Royal Decameron resort. Farther away, on the Bay of Banderas's northwest side, are petite Playa Manzanillo (at the Hotel Piedra Blanca) and Playa Anclote at Punta Mita, with good *palapa* restaurants, snorkeling and surfing nearby, and excursions to offshore Islas Marietas.

Another favorite beach on the Nayarit Coast is gemlike Playa Chacala, whose golden sand curves gently around its intimate, palm-tufted half-moon bay.

The first best beach south on the Jalisco Coast is at family-friendly Pérula, on islet-decorated Chamela Bay. Farther south, find RV and tent-camper havens Playa Tenacatita and Playa Boca de Iguanas (trailer park). Finally, those who want it all—good hotels, restaurants, and drowsy, country-Mexico tranquility—choose Melaque.

Best Wildlife Beaches

On the Nayarit Coast, the beaches at San Francisco and El Monteon both are fed by estuaries. This means superb bird-watching, and you may even get to see some of the indigenous species like crocodiles, turtles, or coatis. The beaches are steep, often with thunderous waves and strong undertow. San Francisco has beach restaurants and amenities but El Monteon doesn't.

For pristine isolation, wildlife-watching (egg-laying turtles in the fall), surf fishing, tent camping, and a small hotel with restaurant and clean facilities, no place could be finer than Playa Platinitos just north of Las Varas on the way to San Blas.

Also very lovely and worthwhile is the local country beach haven of Playa el Naranjo, north of Rincón de Guayabitos–La Peñita. It offers *palapa* restaurants, a near-level beach with little undertow, surfing breaks, a mangrove lagoon, crocodiles, plenty of birds, and lots of palm-shaded room for RV or tent camping.

Except on Sundays, you'll most likely have Playa Mayto to yourself.

Best Hidden Beaches

South of Puerto Vallarta, venture off-road to Playa Mayto, accessible from Highway 200 at El Tuito, via jeep or public minivan over about 20 miles of dirt road. Playa Mayto is a three-mile-long golden-sand beach good for virtually all beach diversions, including a comfortable, moderately priced hotel and restaurant with a pool.

Alternatively, go a mile farther south to Tehualmixtle fishing cove, with restaurants and a rustic hotel; add fishing, snorkeling, and scuba diving (with your own equipment) to the family-friendly beach activities.

Most Beautiful Beaches

Gem of gems, Playa Careyes sits on its own petite half-moon bay and offers *palapa* restaurants, informal tent camping or RV parking by the restaurants, surf fishing, fishing trips, and more. A few miles farther, de facto wildlife refuge Playa el Tecuán offers everything: a long pristine strand perfect for beachcombing, powerful rollers for advanced surfers, great surf fishing, even bird- and wildlife-watching in your own kayak on the Tecuán lagoon. The beach has no facilities, however, so bring everything.

▶ A GAY WEEKEND IN PUERTO VALLARTA

When you arrive in Puerto Vallarta, make sure to pick up a copy of the excellent *Gay Guide Vallarta* or visit their website (www.gayguidevallarta.com) for a wealth of information on Puerto Vallarta's many gay-friendly establishments and events. Also recommended is www.discoveryvallarta.com, one of the city's best websites for gay travelers.

The following suggestions will let you ease into your vacation and let you find your own pace before you dive into the adventures that await. Jungle canopies, water tours, exhilarating nightlife, and unique shopping are among the memorable experiences to be had in Vallarta. By the end, you'll be longing for your next visit. Most of the long term residents will tell you that they started looking for property on their second trip!

Day 1

Instead of immediately rushing headlong into everything Puerto Vallarta has to offer, the first day of your vacation is ideal for leaving your daily grind behind by relaxing and getting into a different rhythm.

Most flights arrive in the early afternoon; check into your hotel or villa, change into something comfortable and walk out the door toward the water. By this time it is likely to be mid to late afternoon, so it's up to you whether or not to grab a towel and try to fit in some sun and sand. There are plenty of free *palapas* somewhere in the general area of the famous Blue Chairs resort at Playa los Muertos, the stretch of sand most popular with the gay community. Most hotels and beach clubs are happy to let you use their lounge chairs and facilities with a minimum food or drink purchase of about $200 pesos. Whether you are looking forward to making new friends or just people watching, Playa los Muertos is the place to be.

Every day seems like a holiday on Playa los Muertos.

Garbo is a "don't miss" nightlife spot.

A popular first day tradition with visitors is to head to a beachfront restaurant for a margarita and some freshly made guacamole and catching the first sunset of their vacation. If you are wearing your swimsuit to the beach, bring along a shirt and some shorts to change into in case you want to dine somewhere less casual.

When it's time for dinner, try upscale La Palapa, where you can have a margarita or something from the extensive wine list while considering which type of seafood to try. A local favorite is red snapper, known as *huachinango,* grilled over an open fire. Some nights feature live music, so stick around if that's the case. If not, head back to where you're staying to freshen up and get ready for your first evening out.

Opt for a low-key night to round out your day of relaxation. Check out Garbo, a popular place for businessmen who want to relax after a day at work. The drinks are decent, and the bartender is fully bilingual, as are the cheerful waiters. While this neighborhood piano bar is busy by sundown, it winds down shortly after midnight when people head home or to one of the later venues. If you don't get the opportunity to experience one of the boisterous nights of piano and singing, make sure to stop back by on a busier night. It's one of the most fun bars in Puerto Vallarta.

Day 2

Your first full day in Vallarta is going to take you away from the comfortable Zona Romántica, and you'll be flying through the jungle. Grab a quick breakfast—the coffeehouses in the Zona Romántica are good choices for something fast.

Head to the small town of Las Juntas y Los Veranos, for a canopy tour - a series of zip-lines that zigzag through the trees in the rugged hillside above the river. Experience the freedom of flying while coming into direct contact with the effervescent jungle teeming with energy. Stay for lunch in the friendly *palapa*-covered outdoor bar and restaurant, and take the transportation back into town when you're good and ready.

Back at your hotel, take a siesta to connect with a centuries-old custom where the natural rhythms of the human body were held in great respect. Puerto Vallarta itself seems to snooze between the hours of 2–6 P.M. When you get up, dress for town (for example, long pants and a linen shirt) and be sure to wear comfortable walking shoes, as this afternoon, you'll be wandering around downtown on foot.

Start on Playa los Muertos, and head north along the beach. You can walk along the Malecón once you reach La Palapa restaurant; it will take you all the way to the pedestrian bridge across the Río Cuale toward downtown. Continue on the Malecón, stopping to enjoy the sculptures that line it, all the way past Los Arcos amphitheater across from the main plaza and the Guadalupe church. En route, notice the sand-sculptors and their

Club Mañana offers great dancing, shows, and partying all night long.

careful handiwork, the stone-stackers, and any number of interesting characters, artists, musicians, and locals who take the evening air with their friends or family. Also note the restaurants you pass along the way—you'll be choosing one for your evening meal. When you reach the Millennium sculpture that curves into the evening sky in front of Hotel Rosita, you'll be at the end of the Malecón and your walk.

Return to the Malecón restaurant of your choice for dinner or repast. Watch another legendary Pacific sunset. It seems as though every one is better than the last. ¡Salud!

After eating, head back toward downtown for a tour of some of the art galleries; many stay open until 8 P.M. during the week or later. Don't miss the historic Galería Uno and the energizing Galería Pacífico. (If you're in town on a Wednesday, the downtown art galleries offer a free Art Walk, a self-guided tour with map that runs 6–10 P.M. and includes free wine and canapés.) If all the art has made you thirsty, stop in at the elegant and popular Costantini Wine Bar, located right across from the entrance to Café des Artistes, for a glass of wine from their amazingly extensive wine list and after, check out the gallery across the street and the other to the left of the restaurant.

Now it's time to dive into the town's nightlife scene. Put on your dancing shoes and head for Club Mañana, the one of the hottest gay bars in Vallarta that offers dancing, nightly drink specials, a swimming pool, and outdoor tables. Things don't really get started here until late night so stay until the sun comes up if you like. If you happen to be in town during the high season (November-March), catch Aunt Joanna's hysterical drag show act at 10pm on Tuesday, Thursday and.

Day 3

The Bay of Banderas offers myriad

humpback whale, Bay of Banderas

opportunities for activities from the more active like scuba and snorkeling to stretches of empty sand beaches perfect for day-dreaming or catching up on your recreational reading. You can choose to spend your day on and in the water by diving or snorkeling, and destination options include Las Caletas, former home of the late director John Huston, where you can don a mask and fins or just enjoy the swimming and spa-ing that are at your fingertips. Or, you can take an unguided water taxi trip to Yelapa, an artist haven south of Vallarta accessible only by sea. Make sure you save some room for the famous pie! If you are here during the months of December to March, don't miss taking a whale-watching trip to see the incredible humpback whales up close and personal, guided by marine biologists. Ocean Friendly Whale Watching is a good choice for trips catering to the gay community. The whales come to Puerto Vallarta every year to either mate or give birth and it's likely that even if you've been whale watching

before, you'll get to see some amazing mating behavior from these massive mammals.

If you really want to experience gay life on the water, choose one of the gay tours available, perhaps to one of the private beaches along the south coast.

At night, once you've dried off, get ready for a night out. Tonight try one of the neighborhood bars, such as Frida, Diva's, La Noche, Los Amigos—or all of them. Get to know the neighborhood and your new friends. Since it's your last night, you might want to hit some of the late night clubs like Stereo to dance until dawn.

Day 4

On your final day, have a leisurely breakfast, maybe at the popular Barrio Sur on Calle Pulpito, where Coco serves a menu that makes it worth starting the day early. If you're not ready for a meal, have some caffeine at any one of the great coffee shops on Olas Altas in the Zona Romántica.

A PERFECT DAY FOR ROMANCE

Ask any of the hundreds of brides, grooms and honeymooning couples that visit each year and they'll tell you, Puerto Vallarta is the place for romance. Swaying palms on golden beaches, moonlit walks along the shore, and brilliant Pacific sunsets make the Bay of Banderas the perfect backdrop for weddings, anniversaries, engagements, or just a quick romantic getaway. Here are our suggestions for a perfect romantic day in Puerto Vallarta.

Start your morning with breakfast on your balcony. Order room service and start the day relaxed and unhurried while watching the waves together. When you're ready, get dressed and hail a cab to **New Pier.** From there, enjoy an hour boat ride, viewing the magnificent mansions and villas that line the shore on your way to **Yelapa.**

If it's still early in the day, hike to the waterfall or take a horseback ride into the jungle. When you return, have a light lunch (and a slice of pie) at one of the beachfront restaurants. Go ahead and swim, sunbathe, or buy some trinkets from the local vendors and then catch a return boat back to the pier.

On your way back to your hotel, recharge with a **couple's massage** at a local spa. Tables are set up side by side so you and your sweetie can enjoy the relaxing and healing powers of massage together. For a real treat, buy a package at one of the hotel spas to enjoy steam rooms, sauna, massage, and total pampering. Once back at your hotel, rest for a while before getting dressed for dinner.

There are any number of restaurants along the Malecón where you can watch a spectacular sunset but **Vista Grill, Barcelona Tapas** and **Chez Elena** are elevated and offer a panoramic view of the city as well. Share a dessert and a kiss as the evening fireworks light up the sky at about 10.

If you've still got it in you, head out to **La Bodeguita del Medio, J&B's** or **Roberto's** for some salsa dancing or stop by a **La Playa** liquor store and pick up a bottle of **Chambrulee** sparkling wine for a moonlit stroll along the beach. End your perfect day with a kiss at midnight, your feet buried in the sand and the warm waters of the bay lapping at your ankles.

New Pier at sunset, Playa los Muertos

Check out the hillside restaurants overlooking the Malecón for a great view of the bay.

For the trinket shopper, head to Isla Río Cuale where stalls and more stalls offer all sorts and variety of beads, carvings, onyx, Talavera pottery, silver jewelry, and even dried puffer-fish. Pay in cash and stow the treasures in your bag. For lunch, stop at The River Café or Le Bistro, both located right on the Río Cuale.

If you're into more serious jewelry, spend time at Viva on Basilio Badillo, and stop in at the superb Galleria Dante across the street, or any one of the gorgeous shops on that block.

If you aren't up for shopping, spend your final day on the beach soaking up the sun. Get a henna tattoo, rent a jet ski or find some afternoon activities at your favorite beach club. Afternoon tea parties, bingo and pool dance parties are all happening or forget the beach and spend the afternoon in one of the great spas nearby getting an exfoliating salt scrub and massage.

For your final night, choose a restaurant with a view not only of the city but of the sea for one of the amazing sunsets. A favorite is Vista Grill up in Alta Vista, where the view will take your breath away so much that you may even forget to eat. Another restaurant with a great view is Barcelona Tapas, which offers a panoramic vista of the city and bay as well as an amazing view of the sunset. Share a pitcher of sangria and promise that you'll be back—soon!

PUERTO VALLARTA

It is easy to see how Puerto Vallarta (pop. 350,000) drew the imagination of location scouts looking for just the right setting for John Huston's movie *The Night of the Iguana* and later the Arnold Schwarzenegger sci-fi flick *Predator.* The lush, verdant jungle and the rolling foothills of the Sierra Madres make for a spectacular backdrop, not just for the movies but for life as well.

The pearl of the Mexican Pacific, Puerto Vallarta radiates with the same rare intensity as the gemstone. As miners from inland pueblos traveled to the coastline in search of a spot to send their salt by sea to coastal Mexican towns, they stumbled into the paradise that is now Puerto Vallarta. What they found was perfection: loamy soil fertilized by the many rivers that feed into the sea; cream-colored beaches that stretched endlessly along the abundance of the Bahía de Banderas; and protection from even the worst storms of the Pacific Ocean.

Even today, despite its rapid growth from tiny village to tourist mecca, Puerto Vallarta retains the magic that those miners must have felt as they looked into the Edenic valley. With mild temperatures year-round, stunning white gold beaches, and a dazzling array of exciting recreational opportunities, it is easy to see what draws tourists back to the Bay of Banderas time and time again.

The centerpiece of Puerto Vallarta is the Bay of Banderas, one of the deepest and largest natural bays in the world. Visitors plumb its mysterious depths on scuba trips, delight in its abundance of brightly colored tropical fish on snorkeling tours and, several times a year,

© ROBIN NOELLE

HIGHLIGHTS

(A Walk Along Isla Río Cuale: A lovely shady stroll taking in crafts stalls; sidewalk artists; quaint, swaying suspension bridges; and the John Huston statue. En route, stop for lunch at a riverside restaurant or one of the view *fondas* at the Municipal Crafts Market (page 31).

(El Pitillal: Find great bargains and see how daily life is lived in Puerto Vallarta's most populated neighborhood when you visit Pitillal. Browse tiny shops and stalls, dine on delicious street fare and enjoy the nightly festivities in the square outside of the cathedral (page 35).

(The Malecón: Enjoy an early-evening stroll along the seawall-walkway called the Malecón. Start out enjoying the many amusements by the Los Arcos amphitheater, and continue north, taking your pick of diversions from the parade of lively clubs, bars, shops, and restaurants (page 35).

(Puerto Vallarta Zoo and Vallarta Botanical Gardens: Bring the family and head to the Puerto Vallarta Zoo where visitors can feed many of the animals and have their photos taken with lion and jaguar cubs (page 36).

(Playa los Muertos: Its strand of yellow sand, gentle waves, and lack of undertow make Playa los Muertos a good spot for wading and swimming. Watch the fisherfolk bring in their daily haul at the New Pier or catch the sunset and a margarita as a beachfront restaurant (page 37).

(Diving and Snorkeling at Los Arcos: Los Arcos Marine Sanctuary, offshore from

LOOK FOR **(** TO FIND RECOMMENDED SIGHTS, ACTIVITIES, DINING, AND LODGING.

Mismaloya, is a magnet for both vacationers and fish. The vacationers snorkel while watching the droves of fish graze the seaweed and coral on the submarine slopes of these arched sea rocks. Best go by day cruise (page 39).

compete for the biggest tuna and marlin in international sportfishing tournaments. The bay is also home to several varieties of sea turtles and dolphins. Once a year, April–December, humpback whales arrive to mate or give birth to calves in its sheltered waters.

The Bay of Banderas also provides a plethora of fresh seafood that is available in every restaurant, from the rustic *palapa* huts lining the beach to the high-end gourmet restaurants that

dot the hillside on winding cobblestone streets above Vallarta's city center. Puerto Vallarta attracts international talent to its many exquisite restaurants and is host to an annual international gourmet festival. One thing is certain, Vallartenses (residents of Puerto Vallarta) love good food.

In fact, it is perhaps the Vallartenses that make Puerto Vallarta truly special. Nowhere else in Mexico will you experience the feeling of warmth and welcoming you will in Puerto Vallarta. With homes tucked in between art galleries and trinket shops, the residents will greet you with a smile and a *"buenas noches,"* as they sit outside enjoying an evening breeze. In many areas, you will meet the artisans themselves and experience the pride and joy they take in creating their art and crafts.

This book provides a roadmap for residents and visitors alike, whatever their passions. From the well-known and well-loved Zona Romántica and Isla Cuale, to lesser-known hamlets and everything in between, you are invited to discover what makes Puerto Vallarta, like the pearl, a rare and beautiful treasure.

PLANNING YOUR TIME

Part of the beauty of Puerto Vallarta is the tremendous variety in activities available for a wide range of interests. With such an abundance of things to do, prioritization is key. On an average weeklong trip, there is just too much to do and see for all but the most determined travelers, especially if relaxation is on the agenda. There are two things not to be missed during your trip, however; spending some time on or in the lovely Bay of Banderas and dining at some of the incredible restaurants scattered throughout the city.

Shopping enthusiasts will find innumerable boutiques and shopping centers, many offering authentic Mexican art and handicrafts. Art lovers can spend a couple of days

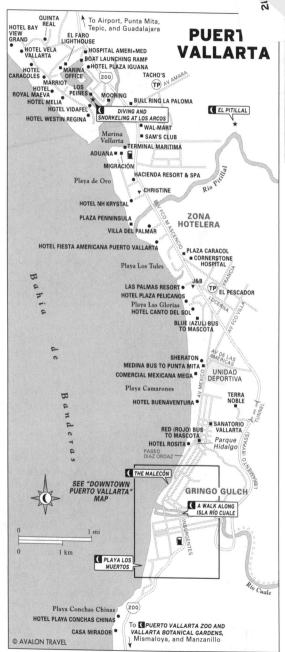

© AVALON TRAVEL

© ROBIN NOELLE

Cruise ships bring millions of visitors to Puerto Vallarta each year.

exploring the variety of fine art galleries and viewing the sculpture and architecture of the city. Adventurers can tromp through the jungle on hikes, horseback rides, or ATV or even fly through the treetops on one of the several canopy tours. Of course, scuba divers and snorkelers will be delighted with the unusual mix of tropical fish and other aquatic life.

Evenings can be spent dining with your feet in the sand at one of the many beachfront restaurants or viewing the glittering lights of the bay and the fireworks show from the **Marigalante Pirate Ship** (tel. 322/223-0309, www.marigalante.com.mx) that takes place every evening, at a hillside restaurant perched above the city with a panoramic view of the surrounding area. Afterward, take a walk along the seaside Malecón and enjoy the sand sculptures, performers, and artists. Later, when the clubs start picking up (after about 11:00 P.M.), you can shake your moneymaker at any number of discos and bars that line the street.

Beyond the Town Limits

For those in town for only a few days or a few hours, you will probably want to spend your time in Puerto Vallarta proper but if you can spare the time, it is well worth a trip just south or north of town. Mismaloya lies to the south and can be traveled to by car, cab, or bus at minimal cost. Enjoy swimming in the calm cove or relaxing in one of the lounge chairs offered by the beach restaurants while dining on fresh shrimp and sipping a margarita. You can walk along a pathway to peer into the now closed set of **John Huston's *Night of the Iguana*** or swim over to the rocky outcropping for some excellent snorkeling. On the way back, stop at **Le Kliff** for a cocktail and appetizer and enjoy the spectacular view of the bay. You can also continue past Mismaloya for trip to the **Vallarta Botanical Gardens** (www.vallartabotanicalgardensac.org) where you can view a wide variety of tropical plants, including a wonderful display of Mexican orchids as well as have a nice lunch at their on-site restaurant.

For more out of town adventure, take one of the many **water taxis** from the pier on Playa los Muertos to the remote and charming **Quimixto, Las Ánimas,** or **Yelapa** on

IF YOU ARE ...

Looking for the one thing not to miss while visiting Puerto Vallarta? Here's the best of the best:

Don't miss these if you are a/an...

- **Animal Lover:** The Puerto Vallarta Zoo

- **Water Enthusiast:** Snorkeling or diving at Los Arcos and Las Marietas

- **Daredevil:** The zip lines at Los Veranos

- **Bird Watcher:** A trip to the Vallarta Botanical Gardens

- **Foodie:** The International Gourmet Festival and Restaurant Weeks

- **Romantic:** Sunset cocktails at Le Kliff

- **Spa Junkie:** A massage at the Grand Velas Spa

- **Sports Nut:** A bucket of shrimp and the game at El Torito

- **Fisherman:** A fishing trip on the Bay of Banderas

- **Shopaholic:** The Mercado Municipal and the Galerías Vallarta

- **Equestrian:** Rancho El Charro horseback riding excursions

- **Surfer:** A day trip to Punta Mita or Sayulita

- **Family:** A trip on the Marigalante Pirate Ship

- **Bargain Hunter:** A trip to El Pitillal

- **Salsa Dancer:** A night dancing at J&B's

the south shore of the bay. While there, take a hike, drench yourself in a waterfall, sun on the beach, and enjoy a good seafood lunch at a beachfront *palapa* restaurant. The more athletic traveler can start at the small fishing village of **Boca de Tomatlán** and take a moderately challenging hike along the water and through the jungle to **Las Ánimas,** stopping at some superb hidden beaches along the way. The trailhead is just over the suspension bridge and heads south along the coastline.

Farther North, South, and Inland

Farther afield, you could spend a day (or two or three, with overnights) busing or driving to hideaways not far north of Puerto Vallarta, such as **Punta Mita** for lunch, sunning, swimming, and maybe surfing; or visit **Sayulita** or **Playa San Francisco** (known as San Pancho to the locals) for the same.

Consider heading farther north and spending two or three more days enjoying the scenic beauty of the northern coast and visiting less touristy havens such as **Chacala** or **San Blas.**

You can also explore to the south for unparalleled beauty and charming beach town stays at **La Manzanilla** or the petite beach resort towns of **Melaque** and **Barra de Navidad.** For those seeking true luxury and have deep pockets, book a few nights at the lavish and secluded **El Tamarindo** resort or the incomparable **El Careyes** hotel and spa.

ORIENTATION

Puerto Vallarta is long and narrow, stretching from about the Riviera-like Conchas Chinas condo headland at the south end to the marina district at the north end. In between, you'll encounter the popular Playa los Muertos and the intimate old Río Cuale neighborhood, joined across the river by the busy (but beachless) central Malecón lined with shopping and restaurants and always bustling with activities. To the north, the beaches resume again at Playa Camarones and continue past the Zona Hotelera (Hotel Zone) string of big resorts to the Terminal Marítima dock where several times a week behemoth cruise ships dock and let forth a stream of daytime tourists. The city technically ends at the International Airport although continuing past that, you will find the small working-class neighborhood of Las Juntas.

Although Nuevo Vallarta is technically in Nayarit, another state from Puerto Vallarta, many new visitors do not realize its distance from the city when booking their stay. Nayarit and Jalisco operate on different time zones, with the official border being the bridge and checkpoint between the two states. Many businesses and people in Nayarit operate on Jalisco time (central standard time in the United States) but it's best when setting an appointment or making reservations, to double-check to avoid confusion.

One basic thoroughfare serves the entire beachfront. Officially Bulevar Francisco Medina Ascencio, it's commonly called the **Carretera Aeropuerto** (Airport Highway), though it changes names three times as it conducts express traffic south past the Zona Hotelera. Narrowing, it first becomes the cobbled Avenida México, then Paseo Díaz Ordaz along the seafront Malecón with tourist restaurants, clubs, and shops, changing finally to Avenida Morelos before it passes the Presidencia Municipal (city hall) and central plaza.

Isla Río Cuale, the tree-shaded, midstream island where the city's pioneers built their huts, marks the change from El Centro to **Zona Romántica** also known as Old Town. It is in this neighborhood that the majority of the quaint shops and art galleries reside and visitors can idle away the hours shopping. This is also home to the majority of the gay-friendly clubs, bars, and shops.

HISTORY
Before Columbus
For centuries before the arrival of the Spanish, the coastal region that includes present-day Puerto Vallarta was subject to the kingdom of Xalisco, centered near the modern Nayarit city of Jalisco. Founded around A.D. 600, the Xalisco civilization was ruled by chiefs who worshipped a trinity of gods: foremost, Naye, a legendary former chief elevated to a fierce god of war; the more benign Teopiltzin, god of rain and fertility; and wise Heri, the god of knowledge.

Recent archaeological evidence indicates another influence: the Aztecs. It seems they left Náhuatl-speaking colonies along the southern Nayarit coastal valleys during their centuries-long migration to the valley of Mexico.

Conquest and Colonization
Some of those Aztec villages still remained when the Spanish conquistador Francisco Cortés de Buenaventura, nephew of Hernán Cortés, arrived on the Jalisco-Nayarit coast in 1524.

In a broad, mountain-rimmed valley, an army of 20,000 warriors, their bows decorated with colored cotton banners, temporarily blocked the conquistador's path. The assemblage was so impressive that Cortés called the fertile vale of the Río Ameca north of present-day Puerto Vallarta the Valle de las Banderas (Valley of the Banners). Thus the great bay later became known as the Bahía de Banderas.

The first certain record of the Bay of Banderas itself is in the log of conquistador Don Pedro de Alvarado, who sailed into the bay in 1541 and disembarked (probably at Mismaloya) near some massive sea rocks. He named these Las Peñas, and they're undoubtedly the same as the present Los Arcos rocks that draw daily boatloads of snorkelers and divers.

For 300 years the Bay of Banderas slept under the sun. Galleons occasionally watered there, and a few pirates hid in its jungle-fringed coves waiting for them.

Independence
The rebellion of 1810–1821 freed Mexico, and a generation later, as with many of Mexico's cities, the lure of gold and silver led to the settlement of Puerto Vallarta. Enterprising merchant Don Guadalupe Sanchez made a fortune here—ironically, not from gold, but from salt for ore processing, which he hauled from the beach to the mines above the headwaters of the Río Cuale. In 1851 Don Guadalupe built a hut and brought his wife and children. Their tiny trading station grew into a little town, Puerto de Las Peñas, at the mouth of the river.

Later, the local government founded the present municipality, which, on May 31, 1918, officially became Puerto Vallarta, in honor of the celebrated jurist and former governor of Jalisco, Ignacio L. Vallarta (1830–1893).

However, the Cuale mines eventually petered out, and Puerto Vallarta, isolated, with no road to the outside world, slumbered again.

Modern Puerto Vallarta

But it didn't slumber for long. Passenger planes began arriving sporadically from Tepic and Guadalajara in the 1950s, and a gravel road was pushed through from Tepic in the 1960s. The international airport was built, the coast road was paved, and tourist hotels sprouted on the beaches. Perhaps most notably, in 1963, director John Huston, at the peak of his creative genius, arrived with Richard Burton, Elizabeth Taylor, Ava Gardner, and Deborah Kerr to film *The Night of the Iguana*. Huston, Burton, and Taylor stayed on for years, waking Puerto Vallarta from its long doze. It hasn't slept since.

Sights

Puerto Vallarta has an abundance of wonderful things to see, from the beautiful sculptures that line the beachfront, to the natural beauty of its beaches and bay. Those who sequester themselves inside their resort miss out on much of what Puerto Vallarta has to offer.

◖ A WALK ALONG ISLA RÍO CUALE

Start at the **Museo Río Cuale,** a joint government-volunteer effort near the downstream tip of Isla Río Cuale. Inside is a fine three-room collection of pre-Columbian ceramics excavated in Jalisco, Nayarit, and Colima, including some especially attractive female sculptures and some charming representations of Colima's famously fetching dogs. The museum's website, www.tiendadelmuseo.com.mx, illustrates a number of for-sale examples. Find the museum open 9 A.M.–2 P.M. and 4–7 P.M. daily. Admission is free.

Head upstream beneath the bridge and enjoy the shady paseo of shops and restaurants. For fun, stroll out on one of the two quaint suspension bridges over the river. Evenings, these are the coolest spots in Puerto Vallarta, as night air often funnels down the Cuale valley, creating a refreshing breeze along the length of the clear, tree-draped river.

Farther upstream, on the adjacent riverbank, stands the **Mercado Municipal Río Cuale,** a

© BRUCE WHIPPERMAN

Swinging suspension bridges cross over the Río Cuale.

honeycomb of stalls stuffed with crafts from all over Mexico. Continue past the upriver bridge (Av. Insurgentes) to **Plaza John Huston,** marked by a pensive bronze likeness of the renowned Hollywood director who helped put Puerto Vallarta on the map with his filming of Tennessee Williams's *The Night of the Iguana* in 1963.

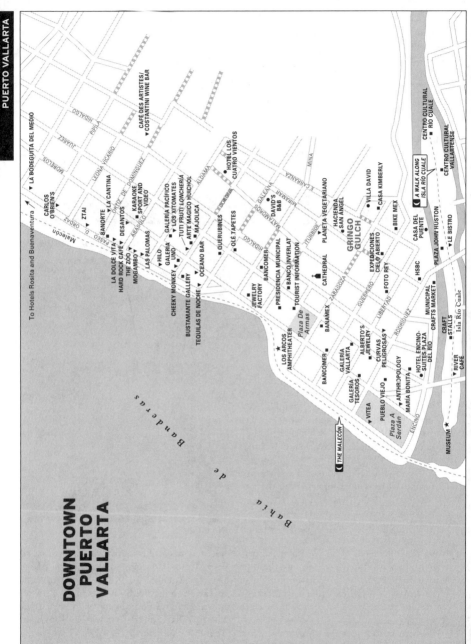

DOWNTOWN
PUERTO
VALLARTA

Bahía de Banderas

To Hotels Rosita and Buenaventura

LA BODEGUITA DEL MEDIO

CARLOS
O'BRIEN'S

CAFÉ DES ARTISTES/
CONSTANTINI WINE BAR

HIDALGO
PIPILA
JUÁREZ
MORELOS
P. OROZCO
Malecón
PASEO DÍAZ ORDAZ

ZTAI
BANORTE
LA CANTINA
DESANTOS
LEONA VICARIO
ORTIZ DE DOMÍNGUEZ
ABASOLO
KARAOKE
SPORT AND
VIDEO

LA DOLCE VITA
HARD ROCK CAFÉ
THE ZOO
MOGAMBO
LAS PALOMAS
HILO

GALERIA
UNO
CHEEKY MONKEY
GALERIA PACÍFICO
TUTI FRUTI LONCHERÍA
LOS XITOMATES
ARTE MÁGICO HUICHOL
MAJOLICA
ALDAMA

HOTEL LOS
CUATRO VIENTOS

OCEANO BAR
QUERUBINES

BUSTAMANTE GALLERY

TEQUILAS DE NOCHE

OLÉ TAPETES

DAVID'S
B&B
MATAMOROS
GALEANA
MIRAMAR
HIDALGO
E. CARRANZA
MINA

HACIENDA
SAN ÁNGEL

PLANETA VEGETARIANO

GRINGO
GULCH

VILLA DAVID

CASA KIMBERLY

BIKE MEX

JEWELRY
FACTORY

PRESIDENCIA MUNICIPAL
BANCO INVERLAT
TOURIST INFORMATION

BANCOMER

CATHEDRAL

ZARAGOZA
GUERRERO
LIBERTAD
RODRÍGUEZ
ENCINO

EXPEDICIONES
CIELO ABIERTO

FOTO REY

HSBC

CASA DEL
PUENTE

PLAZA JOHN HUSTON

LE BISTRO

A WALK ALONG
ISLA RÍO CUALE

CENTRO CULTURAL
RÍO CUALE

CENTRO CULTURAL
VALLARTENSE

BANAMEX

LOS ARCOS
AMPHITHEATER

Plaza De
Armas

BANCOMER

GALERIA
VALLARTA

GALERIA
TESOROS

VITEA

PUEBLO VIEJO

ALBERTO'S
JEWELRY

CURVAS
PELIGROSAS

ANTHROPOLOGY

MARIA BONITA

Plaza A
Serdán

THE MALECÓN

HOTEL ENCINO
SUITES PLAZA
DEL RÍO

MUNICIPAL
CRAFTS MARKET

CRAFT
STALLS

RIVER
CAFÉ

MUSEUM

Isla Río Cuale

Bahía de Banderas

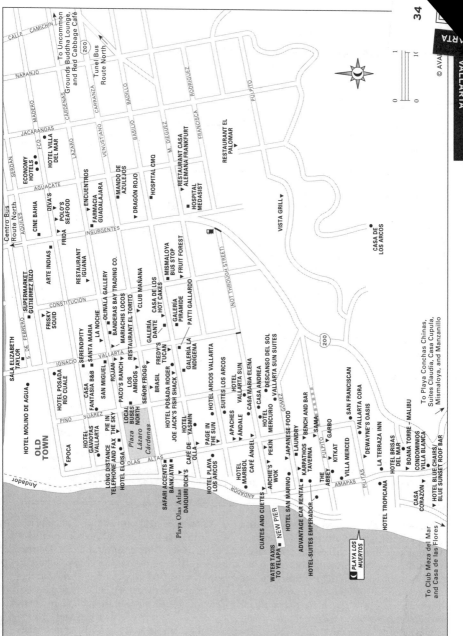

OLD TOWN

To Uncommon Grounds Buddha Lounge, and Red Cabbage Café

Tunel Bus Route North

Centro Bus Route North

CALLE CAMICHIN

NARANJO

JACARANDAS

FCO. VILLA DEL MAR

HOTEL VILLA DEL MAR

ECONOMY HOTELS

DIVA'S

ENCUENTROS

POLO'S SEAFOOD

FRIDA

FARMACIA GUADALAJARA

MANDO DE AZULEJOS

DRAGÓN ROJO

HOSPITAL CMQ

RESTAURANT CASA ALEMANA FRANKFURT

HOSPITAL MEDASIST

RESTAURANT EL PALOMAR

CINE BAHIA

AGUILES

AGUACATE

SERDAN

MADERO

NARANJO

CARDENAS

CARRANZA

LAZARO

VENUSTIANO

BASILIO

M. DIEGUEZ

FRANCISCA

RODRIGUEZ

PULPITO

BADILLO

ARTE INDIAS

SUPERMARKET GUTIERREZ RIZO

FRISKY SQUID

RESTAURANT IGUANA

INSURGENTES

CONSTITUCIÓN

OLINALA GALLERY

BANDERAS BAY TRADING CO.

MARIACHIS LOCOS

RESTAURANT EL TORITO

CLUB MAÑANA

CASA DE LOS HOT CAKES

GALERÍA PIRAMIDE

PATTI GALLARDO

MISMALOYA BUS STOP

FRUIT FOREST

CASA DE LOS ARCOS

VISTA GRILL

SALA ELIZABETH TAYLOR

5 DE FEBRERO

SERENDIPITY

SANTA MARIA

SAN MIGUEL

LA NOCHE

ROJAN

PACO'S RANCH

LOS AMIGOS

SEÑOR FROGS

BRASIL

FREDY'S TUCAN

GALERIA DANTE

GALERIA LA INDIGENA

IGNACIO

VALLARTA

HOTEL MOLINO DE AGUA

CASA FANTASIA B&B

PIE IN THE SKY

HOTEL POSADA RIO CUALE

PINO

SUAREZ

HOTEL GAVIOTAS VALLARTA

EPOCA

HOTEL ELOISA

LONG DISTANCE TELEPHONE AND FAX

Andador

OLAS ALTAS

Plaza Lázaro Cárdenas

JOE JACK'S FISH SHACK

HOTEL POSADA ROGER

HOTEL YASMIN

CAFÉ DE OLLA

PAGE IN THE SUN

APACHES

ANDALE

PEKIN

HOTEL ARCOS VALLARTA

SUITES LOS ARCOS

HOTEL VALLARTA SUN

CASA MARIA ELENA

CASA ANDREA

HOTEL MERCURIO

DESCANSO DEL SOL

VALLARTA SUN SUITES

SAN FRANCISCAN

VALLARTA CORA

SAMA

BENCH AND BAR

GÓMEZ

(200)

(NOT THROUGH STREET)

SAFARI ACCENTS

BANK/ATM

DAIQUIRI DICK'S

Playa Olas Atlas

HOTEL PLAYA LOS ARCOS

HOTEL MARISOL

CAFÉ ANGEL

ARCHIE'S WOK

JAPANESE FOOD

LAUNDRY

KARPATHOS TAVERNA

THE ABBEY

KITKAT

GARBO

VILLA MERCED

DEWAYNE'S OASIS

LA TERRAZA INN

HOTEL BRISAS DEL MAR

BOANA TORRE MALIBU

CONDOMINIOS VILLA BLANCA

To Playa Conchas Chinas, Suites Claudia, Casa Cupula, Mismaloya, and Manzanillo

WATER TAXIS TO YELAPA

CUATES AND CUETES

NEW PIER

ADVANTAGE CAR RENTAL

HOTEL-SUITES EMPERADOR

HOTEL SAN MARINO

HOTEL TROPICANA

CASA CORAZON

HOTEL BLUE CHAIRS/ BLUE SUNSET ROOF BAR

PLAYA LOS MUERTOS

AMAPAS

PILITAS

PULPITO

To Club Meza del Mar and Casa de las Flores

To Playa del Mar and Casa de las Flores

THE NIGHT OF THE IGUANA:
THE MAKING OF PUERTO VALLARTA

The idea to film Tennessee Williams's play *The Night of the Iguana* in Puerto Vallarta was born in the bar of the Beverly Hills Hotel. In mid-1963, director John Huston, whose movies had earned a raft of Academy Awards, met with Guillermo Wulff, a Mexican architect and engineer. For the film's location Wulff proposed Mismaloya, an isolated cove south of Puerto Vallarta. On leased land, Wulff would build the movie set and cottages for staff housing, which he, Huston, and producer Ray Stark would later sell for a profit as tourist accommodations.

Most directors would have been scared away by the Mismaloya jungle, where they would find no roads, phones, or electricity. But, according to Alex Masden, one of Huston's biographers, Huston loved Mismaloya: "To me, *Night of the Iguana* was a picnic, a gathering of friends, a real vacation."

A "gathering of friends," indeed. The script required most of the cast to be dissolute, mentally ill, or both: a blonde nymphet tries to seduce an alcoholic defrocked minister while his dead friend's love-starved, hard-drinking widow keeps a clutch of vulturous biddies from destroying his last bit of self-respect — all while an iguana roped to a post passively awaits its slaughter.

Huston's casting was perfect. The actors simply played themselves. Richard Burton (the minister) came supplied with plenty of booze. Burton's lover, Elizabeth Taylor, who was not part of the cast and still married to singer Eddie Fisher, accompanied him. Sue Lyon (the nymphet) came with her lovesick boyfriend, whose wife was rooming with Sue's mother; Ava Gardner (the widow) became the toast of Puerto Vallarta while romping with her local beach paramour; Tennessee Williams, who was advising the director, came with his lover Freddy; while Deborah Kerr, who acted the only prim lead role, jokingly complained that she was the only one not having an affair.

With so many mercurial personalities isolated together in Mismaloya, the international press flew to Puerto Vallarta in droves to record the expected fireworks. Huston gave each of the six stars, as well as Elizabeth Taylor, a velvet-lined case containing a gold derringer with five bullets, each engraved with the names of the others. Unexpectedly, and partly because of Huston's considerable charm, none of the bullets was used. Bored by the lack of major explosions, the press corps discovered Puerto Vallarta instead.

As Huston explained later to writer Lawrence Grobel: "That was the beginning of its popularity, which was a mixed blessing." Huston nevertheless returned to the area and built a home on the Bay of Banderas, where he lived the last 11 years of his life. Burton and Taylor bought Puerto Vallarta houses, got married, and also stayed for years. Although his Mismaloya tourist accommodations scheme never panned out, Guillermo Wulff became wealthy building for the rich and famous many of the houses and condominiums that now dot Puerto Vallarta's jungly hillsides and golden beaches.

About 100 yards farther on, stop in at the small gallery of the **Centro Cultural Vallartense,** a volunteer organization that conducts art classes, sponsors shows of promising artists, and sometimes invites local artists to meet the public and interested amateurs for informal instruction and idea exchange. Ask the volunteer on duty for more information or see the community events listings in *PV Mirror* or the *Vallarta Tribune,* the local English-language newspapers.

A few more steps upstream at a small plaza stands the headquarters and auditorium of the city-sponsored **Centro Cultural Cuale.** On the left side of the courtyard are the Centro Cultural's graphic and fine arts courses. (Schedule of courses open to the general public posted by the Centro Cultural's office by the auditorium, open 10 A.M.–2 P.M. and 4–7 P.M. Mon.–Sat.)

Walk a few steps farther upstream to the boulder-strewn far point of the island, where you can enjoy the airy river panorama: clear (in dry season) rushing water framed by great riverbank trees, verdant canyon ramparts, and distant cloud-capped mountains.

◖ EL PITILLAL

For those looking for a sample of the truly authentic Mexico that still slumbers behind the glitz of the now cosmopolitan tourist city of Puerto Vallarta, El Pitillal will transport you directly there. Located only three miles or so behind the massive Wal-Mart–Sam's Club shopping center, visitors can take a short cab ride or a bus directly down the road that runs by the shopping center until they reach the petite and ever active central square of Puerto Vallarta's most populated neighborhood.

El Pitillal is home to many of the working people of Puerto Vallarta and you will find that the businesses there cater to their needs instead of tourist desires. As a result, you can find incredible bargains and unusual wares tucked into the warren of streets and storefronts. Lining the streets surrounding the square, you will find leather shops, jewelers, trinket stores, and a mishmash of clothing stores, restaurants, and hardware shops.

During the evening after most people are off from their day jobs of working in hotels and restaurants, the square comes alive, often with live music, assorted street vendors, and a clutch of delicious food stands where you can purchase fresh tamalés, roasted corn on the cob, and tacos.

Spend some time admiring the church, buying your souvenirs, and then take a stroll over to the Río Pitillal. You won't need more than a few hours in Pitillal to get a glimpse of an entirely different side of Puerto Vallarta. You can dine at any one of the local *fondas* tucked back on the streets (look for one that is busy during meal times) or at **Mariscos Tino's** (Calle Avenida 333, tel. 322/225-2171), an original Pitillal favorite just a few blocks uphill from the square.

◖ THE MALECÓN

Several of Puerto Vallarta's other memorable sights lie along the water's edge, on or near the Malecón (seafront walkway). First, let the much-photographed belfry of the main town church be your guide. Named **La Parroquia de Nuestra Señora de Guadalupe,** for the city's patron saint, the church is relatively new (1951) and undistinguished except for the very unusual huge crown atop the tower. Curiously, it was modeled after the crown of the tragic 19th-century Empress Carlota, who went insane after her husband was executed. On the church steps, a native woman sometimes sells textiles, which she weaves on the spot with a traditional backstrap loom (in Mexican Spanish, *tela de otate,* loom of bamboo, from the Náhuatl *otlatl,* bamboo).

Head across the main town square, the Plaza de Armas, flanked by the Presidencia Municipal on its north side, and Los Arcos (The Arches) amphitheater, marked by the arches picturesquely set at the seafront, at the beginning of the Malecón. Although interesting enough by day, Los Arcos frequently forms a backdrop for a colorful flurry of evening snack stalls, sidewalk arts and crafts, playful clowns, and free evening music and dance performances. From there, the Malecón stretches north along the seafront about a mile, toward the Zona Hotelera, which you can see along the curving beachfront.

A number of modernistic sculptures highlight the Malecón; often covered with tourists eager for a photo with the unusual art. All along the walkway you will find street vendors, sand sculptors, and performers such as rock balancers and living statues. On the other side of the street, it is lined with storefronts, restaurants, and time-share salespeople. Beware of anyone asking how long you will be in town!

The Malecón action regularly climaxes in the evening, and especially Saturday nights around 10 P.M. when everyone in town seems be on the Malecón either strolling the sidewalk or riding in a car. This is when the people-watching is at its best. Cruisers come out to show off their cars, young people gather in groups for flirting, and of course, tourists from all over the world marvel at the sights.

TERRA NOBLE

An artistic oasis created by owner-artist Jorge Rubio, Terra Noble (9 A.M.–4 P.M. Mon.–Sat., free admission), blends into the jungle perfectly on a vista hilltop above the middle of town. It's an art and healing center offering workshops, a traditional *temascal* sweat lodge experience, and spa treatments, including a delicious chocolate body treatment. The view from the top is amazing, a panoramic vista of the entire city and bay. Terra Noble spreads downhill through a breathtakingly scenic, tropical deciduous forest at the western edge of the Agua Azul Nature Reserve. The villa on site can be rented by the night or for longer periods and is family and pet friendly. Rates start at about $600 per night. For architectural details of the unique villa, handcrafted by clay sculptor Suzy Odom, see the Terra Noble feature story in *Architectural Digest,* July 1996.

Besides its singular building and parklike grounds, Terra Noble is a serious healing center. A variety of treatments are available from a single massage to an all day experience in the blissful open-air treatment rooms, each with amazing views of their own. Terra Noble is a favorite for weddings and special events and the spa can handle groups of up to nine people at once.

Regardless of whether you get the full treatment, Terra Noble is worth a visit, if for nothing more than a look around and a picnic (pack a lunch). Contact Terra Noble ahead of time to verify hours (tel. 322/223-0308, fax 322/222-5400, www.terranoble.com). Get there by car, taxi, or any local bus that follows the *libramiento* (bypass road) through the hills east of town. Follow the side road, signed Par Vial Zona Centro, about 100 yards south of the summit tunnel (not the short tunnel at the south end), on the west (ocean) side of the *libramiento.* After about a half mile curving uphill, you'll see the Terra Noble entrance sign on the view side of the road.

◖ PUERTO VALLARTA ZOO AND VALLARTA BOTANICAL GARDENS

Headed south of Puerto Vallarta on the main highway brings to a pair of hidden treasures

Check out the incredible vista from the Terra Noble healing center.

COURTESY OF TERRA NOBLE

tucked back into the jungle. The first is the **Zoologico de Vallarta** (Camino al Eden 700, Mismaloya, tel. 322/228-0501, www.zoologicodevallarta.com, $10), where for a small additional fee visitors can purchase a small bag of food to feed the animals. The bag costs $5 and contains five different foods along with a handy chart of which animals eat what. Unlike American zoos, the Puerto Vallarta zoo has no plexiglass or safety moats; the animals are right there for you to see and touch. Toss peanuts to the monkeys on the island or hand feed the flamingos that wade in the water at arm's reach. You can even feed animal crackers to the sweet-tempered black bears.

The zoo, which was once private, does brisk business in trading big cat cubs with other zoos, which is why throughout most of the year, there are cubs for you to hold and play with. For another $10, you can spend 10 minutes getting your picture taken or frolicking with a month old white tiger or jaguar cub. While some of the enclosures seem cramped, the staff members at the zoo are always working hard to improve conditions. They can only do that with the support of visitors and the community.

Farther south, past the zoo and Mismaloya is the **Vallarta Botanical Gardens** (Hwy. 200, mile marker 24, tel. 322/223-6182, www.vallartabotanicalgardensac.org, 9 A.M.– 5 P.M. Tues.–Sun., $5), 20 acres of jungle property that houses more than 3,000 different species of plants. Wind your way through the blue agave hills where more than 6,000 of these cacti grow or check out the amazing Mexican orchid collection. There's a fantastic assortment of both birds and butterflies that call the Botanical Gardens home, so make sure to bring your binoculars and camera.

After you've had your fill of the amazing grounds, head toward the massive Hacienda de Oro visitors center where you can purchase locally made arts and crafts or have a tasty lunch of wood-fired pizza and a vanilla mojito. The view from the restaurant is amazing and don't be surprised when a chattering flock of parakeets comes by to see what you are up to.

Beaches

The beaches along the Bay of Banderas are truly wonderful. Long stretches of golden sand line the Puerto Vallarta area while they are spun into white gold just south of town at Las Gemelas. There are beaches that are right for anyone; secluded and empty beaches lie to the north and south while the perfect for people-watching Playa Los Muertos is at the heart of the action.

◖ PLAYA LOS MUERTOS
Easily the most popular beach in Puerto Vallarta, Playa los Muertos, is the strand of yellow sand that stretches for a mile south of the Río Cuale. This is the best beach for people-watching and making new friends, as there are always people fishing, sunbathing, strolling, and just enjoying the beautiful weather. Vacationers in this area vary from mild to wild

so this might not be the best beach choice for the highly conservative.

There are many beach clubs and restaurants lining Los Muertos and most establishments allow you the use of their lounge chairs with a minimal food or beverage purchase. Sip a margarita and watch the anglers at **New Pier** (foot of Francisca Rodriguez) pull in the day's catch.

Fishing is even better off the rocks on the south end of the beach. *Lisa* (mullet), *sierra* (mackerel), *pargo* (snapper), and *torito* are commonly caught anywhere along close-in beaches.

Gentle waves and lack of undertow make Playa los Muertos generally safe for wading and good for swimming beyond the close-in breakers. The same breakers, however, eliminate Los Muertos for bodysurfing, boogie boarding, or surfing (except occasionally at the far south end).

© BRUCE WHIPPERMAN

Shady palms and a broad walkway border Playa los Muertos.

PLAYA CONCHAS CHINAS

Playa Conchas Chinas (Chinese, or "Curly," Shells Beach) is not one beach but a series of small sandy coves dotted by rocky outcroppings beneath the condo-clogged hillside that extends for about a mile south of Playa los Muertos. A number of streets and driveways lead to the beach from the Manzanillo Highway 200 (the extension of Insurgentes) south of town. Drive, take a taxi, or ride one of the many minibuses marked Mismaloya or Boca that leave from the corner of Constitución and Calle Basilio Badillo, just below Insurgentes, or hike along the tidepools from Los Muertos.

Fishing off the rocks is good here; the water is even clear enough for some snorkeling. Bring your own gear, however, as there's none for rent. The usually gentle waves make any kind of surfing very doubtful.

BEACHES JUST SOUTH OF TOWN

Beach lovers can spend a month of Sundays poking around the many little beaches south of town. Drive, take a taxi, or hop a Mismaloya or Boca minibus from the corner of Calle Basilio Badillo and Constitución.

Just watch out the window, and when you see a likely spot, ask the driver to stop. Say *"Pare* (PAH-ray) *por favor."* The location will most likely be one of several lovely *playas:* **El Gato** (Cat), **Los Venados** (Deer), **Los Carrizos** (Reeds), **Punta Negra** (Black Point), **Garza Blanca** (White Heron), or **Gemelas** (Twins).

Although many of these little sand crescents have big hotels and condos, it doesn't matter because beaches are public in Mexico up to the high-tide line. There is always some path to the beach used by local folks. Just ask *"¿Dónde está el camino* (road, path) *a la playa?"* and someone will probably point the way.

MISMALOYA AND LOS ARCOS

If you ride all the way to Playa Mismaloya, you will not be disappointed, despite the over-sized Hotel Jolla de Mismaloya (which does offer beach and all-inclusive day passes) crowding the beach. Follow the dirt road just past the hotel to the intimate little curve of sand

and lagoon where the cool, clear Mismaloya stream meets the sea. A rainbow of fishing *lanchas* (boats) lie beached around the lagoon's edges, in front of a line of beachside *palapa* restaurants.

Continue a few hundred yards past the *palapas* to the ruins of the movie set of *The Night of the Iguana*. Besides being built for the actual filming, the rooms behind those now-crumbling stucco walls served as lodging, dining, and working quarters for the dozens of crew members who camped here for those eight busy months in 1963.

Stop for food (big fish fillet plate, any style, with all the trimmings, $8, or breakfast eggs from the restaurant's own hens) or a drink at the **Restaurant las Gaviotas** *palapas* across the river.

For still another Mismaloya treat, visit nearby **Chino's Paradise** (11 A.M.–5 P.M. daily). Follow the riverside lower road that forks upstream at the north end of the bridge across the road from the hotel. Arrive in the midmorning (around 10) or late afternoon (around 3) to avoid the tourbus rush. Chino's streamside *palapas* nestle like big mushrooms on a jungle hillside above a cool, cascading creek. Adventurous guests enjoy sliding down the cascades (be careful—some have injured themselves seriously), while others content themselves with lying in the sun or lolling in sandy-bottomed clear pools. Beneath the *palapas,* Chino's serves respectable but uninspired seafood and steak plates and Mexican *antojitos.*

For a more rustic alternative, follow the road another mile uphill to **El Edén** (until about 5 P.M. daily), a jungle swimming hole, complete with food, *palapas,* a natural pool, a Tarzan-style rope swing, and a forest canopy ride.

Fishing, especially casting from the rocks beneath the movie set, and every other kind of beach activity are good at Mismaloya, except surfing and boogie boarding, for which the waves are generally too gentle.

C Diving and Snorkeling at Los Arcos

North, offshore beyond the Mismaloya cove, rise the green-brushed Los Arcos sea rocks,

a federal underwater park and ecopreserve. The name comes from the arching grottoes that channel completely through the bases of some of the rocks. Los Arcos is one of the best snorkeling grounds around Puerto Vallarta. Get there by hiring a glass-bottomed boat in the lagoon.

Snorkeling near the wave-washed Los Arcos is a Puerto Vallarta "must do." Swirling bunches of green algae and branching ruddy corals attract schools of grazing parrot, angel, butterfly, and goat fish. Curious pencil-thin cornet fish may sniff you as they pass, while big croakers and sturgeon will slowly drift, scavenging along the coral-littered depths.

Similarly, scuba diving at Los Arcos is fantastic for experienced and beginner divers alike. There are shallow reefs to dive as well as the more challenging wall dive of the Devil's Canyon, the lip of the continental shelf that plummets down to about five miles. Los Arcos is also where night dives take place, allowing brave divers to experience the magic of phosphorescent algae, sleeping fish, and night predators like the octopus and lobster at their most active.

BEACHES FARTHER SOUTH

Three miles south of Mismaloya is **Boca de Tomatlán,** a tranquil country village overlooking a broad strip of yellow sand bordering a petite blue bay. *Palapa* restaurants supply enough food and shade for days of easy relaxation.

If you decide to linger, contact Agustín Bas, a personable English-speaking Argentinian expatriate. He and his partner, Marjorie Torrance, offer lodging in their gorgeous two-bedroom, three-bath jungle bayfront **Casa Tango** (tel. 322/224-7398, U.S. tel. 310/494-9970, www.casatango.com). Low-season (May–Sept.) tariffs run about $80 per day, $560 weekly ($120 and $790 high season Oct.–Apr.) for up to six, including airport pickup. Agustín and Marjorie also offer many other vacation rentals and personalized guided snorkeling, fishing, horseback, and other tours, specializing in the verdant Bay of Banderas southern shoreline; for more info visit www.tangorentals.com.

You can continue by *colectivo* water taxi

© BRUCE WHIPPERMAN

Water taxis from New Pier regularly shuttle passengers quickly to Yelapa.

(about $4 pp) to the pristine paradises of Las Ánimas, Quimixto, and Yelapa farther south. **Las Ánimas** has seafood, *palapas,* an idyllic beach, and snorkeling; the same is true for **Quimixto,** which also has a waterfall nearby for splashing.

Yelapa, a settlement nestled below lush palm-crowned hills beside an aquamarine cove, is home to perhaps a hundred local families and a small colony of expatriates. For visitors, it offers a glimpse of South Seas life as it was before the automobile. Since Yelapa is accessible only by sea, residents get around on foot or horseback. A waterfall cascades through the tropical forest above the village, and a string of *palapa* restaurants lines the beach.

One of the highlights of Yelapa is the pie. Yelapa's pie ladies roam the beaches until about 4 P.M. daily, selling freshly baked pies (and slices) to people on the beach. The pie is fantastic and comes in yummy flavors like chocolate, fresh coconut, lime, and mango. A hefty slice will run you about $2, so don't forget your wallet.

Lodging is available through either hotels or rental homes, with the majority of the property in Yelapa being for rent. Try the *palapa-*roofed cabanas of the rustic **Hotel Lagunita** (tel. 322/209-5055 or 322/209-5056, www.hotel-lagunita.com, $70 d low season, $120 high). Reservations are especially recommended during the winter high season. For a high-end ecoresort experience, visit the unique **Verana** resort (U.S. tel. 866/687-9358, www.verana.com, starting at $320 d plus meal plan), perched high up on the hill overlooking the bay. To reach the resort, guests must make the 25-minute hike while their luggage is delivered by burro up the mountain. Once there, the view is incredible but the property is still etched into the hillside so this is not a good choice for the unathletic or infirm. While the meal plan is mandatory ($80 d pp) and drinks are not included, you will not be disappointed by the food, which is flavorful, fresh, and inspired. Verana has two spas, one on-site at the resort and a day spa down below near the water line. Either one is well worth a visit.

NORTH-END (ZONA HOTELERA) BEACHES

These are Puerto Vallarta's cleanest, least-crowded in-town beaches, despite the many hotels that line them. Beginning at the Hotel Rosita at the north end of the Malecón, **Playas Camarones, Las Glorias, Los Tules,** and **de Oro** form a continuous three-mile strand to the marina. Stubby rock jetties about every quarter-mile have succeeded in retaining a 50-yard-wide strip of golden sand most of the way.

The sand is grainy, midway between coarse and fine. The waves are usually gentle, breaking right at the water's edge, and the ocean past the breakers is fairly clear (10- or 20-foot visibility) and blue. Stormy weather occasionally dredges up clam, cockle, limpet, oyster, and other shells from the offshore depths.

Fishing by pole, net, or simply line is common along here. Surfing, bodysurfing, and boogie boarding, however, are not. All other beach sports, especially the high-powered variety, are available at nearly every hotel along the strand.

Farther north, along the shore past the Terminal Marítima–Marina Harbor entrance, the beach narrows to a seasonally rocky strip at the oceanfront of a row of big resort hotels.

Should you be staying somewhere other than the beach, rest assured that for now, there is plenty of free beach access in Puerto Vallarta. If you are driving, most free access points in the hotel zone offer parking, and where there is parking, there is usually someone to watch and wash your car for a small fee.

Almost all of the beachfront hotels offer two types of passes for nonguests. The most basic is usually a facilities pass, allowing you use of towels, the pool, gym, and beach for the day. These normally run in the $10–20 range. If the hotel is all-inclusive, then the pass is more expensive but allows for unlimited food and national drinks (think well liquor) normally between the hours of 10 A.M. to 5 or 6 P.M. Those passes run from $50 per person up to $180 per person (for the exquisite Grand Velas Hotel and its gourmet restaurants).

© ROBIN NOELLE

Hikers can walk from Boca de Tomatlán to Las Ánimas along the water.

BEACH HIKES

A pair of good close-in hikes are possible. For either of them, don't forget a sun hat, sunscreen, bug repellent, a shirt, and some light shoes. On the south side, walk from Playa los Muertos about 1.5 miles along the little beaches and tidepools to Playa Conchas Chinas. Start at either end and take half a day to swim, snorkel, sun, and poke among the rocks.

The more ambitious can hike the entire three-mile beach strip from the northern end of the Malecón to the marina. If you start by 9 A.M. you'll enjoy the cool of the morning with the sun at your back. Stop along the way at the showplace pools and beach restaurants of hotels such as the Sheraton, the Canto del Sol, the Fiesta Americana Vallarta, and NH Krystal. Walk back, or opt for a return by taxi or city bus.

WATER TAXIS

Puerto Vallarta visitors can also reach the little southern beaches of Quimixto, Las Ánimas, and Yelapa from Puerto Vallarta itself. You have two options: fast water taxis or one of several all-day tourist cruises. The water taxis (about $20 round-trip), which allow you more time at your destination, customarily leave the Playa los Muertos New Pier three times in the morning, at about 10:30, 11 and 11:30 A.M. high season (11 and 11:30 A.M. low season). In the afternoon, they return twice, at around 4 and 4:30 P.M. high season (but once only, at around 4 P.M., low season). The morning departures

allow about three hours for lunch and swimming at either the Quimixto or Yelapa waterfalls. For more information and tickets call the New Pier water taxi office (tel. 322/222-0680) or email water taxi manager Lucas Donahue at businessyelapa@hotmail.com.

The more leisurely tourist cruises leave around 9 A.M. (returning by mid- to late afternoon) from the Terminal Maritima (cruise ship dock) on the north-side marina harbor complex.

Entertainment and Events

Puerto Vallarta is a town full of entertainments, most of them spontaneous. The glowing sunsets, the balmy evening sea breeze, the crowds of relaxed folks out and about, and the abundance of sidewalk stands, selling everything from paintings to popcorn, are sources of continuous impromptu diversions. Add to that the more formal entertainments, such as the Malecón-front nightclubs, Mexican fiesta tourist shows, quiet refined side-street bars, plus all the traditional festivals—Virgin of Guadalupe, Mexican Independence, Carnival and much more—and there's enough to enjoy a party for every day you spend in Puerto Vallarta.

ARTS AND MUSIC COURSES

The private, volunteer **Centro Cultural Vallartense** periodically sponsors theater, modern dance, painting, sculpture, aerobics, martial arts, and other courses for adults and children. From time to time it stages exhibition openings for local artists, whose works it regularly exhibits at the gallery/information center at Plaza del Arte on Isla Río Cuale. For more information, look for announcements in the events pages of *Vallarta Today* or the *Vallarta Tribune,* or drop by and talk to the volunteer in charge at the Plaza del Arte gallery and information center, at the upstream end of Isla Río Cuale.

Sharing the Plaza del Arte is the **Centro Cultural Cuale** building and adjacent classrooms, where, late weekday afternoons, you

may hear the strains of students practicing the violin, guitar, piano, flute, and pre-Columbian instruments. Such lessons are open to the general public; apply in person during the late afternoon or early evening.

TOURIST SHOWS

Visitors who miss real-life fiestas can still enjoy one of several local **Fiesta Mexicana** tourist shows, which are as popular with Mexican tourists as they are with foreigners. The evening typically begins with a sumptuous buffet of salads, tacos, enchiladas, seafood, barbecued meats, and flan and pastries for dessert. Then begins a nonstop program of music and dance from all parts of Mexico: a chorus of revolutionary *soldaderas* and their Zapatista male compatriots; raven-haired senoritas in flowing, flowered Tehuántepec silk dresses; rows of dashing Guadalajaran *charros* twirling their fast-stepping *chinas poblanas* sweethearts, climaxing with enough fireworks to swab the sky red, white, and green.

The south-of-Cuale **Restaurant Iguana** (Calle Lázaro Cárdenas 311, btwn. Insurgentes and Constitución, tel. 322/222-0105) stages a very popular and *auténtico* show Thursday and Sunday around 5 and 7 P.M. (Sun. only in the low season, call ahead to confirm). Another Zona Romántica show is at **Playa Los Arcos** (Olas Altas 380, tel. 322/226-7100), which offers a buffet dinner for $18 and **Folklorico Mexicano** show nightly.

© BRUCE WHIPPERMAN

Fiesta Mexicana tourist shows are put on weekly by many Puerto Vallarta hotels.

Other good tourist-show bets are at the **Hotel NH Krystal** (tel. 322/224-0202, Tues. at 7 P.M.) and the **Sheraton** (tel. 322/226-0404, Thurs.). The tariff for these shows typically runs $40–50 per person with open bar. During holidays and the high winter season reservations are generally necessary; best to book through a travel or tour desk agent.

LIVE MUSIC

Free music concerts are often held at the bayside **Los Arcos** amphitheater. For more information on these and other live-music listings, check out the events calendars and nightlife pages in *Vallarta Today* or *Vallarta Tribune*.

Cover charges are not generally required at the hotel bars, many of which offer live music and dancing. Among the most reliable venues are the **Sheraton** (tel. 322/224-0202), the **Marriott** (tel. 322/226-0000), the **Fiesta Americana** (tel. 322/226-2100), and the **Playa los Arcos** (tel. 322/226-7100). Be sure to phone ahead to check programs.

Many Puerto Vallarta restaurants also offer live music accompaniment with your evening meal. For example, for Latin music try **La Palapa** (tel. 322/222-5225), on Playa los Muertos just south of New Pier. For jazz, go to **Cuates y Cuetes** (Latin jazz, tel. 322/222-9511), also on Playa los Muertos, or the **River Cafe** (tel. 322/223-0788) on Isla Río Cuale below the downstream Avenida Vallarta bridge.

Local rock bar **Club Roxy** (Ignacio Vallarta 217, tel. 322/223-2404) offers live and loud rock music nightly, often to a full house of locals and tourists. The dance floor is usually packed as the crowd rocks out to classic rock, Motown, and blues.

MOVIES

A number of movie houses entertain residents and visitors. Movies change every Friday and cost about $4 per adult. South of Cuale, find the **Cine Bahía** (Insurgentes 63, btwn. Madero and Serdán, tel. 322/222-1717), which remains a typical 1950s-style small-town movie house. There are several other modern theaters in town that offer reclining seats, air-conditioning and cheap treats, including **Cinépolis** (Francisco Villa 1642 in the Soriana shopping center, tel. 322/293-6763), **Cinemark** (in Plaza Caracol on the main highway, tel. 322/224-8927), and the newest and slightly more expensive **MM Cinemas** (Galerìas Vallarta, tel. 322/221-0095). You can get movie listings from *Vallarta Today* or *Vallarta Tribune* newspapers or online at www.virtualvallarta.com.

NIGHTLIFE

The popularity of Puerto Vallarta's nightlife scene has given it an extra touch of sophistication that many other beach destinations don't share. There's something for everyone here: The offerings range from quiet neighborhood bars and numerous terraces with ocean-view tables to ultracool rooftop lounges and pounding dance clubs. Since Puerto Vallarta is a top destination for Mexicans and foreigners alike, you can expect to find an international clientele at many of the trendy nightspots.

For the visitor this means that a night out

Many fairs offering live entertainment take place in the parks at either end of the Malecón.

isn't the inexpensive fun it once was. It's much harder on the wallet these days, but on the other hand, you won't have any trouble finding a bartender who will pour you a wicked cosmopolitan or offer a lengthy martini or margarita menu with flavors that you hadn't dreamed existed. You'll need to dress up more than you might when clubbing in other beach destinations, but don't forget to wear comfortable shoes: There aren't just the long nights of dancing to consider, there are also the cobblestone streets. But some things are the same as the rest of Mexico: The action doesn't really start until after midnight.

The night scene isn't just for drinking and dancing anymore. In earlier decades, late-night dining options consisted of the corner taco stand or the other corner taco stand. Now the growing popularity of nightclubs with food on premises allows you more than just a toss-it-down snack. Whether it's sushi or tapas, it may be just what you needed to catch that second (or third) wind.

While the actual number of nightclubs is limited, nearly every restaurant on the Malecón offers either live or recorded music in the evenings. Restaurants like **deSantos** and **Ztai** turn from restaurant to dance club around 11 P.M. nightly.

As the hot spot for gay travelers in Mexico, Puerto Vallarta has seen an increase in the range and refinement of the gay nightlife choices as well. There are drag shows and friendly local bars, along with the pick-me-up, toss-me-down, shake-it-loose joints and strip clubs. The Zona Romántica, the area south of the Río Cuale in downtown Puerto Vallarta, is home to most of the area's gay bars. Of course, that doesn't mean that heterosexual singles or couples aren't welcome. In fact, several of the most fun bars in Puerto Vallarta are mixed crowds where the gay and straight mingle. With streetside coffee shops, restaurants, clubs, shops, and boutiques, it's also a great place to spend the evening just walking around the casual streets of the neighborhood.

All this sophistication doesn't mean that people looking for the serious party scene will be disappointed. Puerto Vallarta has a lot of raucous nightspots, especially along the Malecón during spring break and the student month of June. Whatever your taste, you're bound to find something fun. Just get out there: The night lasts forever and the sun comes up late in Vallarta.

Bars and Lounges

Romantics might enjoy whiling away some time at the **Oceano Bar** (corner of Corona, upstairs, overlooking the Malecón), once the bar of the long-gone Oceano Hotel, Puerto Vallarta's first deluxe hostelry. Enjoy the ocean view and even maybe a palm-silhouetted sunset and dream about those days long ago when lovers Richard Burton and Elizabeth Taylor enjoyed the same view when they stayed together in the hotel.

Farther north another block, traditionalists often enjoy **Restaurant Las Palomas** (corner of Aldama, tel. 322/222-3675), which features live marimba music 7–10 P.M. and a mariachi guitar trio after that. The bar features an authentic Mexican atmosphere and cuisine.

Italian restaurant **La Dolce Vita** (corner of Domínguez, tel. 322/222-3852, 10 A.M.–midnight daily in season) entertains dinner customers with live Latin and Cuban music. A popular favorite with the younger crowd is **Ztai** (Morelos 737, Centro, tel. 322/222-0306, www.ztai.com, 6 P.M.–4 A.M. daily) which offers a quiet restaurant on one side and an open garden lounge on the other. Friday night is ladies night with open bar and no cover charge for the females. Men pay $250 pesos. You can order from the full menu of international cuisine in the bar while you dance to the latest techno beats.

For that romantic tête-à-tête, there's simply no place like **Costantini Wine Bar** (Guadalupe Sánchez 740, Centro, tel. 322/222-3228, www.cafedesartistes.com, 6 P.M.–1 A.M. daily): Its dark red interior with high-backed banquettes holds many hidden corners. There is usually live music in the evenings, piano and jazz. Free wine-tastings are offered on Thursday nights (6–7 P.M.), giving you the chance to discover new favorites from the unmatched wine list, accompanied by a full selection of *botanas* (snacks). This is also a downtown hot spot for business cocktails and can be a fun gathering place for friends or coworkers.

Founded by one of the band members of the international group Maná, **de Santos** (Morelos 771, Centro, tel. 322/223-3052, www.desantos.com.mx, 10 P.M.–6 A.M. Wed.–Sat.) tends to draw names—both recognized and not—from Mexico and abroad. Although it's also known as a restaurant, de Santos is one of the best nightspots in town. Relax with a cocktail at one of the prime tables or the long-mirrored bar on the first floor, or climb the stairs to the upper terrace, where you can sip your martini on a gauze-curtained bed under the stars and the house music keeps things cool. Modern, trendy, and the place to be seen, de Santos also draws the late-night dance crowds with the hottest DJs.

Located just a block off the Malecón on Morelos, **La Cantina** (Morelos 709, Centro,

tel. 322/222-1629, www.etcbeach.com, 11:59 A.M.–2 A.M. Sun.–Tues., 11:59 A.M.–4 A.M. Wed.–Sat.) is a popular hangout for the younger Mexican crowd and is known to get quite raucous at night. Bar altercations and people dancing on tables are not uncommon here. La Cantina is genuine and doesn't give a thought to tourists, since not many of them find their way here. The dark interior feels homey, and the canned music, which ranges from *banda* to mariachi to ballads, adds to the very Mexican ambience, while the high ceilings lend a '40s-hacienda atmosphere. This place is best for talking with groups of friends rather than dancing or clubbing.

The increasingly popular small entertainment district, spread along I. Vallarta, near the corner of L. Cárdenas, has acquired a number of lively spots, among them the popular **Mariachis Locos** bar/restaurant (tel. 322/223-2205). Inside, a mostly local straight clientele enjoys a lively nonstop mariachi show nightly from about 11 P.M. to the wee hours.

For good food with your entertainment, continue south on I. Vallarta a block, to the corner of Vallarta and Carranza and the longtime favorite **Restaurant El Torito** (tel. 322/222-3784, 10 P.M.–5 A.M. nightly); try a bucket of fresh shrimp among friends and catch all of the latest sports games on the TV.

For good food with your entertainment, continue south on I. Vallarta, to the corner of Vallarta and Carranza and the longtime favorite **Restaurant El Torito** (tel. 322/222-3784, 10 P.M.–5 A.M. nightly); try a bucket of fresh shrimp among friends and catch all of the latest sports games on the TV.

A number of popular bars and nightspots entertain folks along Avenida Olas Altas. For example, many folks' nights wouldn't be complete without stopping in at the **Ándale** Mexican pub (Olas Altas 425, tel. 322/222-1054, open until around 2 A.M.), a quiet and respectable restaurant during the day and a rowdy, raucous bar known for its sing-alongs at night.

Garbo (Púlpito 142, Zona Romántica, tel. 322/229-7309, www.bargarbo.com, 6 P.M.–2 A.M. daily) is one of the most popular and fun bars in Puerto Vallarta. Located in the trendy Olas Altas area, Garbo caters to a mixed crowd of straight, gay, women, and men. You can sit at the bar and chat with the lively bartender and your neighbors or find a quiet table in the corner and enjoy the nightly piano music. You'll find the clientele and staff very friendly and the drink list exquisite.

Dance Clubs

Carlos O'Brian's (Paseo Díaz Ordaz 796, Malecon, tel. 322/222-1444, www.carlos-obrians.com, 11 A.M.–4 A.M. daily) is a local institution on the Malecón. They used to say if you haven't been here, you haven't been to Vallarta. Today, it continues to be a popular place for tourists who want to party with people they don't know. The age range spans college-age youngsters to middle-aged empty nesters. Like other tourist traps, mysteriously colored shots are handed out by scantily clad cocktail servers and the dance floor is always packed with tourists, from cruise ship passengers to frat boys. The prices are inflated and the atmosphere is cartoonish but its high energy and party 'til dawn mentality keeps the place full day after day.

At the time it was built, **Christine** (NH Krystal Hotel, Zona Hotelera, tel. 322/224-6990, 10 P.M.–6 A.M. daily; cover varies) was the best modern disco in town, and served tourists and visitors more than the local community. While still chic, Christine is now more democratic, but prices can still be high for locals. The indoor auditorium-style design allows for viewing the dance floor from any angle but don't be alarmed when the fog machines start blasting. The clientele is mostly younger here which probably stems from the fact that it's nearly empty until at least midnight.

When **Hilo** (Paseo Díaz Ordaz 588, Malecón, tel. 322/223-5361, www.hilobardance.com, 4 P.M.–4 A.M. daily) opened across from the Malecón, the two-floor-high sculpture of a woman leaning out to peer toward the sea caused a sensation. The oceanview tables here are great for a drink at sunset. A high second-floor mezzanine might cause vertigo,

but climb up to find yourself above the very Mexican sculptures. The dance floor gets crowded with tourists sometime after midnight, and the music pounds into the night at this fun club. Like most dance clubs in this area, the music is extremely loud so don't plan on having conversations without yelling.

Pronounced ho-ta-bei for the letters JB in Spanish, **J&B** (Fco. M. Ascencio 2043, Zona Hotelera, tel. 322/224-4616, www.jbdiscoclub.com, 10 P.M.–6 A.M. daily, cover $9) offers the best ambience for dancing to Latin music with locals. (The club actually opens at 8 P.M. for dance classes during the week. See www.tangobar-productions.com for information.) The night usually starts with DJ-spun music, but on weekends it alternates with live music. Try out your steps in salsa, rumba, merengue, cha-cha, tango, and more in this true community spot where most people get on the floor and dance. If you're part of a group, buy an entire bottle of liquor with mixers for a better deal. Even if you aren't a dancer, watching the incredible talent that dances here nightly can be a real treat.

Cuba staunchly holds its own in downtown Puerto Vallarta with **La Bodeguita del Medio** (Paseo Díaz Ordaz 858, Malecón, tel. 322/223-1585, 11 A.M.–1 A.M. daily), which serves up not only the best *mojitos* in town but also the hottest live Latin music. The tiny dance floor doesn't deter reveling regulars. Revolutionary Cuba is reflected in the huge one-star flag that covers one wall, while the other walls are scribbled with notes, signatures, and epithets in pre-revolutionary style.

When you want to dance and conga line with strangers, the **Zoo** (Paseo Díaz Ordaz 630, Malecón, tel. 322/222-4945, www.zoobardance.com, 11 A.M.–6 A.M. daily) is the perfect spot to release inhibitions that were in hiding until a couple of tequila shots jolted them loose. A 200-pound costumed gorilla may meet you on the street to invite you in, where a party of tourists will most likely become your new best friends. The decor of mounted animal heads and other zoolike paraphernalia lives up to this nightspot's name.

The young and club-crazy will enjoy **Stereo** (Lazaro Cardenas 261, www.myspace.com/stereopv, 9 P.M.–4 A.M.), a small after-hours dance club that caters to a younger and more local crowd, many of whom are active in the gay scene.

Adult Clubs

Puerto Vallarta is host to a number of adult clubs, both gay and straight, and varying from the upscale to the raunchy. A popular favorite for both men and women is the posh **Aquah** (Fco. M. Ascencio 2600, tel. 322/221-2071, 8 P.M.–6 A.M. daily). Another choice is **Prestige Men's Club** (Fco. M. Ascencio 2033, tel. 322/225-6941 8 P.M.–6 A.M. daily). As a good rule of thumb, pay cash as you go and do not run a tab to avoid surprises at the end of the night. Most clubs charge a cover fee (unless you are local with an ID) and offer VIP lounges and private back rooms. For visitors, the cover charge usually runs about $25 and includes 1–2 free national drinks.

FESTIVALS AND EVENTS

Puerto Vallarta residents enjoy their share of local fiestas. Preparations for **Semana Santa** (Easter week) begin in February, often with a **Carnival** parade and dancing on Shrove Tuesday, and continue for the seven weeks before Easter. Each Friday until Easter, you might see processions of people bearing crosses filing through the downtown for special Masses at neighborhood churches. This all culminates during Easter week, when Puerto Vallarta is awash with visitors, crowding the hotels, camping on the beaches, and filing in somber processions, which finally brighten to fireworks, dancing, and food on Domingo Gloria (Easter Sunday).

If you are looking for a relaxing vacation, Semana Santa is not the time to come to Puerto Vallarta. The beaches are literally covered with families camping, partying, and BBQing from dusk to dawn and the streets are lined with cars as thousands of Mexican nationals pour in from Guadalajara and other inland cities. While the festival atmosphere can be exciting

A little boy dresses like Juan Diego for the Festival of the Virgin of Guadalupe.

© ROBIN NOELLE

and fun for some, the traffic, crowds, and resulting litter and noise can be a overwhelming for others.

The town quiets down briefly until the **Fiesta de Mayo,** a countrywide celebration of sports contests, music and dance performances, art shows, parades, and beauty pageants.

On the evening of **September 15,** the Plaza de Armas (City Hall plaza) fills with tipsy merrymakers who gather to hear the mayor reaffirm Mexican independence by shouting the Grito de Dolores—"Long Live Mexico! Death to the Gachupines!"—under booming, brilliant cascades of fireworks.

Celebration again breaks out seriously during the first 12 days of December, when city groups—businesses, families, neighborhoods—try to outdo each other with music, floats, costumes, and offerings all in honor of Mexico's patron, the Virgin of Guadalupe. The revelry climaxes on **December 12,** when people, many in native garb to celebrate their indigenous origins, converge on the downtown church to receive the Virgin's blessing. If you miss the main **Festival of the Virgin of Guadalupe,** you can still enjoy a similar but smaller-scale celebration in El Tuito a month later, on January 12.

Puerto Vallarta is also home to a number of annual events for locals and tourists alike. Two foodie favorites include the **Festival Gourmet** each November (www.festivalgourmet.com for dates) and **Restaurant Week** each

May (www.virtualvallarta.com for dates). The Festival Gourmet is the pricier of the two, offering special culinary exhibitions and tastings as well as special menus at many of Puerto Vallarta's top restaurants featuring guest chefs from around the world. The more reasonable Restaurant Week in May also offers special prix fixe menus but at the price points of $16 and $29 per person and offers a no less delightful culinary experience.

Shopping

Although Puerto Vallarta residents make few folk crafts themselves, they import tons of good—and some very fine—pieces from the places where they *are* made. Puerto Vallarta's scenic beauty has become an inspiration for a growing community of artists and discerning collectors who have opened shops filled with locally crafted sculpture, painting, and

© BRUCE WHIPPERMAN

Puerto Vallarta galleries and stalls offer an abundance of paintings, drawings, and sculpture.

museum-grade handicrafts gathered from all over Mexico. Furthermore, resort wear needn't cost a bundle in Puerto Vallarta, where a number of small boutiques offer racks of stylish, comfortable Mexican-made items for a fraction of stateside prices.

ZONA ROMÁNTCA

The couple of blocks of Avenida Olas Altas and side streets around the Hotel Playa los Arcos are alive with a welter of T-shirt and *artesanías* (crafts) stores loaded with the more common items—silver, onyx, papier-mâché, pottery—gathered from all over Mexico.

A few shops stand out, however. On Avenida Olas Altas, a block north of Hotel Playa los Arcos, find **Safari Accents** (Olas Altas 224, tel. 322/223-2660, 10 A.M.–10 P.M. daily). Inside, peruse a delightful trove of the baroque, including brilliant designer candles, angelic icons, bright metal-framed mirrors, a rainbow of glass lampshades, and gleaming candelabras.

For a different kind of excellence, head along Badillo. After a block and a half, on the south side of the street, step into **Galería La Indígena** (tel./fax 322/222-3007, 10 A.M.–8 P.M. Mon.–Sat.) for a brilliant display of fine native ceremonial crafts. Here, you can appreciate bright Huichol yarn paintings and masks; Tarascan art from Ocumichu, Michoacán; Nahua painted coconut faces from Guerrero; a host of masks, both antique originals and new reproductions;

SHOPPING FOR ARTS AND HANDICRAFTS

Puerto Vallarta has become an excellent shopping ground for handicrafts, fine art, resort wear, and home furnishings. Both the large selection of goods and the reasonable prices add to the temptation to do all your holiday gift shopping in Puerto Vallarta, regardless of the season. For the more common, low-priced (but nevertheless attractive) items, be sure to visit the Municipal Crafts Market by the upstream Río Cuale bridge, preferably early in your tour.

Although virtually all Mexican handicrafts are available in Puerto Vallarta, most of the stores listed below are especially well stocked in certain categories.

CLOTHING

For both resort wear and traditional clothes for women, head to **María Bonita** (Juárez 136) **Luisa's,** (322/222-5042, 10 A.M.-8 P.M. Mon.-Sat.), and **Querubines**.

GLASS

You'll find some excellent selections of Mexican glass at **Safari Accents** and **Mundo de Cristal**.

HUICHOL ART

Some of the best Huichol art can be found at **Galería La Indígena**, **Galería Pirámide** (Basilio Badillo 272) and **Arte Mágico Huichol**.

JEWELRY

Head to **Viva** (274 Basilio Badillo), **Alberto's,** and **Regina Jewelry Factory** for excellent selections of Mexican jewelry.

LEATHER

You'll find fine leather goods at **Huarachería Fabiola**.

METALWORK

Safari Accents and **Querubines** offer selections of beautiful metalwork.

PAINTING

For Mexican paintings, head to **Galería Vallarta, Galería Uno,** and **Galería Pacífico**.

PAPIER-MÂCHÉ

You'll find beautiful papier-mâché handicrafts at **Cabaña del Tío Tom** in Mercado Municipal.

SCULPTURE

If you're looking for serious Mexican sculpture, head to **Galleria Dante** and **Sergio Bustamante**.

TILE AND CERAMICS

For tile and ceramics, check out **Mundo de Azulejos, Querubines,** and **Majolica**.

WOOD CARVINGS AND MASKS

Olinalá Gallery and **Galería La Indígena** are good places to look for traditional word carvings and masks.

WOOL WEAVINGS

You'll find a good selection of Mexican wool weavings at **Querubines** and especially at **Olé**.

You can find a variety of handicrafts from all over Mexico in Puerto Vallarta.

pre-Columbian replicas; and Oaxacan fanciful wooden *alebrijes* (animal figures).

Walk a few doors uphill and across the street to view the eclectic sculpture collection at **Galleria Dante** (269 B. Badillo, tel. 322/222-2477, fax 322/222-6284, www.galleriadante.com, 10 A.M.–5 P.M. Mon.–Fri., 10 A.M.–2 P.M. Sat.). Exquisite wouldn't be too strong a description of the many museum-quality pieces, from neoclassic to abstract modern. Head farther up the street to **Lucy's Cucú Cabaña** (295 Basilio Badillo, tel. 322/222-1220) to see a charming and colorful mix of authentic Mexican handicrafts. While you are there pick up one of co-owner **Gil Gevin's** humorous books about life in Puerto Vallarta. He might even sign it for you if he's there.

Nearby on Ignacio Vallarta, stop into **Galería Alpacora** (tel 322/222-4179, www.galeriaalpacora.com), where you will see some incredibly vibrant wall hangings and rugs imported from South America and made with alpaca wool. **Cuban cigars** are forbidden in the United States, but if you want to pick some up for your stay in Mexico, be sure to drop into **El Gato Gordo** (Ignacio Vallarta 226, tel. 322/223-5282). If Rogelio isn't busy, he can give quite the lesson on how to spot a fake Cuban cigar.

Continue north on Vallarta to **Xunaaxi** (Ignacio Vallarta 139, tel. 322/222-2119) for some great cotton clothing and fun, affordable Mexican handbags.

Tucked away on a quiet residential street a block uphill from Insurgentes, find **Mundo de Azulejos** (Carranza 374, tel. 322/222-2675, fax 322/222-3292, www. talavera-tile.com, 9 A.M.–7 P.M. Mon.–Fri., 9 A.M.–2 P.M. Sat.). It offers a treasury of made-on-site tile and Talavera-style pottery at reasonable prices. Unique, however, are the custom-made tiles—round, square, oval, inscribed, and fired as you choose—with which you can adorn your home entryway or facade.

If you are looking for furnishings, either authentic or custom made, stop into **Banderas Bay Trading Company** (Cardenas 263, tel. 322/223-4352, www.banderasbaytradingcompany.com) where Tari and Peter Bowman have displayed their massive collection of Mexican furniture, art and decor. The Bowmans, who also own Daiquiri Dick's, travel throughout Mexico, attending fairs and purchasing goods directly from the artisans.

For a big selection of glassware, visit **Mundo de Cristal** (Insurgentes 333, tel. 322/222-4157) for an all-Mexico selection, including glasses, goblets, vases, mirrors, lamps, and much more, all at reasonable prices.

ALONG THE RÍO CUALE

For the more ordinary, yet attractive, Mexican handicrafts, head any day except Sunday (when most shops are closed) to the Mercado Municipal at the north end of the Avenida Insurgentes bridge. Here, most shops begin with prices two to three times higher than the going rate. You should counter with a correspondingly low offer. If you don't get the price you want, always be prepared to find another seller. If your offer is fair, the shopkeeper will often give in as you begin to walk away. Theatrics, incidentally, are less than useful in bargaining, which should merely be a straightforward discussion of the merits, demerits, and price of the article in question.

The Mercado Municipal is a two-story warren of dozens upon dozens of shops filled with jewelry, leather, papier-mâché, T-shirts, and everything in between. The congestion can make the place hot; after a while, take a break at a cool riverview seat at one of the *fondas* (permanent food stalls) on the second floor.

One of the most unusual Mercado Municipal stalls is **Cabaña del Tío Tom** (Uncle Tom's Cabin), whose menagerie of colorful papier-mâché parrots are priced a peg or two cheaper than at the tonier downtown stores.

It's time to leave when you're too tired to distinguish silver from tin and Tonalá from Tlaquepaque. Head downstream to the **Pueblo Viejo** complex on Calle Augustín Rodríguez between Juárez and Morelos, near the Avenida I. Vallarta lower bridge. This mall, with individual stores rather than stalls, is less crowded

owned Supermarket Gutiérrez Rizo. Comercial Mexicana's biggest local branch is the **Megastore** (tel. 322/222-7708 or 222-7709, 7 A.M.–10 P.M. daily), a quarter mile south of the Hotel Sheraton. The other branch is at **Plaza Marina** (Km 6.5, Hwy. 200, a few blocks south of the airport, beneath the McDonald's sign, tel. 322/221-0053 or 322/221-0490, open same hours). Rizo's has a location in Zona Romantíca at Aquiles Serdán and Constitución and another less pricey store in Pitillal on Revolución, just west of the main street that passes by the church.

The popular **Plaza Península** (Francisco Medina 2485) houses a Starbucks, Chili's, and several other eateries as well as some upscale retail stores and a casino and sportsbook. There are also branches for most of the banks available in Mexico. Special events open to the public and music are common on weekend evenings.

Recent years have seen tremendous development in Puerto Vallarta and with that the addition of an upscale mall, **Galerías Vallarta** (next door to Wal-Mart, across from the cruise ship terminal) which houses a new Liverpool

department store. Inside the mall you can find a number of higher priced retail stores, several restaurants, a large movie theater, and even another casino and sportsbook.

Central to the Hotel Zone is **Plaza Caracol** (Km 2.5, Hwy. 200, www.plazacaracolpv.com) which houses another massive grocery store, Soriana. Inside the plaza are a number of small boutiques, nail salons, electronics stores, and eateries. Upstairs is a movie theater, food court, and arcade for the kids. Inside of the Soriana grocery store, you will find **The Bookstore** (tel. 322/224-1872, 9 A.M.–9 P.M.), if you need to pick up some English language books.

MARINA DISTRICT

On the walkway that circles the Puerto Vallarta marina, you will find a number of small shops, spas, art galleries, and restaurants. At **Galería EM** (tel. 322/221-2228), artist Mariano Pérez creates unique stained glass art, beautiful crystal lenses encased in metal and other treasures. You can also order custom stained glass windows and doors.

Sports and Recreation

Some people believe that the weather in Puerto Vallarta is too hot for sports, but that's not necessarily the case, especially since water sports couldn't be more perfect during the warm midday, while jogging, tennis, and golf are best enjoyed in the early mornings and late afternoons. Whatever the case, Puerto Vallarta affords plenty of opportunities for exercising your bliss.

WATER SPORTS
Swimming, Surfing, and Boogie Boarding

While Puerto Vallarta's calm waters are generally safe for swimming, they are often too tranquil for surfing, bodysurfing, and boogie boarding. Sometimes strong, surfable waves rise along the southern half of **Playa los Muertos.** Another notable possibility is at the mouth of

the Río Ameca (north of the airport) where, during the rainy summer season, the large river flow helps create bigger than normal waves. Surfing is more common at Bucerías and Punta Mita. It should be noted that crocodiles are native to the area and river mouths are a popular place for these creatures to spend the day sunning. Attacks on humans are rare but keep your eyes peeled if you are planning on swimming or surfing in these areas.

Sailboarding

A small but growing nucleus of local sailboarding enthusiasts practice the sport from Puerto Vallarta's beaches. They sometimes hold a **sailboarding tournament** during the citywide Fiesta de Mayo in the first week of May. For more information, contact Puerto Vallarta tourist information (tel. 325/223-2500, ext. 230 or 232).

SPLENDID ISOLATION

A sprinkling of luxuriously secluded upscale miniresorts, perfect for a few days of quiet tropical relaxation, have opened in some remote corners of the Puerto Vallarta region. Being hideaways, they are not always easily accessible. But for those willing to make an extra effort, the rewards are rustically luxurious accommodations in lovely natural settings.

In order of proximity to Puerto Vallarta, first comes the minihaven **Majahuitas Resort** (tel. 322/293-4506 or U.S. tel. 831/336-5036, www.mexicanbeachresort.com, or contact Mexico Boutique Hotels, toll-free U.S./Can. tel. 800/728-9098, www.mexicoboutiquehotels. com), tucked into a diminutive palm-shaded golden strand on the bay between Quimixto and Yelapa. Here, guests have their choice of seven uniquely decorated cabanas ($250 for two, meals included, low season, $375 high), including a honeymoon suite. Solar panels supply electricity, and a luxuriously appointed central house serves as dining room and common area. A spring-fed pool, sunning, snorkeling, and horseback and hiking excursions into the surrounding tropical forest provide diversions for guests. Get to Majahuitas by water taxi, from the beach at Boca de Tomatlán, accessible by car or the "Boca"-marked buses that leave Puerto Vallarta from the south-of-Cuale corner of Basilio Badillo, one block downhill from Insurgentes.

The following three splendidly isolated small resorts are tucked along the Jalisco Coast south of Puerto Vallarta and are road accessible from Highway 200. (They are also described in the *Jalisco Coast* chapter, which you should consult for more detailed contact and access information.)

Find **Hotelito Desconocido** (toll-free Mex. tel. 01-800/013-1313, toll-free U.S./Can. tel. 800/851-1143, www.hotelito.com, $340 d Apr. 15-Dec. 20 low season, $450 d high season, includes breakfast and all activities) basking on a pristine lagoon and beach two hours south of Puerto Vallarta. Here, builders have created a colony of thatched designer houses on stilts. From a distance, it looks like a native fishing village. However, inside the houses (called *palafitos* by their Italian creator), elegantly simple furnishings – antiques, plush bath towels, and

artfully draped mosquito nets – set the tone. Lighting is by candle and oil lantern only. Roof solar panels power ceiling fans and warm showers. Outside, nature blooms, from squadrons of pelicans wheeling above the waves by day to a brilliant overhead carpet of southern stars by night. In the morning, roll over in bed and pull a rope that raises a flag, and your morning coffee soon arrives. For the active, a full menu, including volleyball, billiards, bird-watching, kayaking, and mountain biking, can fill the day. Reservations are strongly recommended.

About 30 miles farther south, the small sign at Km 83 shows the way to **Las Alamandas** (toll-free U.S./Can. tel. 888/882-9616, www. alamandas.com), where Isabel Goldsmith, daughter of the late British tycoon Sir James Goldsmith, has created an idyllic isolated resort. Guests (28 maximum) enjoy accommodations that vary from luxuriously simple studios ($425 low season, $520 high) to entire villas that sleep six ($1,600 low season, $2,200 high), all with full breakfast. Activities include a health club, tennis, horseback riding, bicycling, fishing, and lagoon and river excursions.

Alternatively, you can enjoy isolation at more moderate rates at **Hotel Punta Serena** (reservations through Blue Bay Club Los Angeles Locos, tel. 315/351-5020, ext. 4013 or 4011, fax 315/351-5412, www.puntaserena.com, $170 d low season, $200 d high), perching on a high headland overlooking the blue Bay of Tenacatita. From the hotel lobby, walkways meander to the tile-roofed lodging units, spread over a palmy parklike garden. The lodging units themselves (all with a/c) are designer-spartan, in white and blue, with modern baths, high ceilings, and broad ocean vistas from view balconies.

Here you can enjoy it all: an adults-only romantic retreat, with all meals and in-house activities – a big blue oceanview pool patio, sauna, sea-vista hot tub, gym, clothing-optional settings – included at no extra cost. Added-cost amenities include native Mexican *temazcal* hot room, and massage and spa services. Additionally, at no extra cost, you can also enjoy all of the lively sports, disco, and beach action at the Blue Bay Club Los Angeles Locos on the beach downhill.

Personal Watercraft, Waterskiing, and Parasailing

These are available right on the beach at a number of the north-side resort hotels, such as the Sheraton, Las Palmas Resort, Fiesta Americana Puerto Vallarta, and NH Krystal.

The same sports are also seasonally available south of Cuale on Playa los Muertos, in front of the Hotels Playa los Arcos and Tropicana. Expect to pay about $50 per half hour for a personal watercraft, $75per hour for waterskiing, and $25 for a 10-minute parasail.

SNORKELING AND SCUBA DIVING

All of the local tour companies offer diving and snorkeling trips around the bay. The two largest, and by extension, most crowded are **Vallarta Adventures** (tel. 322/297-1212, U.S. tel. 888/303-2653, www.vallarta-adventures.com) and **Chico's Dive Shop** (Malecón at Díaz Ordaz 770, btwn. Pípila and Vicario, tel. 322/222-1895, fax 322/222-2210, www.chicosdiveshop.com, 8 a.m.–10 p.m. daily).

For those who prefer a small group of usually less than 10 people, try **PV Scuba** (tel. 322/306-0806, www.pvscuba.com). Dive instructor Alex Vega offers a full range of certifications from PADI Open Water to Divemaster. Those who have never tried diving before can book a Discover Scuba Diving class ($115) which includes a pool class and a two-tank open water dive. Because of the quality of the equipment, strong attention to detail and safety and diving experience, PV Scuba is my personal choice when I dive in the Bay of Banderas.

Another quality company that offers smaller personalized trips for those eschewing cattle boat operations is **Local Divers** (tel. 322/221-6429, www.puertovallartadivers.com). Leslie and her husband Nacho consistently get great word of mouth and referrals for offering small group trips and superb service, especially for dives around Nacho's hometown of Chimo, known for frequent sightings of Giant Pacific manta rays.

Los Arcos marine park is wonderful for scuba or snorkeling as are the gentle spots of **Majahutas** and **Quimixto.** For those divers looking for more advanced or challenging

© ROBIN NOELLE

Los Arcos offers shallow reef or deep wall dives for novices and experts alike.

FAMILY FUN: VALLARTA WITH KIDS

Mexico is a very child-friendly country, indeed children are practically revered by men and women alike. Holidays like Children's Day (April 30) and Mother's Day (May 10) are widely celebrated with fiestas and parties plus presents for the honored guests. On Mother's Day, moms can expect to be greeted with hugs and congratulations on being a mother, even from barely known acquaintances.

Children adapt very easily to Mexico and will soon make friends with the Mexican children in your neighborhood or at your hotel, despite any language barriers. Don't be surprised when your young child is teaching you Spanish words and phrases at the end of your trip. Bringing along some toys to share or inexpensive gifts like coloring books and crayons is an excellent way to help shyer children make new friends.

If you are traveling with small children, often the large resorts are the way to go. They have special areas with shallow swimming pools for the children plus kid's clubs and daily activities where the children can interact with others in their age group. Some of the best child-friendly resorts are the **Hotel NH Krystal** (Av. de las Garzas s/n, tel. 322/224-0202, toll-free Mex. tel. 01-800/903-3300, U.S. tel. 888/726-0528, Can. tel. 866/299-7096, fax 322/226-0738, www.nh-hotels.com) and the **Hotel Buenaventura** (Av. México 1301, tel. 322/226-7000, toll-free Mex. tel. 01-800/713-2888, U.S. tel. 888/859-9439, fax 322/222-3546, www.hotelbuenaventura.com.mx).

There are many tours and activities that children can enjoy from the **Marigalante Pirate Ship** (Paseo Diaz Ordaz No. 770-21, tel. 322/223-0309, www.marigalante.com.mx) which is good for older children but can be scary for some small children, to swimming with the dolphins at **Vallarta Adventures** (tel. 322/297-1212, U.S. tel. 888/303-2653, www.vallarta-adventures.com). Other popular activities for children include zip-line tours for the older children and snorkeling for children of all ages.

If you've got little animal lovers in your group, you can't miss the **Puerto Vallarta Zoo** (Camino al Eden #700, Mismaloya, tel. 322/228-0501, www.zoologicodevallarta.com, $10) where you can feed many of the animals including giraffes, flamingos, and zebras. For a small fee you can even hold and play with lion and jaguar cubs (seasonal) while you get your photo taken.

Feeding your children shouldn't be too rough depending on how picky they are. Most restaurants are happy to provide quesadillas, chicken fingers, and other kid-friendly cuisine even if they don't have a kid's menu. Tourist venues like **Carlos O'Brian's** (Paseo Díaz Ordaz 796, Malecón, tel. 322/222-1444, www.carlos-obrians.com, 11 A.M.–4 A.M. daily) cater to children during the day and offer a fun atmosphere and special menus.

If you are traveling with small children, you might want to take advantage of **Lots for Tots** (tel. 322/175-0081, www.lotsfortotsmexico.com) selection of rental equipment. Owner Anjalla Berttall provides delivery of every type of baby gear imaginable right to the door of your hotel or condo before you arrive. Order strollers, playpens, cribs, and even diapers and baby food.

---

dives, check out **Chimo, Las Marietas** or **El Moro.** For expert divers looking for an all-day adventure, head out to popular fishing spot La Corbeteña to see larger sealife including, occasionally, a shark or two.

DAY CRUISES

Tickets for the popular booze cruises are available nearly everywhere but the best deal is to buy them directly at the Maritime Terminal.

Beware of time-share sellers offering free tours and cruises in exchange for attending a time-share presentation. While free tickets are nice, with some haggling you can earn enough money to buy your own tickets and then some. Booking online through the operator's website can also net you discounts. For all cruises wear your bathing suit and bring a towel and lots of sunscreen. Beware of drinking too much free booze and spending time in the sun.

SPAS, SPAS, SPAS

Being a spa junkie myself, one of my favorite things about visiting Mexico is the low prices on spa treatments and massages. It's common to find specials at the dozens of spas throughout Puerto Vallarta, especially during low season (April-November). An hour massage at a discount spa will run you somewhere around $45/hour during high season and $30/hour during low. Make sure to ask about packages if you want multiple treatments to take advantage of further discounts and don't forget a 10% tip if you receive good service.

For affordable spa treatments in a fairly bare bones but clean, pleasant atmosphere, try **Massage Lily** (Carranza 235, tel. 322/222-1723, open daily) in the Zona Romantíca, just a few blocks from the beach. In *El Centro,***Healing Hands** (Pipila 240, tel. 322/222-8441, diagonally from Pipi's restaurant) is a good bet for a relaxing no-frills massage.

In the Vallarta Marina, you can get a little more upscale at **Day Spa Specialty Massage Clinic** (tel. 322/221-0176, a few doors west of the El Faro lighthouse). They offer good package deals and the ambiance is peaceful and relaxing with private rooms and aromatherapy service.

For an unforgettable splurge, try one of the top spas in the world at the **Grand Velas Spa** (Av. Cocoteros 98 Sur, tel. 322/226-8045,

Vallarta.grandvelas.com) in Nuevo Vallarta. Expect to pay top dollar for a first-class experience at this luxury spa. Arrive an hour prior to your appointment to experience the full process of steam room, warm and cool dipping pools, foot hydrotherapy and more. The treatment rooms are opulent and most massages begin with a decadent foot cleansing ritual.

For truly luxurious, tropical spa experiences, there's two excellent choices. The first is the incomparable **Terra Noble,** (tel. 322/223-0308, www.terranoble.com) where your treatment room is open to the jungle and a magnificent panoramic view of the city and bay. Terra Noble offers massage, a divine Chocolate Body Treatment (among others) and a traditional Aztec steam bath.

Verana Day Spa (tel. 322/222.0878, dayspa.verana.com) offers a great day package that includes round-trip transportation to the Yelapa-based spa from Boca de Tomatlá and three treatments, approximately $120 US. Once on-site, you can spend the day enjoying the pool and other facilities as well as their fantastic spa restaurant. Single services are also available. If you want more than a day trip, you'll need to commit to the five-day minimum stay at the stunning Verana luxury resort at the top of the hill.

The most reliable of the tourist cruises are offered by **Princess Cruises.** They operate four boats, which each follow separate routes. Itineraries do vary from time to time; call 322/224-4777 or visit www.cruceros-princesa.com.mx for current details and reservations. The package for all daytime cruises includes light breakfast, fish or chicken lunch, open beer-and-soft-drink bar, on-board live music show, and dancing for about $50 per person.

The roomiest boat is the *Princess Yelapa,* a triple-decked steel tub with space for hundreds. The route follows the south coastline, passing for a view of Los Arcos sea rocks and continuing to idyllic Majahuitas for an hour

of snorkeling. Later, at Yelapa, passengers disembark for about two hours to sun on the beach or hike to the waterfall (by horseback, if desired).

Princess Cruises also runs the *Sarape,* a smaller motor cruiser accommodating around 60 people, for snorkeling at Los Arcos, continuing to Las Ánimas and Quimixto for a hike (or horseback ride) and swimming at a waterfall.

Other variations are offered by the midsize cruiser *Vagabundo* (snorkeling at Los Arcos and sunning and snorkeling at Las Ánimas) and the larger *Princess Vallarta,* a scaled-down version of the *Princess Yelapa,* for snorkeling and wildlife-viewing at the Islas Caletas and sunning on creamy Playa Blanca on the Bay of Banderas's north shore.

For romantics, the *Princess Vallarta* also offers a 6–9 P.M. sunset cruise, with snacks, open bar, and live music for dancing, also for about $50 per person.

If you tend toward seasickness, fortify yourself with Dramamine before these cruises. Also note that destination disembarkation at Las Ánimas, Quimixto, and Yelapa is by motor launch and can be difficult for travelers with disabilities.

BOATING

The superb 350-berth **Marina Vallarta** (P.O. Box 350-B, Puerto Vallarta, Jalisco 48300, tel. 322/221-0275, fax 322/221-0722) has all possible hookups, including certified potable water, metered 110–220-volt electricity, phone, fax, showers, toilets, laundry, dock lockers, trash collection, and pump-out. Other amenities include 24-hour security, a yacht club, and complete repair yard. It is surrounded by luxurious condominiums, tennis courts, a golf course, and dozens of shops and offices. Slip rates run around $0.75 per foot per day for 1–6 days, $0.60 for 7–29 days, and $0.50 for 30 or more days.

You can also drop by the marina office, open 9 A.M.–2 P.M. and 4–7 P.M. Monday–Friday and 9 A.M.–2 P.M. Saturday. Get there from the airport boulevard, northbound, by turning left at the main marina turnoff (marked by the huge Neptune sculpture on the building to the left). After two blocks, bear left at the fork, onto Paseo Marina. Timón is the next street on the left. The marina office is at the foot of Timón, on the left, beneath the embarcadero-front portal.

The marina also has a **public boat-launching ramp** where you can float your craft into the marina's sheltered waters for a nominal fee. If the guard isn't available to open the gate, call the marina office for entry permission. To get to the launch ramp, follow the street marked Proa, next to the big pink-and-white disco, one block south of the main Marina Vallarta entrance (below the

monumental Neptune sculpture on the corner building).

There is another yacht club farther north in Nuevo Vallarta that serves that marina. **Vallarta Yacht Club** (Paseo de los Cocoteros, next door to the Paradise Village Resort, tel. 322/297-2222, www.vallartayachtclub.com) offers reciprocal arrangements with many yacht clubs around the world and offers nonmembers two free visits. Club amenities include a full service staff, swimming pool, BBQ area, and member's pricing at the very good and reasonably priced restaurant. The club emphasizes social activities and offers a junior sailing program. Members can participate in the several regattas and other events that take place throughout the year.

Sailing

Sail Vallarta (tel. 322/221-0096 or 221-0097), which operates from Marina Vallarta, takes parties out on sailing excursions, as does **Vallarta Adventures** (tel. 322/297-1212, U.S. tel. 888/303-2653, www.vallarta-adventures.com) for $160 for two. Ask for a low-season discount.

If you're seriously interested in learning to sail, check out **Vallarta Explorer** (cell in Puerto Vallarta 044-322/779-7526, www.vallartaexplorer.com), who, in addition to taking you on a sailboat ride, offers comprehensive how-to-sail instruction. Another option is **J World** (tel. 800/910-1101 or 322/226-6767, www.sailing-jworld.com), which offers charters, sailing lessons, and certifications.

SPORTFISHING

At their present rate of attrition, sailfish and marlin will someday certainly disappear from Puerto Vallarta waters. Some captains and participants have fortunately seen the light and are releasing the fish after they're hooked in accordance with IFGA (International Fish and Game Association) guidelines.

You can hire a *panga* (outboard launch) with skipper on the beach in front of several hotels, such as Los Arcos on Playa los Muertos; the Buenaventura and Sheraton on

Playa los Camarones; the Plaza Pelícanos, Las Palmas Resort, and Fiesta Americana Puerto Vallarta on Playa las Glorias; and NH Krystal on Playa de Oro. Expect to pay about $25 per hour for a two- or three-hour trip that might net you and a few friends some jack, bonito, *toro*, or dorado for dinner. Ask your favorite local-style restaurant to fix you a fish banquet with your catch.

Another good spot for *panga* rentals is near the **Peines** (pay-EE-nays) docks, where the anglers keep their boats. You may be able to negotiate a good price, especially if you speak Spanish. Access to the Peines is along the dirt road to the left of the Isla Iguana entrance (just adjacent, south, of the fake roadside lighthouse a mile north of the Terminal Maritima). The fisherfolk, a score or so members of the Cooperativa de Deportes Aquaticos Bahía de Banderas, have their boats lined up along the roadside channel to the left, a few hundred yards from the highway.

At the end-of-road dock complex (the actual Peines), behind the entrance gate lie the big-game sportfishing boats that you can reserve only through agents back in town or at the hotels. Agents such as **American Express** (tel. 322/223-2910, 322/223-2927, or 322/223-2955, fax 322/223-2926) customarily book reservations during high season on the big 40-foot boats. They go out mornings at 7:30 and return about seven hours later with an average of one big fish per boat. The tariff runs around $100 per person; food and drinks are available but cost extra. Big boats generally have space for 10 passengers, about half of whom can fish at any one time. Most everyone usually gets something, if not a big sailfish or marlin.

Another agency that rents sportfishing boats is the **Sociedad Cooperativa Progreso Turístico** (north end of the Malecón at 31 de Octubre, across from Hotel Rosita, tel. 322/222-1202), which has four boats, ranging 32–40 feet. Rentals run $350–450 per day for a completely outfitted boat. It's best to talk to the manager, who is usually there 8 A.M.–noon and 4–8 P.M. Monday–Saturday.

A number of local English-speaking captains regularly take parties out on their well-equipped sportfishing boats. Alex Gómez, known as **Mr. Marlin** (at the Tennis Club Puesta del Sol deli, tel. 322/221-0809, www.mrmarlin.com), record holder of the biggest marlin catch in Puerto Vallarta, acts as agent for more than 40 experienced captains. Prices begin at about $300 for a 26-foot boat and $575 for a 35-foot boat, for a full day, including bait, ice, and fishing tackle.

Alternatively, go **Fishing with Carolina** and Captain Juan (call Candace Caroline Shaw for information and reservations at 322/224-7250, cell tel. 044-322/292-2953, www.mexonline.com/fishingwithcarolina.htm), who offers sportfishing, whale-watching, and snorkeling expeditions on their fully equipped diesel boat. Two anglers go all day for $125 per person, three for $350.

Call Mr. Marlin if you'd like to enter the Puerto Vallarta **Sailfish Tournament** (tel. 322/221-0809, www.fishvallarta.com); it's held annually in November (2007 marks the 52nd). The registration fee runs about $1,200 per participant, which includes the welcome dinner and the closing awards dinner. The five grand prizes usually include automobiles. The biggest sailfish caught was a 168 pounder in 1957.

Freshwater bass fishing is also an option, at lovely foothill Cajón de Peñas Reservoir (see the *Jalisco Coast* chapter), on your own or with **Viva Tours** (tel. 322/224-0410 or 322/224-0826, tel./fax 322/224-0182). For about $150 per person, minimum four persons, you get all transportation, breakfast and lunch, fishing license, guide, and gear. The lake record is 13 pounds.

LAND SPORTS
Bicycling
Bike Mex (Guerrero 361, tel. 322/223-1834, www.bikemex.com) offers mountain biking adventures in surrounding scenic country locations. It tailors trips according to individual interests and ability, from beginning to advanced levels. More advanced trips include

outback spots Yelapa and Sayulita and mountain destinations, such as San Sebastián, Mascota, and Talpa. Participants enjoy GT full suspension or Kona mountain bikes (27 gears), helmets, gloves, purified water, and bilingual guides. Alternatively, contact **Ecoride** (Miramar 382, tel. 322/222-7912, www.ecoridemex.com), which, among others, offers an advanced but super-scenic bike trip around San Sebastián, in the mountains above Puerto Vallarta.

Tennis and Golf

The friendly **John Newcombe Tennis Club** (Hotel Canto del Sol, tel. 322/226-0123, $16/hr) rents eight courts—four outdoor clay, four indoor. A sign-up board is available for players seeking partners. Also available are massage, steam baths, equipment sales and rentals, and professional lessons ($35/hr).

The **Hotel NH Krystal** (tel. 322/224-0202 or 322/224-2030, $15/hr) has several lighted courts for nighttime play. The NH Krystal club also offers equipment sales, rentals, and professional lessons ($20/hr). Other clubs, such as at the **Sheraton** (tel. 322/223-0404, 7:30 A.M.–dusk daily, $10/hr), also rent their courts to the public.

There are many championship and celebrity-designed golf courses in Puerto Vallarta and the Bay of Banderas. In fact, it's possible to play a different course every day of the week. The 18-hole, par-71 **Marina Vallarta Golf Course** (tel. 322/221-0073, www.marinavallartagolf.com), designed by architect Joe Finger, is one of Mexico's best. It is open to the public for $129 for morning, $98 for afternoon, which includes greens fee, caddy, and cart.

Alternatively, try **Vista Vallarta** (tel. 322/290-0030, www.vistavallartagolf.com), with two 18-hole golf courses in the country east of the marina about three miles. Greens fees run about $183 for morning, $129 after 2 P.M. There are two golf courses at this location, one designed by Tom Weiskopf and the other by Jack Nicklaus.

If you are staying in Nuevo Vallarta or don't

mind the drive, you can take on **El Tigre** (tel. 322/297-0773, www.eltigregolf.com)—an 18-hole, par-72 course, which while mostly flat makes use of water and sand to make things interesting. Many national and international tournaments take place at El Tigre. Green fees are $116 for morning and $80 for afternoon.

The green, palm-shaded 18-hole **Los Flamingos Golf Course** (Km 145, Highway 200, 8 mi/13 km north of the airport, tel. 329/296-5006, www.flamingosgolf.com.mx, 7 A.M.–5 P.M. daily) offers an alternative. Open to the public, Los Flamingos services include carts, caddies, club rentals, a pro shop, restaurant, and locker rooms. The greens fee of $121 for morning and $77 for afternoon includes the cart.

Horseback Riding

A pair of nearby ranches give visitors the opportunity to explore the Puerto Vallarta region's gorgeously scenic tropical forest, river, and mountain country. Options include English or Western saddles, and rides ranging from two hours to a whole day or a whole week. Contact either **Rancho Ojo de Agua** (tel. 322/224-0607, www.mexonline.com/ranchojo.htm) or **Rancho El Charro** (tel. 322/224-0114, www.ranchoelcharro.com).

GYMS

Puerto Vallarta has a number of good exercise gyms. One of the best is the women-only **Total Fitness Gym** (at the marina, Tennis Club Puesta del Sol, tel. 322/221-0770), offering 40 machines, complete weight sets, professional advice, and aerobics workouts. Similar facilities and services are available for both sexes at the **Hola Puerto Vallarta** hotel and spa (tel. 322/226-4600, $15/day).

Many hotels offer yoga in the mornings but the quality of the instructors at many resorts is suspect. If you are interested in yoga while in Puerto Vallarta, try classes at **Yoga Vallarta** (Basilio Badillo 325, tel. 322/116-5809, www.yogavallarta.com) or **Árbol del Yoga** (tel. 322/140-3201) in Plaza Genovesa in the hotel zone.

SPORTING GOODS

Given the sparse and pricey local sporting goods selection, serious sports enthusiasts should pack their own equipment to Puerto Vallarta. A few stores carry some items. Among the most reliable is **Deportes Gutiérrez Rizo** (corner of Av. Insurgentes and A. Serdán, tel. 322/222-2595, 9 A.M.–7 P.M. and 4–8:30 P.M. Mon.–Sat.). Although fishing gear—rods, reels, line, sinkers—is its strong suit, it also stocks a general selection including sleeping bags, inflatable boats, tarps, pack frames, wet suits, scuba tanks, and water skis.

TOURS
Adventure Tours

A number of nature-oriented tour agencies lead off-the-beaten-track Puerto Vallarta–area excursions. **Vallarta Adventures** (tel. 322/297-1212, U.S. tel. 888/303-2653, www.vallarta-adventures.com) offers boat tours to the Islas Marietas wildlife sanctuary (sea turtles, manta rays, dolphins, whales, seabirds), a dozen airplane excursions, and a rugged all-day Mercedes-Benz truck ride (canyons, mountains, crystal streams, rustic villages) into the heart of Puerto Vallarta's backyard mountains. You can also book dolphin and sea lion encounters, zip-line tours and other outdoor adventures. Discounts are available when booking online.

The offerings of unusually ecologically aware **Expediciones Cielo Abierto** (Open Sky Expeditions, 339 Guerrero, two blocks north of the riverside Municipal Crafts Market, tel. 322/222-3310, U.S./Can. tel. 866/422-9972, www.vallartawhales.com) include snorkeling around Punta Mita, hiking in the Sierra Cuale foothill jungle, bird-watching, cultural tours, dolphin encounters, and whale-watching. The whale-watching tour is the best in Puerto Vallarta, offering up close and personal viewing of the whales from a semi-inflatable boat. The guides are all marine biologists and provide lots of interesting facts and trivia about the whales of Vallarta. The best part is that they are extremely sensitive to the whales and unlike other tours, do not disclose the location

of whale pods over the radio, limiting the number of boats viewing them at one time.

Ocean Friendly Whale Watching (tel. 322/225-3774, www.oceanfriendly.com) is available for private tours or group trips and is also dedicated to responsible whale-watching. Marine biologist Ocsar Frey is dedicated to spreading the word about responsible whale-watching and does extensive research on the humpback whales each year. You are sure to learn a lot you didn't know about whales on one of Oscar's tours and he's also an expert photographer so if you ask nicely, you may be able to take home some beautiful photos to remember the trip by.

Viva Tours (tel./fax 322/224-0410, www.vivatours-vallarta.com) organizes a number of off-the-beaten-track adventures, including horseback riding, hiking, biking, fishing, and much more.

Finally, if you want to see a listing of all adventures possible in Puerto Vallarta, visit www.puertovallartatours.net, the creation of web-savvy agents John and Sandra, who offer a long list of options, from booze cruises and golf to visits to remote Huichol mountain villages and hot-air ballooning.

Jungle Canopy Tours

At **Canopy Tour Los Veranos** (tel. 322/223-6060, www.canopytours-vallarta .com, $79) you'll enjoy a bird's-eye view and plenty of thrills as you zip from tree to tree through the jungle on cables. Reach it by car or bus, via Highway 200 south, three miles (5 km) past Boca de Tomatlán. At Las Juntas y Los Veranos, turn right onto the dirt side road. Continue about a mile to Canopy Tour Los Veranos at the end of the road.

Alternatively, **Vallarta Adventures** (tel. 322/297-1212, U.S. tel. 888/303-2653, www .vallarta-adventures.com, adults $79) offers perhaps the best of all canopy tours, at its camp nestled in the vine-hung tropical forest foothills along the road to San Sebastián. The actual canopy tour takes you through about 10 sturdy forest perches, via 100- or 200-yard cable rides from perch to perch in a total of about an hour and a half.

TATTOOS

Chances are you'll see a lot of tattoos if you spend much time on the beaches of Puerto Vallarta. There are at least a dozen tattoo parlors in town, frequented by locals and tourists alike. The same rules apply when selecting a tattoo shop in Mexico as do in the United States and elsewhere; make sure the shop is clean, ask to see a portfolio of prior work and watch the artist use a clean needle and appropriate sanitation techniques. All of the tattoo parlors I've personally visited in Puerto Vallarta have met these conditions and I've had some of my own work done right here in town.

As a side note, if you prefer not to have such a permanent reminder of your Puerto Vallarta vacation, you can always get a henna tattoo from one of the wandering beach vendors. Keep in mind that the black henna has been known to cause allergic reactions in some people, including red, scaly patches and intense itching. Of course, by the time you've gotten the tattoo and the henna has dried, it will be too late.

If you are overly concerned about your reaction, ask for a small daub in an inconspicuous spot. If you have no adverse effects within 24 hours, you should be okay for a full tattoo of your choosing the next day. To make sure that your tattoo lasts, you can negotiate with the artist to return the morning of your departure to touch it up. I've never had anyone fail to show up at the appointment time and place and the tattoo should last for a week or two after you return home.

Some of the more popular tattoo studios include:

- **Mystique Tattoo,** (Guerrero 169, tel. 322/222-9500) located in El Centro, two blocks south of the Plaza de Armas.

- **Mayas Tattoo,** (Plaza las Glorias, next door to Gold's Gym, tel. 322/137-2678) in the hotel zone.

- **Chapa Tattoo,** (Basilio Badilla 313, tel. 322/222-4155) in the Romantic Zone.

- **Rasta Tattoo,** (Av. Mexico 1108, tel. 322/222-1952) in El Centra, one block south of Ley's.

Accommodations

In Puerto Vallarta you can get any type of lodging you want at nearly any price. The location sets the tone, however. The relaxed, relatively tranquil but charming neighborhood south of the Río Cuale (especially around Avenida Olas Altas) has many budget and moderately priced hotels, apartments, and condos within easy walking distance of restaurants, shopping, and services. Virtually all hotels welcome guests regardless of race, religion, or sexual preference. A very few do not accept families with young children. Many of the best-buy small hotels are very close to, if not right on, lively Playa los Muertos. While no strict dividing line separates the types of available lodgings, hotels generally offer rooms with maximum service (front desk, daily cleaning, restaurant,

pool) but no kitchens for shorter-term guests, while apartments and condos virtually always offer multiple-room furnished kitchen units at greatly reduced daily rates for longer stays. If you're staying more than two weeks, you'll save money and also enjoy more of the comforts of home in a good apartment or condo rental. You can often find good deals and last minute specials on popular rental sites like www.vrbo.com or on the PuertoVallarta Craigslist website at pv.craigslist.org.

One thing to note is that in Mexico, the beds are hard. You may find little difference between beds at a $50 per night hotel versus a $200 per night hotel, save for the linens. At the higher end hotels, they may offer egg-crate foam pads for the mattress, but if you are used to a soft mattress or a sensitive sleeper, you should call ahead to make sure and skip the low budget hotels.

ZONA ROMANTÍCA
Under $50

On Avenida Fco. I. Madero, just downhill from the corner of Jacarandas, stand Puerto Vallarta's most recommendable economy hotels. These bare-bulb—but respectable and clean—one-star hostelries have tiers of interior rooms with few amenities other than four walls, a shower bath (check for hot water), and a double bed. The prices, however, are certainly right. The best of the bunch are probably **Hotel Ana Liz** (Madero 429, tel. 322/222-1757, $25 s, $35 d) and **Hotel Bernal** (tel. 322/222-3605, $28 s, $33 d), next door. Also, you might check out **Hotel Cartagena** (Madero 426, tel. 322/222-6914, $28 s, $32 d), across the street.

Also especially worthy is the slightly pricier **Hotel Villa del Mar** (Madero 440, tel. 322/222-0785, www.hvilladelmar.com), whose longtime loyal patrons swear by it as the one remnant of Puerto Vallarta "like it used to be." The austere dark-wood lobby on the corner of Madero and Jacarandas leads to a double warren of clean upstairs rooms, arranged in interior and exterior sections. (Above that is a top-floor cluster of attractive budget-priced studio kitchenette apartments. The 30 or so exterior-facing rooms (about $30 s, $36 d, $42 t year-round) are generally the best, with nondeluxe but comfortable amenities including queen-size beds, traditional-style dark-wood decor, ceiling fans, more light and quiet, and in some cases even private street-view balconies. The less desirable interior-wing rooms (about $28 s, $32 d, $38 t year-round), by contrast, have windows that line walkways around a sound-reflective, and therefore often noisy, interior tiled atrium, and guests must draw curtains for quiet and privacy. Rooms vary, so inspect a few before you decide. No TV, phones, or pool are available, and credit cards are not accepted.

The **Hotel Yasmín** (B. Badillo 168, tel. 322/222-0087, about $50 s, $60 d with fan, add $10 for a/c, year-round), downhill at Pino Suárez, a block from the beach, offers another budget choice. The Yasmín's positives are its plant-festooned inner patio and Café de Olla, a good restaurant next door. Its negative (whenever I've been there) is its glum management. Although the three stories of plain rooms are clean, many are small. Inspect before you pay. You can compensate by renting one of the lighter, more secluded sunny-side upper rooms.

$50-100

Just across the Avenida Vallarta (downstream) bridge stands the renovated **Hotel Encino-Suites Plaza del Río** (Av. Juárez 122, tel. 322/222-0051 or 322/222-0280, toll-free Mex. tel. 01-800/326-3600, fax 322/222-2573, www.hotelencino.com). The lobby opens into a pleasant patio with tropical fountain, enfolded by tiers of 75 rooms that go for about $56 s, $62 d high season; ask for a low-season *paquete* (discount package). Inside, the rooms are tastefully decorated in blue and white, many with ocean or city-hill views. Many large, similarly appointed one- and two-bedroom kitchenette suites (about $82 low season, $110 high) are available in an adjoining building. The hotel climaxes at the rooftop pool and sundeck, where guests enjoy a panoramic view of the surrounding jungly hills above the white-stucco-and-tile Old Town, spreading to the blue, mountain-rimmed bay. Monthly rental discounts can run as much as 50 percent, and amenities include air-conditioning in rooms (no a/c in suites), phones, security boxes, and restaurant/bar.

A few blocks farther south on Playa los Muertos, the seven-story apartment-style **Hotel-Suites Emperador** (Amapas 114, tel. 322/222-5143, fax 322/222-1767, www.hotelemperadorpv.com) offers oceanview lodgings at moderate prices. Although the hotel fronts the beach, it has no beach entrance nor beach facilities. It does, however, offer guests a small but inviting pool and patio half a block away. The hotel, in two sections (formerly Hotel Las

Glorias and Suites Emperador, respectively) on opposite sides of Amapas, offers either hill views or ocean views ($72 d standard–$243 d master suite high season), with air-conditioning, phones, TV, and credit cards accepted.

Head directly upstream to the Avenida Insurgentes bridge and you'll find **Casa del Puente** (Av. Insurgentes, tel. 322/222-0749, U.S. tel. 415/513-5313 or 888/666-9540, www.casadelpuente.com) tucked on the north riverbank upstream from a bridge-front sidewalk restaurant. The elegant villa/home of Molly Stokes, grandniece of celebrated naturalist John Muir, Casa del Puente is a lovely home away from home. Antiques and art adorn the spacious, high-beamed-ceiling rooms, while outside its windows and around the decks great trees spread, tropical birds flit and chatter, jungle hills rise, and the river gurgles, hidden from the city hubbub nearby. Molly offers three lodging options: an upstairs riverview room with big bath and double bed ($40 low season, $60 high), a spacious one-bedroom/one-bath apartment ($50 d low season, $90 d high), and a two-bedroom/two-bath apartment ($60 d low, $95 d high), with wireless Internet access. Discounts may be negotiated, depending upon season and length of stay. Reserve early for the winter season.

Right across the street, check out **Casa María Elena** (Francisca Rodríguez 163, tel. 322/222-0113, fax 322/223-1380, mariazs@prodigy.net.mx, $50 low season, $75 high). Here, eight attractive fan-only brick-and-tile units stand in a four-story stack on a quiet, cobbled side street just a block and a half from the beach. The immaculate, light, and spacious units have living room with TV, bedroom, and modern kitchenettes (toaster oven and coffeemaker). A one-week rental gets a 10 percent discount; longer-term discounts are negotiable. Guests also enjoy the option of in-house Internet access and three weekly hours of free Spanish language or cooking lessons taught by the owner, María Elena Zermeño.

Recent renovations have boosted the venerable ◖ **Hotel Eloisa** (Calle Lázaro Cárdenas 170, tel./fax 322/222-6465, 322/222-0286, or 322/223-3650, www.hoteleloisa.com) from ho-hum to invitingly attractive. Find it two blocks south of the river, on the quiet, bus-free north (cul-de-sac) side of Plaza Lázaro Cárdenas. The hotel's five floors of approximately 75 rooms ($55 d low season, $75 d high for rooms with a/c) and kitchenette studios and suites ($20 more) enclose an appealingly light and airy inner atrium. Downstairs, past the small lobby, guests enjoy a modest restaurant/bar and a small but inviting pool patio. Upstairs, standard-grade rooms are decorated with white tile floors, pastel bedspreads, king-size (or a pair of double) beds, modern shower baths, and pleasingly traditional wood furniture and doors. Many rooms open to sunny balconies with a view of the plaza. Studios and suites are similarly decorated but larger, with kitchenettes, one or two bedrooms, and a living/dining room. A breezy rooftop sundeck with a view completes the attractive picture. All rooms have satellite TV and air-conditioning or fans (or both), and it's only a block from the beach. Discounts for long-term rentals are negotiable.

Another good choice, two blocks uphill from the beach in the heart of the Olas Altas neighborhood, is the **Hotel Vallarta Sun** (Francisca Rodríguez 169, tel./fax 322/223-1523, vallartasun@usa.net, $65 d daily, $1,200/month year-round). Here, about 20 spacious rooms with balconies overlook a sunny pool patio. Inside, rooms are clean, attractive, and comfortable, with modern bathrooms and queen-size beds.

The **Hotel Los Arcos Vallarta** (M. Dieguez 171, tel. 322/222-0712, www.playalosarcos.com/losarcosvallarta, $62 d low season, $99 d high) is two blocks south, on a quiet cul-de-sac. Its amenities include a rooftop pool patio with a city and hill view. The Arcos Vallarta (formerly Hotel Fontana) is a sister property of (and is reservable through) the Hotel Playa Los Arcos (described later in this section), and has 42 thoughtfully furnished pastel rooms built around a soaring interior atrium; credit cards are accepted.

Vacationers who need beachfront ambience often pick the all-inclusive **Hotel San Marino**

(Rudolfo Gómez 111, tel. 322/222-1555 or 322/222-3050, www.hotelsanmarino.com), right in the middle of the Playa los Muertos action. The San Marino's soaring *palapa* restaurant patio opens to an oceanfront pool and courtyard with a sundeck. Occupants of all 160 renovated, marble-floored, pastel-and-white rooms ($90 d low season, $100 d high) and suites ($110 d low season, $125 d high) enjoy city, mountain, or ocean views, with air-conditioning, cable TV, phones, and access to the bar and two restaurants.

A major Olas Altas neighborhood activity hub is the **Hotel Playa Los Arcos** (middle of the block between Calles Basilio Badillo and M. Dieguez), a favorite of a generation of savvy American and Canadian winter vacationers. The Playa Los Arcos (Olas Altas 380, tel. 322/222-0583 or 322/222-7100, U.S. tel. 800/648-2403, Can. tel. 888/729-9590, fax 322/222-7104, www.playalosarcos.com) is the flagship of a triad that includes the nearby Hotel Los Arcos Vallarta and the apartments at Suites Los Arcos; it handles bookings for all three and guests are welcome to enjoy all of the Playa Los Arcos's leisurely beachfront facilities.

All three of these lodgings have swimming pools and many comfortable, tastefully decorated, air-conditioned rooms with TV, phones, and small refrigerators in many rooms. The mecca, however, is the bustling Playa Los Arcos, with its compact palm- and vine-decorated inner pool patio, restaurant with salad bar, live music every night, and beach chairs in the sand beneath shady palms or golden sun. The Hotel Playa Los Arcos's 175 rooms rent from about $90 d low season, approximately $100 d high season, for economy-grade rooms. More spacious superior-grade rooms, some with ocean views, run about $117 d low season, $125 d high season; credit cards are accepted. Many guests pay much less by pre-booking bargain air-hotel packages through travel agents or the Internet. Moreover, during low season (May–mid-July, Sept., Oct., and sometimes Nov., and even Jan.) all three hotels often offer special promotions, such as a 20

percent senior discount, two kids under 12 free when sharing a room with parents, long-term discounts, or third night free.

The family-friendly 🅒 **Hotel Tropicana** (Amapas 214, tel. 322/222-0912, fax 322/222-6737, www.hoteltropicana.com, standard room $95 d low season, superior $20 more, with breakfast; add about 15 percent high season) is one of the plushest hotels on Playa los Muertos. Guests benefit both from spacious rooms in a brand-new wing and an airy pool patio and a flock of beachfront amenities—sundeck, restaurant, volleyball, and shady *palapas*—that spread all the way to the surf. Upstairs, virtually all of the comfortable, older semideluxe standard-grade rooms and the newer superior-grade deluxe rooms enjoy private balconies and ocean vistas. All rooms have air-conditioning and cable TV, and credit cards are accepted. It won't hurt to ask for a promotional price *(promoción)*, especially weekdays and low season.

Over $100

The all-inclusive family-friendly **Club Meza del Mar** (Amapas 380, tel. 322/222-4888, fax 322/222-2308, www.clubmeza.com) that stairsteps uphill from Playa los Muertos is a good choice for those looking for an affordable resort experience. A host of longtime returnees swear by the hotel's food, service, and friendly company of fellow guests, who, during the winter, seem to be divided equally between Americans and English- and French-speaking Canadians. The Meza del Mar's 127 rooms and suites are distributed among two adjacent buildings: the Main Tower, a high-rise with view overlooking the pool deck, and the Ocean Building, a three-story tier with views right over the beach. Guests in the preferred rooms, most of which are in the Ocean Building, enjoy private balconies and the sound of the waves outside their window. Other guests are quite happy with the expansive ocean view from the top floors of the Main Tower.

The rooms themselves, while not super deluxe, are comfortably furnished, many in the Mexican *equipal* style of handcrafted leather furniture. All rooms have air-conditioning, but no TV or phones, and only limited wheel-chair access; all are clean and semideluxe, but they vary, so ask to see others if your assignment isn't satisfactory. Rates vary according to season and grade of room and include all food (not gourmet, but wholesome), drinks, and entertainment in the hotel's restaurants, bars, pools, and beachfront club. All-inclusive rate during the high season runs about $102 per person per night for double occupancy for a comfortable standard-grade room and $126 per person per nightfor a semideluxe oceanview one-bedroom suite. The Meza del Mar website offers many promotions and discounts for both high and low season.

Back near Avenida Olas Altas, find the apartment-style **Suites Los Arcos** (on M. Dieguez, book through Hotel Playa Los Arcos, $113 d low season, $135 d high), with a long blue pool patio and an airy sitting area to one side of the lobby. Upstairs are 15 studio apartments, simply but attractively furnished in tile, wood furniture, and pastel-blue sofas and bedspreads. All have baths (some with shower bath), king-size beds, furnished kitchenette, air-conditioning, TV, and private balcony.

EL CENTRO

Hotels generally get more luxurious and expensive the farther north of the Río Cuale you look. The far northern section, on the marina's ocean side, with a line-up of several big international chain hotels, is isolated several miles from downtown and has only a narrow beach, often with more rocks than sand. Most of the central part of downtown, which begins at the Río Cuale and stretches for about a mile north along the Malecón, has no good beach except at the far north end and is generally too noisy and congested for comfortable lodgings, with some exceptions.

$50-100

One of the sprinkling of good downtown hotel options is the longtime **Hotel Los Cuatro Vientos** (Matamoros 520, tel./fax 322/222-0161 or 322/222-2831, www.che-zelena.com), perched in the quiet, picturesque

hillside neighborhood above and a few blocks north of the main town church. The 16 rooms and suites are tucked in tiers above a flowery patio and restaurant Chez Elena, and beneath a rooftop panoramic-view sundeck. The fan-only units are simply but attractively decorated in colonial style, with tile, brick, and traditional furniture and crafts. Rates (excluding Dec. 15–Jan. 6) run about $68 s or d, $78 for a suite October 15–June 15, $35 and $50 other times, with continental breakfast (during Oct.–June high season only) and a small pool; credit cards are accepted. Rooms vary, so check more than one before paying.

Located right on the main highway at the southern end of the Malecón is the **Rio Hotel** (Morelos 70, tel. 322/222-0366, www.hotel-rio.com.mx). Significant remodeling was happening during my visit, but the rooms seemed simple and clean. The courtyard offers a nice swimming pool and the popular **Coexist Café** is located here, a good place to enjoy a happy hour drink or a traditional Mexican breakfast. The rooms include air-conditioning, telephones, and cable TV. Some rooms are available with kitchenettes for longer stays. Noise, both construction and traffic, are likely here but the price is hard to beat. Rooms start at $50 during the high season and place you in the heart of the action of both the Romantic Zone and the Malecón.

At the north end of the Malecón stands one of Puerto Vallarta's popular old mainstays, the homey beachfront **Hotel Rosita** (Díaz Ordaz 901, corner of 31 de Octubre, tel./fax 322/223-2185, 322/223-2000, or 322/223-2151, www.hotelrosita.com). It's centered around a grassy, palm-shadowed oceanview pool, patio, and restaurant, with plenty of space for relaxing and socializing. Most of the spacious rooms, of *típica* Mexican tile, white stucco, and wood, either look out to the ocean, or down upon the tranquil patio scene, while some, to be avoided if possible, border the noisy, smoggy main street. An unfortunate, but probably necessary, wire security fence mars the ocean view from the patio. Egress to the nearest beach, Playa Camarón, is through a south-side gate.

The Rosita's 115 rooms ($66–95 d low season, $95–140 high, depending on location) include fans or air-conditioning, security boxes, and a bar; credit cards are accepted.

$100-150

The **Hotel Buenaventura** (Av. México 1301, tel. 322/226-7000, toll-free Mex. tel. 01-800/713-2888, U.S. tel. 888/859-9439, fax 322/222-3546, www.hotelbuenaventura.com.mx), on the beach several blocks farther north, where the airport boulevard narrows as it enters Old Town, is one of Puerto Vallarta's few north-side close-in deluxe hotels. The lobby rises to an airy wood-beamed atrium and then opens toward the beach through a jungle walkway festooned with giant hanging leafy philodendrons and exotic palms. At the beachfront Los Tucanes Beach Club, a wide, palm-silhouetted pool patio borders a line of shade *palapas* along the creamy yellow-gray-sand beach. Most of the smallish rooms, decorated in wood, tile, and earth-tone drapes and bedspreads, open to petite, private ocean-facing balconies. The 236 rooms ($130 d low season, $180 d high) include air-conditioning, phones, buffet breakfast, restaurant, bar, and live music in season; credit cards are accepted.

Over $150

Directly next door is the sister property of the Buenaventura, the **Villa Premiere Hotel** (tel. 322/226 7040, www.premiereonline.com.mx). The Villa Premiere is an adults-only hotel, with no one under 16 years of age admitted. The rooms are very comfortable and tastefully decorated and include such upscale luxuries as a pillow menu, aromatherapy selection, and plasma televisions. The hotel is very peaceful, with trickling fountains and staff masseuses on hand to give complimentary five-minute massages to guests. Rates begin at about $308 for the European plan during high season. Add an additional $80 per day per person for all-inclusive, which includes the restaurants at the Buenaventura as well.

Only superlatives can possibly describe the ▐ **Hacienda San Ángel** (Miramar 336,

tel. 322/222-2692 or 322/221-2277, U.S. tel. 415/738-8220, fax 322/223-1941, www.haciendasanangel.com), life project of personable owner-manager Janice Chatterton. She invites her guests to enjoy her Hacienda, once the house of celebrated actor Richard Burton, as their home away from home in Puerto Vallarta. Beginning in the early 1990s, Janice bought the three adjacent houses, which, with consummate design and decorative skill, she integrated into her present grand mansion.

Janice has spared little to adorn her abode with a heavenly choir of cherubs, saints, adored Madonnas, and a veritable museum of handsome old-world antique furnishings. She and her four-dog family invite visitors to enjoy any one of 14 uniquely designed and decorated suites ($320–700 d high season), many with airy town and ocean vistas. She also offers a cluster of four of her rooms as Villa La Luna, for a group of up to 10 people. Call for rates. All accommodations come with fans, air-conditioning, cable TV, DVD player, phone, continental breakfast, wireless Internet, and a load of luxurious extras, including a full-service gourmet restaurant and two lovely heated pools. Sorry, no children under 16. (You may also reserve at Hacienda San Ángel through Mexico Boutique Hotels, toll-free Mex. tel. 01-800/508-7923, U.S./Can. tel. 800/728-9098, www.mexicoboutiquehotels.com.)

ZONA HOTELERA

Near the north end of the downtown Malecón, where the good beach resumes at Playa Camarones, so do the beachfront hotels. They continue, dotting the tranquil, golden strands of Playa las Glorias, Playa los Tules, and Playa de Oro. On these beaches are the plush hotels (actually self-contained resorts) from which you must have wheels to escape to the shopping, restaurants, and the piquant sights and sounds of old Puerto Vallarta.

Puerto Vallarta's plush hostelries vary widely, and higher tariffs do not guarantee quality. Nevertheless, some of Pacific Mexico's best-buy luxury gems glitter among the 20-odd hotels lining Puerto Vallarta's north-end Zona

Hotelera beaches. The prices listed are rack rates—the highest prices paid by walk-in customers. Much cheaper—with as much as a 50 percent discount—airfare-lodging packages are often available, especially during low season (Jan., May and June, and Sept.–Nov.). Get yourself a good buy by shopping around among hotels, the Internet, and travel agents several weeks before departure.

$50-100

At the far north end, just before the cruiseship Terminal Maritima, stands the neocolonial **Hacienda Hotel and Spa** (Paseo de la Marina, tel. 322/226-6667, fax 322/226-6672, www.haciendaonline.com.mx). One of the Zona Hotelera's best-buy options, the Hacienda offers a load of amenities at moderate rates. Its 155 rooms ($90 d low season, $135 d high; all-inclusive option is currently $35/day pp additional), arranged in low-rise tiers, enfold a leafy green patio/garden, graced by a blue free-form pool and a slender, rustic shade *palapa*. On one side, water gurgles from a neo-antique aqueduct, while guests linger at the adjacent airy restaurant. The rooms are spacious, with high hand-hewn-beam ceilings, marble floors, and rustic-chic tile-and-brick baths, and include air-conditioning, phones, cable TV, some wheelchair access, and credit cards accepted. The only slight drawback to all this is guests must walk a couple of short blocks to the beach. Spa services, such as a *temascal* sauna, facials, many massage options, reflexology, and aromatherapy, are abundant but cost extra.

$100-150

The majority of the hotels in the Hotel Zone will fall into this price range, especially if you book in advance online. You can often get airfare and lodging specials through travel websites that offer big discounts at resorts and usually include the all-inclusive package. One all-inclusive resort to consider is **Las Palmas by the Sea** (Km 2.5 Blv. Fco. Medina Ascencio, tel. 322/226-1220, fax 322/226-1268, www.laspalmasresort.com).

Past the reception, an airy, rustic *palapa* shelters the lobby, which opens to a palmy beachside pool patio. Here on the wide, sparkling Playa las Glorias, opportunities for aquatic sports are at their best, with the hotel's sport shop (snorkeling, fishing, Hobie Cat sailboats, parasailing) right on the beachfront. The 225 rooms, with all food, drinks, and in-house entertainment, run about $90 per person low season, $177 high; kids are discounted depending on their ages. Guests in most rooms enjoy private oceanview balconies and comfortable semideluxe furnishings, with air-conditioning, phones, TV, restaurant, snack bar, bars, pool, and parking; credit cards are accepted. Check the website for promotional packages, such as kids under nine free, or third night free during times of low occupancy (Sept.–Nov. and May–June).

A couple of blocks farther south, the **Hotel Plaza Pelícanos** (Called Diego Rivera 120, , tel. 322/224-1010, toll-free Mex. tel. 01-800/713-2152, fax 322/224-3618, www.plazapelicanos.com.mx), a Mexican-owned hotel, caters mostly to North American clientele during the winter, and Mexican tourists during national holidays, before Easter week, and in August. The Hotel Plaza Pelícanos is divided perfunctorily into sections I and II. Although tariffs are the same in both, the preferred section is II (the graceful, former Hotel Plaza las Glorias), where a blue swimming pool meanders beneath a manicured patio/grove of rustling palms. Behind the Spanish-style stucco, brick, and tile facade, the luxurious rooms overlook the patio and ocean from small view balconies, and are tile-floored, with decor in dark wood, white stucco, and blue and pastels. All 237 rooms rent, all-inclusive only, for about $145 s, $130 d per person low season, and $170 s and $155 d high, with air-conditioning, cable TV, two pools, bars, beachfront jogging track, restaurants, and parking.

Next door to the south, find the **Hotel Canto del Sol** (Jose Clemente Orozco 125, tel. 322/226-0123, ext. 4142, 4143, or 4144, fax 322/224-4437 or 322/224-5236, www.cantodelsol.com). During the high winter season, Hotel Canto del Sol (formerly Hotel Continental Plaza) bustles all day with tennis in the eight-court John Newcombe Tennis Club next door; aerobics, water polo, and volleyball in the big central pool; and parasailing, jetboating, and sailboarding from the golden Playa las Glorias. The luxurious but smallish rooms ($120 d low season, $150 d high, all-inclusive), decorated in soothing pastels, open to balconies overlooking the broad palm-decorated patio. All-inclusive packages cover all in-house food, drinks, and entertainment. Fourth night is often gratis, especially during the May–June and September–October low seasons. Amenities include air-conditioning, shows, water aerobics, tennis, kid's club, restaurants, bars, sauna, hot tub, exercise room, wheelchair access, and parking.

For another bountiful option, return a mile north to the **Hotel NH Krystal** (Av. de las Garzas s/n, tel. 322/224-0202, toll-free Mex. tel. 01-800/903-3300, U.S. tel. 888/726-0528, Can. tel. 866/299-7096, fax 322/226-0738, www.nh-hotels.com). Stay here and you get more than a mere hotel: This palmy, roomy low-rise resort-village (one of the few Puerto Vallarta luxury resorts designed by and for Mexicans) is exactly what a Mexican Walt Disney would have built. Don't be put off by the rather gloomy lobby (the new European owners are trying to save electricity), just feast your eyes on the amenities spread over its 34 beachside acres: a flock of deluxe garden bungalows that open onto private pool patios, a Porfirian bandstand that stands proudly at the center, while nearby a colonial-style aqueduct gushes water into a pool at the edge of a serene, spacious palm-shaded park. Guests who prefer a livelier environment can have it. Dancing, in season, goes on in the lobby or beside the huge meandering beachside pool, where the music is anything but serene. The NH Krystal's 460 deluxe rooms and suites ($91 d low season, $150 d high, two kids under 12 free) include air-conditioning, phones, cable TV, 44 pools (no joke), multiple restaurants, and all sports.

Over $150

Half a mile south, the ◖ **Hotel Fiesta Americana Puerto Vallarta** (P.O. Box 270, Puerto Vallarta, Jalisco 48300, tel. 322/226-2100, U.S./Can. tel. 800/FIESTA-1 or 800/343-7821, fax 322/224-2108, www.fiestaamericana.com) is for many the best hotel in town. The lobby *palapa,* the world's largest, is an attraction unto itself. Its 10-story palm-thatch chimney draws air upward, creating a continuously cool breeze through the open-air reception. Outside, the high-rise rampart of oceanview rooms ($150 d low season, $250 d high, two kids under 12 free) overlooks a pool and garden of earthly delights, complete with a gushing pool fountain, water volleyball, swim-up bar, and in-pool recliners. Beyond spreads a 150-foot-wide strip of wave-washed yellow sand. Amenities include air-conditioning, TV, phones, all sports, aerobics, three restaurants, huge pool, three bars, wheelchair access, and parking.

Next door to the north, the all-inclusive **Hola Puerto Vallarta,** formerly the Qualton Club (Km 2.5, Av. de las Palmas s/n, tel. 322/224-4446, toll-free Mex. tel. 01-800/327-0000, fax 322/224-4447, www.holapuertovallarta.com), offers an attractive all-inclusive option for vacationers who enjoy lots of food, fun, and company. On a typical winter-season day, hundreds of fellow sunbathing guests line the rather cramped poolside, while a few steps away dozens more relax beneath shady beachfront *palapas.* Nights glow with beach buffet theme dinners—Italian, Mexican, Chinese, and more—for hundreds, followed by shows where guests often become part of the entertainment. The list goes on—constant food, open bars, complete gym and spa, tennis by night or day, scuba lessons, volleyball, water sports, free disco, golf privileges, stress therapy, yoga, aerobics galore—all included at no extra charge. If you want relief from the hubbub, you can always escape to the greener, more spacious Fiesta Americana poolside next door. The hotel's 320 rooms ($110 pp low season, $140 high, kids 7–11 $30, 12–17 $50), all with private view balconies, are luxuriously decorated in pastels and include air-conditioning, cable TV, phone, and wheelchair access; credit cards are accepted.

SOUTH OF TOWN
$50-100

Take a bus or drive the Manzanillo Highway 200 (the southward extension of Insurgentes) about a mile south of town and your reward will be the **Hotel Playa Conchas Chinas** (P.O. Box 346, Puerto Vallarta, Jalisco 48390, tel./ fax 322/221-5770 or 322/221-5763, www.hotelconchaschinas.com), which offers a bit of charm and luscious seaside ambience at moderate rates. The stucco-and-brick complex rambles several levels down a palm-shaded hillside (with dozens of stairs) to a petite pool patio overlooking an intimate cove on Conchas Chinas beach. Here, gulls soar, pelicans dive, palm trees sway, and sandy crescents nestle between tidepool-dotted sandstone outcroppings. The 19 lodgings themselves come in two grades. Studio superior rooms ($90 d low season, $110 d high) are spacious, decorated in Mexican traditional tile-brick, and furnished in brown wood with kitchenette and tub bath; most have an ocean view. Studio deluxe grade ($115 d low, $130 d high) adds a bedroom, oceanview patio/balcony, and a whirlpool tub. Amenities include air-conditioning, phones, and the romantic El Set sunset restaurant above and a beachfront breakfast café below; there is no elevator or wheelchair access. Credit cards are accepted. Low-season discounts, such as one day free for a four-day stay or two days free for a one-week stay, are sometimes offered.

Over $100

Another mile south, you can enjoy the extravagant isolation of the **Dreams Puerto Vallarta Resort and Spa** (reserve at Playa de las Estacas, tel. 322/226-5000, U.S./Can. tel. 866/2DREAMS, fax 322/221-6000, www.dreamsresorts.com) at correspondingly extravagant prices. The region's first world-class hotel, the Dreams Puerto Vallarta (formerly the Hotel Camino Real) has aged gracefully. It's luxuriously set in a lush tropical valley, with polished wooden walkways that wind along a beachside garden intermingled with blue swimming pools. The totally self-contained resort on a secluded, seasonally narrow strip of golden-white sand offers a host of vacation delights: luxury view rooms in the main tower ($190 s low season, $265 high) or the Royal Beach Club tower (about $70 more per adult), all in-house food and drinks, water sports, restaurants, bars, live music every evening, shows, and supervised children's activities for one all-inclusive price. Rooms in the Royal Beach Club tower have hot tubs and wheelchair access.

APARTMENTS AND CONDOMINIUMS

Puerto Vallarta abounds with apartments and condominiums, mostly available for one week or more. Many of the best-buy Puerto Vallarta apartments and condos are concentrated in the colorful Olas Altas–Conchas Chinas southside district and high-season rates run from about $500 per month for modest studios to $1,000 and more for three-bedroom houses.

One of the most recommendable local apartment and condo rental agents is friendly **Bayside Properties** (F. Rodríguez 160, tel. 322/223-0898 or 322/223-4418, fax 322/223-0898, dosgatos@pvnet.com.mx, www.baysidepropertiespv.com), a few doors uphill from Avenida Olas Altas in the heart of the Olas Altas district.

Other well-established south-of-Cuale rental agencies that you may find useful are **Tropicasa Realty** (Pulpito 45A, corner of Olas Altas, tel. 322/222-6505, fax 322/222-2555, www.tropicasa.com) and **Tango Rentals** (tel. 322/224-7398, U.S./Can. tel. 310/494-9970, www.tangorentals.com), run by personable Agustín Bas and his partner, Marjorie Torrance. They offer a wide range of vacation rentals, from modest condos to luxurious villas, especially in the intimate south-of-Cuale neighborhood.

Furthermore, a number of U.S.-based agencies specialize in the more luxurious rentals scattered all over the city.

Other apartments are rentable directly

through local managers. The best place to look for rental homes and apartments is **Vacation Rentals by Owner** (www.vrbo.com) or the local Craigslist page under "Vacation Rentals" (pv.craigslist.org). If you are looking for longer term housing or unfurnished places, try the local Spanish language classified guide *Mano a Mano* (www.manoamano.com.mx) which comes out every Thursday and can be purchased at any local newsstand or OXXO convenience store for three pesos.

TRAILER PARKS AND CAMPING

Puerto Vallarta visitors enjoy two good trailer parks. The smallish palm-shaded **Trailer Park El Pescador** (Francia 143, tel. 322/224-2828) is two blocks off the highway on Francia at the corner of Lucerna, a few blocks north of the *libramiento* downtown bypass fork. The 65 spaces (4 blocks from the Playa las Glorias) rent for about $24 per day, with one free day per week, one free week per month; with all hookups, including showers, toilets, long-distance phone access, and launderette. Pets are okay. Luxury hotel pools and good restaurants are nearby.

Farther out, but much more spacious, is **Tacho's Trailer Park** (P.O. Box 315, Puerto Vallarta, Jalisco 48300, tel. 322/224-2163), half a mile from Highway 200 on Avenida Aramara, the road that branches inland across the airport highway from the cruise-ship dock. Tacho's offers a large grassy yard with some palms, bananas, and other trees for shade. The 100 spaces run about $26 per day (one free week on a monthly rental), including all hookups and use of showers, toilets, laundry room, pool and *palapa*, and shuffleboard courts. Pads are paved, and pets are okay.

Other than the trailer parks, Puerto Vallarta has precious few campsites within the city limits. Plenty of camping possibilities exist outside the city, however. Especially inviting are the pearly little beaches, such as Las Ánimas, Quimixto, Caballo, and others that dot the wild coastline between Boca de Tomatlán and Yelapa. *Colectivo* water taxis regularly head for these beaches for about $5 per person from Boca de Tomatlán. Local stores at Quimixto, Las Ánimas, and Boca de Tomatlán can provide water (bring water purification tablets or filter) and basic supplies.

Food

What a lot of people don't realize about Puerto Vallarta is that the city is home to a tremendous number of superb restaurants. Not just the regional specialties of fresh seafood and authentic Mexican food, but of all types. Home to two separate food events during the year, Puerto Vallarta is developing a well-deserved reputation for being a foodie town. From five-star dining to the local corner taco stand, there is something for everyone when it comes to dining in Puerto Vallarta.

Vacationers should avoid the all-inclusive plan at the local resort and opt instead to sample some of the regional fare. While it's easy to find traditional favorites that are common in U.S. restaurants, be sure to try more authentic Mexican food such as the delicious *pozole,* a

soup that you can find in nearly any Mexican restaurant, especially on weekends. Made from chicken and cracked corn and topped with cabbage, cilantro and onion, it can be as much as a meal as it is a soup.

COFFEEHOUSES AND BREAKFAST
Zona Romantíca

Good coffee is plentiful in Puerto Vallarta, where many cafés roast from their own private sources of beans. The best coffeehouses are sprinkled along Avenida Olas Altas, just a block from Playa los Muertos. Here, coffee and book lovers get the best of both worlds at **Page in the Sun** (corner of Olas Altas and M. Dieguez, tel. 322/223-1273, 7 A.M.–midnight daily), diagonally across from Hotel Playa Olas Altas. At Page in the Sun, longtimers sip coffee and play chess while others enjoy their pick of lattes, cappuccinos, ice cream, muffins, and walls of used paperbacks and magazines.

Exactly one block farther up Olas Altas, take a table at the **Café San Ángel** (corner of Rodríguez, 8 A.M.–10 P.M. daily, $3–5) and soak up the sidewalk scene. Here, you can enjoy breakfast, a sandwich, or dessert and good coffee in a dozen varieties.

For fancier offerings and refined ambience, go to the Old Europe–style **Café Maximilian** (380 Olas Altas, tel. 322/222-5058, 8 A.M.– midnight daily, closed Sun. in low season) on the sidewalk in front of Hotel Playa los Arcos. For breakfast, **La Casa de Los Hot Cakes** (Basilio Badillo 289, btwn. I. Vallarta and Constitución, tel. 322/222-6272, 8 A.M.–2 P.M. Tues.–Sun., $4–6), skillfully orchestrated by personable travel writer turned restaurateur Memo Barroso, has become a Puerto Vallarta institution. Besides bountiful Mexican and North American breakfasts—orange juice or fruit, eggs, toast, and hash browns for about $5—Memo offers an indulgent list of pancakes. Try his nut-topped, peanut butter–filled O. Henry chocolate pancakes, for example. For lighter eaters, vegetarian and less indulgent options are available. Memo's latest love is coffee. If you're lucky enough to be near La Casa de Los Hot Cakes at the right time, simply follow your nose to the source of the heavenly aroma of his roasting beans—premium estate-grown only, from Oaxaca, Chiapas, and Veracruz.

Enjoy an affordable and authentic Mexican breakfast at **Fredy's Tucán** (next door to Hotel Posada de Roger, on the corner of Basilio Badillo and Vallarta, tel. 322/223-0778, 8 A.M.–4 A.M. daily). Fredy's is a favorite of locals and tourists alike, frequently voted "best breakfast" in Puerto Vallarta. Although they do serve lunch and dinner as well as have a full bar, breakfast is the favorite and is served until 2:30 P.M. every day.

El Centro

Just behind the Blockbuster video on Highway 200 is **Café Canela** (Lucerna 107, tel. 322/293-5423) where you can enjoy a variety of coffee drinks in their comfortable lounge setting. **Café Van Gogh** inside of Plaza Caracol is another good bet for fresh deli sandwiches, steaming espresso drinks and free Wi-Fi with purchase.

Marina

Along the walkway surrounding the marina, you will find two coffee shops that serve light meals and freshly made coffee drinks. The first is **The Coffee Cup** (tel. 322/221-2517) which also houses some beautiful art. Customers are invited to use the free computers and Internet available, make long distance calls at reduced rates, and view the lively and interesting art adorning the walls. A bit farther along the marina Malecón is **Once Upon a Bean,** a used bookstore and coffee shop that also offers Internet and computers for customer use.

STALLS AND SNACKS
Zona Romantíca

A number of food stalls concentrate along Avenida Constitución, Francisco Madero, and Pino Suárez just south of the Río Cuale; several others cluster on the side-street corners of Avenida Olas Altas a few blocks away.

One of the stalls, the **Calamar Aventurero** (The Frisky Squid, tel. 322/222-6479, 9 A.M.–7 P.M. Mon.–Sat., $2–6), has become a very popular open-air seafood restaurant, at the corner of Aquiles Serdán and Constitución. Choose from smoked marlin tacos, ceviche, fish burritos, and much more.

Some of the most colorful, untouristed places to eat in town are, paradoxically, at the tourist-mecca Mercado Municipal on the Río Cuale, at the Avenida Insurgentes bridge. The *fondas* (7 A.M.–6 P.M. daily) tucked on the upstairs floor (climb the street-side staircase) specialize in steaming homestyle soups, fish, meat, tacos, *moles,* and chiles rellenos ($2–4). Point out your order to the cook and take a seat at the cool, riverview seating area.

Mango-on-a-stick makes a delicious Puerto Vallarta treat.

For some light Asian fare, stop into Plaza Romy (Vallarta 228, corner of Madero) and get some pot stickers or salad rolls at **Mami's Cucina Asiatica.** Mami's also serves up shrimp and chicken tacos, teriyaki chicken and other lunch or snack fare.

El Centro

Although food stalls are less numerous north of the Río Cuale, you can fill up quite well with the sprinkling of evening taco, hot dog, and sweet corn *(elote)* stands around the downtown plaza.

Alternatively, try **Tuti Fruti** *lonchería* (corner of Morelos and Corona, tel. 322/222-9621, 8 A.M.–11 P.M. Mon.–Sat., $3–4), an inviting nook (bus noise notwithstanding) for a refreshing snack, especially while sightseeing or shopping around the Malecón. You could even eat breakfast, lunch, and dinner there, starting with juice and granola or eggs in the morning, a *torta* and a *licuado* during the afternoon, and an *hamburguesa* for an evening snack.

Pepe's Tacos (Honduras 173, tel. 322/223-1703, across from the Pemex gas station, 1 P.M.–6 A.M. rumored to have the b Puerto Vallarta. This taurant offers many (all at a reasonable pric. try the tacos. *Tacos al pastor* are ma slow roasted rotisserie pork and served with a bit of roasted pineapple, onions and cilantro. Top with fresh salsa. At less than $1 a taco, a family can have a very affordable lunch here. Pepe's is also open late night and is a great place to grab some tacos on the way home from the clubs.

Directly next door to Pepe's is **El Tacón de Marlin** (corner of Honduras and Peru) where seafood lovers cannot miss the *robalo con camaron* burrito; a large flour tortilla stuffed with bacon-wrapped marlin and fresh shrimp ($7). Tacón de Marlin has two other locations as well; one is directly across from the airport on the main highway and great to stop in to before you hop on a flight home.

Zona Hotelera

Just down the street from Wal-Mart on Avenida Prisciliano Sánchez is **Taquitos Roque** (across from Elektra, under the yellow awning) another safe bet for delicious *tacos al pastor* and *queso fundido*. Stop here on your way to or from Pitillal.

Marina

While in the marina, be sure to stop at **Marisma Fish Taco** on the corner of Popa, behind Plaza Neptune. Enjoy crispy, fresh tacos made from deep fried shrimp, dorado, or calamari and wash it down with a frozen lemonade to keep you cool. The tacos are served with lettuce, mayo, and four salsas for you to pick from. Marisma's serves other Mexican food as well, but you can't go wrong with the tacos which are some of the best in town.

RESTAURANTS

If you're coming to Puerto Vallarta mainly for its gourmet offerings, avoid, if possible, September and October, when some of the best restaurants are closed.

Romantíca

Café de Olla (Basilio Badillo 168, tel. 322/223-1626, 9 A.M.–11 P.M. daily except Tues., $6–10) serves affordable and delicious Mexican breakfast, lunch, and dinner. During high season it will be recognizable by the flock of evening customers waiting by the door. Café de Olla serves Mexican food the way it's supposed to be, starting with enough salsa and *totopos* (chips) to make appetizers irrelevant. Your choice comes next—either chicken, ribs, and steaks from the street-front grill—or the savory *antojitos* platters piled with tacos, tostadas, chiles rellenos, or enchiladas by themselves or all together in its unbeatable *plato mexicano*. Prepare by skipping lunch and arriving for an early dinner to give your tummy time to digest it all before bed.

Archie's Wok (Francisca Rodríguez 130, btwn. Av. Olas Altas and the beach, tel. 322/222-0411, 2–11 P.M. Mon.–Sat.) is the founding member of a miniature "gourmet ghetto" that is flourishing in the Olas Altas neighborhood. The founder, now deceased, was John Huston's longtime friend and personal chef. However, Archie's widow, Cindy Alpenia, carries on the culinary mission. A large local following swears by her menu of vegetables, fish, meat, and noodles. Favorites include Thai coconut fish, barbecued ribs Hoisin, and spicy fried Thai noodles ($8–15). Make up a party of three or four, and each order a favorite. Arrive early—there's usually a line by 7:30 P.M. for dinner; Visa is accepted.

Next door to Archie's Wok, **Restaurant Peking** (F. Rodríguez 136, tel. 322/222-2264, noon–10 P.M. daily, $6–8) adds a new, refined version of Chinese cooking to Puerto Vallarta's already rich gastronomic treasury. Perhaps the promise of "the only Chinese-born chef in Puerto Vallarta" is its secret to success, but the food, whether a light lunch of spring rolls and wonton soup or a dinner of stir-fried scallops, kung pao chicken, and a whole fish, is bound to please.

For Mexican food with a twist, try **Banana Cantina** (Amapas 147, above ChocoBanana, tel. 322/222-2114, www.bananacantina.com, 8 A.M.–11 P.M. daily). The shrimp spring rolls make a great shared appetizer ($9) while you'll probably want the bowl of tortilla soup ($6), heaped with fresh avocado, all to yourself. Try the unique brie and papaya quesadillas ($8) or coconut shrimp ($15) for a tropical delight. Owner Debbi Egan routinely holds Wednesday night charity dinners for local nonprofit groups, so be sure to check the website for dates.

If you are looking for the best Baja-style fish tacos in Puerto Vallarta, look no further than **Joe Jack's Fish Shack** (Basilio Badillo 212, tel. 322/222-2099, 12 P.M.–1 A.M. daily). This deceptively small looking restaurant offers a fun, casual atmosphere and two-for-one mojitos in various flavors during happy hour. The fish taco plate is massive ($9) and offers three huge pieces of breaded fish (or you can have it grilled) on flour tortillas. Joe Jack's also has all-you-can-eat fish and chips on Friday. If the downstairs bar is too crowded, don't worry, they have a second level for dining as well.

For some of the best seafood in Vallarta, try **Mariscos Polo's** (Francisco Madero 376 between Insurgentes and Aguacate, tel. 322/306-8944, 12 P.M.–10 P.M., closed Tuesday). Here you will find a dazzling array of seafood dishes to choose from including garlic octopus, fish fillet with mushrooms and white wine, coconut shrimp, and shrimp ceviche. The food is fresh and delicious, and the service is impeccable.

Another good place to feast is **Hacienda Alemana Frankfurt** (Basilio Badillo 378, one-half block uphill from Insurgentes, tel. 322/222-2071, 11 A.M.–10 P.M. daily), the closest thing to a German *biergarten* south of New Braunfels, Texas. Brainchild of master chef Michael Pohl, who started out with a budget hotel in 1995 (which he still operates) and expanded to a garden restaurant a few years later, works his miracle with aplomb. Besides all of the German favorites, such as smoked pork chops with sauerkraut, Wiener schnitzel, bratwurst ($8–13), and melt-in-your-mouth *apfel strudel,* Michael also offers popular French, Italian, and vegetarian specialties. If you can manage to skip lunch, go for the best of all, Michael's all-out effort—a genuine Bavarian buffet (about $18, served Nov.–Apr., 6–10 P.M. Mon., Wed., and Sat., call to confirm).

Encuentros (Lázaro Cárdenas 312, tel. 322/222-0643, www.encuentrosbarlounge.com, 6 P.M.–2 A.M.) offers delicious thin crust pizzas and other delicious options in a refined and relaxed atmosphere. The small tables and quiet setting welcomes conversation and romantic dining. They have an extensive drink menu with a variety of cocktails and martinis. Happy hour is offered daily with two-for-one drinks. Air-conditioned and friendly, Encuentros is cash only.

Tucked back along the Río Cuale is hidden favorite **Red Cabbage Café** (Rivera del Río 204a, tel. 322/223-0411, 5 P.M.–11 P.M.). A small restaurant decorated with a vibrant and eclectic mix of Frida themed decor, the menu is focused on items served at Frida and Diego's wedding feast. Everything is superb but the *chiles en nogada* and chicken mole are widely recognized as divine. The restaurant is smoke-free and cash only. If you are looking for truly authentic Mexican food at a reasonable price, don't miss the Red Cabbage.

A number of good restaurants offer both leisurely ambience and good food right on the bank of the Río Cuale. Moving upstream, start at the **River Café,** beneath the downstream Avenida Vallarta bridge (tel. 322/223-0788, 9 A.M.–10 P.M. daily). The owners have earned a solid reputation with a gorgeously tranquil streambank location, tasty international-style cuisine, and attentive service. Here, breakfast, lunch and sandwiches, and supper (ribs, fish, and Mexican specialties $14–25) are equally enjoyable. During the day, especially when there are cruise ships in port, you will find large groups and families enjoying the restaurant. Relaxing instrumental music afternoons and subdued jazz evenings complete the River Café's attractive picture.

For indulgently rich but good food and luxuriously leafy atmosphere, the showplace **Le Bistro** (Isla Río Cuale 16A, tel. 322/222-0283, 9 A.M.–11:30 P.M. Mon.–Sat., $10–20) is tops, just upstream from the Avenida Insurgentes bridge. The atmosphere is European and elegant and decidedly more upscale and refined than the River Café. The river gurgles past outdoor tables, and giant-leafed plants festoon a glass ceiling, while jazz CDs play so realistically that you look in vain for the combo. Try the *roles supremo* ($9) as an appetizer and if there's room, the chicken crepes are delicious ($11).

For a great beachfront option for breakfast, lunch, or dinner, you can't go wrong with **Daiquiri Dick's** (Olas Altas 314, tel. 322/222-0566, www.ddpv.com, 9 A.M.–11 P.M. daily). Dine outside on the beachfront patio and watch the people enjoying Playa los Muertos. The restaurant is spacious with a comfortable but upscale atmosphere. Daiquiri Dick's often has live music whether it's a mariachi band in the evenings or the soft sounds of live harp music during Sunday brunch. Lunch prices range from $8–15.

Another excellent beach restaurant choice is **época** (Aquiles Serdán 174, tel. 322/222-2510, www.epoca-pv.com, 8:30 A.M.–11:30 P.M. daily, check hours during low season). Here diners can enjoy a beautiful sunset while enjoying an inspired menu of Mexican and seafood favorites. época offers beach seating as well as tables inside the restaurant, so dig your toes in the sand and enjoy a hearty bowl of standout tortilla soup, a shrimp cocktail, or some delicious tuna tacos.

Your stay in Puerto Vallarta would not be complete without sunset cocktails and dinner beneath the stars at one of Puerto Vallarta's south-of-Cuale hillside view restaurants. Of these, the **Vista Grill** (formerly Señor Chico's, Púlpito 377, tel. 322/222-3570, 5–11 P.M. daily, reservations recommended, $10–25) continues as a visitor favorite for its romantic atmosphere and airy town and bay view. Soft guitar solos, flickering candlelight, pastel-pink tablecloths, balmy night air, and the twinkling lights of the city below are virtually certain to make your Puerto Vallarta visit even more memorable. It's best to get there by taxi. If you drive yourself, turn left at Púlpito, the first left turn possible uphill past the gasoline station as you head south on Highway 200 out of town. After about two winding blocks, you'll see the Vista Grill on the left as the street tops a rise. Winter nights it's best to bring a sweater or jacket. The offshore breeze by 9 P.M. may be a bit cool.

El Centro

Within the bustle of the Malecón restaurant row stands the longtime favorite **Las Palomas** (Malecón at Aldama, tel. 322/222-3675, 8 A.M.–10 P.M. Mon.–Sat., 9 A.M.–5 P.M. Sun., moderate). Soothing suppertime live marimba music and graceful colonial decor beneath a towering big-beamed ceiling afford a restful contrast from the sidewalk hubbub just outside the door. Both the breakfasts and the lunch and dinner entrées (nearly all Mexican style, $5–12) are tasty and bountiful.

A pair of formerly up-and-coming restaurants, de Santos and Los Xitomates (heetoh-MAH-tays), on Morelos, have achieved solid success. Both rely on the current popularity of innovative Mexican cuisine. At **Los Xitomates** (Morelos 570, btwn. Aldama and Corona, tel. 322/222-1695, 6 P.M.–midnight daily, $10–18), soft music and flickering candles set the stage, while good wine and continental–North American–Mexican fusion cuisine provide the performance. For example, you might start off with romaine-avocado salad dressed with roquefort, accompanied by a glass of Chilean Calixa chardonnay ($5), followed by either barbecued breast of chicken, grilled rib eye steak, or rice with wild mushrooms and chile serrano. My pick was the steak, which was cut thin, accompanied by a glass of good red Chilean Concordia shiraz ($4). Reservations recommended, especially weekends.

At **Restaurant de Santos** (Morelos 771, tel. 322/223-3052 or 322/223-3053, 5 P.M.–2 A.M. daily, $6–23, reservations strongly recommended), a couple of blocks farther north and across the street, the atmosphere is young, lively, and often crowded. This is a restaurant where the crowds gather in the later evening, so for early diners, reservations are not required. There are many tasty items to choose from on the menu at de Santos, but the spicy lobster ravioli is probably my favorite. The ambience is relaxed and peaceful during the early evening but after 11 when the crowds start arriving, the soft music is replaced by loud DJs.

Good macrobiotic and vegan cuisine is getting a foothold in Puerto Vallarta in a number of locations. For a very worthy alternative, go to **Planeta Vegetariano** (Iturbide 270, near the corner of Hidalgo, tel. 322/222-3073, 8 A.M.–10 P.M.) located downtown, near the south side of the church. The very affordable buffet ($6) mixes a cold salad bar with hot options like soups, curries, and other delicious veggie dishes. The owners (with just 10 tables) have achieved renown with a healthy and delicious offering for Puerto Vallarta's growing cadre of health-conscious visitors and locals. It's easy to imagine some visitor-devotees eating all their meals there, and being amply rewarded. It is a self-serve restaurant so pay in advance and then help yourself.

Another great lunch spot is the oceanfront bistro, **Vitea** (on the Malecón, corner of Libertad, tel. 322/222-8703, open daily for breakfast, lunch, and dinner). Vitea offers great people-watching and great service. They have a delicious French onion soup and grilled vegetable sandwich among other Mediterranean-inspired dishes. The atmosphere is upscale casual, so no beachwear!

Perched on the hill with a great view of the bay is **Barcelona Tapas** (Matamoros and 31 de Octubre, just up from Woolworth's, tel. 322/222-0510, www.barcelonatapas.net, noon–11:30 P.M. daily). An authentic Spanish tapas restaurant, Barcelona offers fantastic service and superb food. In addition to tapas, hungry diners can try the seafood paella ($22) or the chef's surprise tasting menu, six courses selected by the chef including soup, salad, hot and cold tapas and dessert ($29). Be sure to grab one of the coupons available on the Barcelona website for a discount on your meal or a free dessert. Note that you must climb four flights of stairs to dine here but the view is worth it!

There's a trio of romantic hillside dining options, listed from north to south. Start out one evening at the striking castletower of **Restaurant Café des Artistes** (Guadalupe Sanchez 740 at Leona Vicario, tel. 322/222-3228 or 322/222-3229, 6–11:30 P.M. daily, reservations mandatory, latest at 10:30 P.M.) that rises above the surrounding neighborhood. Romantics only need apply.

Candlelit tables, tuxedoed servers, gently whirring ceiling fans, soothing live neoclassical melodies, and gourmet international cuisine all set a luxurious tone. You might start with your pick of soups, such as chilled cream of watercress or cream of prawn and pumpkin, continue with a salad, perhaps the smoked salmon in puff pastry with avocado pine nut dressing. For a finale, choose honey- and soy-glazed roast duck or shrimp sautéed with cheese tortellini and served with a carrot custard and a spinach-basil puree. (Entrées $10–30, most around $20.)

Higher up the slope is the longtime favorite midpriced **Restaurant Chez Elena** (Matamoros 520, tel. 322/222-0161, 6–10 P.M. daily, $8–14, reservations recommended, closed Aug.–Sept.), on a quiet side street a few blocks above and north of the downtown church. Soft live guitar music and flickering candlelight in a colonial garden terrace set the tone, while a brief but solid Mexican-international menu, augmented by an innovative list of daily specialties, provides the food. On a typical evening, you might be able to choose between entrées such as *cochinita pibil* (Yucatecan-style shredded pork in sauce, $9), banana leaf–wrapped Oaxacan tamales ($6), or dorado fillet with cilantro in white sauce ($14). Chez Elena guests often arrive early for sunset cocktails at the rooftop panoramic view bar and then continue with dinner downstairs.

Finally, highest on the hill, treat yourself to dinner at Puerto Vallarta's most uniquely private restaurant, at the elegant, boutique 15-room **Hacienda San Ángel** (Miramar 336, tel. 322/222-2692 or 322/221-2277, dinner 6–10 P.M.). Personable owner Janice Chatterton initially created her restaurant for her in-house guests, but now extends her invitation to all lovers of fine fusion Mexican–continental–North American cuisine. Some of her favorite recommendations include, for starters, smoked salmon *carpaccio* ($9) and/or grilled vegetables ($7). Continue with shrimp coconut cream soup ($7) and climax it all with roasted half chicken, stuffed with *cuitlacoche* ($15). For more of her suggestions, visit www.haciendasanangel.com.

Marina

Sister restaurant to the Vista Grill and La Palapa, **Tikul** (Paseo de la Marina, just east of the El Faro lighthouse, tel. 322/209-2010, www.tikul.com) is an equally elegant option for those who wish to dine among the fishing boats and yachts of the marina. Choose from outdoor or indoor (air-conditioned) dining and enjoy watching the people stroll on the walkway. With stained glass and marble lamps, a stone bar carved from *tikul,* the inspiration for the restaurants' name, the setting is classic and refined. Live jazz is provided to set the mood. With an emphasis on Pacific cuisine, Tikul offers a wide assortment of delicious dishes to meet the desire of seafood and meat lovers. The boneless short rib cannot be missed. Other standouts include the curry and ancho shrimp and the Chilean sea bass.

Another dining option in the marina is **Gazebo** (just east of Tikul, tel. 322/221-3700) where most nights you will be enticed in by the owner himself. Gazebo offers one of the best deals for dinner in the surrounding area, a three course dinner for about $22. The regular menu offers an array of Italian and Mexican dishes as well as fresh seafood.

With three locations to choose from, carnivores can pick their favorite to enjoy a festival of meat at **Brasil.** Brasil has a location in the Romantic Zone (Carranza and Vallarta), the marina, and still another in Paradise Village in Nuevo Vallarta. A traditional Brazilian steakhouse, the meat doesn't stop coming until you say so. Prices are $16 for women and $21 for men and include unlimited servings of grilled meats brought to your table by waiters and a large selection of side dishes. The meats range from chicken wings to cuts of tender filet mignon and all are delicious.

SUPERMARKETS, BAKERIES, AND ORGANIC GROCERIES
Zona Romantíca

For imported foods and favorites from back home try locally owned **Supermarket Gutiérrez Rizo** (Constitución and Vallarta, just south of the Río Cuale, tel. 322/222-0222 or 322/222-6701, 6:30 A.M.–10 P.M. daily),

NOPAL

If you visit any supermarket while in Puerto Vallarta, you are sure to see a stand laden with cactus pads while in the produce section. You'll also see cactus being prepared and sold in outdoor markets, from street vendors and on menus of local restaurants. This cactus is called **nopal**, but you might know it better as prickly pear.

Nopal is a common ingredient in its native homeland of Mexico but it's also very popular in the Southwestern states in the United States (where it's commonly used in jelly and margaritas). It has been a part of Mexican cuisine since long before the Spanish arrived in Mexico and it is thought that the Aztecs may have named Tenochtitlán, which means "place

of the cactus," (now Mexico City) after the hearty plants that were so important to the ancient civilization.

Once the pads of the nopal have been cut, they are called "nopalitos" and are used in a variety of dishes, including huevos con nopal and tacos de nopales. You'll also find it in salads and mixed into other dishes with other vegetables.

Because nopal is so high in fiber and nutrients; it has been investigated over the last twenty years for its curative properties. It's said that nopal can lower cholesterol, reduce arterial plaque, as well as help with certain liver problems, diabetes, and even colon cancer.

a remarkably well-organized dynamo of a general store. Besides vegetables, groceries, film, socks, spermicide, and sofas, it stocks one of the largest racks of English-language newspapers and magazines (some you'd be hard-pressed to find back home) outside of Mexico City.

South of Cuale, don't miss stopping by the charming neighborhood bakery, **Pays de Catalina** (Basilio Badillo 317, tel. 322/223-2682, 8 A.M.–10 P.M. daily), a few doors up the street from Casa de Los Hot Cakes. Here, the longtime owner-baker continues to put out a scrumptious menu of goods, from big, crunchy cookies and cinnamon rolls to get-'em-while-they're-there croissants and crisp apple tarts.

For fresh organic produce as well as some imports, head over to the **Fruit Forest** (Constitucion 363, tel. 322/222-0606). On

a good day, you can even find half-and-half there. Other treats include fresh lemons and exotics like dragon fruit.

Zona Hotelera

On the north side of town, **Panadería los Chatos** (8 A.M.–8 P.M. Mon.–Sat.) offers a fine selection at two locations: in the Hotel Zone (Fco. Villa 359, tel. 322/223-0485) across from the Hotel Sheraton, and farther north in the marina (tel. 322/221-2540).

Health-food devotees have an excellent option in **Agro Gourmet** (Francisco Medina Ascencio 2820, across from the marine terminal, tel. 322/221-2656, 8 A.M.–8 P.M. Mon.–Sat. and 9 A.M.–6 P.M. Sun.). Besides home-grown lettuces and other vegetables and herbs, it also offers a trove of hard-to-get cheeses, breads, ravioli, pesto, tahini, hummus, and much more.

Puerto Vallarta for Gay Travelers

Puerto Vallarta has long been popular with gay travelers, many of whom end up purchasing homes and returning year after year. There is a large and vibrant gay community within Zona Romántica, making it easy for newcomers to make friends and feel welcome when visiting for the first time. While Zona Romántica is where the majority of the gay-friendly and gay-owned businesses reside, its popularity is not exclusive to the gay community. Indeed, visitors of all lifestyles will find plenty to do and see when visiting this quaint and charming area; from live music and art galleries to rooftop parties and after-hours dance clubs.

While most of the gay bars and accommodations are located in Zona Romántica, don't feel as though you must limit your choices to that area. Indeed, gay travelers are generally welcomed with open arms throughout Puerto Vallarta. Despite the conservative and religious beliefs of many of the residents, Vallarta is very

live and let live in their approach to differences whether it's someone of another race, religion or sexual orientation. Still, it is best to remember that culturally, Mexico is conservative and over the top displays of public affection will be frowned upon whether it is of the gay or heterosexual variety.

RECREATION
Gay Tours
There's a variety of tours and cruises to select from throughout the city so don't feel restricted to only selecting from those that cater to the gay community. However, if you are looking for an exclusively gay tour, there are several great ones to choose from. **PVRPV** (tel. 322/222-0638, www.pvrpv.com, $70 US) offers a gay cruise every Friday that includes breakfast, lunch and an open bar. They will also provide snorkeling equipment. Depending on the time of year, you will likely see sea turtles and dolphins

© ROBIN NOELLE

Many whale-watching tours are gay-friendly in Puerto Vallarta.

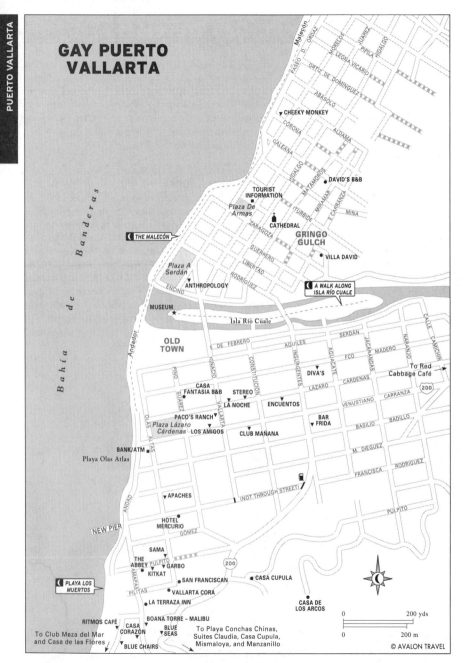

GAY PUERTO VALLARTA

Malecón

PASEO D. ORDAZ

MORELOS
JUAREZ
PIPILA
HIDALGO
LEONA VICARIO
ORTIZ DE DOMINGUEZ
ABASOLO

● CHEEKY MONKEY

CORONA
ALDAMA

GALEANA

HIDALGO
MATAMOROS
● DAVID'S B&B
MIRAMAR
E. CARRANZA
MINA

TOURIST
INFORMATION
Plaza De
Armas
ZARAGOZA
CATHEDRAL
ITURBIDE

GRINGO
GULCH

◖ THE MALECÓN

GUERRERO

● VILLA DAVID

LIBERTAD

Plaza A
Serdán
RODRIGUEZ

ENCINO
● ANTHROPOLOGY

◖ A WALK ALONG
ISLA RÍO CUALE

MUSEUM ★

Isla Río Cuale

Bahía   de   Banderas

Andador

OLD
TOWN

5 DE FEBRERO
IGNACIO

AQUILES
SERDÁN

JACARANDAS
NARANJO
MADERO

CALLE CAMICHIN

To Red
Cabbage Café
(200)

INSURGENTES
AGUACATE
FCO

DIVA'S ●
CARDENAS

CONSTITUCIÓN
CASA
FANTASIA B&B ▼
VALLARTA
STEREO ●
● LA NOCHE
ENCUENTOS
LÁZARO

VENUSTIANO
CARRANZA

PACO'S RANCH ▼
Plaza Lázaro
Cárdenas   LOS AMIGOS ▼
CLUB MAÑANA ●
BAR
▼ FRIDA
BASILIO
BADILLO

PINO SUAREZ
OLAS ALTAS

BANK/ATM ■
Playa Olas Atlas

M. DIEGUEZ

FRANCISCA
RODRIGUEZ

ANDAD

▼ APACHES

(NOT THROUGH STREET)

PULPITO

NEW PIER
HOTEL
MERCURIO
GOMEZ

(200)

SAMA ▼
THE
ABBEY ▼ PULPITO
AMAPAS ▼ GARBO
KITKAT ▼

● SAN FRANCISCAN
● CASA CUPULA

PILITAS

◖ PLAYA LOS
MUERTOS

● VALLARTA CORA

● LA TERRAZA INN

CASA DE
LOS ARCOS

RITMOS CAFÉ ▼
BOANA TORRE – MALIBU
CASA
CORAZON ▼
BLUE ▼
SEAS
To Club Meza del Mar
and Casa de las Flores
BLUE CHAIRS
To Playa Conchas Chinas,
Suites Claudia, Casa Cupula,
Mismaloya, and Manzanillo

0   200 yds
0   200 m

© AVALON TRAVEL

on your cruise, maybe even whales or a Giant Pacific Manta Ray. Make sure you bring your sunscreen!

While **Diana's Tours** (tel. 322/222-1510, www.dianastours.com, $75 US) started out offering day cruises catering to women, they now offer gay cruises open to all. Thursday is the main day for the cruise but during high season, they may offer Friday tours as well.

Marine biologist Oscar Frey of **Ocean Friendly Whale Watching** (tel. 322/225-3774, www.oceanfriendly.com) is available for private tours catering to the gay community. While most other tours are gay-friendly, there's nothing wrong with having a professional gay guide who is dedicated to responsible whale watching and research. He specializes in groups so if you have one, call him first. You are sure to learn a lot you didn't know about whales on one of Oscar's tours and he's also an expert photographer so if you ask nicely, you may be able to take home some beautiful photos to remember the trip by.

If you prefer to keep your feet dry, there are plenty of land-based tours to choose from. **Boana Horseback Riding** (tel. 322/222-0999, www.boana.net/tours.htm, $40 US) is a great way to get to know the area beyond the highway, bars, and beaches—the lushness of the jungle once you go beyond the beaten track is breathtaking. Take a scenic afternoon ride along the river and into the hills. Their tour includes transportation to their mountain ranch, snacks and drinks.

Unique ATV Tours (tel. 322/223-6182) can arrange tours for groups or private parties to some little known areas in the mountains and jungle or swing through the trees on a zip line tour with **Canopy Chico's** (tel. 322/222-0501) at the luscious Los Veranos zip line site.

Whether or not you're staying at the Blue Chairs Resort, the **Blue Chairs Concierge** (Blue Chairs Resort, tel. 322/222-5040, www.blue-chairs.com) is more than happy to help you find the gay tour or outing you're looking for to pass the time, get to know the area, or just meet new friends. They can arrange for anything from home-visit massages to horseback rides.

Beach Clubs

The most popular and well known beach club and resort within the international gay community is the **Blue Chairs Beach Resort,** perched on the south side of breezy Playa los Muertos (Malecón 4, tel. 322/222-5040, U.S./Can. tel. 866/514-7969, www.blue-chairs.com). During the busy winter season, you can join the hotel's buzz of activity, starting with a friendly crowd that congregates in the hotel's famous beachfront blue chairs, and continuing with anything from bingo and karaoke to laughing with the crowd at drag shows and theme parties up on the rooftop terrace.

Located just near the famous **Blue Chairs** is the **Blue Seas** (tel. 322/226-8152, www.blueseaspuertovallarta.com). The newest gay beach resort to open in Puerto Vallarta recently added a separate beach lounge where guests of the resort or those just wishing to spend the day are able to relax in high quality and comfortable lounge chairs under the palapas or enjoy the bar and spa services. They offer an elegant, spa-like atmosphere and the beachside restaurant has a solid menu and decent wine list to select from.

Also adjacent to the Blue Seas and the Blue Chairs is the Green Chairs located in front of **Ritmos Beach Café** (tel. 322/222-1371, www.ritmoscafe.com) which offers live music in the afternoons and evenings. Dine at the restaurant or enjoy the bar menu while lounging on the beach. All three of the beach clubs have their own dedicated clientele and it's up to you to decide which location appeals to you.

Dance Clubs

One of the most popular gay discos, **Club Paco Paco** is now under new management and has changed its name to **Paco's Ranch** (Ignacio Vallarta 278, tel. 322/222-1899, 6 P.M.–6 A.M.) but you'll still find the same fun-loving clientele. It's one of the oldest gay bars and clubs in Puerto Vallarta, offering several bars and dance floors including a rooftop bar and outside terrace. Here you can dance until the wee hours of the morning to a mix of techno, hip hop and disco. There are late night drink specials and drag shows on the weekend.

When **Club Mañana** (Venustiano Carranza 290, Zona Romántica, tel. 322/222-7772, www.manana.com.mx, 10 P.M.–6 A.M. daily) opened, even local politicians showed up. It's the first club of this category that has been able to break into the local scene, changing it forever. The charming hacienda has a private garden with patios; a swimming pool; air-conditioned disco; great shows featuring singers, drag queens, and strippers; VIP lounge; drink specials; and more. Things really pick up here in the late evening and early morning hours and Mañana is considered *the* place to see and be seen. Their prime location in the Zona Romántica places it within walking distance to many popular hotels and condos.

A favorite after hours hot spot with the local young gay crowd is the little dance club **Stereo** (Lazaro Cardenas 261, www.myspace.com/stereopv, 9 P.M.–4 A.M.).

Anthropology (Morelos 101, Centro, 9 P.M.–4 A.M.) is a men-only strip club offering shows nightly. There's a busy upstairs bar as well as a quieter rooftop bar if you prefer conversation. There's no cover charge so if you're in the mood for eye candy, this is the place to go.

Events

Puerto Vallarta is home to a number of popular annual events for the gay community. **Women's Week** takes place in February each year (www.vallartaheat.com for more information on dates for 2010) and draws a huge lesbian crowd for some fun in the sun. Like most weeklong events, there are scheduled activities to choose from as well as lodging packages from participating venues.

Still going strong after eleven years is the **Annual Latin Fever** weekend which usually takes place over the American Thanksgiving holiday in November. Organizer Will Gorges (www.willgorges.com) also hosts an annual **New Year's Eve** event in Puerto Vallarta.

At the end of January, you will find **Steve Buczek's Annual Leather and Bear Week** in full effect. Scheduled events include pool

parties, booze cruises, beach dance parties and adventure tours like zip lines and ATVs. Special lodging and airfare packages are available to those registered for the event (www.beefdip.com).

FOOD AND NIGHTLIFE

A comfortable street-side neighborhood bar, **Apaches** (Olas Altas 439, Zona Romántica, tel. 322/222-5235, apaches2000@yahoo.com, 4 P.M.–1 A.M. Mon.–Sat.) is a favorite with both gay and lesbian patrons as well as somewhat mixed crowd. A longtime favorite of locals and repeat visitors to Vallarta, this lesbian-owned establishment always treats you like you matter. While it sometimes might be a bit dusty around the edges, it's always a great place to spend the afternoon or evening.

Los Amigos (Venustiano Carranza 239, Zona Romántica, tel. 322/222-7802, www.losamigosbar.com, 6 P.M.–4 A.M. daily) caters to a slightly more mature and sometimes blue collar crowd. The cantina atmosphere and the friendly service convinces patrons to stick around this laid-back neighborhood hangout, despite the draw of two popular gay hangouts next door. Daily specials offered 6–8 P.M. include 20-peso cocktails and 10-peso beers.

Primarily serving the guests of the Blue Chairs Resort, **Blue Sunset Roof Bar** (Hotel Blue Chairs Resort, Zona Romántica, tel. 322/222-5040, www.bluechairs.com, 7 P.M.–11 P.M. daily) is nevertheless accessible by elevator to the passing public. If you don't already have the event calendar from their website or the latest Gay Guide, ask about the entertainment—frequently a visiting chanteuse or reigning drag queen will put on a show on the weekends during the busy season. In addition to live entertainment, this popular hangout always has something going on from bingo to karaoke. This is a favorite spot for nightly sunset viewing.

The Cheeky Monkey (Corona at the Malecón, www.cheekymonkeypv.com, noon–4 A.M. daily) is the only gay-owned restaurant and bar located on the popular Malecón in downtown Vallarta. Climb to the third floor

© CARLOS A. VASQUEZ

Garbo

after locating the side-door on Corona, just in from the corner of Paseo Díaz Ordaz. It's a mixed crowd so there's no problem with bringing your straight friends along. Don't expect a wild, raunchy evening here. Instead enjoy the food, people watching and $2 margaritas.

With lipstick-red interiors adorned with black-and-white Hollywood glossies from earlier days, the quiet and relaxed **Diva's** (Fco. Madero 388, Zona Romántica, tel. 322/222-7774, www.divaspv.com, 6 P.M.–2 A.M. daily) is a great place to go alone or with friends early in the evening before hitting the nearby dance clubs. The drinks are good, and the service is at your elbow without being in your face. You don't have to worry about offending anyone if you don't feel like chatting up the loyal crowd of regulars. This is a great place to go if you prefer conversation over pounding techno. You may have to search for the bar, however, as it's nearly hidden on a side street at the exit of the once popular Cine Bahía.

Frida (Insurgentes 301, Zona Romántica, no phone, www.fridaunbar.com, 1 P.M.–2 A.M. daily) recently relocated to a great two-story corner location but it's still a nice, quiet bar— a good place to go with old friends. The pool table takes your mind off the drink in your hands, but the jukebox can sometimes make it difficult to talk. Beer is the beverage of choice and rugged jeans are the preferred attire among the crowd here, primarily older locals and their young friends. Cheap drinks and a fun atmosphere make Frida's an enjoyable hangout.

There are few places like **◖ Garbo** (Púlpito 142, Zona Romántica, tel. 322/229-7309, www.bargarbo.com, 6 P.M.–2 A.M. daily), where you can sit and chat with friends in comfort or flirt with your neighbor with ease in the same breath. A regular spot for many local professionals, usually during happy hour, Garbo's gives you space and respect but you're always welcome to join the party. Sit at the high bar or find a quiet four-top with chairs or banquets. Weekends and evenings bring the added benefit of live music, usually on piano, which often results in rousing sing-alongs. The mixed crowd, charming servers and superb martini menu make Garbo's a "don't miss" venue and a favorite of locals and tourists alike.

Just up the street from Garbo's is **Kitkat** (Púlpito 120, Zona Romántica, tel. 322/223-0093, 6 P.M.–2 A.M. daily). This dramatic New York style lounge offers an international menu and extensive cocktail menu. With an art deco atmosphere, KitKat is one of the more cosmopolitan restaurant lounges in Puerto Vallarta. You'll find locals and visitors enjoying martinis and dining in the late evening hours.

La Noche (Lázaro Cárdenas 257, Zona Romántica, tel. 322/222-3364, www.lanochepv.com, 6 P.M.–3 A.M. daily, opens later off-season),offers quiet corner booths for conversation or a romantic drink as well as more central seating for more social groups. The dimly lit air-conditioned interior removes you from the busy world and the music is enjoyable and not overbearing. Sexy videos play on the wall-mounted TVs throughout this petite bar. A hangout for a crowd neither too young or too veteran, you'll find a great drink menu, friendly service and nightly specials plus lots of delicious eye candy.

When you're wandering around and just want to sit down and put up those feet, stop in at **Sama** (Olas Altas 510, Zona Romántica, tel. 322/223-3182, 5 P.M.–2 A.M. Tues–Sun.), a sidewalk cocktail bar with shaded tables and nibbles to eat in case you're hungry. Service is quick and friendly, and the drinks are good and strong. You'll find Sama quite popular with the young crowd.

Overstuffed couches, large bronze sculptures of goddesses, and a breezy interior cooled by huge fans give the **Uncommon Grounds Buddha Lounge** (Lázaro Cárdenas 625, Zona Romántica, tel. 322/223-3834, www.uncommon-grounds.com, 4 P.M.–close Tues.–Sun.) a comfortable feel. Stop in for a drink and chat with the owners, a vivacious lesbian couple from New Jersey who fell in love with Vallarta—these friendly women give this popular spot its character. Daily drink specials include such toothsome drinks as raspberry *mojitos* and mango margaritas. This is a good place to go either to meet friends for a drink early in the evening or to get to know someone new. If you're going to be in town for a while, sign up for their email event listings.

Encuentros (Lázaro Cárdenas 312, tel. 322/222-0643, www.encuentrosbarlounge.com, 6 P.M.–2 A.M.)is a great spot to grab some pizza or other nosh during the evenings. The refined and relaxed atmosphere welcomes conversation and intimate settings. They have delicious thin crust personal sized pizzas and an extensive drink menu. Happy hour is offered daily with 2 for 1 drinks. Air conditioned and friendly, Encuentros is cash only.

Tucked back along the Río Cuale is hidden favorite **Red Cabbage Café** (Rivera del Rí 204a, tel. 322/223-0411, 5 P.M.–11 P.M.). A small restaurant decorated with a vibrant and eclectic mix of Frida themed dé cor, the menu is focused on items served at Frida and Diego's wedding feast. Everything is superb but the chiles en nogada and chicken mole are widely recognized as divine. The restaurant is smoke-free and cash only.

ACCOMMODATIONS

Puerto Vallarta offers a wide variety of gay-friendly hotels, villas, and B&Bs. All of the properties listed below advertise in the local gay media and the majority, if not all, are gay-owned. Many are located in the Zona Romántica, an appealing gay-friendly neighborhood south of the Río Cuale in downtown Puerto Vallarta. Of course, just because a hotel or resort isn't listed here doesn't mean that you won't be welcome. Many gay visitors book their first trip into the hotel zone, which is comprised mostly of large beach resorts. Once they realize that the majority of gay bars and clubs are south of the Río Cuale, they usually stay in that part of town for their next trip. There's a wide variety of places to choose from in all different price points so whether you are looking specifically for a gay hotel or just want to be away from the big resorts, Zona Romántica has something for you.

$50-100

Climb the hill to find your private apartment-like room at **La Terraza Inn** (Amapas 299, Amapas, tel. 322/223-5431, www.terrazainn.com, $55–60 d low, $85–90 d high), a friendly gay-owned inn just a block up from Playa los Muertos on Amapas. Upper terrace rooms have a bit of a view beyond the high-rise in front, but each of the 10 rooms, are spacious and comfortable and have a terrace complete with lounge furniture for sunning. Some rooms with kitchenettes allow you to eat at home. Guests also have access to the inn's laundry, Wi-Fi, dining services, and on-call massage service. Pets are allowed and, in fact, if you leave your window open, neighborhood cats may just pop in for a peek. All of the rooms have ceiling fans but if you are visiting during the steamy summer, make sure you book a room with an air conditioner. A new breakfast café is available on the lower floor.

When a carefree vacation is on the horizon, the young and restless choose the men-only **Vallarta Cora** (Pilitas 174, Zona Romántica, tel. 322/223-2815, www.vallartacora.com, $95 d high, special rates by email), which has earned a well deserved reputation as a party place. The four-story white stucco tower houses 14 clean tiled rooms with basic amenities, living room, dining room, kitchenette, air-conditioning, balcony, and oval-shaped bathtub. There are also small safes to store your valuables. The happening pool area is open to the public for weekly pool parties while the hot tub can accommodate up to 60 people, all clothing-optional. Two-for-one happy hours and the new behind-the-bar steam room keep this place hopping. Wi-fi is available throughout the premises.

Back downhill in the Olas Altas neighborhood, on a quiet uphill side street, stands the modest but well-managed gay and lesbian resort **Hotel Mercurio** (Francisca Rodríguez 168, tel./fax 322/222-4793, www.hotel-mercurio.com, $57 s or $67 d low season, $64 s or $73 d high, studio with kitchenette $71 s or d low, $112 s or d high). The small lobby leads to an intimate leafy pool patio, enclosed by three tiers of rooms simply decorated in rustic wood, tile, and stucco, with TV, air-conditioning, and shower bath; credit cards are accepted. During times of low occupancy, the Mercurio sometimes offers promotions, which you can read about online at their website. Although the Mercurio is gay-friendly, straight visitors are welcome too but it's adults only so no one under 18 is allowed on site.

Directly above the Playa los Muertos south shoreline, the breezy plant-decorated room tiers of **Casa Corazón** (Amapas 326, tel./fax 322/222-6364 or 322/222-2738, U.S./Can. tel. 866/648-6893, www.casacorazonvallarta.com, small rooms $37 s, $53 d low season, $69 s, $100 d high; large rooms with kitchenette can be rented by the month) stairstep down its beachfront hillside. Tucked on one of the middle levels, a homey open-air restaurant and adjacent soft-couch lobby with a shelf of used paperbacks invite relaxing, reading, and socializing with fellow guests. No TVs, ringing phones, or buzzing air-conditioners disturb the tranquility; the people and the natural setting—the adjacent lush garden and the boom and swish of the beach waves—set the tone. The 42 rooms, while not deluxe, are varied and comfortably decorated with tile, brick, and colorful native arts and crafts. Guests in some of the most popular

rooms enjoy spacious, sunny oceanview patios. While not gay owned, it is certainly gay friendly and is a much more family orientated atmosphere than some of the other hotels in the area. Check the website for specials.

$100-150

The modern ten-floor tower of **Boana Torre-Malibu** (Amapas 325, Zona Romántica, tel. 322/222-6695, www.boana.net, $40–70 d low, $100–125 d high) offers special rates for longer stays, giving you the option of experiencing condo living right in the Zona Romántica just across from the gay beach at Playa los Muertos. You can take virtual tours of almost all of the units from their website because they do vary in style and amenities. All apartments have one or two bedrooms with a separate kitchen and living area with balcony, air conditioning and guests have access to what is called "the largest gay pool in the city." The on-site travel agency will book tours and day cruises for you, although finding something to do shouldn't be a problem here—the location puts you within easy walking distance of the best restaurants, coffee shops, and bars. Billed as a "straight-friendly" condo-hotel, all are welcome.

Casa de las Flores (Calle Santa Barbara 359, Zona Romántica, tel. 322/120-5242 or U.S. tel. 510/763-3913, www.casadelasfloresspv.com, $80–250 d low, $150–325 d high, $180–450 d holiday) is a much-photographed quirky bed-and-breakfast that allows pets and children. This property has a rambling, homey atmosphere with some air-conditioned rooms, Internet access, fully equipped kitchen and bar, dipping pool for the main house, maid service, and cable TV. Located within walking distance from Playa los Muertos, the casa offers impressive views of the bay from its terraces. While not focused solely on the gay community, Las Flores is gay-owned. Long-term rates are available May–October and the minimum stay at any time is seven nights.

The interior-focused **Casa Fantasia B&B** (Pino Suárez 203 at Francisco Madero, Zona Romántica, tel. 322/223-2444, www.mexonline.com/casafantasia.htm, $60–80 d low, $120–150 d high) offers a haven from the busy streets and beaches of the Zona Romántica. With more than 10,000 square feet of space, this three house hacienda style B&B is handsomely decorated with antiques and art. Gay couples are the preferred guests of choice and unregistered guests are not allowed into the rooms. The champagne happy hour and full breakfast at the sunny poolside are de rigueur. Full breakfast is served daily. Only a block from the beach, this gay-owned guest house is spacious yet welcoming.

The deluxe men-only, clothing-optional **Villa David** (Galeana 348, Gringo Gulch, tel. 322/223-0315, from the U.S. 877/832-3315, www.villadavidpv.com) is the only gay lodging choice in the tony Gringo Gulch area. It offers an inviting and home-like atmosphere. Villa David's ten rooms enfold an intimate, leafy tropical pool patio overlooking panoramic vistas of Puerto Vallarta, bay, and mountains. The rooms, decorated with 19th century–style traditional hardwood furniture, embellished with reading lamps and hand-hewn bedspreads, likewise all enjoy bay views. Rates for the rooms run about $93 d low season, $109 high; larger suites go for $119 d low and $139 d high, all with private baths, fans, air conditioning and hearty buffet breakfast. Other amenities include a common kitchen and living room with TV and DVD, in-house wireless Internet, roof-top viewing deck, and a hot-tub deck with bar. Guests enjoy easy walking access to both Río Cuale and Malecón sights, galleries, shops, and restaurants.

Over $150

Forty-two rooms and 12 suites make up **Abbey Hotel Vallarta** (Púlpito 138, Zona Romántica, tel. 322/222-4488, www.abbey-hotelvallarta.com, $160–240 d high), a modern tower-style hotel right on the gay beach in the Zona Romántica and just around the corner from local hot spots like **Garbo** and **KitKat**. All rooms are invitingly furnished, with immaculate tile floors, modern hardwood furniture, and private town- or oceanview balconies. Amenities

include an in-room safety deposit box, air-conditioning, telephone, cable TV, and high-speed Internet access. Suites include kitchenettes and a large living room with dining area. Other on-site offerings include a reserved beach area, swimming pool, and Jacuzzi as well as restaurant and bar. For an additional charge, VIP airport pickup, in-room massage, and your choice of local tours and outings are also available.

When you need to feel the comfort and services of the international gay community, head to the **Blue Chairs Beach Resort,** perched on the south side of breezy Playa los Muertos (Malecón 4, tel. 322/222-5040, U.S./Can. tel. 866/514-7969, www.bluechairs.com). Gay-owned for six years, the hotel, which advertises itself as the world's largest gay-and-lesbian beachfront resort, is a six-story stack of about forty comfortably furnished rooms and suites, many with private sea-view balconies. During the busy winter season, you can join the hotel's buzz of activity, starting with a friendly crowd that congregates in the hotel's famous beachfront blue chairs, and continuing with anything from bingo and karaoke to laughing with the crowd at drag shows and theme parties. Lodging prices vary, from the most economical room (with partial ocean view) for about $70 s or d low season, $110 s or d high, to a kitchenette junior suite with ocean view ($120 s or d low season and $240 s or d high), and at the top of the scale one-bedroom oceanview villa ($127 s or d low, $250 s or d high); add $20 per additional person. All lodgings come with private baths, fans, air-conditioning, and cable TV, as well as use of the rooftop restaurant and pool.

The ever popular **Casa Cúpula** (129 Callejon de la Igualdad, Zona Romántica, tel. 322/223-2484, www.casacupula.com, $160–279 d regular, $195–310 d high, suites $275–375) is considered one of the best gay-friendly guest houses in Puerto Vallarta. The gay-owned and managed bed-and-breakfast promises you personal service, and you will not only feel cared for but pampered while staying in one of the 10 rooms. Each room is uniquely decorated with comfortable beds and other luxury touches. Rooms include double showers, fluffy towels, mini bars, AC and DVD players. Located above the highway in a quiet area surrounded by the peaceful jungle, it's the sort of place where you'll see hummingbirds flitting around the relaxing lounge area and pool. Chef Jim Jardine comes from San Francisco and serves up relaxed home-style gourmet cuisine. **Casa de Los Arcos** (Hortensias 168, Alta Vista, tel. 322/222-5990, www.casadelosarcos.com, $100–200 d low, $150–275 d high, weekly rates), a four-casita hillside villa, allows the option of renting the entire place for groups of family or friends, or, when available, renting a separate casita. Each casita features its own living room, dining area, kitchen and private terrace with air-conditioning in the closed areas. The house is fully staffed Monday through Saturday; the cook is available Sunday for an extra charge. What's great about this residence is that you and a group of friends can all stay in one place, but you'll have your privacy when you need it, as well as large common living areas. The atmosphere has a very Mexican flavor, and the open-air *palapa* roof and private terraces will help you relax. Well behaved pets are welcome.

A boutique condo-hotel located right in the Zona Romántica, the **San Franciscan** (Pilitas 213, Zona Romántica, tel. 322/222-6473, www.san-franciscan.com; $98–140 d low, $130–285 d high, 4 bdrms $270 d low, $360 d high) offers a protected haven with 20 rooms and easy access to any of the services outside the gates. The five floors host five types of suites, including four bedroom suites that can accommodate groups of up to six or eight. Amenities and services include free long-distance calls to the United States and Canada, free Internet access, no rate increase for regular registered customers for ten years, air-conditioning, kitchens with microwaves, cookware, silverware, and china—and just about anything else to make your stay comfortable. The San Franciscan just recently added a comedy club to the premises. Adults only, no pets.

Real Estate Brokers

Bayside Properties (Francisca Rodríguez 160, tel. 322/222-8148, www.baysidepropertiespv.com), a gay-friendly rental and real estate sales operation owned by two women, handles many of the downtown and south-side apartments and condominiums.

Another gay-friendly establishment, **Cochran Real Estate** (Leona Vicario 230-D, Zona Romántica, tel. 322/221-6146, www.vallartaliving.com) focuses on service both in rentals and real estate sales.

Home mortgages are increasing in popularity among both foreign buyers and local residents. Gay-owned **Mexlend** (tel. 322/222-7377, www.mexlend.com) is one of the leading lenders and can arrange for loans on many property types anywhere in Mexico. They offer both US dollar loans and peso loans for Mexican nationals or expats who decide to live and work in Mexico full time.

One of the partners of **Paradise Properties** (Atún 118, Las Gaviotas, tel. 322/224-5416, www.paradisepropertiespv.com) is gay; this agency focuses on personal service in sales and rentals.

The founder and many of the staff of **Puerto Vallarta Rentals Premier Vacations** (Francisca Rodríguez 152, Zona Romántica, tel. 322/222-0638, www.pvrpv.com) are gay. This successful rental operation handles villas as well as tours and other services.

Gay-owned **Timothy Fuller & Associates** (Rodolfo Gómez 122, Zona Romántica, tel. 322/222-1535, www.timothyfuller.com) is a partnership of well-trained rental and real estate professionals.

The founding partner of extremely successful **Tropicasa** (Púlpito 145-A, Zona Romántica, tel. 322/222-6505, www.tropicasa.com) is an active member of the gay community as well as the president of the local real estate association and the local Make a Wish foundation.

Information and Services

Since Puerto Vallarta is an up-to-date city, information is as close as your hotel telephone (or, if you don't speak Spanish, your hotel desk clerk) or one of the hundreds of publicly available Internet connections. A plethora of banks with ATMs, street telephones, Internet stores, pharmacies, doctors, hospitals, and much more are available, ready to smooth your Puerto Vallarta visit.

TOURIST INFORMATION OFFICES

The downtown tourist information office (tel. 322/223-2500, ext. 230 or 232, fax ext. 233, 8 A.M.–9 P.M. Mon.–Fri., 9 A.M.–2 P.M. Sat.) is on the northeast corner of the central plaza. They provide assistance, information, and dispense whatever maps, pamphlets, and copies of *Vallarta Today* and *Puerto Vallarta Lifestyles* they happen to have.

PUBLICATIONS

New books in English are not particularly common in Puerto Vallarta. Nevertheless, **Supermercado Gutiérrez Rizo** (south of Cuale, corner of Constitución and Aquiles Serdán, tel. 322/222-0222) stocks an excellent American magazine selection, some new paperback novels, and newspapers, including the *Miami Herald* Mexico edition and sometimes *USA Today* and the *Los Angeles Times*. Also, a number of small stores and stalls, such as the no-name **newsstand** (Olas Altas 420, until 9 or 10 P.M. daily), regularly sell at least one U.S. newspaper.

Vallarta Today (tel. 322/225-3323, fax 322/224-1186, www.vallartatoday.com), *Vallarta Tribune* (tel. 322/223-0585 or 322/223-1302, www.vallartatribune.com), and the *PV Mirror* (www.pvmirror.com) are all informative tourist papers and handed out free at the airport and travel agencies, restaurants, and hotels all over town (contact them directly if you can't find a copy). Besides detailed information on hotels, restaurants, and sports, they

include a local events and meetings calendar and interesting historical, cultural, and personality feature articles.

Puerto Vallarta Lifestyles (Calle Timón 1, tel. 322/221-0106, 9 A.M.–7 P.M. Mon.–Fri.), the quarterly English-language magazine, features unusually detailed and accurate town maps as well an overwhelming number of real estate ads. Refer to the dining guide in the magazine for a peek at the menus of Vallarta's most upscale restaurants. Other useful information includes art gallery listings and usually profiles of outlying areas. If you cannot find a copy at the airport or your hotel contact *Lifestyles* directly or pick one up at their office in the marina.

Also very useful is the class-act **Gay Guide Vallarta** that lists many gay and gay-friendly hotels, restaurants, real estate offices, and bars and nightclubs, plus a calendar and much more. Visit the website, www.gayguidevallarta.com, or pick up a copy at one of their advertisers, notably the Blue Chairs Beach Resort (tel. 322/222-2176 or 322/222-5040) on Playa los Muertos, south end, or contact the editor (tel. 322/222-7980, editor@gayguidevallarta.com).

The **Puerto Vallarta Library** (Francisco Villa 1001 in Colonia Los Mangos, director Ricardo Murrieta tel. 322/224-9966 or Jimmie Ellis tel. 322/222-1478), built and now operated by the volunteer committee Pro Biblioteca Vallarta, has accumulated a sizable English and Spanish book collection. Get there by taxi or car, several blocks along Villa, which runs at a diagonal north and inland at the sports field across the airport boulevard from the Hotel Sheraton. Or take a bus marked Pitillal and Biblioteca.

You can find new English language books at **The Bookstore** in Plaza Caracol, **NW Bookstore** in Paradise Village and at Costco in Fluvial.

MONEY

Banking has come to the Olas Altas district, with the branch of **Banorte** (Av. Olas

IS IT SAFE?

At the time of this writing, Puerto Vallarta among other places in Mexico, has been receiving a tremendous amount of coverage in the news. The majority of this coverage has been focusing on the violent and public war between the narcotics traffickers and the military and police. Many people, especially those who have never been to Mexico or do not visit regularly, wonder if it is still safe to travel.

The majority of the violence is along the Mexico-America border and although there have been tragic instances of innocents being caught in the crossfire, the majority of causalities remain drug dealers and those trying to catch them. Puerto Vallarta, and many other tourist areas have a strong, vested interest in maintaining a safe and hospitable atmosphere as the entire livelihood of the people and city itself lies within the tourism industry. While the increased military presence may frighten some people, the police with the large machine guns are actually there to lend an air of security, not intimidation; unless that intimidation is of would-be rabble-rousers.

As many residents and frequent visitors will attest, there is still a very low crime rate in Puerto Vallarta, especially when compared with a U.S. city of comparable size and socio-economic background. The majority of crimes are nuisance crimes: vandalism, pickpockets, and simple burglary (usually of unattended belongings that present an irresistible temptation to the people who live in poverty here).

By far, the biggest dangers to out of town visitors remain sunburn, overimbibing, and other typical vacation woes.

Altas btwn. Basilio Badillo and Carranza, tel. 322/222-4040, 9 A.M.–4 P.M. Mon.–Fri., 10 A.M.–2 P.M. Sat.). After hours, use its ATM. Additionally, you can use the HSBC bank ATM on upper Olas Altas (corner of Rodríguez, two blocks south of Hotel Playa Los Arcos).

Most downtown banks cluster along Juárez, near the plaza. One exception is **HSBC** (tel. 322/222-0027 or 322/222-0277, 8 A.M.–7 P.M. Mon.–Sat.), on Libertad, corner of Carranza, just north of the Insurgentes bridge and open the longest hours of all.

Banamex (Zaragoza 176, at Juárez, south side of the town plaza, tel. 322/222-0911) changes U.S. and Canadian cash and travelers checks at the best rates in town. For money exchange, go to the special booth (9 A.M.–4 P.M. Mon.–Fri., 10 A.M.–2 P.M. Sat.) to the left of the bank's main entrance.

If the lines at Banamex are too long, try **Scotiabank Inverlat** (Juárez, half a block north of the plaza, tel. 322/223-1224, money exchange hours 9 A.M.–5 P.M. Mon.–Fri.) or **Bancomer** across the street (corner of Juárez and Mina, tel. 322/222-1919 or 322/222-3500, 8:30 A.M.–4 P.M. Mon.–Fri.).

Additionally, scores of little *casas de cambio* (exchange windows) dot the cobbled Old Town streets, especially along the south end of the Malecón downtown, and along Avenida Olas Altas and Insurgentes south of the Río Cuale. Although they generally offer about $2 per $100 less than the banks, they compensate with long hours, often daily 9 A.M.–9 P.M. In the big hotels, cashiers will generally exchange your money at rates comparable to the downtown exchange booths.

The local **American Express** (Morelos 160, corner of Abasolo, tel./fax 322/223-2955 or 322/223-2910, 9 A.M.–6 P.M. Mon.–Fri., 9 A.M.–1 P.M. Sat.) cashes American Express travelers checks and offers full member services, such as personal-check cashing (up to $1,000 every 21 days; bring your checkbook, your ID or passport, and your American Express card). The office is downtown, one block inland from the Hard Rock Cafe.

COMMUNICATIONS

Puerto Vallarta has a number of branch post offices. The main *correo* (Mina 188, tel. 322/223-1360, 9 A.M.–5 P.M. Mon.–Fri.,

9 A.M.–1 P.M. Sat.), with secure Mexpost mail service, is downtown, two blocks north of the central plaza, just off Juárez. There's a branch at the Edificio Maritima (Maritime Building), near the cruise-ship dock (tel. 322/224-7219, 8 A.M.–2 P.M. Mon.–Fri., 9 A.M.–1 P.M. Sat.), but the airport has lost its post office branch; deposit postcards and letters in the airport mailbox *(buzón)*.

The cheapest and often most convenient telephone option that isn't voice over IP (VoIP) is to buy a *tarjeta de teléfono* (Ladatel public phone card) and use it at street telephones. Lacking a telephone card, call from your hotel. Lacking a hotel (or if you don't like its extra charges), go to one of the many *casetas de larga distancia* (long-distance telephone offices), sprinkled all over town.

Puerto Vallarta has a flock of public **Internet** cafés. However, they change as often as the Puerto Vallarta breeze. At this writing, there were many, mostly concentrated downtown: several south of the Río Cuale, along Avenida Olas Altas, and several more north of the Río Cuale along Juárez. Ask your hotel desk clerk for the closest one.

Many locations offer free wireless Internet services, from bars and restaurants to the local shopping centers. If you have your laptop, you probably aren't far from a free signal. **Starbuck's** in Plaza Peninsula and downtown in the *zocolo* (town square) both offer free Internet with purchase. While wireless access in your hotel room is rare, even the smaller hotels often offer it in the lobby or other public areas. Use a program like Skype (www.skype.com) to make calls from your computer for as little as .02 cents per minute to the U.S.

HEALTH AND EMERGENCIES

If you need emergency care, go to one of the Puerto Vallarta hospitals that have 24-hour service: **Amerimed** (in the marina, tel. 322/221-0023), **Medasist** (south of Cuale, tel. 322/223-0444), and **San Javier** (also in the marina, tel. 322/226-1010).

If, however, you prefer to go to Puerto Vallarta's newest hospital, with a load of diagnostic equipment and a raft of specialists to use it, go to **Cornerstone Hospital** (tel. 322/224-9400), behind the Gigante store at north-side Plaza Caracol. Alternatively go to the respected **Hospital CMQ** (Centro Médico Quirúrgico, Basilio Badillo 366, btwn. Insurgentes and Aguacate, tel. 322/223-1919 ground floor or 322/223-0011 second floor), south of the Río Cuale.

For an American-trained English-speaking doctor, Puerto Vallarta visitors enjoy the services of at least two IAMAT (International Association for Medical Assistance to Travelers) doctors: Consult either Dr. Alfonso Rodríguez (Lucerna 148, tel. 322/293-1991) or Dr. Mark Engleman (Amerimed Hospital, on the airport boulevard, in the marina, tel. 322/293-1991).

For round-the-clock prescription service, call or go to the well-stocked 24-hour **Farmacia Guadalajara** (on the Av. Insurgentes corner of Av. Lázaro Cárdenas, south of Cuale, tel. 322/222-0101). Alternatively, try one of the five branches of **Farmacia CMQ,** such as south of Cuale (Basilio Badillo 367, tel. 322/222-1330 or 322/222-2941) or on the north side (Peru 1146, tel. 322/222-1110).

Furthermore, a legion of loyal customers swears by the diagnostic competence of Federico López Casco, of **Farmacia Olas Altas** (Av. Olas Altas 365, tel. 322/222-2374), two blocks south of Hotel Playa Los Arcos, whom they simply know as "Freddy." Although a pharmacist and not a physician, his fans say he is a wizard at recommending remedies for their aches and pains.

For **police** emergencies, call the emergency number, 322/290-0507 or 322/290-0512. In case of fire, call the *bomberos*—the fire department (tel. 322/224-7701).

IMMIGRATION, CUSTOMS, AND CONSULATES

If you need an extension to your tourist card, you can get a total of 180 days at the local branch of **Instituto Nacional de Migración.** Present your existing tourist card at the office on the cruise-ship dock entrance road (upstairs at street number 2755, tel. 322/224-

7653 or 322/224-7970, fax 322/224-7719, 9 A.M.–1 P.M. Mon.–Fri.) next to the Pemex gas station, or the office at the airport (tel. 322/221-1380, fax 322/224-7719, 322/224-7653, or 322/224-7970). If you lose your tourist card, go to Migración with your passport or identification, and some proof of the day you arrived in Mexico, such as a copy of the original permit or your airplane ticket.

Both the U.S. and Canadian consuls have moved out of downtown. They have retained their local Puerto Vallarta telephone numbers, however. The U.S. consul issues passports and does other essential legal work for U.S. citizens and is located on the main Nuevo Vallarta beachfront boulevard (Plaza Paraíso, Paseo de los Cocoteros 1, tel./fax 322/222-0069 or 322/223-0074, 8 A.M.–12:30 P.M. Mon.–Fri.). In an emergency after hours, call the U.S. Consul General in Guadalajara (tel. 33/3268-2100 or 33/3268-2200).

The Canadian honorary consul, who has moved to the hotel zone on the airport boulevard (Edificio Obelisco, Suite 108, Blv. Francisco Ascencio 1951, tel. 322/293-0098 or 322/293-0099, fax 322/293-2894, 9 A.M.–3:30 P.M. Mon.–Fri.), provides similar services for Canadian citizens. In an emergency or after hours call the Canadian Embassy in Mexico City (toll-free Mex. tel. 01-800/706-2900).

SPANISH INSTRUCTION

The **University of Guadalajara Study Center for Foreigners** (Libertad 105, tel. 322/223-2082, fax 322/223-2982, www.cepe.udg.mx) offers one-, two-, and four-week total-immersion Spanish-language instruction, including home stays with local families.

VOLUNTEER WORK

A number of local volunteer clubs and groups invite visitors to their meetings and activities. Check with the tourist information office or see the events calendar and directory pages in *Vallarta Today* or *Vallarta Tribune.*

The International Friendship Club, or **Club Internacional de la Amistad** (Parian del Puente office complex, local 13, P.O. Box 604, Puerto Vallarta, Jalisco 48350, tel. 322/222-5466, www.pvmexico.com, 8:30 A.M.–12:30 P.M. Mon.–Fri.), an all-volunteer service club, sponsors a number of health, educational, and cultural projects. It welcomes visitors to the (usually second Monday) monthly general membership meeting. For more information, see the events calendar section of *Vallarta Today,* the directory page of the *Vallarta Tribune,* or drop by the office behind the HSBC bank, above the north bank of the Río Cuale Avenida Insurgentes (upper) bridge.

The **Ecology Group of Vallarta,** a group of local citizens willing to work for a cleaner Puerto Vallarta, welcomes visitors to its activities and regular meetings. Contact Ron Walker (tel. 322/222-0897, rc_walkermx@yahoo.com. mx) for more information.

The **S.O.S. Animal** (tel. 322/227-5519 or 322/221-0078) protection association is working to humanely reduce the number of stray and abandoned animals on Puerto Vallarta streets. Call for more information, or see the directory page of the *Vallarta Tribune.*

Children of the Dump, a local nonprofit who has been working for more than 10 years on proving education and assistance for the children in Puerto Vallarta's poorest neighborhood is always in need of classroom helpers or teachers. For those willing to commit several months of time, a small stipend available. Children of the Dump also offers free tours of the neighborhoods surrounding the municipal dump. During the tours you will see how the other side of Puerto Vallarta lives, participate in the hot lunch program, and meet the children who attend the **School of Champions,** the free after-school program for children ages 5–13. Tours can be arranged through Arthur Fumerton (tel. 322/223-4311, www.childrenofthedumpvallarta.org).

Getting There

Dozens of air departures, hundreds of long-distance buses, and a good paved highway network speed thousands of travelers to and from Puerto Vallarta daily.

BY AIR

Several major carriers connect Puerto Vallarta by direct flights with United States and Mexican destinations.

Mexicana Airlines (reservations tel. 322/221-1266 or toll-free Mex. tel. 01-800/502-2000, flight information tel. 322/224-8900) flights connect daily with Mexico City and Guadalajara. **Aerocalifornia Airlines** (tel. 322/209-0328) connects with Los Angeles and Mexico City. **Aeroméxico** (tel. 322/224-2777) flights connect daily with Los Angeles, Tijuana, Guadalajara, Acapulco, León, Monterrey, and Mexico City.

Alaska Airlines (reservations toll-free Mex. tel. 01-800/426-0333) flights connect with Los Angeles, San Francisco, San Jose, and Seattle; for arrival and departure information call the airport (tel. 322/221-1350 or 322/221-2610.)

American Airlines (toll-free Mex. tel. 01-800/362-7000) flights connect with Dallas-Ft. Worth and Chicago seasonally. **U.S. Airlines,** formerly America West Airlines (reservations in Mexico toll-free U.S. tel. 800/235-9292, flight information tel. 322/221-1927 or 322/221-1333) flights connect with Phoenix and Los Angeles.

United Airlines (reservations toll-free Mex. tel. 01-800/003-0777, flight information tel. 322/222-3264) flights connect with San Francisco.

Frontier Airlines flights connect with Denver. For reservations and information, contact a travel agent, such as American Express (tel. 322/223-2955 or 322/223-2910).

Aerocalafia Airlines connects with Los Cabos (reservations toll-free Mex. tel. 01-800/560-3949, flight information tel. 322/221-1333). **Aviacsa** airlines connects with Mexico City (reservations toll-free Mex. tel. 01-

800/560-3949, flight information tel. 322/221-3095 or 322/221-2624).

Continental Airlines (tel. 322/221-1025 or toll-free Mex. tel. 01-800/900-5000) flights connect daily with Houston.

West Jet and Air Tran (call Noli Tours, tel. 800/666-8881) charter flights connect with several Canadian cities (Toronto, Winnipeg, Saskatoon, Regina, Calgary-Edmonton, and Vancouver), mostly during the winter. **Other charters** that connect with Puerto Vallarta from a number of U.S. cities seasonally are USA 3000, Transmeridian, and Apple Vacations. Contact a local travel agent.

Airport Arrival and Departure

Air arrival at Puerto Vallarta Airport (code-designated PVR, officially Gustavo Díaz Ordaz International) is generally smooth and simple. After the cursory (if any) customs check, arrivees can avail themselves of two 24-hour ATMs and a money-exchange counter open 9 A.M.–6 P.M. daily.

A lineup of car rental booths includes **Advantage** (tel. 322/221-1499, advantagepvr@prodigy.net.mx), **Alamo** (tel. 322/221-3030), **Avis** (tel. 322/221-1112), **Budget** (toll-free Mex. tel. 01-800/700-1700), **Dollar** (tel. 322/223-1354), **National** (tel. 322/209-0356), and **Thrifty** (tel. 322/321-2984, 322/321-2485, or toll-free Mex. tel. 01-800/021-2277). You might also save money with an air-and-car package or by reserving with a discount (such as AARP, AAA, senior, airline, credit card, or others) before you leave for Mexico.

Transportation to town is easiest by *colectivo* (collective taxi-vans) or *taxi especial* (individual taxi). Booths sell tickets at curbside. The *colectivo* fare runs about $6 per person to the northern hotel zone, $7 to the center of town, and $8 or more to hotels and hamlets south of town. Individual taxis (for up to four passengers) run about $15, $16, and $25 for the same rides.

Taxis to more distant northern destinations,

such as Sayulita (30 mi/50 km), San Francisco (32 mi/53 km), Rincón de Guayabitos (39 mi/62 km), and San Blas or Tepic (100 mi/160 km), run about $50, $60, $108, and $170, respectively. A much cheaper alternative is to hire a taxi (no more than $10) from the airport to the new bus terminal a mile north of the airport, where you can continue by very frequent buses.

Airport departure is as simple as arrival. Save by sharing a taxi with departing fellow hotel guests. Agree on the fare with the driver before you get in. If the driver seems too greedy, hail another taxi.

If you've lost your tourist card, arrive early and be prepared with a copy or you may have to pay a fine unless you've gotten a duplicate through Migración. In any case, be sure to save enough pesos or dollars to pay your **$12 departure tax** (unless your ticket already includes it).

BY CAR OR RV

Three road routes connect Puerto Vallarta north with Tepic and San Blas, east with Guadalajara, and south via Melaque-Barra de Navidad with Manzanillo.

To Tepic, **Mexican National Highway 200** is all asphalt and in good condition most of its 104 miles (167 km) from Puerto Vallarta. Traffic is ordinarily light to moderate, except for some slow going around Tepic, and over a few low passes about 20 miles north of Puerto Vallarta. Allow three hours for the southbound trip and half an hour longer in the reverse direction for the winding 3,000-foot climb to Tepic.

A shortcut connects San Blas directly with Puerto Vallarta, avoiding the oft-congested uphill route through Tepic. Heading north on Highway 200, at Las Varas turn off west onto Nayarit Highway 16 to Zacualpan and Platanitos, where the road continues through the coastal tropical forest to Santa Cruz village on the Bay of Matanchén. From there you can continue along the shoreline to San Blas. In the opposite direction, heading south from San Blas, follow the signed Puerto Vallarta turnoff

to the right (south) a few hundred yards after the Santa Cruz de Miramar junction. Allow about three hours, either direction, for the entire San Blas–Puerto Vallarta trip.

The story is similar for Mexican National Highway 200 along the 172 miles (276 km) to Manzanillo via Barra de Navidad (134 mi/214 km). Trucks and a few potholes may cause slow going while climbing the 2,400-foot Sierra Cuale summit south of Puerto Vallarta, but light traffic should prevail along the other stretches. Allow about four hours to Manzanillo, three from Barra de Navidad, and the same in the opposite direction.

The Guadalajara route is nearly as easy. From Puerto Vallarta, follow Highway 200 as if to Tepic, but, just before Compostela (80 mi/129 km from Puerto Vallarta) follow the 22-mile (36 km) Guadalajara-bound *cuota* (toll) shortcut east, via Chapalilla. From Chapalilla, connect seamlessly east via **Mexican National Highway 15 D** *cuota autopista*. Although expensive (about $20 per car, much more for motor homes), the expressway is a breeze compared to the narrow, winding, and congested *libre* Highway 15. Allow around five hours at the wheel for the entire 214-mile (344 km) Guadalajara–Puerto Vallarta trip, either way (seven hours by the old *libre* route).

BY BUS

Many bus lines run through Puerto Vallarta. The major long-distance bus action is at the new **Camionera Central** (Central Bus Station) about a mile north of the airport. Reservations and ticketing are efficiently computerized, and most major lines accept credit cards. The shiny, air-conditioned complex resembles an airline terminal, with a cafeteria, juice bars, a travel agency, a long-distance telephone and fax service, luggage storage lockers, a gift shop, and a hotel reservation office (tel. 322/290-1014). The buses are usually crowded; don't tempt people with a dangling open purse or a bulging wallet in your pocket.

Mostly first- and luxury-class departure ticket counters line one long wall. First-class **Elite** and its parent **Estrella Blanca** (tel. 322/290-1001), with its affiliated lines Turistar, Futura, Transportes Norte de Sonora, and Transportes Chihuahenses, connect the entire northwest–southeast Pacific Coast corridor. Northwesterly destinations include La Peñita (Rincón de Guayabitos), Tepic, San Blas, Mazatlán, all the way to Nogales or Mexicali and Tijuana on the U.S. border. Other departures head north, via Tepic, Torreón, and Chihuahua to Ciudad Juárez, at the U.S. border. Still others connect northeast, via Guadalajara, Aguascalientes, Zacatecas, and Saltillo, with Monterrey, where quick connections are available with the east Texas border at Matamoros. In the opposite direction, departures connect with the entire southeast Pacific Coast, including Melaque–Barra de Navidad, Manzanillo, Playa Azul junction, Lázaro Cárdenas, Ixtapa–Zihuatanejo, and Acapulco (where you can transfer to Oaxaca-bound departures). Additionally, **Transportes Norte de Sonora** (TNS) departures connect north with San Blas via the coastal (Tepic bypass) shortcut.

New competing first-class line **TAP** (tel. 322/290-0119 or 322/290-1001), Transportes y Autobuses del Pacífico, provides about the same first-class northwest Pacific service as both Elite and Transportes Pacífico.

Transportes Pacífico (tel. 322/290-1008) offers first-class departures (for cash only) that also travel the northwest Pacific route, via Tepic and Mazatlán to Nogales, Mexicali, and Tijuana. Transportes Pacífico provides additional first-class connections east with Guadalajara and Mexico City direct, and others to Guadalajara by expressway shortcut (*corta*).

Transportes Pacífico also provides very frequent second-class daytime connections north with Tepic, stopping everywhere, notably Bucerías, Sayulita, Guayabitos, La Peñita, Las Varas, and Compostela en route. The Bucerías bus fare should run less than $2, Sayulita $4, Guayabitos about $5, and Tepic or San Blas $7 (for San Blas, go by Transportes Norte de Sonora direct or Transportes Pacífico second-class and transfer at Las Varas).

Affiliated lines **Autocamiones del Pacífico** and **Transportes Cihuatlán** (tel. 322/290-0994) provide many second-class and some first-class departures along the Jalisco coast. Frequent second-class connections stop at El Tuito, Tomatlán, El Super, Careyes, Melaque, Barra de Navidad, and everywhere in between. They also connect with Guadalajara by the long southern route, via Melaque, Autlán, and San Clemente (a jumping-off point for Talpa, Mascota, and San Sebastián). Primera Plus, its luxury-class line, provides a few daily express connections southeast with Manzanillo, with stops at Melaque and Barra de Navidad.

A separate luxury-class service, a subsidiary of Flecha Amarilla, also called **Primera Plus** (tel. 322/290-0716 or toll-free Mex. tel. 01-800/375-7587), also provides express connections southeast with Melaque, Barra de Navidad, Manzanillo, and Colima. Other such Primera Plus departures connect east with Lake Chapala and Guadalajara, continuing to Aguascalientes, Irapuato, Celaya, Querétaro, and León. Affiliated line **Autobuses Costa Alegre** provides frequent second-class connections southeast along the Jalisco coast, via El Tuito, El Super, Careyes, Melaque, Barra de Navidad, and all points in between.

Additionally, **ETN** (Enlaces Transportes Nacional, tel. 322/223-2999 or 322/290-0997) provides first-class departures connecting east with Guadalajara and Mexico City, offering continuing connections in Guadalajara with several Michoacán destinations.

Getting Around

BY BUS

Since nearly all through traffic flows along one long thoroughfare, Puerto Vallarta bus transportation is a snap. Puerto Vallarta is blessed by a large squadron of buses, operated by both private companies and bus drivers' cooperatives. They run north–south, beginning at their south-of-Cuale terminus on the east (Calle Pino Suárez) side of Plaza Lázaro Cárdenas. From Plaza Lázaro Cárdenas, all buses head north. Most of them (marked "Centro") pass through the downtown center northbound along Avenida Juárez. A few other buses, marked "Tunel," bypass the downtown center via a tunnel uphill, east of downtown, and continue along the foothill *libramiento* boulevard and rejoin the main-route buses on the northbound side of thoroughfare Bulevar Francisco Ascencio at the Zona Hotelera. From there, the major bus terminals (marked prominently on the bus windshields) are at Pitillal (at the north end of the Zona Hotelera), the marina, and the Las Palmas, Juntas, and Ixtapa suburbs, farther north.

The Puerto Vallarta bus system is a simple learn-as-you-go (no tourist passes, transit maps, nor set schedules) expanded version of the original village system of two generations ago. However, it's efficient and very safe, except perhaps for an occasional pickpocket when crowded. Be sure to keep your purse buttoned and your wallet secure in your waist belt.

Buses run daily between about 5:30 A.M. and 10 P.M., at two-minute intervals during peak hours, five-minute intervals nonpeak. Have enough coins *(monedas)* in hand to pay your $5.50 peso tariff to the driver, who can usually change small bills. All buses eventually return to their south-end terminus, at Plaza Lázaro Cárdenas a few blocks south of the Río Cuale.

© ROBIN NOELLE

Traveling to nearby beaches like Mismaloya is cheap and easy by bus.

Northbound, from Plaza Lázaro Cárdenas, buses retrace their routes to one of several important stops scrawled across their windows. Destinations on the north side, from closest in to farthest north, are the Centro (town center, 1–2 miles, 5 minutes), Zona Hotelera (Hotel Zone, 3–5 miles, 10–15 minutes), Pitillal (5 miles, 15 minutes), Marina Vallarta (7 miles, 20 minutes), the airport (8 miles, 22 minutes), Camionera Central (long-distance bus station, 10 miles, 24 minutes), Las Palmas (11 miles, 25 minutes), Juntas (13 miles, 28 minutes), and Ixtapa (15 miles, 33 minutes). Since the buses headed to the destinations farthest north stop at all of the intermediate destinations, you can go everywhere you are likely to want to go by hopping on buses marked "Las Palmas," "Juntas," or "Ixtapa."

Hint: If you're headed to the downtown north of the Río Cuale, be sure to take a "Centro"-marked bus. (And not a "Tunel"-marked bus that bypasses the town center by going through the tunnel and along the uphill *libramiento* bypass.) On the other hand, from south of Cuale, if you want to get to north-side destinations (Zona Hotelera, marina, airport) in a hurry, you should take the "Tunel"-marked bus.

Two other **local bus terminals** serve Puerto Vallarta. For south-end destinations of Mismaloya and Boca de Tomatlán catch one of the minibuses marked "Mismaloya" or "Boca" that leave from the south-of-Cuale corner of Constitución and Calle Basilio Badillo, just below Insurgentes.

On the other hand, for the northwesterly Bay of Banderas destinations of Bucerías, Cruz de Huanacaxtle, and Punta de Mita, go by **Autotransportes Medina** buses that you can conveniently catch either at their downtown north-side station (1410 Brasil, tel. 322/212-4732 or 322/222-7279) or on the main boulevard, northbound side, across from the Hotel Sheraton.

BY CAR

Congestion and lack of parking space (or even parking garages) reduces the desirability of doing much driving of your own car or a rental car around downtown Puerto Vallarta. Nevertheless, for excursions outside of town, a car adds flexibility, convenience, and economy over the price of a guided tour, especially if you share costs with other passengers. Expect to pay about $50–65 a day for the cheapest rental, including legally required liability insurance. Car rental companies have booths at the airport. See *Airport Arrival and Departure* under *Getting There* earlier in this chapter.

If you must drive and park downtown, avoid driving along the very congested downtown Malecón southbound. If you're coming into town along the ingress boulevard from the north, instead follow the *libramiento* downtown bypass that forks left at the big Barra de Navidad sign over the boulevard. It leads you quickly to the less-congested south-of-Cuale old town neighborhood. There, either park your car and walk, or take a taxi. If you still insist on driving, go north along one-way Avenida Insurgentes, cross the Río Cuale bridge, bear left three blocks along Libertad, then right into the town center along Juárez, where you will eventually be able to find a parking place.

There are several parking garages now in place, although hours vary. Some are open 24 hours and others close late night. Be sure to check before you leave the garage. The garages are: Parque Hildalgo at the northern end of the Malecón, Juárez parking garage at the south end of the Malecón and one more in Zona Romantía, under the Parque Lazaro Cardenas. Rates run about $1 an hour and several restaurants and businesses offer parking validation for the Juárez garage (see cashier for a list). Due to the major construction that happens throughout the city, for large cars and trucks especially, parking in a garage is a smart choice.

BY TAXI

Taxis are all private, convenient, and safe, but not cheap (about $4–8 per trip within the city limits, verify rates at your hotel desk). Most taxi drivers will quote you the correct going rate. If not, bring him to his senses by hailing another taxi. Under any circumstances, don't get in until the price is settled.

WALKING AND BIKING

Walking is by far the best alternative for getting around downtown Puerto Vallarta. The heart of the Old Town, north and south of the river, stretches barely a mile and a half (2.5 km), a 30-minute walk north–south, and a half mile (0.6 km) 10-minute walk east–west. Bicycles, while available for rent ($10/day) downtown, are not a very safe alternative, given the many buses and fast drivers, who either don't see or ignore bicycles. Moreover, bicycles are a burden in Puerto Vallarta's hilly Old Town neighborhoods.

PUERTO VALLARTA

AROUND THE BAY OF BANDERAS

It used to be that Puerto Vallarta was *the* destination for tourists and snowbirds but with the city's explosive development and limited space due to the buttress of mountains at its back, growth along the sandy shores of the Bay of Banderas was inevitable. Now more people than ever skip the decidedly more urban setting of Puerto Vallarta for the bucolic towns that ring the bay and nestle into the majestic mountain range.

In these tiny hamlets, the accommodations and services, while limited, trend toward a more authentic and affordable experience. The beaches are less crowded and the outdoor recreational opportunities are just as abundant. Many of these small towns offer a glimpse of what Puerto Vallarta used to be like, before becoming one of the top three tourist destinations in Mexico.

The golden northwestern beaches and boutique resorts of Bucerías, La Cruz de Huanacaxtle and Punta Mita beckon within sight of downtown Puerto Vallarta. They decorate the long shoreline that curves north and west, to the Bay of Banderas's farthest point, at Punta de Mita. With the recent onslaught of condominium complexes and megaresorts, it's difficult to believe that you can still find an empty stretch of beach to call your own, but it's true (during the week). There's plenty of opportunity for surfing, sailing, snorkeling, fishing, and swimming or just spend the day browsing tiny shops and sipping a cool margarita under a beachside *palapa* and watch the world go by.

On the other hand, the Sierra Cuale, which rises easterly from Puerto Vallarta's downtown streets, offers unique opportunities for

© ROBIN NOELLE

HIGHLIGHTS

Playa Anclote: Half the fun of visiting this beach in Punta Mita is getting there. Once you've arrived, spend the day lounging on the beach, enjoy a surfing lesson, or take an excursion to the Islas Marietas for bird-, dolphin-, and whale-watching (page 114).

Islas Marietas: An aquatic wonderland, this protected marine park provides myriad opportunities for swimming, snorkeling, scuba and viewing rare Blue Footed Boobie birds (page 115).

San Sebastián: This hidden mountain hamlet can be visited in a day by car or bus. Spend a few hours strolling the little plaza and the cobbled streets, as well as visiting the Hacienda Jalisco, a coffee farm, and perhaps an old gold mine (page 117).

Mascota Museum and Casa de Cultura: Admire the Mascota Museum's lovingly displayed memorabilia collection, and the Casa de Cultura's fascinating 3,000-year-old ceramics. Afterward, stroll the plaza, then enjoy a picnic at nearby Corinches Reservoir (page 126).

Laguna Juanacatlán: Make a gem of an excursion out of Mascota to this clear mountain lake by sturdy car. Ideally, enjoy an overnight at the Sierra Lago Resort and Spa on the luscious spruce-tufted lakeshore. It's best to do this trip in the late spring, summer, or fall (page 132).

Virgin of Talpa Basilica: Visit the

LOOK FOR (TO FIND RECOMMENDED SIGHTS, ACTIVITIES, DINING, AND LODGING.

Virgin of Talpa in her basilica and the nearby museum. If possible, attend one of Talpa's four tumultuous annual festivals that honor the Virgin, but be sure to make hotel reservations far in advance (page 134).

adventurous travelers. In and around the petite mountain-country towns of San Sebastián, Mascota, and Talpa you can explore old gold mines and picturesque hidden villages, camp or lodge at pine-shadowed lakes and streams, trek by foot or horseback through sylvan wildlife-rich mountain valleys by day and relax in comfortable small hotels and luxurious haciendas by night—all these await travelers who venture into Puerto Vallarta's backyard mountains.

PLANNING YOUR TIME

For the **northwestern bay beaches** the key is to follow Highway 200 north by car, bus, or tour. If you're on a short time budget, go for a day to **Bucerías,** a medium sized town just 25 minutes north of Puerto Vallarta. There you can shop in the little marketplace stalls near the town square, swim or beachcomb the several miles of burnt sugar beaches and end your day with crab enchiladas and a dazzling

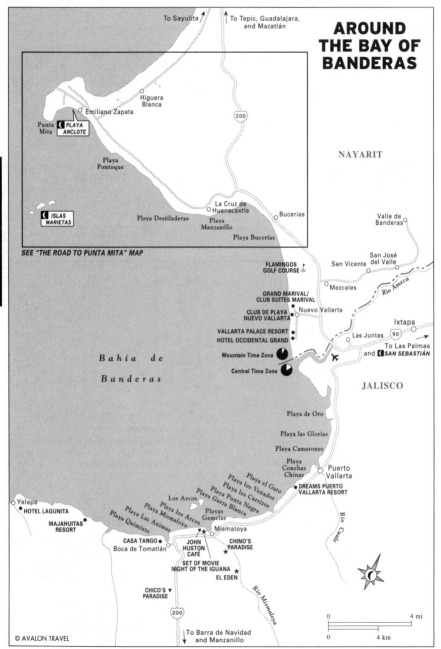

AROUND THE BAY OF BANDERAS

To Sayulita

To Tepic, Guadalajara, and Mazatlán

Higuera Blanca

Emiliano Zapata

Punta Mita

PLAYA ANCLOTE

Playa Pontoque

200

NAYARIT

ISLAS MARIETAS

La Cruz de Huanacaxtle

Bucerías

Valle de Banderas

Playa Destiladeras

Playa Manzanillo

Playa Bucerías

SEE "THE ROAD TO PUNTA MITA" MAP

San José del Valle

San Vicente

FLAMINGOS GOLF COURSE

Mezcales

Río Ameca

GRAND MARIVAL/ CLUB SUITES MARIVAL

Nuevo Vallarta

CLUB DE PLAYA NUEVO VALLARTA

VALLARTA PALACE RESORT
HOTEL OCCIDENTAL GRAND

Ixtapa

Las Juntas

90

To Las Palmas and **SAN SEBASTIÁN**

Mountain Time Zone

Central Time Zone

Bahía de Banderas

JALISCO

Playa de Oro

Playa las Glorias

Playa Camarones

Playa Conchas Chinas

Puerto Vallarta

Playa el Gato

Playa los Venados

Playa los Carrizos

Playa Punta Negra

Playa Garta Blanca

Playas Gemelas

DREAMS PUERTO VALLARTA RESORT

Los Arcos

Playa los Arcos

Playa Mismaloya

Playa Las Animas

Playa Quimixto

Mismaloya

Río Cuale

Yelapa

HOTEL LAGUNITA

MAJAHUITAS RESORT

CASA TANGO

Boca de Tomatlán

JOHN HUSTON CAFÉ

CHINO'S PARADISE

SET OF MOVIE NIGHT OF THE IGUANA

EL EDEN

CHICO'S PARADISE

200

Río Mismaloya

To Barra de Navidad and Manzanillo

0   4 mi

0   4 km

© AVALON TRAVEL

BAY OF BANDERAS TIME CHANGE

On the road to Nuevo Vallarta, Bucerías, and Punta Mita, the northern curve of the Bay of Banderas begins as Highway 200 crosses the Río Ameca and enters the state of Nayarit. Here clocks shift from central to mountain time; heading north, **set your watch back one hour.** Most businesses around the bay operate on Jalisco time but it's a good idea to double-check with the hotel or restaurant to make sure so that you don't miss your check out time or dinner reservation.

Pacific sunset at a beachfront restaurant like **Mar y Sol.**

With a day or two more, you might grab a room at one of the local hotels or B&Bs and stay a while or head a bit farther around the bay to **La Cruz de Huanacaxtle,** the latest village to be targeted for development with its spanking new marina. The once pristine and isolated **Punta de Mita** has become host to a slew of high-end luxury resorts but there are still several beaches available for public access and it's well known for being a top surf destination in the area. Splurge on a luxury room on the beach or opt for one of the still affordable, more spartan hotels just off the beach.

For Puerto Vallarta's **mountain country,** go by either bus, sturdy passenger car or SUV, or charter flight tour. In one long day, you can visit **San Sebastián,** enjoy lunch, stroll around the village square, visit a historic hacienda or an old gold mine, and return to Puerto Vallarta.

If you have two or more days, you can continue on to **Mascota** for an overnight or two in one of its comfortable hotels. Stroll around the town, visit the **Raoul Rodríguez Museum** and the **Casa de Cultura,** and maybe camp on the pine-shaded shoreline of **Corinches reservoir.** Spend another day visiting the picturesque villages of **Yerbabuena, Cimarron**

Chico, and **Navidad.** Alternatively, drive out in a different direction from Mascota and spend a day, maybe an overnight, at pristine high-sierra **Laguna Juanacatlán** and Sierra Lago Resort and Spa.

With another day, continue on to the fascinating pilgrimage town of **Talpa.** Visit the **Virgin of Talpa Basilica,** adored by hundreds of thousands of yearly pilgrims. Afterward, if you have another day, spend a restful overnight at **Hacienda Jacarandas** bed-and-breakfast before returning to Puerto Vallarta.

GETTING TO NUEVO VALLARTA, BUCERÍAS, AND PUNTA MITA

Autotransportes Medina (1410 Brasil, tel. 322/212-4732 or 322/222-7279) buses complete a flood of daily round-trips between Playa Anclote (Restaurant El Dorado terminal) and the Puerto Vallarta station, north of the Malecón. In Puerto Vallarta, walk or hire a taxi to the terminal, or catch the bus as it heads

Virgin of Talpa Basilica

BAY OF BANDERAS BY BOAT

In addition to the thousands of people who visit Puerto Vallarta and charter sailing or fishing boats each year, hundreds of people sail and cruise down the Pacific Coast of Mexico to stay for a little or long while as well. The coastline is scenic, the waters calm, and Pacific Mexico is well known for its wonderful sportfishing opportunities.

In addition to the fishing and recreational boating opportunities, you'll find that there are boat shows, fishing tournaments, and sailing regattas to partake in as well. Find out additional information from the four marinas that serve the Puerto Vallarta and Bay of Banderas areas:

· **Marina Vallarta:** Quite possibly one of the largest marina complexes in Mexico, Marina Vallarta is set on almost 500 acres of land that includes a 500-slip marina, an 18-hole golf course, multiple fine hotels, and a marina-side Malecón with galleries, restaurants, spas, and boutiques. It's located just south of the Puerto Vallarta airport at the large statue of Neptune.

· **Marina Nuevo Vallarta:** Located in the tony Nuevo Vallarta area just over the border of Nayarit, the petite Marina Nuevo Vallarta (www.marinanuevovallarta.com) is another option for cruisers stopping off in the Bay of Banderas. It offers 80 berths with services like showers, electric, water, and Wi-Fi Internet access.

· **Paradise Village Marina:** Paradise Village is home to a 200-slip marina (www.paradisevillagemarina.com), a luxury resort complex, and the **Vallarta Yacht Club.** Fuel is not available on-site; you must go to nearby Marina Vallarta for that, but there are plenty of opportunities for shopping, dining, and recreation.

· **Marina Riviera Nayarit:** Based in the little but growing village of **La Cruz de Huanacaxtle,** Marina Riviera Nayarit (www.marinarivieranayarit.com) is the newest marina in the Bay of Banderas area. While the 351-slip marina is complete, along with the brand new yacht club, sky bar, and fuel station, there are still plans to add a five-star hotel, several condo towers, and retail commercial spaces to the complex.

the new marina at La Cruz de Huanacaxtle

north along the airport boulevard through the Zona Hotelera. Stops en route include Nuevo Vallarta, Bucerías, La Cruz de Huancaxtle, Piedra Blanca, and Destiladeras. The last bus returns to Puerto Vallarta at about 9 P.M.

Taxis are available but outrageously expensive with fares running as much as $75 or more for a one-way trip to Punta Mita. The shared white minivans are slightly more affordable and can be waved down near Wal-Mart or the airport or nearly anywhere on the highway. For a more leisurely or extended trip, a rental car would be a good investment (approx. $60 per day from the airport).

Nuevo Vallarta

When planning a trip to Puerto Vallarta new visitors sometimes mistakenly believe that Nuevo Vallarta is part of or even close to Puerto Vallarta. This is not the case. Nuevo Vallarta lies 15–20 minutes north of Vallarta just off of Highway 200, once you've crossed the river into the state of Nayarit. With few exceptions, there is little to do and see in Nuevo Vallarta outside of the mega beach resort complexes and golf courses. Nuevo Vallarta is a bit like the Disneyland version of Mexico—perfectly paved streets, lush tropical landscaping, guarded gates, and the only Mexicans one tends to see speak very good English and wear uniforms. You'll find very little to remind you of the more authentic Mexico that you will experience if you stay in less manufactured environments.

GOLF

The centerpiece of Nuevo Vallarta is **El Tigre** (tel. 322/297-0773, www.eltigregolf.com), an 18-hole, par-72 course, which while mostly flat makes use of water and sand to make things interesting. Many national and international tournaments take place at El Tigre. Greens fee is $116 for morning and $80 for afternoon.

A bit farther north, the green, palm-shaded 18-hole **Los Flamingos Golf Course** (Km 145, Hwy. 200, 8 mi/13 km north of the airport, tel. 329/296-5006 from Puerto Vallarta, www.flamingosgolf.com.mx, 7 A.M.–5 P.M. daily) offers an alternative to El Tigre. Open to the public, Los Flamingos services include carts, caddies, club rentals, a pro shop, restaurant, and locker rooms. The greens fee of $121 for morning and $77 for afternoon includes the cart.

SAILING

Vallarta Yacht Club (Paseo de los Cocoteros, next door to the Paradise Village Resort, tel. 322/297-2222, www.vallartayachtclub.com) offers reciprocal arrangements with many yacht clubs around the world and offers nonmembers two free visits. Club amenities include a full service staff, swimming pool, BBQ area, and member's pricing at the very good and reasonably priced restaurant. The club emphasizes social activities and offers a junior sailing program. Members can participate in the several regattas and other events that take place throughout the year.

For those looking to charter a sailboat or even take sailing lessons, **J World** (tel. 800/910-1101 or 322/226-6767, www.sailing-jworld.com) can be found in Paradise Village. Head through the gates and past the caged tigers, down toward the water to find their offices.

SHOPPING

Other than hotel gift stores and beach vendors, there isn't a lot of shopping in Nuevo Vallarta, save for the large **Paradise Village** mall. Inside you will find a number of fast food joints, restaurants, a small grocery store, and several bank branches. There are many shops to browse but none of them offer anything truly unique and it is all marked up considerably from what you would pay for similar items in Puerto Vallarta. So unless you plan on skipping Puerto Vallarta altogether, which would be a shame, save your pesos for a trip into town.

ACCOMMODATIONS

Nearly all of the hotel offerings in Nuevo Vallarta are both expensive and offer timeshares. This means that you will mostly likely be invited to their "welcome gathering" or a free tour of the hotel and breakfast for at least one of the days that you are there. If you do not wish to be party to the hard-sell presentations, simply decline the invitation. Many hotels will offer free gifts for attending these presentations and the quality of the gift is entirely dependent on the attendee's negotiating skills. Tough negotiators will walk out with cold, hard cash or at the very least, a pair of expensive tour tickets.

No one wants to pay the rack rate on these hotels, so be sure to book in advance. Normally, you can get a good discount by purchasing an air-inclusive package or booking directly from the website of the hotel where promotions and specials are listed.

$100-300

Nuevo Vallarta's first world-class hotel is a palmy Mediterranean-style French-Canadian–owned twin development. Its older (circa 1990) section, the **ClubSuites Marival** (Blvd. Nuevo Vallarta, esq. Paseo Cocoteros, tel. 322/297-0100 or 322/226-8200, toll-free Mex. tel. 01-800/326-6600, fax 322/297-0160, www.go-marival.com), sits beside the new, shinier **Grand Marival**. The hotels sometime invite the public to drop in on their continuous party ($50/day pp), which includes sports, crafts, games, and food and drink. If you take a room in the Grand Marival, the all-inclusive food, lodging, and activities run about $200 per day for two in low season, $400 high. The Club section, being a half a block from the beach, is cheaper by about $10 per person. If you reserve through an agent, be sure to ask for a package or promotional price.

Along the beach boulevard, Paseo de Cocoteros, about two miles south of the original development, a line of big new hotels woos

vacationers with a plethora of facilities and long, velvety beaches. The 344-room **Vallarta Palace Resort** (Paseo de los Cocoteros 19, tel. 322/226-8470, toll-free Mex. tel. 01-800/672-5223, fax 322/226-8471, www.palaceresorts.com) is the most established. Arrival there feels like approaching a small Elysium. Above the reception area rises an airy, angular atrium. Nearby, a garden of lovely ceramic fruits decorates whitewashed stairs leading down to a buffet loaded with salads, fruit, poultry, fish, meats, and desserts spread on one side of a spacious, guest-filled dining area. Outside are pools beneath palm trees along the beach, where crowds enjoy nightly dancing and shows. By day, guests lounge, swim, and frolic amid a varied menu of activities, from water aerobics and yoga to beach volleyball, bicycling, and kayaking.

Rates include all food, drinks, activities, and a deluxe oceanview room with everything. For walk-in guests, prices begin at about $380 for two, kids 4–17 about $120. If the season is right, you may be able to secure a reduced-rate package via the Internet or a travel agent. Be aware that this is partly a time-share property and the management is always interested in selling you a time-share.

Next door to the south, the **Occidental Allegro Nuevo Vallarta** (Paseo de los Cocoteros 18, tel. 322/297-0400, toll-free Mex. tel. 01-800/907-9500, toll-free U.S./Can. tel. 800/858-2258, fax 322/297-0082, www.occidental-hoteles.com) offers a similar all-inclusive vacation package for about $300 for two in low season, $470 high. Children under 6 stay free, kids 6–12 stay for $50 in low season, $70 high. Day passes, including all in-house food, drinks, sports, and entertainment, run about $40 per adult; night passes are about $50. Bargain packages are often available by Internet reservation or through agents during nonpeak seasons.

FOOD

Outside of the hotels and the Paradise Village mall, there aren't a ton of places to eat in Nuevo Vallarta and of course, the very best dining is in Puerto Vallarta. There are however, a few standouts. Tucked around the corner on a quiet street at the south end of the development, **Nopal Beach** (Boulevard de Nayarit 70, tel. 322/297-4568) is a hidden gem. With simple outdoor seating and a casual menu of Mexican favorites, Nopal Beach is a favorite place for locals and tourists alike. For breakfast try the breakfast burrito, made with your choice of ingredients and wrapped inside a large flour tortilla. For lunch, grab some guacamole and chips and the fish tacos. Dishes run from $5–$10.

Just around the corner from Nopal Beach as you head back toward the highway is **Guido's** (Boulevard de Nayarit, across from the cab stands, tel. 322/297-1061, www.guidos-vallarta.com.mx) where you can find authentic Italian food prepared by the owner/chef Guido Morelli. Guido's offers a nice selection of pastas and Italian dishes, a good wine list and fine service.

On the other side of Nuevo just off the highway is local Mexican favorite and a meat lover's paradise **La Parrilla de Villa** (Av. Ingreso Norte, tel. 322/297-7915). For $60, you and three friends can share a platter of four grilled meats including chorizo and carne asada, as well as a bottle of tequila or 20 beers. As expected, La Parrilla is a party kind of place. There's not much for vegetarians to choose but there are vegetarian fajitas on the menu ($9). Carnivores not traveling in a pack can order from a selection of grilled meats including some good BBQ ribs ($11). Most plates come with beans, baked potato, tortillas, and grilled onions. There's a playhouse for the kids to enjoy while adults dine, a live lounge singer who entices diners to sing along with popular Mexican favorites, and a full bar.

Bucerías

Bucerías (Place of the Divers) doesn't look like much from the highway, just a long stretch of rundown buildings and shabby businesses but looks are deceiving. Situated 12 miles (19 km) north of the Puerto Vallarta airport, Bucerías (pop. 5,000) features a lovely golden beach, a clutch of wonderful restaurants, and several comfortable lodging choices. There's a number of places offering live music and the town square often hosts events or small carnivals. There's even a weekly art walk. Local people have long flocked to Bucerías on Sunday for beach play, as well as for fresh seafood from one of several beachfront *palapa* restaurants.

Bucerías is a popular choice for retirees due to its inexpensive and quiet nature. Popular with Canadians, there's a sizeable community of expats, many of whom run B&Bs, restaurants, or other small businesses. The town has developed continuously from its beginning as a fishing village of a few long dusty streets running parallel to the beach. Visitors from Puerto Vallarta began arriving and the town gradually acquired a sprinkling of small businesses—grocery stores, bakeries, and local-style restaurants. Now as the space becomes more limited, Bucerías has started to spread to the north with the addition of several large condo complexes and new little strip malls. The largest and most popular addition to the area is the massive supermarket **Mega Commercial** which sits just south of the town on the main highway. Here residents and tourists alike can do the majority of their shopping for groceries and sundries. Several new businesses are slated to open in the large plaza including several services and retail shops.

Despite its burgeoning popularity, some the original charm of Bucerías remains: lots of old-fashioned local color, especially around the lively town-center market and the adjacent rickety midtown footbridge over the creek (that blocks through traffic and divides Bucerías into a pair of subvillages), and the seemingly endless beach, with slowly breaking waves and soft golden-white sand, perfect for swimming,

BAY OF BANDERAS

bodysurfing, boogie boarding, surfing, and surf fishing. Tent camping is customary on the beach, especially during the Christmas and Easter holidays.

ENTERTAINMENT AND EVENTS
Nightlife and Live Music

For what's pretty much a quiet little town just north of Puerto Vallarta, Bucerías does have a few venues for live music and nighttime socializing. At night the square downtown in front of the church comes alive with Mexican families, courting sweethearts, tourists, and teens all gathering in and around the gazebo to mix and mingle. Street vendors and food stands appear as if by magic around dusk and sometimes the occasional musician or street performer will materialize to entertain the masses as well. This is definitely where the action is.

For those looking for the most popular bars, you'll usually find a good crowd at **The Shamrock Pub** (Av. Mexico 22, tel. 329/298-3073), particularly on St. Patrick's Day.

Two blocks south, you will find **The Twisted Rose** (corner of Mexico and Hildalgo, tel. 322/146-3023), which offers live music on many nights as well as special events for holidays. Just around the corner is **Bucerías Gardens** (corner of Mexico and Hildalgo, north of the church), another popular live music venue.

On the south side of town you can stop by **El Gecko Pub** (Morelos 8, across from Casa Tranquila) for some billiards and a cold one. El Gecko is less of a tourist hangout and more of a worker's bar, so enjoy the local flavor!

ACCOMMODATIONS
North Side of Town

At the town's serene north end is the Playas de Huanacaxtle subdivision, with big flower-decorated villas owned by well-heeled Mexicans and North Americans. Sprinkled among the intimate, palm-shaded *retornos* (cul-de-sacs) are a number of good bungalow-style beachside lodgings. As you move southward from the north edge of town, the top-value accommodations

begin with the **Vista Vallarta Suites** (Av. de los Picos s/n, Playas de Huanacaxtle, tel. 329/298-0361 or 329/298-0360, toll-free Mex. tel. 01-800/570-7292, toll-free U.S./Can. tel. 888/888-9127, www.vistavallartasuites.com). Here, three stories of comfortably furnished stucco-and-tile apartments cluster intimately around a palm-tufted beachside pool and patio. A loyal cadre of longtime guests—mostly U.S. and Canadian retiree-couples—return year after year to enjoy the big blue pool, the *palapa* restaurant, walks along the beach, and the company of fellow vacationers. All enjoy fully furnished two-bedroom suites with dining room, kitchenette, living room, cable TV, and private ocean-view balconies. Maids clean rooms daily, while downstairs friendly English-speaking clerks manage the desk and rent cars, boogie boards, and surfboards. High-season rates run $99 d, $178 q; low season $70 d, $130 q. Discounts may be negotiable for long-term rentals.

A block south, the family-style **Bungalows Princess** (Retorno Destiladeras, Playas de Huanacaxtle, tel. 329/298-0100 or 329/298-0110, fax 329/298-0068, www.vallarta-info.com/rentals/princess.html) looks out on the blue Bay of Banderas beneath the rustling fronds of lazy coco palms. Their several two-story detached beachfront bungalows provide all the ingredients for a restful vacation for a family or group of friends. Behind the bungalows, beside an interior pool patio, a stone's throw from the beach, a motel-style lineup of rooms and suites fills the economy needs of couples and small families.

A total of 36 bungalows, suites, and rooms are available. The big, semideluxe (2-bedroom, 2-bath) beachfront housekeeping bungalows rent for about $200 high season, $160 low. A row of about six interior beachfront poolside (2-bedroom, 2-bath) housekeeping bungalow apartments go for about $165 high season, $120 low. Away from the beach, facing a second pool patio, a lineup of junior suites and rooms rent, respectively, for about $110 high season, $90 low, and $75 high, $55 low. Discounts and cheaper long-term rates are often available during the low months of January, May–June, and

September–November. All rooms feature TV with HBO, phone, and air-conditioning; hotel amenities include desk service, a minimarket, and two pools. Credit cards are accepted. Continuing south, nearby **Bungalows Los Picos** (Av. los Picos and Retorno Pontoque, Playas de Huanacaxtle, tel. 329/298-0470, fax 329/298-0131, www.lospicos.com.mx) shares the same palm-shadowed Bucerías beachfront. The rambling, Mexican family–style complex centers around a big inner pool patio, spreading shoreward, to a second motel-style bungalow wing beside a breezy beachside pool area. The most desirable units are the big three-bedroom oceanfront kitchenette bungalows (about $230 high, $180 low, with choice of a/c or fans, sleeping up to eight). Other units, off the beach, around a nevertheless inviting interior pool patio include one-bedroom kitchenette apartments (about $132 high, $110 low, with choice of fans or a/c, sleeping four); and adjacent, smaller four-person kitchenette suites ($105 high, $85 low, all with a/c). A few smaller fan-only rooms ($55 high, $48 low) are also available. All units are clean and comfortably furnished. Amenities include cable TV, snack restaurant, lounge, Internet café, two pools, parking, and credit cards accepted. During low seasons, the management sometimes offers such promotions as three nights for the price of two; discounts for long-term rentals are usually available.

South Side of Town

About a mile away, near the good restaurants, just a block from the beach, consider the inviting, moderately priced **Casa Tranquila** (Morelos 7A, tel. 329/298-1767, cell 044-322/728-7519, www.casatranquila-bucerias.com). Welcoming owners Patricia Mendez and Joann Quickstad offer five compact one-bedroom kitchenette apartments that open to a lovely tropical garden pool patio. All of the apartments are clean, comfortable, and individually decorated (in Aztec, Gringo, Vaquero, Suzie Wong, and Quimixto styles). Rates range from about $55 d to about $70 d, depending on season and whether you prefer air-conditioning or fan. Light sleepers should opt for the

downstairs units as the bar across the street can get noisy sometimes.

Attached to the hotel is **Gringo's Books & Coffee,** an excellent place for trading in your paperbacks and finding new beach reads. You can also find a variety of books written by local authors or having to do with the subject of Mexico. There's even a small French language section. If you are in need of a serious massage by a trained professional, be sure to book an hour with Joann in her relaxing and comfortable massage studio ($45/hr).

Around the corner, less than a block away, find the inviting **Hotel Palmeras** (35 Lázaro Cárdenas, tel./fax 329/298-1288, U.S./Can. tel. 647/722-4139, www.hotelpalmeras.com). Located near restaurants, art galleries, and just a stone's throw from the beach, you can easily spend a week here for an affordable tropical vacation. In the center of the hotel is a lushly landscaped pool area and the rooms are clean and comfortable, especially the recently added suites in the new building. One bedrooms in the old wing run about $35 low season, $65 high, two bedrooms about $75 low, $120 high for four persons, all with air-conditioning, fans, and kitchenettes. The new-wing apartments, all either studios or one bedroom, run about $65 low season, $100 high, all with air-conditioning, fans, cable TV, and private patios or sitting areas. Amenities include lounge with satellite TV, wireless Internet, beach towels, and daily maid service.

About four blocks farther south is the popular **Bungalows Arroyo** (500 Lázaro Cárdenas, tel./fax 329/298-0076, bungalowsarroyo@hotmail.com). The dozen-odd roomy two-bedroom apartments are clustered beside a palmy swimming pool and garden half a block from the beach. The units are comfortably furnished, each with king-size beds, private balcony, kitchen, and living and dining room. Units rent for about $100 low season, $120 high, with discounts available for monthly rentals. They're popular; get your winter reservations in months early.

For a wonderful B&B experience try Brian and Sandi Barkwell's beautiful **Casa Cielito**

Lindo (Calle Fibba #12, tel. 329/298-2440, www.waterfrontdreamvacations.com) located just a few blocks from the beach. There are four lodging choices, the newest being the Mirador suite located on the third floor with views of the ocean. The rooms are comfortable and well appointed with authentic Mexican touches and decor. High season rates start at $100 per night for the Sunflower or Eclipse rooms and go up to $175 per night for the Palapa Retreat Suite which includes a full kitchen. Some suites can be combined for larger groups and there's a one week minimum during the holiday season. The rates include a full, hot breakfast and access to the home's amenities including the fourth floor *palapa* for sunset viewing, the swimming pool, and the common areas. In residence are Sandi and Brian's treasured golden retrievers so this is not a good choice for those who don't care for the occasional wet nose.

Trailer Parks and Camping

There aren't many options for trailer and RV camping in and near Bucerías, however, the **Altarose Rancho RV Park** (Valle de Banderas, Jalisco, tel. 322/148-7031, www.rvparkvallarta.com $20/day or $450/mo) is located 15 minutes south of Bucerías on the way to Puerto Vallarta. Turn at the stoplights at the Mezcales intersection on Highway 200 and head inland, following the signs for Valle de Banderas. This new park offers country camping with a view of the mountains and while the newly planted trees don't offer much shade at the time of this printing, over time the park will be shaded and quite pleasant. Amenities include large lots with water, power and sewer. Outdoor activities are available and services and supplies can be had in the nearby town.

FOOD

A number of good restaurants serve Bucerías's cadre of discriminating diners. A large selection of restaurants lie between the cross streets of Galeana and Morelos, along Calle Lázaro Cárdenas, the street that runs parallel to the beach, beginning just south of the town-center Puente de los Besos (Bridge of the Kisses). On

the other side of the bridge along the beach is a strip of popular seafood restaurants, all offering fresh fish and an opportunity to dip your toes into the sand and watch the sunset. Heading north on Avenida Mexico you will find a number of more eclectic choices from pizza to a new wine bar and tapas restaurant.

One of the most popular restaurants is Sandrina's. Find ◖ **Sandrina's** (btwn. Galeana and Morelos, tel. 329/298-0273, 3–10:30 P.M. Wed.–Mon.) just south of Hotel Palmera. The labor of love of Victoria, British Columbia expatriates Andrew and Sandra Neumann, they serve a varied late-lunch and dinner Mediterranean fusion menu with lots of Greek specialties (antipastos, salads, souvlaki, lasagna) and exquisite mahimahi fish fillet dinners ($8–15) in a beautifully artistic inside-outside garden setting.

Especially popular and equally enjoyable for lunch or dinner, ◖ **Claudio's Meson Bay** (tel. 329/298-1634, 2–10 P.M. daily) is a block farther north on the beach side. Here the welcoming owner has everything in place in his large airy beachfront *palapa,* perfect for happy-hour sunsets. Offerings include super-fresh catch-of-the-day fish, lobster, prawns, clams, and oysters ($8–14), plus a bountiful meat barbecue ($8–18) and a generous salad bar ($5). This all climaxes every Wednesday night with an overflowing all-you-can-eat barbecue ($15).

After trying the above, you might also check out a number of other reliably recommended restaurants in the same neighborhood. Located right on the beach, **Karen's Place** (corner of Lázaro Cárdenas and Juárez, tel. 329/298-1499, 8:30 A.M.–10 P.M. Mon.–Sat., 8:30 A.M.–3 P.M. Sun., $5–12), in the big Costa Dorada condo complex, serves breakfast, lunch, early dinner, and Sunday champagne brunch under the shade a large *palapa*. While all of the seatings here offer delicious food, the brunch is one of the best deals in town for only $9 without and $14 with alcohol. Karen's has very good eggs Benedict.

In their new location just two blocks up from Bungalows Arroyo, **Espressions** (Agustin Melgar 265, tel. 329/298-0749, Mon.–Sat., www.espressionscafe.com, $12–14) does a great job with comfort food, select Asian-inspired dishes, and daily specials. They have a loyal following of regular customers who enjoy dining in the cool garden or on the porch of this renovated home. Local guitarist vocalist Antonio Marquez plays nightly during the high season starting at 7 P.M.

Headed back along Lázaro Cárdenas is the **Red Apple** (corner of Morelos, tel. 329/298-1235, 8:30 A.M.–10 P.M. Mon.–Sat., 8 A.M.–4 P.M. Sun.), an upstairs oceanview *palapa* specializing in garlic shrimp, fajitas, and hearty *ranchero* breakfasts ($5–15). If you are looking for a beer and a pool table, try the **El Gecko Pub** (half a block east on Morelos) where many of the local Mexican residents hang out. Just across the street is **Gringo's Books & Coffee,** run by Joann and Patricia of **Casa Tranquila.** Grab an espresso and fresh baked cookie while browsing through the extensive collection of used books.

From the town square there is a series of similar Mexican seafood restaurants to choose from. Of all of the beachfront restaurants **Mar y Sol** (Av. Pacifico, daily) is my personal favorite, with their spicy and delicious crab tacos and sparkling fresh squeezed lemonade. The staff are friendly and competent and have a good mastery of English for those who don't speak Spanish. Grab some oysters on the half shell or BBQ ribs and enjoy the music from the traveling mariachis.

There is a series of good dining choices along Avenida Mexico, the street running north from the square just past the church. Grab a slice of pizza at **Yo Yo Mo's** or for a more refined ambiance do some wine-tasting and enjoy a light meal of tapas at newcomer **El Buen Vino** (Av. Mexico 27, tel. 329/298-3970, 6 P.M.–1 A.M. Tues.–Sat.). This beautifully appointed wine bar offers delicious gourmet cheese plates, fresh sushi, and an extensive wine list with selections from around the world. Outdoor seating is available in the garden patio and there's live music on select afternoons and evenings. Wine-tastings are Tuesday night at 6 P.M. and are increasing in popularity so call ahead for reservations.

Tapas del Mundo (corner of Av. Mexico & Hildalgo, tel. 329/298-1194, www.tapasdelmundo.com) offers a wide variety of tasty tapas for discerning guests. Enjoy the show as friendly owner/operator Jorge whips up his amazing Caesar salad from scratch and make sure not to miss the Cuban sausage with white sauce. There's something for everyone on the menu, from sizzling garlic shrimp to the vegetarian potato cakes. Jorge also offers cooking classes. Once you've had your fill of tapas, head upstairs to **The Bar Above** to sample one of Buddy's mouthwatering chocolate soufflés and a Spanish coffee. Enjoy the view from the 4th-floor *palapa* while you watch the evening fireworks over the bay.

BAY OF BANDERAS

The Road to Punta Mita

A day trip on the road to Punta Mita used to take you past white-sand beaches, fishing villages, and waterfront *palapa* restaurants but now you are more likely to be driving past construction sites and new condos. A few miles north of Bucerías the Punta Mita highway splits left (west) and passes over Highway 200. The first town you arrive at is the little town of **La Cruz de Huanacaxtle** complete with its brand new luxury marina. There's a handful of good restaurants and a few lodging choices here but the beach isn't anything special and you'll find nicer sand and surf farther along the highway.

LA CRUZ DE HUANACAXTLE

As you turn to follow the gentle curve of the Bay of Banderas toward Punta Mita, you will find yourself in the once little village of La Cruz de Huanacaxtle. Once hardly more than a flyspeck on a map, La Cruz has begun its transition into

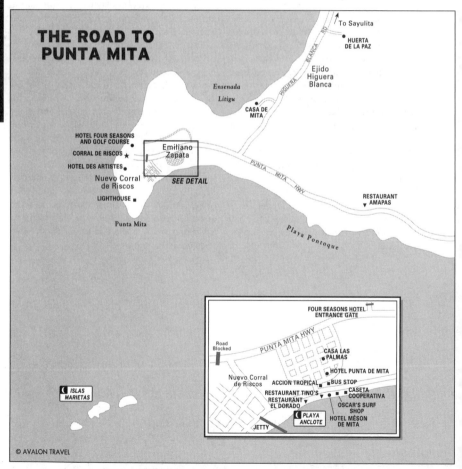

a popular vacation spot for those who find that even Bucerías has gotten too big for their taste. The addition of a brand new, modern marina has brought an upscale element to La Cruz, however you'll find it's not nearly as spendy as say Punta Mita or Sayulita. Some say that La Cruz is "the next big thing" to hit Riviera Nayarit.

Accommodations

Your best option for accommodations outside of renting a house or condo is the darling **La Cruz Inn** (Calle Marlin #36, tel. 329/295-5849, www.lacruzinn.com), where you can rent one of

the five available rooms for about $100 d year-round. The rooms are comfortable and tastefully decorating with carved wooden furniture and Mexican handicrafts. Four of the rooms have lovely outdoor kitchens and private patios. All rooms have both fans and air-conditioning. The rooms open onto a shared courtyard where guests can enjoy a swim in the pool and there is an on-site restaurant **Arriba** that specializes in comfort food. Wi-Fi is available throughout the hotel.

Food

Whether or not you decide to stay overnight in

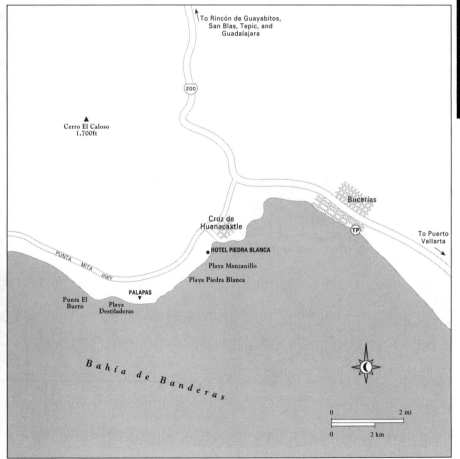

La Cruz, there are couple of restaurants you won't want to miss. At **Frascati** (Av. Langosta 10, tel. 329/295-5154, 5 P.M.–11 P.M. daily, $11–20) diners can enjoy wood-fired pizzas or freshly made pasta with savory sauces. If you enjoy alfredo sauce, this is the place to order it. The garden-like interior setting is beautiful and the waiters are attentive without being overbearing.

If you are looking for the expat crowd, you can try **Philo's** (Calle Delfin 15, tel. 329/295-5068, 8 A.M.–1 A.M., Tues.–Sat.) which is as much a social club and community center as it is restaurant and rock bar. It's especially popular with cruisers who dock at the nearby marina. There's live music on the weekends and you never know when Philo and his band will grace the stage throughout the week. Pizza and ribs are the specialty but the menu includes burgers, salads, and sandwiches as well.

Arriba (Calle Marlin 36, tel. 329/295-5849, www.lacruzinn.com, Mon.–Fri.) is the restaurant located at La Cruz Inn where the owners, John and Carol offer a selection of comfort food and Indian dishes. Try the Steak & Ale pie ($14) or the selection of homemade curries ($12–15). Dining is outside under the large *palapa* on the second floor offering a view of the town square.

Arguably the most popular and well-known dining option in La Cruz is **Tacos on the Street** (Calle Huachinango 9, 5 P.M.–11 P.M., Wed., Sat. and Sun.). This casual restaurant is in front of a local family's house and serves tacos and quesadillas. Some say the best tacos in Mexico. Seating is outside at plastic tables and chairs and guests are welcome to bring their own beer or wine. Soft drinks and Jamaica water are available. Make sure to grab a piece of flan for dessert.

Playa Manzanillo and Hotel Piedra Blanca

Half a mile (at around Mile 2/Km 3) farther past the center of La Cruz, a rough side road to the left leads to beautiful Playa Manzanillo and the Hotel Piedra Blanca. The beach itself, a carpet of fine golden-white coral sand, stretches along a little cove sheltered by a limestone

Playa Destiladeras is a miles-long coral-strewn strand.

© BRUCE WHIPPERMAN

headland—thus Piedra Blanca (White Stone). This place was made for peaceful vacationing: snorkeling at nearby **Playa Piedra Blanca** on the opposite side of the headland; fishing from the beach, rocks, or by boat launched on the beach or hired in the La Cruz de Huanacaxtle harbor.

The **Hotel Piedra Blanca** (Alcatraz 36, Cruz de Huanacaxtle, tel. 329/295-5489 or 329/295-5493, reserva_hotelpblanca@hotmail.com) is an unpretentious family-managed resort. The best of the big, plain but comfortable suites offer upstairs ocean views. All the ingredients—a tennis court, a shelf of used paperback novels, and a rustic *palapa* restaurant beside an inviting beachview pool and patio—are perfect for a season of tranquil relaxation. The 41 suites ($100 d year-round, $80 d for stays of more than two weeks, $1,000 per month) have kitchenettes, air-conditioning, and cable TV; credit cards are not accepted.

Past Piedra Blanca, the highway winds for 12 miles (19 km) to Punta Mita through the bushy summer–fall green-jungle country at the foot of the Sierra Vallejo. Although pristine only a few years ago, this stretch is now pocked with condo and villa developments that unfortunately restrict access to the emerald-forested and coral-studded shoreline.

Rock coral, the limestone skeleton of living coral, becomes gradually more common as you move west along the Punta Mita coast, thus tinting the water aqua and the sand white. As the highway approaches Punta Mita, the living reef offshore becomes intact and continuous.

Playa Destiladeras

A pair of oceanside *palapa* restaurants (at Mile 5/Km 8) mark Playa Destiladeras, a beach-lover's heavenly mile of white sand. Two-to-five-foot waves roll in gently, providing good conditions for bodysurfing and boogie boarding. Surfing gets better the closer you get to the end of the headland at **Punta el Burro** (known also as Punta Veneros), where good left-breaking waves make it popular with local surfers.

The intriguing label *destiladeras* originates with the fresh water dripping from the cliffs past Punta el Burro, collecting in freshwater pools right beside the ocean. Campers who happen upon one of these pools may find their water problems solved.

Punta Mita

In the early 1990s, the Mexican government concluded a deal with private interests to build the Four Seasons resort development at Corral de Riscos, at the end of the Punta Mita highway. The idyllic Corral de Riscos inlet, however, was *ejido* (communally owned) land and base of operations for the local fishing and boating cooperative, Cooperativa Corral de Riscos. In 1995 the government moved the people, under protest, into modern housing beside a new anchorage at nearby Playa Anclote. Now more than 10 years later there seems no end to the development plans for this once isolated and lovely area. The *ejido* people are challenging the government and developers but it's likely that plans for more condos and another championship golf course will continue. At approximately Mile 12, a private gate on the right leads to the super-exclusive 18-hole golf course and 100-room Four Seasons Hotel.

Despite the accumulation of high-end resorts and housing developments and the restricted access to the beaches of the area, Punta Mita can still feel like a funky beach town. There's a clutch of rustic economy hotels and affordable *palapa* restaurants amid the wealth of the new residents, keeping Punta Mita a viable option for traveling surfers looking to ride waves that can last for more than half a mile.

The name Punta Mita (actually Punta de Mita) encompasses the entire northwestern headland of the Bay of Banderas. Important sections include the Emiliano Zapata village (pop. about 1,000) on the bluff above the beach; Nuevo Corral de Riscos (pop. about 500), the new town that the government built for the displaced *ejido* people, west of Emiliano Zapata; and the boat harbor and beachfront *palapa* restaurant strip, called Playa Anclote, or simply "Anclote," by local folks.

The hotel people are trying to erase Corral de Riscos, the lovely west-side fishing inlet and location of the original *ejido* village, from memory. "Corral de Riscos doesn't exist," they claim.

🅲 PLAYA ANCLOTE

Head left, downhill, at the highway's end (Mile 13/Km 21) toward Playa Anclote (Anchor Beach), which gets its name from the galleon anchor displayed at one of the beachside *palapa* restaurants. The beach itself is a broad, half-mile-long curving strand of soft, very fine coral sand. The water is shallow for a long distance out, and the waves are gentle and long-breaking, good for beginning surfing, boogie boarding, and bodysurfing.

A few hundred yards downhill from the highway, a block left of the road T at the bottom, stands the **Caseta Cooperativa Corral de Riscos Servicios Turísticos** (Av. Anclote 17, tel./fax 329/291-6298, cooperativapuntamita@prodigy.net.mx). This former fishing cooperative, now tourism provider, offers a number of services, such as sightseeing and snorkel tours at the Islas Marietas, an hour offshore; fishing for good-eating dorado and tuna ($40/hr); whale-watching (Dec.–Mar.); and surf instruction. One of the guiding lights of the Cooperativa whom you might ask for at the office is personable Austrian-English-German-Spanish guide Rudi Hofer, who among other things leads visitors on sea-mammal, bird-watching, snorkel, and fishing excursions ($100 for 2–8 people), especially during the wildlife-rich winter months.

Alternatively, look up the veteran surf instructor and guide **Eduardo del Valle Ochoa** (Langostina 3, Cruz de Huanacaxtle, tel. 329/295-5087 or in Punta Mita 329/291-6633, www.acciontropical.com.mx), who welcomes visitors daily across the street west of the Cooperativa office. Besides offering

Playa Anclote

surfing lessons, Eduardo arranges sportfishing launches (Dec.–May, three hours, $150, including fishing tackle and bait) and snorkeling, wildlife-watching, and photography boat tours to the pristine offshore wildlife sanctuaries of Islas Marietas. During a typical half-day trip, visitors may glimpse dolphins, sea turtles, and often whales, as well as visit breeding grounds for brown and blue-footed boobies, Heermann's gulls, and other birds.

There are other surf lesson options such as veteran surf instructor Oscar, whose surf equipment rental shop, **Oscar's Rentals** (www.puntamita.com/oscarrentals.htm), is next door to the Caseta Cooperativa Corral de Riscos. Or try **Mictlan Surf School** (tel. 329/291-5413, www.mictlansurf.com), a group of young but experienced surfers who offer lessons and excursions for all levels as well as rentals and sales of surf equipment and accessories right on the main beach road.

◖ ISLAS MARIETAS

Las Marietas Islands biosphere reserve and national park were originally made famous by **Jacques Yves Cousteau,** who studied the area because of the vast variety of species found there. Technically, Las Marietas is an archipelago, located three miles from Punta Mita. This archipelago is formed by two islands, volcanic in origin. The reefs are extensive and range 15–90 feet in depth with volcanic tubes running throughout the underwater area of the islands. This is the second most popular place for local scuba diving and snorkeling aside from Los Arcos. Make sure to go with a guide if you plan on diving because the currents can get very strong in some places.

The reason for the popularity of the island is the numerous species of coral, marine mammals, birds, and fish. Particularly, the islands are known for the large population of **blue-footed boobies.** There are sheltered areas for swimming and several small, sandy areas for relaxing and sunbathing. Whether or not you dive or snorkel, the trip out to the island is worth it because you are almost assured to see wild dolphins and Giant Pacific manta rays.

ACCOMMODATIONS

If you decide to stay, Punta Mita offers a number of comfortable accommodations.

Under $50

The downscale **Hotel Punta de Mita** (Hidalgo 5, Fracc. E. Zapata, tel. 329/291-6269, www.hotelpuntamita.com) overlooks the bay in Emiliano Zapata. Here, what you see is what you get: about 15 small, plain motel-style rooms around an inviting kid-friendly grassy pool patio. Rates run about $40 per room ($50 w/kitchen), with air-conditioning, bunk beds for the kids, and hot showers.

Informal tent **camping** and **RV** parking around Punta Mita is possible when not prohibited by the government because of local construction; ask at the Playa Anclote restaurants if it's okay to camp under big trees at either end of the beach. Stores nearby and on the highway in Emiliano Zapata (commonly known as Punta Mita) a quarter-mile east can furnish the necessities, including drinking water. Camping is also available at **Hotel Meson de Mita** on the beach.

$50-100

In the town of Emiliano Zapata, on the bluff above Playa Anclote, you have several choices. Most comfortable is **Casa Las Palmas** (Calle Francisco Madero, Emiliano Zapata, tel. 329/291-6304, www.casalaspalmas.net), tucked on a quiet side street. Owner/builders David and Irene Forbes offer about 10 spacious apartments in two sections, one built around an inviting inner garden on one side of the street and an inviting pool patio on the other. Inside, the immaculate, commodious one-bedroom ($50 d low season, $75 d high) and two-bedroom ($75 d low season, $95 d high) apartments are finished in pleasingly rustic brick and stucco, with soft chairs, gleaming bathrooms, and soft beds. Discounts are available for long-term rentals. Guests are welcome to use their beautiful blue pool and hot tub across the street.

If you must stay on the beach, you can do it, at luscious Playa Anclote's first beachfront hotel, the **Hotel Mesón de Mita** (Av. Anclote, Corral de Riscos Nuevo, tel. 329/291-6330, mesondemita@yahoo.com.mx). Owners offer eight spacious, comfortably furnished rooms for $65 d low season, $80 d high, with shiny baths and air-conditioning. Some have ocean views, all overlooking the hotel's beach and pool patio. Camping is available for the price of $10 per person and campers have use of the facilities including the pool.

Over $100

Increased visitor arrivals now support a sprinkling of mid- to high-end accommodations. Among the loveliest is **Casa de Mita,** formerly known as Casa Las Brisas, (Playa Cayero, tel. 329/298-4114 or 866/740-7999, fax 329/298-4112, www.casademita.com) of friendly owner/manager/builder Marc Lindskog. Marc personally makes sure that his guests enjoy the best of all possible tropical worlds: a breezy, usually deserted white-sand beach, gourmet cuisine, fine wines, spacious art- and antiques-decorated rooms, and plenty of peace and quiet, around an azure pool patio. For the active, Marc provides a universal gym station and optional fishing, horseback riding, surfing, golf, and more. All this for about $485 for two, all lodging, food, and drinks included. You may also reserve Casa de Mita accommodations through Mexico Boutique Hotels (toll-free Mex. tel. 01-800/508-7923, toll-free U.S./Can. tel. 800/728-9098, www.mexicoboutiquehotels.com). Additional fees apply for stays less than three nights.

For a beachfront resort right on the main strip, try the newly opened **Hotel des Artistes,** a condo-hotel and beach club opened by local restaurateur Thierry Blouet (Av. El Anclote 5, tel. 329/291-5005 or toll-free Mex. tel. 866/628-2693, www.hoteldesartistesdelmar.com). The two-bedroom ($390–450 high) and three-bedroom ($590 high) deluxe suites are luxurious and comfortable, with full kitchens, laundry rooms, and large ocean-facing terraces. The athletic club offers daily and

monthly memberships if you just feel like using the facilities ($52/day). On-site is the **Café des Artistes del Mar,** a second location of the popular Puerto Vallarta gourmet restaurant.

Rental Agents

A number of real estate agents handle villa, house, and condo rentals in Punta Mita. If you're looking for a high-end villa ($200/day and up), you might check out **Punta Mita Realty** (tel. 329/291-6420, fax 329/291-6421, www.puntarealty.com), on beachfront Avenida Anclote by the restaurant El Dorado. For more affordable ($40 and up) apartments, condominiums, and houses, visit **www.puntamita.com,** which lists more modest owner-managed rentals. Bucerías rental agents also manage Punta Mita rentals, so check their listings in the *Bucerías* section of this chapter.

FOOD

On the beachfront street, you'll find one of Playa Anclote's oldest and best seafood restaurants, **El Dorado** (tel. 329/291-6296 or 329/291-6297, 9:30 A.M.–9:30 P.M. daily). Take a table in the airy upstairs oceanview seating area. The menu ($5–18) is based on meat, poultry, and the bounty of super-fresh snapper, scallops, oysters, and lobsters that local fisherfolk bring onto the beach.

For something a bit fancier, try **Tino's** (tel. 329/291-6473, 11 A.M.–9:30 P.M. daily, $6–22), next door to El Dorado. The latest in this popular chain of restaurants, the food is just as delicious here as it is in the orginal location in Pitillal. Here it's nearly all seafood, from marlin tacos and shrimp salad to mixed fish kebab and oysters.

The second location of the popular high-end Puerto Vallarta restaurant **Café des Artistes** (tel. 329/291-5415 for reservations) is located in the lobby of the Hotel des Artistes on the beach. Avant-garde cuisine, an extensive wine list, and the luxurious setting make this a popular choice for a romantic dinner, special occasion, or just a night out to treat yourself.

Into the Mountains

Although the little mountain enclaves of San Sebastián, Mascota, and Talpa are, as the bird flies, not very far from Puerto Vallarta, they are a world apart from the coast and very distinct from each other. All are accessible directly from Puerto Vallarta by highway or horseback, or light-airplane charter flights.

San Sebastián is a half-forgotten former mining town, with a noble plaza and fine colonial-era houses and buildings, notably the Hacienda Jalisco, that appear as they did a century and a half ago. Some old mines, now in ruins, can still be visited, preferably in the company of local guides. Guides can also lead you on foot or horseback through verdant mountain country for day-trip explorations or to overnight campsites. There you can enjoy the sunset, relax around an evening campfire, savor the forest's quiet natural sounds, and marvel at the brilliance of a truly dark night sky.

Mascota, the hub of a rich farm valley, enfolded by lush pine- and oak-forested ridges, is a departure point for outdoor excursions and explorations of the idyllic villages of Yerbabuena,

Cimarrón Chico, and Navidad and the pristine high-sierra **Laguna Juanacatlán.**

Talpa, tucked in its own lush valley, is famous throughout Mexico for its colorful village ambience. Its towering baroque basilica and surrounding plaza are magnets for hosts of visitors who flock to pay respects to the adored **Virgin of Talpa,** one of the renowned Three Sisters virgins of Mexico.

◖ SAN SEBASTIÁN

San Sebastián's upland valley was the heartland of the Náhuatl- (Aztec-) speaking chiefdom of Ostoticpac, which translates roughly as "hollow in the highlands." The people, known as the Texoquines, worshipped the gods of sun and fertility, cultivated corn and cotton, and extracted gold and silver from local deposits. Although the Texoquines initially accepted Christianity peaceably, they later rose in revolt, possibly in reaction to the rapacious excesses of renegade conquistador Nuño de Guzmán. Then-governor Francisco Vásquez de Coronado, reinforced with soldiers from

BAY OF BANDERAS

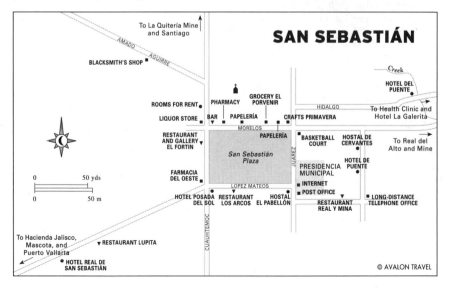

SAN SEBASTIÁN

To La Quitería Mine and Santiago

BLACKSMITH'S SHOP

AMADO AGUIRRE

Creek

HOTEL DEL PUENTE

ROOMS FOR RENT

PHARMACY

GROCERY EL PORVENIR

HIDALGO

To Health Clinic and Hotel La Galerita

LIQUOR STORE   BAR   PAPELERÍA   CRAFTS PRIMAVERA

MORELOS

RESTAURANT AND GALLERY EL FORTIN

PAPELERÍA

San Sebastián Plaza

JUAREZ

BASKETBALL COURT

HOSTAL DE CERVANTES

To Real del Alto and Mine

HOTEL DE PUENTE

PRESIDENCIA MUNICIPAL

FARMACIA DEL OESTE

LOPEZ MATEOS

INTERNET

POST OFFICE

HOTEL POSADA DEL SOL

RESTAURANT LOS ARCOS

HOSTAL EL PABELLÓN

RESTAURANT REAL Y MINA

LONG-DISTANCE TELEPHONE OFFICE

0   50 yds
0   50 m

CUAUHTEMOC

To Hacienda Jalisco, Mascota, and Puerto Vallarta

RESTAURANT LUPITA

HOTEL REAL DE SAN SEBASTIÁN

© AVALON TRAVEL

Guadalajara, marched from the Bay of Banderas into the mountain domain of Ostoticpac, and after a bloody campaign against a determined force of 5,000 warriors, vanquished the Texoquines. The defeated people returned to their homes and fields, and for hundreds of years of Spanish-supervised peace contributed their labor to the church and hacendados, who grew rich from cattle, gold, and silver.

One glance around the present plaza tells you that San Sebastián (pop. 700, elev. 5,250 ft/1,600 m) is unique. Once the most important mining town in the state of Jalisco, the hamlet seems near deserted and tranquil except when the tour buses from Puerto Vallarta arrive. If you wish to avoid the throngs of tourists, make your trip in the morning or late afternoon. The town's cobbled hillside plaza, lined by dignified white buildings and a steepled cathedral, and enclosing a correct Porfirian bandstand, presents a perfect picture of old-world gentility. Such a scene, incongruously tucked at the far end of a winding mountain road, requires explanation.

San Sebastián was once a seat of wealth and modern living, its population exploding during the early 1600s and maintaining decent numbers until the 1930s. The area, rich with gold and silver, gems and agriculture employed more than 30,000 people until the mines closed. Now less than a thousand remain. San Sebastián—officially San Sebastián del Oeste (Saint Sebastian of the West) to distinguish it from a host of other similarly named towns—now earns its living in other ways. In addition to the traditional corn and cattle, local folks cultivate coffee, whose red berries they harvest from the acres of bushes that flourish beneath shady mountainside pine groves. Make sure to pick up some of the locally grown coffee at **La Quinta** located on your left just past the tourism office as you exit town.

San Sebastián Plaza

The most important sights in San Sebastián are visible from the central plaza. The road into town from Puerto Vallarta comes in on the west side of the plaza. Far above the opposite side,

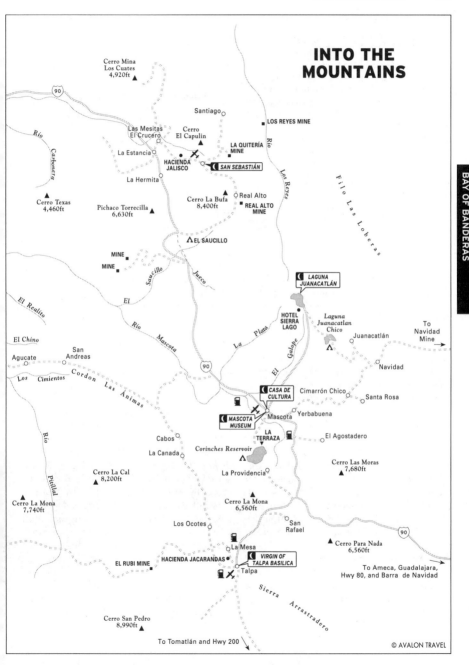

INTO THE
MOUNTAINS

Cerro Mina
Los Cuates
4,920ft

90

Río Carbonera

Santiago

LOS REYES MINE

Las Mesitas
El Crucero

Cerro
El Capulin

**LA QUITERÍA
MINE**

La Estancia

**HACIENDA
JALISCO**

SAN SEBASTIÁN

La Hermita

Cerro Texas
4,460ft

Pichaco Torrecilla
6,630ft

Cerro La Bufa
8,400ft

Real Alto

**REAL ALTO
MINE**

Río Los Reyes

Filo Las Loberas

EL SAUCILLO

MINE

MINE

Saucillo

Jueco

El Realito

El

Río Mascota

La Plata

**LAGUNA
JUANACATLÁN**

**HOTEL
SIERRA
LAGO**

Laguna
Juanacatlan
Chico

Juanacatlán

To
Navidad
Mine

El Chino

Agucate

San
Andreas

Los Cimientos

Cordon Las Ánimas

El Galope

Navidad

90

**CASA DE
CULTURA**

Cimarrón Chico

Santa Rosa

**MASCOTA
MUSEUM**

Mascota

Yerbabuena

Río Pitillal

Cabos

La Canada

Corinches Reservoir

**LA
TERRAZA**

El Agostadero

Cerro La Cal
8,200ft

La Providencia

Cerro Las Moras
7,680ft

Cerro La Mona
7,740ft

Cerro La Mona
6,560ft

Los Ocotes

San
Rafael

Cerro Para Nada
6,560ft

90

EL RUBI MINE

HACIENDA JACARANDAS

La Mesa

**VIRGIN OF
TALPA BASILICA**

Talpa

To Ameca, Guadalajara,
Hwy 80, and Barra de Navidad

Sierra Arrastradero

Cerro San Pedro
8,990ft

To Tomatlán and Hwy 200

© AVALON TRAVEL

THE FESTIVALS OF SAN SEBASTIÁN

The lovely mountain town of San Sebastián makes for a wonderful day or overnight trip from Puerto Vallarta. The several hour drive on windy but well-paved roads is scenic, punctuated by breathtaking vistas and rolling fields of blue agave. Once you arrive, you may be surprised by the tranquil and timeless atmosphere of the small mountain towns. So whether you simply want to experience a wonderful cultural event or are looking for something more social to do during your visit, visiting during one of the many annual festivals is a great time to travel. Each of the mountain hamlets have their own festival calendars so be sure to check the dates when planning your trip!

- **Festival of Patron San Sebastián Martyr:** January 19-21

- **San Sebastián Silver Festival:** Late May

- **Festival of the Virgin of the Asunción:** August 15

- **Mexican Independence Celebration:** September 15-16

- **Festival of the Virgin of the Rosary:** October 7

- **Festival of the Virgin of Guadalupe:** December 12

the landmark mountain **La Bufa** (elev. 8,400 ft/2,560 m) crowns the eastern ridge. Beyond the north edge of the plaza rises the town **church,** dedicated to San Sebastián, who is adored for his martyrdom in Rome in A.D. 288. The church, restored during the 1980s, replaced an earlier 17th-century structure destroyed in an 1868 earthquake. The main altar of the present church holds a pious, heavenward-gazing image of San Sebastián dedicated in 1882. Local folks celebrate the saint's martyrdom during their major local fiesta on January 20.

Near the northeast corner of the plaza, visit the **papelería** and general store of María Francisca Perez Hernández, the local poet who wrote *La Caída de los Cedros,* lamenting the chainsawing of old cedars that decorated the plaza before its renovation in 1984. Pamphlets of her poetry and the local history of chronicler-priest Gabriel Pulido Sendis are for sale inside.

Sights Outside of Town

The road angling downhill past the northwest corner of the plaza marks the route to **La Quitería mine,** the most famous local dig site. About five miles (8 km) from town, at the end of a jeep-negotiable dirt road, lie the ruins. Stripped of machinery by local people, the bare walls, gaping processing pits, and great

ore tailings are all that remain of a mine that produced millions in gold and silver before closing around 1930.

Head out of town along the west (Puerto Vallarta) road; after about two downhill miles (3 km), a signed gate on the right marks the driveway to **Hacienda Jalisco,** the lifelong project of American expatriate Bud Acord. Close the gate after you enter and continue another half mile to the Hacienda.

If, like many visitors, you arrive by plane, you won't be able to avoid seeing the Hacienda Jalisco, because the airstrip is on its land. Bud moved into the dilapidated 1840-era estate during the late 1960s and Hacienda Jalisco became host to dozens of celebrities over time, especially during the heyday of Puerto Vallarta in the 1970s and 1980s. Although Bud recently passed, the management of the guesthouse continues and curious visitors can view historical memorabilia related to the mining operation such as maps and accounting ledgers. The museum (entrance fee $2.50) leads to a baronial *sala* and a porticoed veranda and flowery courtyard. Don't miss the opportunity to stay at least one night at Hacienda Jalisco.

Shopping

For local handicrafts, stop by **La Primavera**

Travel back in time at the authentic Hacienda Jalisco in San Sebastián.

(tel. 322/297-2856, 10 A.M.–3 P.M. and 6–10 P.M. daily). Friendly craftsperson Luz María Preciado crafts many of her offerings by hand, which include a big family of handmade dolls, embroidered pillows, sewing baskets, and *ponche de guayaba* (guava punch).

Accommodations

San Sebastián's most distinguished lodging is **⟨** **Hacienda Jalisco** (reservations through Pamela Thompson in Puerto Vallarta, tel. 322/222-9638 or 322/107-7007, www.haciendajalisco.com), a mining-era hacienda that will make you feel as though you've stepped back in time. The cavernous rooms are decorated with antiques and are lit with oil lamps and individual fireplaces as there is no electricity on-site. Unless there is a full moon, there is virtually no light in the country so guests are encouraged to bring flashlights. Mosquito repellent is also highly recommended. Classic movie buffs are especially welcome—as guests of the hacienda have included John Huston, Richard Burton, Elizabeth Taylor, and Ava

THE HACIENDA TRAIL

Puerto Vallarta's **Rancho el Charro** (Francisco Villa 895, Fracc. Las Gaviotas, tel. 322/224-0114, www.ranchoelcharro.com) offers complete horseback package tours to and from San Sebastián, Talpa, and Mascota. Participants can sign on, with meals and lodging included, for about $2,200 per person for a seven-day trip. Other packages are available and start at about $150 per person, per day.

Tours typically include guided backcountry riding and at least one night camping out on the trail. In addition to exploring San Sebastián, Mascota, or Talpa and neighboring villages, you'll enjoy swimming and hot-tubbing, hearty dinners and cozy evenings at comfortable haciendas and country inns, and, when available, local fiestas. At least one authoritative naturalist/guide accompanies the tour, enriching the experience with expert commentary on trailside flora and fauna.

If horseback riding isn't your thing or you aren't looking for an overnight adventure, try **Wild Mex's** (tel. 322/107-0601, www.wildmex.com) day tours from San Sebastián to Las Palmas (near Puerto Vallarta) via mountain bike. The tour includes transportation from Las Palmas to San Sebastián, bike rental, helmet, water, a guide, and snacks. It starts early in the morning and the ride is about 5-6 hours in length, starting at $110 per person for two or more riders.

Gardner. Hacienda Jalisco's rates, including a hearty breakfast and dinner, run about $82 per person per night.

In the morning manager Joe Thompson will give you a short tour of the property giving some history of the hacienda and pointing out the remains of the mining operation. Instead of mining equipment, the land now holds a vast and varied array of fruit trees and gardens and there are plans to start selling site-grown coffee during the next season.

Another good option is **Hostal El Pabellón** (López Mateo 1, tel. 322/297-0200, $22 s, $39 d, $55 t). Here, you seem to be stepping into an earlier age. Past the entrance, a graceful *sala* leads to a patio garden of fragrant orange trees surrounded by doorways opening into spacious, high-ceilinged rooms; you can easily imagine that, long ago, El Presidente once slept here. The nine rooms have private hot-water shower baths.

On the southeast side of town, find the **Hotel del Puente** (Lerdo de Tejada 3, tel./fax 322/297-2834 or 322/297-2859, $12 s, $24 d, $36 t), a former family house that dates from not long after the town's founding in 1605, past the plaza corner adjacent downhill to the Presidencia Municipal. Here, the long-established Trujillo family has renovated an ancestral home and decorated it with handsome rustic furniture, attractive tile highlights, and wall art. All seven rooms open to a quiet, sunny inner patio garden. Options include rooms, all with private baths and hot-water showers, with 1–5 beds.

Another budget choice on the same street is the quiet and cozy **Hostal de Cervantes** (Lerdo de Tejada 13, tel.322/297-2902) where for $30 s, or $45 d you can get a simple but clean room with bath. Some of the rooms in the back have a bit of a view and there's an on-site restaurant and bar open all day for authentic Mexican cooking or sipping a cold beer.

On the west side of town, on the right side, uphill, off the Puerto Vallarta ingress road, is the redecorated **Hotel Real de San Sebastián** (Calle Zaragoza 41, tel. 322/297-3223 or 322/297-3224, www.sansebastiandeloeste.com.mx). Here the former plain Hotel El Pedregal has been converted into a boutique-style hotel. There are six clean but small and dark rooms, embellished with antique-chic lace, scrolly bedspreads, and shiny new table lamps, for local high-end rates of $52 s, $68 d, with breakfast.

A higher end choice is **La Galerita de San Sebastián** (tel. 322/297-2967, www.lagalerita.com.mx, $150 d, with breakfast), a lovely stone-and-wood rustic home on the northeast

side of the plaza, two blocks past Hotel del Puente. Owners offer three simply but invitingly decorated suites, with bath, including private patio and breakfast. Internet and cable TV are provided.

If nothing else is available, you'll probably be able to stay at **Hotel Posada del Sol** (López Mateos 15, tel. 322/297-2854, $12 s, $22 d), on the town plaza's southwest corner (on the right as you enter town), distinguished by its arch-decorated high front porch. Here you can drink in the entire scene—plaza, church, mountain backdrop—by day and sleep in an 18th-century room by night. The hotel's fortunate deviation from 18th-century furnishings is its clean rooms, with electric lights and private hot-water bathrooms. Rooms surround a homey hillside patio garden decorated with flowers and fruit trees, all overseen by the kindly management of owner Margarita García.

Food and Drink

For store-bought food, try the limited selections of either the grocery **Porvenir** (7 A.M.–11 P.M. daily), on the north side of the plaza, or the small ramshackle corner produce and grocery store, **La Republica** (9 A.M.–2 P.M. and 4–9 P.M. Mon.–Sat.), half a block beyond the northeast plaza corner, past the basketball court. If you're going to need good fresh produce, best stock up, especially during the winter season, in either Puerto Vallarta or Mascota before departure.

Just about the most reliable of local restaurant choices is **Restaurant Lupita** (tel. 322/297-2903, 7 A.M.–11 P.M. daily) about four blocks west of the plaza, on the left, along the Puerto Vallarta road out of town. The friendly, motherly owner cooks just what she would be cooking for her family—eggs, hotcakes, or pork chops for *desayuno* ($2–5) and a four-course *comida* of soup, rice, *guisado* (savory meat or chicken stew), and dessert ($4–5). Evenings, you can usually count on her hearty *pozole* (shredded chicken or pork over hominy in broth), with chopped onions and cabbage, and crispy *totopos* (roasted corn tortillas) on the side ($3).

Alternatively, try **Restaurant El Fortín and Gallery** (tel. 322/297-2856, 9 A.M.–9 P.M. Tues.–Sat.), whose welcoming owner has introduced Italian-Mexican fusion food to San Sebastián. Both inside and outdoor seating make this a nice choice for either escaping the heat of the day or people-watching in the square. Choices include tomato and vegetable salad ($5), cream of *cuitlachoche* with red wine ($5), and red pepper and rosemary pasta ($8). The chicken curry here is surprisingly good.

For authentically Italian choices, go to **Restaurant Real y Mina** (tel. 322/297-2883, 2:30–10:30 P.M. daily except closed on alternate Mon. and Tues.), a block east, past the plaza's southeast corner, and run by husband-wife team Walter Cappelli and Coco Gil. Here, you can have it all, including homemade breads, pastas, gnocchi, lasagna, and much, much more (about over $15 including salad).

Before or after dinner, be sure to stop by town hangout **La Barrondila bar** (9 A.M.–midnight daily, at the northwest corner of the plaza). Join the locals and select from a dozen tequilas and the *raicilla* (mescal liquor) of the bartender's nephew, lined up on the bar. Relax with some dominoes beneath the portico out front, and if hard liquor is not your thing, simply enjoy a cooling Corona and play a tune on their jukebox.

Information and Services

San Sebastián's small *correo* (tel./fax 322/297-2888) is in the Presidencia Municipal (town hall), on the east side of the town plaza. The town *larga distancia* (tel. 322/297-2902, 322/297-2903, or 322/297-3905, fax 322/297-3904, 7 A.M.–2 P.M. and 4–8 P.M. daily) is directly uphill and left, around the corner, a block behind the Presidencia Municipal. If the *larga distancia* is closed, there is a Ladatel card–operated telephone on the front wall of the Presidencia Municipal. There is also an ATM machine here which is good because few local businesses take credit cards. Make sure to carry cash with you for dining and shopping particularly.

If you get sick, go to the local **Centro de Salud** (Health Clinic), about three blocks east, uphill, from the plaza. For minor illnesses, consult the town pharmacy, **Farmacia del Oeste** (tel. 322/297-2833, 11 A.M.–3 P.M. and 5–10 P.M. Mon.–Sat.) at the southwest plaza corner, adjacent to the Puerto Vallarta road.

One of the most highly recommended **guides** in town is English-speaking Obed Dueñas (tel. 322/297-2864), with a car. Also highly recommended, if you can supply the wheels, are a pair of competent Spanish-only speaking guides (bring along someone to translate). They are Ramon Ramos Peña, who lives on the extension of Calle Hidalgo, about a kilometer east of the plaza, and blacksmith *(herrador)* Pedro González Traigos (Amado Aguirre 33), who leads visitors on explorations of local mines. Pedro gained his extensive practical knowledge from his father, a longtime blacksmith at the Quitería mine. A visit to Pedro's shop is worthwhile in itself; you may find him forging red-hot iron into horseshoes. (Perhaps Pedro could recommend someone to translate.)

Pamela Thompson, reservations manager of Hacienda Jalisco, also recommends a guide, Juan, who regularly shows Hacienda Jalisco guests and others to local interesting sights. These often include, besides the in-town sights, the La Quinta coffee farm and processing center, Santa Gertrudis Mine, and La Taberna *raicilla* (mezcal liquor) distillery. Contact her (tel./fax 322/222-9638 or 322/226-1014, info@haciendajalisco.com or pmt15@hotmail.com) and she will forward your message to Juan.

Getting There

By Bus: Road and weather conditions permitting, a sturdy red *(rojo)* ATM (Autotransportes Guadalajara Talpa Mascota, www.talpamascota.com) bus connects Puerto Vallarta with the San Sebastián crossroad at La Estancia, continuing to Mascota and Talpa. It departs daily in the early morning (with an afternoon departure around 4:30 P.M. from the north side of Puerto Vallarta's Parque Hidalgo a couple of blocks north of the Malecón. Check the departure schedule and buy your reserved ticket ahead of time at the little store (tel. 322/222-4816, 9 A.M.–3 P.M. and 6–9 P.M. daily) at the corner of Argentina and Guadalupe Sánchez, two short blocks uphill, east of the bus stop. Under good conditions, the morning bus arrives at the San Sebastián stop around 9 A.M., Mascota at 11 A.M., and Talpa at 2 P.M. The daily morning return trip follows the reverse route, departing Talpa early morning. (Afternoon departure around 3 P.M.), arriving Mascota around 8 A.M., San Sebastián (La Estancia) 10 A.M., and arriving in Puerto Vallarta about 1 P.M. Take drinks and food; little or nothing is available en route.

Note: The *rojo* bus does not go all the way into San Sebastián, but drops off and picks up passengers at the La Estancia crossing, about seven miles from town. Local trucks and taxis then ferry passengers to and from town.

Furthermore, a **van** customarily connects San Sebastián with Mascota. It leaves around 7 A.M. from the San Sebastián plaza, and passes through La Estancia in time for passengers to meet the Puerto Vallarta–bound bus from Mascota. The van continues, arriving in Mascota around 9 A.M. On the return trip it leaves Mascota around noon and arrives in San Sebastián around 2 P.M. This cost is about $4 US.

By Car: Despite the ready bus access, driving your own car or a rented vehicle to San Sebastián on the newly paved all-weather highway from Puerto Vallarta is even easier, and also affords you added independence and flexibility to boot. The direct route from Puerto Vallarta is via the small town of **Las Palmas,** inland, an hour northeast of Puerto Vallarta. Be sure to fill up with gas in either Puerto Vallarta or the Pemex just past the turn to Las Palmas—there are no gas stations around San Sebastián (although unleaded Magna is available from drums) until you reach Mascota. Drive north past the Puerto Vallarta airport along Highway 200. At the signed Highway 70 right turnoff to Ixtapa and Las Palmas a few miles north of the Puerto Vallarta airport, continue along the excellent (but slow, watch for speed bumps) paved road about 15 miles (24 km) to Las Palmas.

Mark your odometer at the signed fork (where you continue straight ahead for San Sebastián, go left for Las Palmas town).

The highway continues smoothly (except for a few construction detours), winding uphill, providing stunning vistas of the valleys and mountains and passing a few hardscrabble ranchos. There are a couple of places to make a pit stop along the way including the occasional tequila distillery and roadside restaurant or two. At Mile 19, you reach **La Estancia** village crossing, with a restaurant and stores. Continue ahead for Mascota, or turn left for San Sebastián. At La Mesita rancho, at Mile 22 (Km 35), turn right for San Sebastián. At Mile 24 (Km 38), pass the Hacienda Jalisco signed gate on the left. Continue another mile to San Sebastián plaza, at Mile 25 (Km 40).

MASCOTA

Mascota is a contraction of the Aztec name Mazocotlan, meaning "place of the deer and pines," a translation depicted by Mascota's traditional hieroglyph of an antlered deer head in profile beneath a three-limbed pine tree.

a deserted street in the mountain town of Mascota

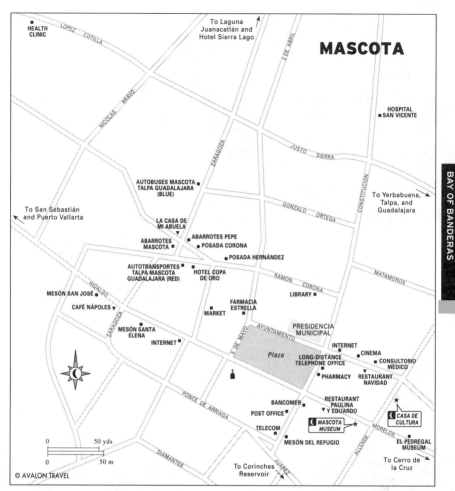

HEALTH CLINIC

LOPEZ COTILLA

To Laguna Juanacatlán and Hotel Sierra Lago

2 DE ABRIL

MASCOTA

NICOLAS BRAVO

ZARAGOZA

HOSPITAL SAN VICENTE

JUSTO SIERRA

CONSTITUCIÓN

AUTOBUSES MASCOTA TALPA GUADALAJARA (BLUE)

GONZALO ORTEGA

To Yerbabuena, Talpa, and Guadalajara

To San Sebastián and Puerto Vallarta

LA CASA DE MI ABUELA

ABARROTES PEPE

ABARROTES MASCOTA

POSADA CORONA

POSADA HERNÁNDEZ

AUTOTRANSPORTES TALPA MASCOTA GUADALAJARA (RED)

HOTEL COPA DE ORO

RAMON CORONA

MATAMOROS

HIDALGO

MESÓN SAN JOSÉ

LIBRARY

CAFÉ NÁPOLES

FARMACIA ESTRELLA

ZARAGOZA

MARKET

MESÓN SANTA ELENA

AYUNTAMIENTO

PRESIDENCIA MUNICIPAL

INTERNET

5 DE MAYO

Plaza

LONG-DISTANCE TELEPHONE OFFICE

INTERNET

CINEMA

CONSULTORIO MÉDICO

PHARMACY

RESTAURANT NAVIDAD

PONCE DE ARRIAGA

BANCOMER

RESTAURANT PAULINA Y EDUARDO

POST OFFICE

CASA DE CULTURA

TELECOM

MASCOTA MUSEUM

MORELOS

ALLENDE

EL PEDREGAL MUSEUM

MESÓN DEL REFUGIO

DIAMANTES

JUAREZ

To Cerro de la Cruz

0   50 yds
0   50 m

To Corinches Reservoir

© AVALON TRAVEL

BAY OF BANDERAS

Although local gold and silver deposits drew early Spanish colonists, agriculture has proved to be the real treasure of Mascota. Its 4,300-foot (1,300-m) altitude brings a refreshingly mild, subtropical climate and abundant moisture to nurture a bounty of oranges, lemons, avocados, apples, grapes, and sugarcane in the surrounding farm valley. Even during the dry winter months, many fields remain lush, irrigated by the Río Mascota, which eventually meanders downhill through its deep gorge to join its sister stream, the Ameca, near Puerto Vallarta.

Mascota (pop. 13,000) is the metropolis of Puerto Vallarta's mountains, offering such services as hotels, restaurants, markets, banks, doctors, and hospitals to local residents and visitors. It's the seat of the local *municipio* of the same name, which spreads beyond the Mascota Valley to a number of idyllic villages tucked away in their own remote emerald vales.

Quiet streets lined with original adobe homes, for the most part well maintained, lend the town an almost European old world charm. The streets and town square are impeccably free of garbage and debris. Signs have been posted reminding residents to keep the town clean and garbage receptacles can be found throughout the city. Now if only more towns would follow suit!

Orientation and Sights

The town spreads out along roughly north–south and east–west lines from the central plaza. The Presidencia Municipal occupies the north side of the plaza; facing it, streets on your right run east, converging on Avenida Justo Sierra, which at the edge of town becomes the Talpa–Guadalajara road. In the opposite direction, running from the south side of the plaza past the church, Avenida Hidalgo heads west toward San Sebastián and eventually Puerto Vallarta. The town church, dedicated to the Virgen de los Dolores (Virgin of Sorrows), was begun around 1780 and not finished until 100 years later. It replaced an earlier church built in 1649.

Looking east from the plaza you'll see the **Cerro de la Cruz,** site of Mascota's biggest yearly party, rising at the edge of town. On May 3, the national **Día de la Cruz** (Day of the Cross), nearly everyone climbs the hill for a high Mass, followed by picnicking, mariachis, and evening bonfires.

Late afternoon is a good time to make the 20-minute climb to the summit, where you can enjoy the cool breeze and the sunset view. On the hilltop, look north across the green valley to see a road winding over a forested ridge. This ridge conceals Mascota's gems—the picturesque hamlets of Yerbabuena, Cimarrón Chico, and Navidad.

📻 Mascota Museum and Casa de Cultura

Don't miss Mascota's museum (on Morelos, one block west of the southwest plaza corner, tel. 388/386-0189, 10 A.M.–2 P.M. and 5–8 P.M. daily), the labor of love of retired teacher Raoul Rodríguez. Here, Señor Rodríguez, who gives a personal guided tour (in Spanish, bring a friend along to translate), exhibits his fascinating personal collection of Mascota memorabilia.

Highlights include mementos of Mascota native daughter Ester Fernández, star of what has become the golden age of Mexican cinema. Other displays highlight the devotion of Mascota priest José María Roble, who was martyred during the Cristero rebellion of the late 1920s. A third section exhibits the oil paintings of noted Mascota landscape painter Gilberto Guerra.

The Mascota Casa de Cultura (Allende 115, 10 A.M.–2 P.M. and 4–7 P.M. Mon.–Sat., 10 A.M.–2 P.M. Sun.), half a block north of the museum, features a permanent exhibit of photos of some of the 12,000 petroglyphs discovered locally in 1999 and 2000. The rock carvings appear to represent rites of sun, water, and fertility. In three other rooms, a number of professionally arranged and labeled displays reveal a fascinating trove of handsome human- and animal-motif ceramic sculptures, dating from about A.D. 1000. All of these finds were excavated during recent years by a team led by Professor Joseph Mountjoy of the University of North Carolina.

For more history and perhaps something a little unusual, stop in at the **El Pedregal** museum (Morelos 64, hours vary, $2 admission) where you can view photos from the town's history as well as an amazing variety of stone-covered objects. Here local author and craftsman Francisco Rodriguez Peña has worked for twenty years to cover nearly everything in his home with rocks and pebbles. From old TVs to an entire bedroom set, the pieces are varied and fascinating. Peña is also the author of a book on the history of Mascota, although it's only available in Spanish.

Entertainment and Events

Other than an occasional public *baile* (dance), *corrida de toros* (bullfight), or *charreada* (rodeo), Mascota people rely on simple diversions. You can join them in a stroll around the town plaza on any evening (especially Sat. and Sun.) or a climb to the top of Cerro de la Cruz.

Mascota life heats up during a number of regionally important fiestas. **Fiestas Patrias** kick off around September 10 with the crowning of a queen, and merrymaking continues during a week of performances, competitions, and patriotic events. On September 13, folks gather to solemnly honor the bravery of the beloved Niños Héroes; then, two days later, fireworks paint the night sky above the plaza as the crowd joins the mayor in a shouted reenactment of Father Hidalgo's Grito de Dolores. Concurrent with the patriotic tumult, the festival of Mascota's patron, La Virgin de Dolores, continues with processions, pilgrimages, high Masses, and an old-fashioned carnival to boot.

Besides participating in all of above, the nearby hamlets of Yerbabuena, Cimarrón Chico, and Navidad stage their own celebrations. Yerbabuena's patron saint is the Virgin of Guadalupe, and the town honors her with native costumes, folk dances, and processions climaxing in a special Mass on December 19. Neighboring Cimarrón Chico celebrates its patron saint in a harvest-style fiesta September 20–29. Navidad honors patrons San Joaquín and Santa Ana with processions, dancing, and fireworks that climax on July 26.

Accommodations

For a more bucolic lodging option that is still close to town, try the **Hotel Rancho La Esmerelda** (tel. 388/386-0953, www.rancholaesmeralda.com.mx), which offers ranch-style accommodations of four cabins and five rooms in a country setting with a view of the surrounding mountains. Simple country furnishings make the rooms homey and comfortable. The cabins are a great deal for larger parties as they sleep up to six people and have a fully equipped kitchenette. Rooms are $48 d and cabins $98 d. To get to the hotel, follow the signs from the Pemex gas station as you enter town. Make a left from the main highway and the hotel is ahead about 300 yards.

For lodging in the heart of the town, a trio of good country hotels line Calle Corona, two short blocks from the town plaza's northwest corner. Walk a block north to Corona, then west another block to the **Posada Corona** (Ramón Corona 72, tel. 388/386-0250, fax

388/386-0460, analuzsd@hotmail.com). Inside, past the immaculate tiled lobby, you'll probably meet the hotel's manager, Analuz Díaz, who carries on the mission of her dynamic but now semiretired mother, "Cuca" Díaz. Most of their 32 rooms—very clean and comfortably furnished with twin or double beds, reading lamps, ceiling fans, and hot-water shower baths—line plant-decorated upstairs corridors. Rates run about $16 s, $30 d, add $5 for additional people, except during the Talpa festivals (around Feb. 2, Mar. 10–19, May 12, and Sept. 10–19), when reservations are mandatory.

Two doors east is the similarly clean and comfortably furnished **Posada Hernández** (Ramón Corona 66, tel. 388/386-0049, $16 d, $30 t). Efficiently managed by owner Esther Hernández, the hotel's 10 rooms surround a leafy, tranquil inner patio. A cabin suitable for up to 10 people is available for $64 per night.

Across the street stands the **Hotel Copa de Oro** (Ramón Corona 75, tel. 388/386-0016, $16 s, $26 d, $34 t). The front desk leads to an open-air interior courtyard, enclosed by ground- and upper-level floors of simply furnished but clean rooms. Owners have brightened up the hotel with paint, polish, and a sprinkling of new furnishings throughout. Expect higher rates during fiesta days.

Mascota's three deluxe hotels, two of which are historic buildings, stand on opposite sides of the central plaza. The more traditional of the three is ◖ **Mesón del Refugio** (Independencia 187, tel. 388/386-0767, mesondelrefugio@yahoo.com). The owners, working with Jalisco tourism's Haciendas and Casas Rurales promotion program, have renovated a distinguished Mascota hotel. The handsome result is 15 high-ceilinged, airy rooms on two floors around a tranquil, inviting inner patio. The rooms ($50 d) and suites ($75 d or t), furnished with designer-rustic tiled floors, hand-loomed bedspreads, handmade wood and leather furniture, original wall paintings and etchings, and bright Talavera-tiled bathrooms, complete the lovely picture. Some even larger, pricier suites have two or three beds and sleep up to six. Amenities include cable TV in the rooms and a bar downstairs.

On the opposite side of the plaza, consider spending your Mascota time in luxurious comfort in the **Mesón de Santa Elena** (Hidalgo 155, tel. 388/386-0313, www.mesondesantaelena.com). The hotel's 12 accommodations, which all enfold a graceful plant-bedecked interior patio, are elaborately decorated with handsomely crafted traditional furniture, decorator lamps, soft carpets, and shiny deluxe tiled baths. All this for a mere $55 d in a standard room; $70 d for larger suites, with cable TV, rooftop panoramic view terrace, restaurant, and comfortably furnished sitting rooms for resting and relaxing.

Half a block away is **Mesón de San José** (Hidalgo 165, tel. 338/386-1501 or 338/386-1502, www.mesonsanjose.com.mx, $35–70 d). Although, like Mesón del Refugio and Meson de Santa Elena, this was a renovation of an existing structure, the rebuilding converted an old house into something nearly completely modern. Downstairs, past the reception and intimate smallish inner patio, is an inviting restaurant, furnished in luxurious shiny all-oak furniture. Upstairs the 14 rustic-deluxe rooms are completely up-to-date, gleaming with new furnishings and fixtures. The owner's pride and joy is a room in the rear, with an expansive private patio, commanding a panoramic over-the-rooftops mountain sunset view. For all this luxury, prices are reasonable.

For an unusually luxurious mountain-lake lodging option, see Sierra Lago Resort and Spa in the *Laguna Juanacatlán* section later in this chapter.

Camping

Local camping opportunities are excellent at **Corinches Reservoir** near Mascota. Here, authorities have built a fine facility, now known locally as La Terraza. For starters, you can enjoy bass and carp dinners from a lake-view *palapa* restaurant with mariachi entertainment Saturday and Sunday afternoons. Alternatively, you can enjoy your own picnic beneath one of several airy picnic shelters, complete with car

pad, useable for self-contained RV parking and camping. Launch your own boat at a good boat ramp downhill, and swim in the cool, freshwater lake to your heart's content.

Moreover, wilderness camping is permitted all around the reservoir's gorgeous five-mile pine-and-oak-studded shoreline. Get there by car or taxi from the Mascota plaza, southeast corner. Follow Calle Constitución south one block. Turn left on Juárez and follow the signs about three miles (5 km) to Restaurant La Terraza on the lakeshore.

The surrounding mountains offer still more wilderness camping opportunities. Pine-bordered volcanic crater Lake Juanacatlán Chico, accessible from Navidad, is a good spot to set up a tent and enjoy a bit of fishing, swimming, and hiking.

Food

The fruits and vegetables are local and luscious at the town **market** (Prisciliano Sánchez at the corner of Hidalgo), a block west of the plaza. For general groceries, go to the big **Abarrotes Mascota** at the corner of Corona and Degollado, a half block west of the Posada Corona. If it doesn't have what you want, Pepe Díaz, owner of **Abarrotes Pepe** (Corona 94, tel. 388/386-0374, 7 A.M.–3 P.M. and 4–9 P.M. Mon.–Sat., 7 A.M.–4 P.M. Sun.) across the street, probably will.

Moreover, Mascota offers a bounty of regional sweets. Check out **Dulces de Mascota** in front of Posada Hernández (Ramón Corona 72, tel. 388/386-0049, 8 A.M.-3 P.M. and 4–9 P.M. Mon.–Sat., 8 A.M.–3 P.M. Sun.). Here, select from a delicious assortment (mango, guava, pineapple) of homemade *conservas* (jams), *empanadas* (fruit turnovers), and crisp locally famous *galletas* (cookies), plus much more.

For an even more exotically unusual treat, walk a block west along Corona to the corner of Zaragoza, across the street from Abarrotes Pepe, to **Mar Carlos** shaved-ice stand. A lineup of large glass jars reveals their scrumptious contents: wild, hand-gathered fruits, from dark red *faisan* and pink *hocuistle* to yellow plumlike *ciruela* and red *frambueza* (wild cranberry). You needn't worry about sampling the delicacies: The eager crowd of customers and the dozen-year-long reputation that friendly husband-wife owner-operators Carlos and Marta have acquired at this spot is proof enough of the wholesomeness of their offerings.

Moreover, good coffee and pastries are plentiful in Mascota, at cozy family-style **Café Napoles** (corner of Hidalgo and Zaragoza, two blocks west of the plaza church, tel. 388/386-0051). Drop in for a savory cappuccino, mocha, or latte and a slice of cake (chocolate, mocha, *tres leches*) or a turnover (pineapple, banana, mango).

For good breakfasts or snacks, Cuca Díaz's nephew Chole runs the **Lonchería El Cholo** (R. Corona about three doors east of Posada Corona, tel. 388/386-0771, 7 A.M.–3 P.M. and 7–10 P.M. Mon.–Sat.).

For more serious eating, try restaurant ◖ **La Casa de Mi Abuelita** (corner of Corona and Zaragoza, tel. 388/386-1975, 8 A.M.–midnight daily, $2–7), a block north and a block west of the plaza. Owners and chefs at My Grandmother's House (which it really was) are very proud of their food, which is nearly exclusively hearty Mexican country fare. Here, you can feast on the specialties that you can't usually get north of the border. These include yogurtlike *jocoque*, a *chivichanga* (a thin burrito made with a corn tortilla), and a *chingadera* (like nachos, except with meat instead of cheese).

You're in for a treat at **Restaurant Navidad** (on Ayuntamiento, half a block east of the plaza's northeast corner, tel. 388/386-0469 or 388/386-0806, 7 A.M.–11 P.M. daily), where you can find out if your favorite Mexican restaurant back home is making enchiladas, quesadillas, tacos, and burritos (*burros* here) authentically. At Restaurant Navidad, they're all good and all very correct. The cavernous space has two rooms of seating and an attached pizza restaurant in case you wish to try something other than Mexican food. A large plate of four crispy *flautas* and accompanying salad will run you about $4.

Agriculture is the main industry of the area so be sure to stop into some of the many shops tucked into the warren of streets from the main square and purchase some regional products. Fresh cheese can be bought almost anywhere as well as honey, fruit candies, and high-octane *raicilla,* also known as Mexican moonshine.

Information and Services

Get the most pesos for your money at **Bancomer** (tel. 388/386-0387 or 388/386-1463, 8:30 A.M.–4 P.M. Mon.–Fri.), on the southeast plaza corner. After-hours, use the ATM.

Mascota's main health clinic is the first-rate government **Hospital Primer Contacto** (tel. 388/386-0174 or 388/386-1823), on Avenida Justo Sierra, the road to Guadalajara, on the northeast side of town. They have 24-hour emergency services and three doctors, a surgeon, a gynecologist, and a general practitioner on call. For serious illnesses and extraordinary diagnostic services, go either to Puerto Vallarta or one of the big Seguro Social Hospitals in Ameca or Tala, about 80 miles east on the road to Guadalajara.

Additionally, you can consult with friendly, articulate Dr. Victor Díaz Arreola at his **Farmacia Estrella** (northwest corner of the plaza, on Calle Cinco de Mayo, tel./fax 388/386-0285, 9 A.M.–2 P.M. and 4–9 P.M. Mon.–Sat., 9 A.M.–2 P.M. and 7–10 P.M. Sun.).

Find the town *biblioteca* on Ramón Corona at the corner of Constitución, behind the Presidencia Municipal. The *correo* (Independencia 156, tel. 388/386-0197, 8 A.M.–3 P.M. Mon.–Fri.) is half a block south of the plaza's southeast corner.

Larga distancia telephone, public fax, copy services, and Internet access are available at Farmacia Estrella, described earlier in this section. Internet access is also available at the **Internet Cyber Center** (tel. 388/386-0784, 9 A.M.–3 P.M. and 5–11 P.M. daily), a few doors west of the plaza's northeast corner. For public fax and money orders, go to **Telecom** (tel. 388/386-0022, 9 A.M.–3 P.M. Mon.–Fri.), off the plaza's southeast corner, half a block south of Bancomer. Other long-distance telephone, fax, and copy services are available at a small office (8 A.M.–9 P.M. daily) on Constitución, east side of the plaza.

Getting There

By Bus: At least two bus lines serve Mascota. The best equipped is **Autotransportes Guadalajara Talpa Mascota** (ATM, www .talpamascota.com), known locally as the *rojo* (red) bus. It connects Mascota with Puerto Vallarta, Talpa, and Guadalajara. For details of the Puerto Vallarta–Mascota–Talpa bus connection, see *Getting There* in the *San Sebastián* section earlier in this chapter. Tickets and departures in Mascota are available from the curbside Rojo (ATM) bus station (Corona 79, tel. 388/386-0093), adjacent to the Hotel Copa de Oro.

Regular **van service** connects San Sebastián and Mascota. It starts out at the San Sebastián plaza daily in the early morning (check for the time locally). The return van departs from the Rojo (ATM) station in Mascota at around 1 P.M., arriving at San Sebastián plaza around 3 P.M.

The competing **Autobuses Mascota Talpa Guadalajara** (known as the Autobus Azul, or Blue Bus) also connects Mascota with Guadalajara, Talpa, and Puerto Vallarta. Tickets and departure information are available at the small Mascota streetside station (corner of Cotilla and Zaragoza, tel. 388/386-1006), two blocks north of Corona.

By Car: Although buses are cheaper, driving will give you added mobility for exploring Mascota's scenic mountain country and hidden villages. The good, paved, all-weather 80-mile (128-km) route from Puerto Vallarta to Mascota is doable in about three hours under good conditions. From Puerto Vallarta, follow the highway route to San Sebastián described in *Getting There* in the *San Sebastián* section earlier in this chapter. At the La Estancia village intersection, continue straight ahead (instead of turning left toward San Sebastián). Set your odometer at the La Estancia crossing.

Two miles (3 km) farther, pass through Ermita village; continue six more miles (9 km) uphill along a pine-and-oak-shaded ridge to a breezy view pass at Mile 8 (Km 13). A faint jeep road heads left along the summit ridge to La Bufa peak and Real Alto village. Continue downhill, passing over El Saucillo Creek, at about Mile 11 (Km 18) and Palo Jueco Creek, about two miles farther on. Continue over a second oak-studded pass at around Mile 19 (Km 29). Then coast five miles (8 km) more downhill past a former fighting-cock farm on the left, at around Mile 24 (Km 43). Continue to the Mascota town limit (and gas station) about four miles (7 km) farther and, finally, the Mascota plaza at Mile 28 (Km 45).

Mascota has two **gas stations,** one on the west side, about a mile west of the Mascota plaza, and another on the east side, about three miles east of town on the Guadalajara–Talpa road.

EXCURSIONS FROM MASCOTA

Having come as far as Mascota, you might enjoy spending some additional hours or a day or two poking around the idyllic trio of hamlets—Yerbabuena, Cimarrón Chico, and Navidad—and maybe taking in the great outdoors at the spruce-studded high-sierra crater lake, Laguna Juanacatlán. Photographers should bring plenty of film to capture the rolling fields and stunning vistas.

If you're driving, Laguna Juanacatlán requires a full day for the round-trip, but a single graded road safely negotiable by passenger car connects the three hamlets in a leisurely four- or five-hour 25-mile (40-km) round-trip from Mascota. Head out via Avenida Justo Sierra to the road fork at the east edge of Mascota town; the right branch heads to Talpa and Guadalajara, the left fork proceeds to Yerbabuena, Cimarrón Chico, and Navidad. If you're traveling on foot (carry water), you'll find few, if any, public buses heading to Yerbabuena, Cimarrón Chico, and Navidad. You can probably catch a ride with one of the cars and trucks that often head along the road during the day. Stick out your thumb; if someone stops, offer to pay.

Yerbabuena

The latter-day renown of Yerbabuena is the labor of love of its longtime resident and official municipal historian, Father Vidal Salcedo R.:

> *Yerbabuena, idyllic and enchanted little nook, You stand apart from Mascota, the noble and lordly. Whoever ventures to thee and pauses at your door, You beckon through love, both given and received.*

That sentiment, in Spanish, heads the pamphlet that Salcedo offers visitors who arrive at his **Quinta Santa María** *mini-museo* (mini-museum) not far from the town plaza. To get there, bear east at the street (16 de Septiembre) past the east side of the plaza, and continue a couple of blocks until you see a big mill wheel beneath a small forest of spreading tropical trees. Open daylight hours, this informal museum has free admission.

If Salcedo is out, someone else—perhaps his nephew, Hector—will offer to guide you around the flowery grounds, which bloom with the fruits of Salcedo's eclectic, unconventional tastes. Ornaments vary, from pious marble images to rusting antique farm implements.

The grounds are scattered with small one-room buildings displaying Salcedo's painstakingly gathered collections. Highlights include indigenous archaeological artifacts, working models of an ore mill and cane crusher, an ancient typewriter, religious banners and devotional objects, a fascinating coin and bill collection, and a metal step-ramp once used with Mascota's first passenger planes that now leads to an upstairs garden gazebo.

Cimarrón Chico

From Yerbabuena head east again. Don't miss the antique country cemetery about a mile out of town. Next stop is Cimarrón Chico (Little Wild Place), the bucolic valley and hamlet about six miles (10 km) over the next ridge. Despite its name, Cimarrón Chico appears peaceful and picturesque. Adobe farmhouses, scattered about a sylvan mountain-rimmed hollow, surround a neat village center. The

© BRUCE WHIPPERMAN

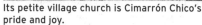
Its petite village church is Cimarrón Chico's pride and joy.

town's pride and joy is its diminutive picture-book **church** at the east edge of the village.

Another don't-miss local stop is the charmingly small and tidy *abarrotería* in the middle of the village. Drop in for good fresh fruits, vegetables, and Jumex brand canned juices. Enjoy a chat with friendly proprietor and community leader Juan López Sandoval. He's a good source of local information, including homes where you might stay overnight, camping spots, and guides for horseback or hiking excursions. He especially recommends that you arrive during the spring (Mar.–May) to enjoy the locally distilled *raicilla* (mescal liquor).

There is one local place to stay. East of town, follow a road fork signed **Rancho Paraíso Cimarrón,** where you'll find a large guest cabana (large enough for a big family) and a small pool. For reservations, call ranch owner Martín Peña (tel. 200/124-7395), who can arrange your stay. The rates are $10 per person, per night.

Continue east, over another scenic pine-clad ridge, four miles (6.5 km) farther to Navidad. Along the way, notice the yellow lichen-daubed volcanic chimney-cliffs towering on the left halfway uphill. Also, at the ridgetop within sight of Navidad, note the cobbled road that forks left, uphill. It leads to the hamlet of Juanacatlán (3 mi, half an hour), as well as Laguna Juanacatlán Chico (jeep only, 5 mi, an hour), and Laguna Jaunacatlán (10 mi, 2.5 rough hours—best go directly from Mascota).

Navidad

The town of Navidad, with a population of about 1,000, is more of a metropolis than either Cimarrón Chico or Yerbabuena. It basks picturesquely on the hillside above a petite green farm valley. Hillside lanes sprinkled with red tile–roofed whitewashed houses and a venerable colonial-era steepled church, dedicated to San Joaquín and Santa Ana, complete the idyllic picture.

At his store across the plaza from the church, friendly English-speaking Juan Arrizon Quintero doubles as the unofficial goodwill ambassador. As he or any of the old-timers lounging in the shade outside his store will tell you, the short supply of *terreno* (land) is a big problem here. Young people must migrate to other parts of Mexico or the United States for jobs. The Navidad mine, still operating several miles farther east, used to employ lots of local people, but now it can hire only a small number of those needing jobs.

Visitors who want to stay awhile or camp nearby can try José's store and one or two local eateries for food. For lodging, check out the guesthouse-style 10-room **Hotel Navidad Dueñas** (tel. 317/385-9895). Friendly owner Hortencia López asks $22 for a simply decorated but comfortable room that opens onto her homey plant-decorated interior patio.

For a wilderness camping opportunity, ask Juan about Laguna Juanacatlán Chico, whose clear 300-foot-deep waters are fine for swimming, kayaking, and trout and bass fishing.

【 LAGUNA JUANACATLÁN

A block north and a block west of the Mascota town plaza, head out Calle Zaragoza by taxi, local minibus, or your own wheels to Laguna Juanacatlán (12 mi/19 km, one hour), a 7,000-foot (2,130-m)-high clear mountain lake framed by steep pine-tufted ridges. Even if you only plan to have lunch in the hotel restaurant and enjoy a stroll around the lake, the stunning drive is well worth the effort, providing you don't have a fear of heights. Following a good cobbled road, climb over a pine-crested ridge and descend into bucolic El Galope river valley, past rustic ranchos and rich, summergreen pastures and cornfields. The steep final 2,000-foot (610-m) ascent is a series of switchbacks and the one-lane road has few turnouts, however at the time of this writing, crews were working to widen several parts of it. Once you reach the apex, the road levels out and winds through a sun-dappled evergreen forest to a lovely view of the lake. A few folks stroll its green grassy banks, small sailboats and kayaks rest by the shore, and smoke curls out of the lakefront lodge stone chimney.

Inside the 【 **Sierra Lago Resort and Spa** (tel./fax 322/224-9350, toll-free Mex. tel. 01-800/725-6277, toll-free U.S./Can. tel. 877/845-5247, www.sierralago.com), the reception leads to a spaciously handsome, beam-ceilinged, knotty-pine rustic dining room and adjacent lakeview lounge and bar. Although the whole hotel layout is luxurious, it's also unpretentiously modest in scale, blending unobtrusively within the gorgeous alpine surroundings.

The 23 accommodations, all offered only on an all-inclusive basis, divide into three categories, all deluxe: ecosuites, actually permanent, open-air tented platforms ($380 d); comfortable standard cabanas ($450 d) with room for families; and cabana suites ($550 d), roomy rustic-chic cabins. Children 4–12 stay for $40 apiece. Amenities include in-suite hot-water shower baths, big bubbling lakeside hot tub, and sauna. The suites include a whirlpool bath and are the only option with fireplaces, so opt for one of these if you plan on staying overnight during the cool winter months. In-house activities include horseback riding, mountain biking, sailing, and kayaking and are included in the price of the room. Massage and spa treatments are available but cost extra.

High prices nothwithstanding, this spot is gorgeous and could be easily worth a splurge for lovers of both comfort and the outdoors. Remember, however, that Laguna Juanacatlán is 7,000 feet (2,130 m) above sea level and during the winter is decidedly cool, even sometimes cold. Then, a dip in the lake would feel very chilly (however, the big steaming lakeside whirlpool bath would feel very welcoming). On the other hand, summer and the drier early to mid-fall would be delightfully temperate at Laguna Juanacatlán.

TALPA

How a petite straw figure can bring hundreds of thousands of visitors a year to lovely but remote little Talpa (pop. about 7,000, officially Talpa de Allende) is a mystery to those who've never heard the tale of the Virgin of Talpa. Back in the 1600s, the little image, believed by many to be miraculous, attracted a considerable local following. The bishop of Mascota, annoyed by those in his flock who constantly trooped to Talpa to pray to the Virgin, decided to have

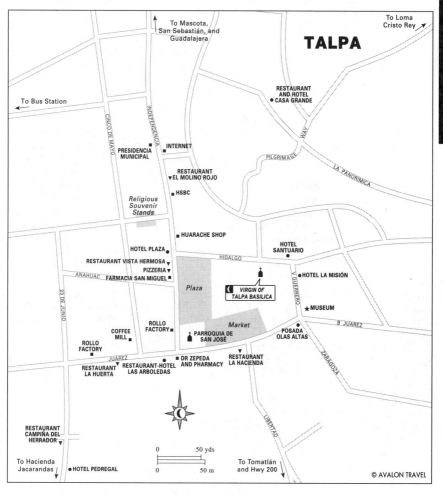

© AVALON TRAVEL

her transported to his Mascota church—and "jailed," some people said. But the Virgin would have none of it: The next morning she was gone, having returned to Talpa.

A few local folks brought the bishop to the outskirts of town, where they showed him small footprints in the road, heading toward Talpa. "Nonsense!" said the bishop. "The Virgin doesn't even have feet, so how could she make such footprints?" So the bishop again had the Virgin brought back to Mascota.

Determined not to be tricked again, the bishop ordered a young campesino to guard the Virgin at night. The Virgin, however, foiled the bishop once more. The young man dozed off, only to wake to the sound of footsteps leaving the church. The frightened young man looked up and saw that the Virgin was indeed gone; later, people found a new set of small footprints heading back toward Talpa.

The flabbergasted bishop finally relented. He left the Virgin in Talpa, where she, now known as the Walking Virgin, has remained ever since.

Virgin of Talpa Basilica

In the pastoral mountain-rimmed Talpa valley, all activity centers on the town square, which spreads from the stately steepled baroque cathedral. Inside, the beloved Virgin of Talpa, flanked by Joseph, Mary, and a pair of angels, occupies the place of high honor. The petite figure stands on her altar, dwarfed by her gleaming silk robe, golden crown, and radiant halo. The faithful, mostly poor folks from all parts of Mexico, stream in continuously—most walking, others hobbling, a few even crawling to the altar on their knees. Music often resounds through the tall sanctuary—either voices, solo or in choir, or instruments, often by mariachis playing mournful, stately melodies.

Back out in the sunshine, sample some of Talpa's other attractions. Head behind the cathedral to Talpa's excellent church-funded **museum** (9 A.M.–3 P.M. daily). Two floors of expertly prepared displays begin with the basics, illustrating—from a strictly Catholic point of view—the miracles and religious significance of the Virgin Mary, continuing with the three "sister" Virgins of Mexico, and description and documentation of a number of latter-day apparitions of the Virgin of Talpa. Upstairs, cases of the Virgin's gilded vestments and other devotional objects decorate the museum's airy atrium.

Sights

After the museum, head to the **market,** downhill at the left (east) side of the plaza. Look over the souvenirs: small sombreros, flowers, and baskets all fashioned of rubbery *chicle,* the basis of chewing gum. There are several local artisans who make traditional leather sandals, **huaraches,** some with gum soles. They take some breaking in but once that is accomplished, are a comfortable option for walking. If you see a bottle filled with a yellow-orange liquid, it's probably *rompope* (rohm-POH-pay), eggnog laced with tequila.

When you feel like getting away from the crowd, climb **Loma Cristo Rey** (Hill of Christ the King), behind and to the left of the church, for some fresh air and panoramic views of the town, valley, and mountains. Back by the plaza, let the sweet perfume of guava fruit lead you to a *rollo* (ROH-yoh) factory. In front of the church, cross Independencia and head left a half block. Before the corner you'll find a shop where machines crush, heat, and stir guava pulp until it thickens like candy, which is then sold in *rollos* (rolls).

Most days the Talpa plaza atmosphere is friendly and pleasantly uncrowded. The action heats up considerably during the **tianguis** (tee-AHN-geese) every other Saturday, when a raft of vendors comes into town to set up their awnings and try to hawk everything from pirated tapes and machetes to snake oil and saucepans. This is a good location, however, to buy cheap housewares like lime squeezers, large hand juicers, tortilla warmers, and more. The Talpa hubbub boils over during four big local fiestas—February 2, March 10–19, May 10–12, and September 10–19—when the fortunate jam hotels or sleep in tents, while everyone else makes do with the sidewalks.

TALPA FIESTAS

Adoration of the Virgin of Talpa climaxes five times during the year. The first, on February 2, coincides with the national festival of Candelaria. While everyone else in Mexico converges upon churches to get their plants, seeds, and candles blessed, Talpa people celebrate by blessing their beloved Virgin.

By far the biggest Talpa event occurs during the week before the feast of St. Joseph on March 19. A million visitors celebrate by downing tons of edible crafts, dancing in the streets, and singing mariachi serenades to the Virgin.

Merrymakers crowd in May 10–12 to celebrate the crowning of the Virgin of the Rosary, accompanied by a glittering carnival, booming fireworks, tasty regional food, and whirling folk dancers.

The prettiest and least crowded of the Talpa celebrations occurs September 10–19, concurrent with the national patriotic Fiesta de Patria. In Talpa, venerable national heroes must share acclaim with the Virgin, whom people bathe, adorn with new jewelry and silks, and parade around the plaza on a flower-petal carpet.

Pilgrims return to the basilica on October 7 for Talpa's fifth and final en masse celebration, of the traditional celebrationof Virgin of the Rosary, in which celebrants fete their beloved Virgin of Talpa with a glittering parade, booming fireworks, and a big carnival.

Accommodations

The most popular accommodations choice is **[** **Hacienda Jacarandas Bed and Breakfast** (tel. 333/447-7366, fax 388/385-0669, www.haciendajacarandas.com, closed Easter–June), the splendidly isolated country inn a couple of miles out of town. Friendly owners Guy Lawlor and Bill Worth can accommodate up to 15 guests in five comfortable guest bedrooms with private baths and one casita that sleeps up to four. Panoramic valley and mountain views can be appreciated from the tiled terraces off of each room. A 55-foot lap pool and hot tub are available for guest use. All this for reasonable rates ($50 s, $75 d), including breakfast.

Get there from town by taxi, on foot, or by car, all via the bridge at the southeast end of town, past Hotel Pedregal, on the eastern extension of Calle 23 de Junio. Cross the bridge. Immediately turn right onto the road that runs west along the river levee. After 0.6 mile (1 km), follow the lane that forks to the left. Continue along the lane uphill for about two miles (3 km) to Hacienda Jacarandas, on the left.

Alternatively, back in town, check out the good hotel choices right on the Talpa plaza. Note: Talpa hoteliers rent rooms by the number of beds, rather than the number of guests. If two of you can fit into one bed, you get the cheapest rate. It makes for cozy traveling.

The most elite choice downtown is the **Hotel La Misión** (corner of Hidalgo and Guerrero, tel. 388/385-0202), behind the cathedral. The hotel's shiny tiled lobby leads past an inviting restaurant/bar, Los Venados, to an intimate fountain and garden tucked in a sunny rear patio. Upstairs, rooms are spacious, clean, and attractively decorated in polished wood furniture and flowery bedspreads. Some of the 40 rooms have private balconies overlooking the cobbled lane below, as well as fans, hot water, and TV. Rentals run a very reasonable $23 one bed, $28 two beds, $39 three beds, except during festivals, when prices rise.

Adjacent to the Hotel La Misión stands the clean, modestly priced **Hotel Santuario** (Hidalgo 12, tel. 388/385-0046). Owners offer 38 modern, attractively furnished rooms, with hot-water shower baths, arranged around an interior patio. Get an upper-rear room for most privacy and quiet, especially during festivals. Rentals cost a reasonable $34 one bed, $47 two beds, and $62 three beds; add $5 during festivals. Amenities include fans or air-conditioning (add $10) and a restaurant.

Alternatively, take a look at the relatively new **Hotel Plaza** (Independencia 20, tel. 388/385-0086), directly in front of the cathedral. Here, 33 shiny white-tiled rooms with bright new furnishings occupy two stories fronting the town plaza. Guests in the street-front rooms enjoy views of the colorful cathedral plaza hubbub below. For peace and quiet, ask for a room in the rear. Rates run about $41 one bed, $46 two beds, and $55 three beds, with fans, TV, and hot water.

Camping is customary around Talpa, especially during festivals. Privacy, however, is not. Unless you find an isolated spot a mile or so away from town, you'll probably have to cope with a flock of curious children. Try to find a spot on the far side of the river that runs south of town.

Camping prospects are much better along the pine-shaded shoreline of **Corinches Reservoir,** near Mascota, about 10 miles north. The principal amenities are a good *palapa* restaurant, space to picnic and/or set up a tent or park an RV, swimming, a boat ramp, and the *lobina* (large-mouth bass) prized by anglers. You can see Corinches Reservoir downhill south and west of the Mascota–Talpa road. Easiest access is from downtown Mascota.

Food

Buy supplies from the several groceries (especially Abarrotes Oasis, in front of the Cathedral) along main street Independencia or the town market on the plaza, west of the cathedral. As for restaurants, the steady flow of pilgrims supports several near the plaza.

For a snack right on the plaza, the **Pizzería San Miguel** (Independencia, next to Hotel Plaza, 8 A.M.–9 P.M. daily, $3–10) puts out good pizza and sandwiches. Next door, second-floor **Restaurant El Campanario** (tel. 388/385-1370, noon–7 P.M. daily, 8 A.M.–9 P.M. daily during fiestas) serves from a broader menu of breakfasts ($3), lunches ($3–4), and dinners ($3–7), while also affording an airy, upstairs view of the plaza.

Get a bit of graceful colonial-era atmosphere with your seafood, tacos, or *hamburguesas*

($3–8) at the old mansion, now **El Molino Rojo** (Red Mill) restaurant. Find it on the main street, by the HSBC bank, a block west of the plaza. Equally serious eaters head the opposite direction—east to the end of the main street and downhill three short blocks farther (two downhill, one left) to **◖ Restaurant Campiña del Herrador** (23 de Junio, across from Hotel Pedregal, tel. 388/385-0376, 8 A.M.–10 P.M. daily, $3–10) for hearty country-style breakfasts, lunches, and dinners.

Information and Services

You'll pass most of Talpa's businesses on Independencia as you enter town from the Mascota–Guadalajara direction.

For simple advice and remedies, consult with Doctora Olga Valencia at her **Farmacia San Miguel** (Independencia 16, across from the plaza, tel. 388/385-0085, 10 A.M.–3 P.M. and 6–11 P.M. daily). Alternatively, visit highly recommended Doctor Daniel Zepeda in his **Farmacia La Parroquia** (at the end of Independencia, half a block south of the plaza's southwest corner, tel. 388/385-0089). His wife speaks English.

If you need to change money, go to the **HSBC** (tel. 388/385-0197, 8 A.M.–7 P.M. Mon.–Fri., 8 A.M.–3 P.M. Sat.) or its 24-hour ATM, a half block west of the plaza. Across the street from the bank, at the Presidencia Municipal, you'll find both the *correo* and **Telecomunicaciones,** if you need to make a long-distance call or send a fax.

Getting There

By Bus: Talpa buses operate from a central terminal two blocks north and three blocks west of the plaza. Bus connection with Puerto Vallarta via Mascota and San Sebastián is best made by **Autotransportes Guadalajara Talpa Mascota** (ATM, tel. 388/3850-0015, www.talpamascota.com) *rojo* buses. They customarily depart daily early mornings and afternoons, via Mascota and the La Estancia (San Sebastián) crossing. From the Puerto Vallarta end, a similar bus leaves daily early mornings and afternoons, from the north side of Parque Hidalgo, two blocks north of the Hotel Rosita on the Malecón. Reserve your ticket ahead of time at the little store (tel. 322/222-4816) at the corner of Guadalupe Sánchez and Argentina, two blocks north of the plaza Hidalgo *rojo* bus stop.

ATM's *rojo* first- and second-class buses also connect Talpa with Guadalajara several times daily, arriving at both the Camionera Nueva station in Guadalajara's southeast suburb and the Camionera Vieja (tel. 333/619-7549) in downtown Guadalajara.

Autobuses Mascota Talpa Guadalajara (tel. 388/385-0701) *azul* buses originate in Mascota, continue to Talpa, then to Guadalajara several times daily, arriving at the old (Camionera Antigua) terminal near the Guadalajara city center.

By Car: Access to Talpa from Puerto Vallarta is via Mascota. From the Mascota plaza east side, follow Calle Constitución north two blocks. Turn right on Calle Justo Sierra, and, a few blocks later, at the country edge of town, bear right at the signed fork to Talpa and Guadalajara. Continue about six miles (9 km) to the Talpa junction. Turn left for Guadalajara, right for

Talpa, and continue along the good paved road another eight miles to Talpa. Unleaded gasoline is customarily available in Talpa at the Pemex *gasolinera* about a quarter mile into town, before you arrive at the town plaza.

A pair of alternate road routes access the Talpa–Mascota region from the south. From the Guadalajara–Barra de Navidad Highway 80, follow the signed turnoff at San Clemente. Continue 48 miles (77 km) (through Ayutla, Cuatla, and Los Volcanes) on paved (but sometimes potholed) roads northwest 44 miles (71 km) to the intersection with Highway 70. Turn left and continue another 14 miles (22 km) to a signed Talpa–Mascota junction. Turn left for Talpa (or continue straight ahead for Mascota and San Sebastián).

The other southern route—a rough, unpaved, and seemingly endless up-and-down backcountry adventure—heads from Highway 200, northeast through Tomatlán. It continues about 80 miles (130 km) via the hardscrabble hamlets of Llano Grande and La Cuesta. Figure about eight hours Tomatlán to Talpa under optimum dry conditions.

THE NAYARIT COAST

Unfortunately, not enough people make the effort to see what lies north of Puerto Vallarta along the beautiful and verdant coastline. This may change however, as the Nayarit tourism board has recently spent a great deal of money promoting "Riviera Nayarit," as the next big tourist destination in Mexico. Riviera Nayarit runs from the modern, upscale Nuevo Vallarta north along the coast to the port city of San Blas. Its beauty—verdant mountain and shoreline forests, orchard-swathed plains, and curving yellow strands of sand—is largely natural. Dotted along in coves and sheltered bays are the hidden beach towns, some lively and thriving and others tranquil and serene. Sayulita, San Francisco, Lo de Marcos, Rincón de Guayabitos, Chacala, and San Blas—each of these towns are distinct from one another and offer different types of lodging, dining, and recreational opportunities. Whether you are looking for a quiet respite from the crowded streets and beaches of Puerto Vallarta or a non-stop beach party with hundreds of potential new friends, there's a place for you just a couple of hours away.

The first stop along the coast is Sayulita, once mostly the home of fishing families and oyster divers. Sayulita is now home to a decent sized group of expats and hosts a large seasonal migration of surfers, sail boarders, and ex-hippy types. While the general feel is that of a funky beach town, Sayulita has been touched with the same upscale element that has taken over other previously hip beach towns like Punta de Mita and La Cruz de Huanacaxtle to the south.

© ROBIN NOELLE

HIGHLIGHTS

(Sayulita: This palm-tufted beachfront village offers abundant opportunities for sunning, surfing, swimming, and snorkeling. Add the good local food, comfortable hotels, a fine beachfront trailer park and campground, and it becomes irresistible (page 143).

(Playa los Muertos: While visiting La Peñita, don't miss a trip to the beachfront graveyard on the northern section of beach. The crypts and tombs along the shore make for a wonderful and unusual photo opportunity (page 156).

(La Peñita *Tianguis*: Spend the morning browsing wares from all over Mexico during this Thursday morning market. Artisans from as far away as Oaxaca and Puebla come to sell handmade rugs, masks, carved bowls and jewelry. (page 158).

(Alta Vista Archaeological Sacred Site: Make the side trip to this fascinating forested site. The petroglyph-decorated trail climaxes in a magnificent wonder-evoking natural spring and stone amphitheater (page 168).

(Playa Chacala: Spend a day or week at this loveliest of beaches, a strip of golden sand that enfolds a petite half-moon bay. A magnificent grove provides shade, good restaurants, and fresh seafood, and either homey or deluxe lodgings provide restful nights (page 168).

(La Tovara Jungle River Trip: Along the river's winding, vine-festooned, orchid-swathed channel, enjoy close-up views of snoozing crocodiles, basking turtles, and fluttering herons and egrets. Top off your tour with lunch and swimming at crystal-clear La Tovara natural springs (page 179).

(Mexcaltitán: From San Blas, make an excursion to the island-village of Mexcaltitán, believed to be the fabled Aztlán homeland of the

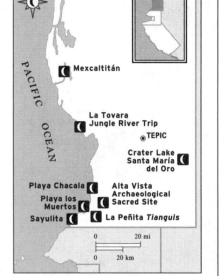

LOOK FOR **((** TO FIND RECOMMENDED SIGHTS, ACTIVITIES, DINING, AND LODGING.

Aztec people. Stroll the automobile-free village lanes, visit the excellent historical museum, and stay at the town's modest hotel (page 192).

(Crater Lake Santa María del Oro: Traveling southeast from Tepic, don't miss idyllic Laguna Santa María, spectacularly set in a dormant now-forested volcanic crater. Swim, kayak, sail, and hike the mountain trails, then camp by tent or RV or stay in a comfortable hotel room or bungalow (page 201).

THE NAYARIT COASAT

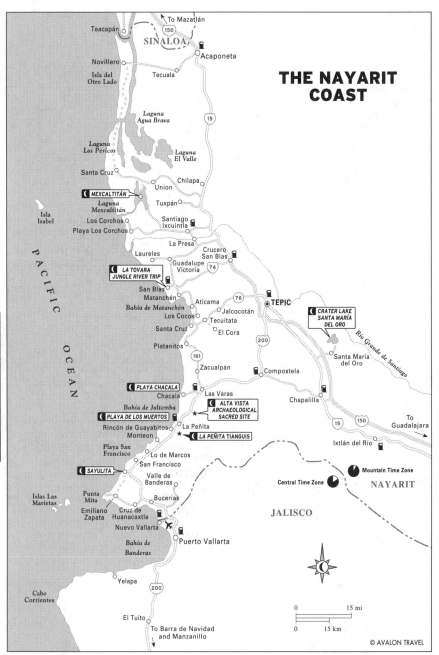

THE NAYARIT COAST

To Mazatlán

Teacapán
SINALOA
15D
Acaponeta

Novillero
Isla del
Otro Lado
Tecuala

THE NAYARIT COAST

Laguna
Agua Brava
15

Laguna
Los Pericos
Laguna
El Valle

Santa Cruz
Chilapa
Union

MEXCALTITÁN
Laguna
Mexcaltitán
Tuxpán

Isla
Isabel
Los Corchos
Playa Los Corchos
Santiago
Ixcuintla

La Presa
Crucero
San Blas

Laureles
Guadalupe
Victoria
74

LA TOVARA
JUNGLE RIVER TRIP
P A C I F I C

San Blas
Matanchén
Aticama
76
TEPIC

Bahía de Matanchén
Jalcocotán
CRATER LAKE
SANTA MARÍA
DEL ORO

Los Cocos
Tecuitata

Santa Cruz
El Cora
Río Grande de Santiago

O C E A N
Platanitos
200

161
Santa María
del Oro

Zacualpán
Compostela

PLAYA CHACALA
Las Varas

Chacala
ALTA VISTA
ARCHAEOLOGICAL
SACRED SITE
Chapalilla

Bahía de Jaltemba
PLAYA DE LOS MUERTOS
15
15D

Rincón de Guayabitos
Monteón
La Peñita
To
Guadalajara

LA PEÑITA TIANGUIS
Ixtlán del Río

Playa San
Francisco
Lo de Marcos
San Francisco

SAYULITA
Valle de
Banderas
Mountain Time Zone

Central Time Zone
NAYARIT

Islas Las
Marietas
Punta
Mita
Bucerías

Emiliano
Zapata
Cruz de
Huanacaxtle
JALISCO

Nuevo Vallarta

Bahía de
Banderas
Puerto Vallarta

Yelapa
200

Cabo
Corrientes

0   15 mi
El Tuito

To Barra de Navidad
and Manzanillo
0   15 km

© AVALON TRAVEL

TOP SURF BREAKS OF RIVIERA NAYARIT

The Pacific Coast of Mexico has been popular with traveling surfers for a long time, long before the beaches were covered with five-star hotels and condominium complexes. The empty expanses of golden beaches, big breaks, beach camping, and cheap dining have continued to bring a seasonal crush of hobbyists, newbies, and pros during the fall and summer months when the tourist crowds have yet to arrive for the winter and the swells are the largest.

Sayulita: Sayulita is one of the most popular places for surfing north of Punta Mita. There's a long right break off of a reef in front of the main beach and another faster left break north of the river mouth. There are year-round waves in Sayulita and it's far from deserted. The popularity of the funky beach town means lots of competition for waves and crowded beaches especially during the winter months.

San Pancho (San Francisco): San Pancho makes for a great day trip if you are staying in Puerto Vallarta or somewhere along the coast. The hard break and big waves means there are few swimmers in the water here so surfers and sometimes sailboarders have the water to themselves. San Pancho features a left beach break.

La Caleta: From Chacala hire a *panga* to take you to Playa la Caleta, where you can find what is often referred to as "the best left." With the exception of when some of the local surf tour companies are there, the area is quiet and uncrowded.

Matanchén Bay: Home to many seasonal surfing championships, Matanchén Bay is known for having the for the longest ride in the world (Guinness Book of World Records) for taking surfers up to a mile and a half on a single wave. May is the month to come if you are looking to tackle this lengthy ride. If you are looking to hook up with other surfers to direct you to some of the other excellent surf spots nearby, check out Stoner's Surf Camp on Playa el Borrego in San Blas.

A few miles farther north, **San Francisco** (or locally, San Pancho) still retains its sleepy beach-village ambience, but is also home to a growing community of well-to-do North American vacationers and retirees. Nestled between the sidewalk restaurants and Internet cafés operated out of local Mexican resident's homes, are art galleries, upscale boutiques and international cuisine restaurants.

The magnet of **Lo de Marcos** is its wide, family-friendly beach, sheltered by headlands on both sides and bordered by a sprinkling of beach bungalows and palm-shaded RV parks and campgrounds. The same is true of **Rincón de Guayabitos,** but even more so. It's the hands-down favorite resort with Mexican families of the entire Nayarit Coast, largely for its many budget but comfortable housekeeping bungalows and tranquil, kid-friendly waves. A battalion of North American winter RV retirees have picked up the same message and stay the winter, fishing, barbecuing, and playing cards with longtime fellow returnees.

The beach list goes on: incomparably lovely **Playa Chacala,** with its creamy half-moon beach, regal palm grove, homey local lodgings, and a pair of rustic-chic hotel-spas; and farther north, the broad **Bay of Matanchén** with its pair of petite beachfront hotels, trailer parks, waterfall hikes, crocodile farm, and world-class surfing at north-end Playa Matanchén.

Next comes **San Blas,** rich in history revealed in its ancient, mossy hilltop fortress and its restored customs house and museum downtown. In the present, San Blas has become itself a jumping-off point for natural adventures. These include jungle boat tours through its orchid-festooned wildlife-rich mangrove wetland, an excursion to offshore marine life sanctuary **Isla Isabel,** and/or an overnight in **Mexcaltitán.** The "Venice of Mexico," it's the ancestral island home of the Aztec people, who wandered east from Mexcaltitán around A.D. 1100 and within 400 years had built one of the world's great cities and conquered Mexico.

And finally, travel to the lush, green summit

of Nayarit's coastal mountains to **Tepic,** the Nayarit state capital, nestled in its fertile volcano-rimmed valley. Tepic is both the rich source of a trove of colorful and uniquely enigmatic Huichol ritual handicrafts and jumping-off point for the idyllic forest-rimmed volcanic crater lake, **Laguna Santa María del Oro.**

PLANNING YOUR TIME

You could spend as little as two days and as much as two weeks or more exploring the Nayarit Coast, depending on your interests. If you have only two days, best go by tour or car, stopping at **Sayulita** or **San Francisco** for lunch and a stroll and sun on the beach, then continue north for an overnight at **Casa Pacífico** or **Mar de Jade** in Chacala. The next day, continue along the Bay of Matanchén, to San Blas, for the unmissable **jungle boat tour** and lunch (four hours) at **La Tovara** spring. Return south through Tepic and, time permitting, enjoy a (two-hour) detour to gorgeous volcanic **Laguna Santa María** en route back to Puerto Vallarta.

With a few more days, you could add an overnight or two at Sayulita and/or San Francisco. Be sure to include a visit to the nearby **Alta Vista Sacred Site** and archaeological zone.

Continuing north to San Blas, between August and December, stop by (two hours for a look, or overnight) at **Playa las Tortugas** vacation home resort and the adjacent turtle conservation center.

Spend a few nights farther north at San Blas, which you can use as an excursion hub

for wildlife-watching, beach swimming, sunning, and strolling, and adventures farther afield to the **Huichol Cultural Center** in Santiago Ixcuintla and the historic and picturesque island-town of **Mexcaltitán** for perhaps an overnight.

Return south, via Tepic, stopping for lunch and shopping for Huichol handicrafts. Continue to **Laguna Santa María** for at least an overnight. Spend your last day swimming and boating on the lake and strolling its lush, forested shoreline.

Getting There

If driving, mark your odometer as you pass the Puerto Vallarta airport so you can anticipate the small signs along Highway 200 that mark many turnoffs. Or take the city bus or hire a taxi to the Camionera Central (central bus station) about a mile north of the airport. There, ride one of the many Transportes Pacífico or Estrella Blanca–affiliated northbound buses. Bus travelers heading all the way to San Blas have two options. The quickest is to ride an early Transportes Norte de Sonora bus (buy your ticket at the Estrella Blanca counter) direct to San Blas. Or you can take Transportes Pacífico's longer route uphill via Tepic. Upon arrival at the Tepic station, transfer to one of several daily Transportes Norte de Sonora buses that connect with San Blas.

You can also go directly to the Nayarit Coast after airport arrival by sharing a taxi ($55–80). A *colectivo,* if available in front of the bus station, would be much cheaper.

Sayulita and Vicinity

Northbound, about a half-hour ride north of Puerto Vallarta, Highway 200 bends away from the Bay of Banderas shoreline and climbs a low range of mountains. Very quickly the roadside foliage turns attractively lush, with grand vine-draped trees that at times create a leafy green tunnel over the highway. Although not strictly a rainforest, this Nayarit coastal forest is a well-watered jungle landscape, festooned with trees, shrubs, and flowering vines that provide a rich habitat for myriad animal species, both common and endangered.

Along the highway, the forest sometimes gives way to a roadside village, decorated with small orchards. Signs at intersections announce the beachfront towns along the way. Once purely fishing villages, they're now growing vacation havens for mostly international travelers during the winter, and Mexican vacationers during traditional holiday seasons.

There's always time for "time out" on the beach in Sayulita.

🄲 SAYULITA

Little Sayulita (pop. 3,000), 22 miles (35 km) north of the Puerto Vallarta airport, was once the kind of spot that romantics hankered for: a drowsy village on a palmy arc of sand, a hidden retreat for those who enjoy the quiet pleasures and local color of Mexico. And while Sayulita still has tranquil moments during low season, you'll find a high energy town jam-packed with surfers and families during the high season.

Once only a destination for Puerto Vallarta day-trippers, Sayulita now is host to a yearly influx of RV retirees and youthful Americans, Canadians, Europeans, and Japanese who have made Sayulita their fall-winter destination of choice. Many have opted to buy full- or part-time homes in the area and the atmosphere of Sayulita has grown to reflect that in the increasingly upscale boutiques and galleries. You will not find many bargains in this little town.

Nevertheless, any time of the year Sayulita's amenities remain: clean waters, fine for swimming, bodysurfing, beginning-to-intermediate

surfing, and fishing; colorful country ambience; and plenty of warm sun during the day and cool offshore breezes at night.

Recreation

While there are probably better places to surf locally, there are few more popular than Sayulita and nearby town Punta Mita. A strong northern swell comes in December through August, so advanced surfers will want to plan their trip during this time. At other times of the year you will still be able to surf on the nearby right-, and left-breaks but the swells will be smaller. Catch up on the local surf conditions on the Sayulita Life website: www.sayulitalife.com/sayulitasurfing.htm.

Veteran surfer/hotelier **Mario Rubio** rents beach chairs, umbrellas, boogie boards, snorkel gear, surfboards, and kayaks and offers surfing lessons, right on the main beach. He also arranges jungle tours, horseback rides, guided

© BRUCE WHIPPERMAN

THE NAYARIT COASAT

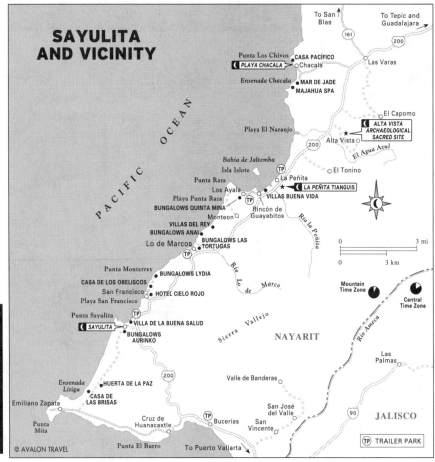

SAYULITA AND VICINITY

hikes, and hotel-surfing packages. Contact him at his Duende Surf Dawgs beach rental stall.

Surfboard and boogie board rentals can be found all along the beach or if you are looking for lessons, try **Pazport Surf School** (tel. 322/149-9251, www.sayulitalife.com) where you can get private or group lessons for between $30–40. **Lunazul** (tel. 329/291-2009, www.sayulita life.com) also offers boogie and surf board rentals and private/group lessons on the beach, just north of Don Pedro's restaurant.

You can also schedule lessons or a local surf trip through **Wild Mex** (tel. 322/107-0601,

www.wildmex.com), which offers various multiday surf packages, surfing day trips, and also mountain biking excursions. Surf day trips start at about $30 for advanced level surfers (two people or more) and run up to $65 for beginners and intermediate.

Meanwhile **Via Yoga** (tel. 800/603-9642, www.viayoga.com) offers six-day yoga and surfing retreats in Sayulita including organized activities and lessons.

If you are looking to do some diving and don't want to travel into Puerto Vallarta, you can take trips or even get your PADI certification at the **Sayulita Diving School** (tel. 322/147-5893, www.sayulitadivingschool.com).

For fishing, surfing, and snorkeling excursions, contact local captain **Fidel Ponce Cruz** and his wife, Leticia (tel. 329/291-3563, www.sayulitalife.com). Sayulita is Fidel's hometown, so he knows the best local spots. Local **Rancho Manuel** (tel. 322/132-7683) offers horseback tours along shady paths through the Sayulita tropical forest. Get tickets at the Restaurant Costeóo on the beach, or at the ranch itself, about four blocks east up Calle Gaviotas, past the town plaza and the church.

Furthermore, **Greg Adams,** manager of Villa Buena Salud (tel. 329/291-3029, see listing in *Accommodations* section), arranges local day tours: to waterfalls, a hot spring, Alta Vista sacred site, La Tovara spring in San Blas, Mexcaltitán, and much more.

Shopping
Among the best of the handicrafts galleries that dot Sayulita's main street is **La Hamaca Gallery** (tel. 322/227-5817, 9 A.M.–8 P.M. daily). Offerings include much fine and decorative ceramics, Day-of-the-Dead curios, and a selection of Huichol art, sales of which benefit the nonprofit Huichol Center for Cultural Survival. Across from the restaurant Don Pedro's, you can stop into the **Ojo de Venado** gallery (Calle Marlin 6, tel. 329/291-2018) of ecological art which features handicrafts and art work from all over Latin America. All of the wares offered for sale conform to Fair Trade standards so if you can't purchase from the artists themselves, you can feel good knowing they were paid fairly.

Surf enthusiasts will love **Sayulita Surf & Art** (Revolucion and Niños de Heroes, tel. 329/291-3761) where they can purchase vintage or used surf boards, locally created surf art and surfboard designs, from signs to painted boards for decoration. They even have a buyback program, so if you want your own board during an extended stay, you can sell it back to them before you leave. Handy!

If you are looking to pick up new, used, or locally written books, stop by **Libreria Sayulita** (Miramar 17A, tel. 322/103-4703, 10 A.M.–8 P.M. daily), a cool bookstore that offers language lessons, Internet services, and local art. There's a nice bakery inside should you get hungry while browsing the stacks. The personable owners stock newspapers such as *USA Today,* the *New York Times,* and the *Miami Herald,* and a number of popular U.S. magazines during the October–May high season.

Accommodations
Under $50: Sayulita's perennial favorite budget accommodations are the economical and clean and comfortable rooms at **Sayulita Trailer Park,** on the north-end beachfront. Besides the clean and comfortable budget rooms ($38 d), you also can opt for one of about a dozen simply but thoughtfully furnished kitchenette bungalows ($60–80 d, one day free per week), four of them smack on the lovely palm-shaded beachfront ($440 d weekly). (Add about $45 per extra person.) During the two weeks before Easter and December 15–31, rates rise about 20 percent and reservations must include a minimum seven-day stay and a 50 percent deposit. Get reservations—for winter, best six months in advance—through the owners, Thies and Cristina Rohlfs, either in Mexico City (office tel. 55/5390-2750, home tel. 55/5572-1335, www.pacificbungalow.com) or in Sayulita directly (tel./fax 329/291-3126, Nov.–May). Rates for the trailer spaces average $18–28 depending on the size of the space.

Another budget option just a block off the beach are the bungalows at **Casa Cansada** (Calle Las Gaviotas, one block from the beach, tel. 322/160-2760) where you can rent one of the three rooms available with a shared bath ($40 d) or one with private bath ($50 d). The rooms are basic but clean and sunny.

The lodging most likely to have a room when everything else is filled is the downscale, emergency-only **Hotel Sayulita,** on the beach. Although the owner, at the hardware store next door, asks about $27 d, $36 t, for 33 very basic rooms around a cavernous interior courtyard, you might be able to bargain for a better price. He accepts no reservations; during the crowded winter season arrive early enough to assure yourself a room.

$50-100: Longtime expatriate resident Adrienne "Tía Adriana" Adams, owner, and son Greg Adams, on-site manager, of the bed-and-breakfast **Villa Buena Salud**, rent about a dozen comfortable, thoughtfully decorated rooms and suites with bath ($50–120 d high season, $30–60 d low), including breakfast high season for two, minimum three nights. Her airy, art-draped, three-story house is a short block from the main Sayulita beachfront. Although her upper-floor rooms are for adults only, families with children are welcome in two downstairs apartments ($110 high season, $55 low,), with kitchen, VCR, and TV. (Adrienne also offers five comfortable lodgings in a hilltop view "Hideaway" designer villa, $40–120 high season.) Adrienne enjoys dozens of repeat customers; get your winter reservations in early. She receives reservations (www.tiaadrianas.com) July–October in California (1495 San Elijo, Cardiff, CA 92007, tel. 760/632-7716, fax 760/632-8585) and November–June in Sayulita (tel./fax 329/291-3029).

On the north side of town, find luxuriously lovely **Villas Sayulita** (tel. 329/291-3065, tel./fax 329/291-3063, www.villasayulita.com) on a quiet street about two long blocks uphill from the beach. Owners offer about a dozen spacious kitchenette suites ($80 d high season, $70 d low), on lower and upper floors, adjacent to an invitingly intimate tropical pool patio, with picnic *palapa*. The suites themselves are lovingly designed and immaculately maintained, with TV, air-conditioning, attractive rustic tile floors, deluxe modern baths, and soaring arched ceilings. Some beds are king-size, with a pullout for kids, other rooms have two double beds.

Back near the town center, the gorgeous *palapa*-chic **◖ Bungalows Aurinko** (Calle Marlin, tel. 329/291-3150, www.sayulita-vacations.com) offers an excellent alternative. Labor of love of its friendly owner/builder Nazario Carranza, Aurinko (sun in the Finnish language) glows with his handiwork: handcrafted

natural wood bedstands and dressers, rustically luxurious whitewashed walls adorned with native arts and crafts, all beneath a handsome, towering *palapa* roof, only a block from the beach. The five one-bedroom units rent from about $81 d in high season, $65 d low. A pair of two-bedroom units go for about $127 d each in high season, $97 d low, and a gorgeous penthouse suite goes for about $106 d high season, $95 d low; all with modern bathrooms, airy patio kitchens, and ceiling fans.

At the end of the south-side beach road, the designer cabanas of hotel **Villa Amor** (tel. 329/291-3010, fax 329/291-3018, U.S. tel. 619/291-3010, www.villaamor.com) dot the leafy headland. Villa Amor offers about 33 owner-designed architecture-as-art rustic *palapa*-chic view dwellings ($110–700, higher Christmas–New Year's and Easter seasons). Accommodations, many open-air, vary from three-bedroom, 2.5-bath house-sized full kitchen suites, down to modest but still deluxe refrigerator-and-sink studios, all enjoying vistas of Sayulita's petite bay, with fans only, no phones, and no TV. Most beds are king- or queen-size; colors range from soft pastels to white. Credit cards are *not* accepted. (The only possible drawback to all this luxury might be the open-air *palapa* architecture of some, but not all, of the accommodations, which although inviting, might be a bit buggy and damp during summer rainy spells or chilly during midwinter cool snaps.)

TRAILER PARKS AND CAMPGROUNDS

RV folks love the north-side **Sayulita Trailer Park** (Dec.–May tel./fax 329/291-3126, year-round fax 55/5390-2750, www.pacificbungalow.com) in a big, sandy palm-shaded lot, with about 36 hookups (some for rigs up to 40 feet) and some room for tents, right on the beach. Guests enjoy just about everything—good clean showers and toilets, electricity, drinking water, a used-book shelf, concrete pads, dump station, pets okay—for about $18 for two people, one day free per week, discounts possible for extended stays. Add about $4 per extra person. Get reservations—for winter, best six months in advance—through the owners, Thies and Cristina Rohlfs (sayupark@prodigy .net.mx).

Trying just as hard is Sayulita's downscale campground, gated and enclosed **Palmar del Camarón** (tel. 329/291-3373, no reservations accepted, always room for one more) in a big palm grove on the gorgeous palm-shadowed north-side beachfront. The environmentally conscious owner, who looks exactly like Harrison Ford and is known locally as "Camarón," offers plenty of grassy spots for tents and smaller self-contained vans needing no hookups. Tent spaces ($5 pp) are first-come, first-served, with showers, toilets, and *palapas* for shelter against sun and rain. Camarón also rents rustic *palapa cabañas* ($30 d), with mosquito nets and private toilet and shower. Other extras include a beachfront *palapa* restaurant and security lockers. Find it as you enter town from Highway 200, by going right at the lane that borders the baseball field. After a block and a half, turn right at the campground gate.

RENTAL AGENTS
Drawn by the quiet pleasures of country Mexico, a number of American, Canadian, and Mexican middle- and upper-class folks have built comfortable vacation homes in and around Sayulita and are renting them out. **Avalos Real Estate** (tel./fax 329/291-3122, www.move2sayulita.com), Sayulita's original real estate agent, lists such properties for rental or sale. For more information and listings, you may also contact their U.S. agent (tel. 805/481-7260 or toll-free fax 800/899-4167).

Alternatively, check out **Garcia Realty** (Revolución 41, tel./fax 329/291-3058, www.sayulita-garciarealty.com or www.sayulita-realestate.com) on the main street, a few doors north of the town plaza. Besides rentals, they list homes and villas for sale.

Food
Vegetables, groceries, and baked goods are available at a pair of stores by the town plaza, or at Abarrotes Doria, just south of the bridge on Revolución, the main ingress street from

the highway. Local-style food is supplied by a lineup of plaza taco stands at night, and some beachfront *palapa* restaurants. Bountiful breakfasts, lunches, and early dinners are the main event at **Choco Banana** (6 A.M.–6 P.M. daily) on the town plaza with lots of hearty American-style breakfasts ($3–5), veggie and meat burgers ($4), fish fillets ($6), carrot cake ($2), and good espresso ($1). Of course, you can't miss out on the frozen chocolate-covered bananas or creamy, blended coffee drinks.

A bit higher up the scale, a number of recommendable restaurants dot Sayulita's streets and beachfront. One of the best established is **Don Pedro's** (tel. 329/291-3090), a once humble, now elegant, seafood *palapa* on the south-end beachfront. Here, the main events are the freshest catches of the day, cooked with European flair, such as mahimahi (dorado) Portofino style, and local oysters, octopus, fish, and shrimp cooked up as bouillabaisse (seafood stew, $10–15).

You can get just as fresh Mexican-style seafood (fish and shrimp any style, fish tacos and tortas, $4–8) at neighboring **El Costeño** restaurant (sometimes known as Ruperto's), also on the Sayulita main beachfront. Don't expect speedy service but the food is worth the wait.

In town, on the main street, Revolución, family-owned **La Fiesta** restaurant is a party ready to happen, especially on weekends. The whole family, including the waiters and the audience, sometimes gets into the act. The spark plug is the father, Miguel, who both emcees and plays the keyboard, often accompanied by his daughter, who sings like a songbird. Besides all this, their lovingly prepared Mexican specialties ($5–10), with bottomless hot, handmade tortillas, are among the best on the Nayarit Coast.

If you are in the mood for something affordable and fast, you can't go wrong with newcomer **Burrito Revolución** (Revolución, just before the main plaza, noon–11 P.M. daily, $5–8). You can have big, luscious burritos with a variety of fillings (try the chili lime chicken) and several sauces to choose from. The informal, open-air bar seating makes this a great place for making friends and people-watching.

For a more refined and tropical experience, try **Calypso** (main plaza, 6–11 P.M.daily, tel. 329/291-3704, $11–22), where you can grab a cold one at the long, curved wooden bar or bring your large group for dinner under the *palapa*. The portions are notoriously huge and the menu offers a nice selection of dishes from salads and pastas to fresh seafood and BBQ chicken.

Return another day, across Revolución, to restaurant-pizzeria **"Si Hay Olitas"** ("Yes, there are some little waves," 7 A.M.–9 P.M. daily, $4–12) for your choice of ribs, hamburgers, chicken, or Mexican specialties such as *molcajete* (cactus leaves and leeks with chicken or beef strips), flaming fajitas, and good in-house pizza.

Owner/chef Miguel Muro of **Sayulita Cafe** (on Revolución, a block south of the plaza, tel. 329/291-3511, 1–11 P.M. daily) has raised the chile relleno (stuffed chile) to a high art. He offers a quartet of delicious variations: cheese, vegetarian, tuna, or chicken ($8). Alternative options include bountiful salads ($5), barbequed ribs ($9), and T-bone steak with baked potato ($12), all served in a tranquil candlelit atmosphere, enhanced by low-volume melodies and whirring ceiling fans.

Information and Services

A number of businesses keep busy serving Sayulita's visitors. For general information, fax, and Internet connection, go to **Garcia Realty** (Revolución 41, tel./fax 329/291-3058, garcia-realty@msn.com) on the main street, a few doors north of the town plaza. They also list vacation rentals and homes and villas for sale.

Change your dollars to pesos at **Casa de Cambio Sayulita,** on the south side of the Sayulita town plaza. Find it open 10 A.M.–2 P.M. and 4–8 P.M. Monday–Saturday.

Spanish-language lessons are also offered by **Total Immersion Language School** (tel. 329/291-3573, U.S. tel. 562/716-6044, info@ sayulita-villas.com), of instructor/owners Steve and Maiira Poole.

The website www.sayulitalife.com amounts to a good community newspaper, chock-full of informative advertisements, from hotels and surf shops, to doctors and horseback rides, plus public service announcements, maps, local news, and an events calendar to boot.

As for laundry, get yours done at the *lavandería* (Revolución 9, 8 A.M.–8 P.M. Mon.–Sat.) a block north of the river bridge.

For remedies and medical consultations, you have at least two choices: Either Doctora Rosa Flores Alegria at her **Farmacia America** (Revolución 14, half a block south of the bridge, 9 A.M.–2 P.M. and 4–8 P.M. daily), where she consults 3–9 P.M. Monday–Saturday and 9 A.M.–4 P.M. Sunday; or **Doctor Miguel de Dios Arroyo** at his pharmacy (Revolución 41, half a block south of the town plaza, tel. 329/291-3555, 9 A.M.–2 P.M. and 4:30–9:30 P.M. Mon.–Sat.).

PLAYA SAN FRANCISCO

The idyllic beach and drowsy country ambience of the little former mango-processing village of San Francisco (San Pancho as locals call it, pop. about 1,000) offers yet another bundle of pleasant surprises. Exit Highway 200 at the road sign 25 miles (40 km) north of the Puerto Vallarta airport and continue straight through the town to the beach.

The broad golden-white expanse of sand enclosed by palm-tipped green headlands extends for a half mile on both sides of the town. Big, open ocean waves (take care—there's often strong undertow) frequently pound the beach for nearly its entire length. Offshore, flocks of pelicans dive for fish while frigate birds sail overhead. At night during the rainy months, sea turtles come ashore to lay their egg clutches, which a determined group of volunteers tries to protect from poachers. Beach *palapa* restaurants provide food and drinks. If you're enticed into staying, a sprinkling of good restaurants, hotels, and bed-and-breakfasts offer food and accommodations.

Sights

San Francisco has acquired a history museum that tells stories of the local past, from

COURTESY OF TAILWIND OUTDOOR

Experience the jungle with luxury camping at Tailwind Outdoor.

the days of the old haciendas to President Luis Echeverría, who came, fell in love with San Pancho, and gave the town its first big boost. Find the museum on Avenida Tercer Mundo, corner of Calle Latina America. Hours vary, depending upon the availability of volunteers.

Grupo Ecológico de la Costa Verde

Founded in 1992, the Grupo Ecológico de la Costa Verde, headquartered in Puerto Vallarta, has been instrumental in rescuing the Puerto Vallarta region's sea turtle populations from the brink of extinction. Spurred on by a dedicated cadre of volunteers, the organization's San Pancho chapter has led the effort, by working to increase the San Pancho olive ridley nesting turtle population tenfold, from about 70 to 700 active yearly nests in five years. The San Pancho chapter (Calle America Latina 102, tel. 311/258-4100, www.project-tortuga.org) welcomes volunteers.

Shopping

A few arts-and-crafts gallery-shops sprinkle main street Avenida Tercer Mundo. In the middle of town, the **Oasis** gift shop sells crafts and T-shirts, profits from which go to the local turtle protection project. Also **Galería Corazón** (9 A.M.–5 P.M. Mon.–Sat., closed July–Sept.), across Avenida Tercer Mundo from Calandria Realty, features an eclectic assortment of locally crafted candles, ceramics, woodcrafts, textiles, and more.

Accommodations

On a quiet, flowery side street, American owners rebuilt a venerable house, thus creating the **Hotel Cielo Rojo** (Red Sky) bed-and-breakfast (Calle Asia 6, tel./fax 311/258-4155, www.hotelcielorojo.com), seemingly perfect for those who appreciate quiet relaxation. A tiled entrance walkway guides visitors indoors, through an artfully decorated small lobby to an airy breakfast garden patio partially sheltered by a gracefully traditional *palapa* roof. A hot tub for guests' enjoyment is tucked on one side.

Stairs lead to three luxuriously open upper-room stories, of six spacious rooms and a larger suite, all tucked beneath a handsomely rustic top-floor *palapa*-roofed two-bedroom suite. The accommodations themselves are simply but elegantly furnished with handcrafted wood furniture, wall arts and crafts, designer lamps, and colorful native-style handcrafted bedspreads. The exquisitely tiled bathrooms are fitted with gleaming modern-standard wash basins, toilets, and showers. The six rooms (with either queen-size bed, or two twins) rent for about $65 d low season, $85 d high; the larger suites (with one queen, one twin each) go for about $85 low season, $95 high. The top-floor two-bedroom suite goes for about $150 high season, $115 low; all with ceiling fans and continental breakfast included.

Lovers of nature and solitude should head north of town (past the Costa Azul Adventure Resort) and continue a mile and a fraction (about 2 km) along the gravel coastal road to a signed driveway leading through the palm-tufted tropical forest. At road's end, find **Bungalows Lydia** (Km 111, Carreterra

THE NAYARIT COAST

© BRUCE WHIPPERMAN

the pool at Costa Azul Adventure Resort in San Francisco

Puerto Vallarta–Tepic, tel. 311/258-4337 or 311/258-4338, www.bungalowslydia.com or www.vrbo.com/8853), the mini-eden and life dream-made-true of sprightly and welcoming Lydia Cisneros Mora. Her (and her sister's) offering consists of four smallish but clean kitchenette studios ($95 low season, $105 high) and two larger one-bedroom bungalow suites (one for $150 high season, $130 low, the other for $190 high, $170 low, for up to four), with hot-water shower baths and simply but thoughtfully decorated in whites and pastels. They're set in a charming oceanfront garden on a spectacularly rocky point buffeted by wild, foaming surf—the place is kept nearly bug-free by the ocean breeze. Discounts are negotiable for longer-term rentals; there's wireless Internet but no phones or TV, and plenty of fresh air, sunsets, and animal friends—coatis, raccoons, armadillos, and squirrels *(ardillas)*—in the neighboring vine-hung tropical forest. Paths lead down to a pair of secluded beaches, separated by a rocky outcropping, naturally equipped with an oceanfront tidepool whirlpool bath.

For another outdoor adventure, continue past Bungalows Lydia to the secluded camping platforms at **Tailwind Outdoor** (tel. 322/100-1585, www.tailwindoutdoor.com). Here Tamara Jacobi and her family have created a luxury camping experience for those who want to experience the serene enjoyment of outdoor living. There are ecobungalows ($75 d) that offer safari tent–style camping on beautiful wooden platforms set into the jungle. The platforms are completely private and offer the comforts of electricity, rustic cooking facilities, king-sized beds, and mosquito nets. Hot showers are provided next to the platforms but those who desire flush toilets will have to trek up to the main headquarters located under a *palapa* at the top of the hillside.

Guests have access to all of the facilities including a shared kitchen and petite swimming pool. There's a wooden viewing platform for nightly sunset watching. For your daytime activity, Tamara leads kayak and nature tours (priced separately) or you can ramble around the five acres on your own, including several moderate-advanced hikes through the jungle and nearby avocado orchards. A pathway leads down the hill to a small, secluded beach. The entire facility can be rented for $375 ($400 holiday, sleeps 8) for families or groups. Check the Tailwind website for retreat and special event listings.

Back on the town main street, a sign on the right marks the good gravel road to the **Costa Azul Adventure Resort.** In-hotel activity centers around the beach and the palm-shaded pool patio and adjacent restaurant-bar. Farther afield, hotel guides lead guests (at extra cost) on kayaking, biking, surfing, and snorkeling trips and naturalist-guided horseback rides along nearby coves, beaches, and jungle trails.

The main hotel building, at the foot of a hillside of magnificent Colima palms, offers 20 large comfortable suites. Uphill, sheltered beneath the palms, stand eight villas (six one bedroom and a pair of two bedroom). Suites in the main hotel building rent, high season, for about $120 d; the one-bedroom villas go for about $160 d, and the two-bedroom villas about $300, for up to six. Up to two children under 12 stay free. Reservations (224 Av. del Mar, Suite D, San Clemente, CA 92672, local Mex. tel. 311/258-4120, fax 311/258-4099, U.S./Can. tel. 949/498-3223 or toll-free U.S. tel. 800/365-7613, U.S. fax 949/498-6300, www.costaazul.com) are strongly recommended, especially in the winter.

Past Costa Azul, north a block or two, turn downhill toward the beach and continue another block north to lovely, secluded **C Casa de los Obeliscos** (tel. 311/258-4315, U.S. tel. 415/233-4252, www.casaobelisco.com). Here, welcoming American owners have created their version of paradise for their guests to enjoy. They offer four super-comfortable airy, art-and-tile decorated suites, two of them with private oceanview patios, all overlooking a luscious hibiscus-decorated pool patio. The tropical garden setting makes for a lovely and relaxed atmosphere and guests can enjoy snacks and drinks at the pool bar. Beach access is just across the street. Rates run $180 d low season, $225 d high ($275 Christmas–New Year's), including a big, delicious breakfast. Sorry, no children under sixteen or pets; closed August and September. Get your reservations in early (by email only, reservations@casaobelisco.com).

RENTAL AGENTS

For the many other San Francisco villa, house, or apartment rentals, consult friendly real estate agents Geno Lamphiear and Elvia Garcia at **Calandria Realty** (Av. Tercer Mundo 50, tel. 311/258-4285, www.calandriarealty.com) in front of Restaurant Ola Rica on the main street. Alternatively, you might also consult **Feibel Real Estate** (Av. Tercer Mundo 91, tel./fax 311/258-4041, www.flffeibel.com), which also lists vacation rentals and for-sale homes.

Food

The growing local community of middle-class Americans, Canadians, and Mexicans and the trickle of Puerto Vallarta visitors support a number of recommendable in-town eateries.

For Mexican supper, start at **Cenaduria Delfin** (on the main street, after 5 P.M.), about a block from the beach. The house specialty is yummy pozole on Saturday and Sunday nights. Look for the small paper plate tacked on the wall that says, *Hay Flan,* for some of the most delicious flan you've ever tried. On another night, head straight to Eva's **Red Chairs** taco stand, past the hospital, at the foot of the hill on the way to Restaurant del Mar.

On the same main street in the middle of town, nearly everyone in San Pancho recommends **C La Ola Rica Restaurant and Bar** (6–11 P.M. Mon.–Sat., $10–24). Welcoming owners Triny and Gloria offer fresh seafood and Mexican supper specialties. For good Italian pasta and pizza, go to *palapa* **Restaurant Pizzeria Galloly** (tel. 311/258-4135, $6–12), on the south side of the main street about four blocks from the beach.

European-tropical fusion cuisine has arrived in San Pancho, at view **C Café del Mar** (5–11 P.M. Thurs.–Tues., closed June–Sept., $10–22) on the hill northeast above the village. Local expatriates rave about the sauces, succulent fish, homemade pasta, exotic drinks ($4), and yummy chocolate cake ($3) that Belgian-born chef Almandine produces daily. Get there by following the street past the hospital (about a quarter mile from the highway); pass Eva's Red Chairs taco stand and follow the signs uphill.

The same owners of Café del Mar have opened a beachfront *palapa* restaurant called **La Perla del Mar** (noon–9 P.M. daily, $5–12) on the beach. Here, get everything—fish, oysters, clams, octopus, shrimp—super-fresh, either for lunch or early dinner beneath the *palapa.*

Bottega de Sapori is the local Italian bakery featuring fresh breads, pizza, lasagna, and desserts. Find it on Calle Latina America, about a block from main street Avenida Tercer Mundo.

Health and Emergencies

San Francisco residents benefit from a modest local general hospital (tel. 311/258-4077), with ambulance, emergency room, and doctors on-call 24 hours. Find it off the main street, to the right (north), about a quarter-mile from the highway.

PLAYA LO DE MARCO

Follow the signed Lo de Marco turnoff 31 miles (49 km) north of the Puerto Vallarta airport (or 8 mi/13 km south of Rincón de Guayabitos). Continue about a mile through the town to the long, sandy beach, dotted with a baker's dozen of seafood *palapa* restaurants. Playa Lo de Marco is popular with Mexican families; on Sunday and holidays they dig into the fine golden sand and frolic in the gentle, rolling waves. The surf of the nearly level, very wide Playa Lo de Marco is good for all aquatic sports except surfing. The south end has a rocky tidepool shelf, fine for bait-casting. During the clear-water late fall–winter season, scuba divers and snorkelers rent boats and head to pristine offshore Isla Islote.

© BRUCE WHIPPERMAN

Playa Lo de Marco is a favorite family beach.

Food

There are the usual taco stands and *fondas* to choose from in Lo de Marco, but most people dine out in nearby Guayabitos or San Francisco. The one standout from the crowd locally is **Benja's Tacos** where people rave about the **tacos al pastor.** You can find Benja's on the main street just before the Comex paint store. Open for lunch and dinner.

Accommodations

There are a number of low to mid-priced accommodations in town, some beachfront. For off-beach lodging, the best by far is **Hotel Bungalows Las Tortugas** (Luis Echevarría 28, tel./fax 327/275-0092, $35 d). The major attraction is the layout of about 18 kitchenette apartments in two stories around a broad, invitingly tropical designer pool and patio, with kiddie pool and hot tub. Inside, the units, all with kitchenettes, TV, dishes and utensils, and fans, are bare-bulb (bring your own lampshade), sparely but comfortably furnished, spacious, and clean. The second-floor apartments, with king-size beds, are more inviting than

some others. Look at more than one before deciding. Asking rates run high, but, except during holidays and some weekends, discounts may be negotiable, so be sure to ask for a *descuento* (days-koo-AYN-toh).

For something fancier, consider the big **Villas and Bungalows Tlaquepaque** (Pie de Av. Luis Echeverría, tel./fax 327/275-0080, villastlaquepaque@prodigy.net.mx). Past the imposing neocolonial front gate and reception spreads a manicured, grassy park, with luxurious blue-pool patio, basketball court, soccer field, and kiddie playground, interspersed among handsome accommodation tiers. Lodgings vary from one-bedroom studios to big three-bedroom, three-bath extended-family suites.

The lodgings themselves are immaculate and handsomely decorated in white stucco, bright Spanish tiles, and traditional handcrafted wooden furniture. A number of the studios are cozy and comfortable, with bright garden views and two double beds. Considering all the family-friendly facilities, the lower-end prices are moderate, beginning at about $33 d for the studios during the low season (Sept.–Dec. 15 and Jan.–Mar.), with breakfast sometimes included, and ranging up to $60 for two-bedroom family suites. Look at the several options before choosing. With plenty of space to run around and only a block from the beach, this is a great place for kids and large groups. Reservations are generally not necessary except July–August and Christmas and Easter holidays and maybe some weekends. Long-term rates are available.

If you prefer to stay closer to the sand and waves, a sprinkling of family-friendly beachfront lodgings appears promising: Check out **Bungalows Margarita** (Emiliano Zapata 22, tel. 327/275-0452, www.bungalowsmargarita.com). Here in a brightly colored apartment-style complex you have your choice of rooms ranging from oceanview suites that sleep up to six adults ($110 d) with kitchens, to rooms that sleep two ($55 d) and everything in between. There's air-conditioning, ceiling fans, and other creature comforts as well as a nice beach *palapa* and BBQ area. Get there by turning left from the main town highway entrance street, at the last road before the beach.

Also on the beachfront, a block north of the main road, you can stay at **Villas del Rey** (U.S. tel. 425/334-6051, www.mexicobeachfrontvillas.com), where local artist Lonney Ford and his wife Stacey have created a lovely garden setting decorated with Lonney's unusual sculptures right on the beach. The main attraction here is the massive villa ($400/day, sleeps 10–12) which is perfect for large groups and family get-togethers. Also available are three charming studios ($80 d) and a one-bedroom ($100 d) unit. All units include a full kitchen, queen beds, and ceiling fans and wireless Internet.

TRAILER PARKS AND CAMPGROUNDS

Lo de Marcos has a number of beachfront trailer parks, popular during the winter with a regiment of American and Canadian RV retirees. Best of the bunch is the good **El Caracol** trailer park and bunglow complex (P.O. Box 89, La Peñita de Jaltemba, Nayarit

63726, tel./fax 327/275-0050, http://elcaracol_mx.tripod.com). The trailer park section offers about 15 concrete-pad spaces in a palm- and banana-shaded grassy park right on the beach. With a small beachfront kiddie pool patio, all hookups, and immaculate hot-shower and toilet facilities. The spaces rent for about $22 d daily, $19 d monthly, $16 d for a 95-day stay; add $4 per day for air-conditioning power. Add $5 per day per extra person. Dogs are not generally welcome. It's popular, so make winter reservations in July or August. Caracol's bungalows are correspondingly well appointed. They are available with one bedroom (for up to three) or two bedrooms (for up to five), all comfortably furnished with all the comforts of Hamburg (the owner is German), including fans, optional air-conditioning, and complete kitchenettes. Daily rates run from $66 for two people in a one-bedroom bungalow, up to about $87 for five people in a two-bedroom bungalow; add $5 for one-bedroom air-conditioning, $10 for two-bedroom. Long term rates, for a three-month rental, can sometimes be negotiated to as low as $25 daily for a one-bedroom and $43 daily for a two-bedroom. Get your reservations in early.

Tent, RV camping, and bungalow lodgings are available at the trailer park **Pequeña Paraíso** (Carretera a Las Miñitas 1938, tel. 327/275-0089), beside the jungle headland at the south end of the beach. Here, the manager welcomes visitors to the spacious, palm-shaded beachside grove. Basic but clean apartments rent for about $220 per week, with kitchenette, hot-water showers, and fans. RV spaces ($18/day, $125/wk, $465/mo) have all hookups, with showers and toilets. Dozens of grass-carpeted, palm-shaded tent spaces rent for about $5 per person per day. Stores in town nearby can furnish basic supplies. Reserve, especially during the winter.

Get to the beachfront bungalows and trailer parks by turning left just before the beach, at the foot-of-the-town main street (which leads straight from the highway). Continue about another mile to El Caracol, on the right, and El Pequeño Paraíso, a hundred yards farther.

If those two are full, a few other trailer parks are recommendable. Best appears to be beachfront trailer park **Pretty Sunset** (tel./fax 327/275-0024 or 327/275-0055), with about 18 complete hookups ($20/day, $450/mo) in a mostly unshaded but spacious beachfront park. Another similarly equipped, but smaller, option along the same beachfront is **Trailer Park and Bungalows Huerta de Iguanas** (tel. 327/275-0089).

If they're all full, you're most likely to get a tent or RV space at the huge, overflow-style **Trailer Park and Campground El Refugio** ($24/day, $525/mo) on the north end of the beach, at big Villas and Bungalows Tlaquepaque (see listing under *Accommodations* this section).

HIDDEN BEACHES

Continuing south along the Lo de Marcos beach road past the trailer parks, you will soon come to two small sandy beaches, **Playa las Miñitas** and **Playa el Venado.** Both of these pretty, rock-enfolded strands, especially El Venado, are likely to be crowded weekends, but mostly empty mid-week, with lots of empty *palapas,* ripe for a tent. Even if for a day, bring your swimsuit, picnic lunch, and snorkeling gear.

Rincón de Guayabitos and La Peñita

Rincón de Guayabitos (pop. about 3,000 permanent, maybe 8,000 in winter) lies an hour's drive north of Puerto Vallarta, at the tiny south-end *rincón* (wrinkle) of the broad, mountain-rimmed Bay of Jaltemba. The full name of Rincón de Guayabitos's sister town, La Peñita (Little Rock) de Jaltemba, comes from its perch on the sandy edge of the bay.

Once upon a time, Rincón de Guayabitos (or simply Guayabitos, meaning Little Guavas) lived up to its diminutive name. During the 1970s, however, the government decided Rincón de Guayabitos would become both a resort and one of three places in the Puerto Vallarta region where foreigners could own property. Today Rincón de Guayabitos is a summer, Christmas, and Easter haven for Mexicans, and a winter retreat for U.S. and Canadian citizens weary of glitzy, pricey resorts.

ORIENTATION

Guayabitos and La Peñita (pop. around 10,000) represent practically a single town. Guayabitos has the hotels and the scenic beach-village ambience, while two miles north La Peñita's main street, **Emiliano Zapata,** bustles with stores, restaurants, a bank, and a bus station.

Guayabitos's main street, **Avenida del Sol Nuevo,** curves lazily for about a mile parallel to the beach. During holidays and the busy winter months, it's almost like a street fair with vendors lining the avenue and throngs of people shopping and dining. From the Avenida, several short streets and *andandos* (walkways) lead to a line of *retornos* (cul-de-sacs). There are literally dozens of hotels to choose from on and within two blocks of the beach, with an emphasis on low to mid-range pricing. Guayabitos might be one of the few beach resort towns where you can still get a $10 hotel room.

SIGHTS
Isla Islote

Only a few miles offshore, the rock-studded humpback of Isla Islote may be seen from every spot along the bay. A flotilla of wooden glass-bottomed launches plies the Guayabitos shoreline, ready to whisk visitors across to the island. For about $20 per hour, parties of up to eight can view fish through the boat bottom and see the colonies of nesting terns, frigate birds, and boobies on Islote's guano-plastered far side. You might see dolphins playing in your boat's wake, or perhaps a pod of whales spouting and diving nearby.

Cerro de la Santa Cruz

Some breezy afternoon, you might enjoy

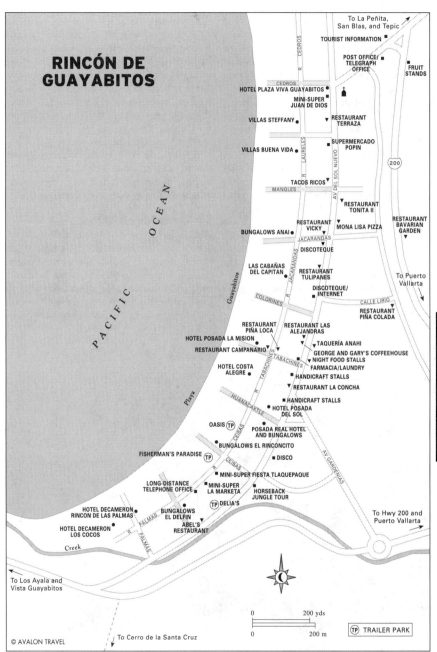

RINCÓN DE GUAYABITOS

OCEAN

PACIFIC

Playa

R. GUAYABITOS

R. CEDROS

CEDROS

R. LAURELES

MANGLES

AV. DEL SOL NUEVO

JACARANDAS

R. JACARANDAS

COLORINES

CALLE LIRIO

R. TABACHINES

TABACHINES

HUANACAXTLE

R. CEIBAS

CEIBAS

AV. GARDENIAS

R. PALMAS

PALMAS

Creek

To La Peñita,
San Blas, and Tepic

TOURIST INFORMATION

POST OFFICE/
TELEGRAPH
OFFICE

FRUIT
STANDS

HOTEL PLAZA VIVA GUAYABITOS
MINI-SUPER
JUAN DE DIOS

VILLAS STEFFANY

RESTAURANT
TERRAZA

SUPERMERCADO
POPIN

VILLAS BUENA VIDA

TACOS RICOS

RESTAURANT
TONITA II

RESTAURANT
VICKY

MONA LISA PIZZA

RESTAURANT
BAVARIAN
GARDEN

BUNGALOWS ANAI

DISCOTEQUE

LAS CABAÑAS
DEL CAPITAN

RESTAURANT
TULIPANES

To Puerto
Vallarta

DISCOTEQUE/
INTERNET

RESTAURANT
PIÑA COLADA

RESTAURANT
PIÑA LOCA

RESTAURANT LAS
ALEJANDRAS

HOTEL POSADA LA MISION

RESTAURANT CAMPANARIO

TAQUERÍA ANAHI

GEORGE AND GARY'S COFFEEHOUSE
NIGHT FOOD STALLS

HOTEL COSTA
ALEGRE

FARMACIA/LAUNDRY

HANDICRAFT STALLS

RESTAURANT LA CONCHA

HANDICRAFT STALLS

HOTEL POSADA
DEL SOL

OASIS (TP)

POSADA REAL HOTEL
AND BUNGALOWS

BUNGALOWS EL RINCONCITO

FISHERMAN'S PARADISE (TP)

DISCO

MINI-SUPER FIESTA TLAQUEPAQUE

LONG-DISTANCE
TELEPHONE OFFICE

MINI-SUPER
LA MARKETA

HORSEBACK
JUNGLE TOUR

(TP) DELIA'S

HOTEL DECAMERON
RINCON DE LAS PALMAS

BUNGALOWS
EL DELFIN

HOTEL DECAMERON
LOS COCOS

ABEL'S
RESTAURANT

To Hwy 200 and
Puerto Vallarta

To Los Ayala and
Vista Guayabitos

To Cerro de la Santa Cruz

200

THE NAYARIT COAST

© AVALON TRAVEL

| 0 | 200 yds |
| 0 | 200 m |

(TP) TRAILER PARK

following the 225-step pilgrimage (May 3 and Easter) path to the summit of Cerro de la Santa Cruz (Hill of the Holy Cross). From the top of La Cruz, as it's locally known, appreciate the ocean, beach, and cloud-tipped mountain panorama of the Bay of Jaltemba. Find the trail at the south end of Guayabitos's main street, Avenida del Sol Nuevo. Turn left at the crossroads and look for the path heading uphill.

BEACHES

The main beach, **Playa Guayabitos-La Peñita,** curves two miles north from the rocky Guayabitos headland and point, growing wider and steeper at La Peñita. The shallow south-end Guayabitos cove, lined by *palapa* restaurants and dotted with boats, is a favorite of Mexican families on Sundays and holidays. They play in the one-foot surf, ride the boats, and eat barbecued fish. During the busy Christmas and Easter holidays, the beach can get a bit crowded and messy from the people, boats, and fishing.

Farther along toward La Peñita, the beach broadens and becomes much cleaner, with surf good for swimming, bodysurfing, and boogie boarding. Afternoon winds are often brisk enough for sailing and sailboarding, though you must bring your own equipment. Scuba and snorkeling are good, especially during the November–May dry season, near offshore Isla Islote, accessible via rental boat from Guayabitos. Local stores sell inexpensive but serviceable masks, snorkels, and fins.

A mile north of La Peñita, just past the palm-dotted headland, another long, inviting beach begins, offering good chances for surf fishing and beginning and intermediate surfing.

◖ Playa los Muertos

Also at the south end of Avenida del Sol Nuevo, follow the crossroad to the right, toward Los Ayala. Just as the road reaches its summit, curving left around the Guayabitos headland, notice a dirt road forking right, downhill. It continues through a cemetery to Playa los Muertos (Beach of the Dead), where the graves come right down to the beach.

© ROBIN NOELLE

Erosion has left tombs sticking out onto the beach in La Peñita.

Ghosts notwithstanding, this is a scenic little sandy cove. On fair days get your fill of safe swimming, sunning on the beach, or tidepool exploring among the clustered oysters and mussels and the skittering crabs. The cemetery makes an interesting backdrop for photos; however, there are plans in the near future to relocate the cemetery to another part of town, so see it here while you can.

Playa los Ayala

Continue along the road about another mile to the once sleepy but now up-and-coming settlement and one-mile yellow strand of Playa los Ayala. Although local-style beachside *palapa* restaurants and bungalow accommodations are blossoming, the long, lovely Playa los Ayala retains its Sunday popularity among local families. All of the beach sports possible at Guayabitos are possible here, with the added advantage of a much cleaner beach.

Like Guayabitos, Los Ayala has its secluded south-end cove. Follow the path up the beach-end headland. Ten minutes' walk along a tropical forest trail leads you to the romantic little jungle-enfolded sand crescent called **Playa del Beso** (Beach of the Kiss). Except during holidays, for hours on end few if any people come here.

Among the best of Los Ayala's accommodations is **Bungalows Quinta Mina** (tel./fax 327/274-1141 or 327/274-1321). This three-story stack of modern kitchenette apartments enfolds an inviting beachfront pool and patio. Here, adults lounge around the small pool, while their kids frolic in a beachside kiddie pool. Upstairs, the dozen or so one-bedroom units, sleeping four, are simply but attractively furnished, with large rustic floor tiles, soft couches, white stucco walls, and shiny shower bathrooms. Low-season rentals run about $53 for up to four, except holidays and *puentes* (long weekends).

If the Quinta Mina is full, check out the Los Ayala branch of the popular Rincón de Guayabitos lodging **Bungalows el Delfín** (Av. Estero 228, tel. 327/274-0971, www.bungalowsdelfin.com).

Playa Punta Raza

Punta Raza is one of the most beautiful beaches along the coast. Tucked back down a three-mile jungle dirt road, you will find miles of dreamy golden sand perfect for beachcombing, lazing in the sun, or frolicking in the surf. Unfortunately, developers have discovered this isolated beach and now closed the area to make way for a megaresort complex. There is still a small area where you can pull off the road and since there is no private ownership of the beaches, visitors are welcome to park and enjoy the beach. There's only space enough for a few cars and at the moment no services are available. You will also be under the watchful eye of the security guard who staffs the guardhouse at the gate. Still, this beach is worth a drive over before the road is paved and the teeming masses of pink, peeling tourists take over and turn El Monteón into the next Nuevo Vallarta.

Three miles south of Guayabitos along Highway 200, turn off west at El Monteón; pass through the village and turn right at Calle Punta Raza just before the pavement ends. Continue along the rough road through the creek and over the ridge north of town. At the summit, stop and feast your eyes on the valley view below, then continue down through the near-virgin jungle, barely scratched by a few poor cornfields. About a mile downhill from the summit, stop to see if the seasonal hillside Hotel and Restaurant Rincón del Cielo on the right is open.

If the **Hotel and Restaurant Rincón del Cielo** is open, it affords the opportunity of enjoying an overnight at Playa Punta Raza without the effort of camping. Pioneering owners María Zavala and Juan Bernal offer eight immaculate and simply but lovingly decorated rooms. Two are at the jungle's edge ($45 d), one is at the ground level in their whimsical, medieval-style stone tower ($55 d), and the two others enjoy airy view perches above the surf ($65). Without electricity, María and Juan and their nighttime guests manage well using gas for light and refrigeration in their restaurant (seafood, salads, and pasta) and candles and hurricane lanterns in the rooms. Make reservations (not usually necessary) by leaving a message with the telephone operator in Monteón (tel. 327/274-7070).

ℂ LA PEÑITA *TIANGUIS*

One thing not to be missed in La Peñita is the weekly open air markets called *tianguis*. While other areas host markets as well, the Thursday morning market in La Peñita includes artisans from all over Mexico, some from as far away as Oaxaca and Puebla, home of the Talavera pottery. The marketplace is brimming with color as the artisans display their wares on tables and spread blankets. Handwoven rugs and baskets, carved Ironwood statues, gruesome and funny wooden masks—you'll find all manner of beautiful and authentic Mexican handicrafts in the square in the center of the market.

You'll see the market to your left where it starts on the south side of the main road into town about four blocks from the beach. The center square is where you will find the majority of artisans and craftpersons. The market is usually shut down by 2 P.M. so make sure to get there early enough to see everything.

In addition to hand painted wooden bowls and handmade jewelry, the *tianguis* is a great place to buy homewares like juicers, tortilla warmers, and lime squeezers. There are produce and fish vendors as well as many taco and ceviche stands for when you get hungry. Don't miss the organic Nayarit coffee and fresh honey!

NIGHTLIFE

Guayabitos's spot for romantics is **Vista Guayabitos** restaurant (noon–10 P.M. daily) on the south edge of town. Little has been spared to afford a perfect spot to enjoy a refreshment and/or snack and the breezy panoramic view of Guayabitos's curving cloud-tipped shoreline. Follow the south road to Los Ayala; at the big hilltop curve, follow the driveway on the right steeply uphill.

While Guayabitos is a bustling and energetic town during the high season, it doesn't have the nightlife options of Puerto Vallarta. A few

© ROBIN NOELLE

fresh honey for sale at the La Peñita *tianguis*

nightspots, findable by the noise they emanate, operate along Avenida del Sol Nuevo. One of the liveliest and longest-lasting is Charley's live music cabaret, at the corner of Tabachines, and the big, booming dance club at the corner of Avenida del Sol Nuevo and Jacarandas (from around 9 P.M. most nights, especially Friday and Saturday).

If oldies but goodies are your thing, the Bavarian Garden restaurant offers live '40s through '70s tunes and country music for dancing, 7–9 P.M. Wednesday and Friday during the November–May high season.

RECREATION

Aquatic sports concentrate around the south end of Guayabitos beach, where launches ply the waters, offering banana (towed-tube) rides and **snorkeling** at offshore Isla Islote. Rent a **sportfishing** launch along the beach. If you want to launch your own boat, ask at the Fisherman's Paradise Trailer Park if you can use their ramp for a fee.

Tours and Guides

A few local guides lead tours into the lush, wildlife-rich Guayabitos hinterland. Most accessible is **Indalesio Muñoz,** who leads horseback nature trail rides directly from his corral on the south end of Avenida del Sol Nuevo, across from the Hotel Bugambilias. Tariff is about $20 per person for a two-hour ride.

Highly recommended English-speaking guide **Esteban Valdivia** (home tel. 327/274-0805, Restaurant Piña Colada tel. 327/274-1211) offers more extensive tours to unusual, untouristed local sites. His itinerary can include such intriguing destinations as hidden Las Miñitas bay and beach near Lo de Marcos, Jamurca hot mineral pools, the Alta Vista Archaeological Sacred Site near Las Varas, the jungle river-boat tour to La Tovara spring in San Blas, and the sylvan volcanic Laguna Santa María, in the Sierra southeast of Tepic.

ACCOMMODATIONS

Rincón de Guayabitos has more far more hotels than any other town in Nayarit, including the state capital, Tepic. Competition keeps standards high and prices, for the most part, moderate. During the low season (Sept.–Dec. 15), most places are more than half empty and ready to bargain. During the winter season, the livelier part of town is at the south end, where the foreigners, mostly Canadian and American RV folks, congregate.

Guayabitos has many lodgings that call themselves "bungalows." This generally implies a motel-type suite with kitchenette and less service, but sleeping more people than most hotel rooms. For long stays or if you want to save money by cooking your own meals, bungalows can provide an attractive option. Note: Virtually all of the following lodgings have a web page on the Guayabitos general website www.guayabitos.com.

Under $50

On the north side of Andando Huanacaxtle, the kindly owner of **Hotel Posada del Sol** (tel. 327/274-0043, fax 327/273-1319, $60) offers 30 tastefully furnished kitchenette bungalows around a palmy garden pool patio. Best are the upper-level units, on the north side, with air-conditioning and garden-view patio-balconies. Economical long-term discounts are negotiable. This charming place, as you would expect, is very popular and full in winter with a crowd of long-time returnees. Get your reservations in early.

A good beachfront choice is the neocolonial-style **Hotel Posada La Misión** (Retorno Tabachines 6, tel./fax 327/274-0357, 327/274-0895, or 327/274-1000, posadamision@prodigy.net.mx), whose centerpiece is a beachview restaurant/bar. Extras include an inviting azure pool and patio, thoughtfully screened off from the parking. Its rooms are high-ceilinged and comfortable except for the unimaginative bare-bulb lighting; bring your favorite bulb-clip lamp shades. Rents range, from the smaller but comfortable economy double-bed rooms for about $40 to larger kitchenette suites sleeping six for about $58, all the way up to a pair of big kitchenette bungalows for about $80, all prices higher during Christmas and

Easter holidays. Amenities include the good El Campanario restaurant out in front, oceanview restaurant/bar, air-conditioning, ceiling fans, and parking; credit cards are accepted.

Bare-bones but clean, budget-conscious travelers can get a real bargain at **Hotel Plaza Viva Guayabitos** (Av. Sol Nuevo, corner of Cedros, tel. 327/274-0647, www.vivaguayabitos.com. mx), where during the low season you can still get a room for $10 s. The rooms are very basic but there's hot water, TV, Internet, and air-conditioning. The hotel offers secure parking, an on-site restaurant, and a pool. Rates run up to $25 s during the high season with discounts available for five nights or more.

$50-100

Among the more economical recommendable lodgings in town is the family-friendly 46-unit **Posada Real Hotel and Bungalows** (Av. Nuevo Sol and Andando Huanacaxtle, tel./fax 327/274-0707, toll-free Mex. tel. 01-800/74-3501, www.guayabitos.com.mx), built around a cobbled parking courtyard jungle of squawking parrots and shady palms, mangoes, and bamboo. The bungalow units are on the ground floor in the shady courtyard; the hotel rooms are stacked in three plant-decorated tiers above the lobby in front. The 20 double-bed hotel rooms rent for about $55 high season, $36 low, with discounts possible for longer-term stays. The 26 four-person bungalows with kitchenette rent for about $65 high season, $60 low. Amenities include ceiling fans, a small pool, and a kiddie pool, waterslide, racquetball, and parking; credit cards are accepted.

Right-on-the-beach **Bungalows El Rinconcito** (Retorno Ceibas s/n and Calle Ceibas, tel./fax 327/274-0229, bws_elrinconcito@hotmail.com) remains one of the best lodging buys in Guayabitos. The smallish whitewashed complex set back from the street offers large, tastefully furnished units with yellow-and-blue-tile kitchens and solid Spanish-style dark-wood chairs and beds. Its oceanside patio opens to a grassy garden overlooking the surf. The seven one-bedroom bungalows rent for about $56 high season, $44 low, with

fans and parking. Three two-bedroom bungalows rent for about $75 high season, $56 low. Discounts are generally negotiable for longer-term stays.

One of the most appealing off-beach Guayabitos lodgings is **Bungalows El Delfín** (Retorno Ceibas and Andando Cocoteros, tel./fax 327/274-0385, www.bunga-lowseldelfin.com), managed by friendly owners Francisco and Delia Orozco. Amenities include an intimate banana- and palm-fringed pool and patio, including recliners and umbrellas for resting and reading. Chairs on the shaded porch/walkways in front of the three room-tiers invite quiet relaxation and conversation with neighbors. The spacious four-person suites are large and plainly furnished, with basic stove, refrigerator, and utensils, rear laundry porches, and big tiled toilet-showers. The 23 bungalows with kitchenette sleep four and rent for about $50 d high season, $40 d low, $28 for one-month rental, with ceiling fans, pool, and parking; small dogs and cats are allowed.

Just as deluxe but more spacious is the all-inclusive beachfront family-oriented **Hotel Costa Alegre** (Retorno Tabachines s/n at Calle Tabachines, tel./fax 327/274-0241, 327/274-0242, or 327/274-0243, toll-free Mex. tel. 01-800/710-5683, www.costaalaegresuites.com), where the Guayabitos beach broadens. Its plusses include a big blue pool and patio on the street side and a broad, grassy oceanview garden on the beach side. Although the rooms are adequate, most of the regiment of kitchenette bungalows are set away from the beach with no view but the back of neighboring rooms. The most scenic choices are the several upper-tier oceanfront rooms, all with sliding glass doors leading to private seaview balconies. Some rooms are in better repair than others; look at more than one before paying. The 30 view rooms run about $55 s all-inclusive with discounts for children; the 80 kitchenette bungalows $75 ($440/week). Amenities include air-conditioning, pool, parking, and restaurant/bar; credit cards are accepted. Frequently pricing specials will be posted outside of the hotel.

Travelers who like lots of ready-made entertainment and an all-inclusive option should consider the compact pool-and-patio ambience of the **Hotel Decameron Rincón de las Palmas** (Retorno Palmas, corner of Calle Palmas, tel. 327/274-0190, fax 327/274-0138). On the south end of the beach, with an airy beachview restaurant and bar for sitting and socializing, this is a lodging for those who want company. Guests may often have a hard time *not* getting acquainted. The smallish rooms are packed in two double parallel breezeway tiers around a pool and patio above the beach. Right outside your room during the high season you will probably have your pick of around 50 sunbathing bodies to gaze at and meet. This hotel, once independent, is owned and operated by its big neighbor **Hotel Decameron Los Cocos**, which handles reservations (in a Bucerías office, tel. 329/298-0226, toll-free Mex. tel. 01-800/011-1111, www.decameron.com), mandatory in winter. Specify the Hotel Rincón de las Palmas (or Cocos II, as it's now known), or you might be put in the oversize Los Cocos. The 40 rooms rent, high season, all-inclusive, for $75 per person double occupancy, with all drinks, food, and in-house entertainment included. Amenities include air-conditioning, pool, TV, tennis court, breezy seaview restaurant and bar, and parking; credit cards are accepted.

For lots of peace and quiet in a deluxe tropical setting, the **Bungalows Anai** (Calle Jacarandas and Retorno Jacarandas, tel./fax 327/274-0245, www.suitesanai.com) is just about the best on the beach. The 12 apartments, each with private oceanview balcony, in three separate four-unit sections, stand graciously to one side. They overlook a spacious plant-bedecked garden, shaded by a magnificent grove of drowsy coconut palms. The garden leads to an oceanview pool patio and whirlpool tub, where a few guests read, socialize, and take in the beachside scene below. Inside, the two-bedroom apartments are simply but thoughtfully furnished in natural wood, bamboo, and tile and come with bath, three double beds, furnished kitchen, fans, air-conditioning, and TV. Rentals run about $76 for two, add about $12 for each additional person; one-week minimum stay. Book your reservations early.

Set back from the road in a tropical parklike setting is **Las Cabañas del Capitan** (Retorno Jacarandas 88, tel./fax 327/274-0304 or 327/274-0901, www.bungalowselcapitan.com) offering quiet rooms with a rustic feel. Guests of the 28 bungalows enjoy full open-air kitchens and private balconies with views of the garden, pool, or ocean. The accommodations are done in an authentic Mexican style with tiles and wooden furniture. There are no phones or TVs in the suites but the bedrooms have air-conditioning. Rentals run about $85 high and $50 low.

Over $100

A few doors south, the deluxe **Villas Buena Vida** (Retorno Laureles 2, tel. 327/274-0231, toll-free Mex. tel. 800/640-3388, fax 327/274-0756, www.villasbuenavida.com) is one of Guayabitos's luxury lodgings. About 40 tastefully appointed oceanview suites rise in three stories above a palm-shaded pool and patio right on the beach. For Guayabitos, the high-season asking rates are correspondingly luxurious: two-bed "villa" apartments run about $152 d high season, junior suites $199, master suites $253. Low-season rates start at $104 d. Discounts are customarily available for long-term stays.

RV Parks

All Guayabitos RV parks are customarily packed wall-to-wall most of the winter. Some old-timers have painted and marked out their spaces for years of future occupancy. The best spaces of the bunch are all booked by mid-October. And although the longtime residents are polite enough, some of them are clannish and don't go out of their way to welcome new kids on the block.

This is fortunately not true at **Delia's** (Retorno Ceibas 4, tel. 327/274-0226, 327/274-0397, 327/274-0398, or 327/274-0399), Guayabitos's homiest trailer park. Friendly owner Delia Bond Valdez and her daughter Rosa Delia have 12

RV park residents on the beach at Rincón de Guayabitos

spaces ($16/night, $425/month all year), some often unfilled even during the high season. Their place, alas, is not right on the beach, nor is it as tidy as some folks would like. On the other hand, Delia offers a little store and a long-distance phone service right next to the premises. She also rents three bungalows for about $500 a month. Spaces have all hookups (but insufficient power for a/c), showers, toilets, and room for big rigs; pets are okay; extra person $5. Space for camper vans costs $250/month with all hookups, tent spaces go for $10/day, $225/month.

Next to the north comes **Fisherman's Paradise Trailer Park** (Retorno Ceibas s/n, tel. 327/274-0014, fax 327/274-0525, paraiso-delpescador@hotmail.com), which is also popular as a mango-lover's paradise. Several spreading mango trees shade the park's 33 concrete pads, and during the late spring and summer when the mangos are ripe, you might be able to park under your own tree. Winter-season spaces rent for about $25 per day for two people, minimum 15-day rental (or $18/day for a three-month rental), with all hookups,

showers, toilets, and lovely pool and patio; pets are okay, and add $4.75 per extra person. Hotel rooms are available as well and start at $65 for up to four people.

Neighboring **Trailer Park Oasis** (Retorno Ceibas s/n, Apdo. 52, tel. 327/274-0361) is among Guayabitos's most deluxe and spacious trailer parks. Its 19 all-concrete, partly palm-shaded spaces are wide and long enough for 40-foot rigs. Pluses include green grassy oceanview grounds, beautiful blue pool, a designer restaurant, and a luxury oceanview *palapa* overlooking the beach. Spaces rent for about $26 per day, with all hookups, showers, toilets, fish-cleaning facility, beautiful beachfront pool, and boat ramp; pets okay.

Residents at the big **La Peñita RV Park** (P.O. Box 22, La Peñita, Nayarit 63727, tel. 327/274-0996, reserve Nov.–Apr. tel. 327/274-1593, June–Oct. U.S. tel. 250/286-1803, U.S. fax toll-free 800/858-0604, www.lapenitarvpark.com) enjoy a breezy oceanview location one mile north of La Peñita; watch for the big highway sign. Its 128 grassy spaces ($25/day, $600/month) are sprinkled over a shady hillside park, overlooking a golden beach and bay, with all hookups; closed May–October. The many amenities include a pool, hilltop terrace club, wireless Internet, taco Tuesdays with free margaritas, hamburger night, laundry, showers and toilets, and surfing, boogie boarding, and surf fishing. Tenters are welcome for $16 per tent for two.

FOOD
Fruit Stands and Minimarkets
The orchard country along Highway 200 north of Puerto Vallarta offers a feast of tropical fruits. Roadside stands at Guayabitos, La Peñita, and especially at Las Varas, half an hour north, offer mounds of papayas, mangos, melons, and pineapples in season. Watch out also for more exotic species, such as the *guanábana,* which looks like a spiny mango, but whose pulpy interior looks and smells much like its Asian cousin, the jackfruit.

A number of Guayabitos *mini-supers* supply a little bit of everything. Try **Mini-super La Marketa** (Retorno Ceibas across from Trailer Park Villanueva, tel. 327/274-0399, 7 A.M.–8 P.M.Mon–Sat., 7 A.M.–2:30 P.M. Sun.) for vegetables, a small deli, and general groceries. Competing next door is **Mini-Super Fiesta Tlaqupaque Fiesta** (tel. 327/274-0434, 8 A.M.–8 P.M. Mon–Sat.). On the north end of Avenida del Sol Nuevo, **Mini-super Juan de Dios** and **Supermercado Popin** (both 8 A.M.–9 P.M. daily) opposite the church and Hotel Peñamar, respectively, stock more, including fresh baked goods.

For larger, fresher selections of everything, go to one of the big main-street *fruterías* or supermarkets in La Peñita, such as **Supermercado Lorena** on main street Emiliano Zapata, in the middle of town (tel. 327/274-0255, 8 A.M.–10 P.M. daily).

Cafés and Restaurants
Several Guayabitos cafés and restaurants offer good food and service during the busy winter, spring, and July–August seasons. Some, however, either close or restrict their hours during the midsummer and September–November low seasons.

By location, moving from the Guayabitos's south end, first find tidy, budget **Abel's Restaurant** *palapa* (south end of Av. del Sol Nuevo, behind Bungalows del Delfín, 7 A.M.–9 P.M. daily). Abel has been providing delicious meals for residents of Guaybitos for more than 22 years. Start off your day right with a home-cooked American-style breakfast ($2–3), such as French toast, pancakes, or eggs any style. Return for lunch or dinner ($3–7), with one of Abel's hearty *burrita* or *azteca* soups, followed by a tasty meat, fish, or chicken plate.

For supper, you can't enjoy a tastier option than the family-run **Taquería Anahi** (middle of Av. del Sol Nuevo, east side, corner of Tabachines, early morning–10 P.M. daily year-round, $1–3). Here, dedicated cooks put out hearty tacos, enchiladas, spicy pozole (shredded pork roast and hominy vegetable stew), and much more.

Right across the street, don't miss **George and Gary's Coffee House** (tel. 327/274-0400, 7 A.M.–9 P.M. daily), for the best morning coffee in town. Later, drop by for a cool-down afternoon treat, such as George's mocha frappe. Master of the show is personable, knowledgeable former professor of veterinary medicine and civic leader **Jorge Castuera.** If there's something you want to know about Guayabitos, Jorge is the person to ask. There's an excellent selection of used paperbacks for trade here, so don't forget to bring those books you've already read!

A few doors north, the clean, local-style **Restaurant Las Alejandras** (tel. 327/274-0488, 8 A.M.–9 P.M. daily in season, $3–7) offers good breakfasts and a general Mexican-style menu.

From Avenida del Sol Nuevo, walk a block toward the beach, to one of Guayabitos's best, the moderately priced **Campanario** (Retorno Tabachines 6 at Calle Tabachines, tel. 327/274-0357, 8 A.M.–9 P.M. daily high season, 8 A.M.–5 P.M. daily low, $5–12), in front of the Hotel Posada la Misión. The menu, a longtime favorite of the North American RV colony, features bountiful fresh seafood, meat, and Mexican plates; credit cards are accepted. (For a variation on a similar comfort-food theme, try equally popular **Restaurant La Piña Loca** across the street.)

A good place to start your day is in a comfortable booth at coffee shop–style, air-conditioned **Restaurant Tulipanes** (Av. del Sol Nuevo, south corner of Jacarandas, tel. 327/274-0575, 8 A.M.–10 P.M. daily). Pick from a long list of hearty breakfast combos ($4–5), including eggs, bacon, hash browns, hotcakes, and French toast. Return at lunch and dinner ($3–7) for guacamole ($3), soups and salads ($3), and pasta, chicken, and fish.

Similar good home-style food and service is available farther north at **Restaurant Tonita** (near the corner of Andando Colorines, 7:30 A.M.–9:30 P.M. Mon.–Fri. in season).

If you are looking for pizza, try **Mona Lisa Pizza** (Av. del Sol Nuevo and Calle Magles, tel. 327/274-0137, 5–10 P.M.) where the specialty is thin crust, wood-fired pizza.

Also highly recommended is the **Restaurant Piña Colada** (Hwy. 200 lateral road, end of Calle Lirio, east of Av. del Sol Nuevo, tel. 327/274-1211 or 327/274-1172) of friendly local guide Estaban Valdivia.

Finally, be sure not to miss Guayabitos's hands-down best restaurant, the ◀ **Bavarian Garden** (on Hwy. 200, at the south-end signal and entrance to town, tel. 327/274-2136, 5 A.M.–9 P.M. Mon.–Sat., 8 A.M.–9 P.M. Sun. with sumptuous morning brunch, Nov.–Easter). Here, you and probably at least a dozen winter-season (reservations recommended) diners will enjoy a feast, with entrées such as *kassler ripchen* (smoked pork chops, $10) or savory Hungarian goulash (substitute German potato pancakes for rice, $9), topped off with homemade *apfel strudel* ($3) and rich espresso coffee. *Wunderbar!* Note: May–October low-season hours are 5 A.M.–9 P.M. Monday–Saturday (except closed Thurs.); 8 A.M.–2 P.M. Sunday for brunch.

INFORMATION AND SERVICES

Nayarit State Tourism maintains an **information office** (tel. 327/274-0693, 9 A.M.–7 P.M. Fri.–Wed.) at the north end of Avenida del Sol Nuevo, by the highway.

If you can't find out what you want at the *turismo,* an excellent alternative source is **Jorge Castuera,** the well-informed, personable, English-speaking former professor of veterinary medicine and owner of George and Gary's Coffee House (Av. del Sol Nuevo, corner of Tabachines). Jorge also runs a launderette and a book exchange: Bring one in, get one back.

Money

Although Guayabitos has no exchange agency as such, some of the minimarkets may exchange U.S. or Canadian dollars or travelers checks. More pesos for your U.S. and Canadian cash or travelers checks are available at the **Bancomer** branch (with ATM) in La Peñita (on the highway, about three doors south of main Av. E. Zapata crossing, tel. 327/274-0237, 9 A.M.–4 P.M. Mon.–Fri.).

Communications

The *correo* (tel. 327/274-0717, 8 A.M.–2 P.M. Mon.–Fri.) and the **Telecom** (8 A.M.–2 P.M. Mon.–Fri.) stand side by side in the park, just north of the town church.

Long-distance telephoning is most conveniently and economically done on public street telephones, with Ladatel phone cards, widely available in stores along Avenida del Sol Nuevo. A $5 Ladatel card will get you about 10 minutes of time to the United States or Canada on a street telephone. Lacking a phone card, go to Jorge Castuera's coffee house; he offers long-distance telephone service.

Connect to the Internet at the **Internet Discoteque,** open daily 10 A.M.–midnight. It's located on Avenida del Sol Nuevo, just north of the corner of Andando Colorines.

Health and Emergencies

Guayabitos has a **paramedic ambulance** (tel. 327/274-1561), operated by the *bomberos* (firefighters) from near the tourist information office, on the north side of the north end of Avenida del Sol Nuevo. If necessary, they can take you in a hurry 14 miles (22 km) south to the small general hospital in San Francisco (tel. 311/258-4077), which offers X-ray, laboratory, gynecological, pediatric, and internal medicine consultations and services, both at regular hours (10:30 A.M.–noon and 4–6 P.M.) and on 24-hour emergency call.

Alternatively, for local medical consultations in La Peñita, go to the highly recommended small, private 24-hour **Clínica Rentería** (Calle Valle de Acapulco, tel. 327/274-0140). A surgeon, a gynecologist, and a general practitioner (Raul Rentería, M.D.) are on call there. For medical consultations and simple remedies in Guayabitos, see Dr. Alfredo Rentería at his pharmacy (Av. del Sol Nuevo a few doors north of Tabachines, tel. 327/274-0747).

GETTING THERE

Transportes Pacífico first- and second-class buses (southbound for Puerto Vallarta, and northbound for Tepic, Guadalajara, and Mazatlán) routinely stop (about twice every daylight hour, each direction) both at the main highway entrance to Guayabitos's Avenida del Sol Nuevo and at La Peñita's main Highway 200 crossing. The same is true of Estrella Blanca buses (Transportes Norte de Sonora), southbound to Puerto Vallarta and northbound to San Blas; and Elite, southbound to Puerto Vallarta, Manzanillo, Ixtapa-Zihuatanejo, and Acapulco, and northbound to Tepic, Guadalajara, Mazatlán and the U.S. border.

At La Peñita, Transportes Pacífico and Estrella Blanca cooperate, sharing a pair of stations (and phone, tel. 327/274-0001) on opposite sides of the main highway crossing corner.

Also at La Peñita, a third bus line, **Primera Plus** luxury buses en route between Puerto Vallarta and Guadalajara, also stops at a separate small station next to the Transportes Pacífico, Transportes Norte de Sonora, and Elite station.

The Guayabitos coast is easily accessible by **taxi** (about $60 for four) from the Puerto Vallarta International Airport, the busy terminal for flight connections with U.S. and Mexican destinations. Buses (which you must board at the Puerto Vallarta bus station, north of the airport) and taxis cover the 39-mile (62-km) distance to Guayabitos in around an hour.

The Road to San Blas

The lush 60-mile (100-km) stretch between Rincón de Guayabitos and San Blas is a Pacific eden of flowery tropical forests and pearly, palm-shaded beaches largely unknown to the outside world. Highway 200 and the coastal bypass highway that connects at Las Varas lead travelers past leafy tropical banana and mango orchards, mangrove-edged lagoons, vine-strewn jungle, and a string of little havens—Playa El Naranjo, Chacala and Mar de Jade, Playa las Tortugas, Platanitos, Paraíso Miramar, Casa Mañana, and Las Islitas—that add sparkle to an already inviting coastline.

PLAYA EL NARANJO

Seven miles (11 km) along Highway 200, north of Guayabitos, a signed, cobbled side road leads through Lima de Abajo village about 2.5 miles (4 km) to the gorgeous golden beach of El Naranjo (The Orange Tree). Several permanent *palapa* seafood restaurants line the beach, a palm grove provides ample space and shade for RV parking and tent camping; a spreading mangrove lagoon beyond the grove nurtures a host of wildlife, including a few crocodiles that bask in the sun at the lagoon's edge. Bugs come out in late afternoon and evening. Campers: Be prepared with insect repellent.

The beach itself is gloriously flat and kid-friendly. About a hundred yards out in the water, rolling billows, good for beginning and intermediate surfing, break gracefully. A platoon of pelicans and frigate birds soar and dive above the waves, while on the beach, little crabs skitter along the sand, pursued by squads of nimble shore birds.

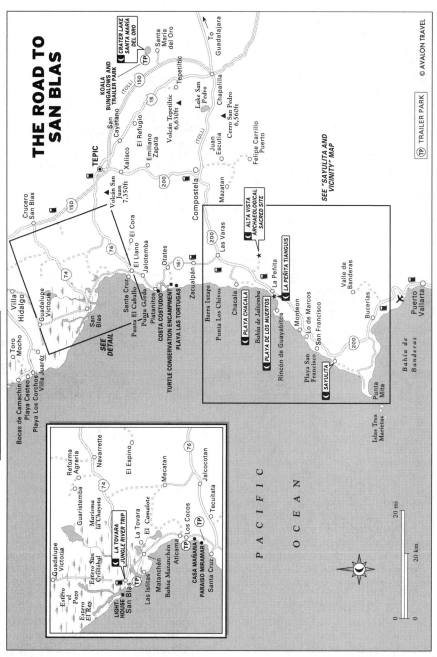

THE ROAD TO SAN BLAS

© AVALON TRAVEL

(TP) TRAILER PARK

CRATER LAKE SANTA MARÍA DEL ORO

Santa María del Oro

KOALA BUNGALOWS AND TRAILER PARK

To Guadalajara

San Cayetano

Tepetiltic

(15D)

(TOLL)

El Refugio

(15)

Volcán Tepetiltic 6,630ft

Lake San Pedro

Chapalilla

TEPIC

Xalisco

Emiliano Zapata

Cerro San Pedro 6,560ft

Juan Escutia

Felipe Carrillo Puerto

(200)

Compostela

Crucero San Blas

Volcán San Juan 7,350ft

(15D)

(TOLL)

(200)

Mazatan

Las Varas

ALTA VISTA ARCHAEOLOGICAL SACRED SITE

SEE "SAYULITA AND VICINITY" MAP

El Cora

El Llano

Jalostemba

(76)

El Caballo

(74)

Guadalupe Victoria

San Blas

Santa Cruz

Punta El Caballo

Platanitos

Punta Gorda

Otates

(161)

Zacualpán

COSTA COSTUDIO

TURTLE CONSERVATION ENCAMPMENT

PLAYA LAS TORTUGAS

La Peñita

LA PEÑITA TIANGUIS

Barra Ixtapa

Punta Los Chivos

Chacala

PLAYA CHACALA

Bahía de Jaltemba

PLAYA DE LOS MUERTOS

Valle de Banderas

SEE DETAIL

Villa Hidalgo

Villa Victoria

Toro Mocho

Bocas de Camachin

Playa Cesteo

Playa Los Corchos

Villa Juárez

Rincón de Guayabitos

Montéon

Lo de Marcos

San Francisco

Playa San Francisco

SAYULITA

Bucerías

(200)

Bahía de Banderas

Puerto Vallarta

Punta Mita

Islas Tres Marietas

PACIFIC

OCEAN

20 mi

20 km

Guadalupe Victoria

Reforma Agraria

Navarrette

El Espino

(74)

Guaristemba

Marisma la Chayota

Mecatan

El Camalote

(76)

Jalcocotan

Estero el Pozo

San Blas

La Tovara

Los Cocos

Tecuitata

LA TOVARA JUNGLE RIVER TRIP

Estero San Cristóbal

Estero El Rey

LIGHT HOUSE San Blas

Las Islitas

Matanchén

Bahía Matanchén

Aticama

Santa Cruz

CASA MAÑANA

PARAISO MIRAMAR

(TP)

(TP)

(TP)

(TP)

(TP)

THE BELLS OF SAN BLAS

Renowned Romantic poet Henry Wadsworth Longfellow (1807-1882) most likely read about San Blas during the early 1870s, just after the town's port was closed to foreign trade. With the ships gone, and not even the trickle of tourists it now enjoys, the San Blas of Longfellow's time was perhaps even dustier and quieter than it is today.

San Blas must have meant quite a lot to him. Ten years later, ill and dying, Longfellow hastened to complete "The Bells of San Blas," his very last poem, finished nine days before he died on March 24, 1882. Longfellow wrote of the silent bells of the old Nuestro Señora del Rosario (Our Lady of the Rosary) church, whose arches, albeit mossy and frail, still rise proudly atop the summit of Cerro San Basilio.

What say the Bells of San Blas
To the ships that southward pass
From the harbor of Mazatlán?
To them it is nothing more
Than the sound of surf on the shore,
– Nothing more to master or man.

But to me, a dreamer of dreams,
To whom what is and what seems
Are often one and the same,–
The Bells of San Blas to me
Have a strange, wild melody,
And are something more than a name

For bells are the voice of the church;
They have tones that touch and search
The hearts of young and old;
One sound to all, yet each
Lends a meaning to their speech,
And the meaning is manifold.

They are a voice of the Past,
Of an age that is fading fast,
Of a power austere and grand;
When the flag of Spain unfurled
Its folds o'er this western world,
And the Priest was lord of the land.

The chapel that once looked down
On the little seaport town
Has crumbled into the dust
And on oaken beams below
The bells swing to and fro,
And are green with mould and rust.

"Is then, the old faith dead,"
They say, "and in its stead
Is some new faith proclaimed,

That we are forced to remain
Naked to sun and rain,
Unsheltered and ashamed?"

Once in our tower aloof
We rang over wall and roof
Our warnings and our complaints;
And round about us there
The white doves filled the air,
Like the white souls of the saints.

"The saints! Ah, have they grown
Forgetful of their own?
Are they asleep, or dead,
That open to the sky
Their ruined Missions lie,
No longer tenanted?

"Oh, bring us back once more
The vanished days of yore,
When the world with faith was filled;
Bring back the fervid zeal,
The hearts of fire and steel,
The hands that believe and build.

"Then from our tower again
We will send over land and main
Our voices of command,
Like exiled kings who return
To their thrones, and the people learn
That the Priest is lord of the land!"

O Bells of San Blas, in vain
Ye call back the Past again!
The Past is deaf to your prayer;
Out of the shadows of night
The world rolls into light;
It is daybreak everywhere.

Among the most inviting of the dozen-odd seafood *palapas* is **Restaurant Keenia** (tel. 322/294-8563, 8 A.M.–7 P.M. daily), run by personable, English-speaking Fidel López. He's especially proud of his *pescado sarandeado* (basted and barbecued fish).

◖ Alta Vista Archaeological Sacred Site

Two miles (3 km) north of the Highway 200 Playa El Naranjo turnoff, a right-side (east) turnoff road signed Alta Vista (the local municipality eight miles uphill) points the way to Santuario Alta Vista Archaeological Sacred Site. There you will find a *palapa* shelter, a caretaker (offer a gratuity of about $2 per person), and a half-mile self-guided trail dotted with dozens of petroglyphs that experts estimate date back at least 2,000 years.

Unlike many other such sites in Mexico, Alta Vista is still actively frequented as a holy place, known traditionally as **Chacalán** by local people. When you reach the end of the path, you'll see flower-adorned impromptu shrines that decorate a magnificent rock amphitheater-like cascade, studded with friendly water-rounded volcanic blocks and crystalline spring-water pools. There seems no doubt that this place, so special that it evokes wonder, has been revered by local folks for untold millennia. For a small fee, camping may be possible near the entrance. For more details, visit www.guayabitos.com.mx.

Get there by foot or by car (preferably a high-clearance jeep or truck) via the Highway 200 gravel turnoff road. After about a mile winding uphill, turn into a tree-lined country lane on the left. If you reach a farmhouse, turn back; you went too far. Continue gradually downhill about half a mile, and turn onto another narrower lane on the right. After about another half-mile downhill, the road will probably become too rough for a passenger car. If so, you may have to walk the additional mile. Continue downhill, bearing right along a creek, to road's end, where the path crosses the creek. Continue on foot, across the creek and straight ahead, to the site.

Blocks of natural volcanic asphalt rock add a kind of mysterious beauty to the Alta Vista Archaeological Sacred Site.

If you prefer, there are guided horseback rides from nearby Chacala that will take about six hours (four hours to the location on horse, viewing time and then a return trip via van).

◖ PLAYA CHACALA

Side roads off Highway 200 provide exotic, close-up glimpses of Nayarit's tangled, tropical woodland, but rarely will they lead to such a delightful surprise as the green-tufted golden crescent of Playa Chacala.

Nineteen miles (31 km) north of Rincón de Guayabitos, follow the six-mile newly paved road to the great old palm grove at Chacala. Beyond the line of rustic *palapa* seafood restaurants lies a heavenly curve of sand, enfolded on both sides by palm-tipped headlands.

Supplied by the beachside restaurants (especially recommended: **Restaurant Las Brisas,** for good breaded shrimp, and **Restaurant Acela**) and the stores in the village, Playa Chacala is ideal for those who are looking for peace and quiet without much of a nightlife.

© ROBIN NOELLE

the petite hamlet of Playa Chacala

Chacala used to be an excellent place for camping and RVs however recently the town has eliminated all camping activities due to waste management problems. Residents have also started a clean beach campaign, asking visitors who come on the daily caravan of tour buses to donate $2 to the cause. Volunteers routinely walk the beaches in the afternoon to remind visiting families to pack out whatever they brought onto the beach. The result is that the beach is much cleaner than it has been especially on weekends and holidays.

A mile farther north, past Chacala village on the headland, the road ends at Playa Chacalilla, Playa Chacala's miniature twin. Due to the recent residential development, public access has been restricted completely for now.

Recreation

Playa Chacala's oft-gentle surf is good for close-in bodysurfing, boogie boarding, swimming, and beginning-to-intermediate surfing. Furthermore, the water is generally clear enough for snorkeling off the rocks on either side of the beach. If you bring your equipment,

kayaking, sailboarding, and sailing are possible. The sheltered north-end cove is nearly always tranquil and safe, even for tiny tots. Fishing is so good many local people make their living at it. Chacala Bay is so rich and clean that tourists sometimes eat oysters right off the rocks.

Boatmen on the beach, or at the dock at the bay's far north end, offer excursions (figure about $20 per hour) to nearby secluded beaches, such as **Playa la Caleta** for surfing and **Playa las Cuevas** (the Caves) for picnicking, swimming, and snorkeling. Be prepared with your own drinks, food, and equipment, however.

Rent a bike for the day ($12) from **Bicicletas Adrian** (tel. 327/219-4116) and take a jungle ride. You can also take guided tours to the lake and other nearby scenic wonders.

Horseback rides along local jungle trails are also available from providers at the beach. **Concha,** owner of Casa Concha (tel. 327/219-4019, conchaguanahani_234@ hotmail.com, offers bird- and wildlife-watching hikes.

Accommodations

◖ **Mar de Jade** (Puerto Vallarta tel. 322/222-1171 or 327/219-4060, Chacala tel. 327/209-4060 or 327/209-4070, fax 327/209-4080, toll-free U.S. tel. 800/257-0532, www.mardejade.com), the holistic-style living center at the south end of Playa Chacala, offers some unique alternatives. Laura del Valle, Mar de Jade's personable and dynamic physician/founder, has worked steadily since the early 1980s building living facilities and a learning center while simultaneously establishing a local health clinic. Now, Mar de Jade offers Spanish-language and volunteer programs for people who enjoy the tropics but want to do more than laze in the sun. A major thrust is interaction with local people. Spanish, for example, is the preferred language at the dinner table.

The semideluxe and deluxe lodgings nestled into a flowery, junglelike hillside garden complex consist of 15 suites and 12 guest rooms, each with ocean views and most with private balconies. The rooms and spacious suites are simply but elegantly decorated with designer rustic tile, rich mahogany furnishings, and cut stone. Stone pathways lead to the beachside main center, which consists of a dining room, kitchen, offices, library, and classroom overlooking the sea.

While Mar de Jade's purpose is nonprofit work that supports the neighboring community, it has nothing against visitors who *do* want to laze in the sun, beachcomb, and soak in the beachfront pool and whirlpool tub. Mar de Jade invites travelers to make reservations and stay as long as they like, for about $120 per person, double occupancy (guest room), to about $145 (suites), November–April, including three meals a day. Tax, gratuity, and alcohol are not included. Children with parents stay for about $30 each; children under six are free. Low season May–October rates run about 25 percent less. Discounts may be negotiable for stays of three weeks or longer.

The core educational program is a three-week Spanish course (fee about $300 for three weeks), although it does offer one- and two-week options for those who can't stay the full three weeks. Volunteer work-study programs, such as organic gardening, kitchen assistance, carpentry, maintenance, arts-and-crafts instruction, and teaching English might be arranged. Sometimes participants volunteer to join staff in local work, such as at the medical clinic or on construction projects.

Civil engineer and builder José Enrique del Valle and his wife, who own the jungle-forest parcel above Mar de Jade, have worked hard to put their land to good use. His dream-come-true, **Majahua Spa Bed and Breakfast** (tel. 327/219-4053, 327/219-4054, or 327/219-4055, www.majahua.com), now regularly receives guests. José, his wife, and his several staff members offer five luxuriously rustic and private accommodations, an open-air restaurant, and a sprinkling of spa services. The lodgings, which blend artfully into the verdant tropical-forested hillside, are all lovingly designed and hand-built of stucco and tile, with various sleeping options (that include double, king-size, and kid-size beds), modern standard baths, and beautiful views.

Accommodations vary from the La Puerta honeymoon suite just above the restaurant and move upward, through mid-sized double suites A and B to the airy top-level view "penthouse," La Torre, big enough for five. In the middle, a small spa section offers massage, facials, and aromatherapy. High-season (Dec. 1–May 30) rates begin at about $125 for two, and run upward to about $275 for the big "penthouse" suite. All lodging prices include breakfast. Add $25 for extra guests.

To get to Majahua turn left at the beach road and pass through the gates into the large palm-grove parking area. Continue along the coastline by staying to the right until you pass into another parking area. Park closest to the eastern side of the lot and then look for the trail leading up to reception. The walk is short and not too difficult, however walking shoes will make it easier. Once you check in, your luggage can be brought up by ATV.

For his more active guests, José offers to lead (or get a guide to lead) all-day wildlife-viewing and hiking excursions, including to a nearby extinct volcano (elev. 750 ft) crater lake.

José, along with the help of many others, notably Susana Escobido, have led Chacala's transition from a drowsy subsistence fishing village to a growing tourist destination. Now, with the help of many U.S. and Canadian volunteers, Chacala people, under the umbrella of the national **Techos de Mexico** (Roofs of Mexico) program (www.techosdemexico.com), have built modern-standard tourist accommodations into their homes. They invite travelers to come and stay at very reasonable rates, ranging $20–40 for two, sometimes including breakfast. Check the website for additional information including photos and prices.

Check out the website www.chacalaescape.com to reserve some of the rooms by phone, email or online. The growing list now includes: **Casa Gracia** (tel. 327/219-4021 or 327/219-4067, sescobido@aol.com); **Casa Aurora** (tel. 327/219-4027 or 327/219-4067, sescobido@aol.com, $35–45), which has four rooms, fan, sea view, and parking; **Casa Beatriz** (tel. 327/219-4005), which has two rooms, fan, sea view, and parking; and **Casa Concha** (tel. 327/219-4019, conchaguanahani_234@hotmail.com, $20–50), which has three rooms, fan, sea view, and parking.

Chacala is a small village; all of the above are within three blocks of the beach and excellent fresh seafood *palapa* restaurants.

Although not part of the Techos de Mexico, the **Hotel las Brisas** (tel. 327/219-4015, www.lasbrisaschacala.com) is locally owned and operated. The rooms (sheltered beneath the rustic *palapa* of a good beachfront restaurant) could be heaven for beach-lovers, smack on the lovely Chacala beachfront. The 11 smallish accommodations, mostly all upstairs, are conveniently removed from restaurant hubbub below. They are attractively decorated in pastels, with private baths, air-conditioning, cable TV, and in-house wireless Internet. Rentals run about $55 nightly and include some meals; with discounts for long-term stays. Get your winter reservations early.

Besides helping lead the Chacala community, spark plug Susana Escobido offers her own

lodging, the lovely seaview **Casa Pacífica** (tel. 327/219-4067, local Chacala cell 044-327/102-0861, U.S. tel. 760/300-3908, www.casapacificachacala.com). Choose from three invitingly comfortable modern-standard rooms with fan, hot-water shower bath, and breakfast. Rentals run $60–70 d high season, $50 d low, with no breakfast low season.

Food

There are plenty of beach *palapa* restaurants to choose from but the best are **Chico's** (first restaurant on the south end of the beach), **Las Brisas** (about midway up the beach), and **Acela** (on the northern end). You'll find more or less the same type of menu at each place, lots of fresh fish, oysters and lobster, grilled meats and full bar menus. Popular with the younger crowd is **Chac Mool** (Islas Canarias 7, tel. 327/219-4097), a new wine bar and café. In addition to coffee drinks, deli sandwiches, and pastries, you can also purchase locally grown and roasted organic coffee.

AROUND THE BAY OF MATANCHÉN

The broad Bay of Matanchén, framed by verdant mountains, sweeps northward toward San Blas, lined with an easily accessible pearly crescent of sand, ripe for campers and beachcombers. Village stores, seafood *palapas*, a palmy vacation-home paradise, turtle conservation center, two beachside trailer parks, and a pair of friendly, small resorts provide the amenities for a day or a month of restful adventuring.

Playa Las Tortugas and Turtle Conservation Center

Playa las Tortugas (Turtle Beach, tel. 322/294-1677, toll-free U.S. tel. 800/320-7769, www.playalastortugas.com) is a petite vacation-retirement community set beneath a magnificent miles-long beachfront palm grove, about 15 miles (24 km) north of the Las Varas turn-off from Highway 200. It's the life project of developer, builder, and Mexico-lover Robert Hancock, whose dream is that wildlife and people can (and should) be able to coexist.

Indeed, he has helped to bring that reality about. Since its beginning in 1999, the very presence of the workers, staff, residents, and visitors to Robert's miniparadise has helped the conservation workers shield thousands of nesting turtles and their hatchlings from poachers and has led to a very viable yearly nesting population of about 2,000 turtles.

His development of mostly midsized, two-story individual houses, with lots of grassy space in between, reflects his vision. At this writing, Turtle Beach has about eight rental houses, which Robert rents part-time for the owners. Although they are all different, the designs—exteriors of muted earth-tone stucco beneath red-tiled roofs, interiors with lots of tile, view balconies, airy vistas, and high ceilings—are variations on a low-key, nature-friendly theme. Sizes vary, but most are modest two- or three-bedroom, two-bath layouts. The completely furnished and equipped rentals begin at about $220 per night for 2–4 adults.

Besides lazing by the blue pool and soaking in the steaming whirlpool tub, residents and guests can enjoy their choice of beachcombing, good surfing, boogie boarding, fishing, horseback riding, kayaking, and wildlife-watching in the ocean and the adjoining mangrove estuary and lagoon. Other times, visitors can help with turtle conservation efforts at the adjacent turtle preserve and hatchery. To get in on the turtle action, arrive during the August–November 15 nesting season, when visitors are welcome to witness turtle releases around 5 P.M. daily.

Get to Playa las Tortugas from Highway 200 via the signed left (northbound) turnoff just past the gas station at the middle of Las Varas. Continue about eight miles, through Zacualpán town. After another five miles (8 km), pass the Otates village turnoff sign on the right, and continue another quarter mile on the main road to the signed Playa las Tortugas dirt side road, between kilometer markers 21 and 22. Turn left and continue another six miles (10 km) to the Playa las Tortugas entrance gate.

Platanitos

Seventeen miles (27 km) along the coastal highway north of Las Varas, orchards and fields give way to a tropical forest at Punta Platanitos (Little Bananas), where a road leads down to a cove lined with the *pangas* and seafood *palapas* of the Platanitos village and fishing cooperative. Local folks, drawn by the yellow sand, gentle blue waves, and super-fresh seafood, have for years flocked here for Sunday outings. You can do likewise, and, if you bring your own equipment, you can also enjoy sailboarding, kayaking to nearby hidden coves, snorkeling, and fishing from headland rocks or by boat (which, most days, you can launch from the beach). Tent or RV camping appears promising (ask if it's okay: *"¿Es bueno acampar acá?"*) in the beachside shade. If you have a sturdy vehicle and a good camera, head past the large paved parking lot and make a left on the dirt track leading up the hill. Once over the rise you'll have a panoramic vista of the estuary and gorgeous blue ocean framed by the gentle swaying palms of Las Tortugas beach.

To the Bay of Matanchén and Paraíso Miramar

From Platanitos, the narrow road plunges into the forest, winding past great vine-draped trees and stands of cock-plumed Colima palms. If you glimpse green citrus fruit among the riot of leaves and flowers, you might be seeing a wild lime, or, if yellow, a guava or passion fruit dangling from its long vine. Now and then, you will pass a ponderous red-barked *papillo* tree, with its bark curling and sloughing off its great ruddy trunk and branches. The *papillo* is sometimes known as the "gringo" tree because it's always red and peeling.

The Bahía de Matanchén begins about five miles past Platanitos, just about when you're first able to see it from the roadside—a spreading, shining vista of mountain, grove, and sea.

Continuing north, and downhill, you reach the end of Nayarit 161 at its intersection with the Tepic highway, Nayarit 76, near the twin villages of Santa Cruz and Miramar (total pop. about 1,000). Continue north about a mile (1.5 km) and you will pass through even tinier Playa Manzanilla village, where a small beachside sign marks the driveway to Paraíso Miramar (Km 1.2, Carretera a San Blas, tel. 323/254-9030 or 323/254-9031, http://intl. hotelparaisomiramar.com).

The spacious, green bayview park is bedecked by palms and sheltered by what appears to be the grandmother of all *higuera* trees (wild fig or banyan in India). On the cliff-bottom beach beneath the great tree, the surf rolls in gently while the blue bay, crowned by jungle ridges, curves gracefully north toward San Blas.

Paraíso Miramar's owners, most of whom live in Tepic, and their hardworking staff offer a little bit for everyone: six simple but clean and comfortable rooms with bath facing the bay and behind that, grassy RV spaces with concrete pads and all hookups, and two kitchenette bungalows sleeping up to six. There are also three fully furnished two-bedroom apartments that rent nightly or by the week ($115/day or $600/wk) A small view restaurant and blue pools—swimming, kiddie, and hot tub—complete the lovely picture.

Rooms rent for about $58 d, all with air-conditioning; bungalows go for about $75 for four people, $90 for six, with hot-water showers, air-conditioning, and satellite TV.

The RV area has expanded considerably with 48 spaces available for all sizes. These range from 16 spaces with full hookups to 12 without water or power. Rates vary depending on the type of vehicle you have so check the website for the most recent information and to make reservations. Prices range from $16–24 per day. For a week's stay, you customarily get one day free and there are long-term discounted rates available.

Casa Mañana

About 2.5 miles farther north (or 8 mi/13 km south of San Blas), the diminutive shoreline retreat 🍴 **Casa Mañana** (P.O. Box 49, San Blas, Nayarit 63740, tel. 323/254-9080 or 323/254-9090, toll-free Mex. tel. 01-800/202-2079, www.casa-manana.com) perches at the south end of breezy Playa los Cocos. Owned and managed by an Austrian man, Reinhardt, and his Mexican wife, Lourdes, Casa Mañana's two double-storied tiers of rooms rise over a homey, spic-and-span beachview restaurant and pool deck and garden. Very popular with Europeans and North Americans seeking South Seas tranquility on a budget, Casa Mañana offers fishing, beachcombing, hiking, and swimming right from its palm-adorned front yard. The 26 rooms rent for about $64 d high season, $53 d low, with air-conditioning and ocean view, or $37 d high, with air-conditioning but no view. All rentals get one day free per week stay. Longer-stay discounts are negotiable, and winter reservations are strongly recommended.

If you're staying at Casa Mañana, you might look into the services of **Seven Sunsets Tours** (www.sevensunsets.com) of photographer-guide John Stewart. His mission is to lead his clients to experience the "real" Mexico via nature-friendly strolls, hikes, and horseback rides to off-the-beaten-track local sites.

Playa los Cocos

From Casa Mañana, Playa los Cocos and its venerable palm grove stretches north past beachfront houses, a couple of very basic lodgings, and a sprinkling of beachside *palapa* restaurants.

Continuing northward, notice that the occasionally heavy surf is gradually eroding the beach, leaving a crumbling 10-foot embankment along a mostly rocky shore. Playa los Cocos is nevertheless balmy and beautiful enough to attract a winter RV colony to **Trailer Park Playa Amor** (Trailer Park Playa Amor, c/o gerente Javier López, Playa los Cocos, San Blas, Nayarit 63740, tel. 323/231-2200), which overlooks the waves right in the middle of Playa los Cocos. Besides excellent fishing, boating, boogie boarding, swimming, and sailboarding, the park offers 30 grassy spaces for very reasonable prices. Rentals run about $12, $13, and $14 for small, medium, and large RVs respectively ($20 for a/c power), with all hookups, showers, and toilets; pets are okay. Tenters with no hookups pay $6. Although you can expect plenty of friendly company during the winter, reservations are not usually necessary.

Waterfall Hikes

A number of pristine creeks tumble down boulder-strewn beds and foam over cliffs as waterfalls *(cataratas)* in the jungle above the Bay of Matanchén. Some of these are easily accessible and perfect for a day of hiking, picnicking, and swimming. Don't hesitate to ask for directions: *"¿Dónde está el camino a la catarata, por favor?"* ("Where is the path to the waterfall, please?"). If you would like a guide, ask, *"¿Hay guía, por favor?"* One (or all) of the local crowd of kids may immediately volunteer.

You can get to within walking distance of the waterfall near **Tecuitata** village either by car, taxi, or the Tepic-bound bus; it's five miles (8 km) miles out of Santa Cruz along Nayarit Highway 76. A half-mile uphill past the village, a sign reading Balneario Nuevo Chapultepec marks a dirt road heading downhill a half-mile to a creek and a bridge. Cross over to the other side ($4 entrance fee), where you'll find a *palapa* restaurant, a hillside waterslide, and a small swimming pool.

Continue upstream along the right-hand bank of the creek for a much rarer treat. Half the fun is the sylvan jungle delights— flashing butterflies, pendulous leafy vines, gurgling little cascades—along the meandering path. The other half is at the end, where the creek spurts through a verdure-framed fissure and splashes into a cool, broad pool festooned with green, giant-leafed *chalata* (*taro* in Hawaii, *tapioca* in Africa). Both the pool area and the trail have several possible campsites. Bring everything, especially your water-purification kit and insect repellent. Known locally as Campamento Arroyo, it is popular with kids and women who bring their washing.

Another waterfall, the highest in the area, near the village of **El Cora,** is harder to get to but the reward is even more spectacular. Again, on the west–east Santa Cruz–Tepic Highway 76, a negotiable dirt road to El Cora branches south just before Tecuitata. At road's end, after about five miles (8 km), you can park by a banana-loading platform. From here, the walk (less than an hour) climaxes with a steep,

rugged descent to the rippling, crystal pool at the bottom of the waterfall.

While rugged adventurers may find their own way to the waterfalls, others rely upon guides Armando S. Navarrete (Sonora 179, San Blas, no phone) and Juan "Bananas" Garcia (tel. 323/285-0462), founder of Grupo Ecológico in San Blas.

Playas Matanchén and Las Islitas

Playa los Cocos gives way at its north end to Aticama village (a few stores and beachside *palapas*) where, northbound, the shoreline road climbs a jungle headland and swoops down to the bay once again. Past a marine sciences school, the beach, a long, palm-studded sand-ribbon washed by gentle rollers and dotted with beachfront *palapa* restaurants and downscale vacation homes, curves gently northwest to the superwide and shallow giant kiddie-pool of Playa Matanchén. A left crossroad (which marks the center of Matanchén village, pop. about 300) leads past a lineup of beachfront *palapa* restaurants to Playa las Islitas, at the bay's sheltered north cove.

The beaches of Matanchén and Las Islitas are an inseparable pair. Las Islitas is dotted by little outcroppings topped by miniature jungles of swaying palms and spreading trees. One of these is home for a colony of surfers waiting for the Big Wave, the Holy Grail of surfing. The Big Wave is one of the occasional gigantic 20-foot breakers that rise off Playa las Islitas and carry surfers as much as a mile and a quarter (an official Guinness world record) to the soft sand of Playa Matanchén.

For camping, the intimate, protected curves of sand around Playa las Islitas are inviting. Check with local folks to see if it's okay to camp. Although few facilities exist (save a few surfing-season food *palapas*), the beach-combing, swimming, fishing from the rocks, shell-collecting, and surfing are often good even without the Big Wave. The water, however, isn't clear enough for good snorkeling. Campers should be prepared with plenty of strong insect repellent.

During surfing season (Aug.–Feb.) the Team

Banana and other *palapa*-shops open up at Matanchén village and Las Islitas to rent surfboards and sell what each of them claims to be the "world's original banana bread."

Ejido de la Palma Crocodile Farm

About three miles (5 km) south of Matanchén village, a sign marks a side road to a *cocodrilario* (crocodile farm). At the end of the two-mile track (trucks okay, car negotiable with caution when dry), you'll arrive at El Tanque, a spring-fed pond, home of the Ejido de la Palma crocodile farm. About 50 toothy crocs, large

and small, snooze in the sun within several enclosures. Half the fun is the adjacent spring-fed freshwater lagoon, so crystal clear you can see half a dozen big fish wriggling beneath the surface. Nearby, ancient trees swathed in vines and orchids tower overhead, butterflies flutter past, and turtles sun themselves on mossy logs. Bring a picnic lunch, binoculars, bird book, insect repellent, and bathing suit. You can also rent a *panga* (small boat) for a tour through the mangroves. Come early in the morning for excellent bird- and wildlife-watching (approx. $10 pp).

San Blas and Vicinity

San Blas (pop. about 15,000) is a small town slumbering beneath a big coconut grove. Life goes on in the plaza as if San Blas has always been an ordinary Mexican village. But once San Blas was anything but ordinary. During its latter 18th-century glory days, San Blas was Mexico's burgeoning Pacific military headquarters and port, with a population of 30,000. Ships from Spain's Pacific Rim colonies crowded its harbor, silks and gold filled its counting houses, and noble Spanish officers and their mantilla-graced ladies strolled the plaza on Sunday afternoons.

Times change, however. Politics and San Blas's pesky *jejenes* (hey-HEY-nays, invisible no-see-um biting gnats) have always conspired to deflate any temporary fortunes of San Blas. The *jejenes's* breeding ground, a vast hinterland of mangrove marshes, may paradoxically give rise to a new, more prosperous San Blas. These thousands of acres of waterlogged mangrove jungle and savanna are a nursery home for dozens of Mexico's endangered species. This rich trove is now protected by ecologically aware governments and communities and admired (not unlike the game parks of Africa) by increasing numbers of ecotourists.

ORIENTATION

The overlook atop the **Cerro de San Basilio** is the best spot to orient yourself to San Blas.

From this breezy point, the palm-shaded grid of streets stretches to the sunset side of **El Pozo** estuary and the lighthouse-hill beyond it. Behind you, on the east, the mangrove-lined **San Cristóbal** river estuary meanders south to the Bay of Matanchén. Along the south shore, the crystalline white line of San Blas's main beach, **Playa el Borrego** (Sheep Beach), stretches between the two estuary mouths.

HISTORY
Conquest and Colonization

San Blas and the neighboring southward-curving Bay of Matanchén were reconnoitered by gold-hungry conquistador Nuño de Guzmán in May 1530. His expedition noted the protected anchorages in the bay and the Esteroel Pozo adjacent to the present town. Occasionally during the 16th and 17th centuries, Spanish traders in their galleons and the pirates lying in wait for them would drop anchor in the *estero* or the adjacent Bay of Matanchén for rendezvous, resupply, or cargo transfer.

By the latter third of the 18th century, New Spain, reacting to the Russian and English threats in the North Pacific, launched plans for the colonization of California through a new port called San Blas.

The town was officially founded atop the hill of San Basilio in 1768. Streets were surveyed;

THE NAYARIT COAST

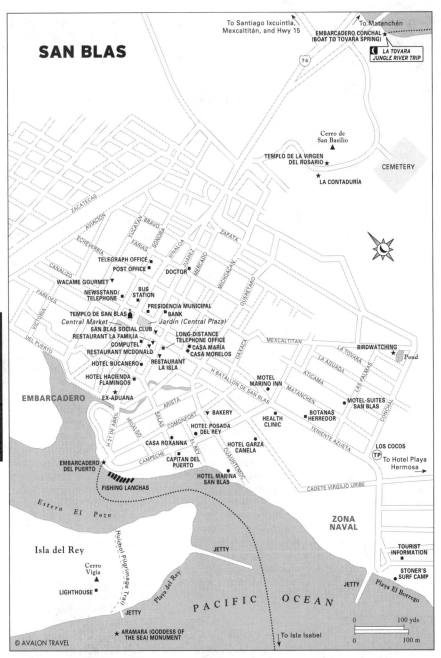

SAN BLAS

To Santiago Ixcuintla,
Mexcaltitán, and Hwy 15

To Matanchén

EMBARCADERO CONCHAL
(BOAT TO TOVARA SPRING)

LA TOVARA
JUNGLE RIVER TRIP

74

Cerro de
San Basilio ▲

TEMPLO DE LA VIRGEN
DEL ROSARIO ★

CEMETERY

★ LA CONTADURÍA

ZACATECAS

AVIACION

ECHEVERRIA

CANALIZO

YUCATÁN BRAVO

FARIAS SONORA

SINALOA

JUAREZ

MERCADO

ZAPATA

MICHOACÁN

QUERÉTARO

PAREDES

VICTORIA

DEL PUERTO

TELEGRAPH OFFICE ■
POST OFFICE ■

DOCTOR ■

WACAME GOURMET ▼

NEWSSTAND/
TELEPHONE ■

BUS
STATION

PRESIDÉNCIA MUNICIPAL
■ BANK

TEMPLO DE SAN BLAS ▼
Central Market ─ Jardín (Central Plaza)
SAN BLAS SOCIAL CLUB ▼
RESTAURANT LA FAMILIA ▼
COMPUTEL ■
RESTAURANT MCDONALD ▼

LONG-DISTANCE
TELEPHONE OFFICE ■
● CASA MARÍA
CASA MORELOS

HOTEL BUCANERO ●

RESTAURANT
LA ISLA ▼

HOTEL HACIENDA
FLAMINGOS ●

★ EX-ADUANA

EMBARCADERO

H 21 DE ABRIL

HIDALGO

SALAS

ARISTA

COMONFORT

CAMPECHE

EL REY

▼ BAKERY

HOTEL POSADA
DEL REY ●

CASA ROXANNA ■

CAPITAN DEL
PUERTO ●

H BATALLON DE SAN BLAS

MEXCALTITAN

BIRDWATCHING
★ Pond

LA TOVARA

LA AGUADA

LAS PALMAS

ATICAMA

MATANCHEN

OAXACA

MOTEL
MARINO INN ●

HOTEL GARZA
CANELA ●

HOTEL MARINA
SAN BLAS ●

CUAUHTEMOC

HEALTH
CLINIC ■

BOTANAS
HERREDOR ■

TENIENTE AZUETA

CONCHAL

MOTEL-SUITES
SAN BLAS ●

LOS COCOS
TP
To Hotel Playa
Hermosa →

CADETE VIRGILIO URIBE

EMBARCADERO ★
DEL PUERTO ●

FISHING LANCHAS

Estero   El   Pozo

Isla del Rey

Cerro
Vigia ▲

LIGHTHOUSE ■

Huichol Pilgrimage Trail

Playa del Rey

JETTY

JETTY

ZONA
NAVAL

TOURIST
INFORMATION ■

STONER'S
SURF CAMP ●

Playa El Borrego

JETTY

JETTY

PACIFIC   OCEAN

★ ARAMARA (GODDESS OF
THE SEA) MONUMENT

To Isla Isabel

0   100 yds

0   100 m

© AVALON TRAVEL

docks were built. Old documents record that more than 100 pioneer families received a plot of land and "a pick, an adze, an axe, a machete, a plow…a pair of oxen, a cow, a mule, four she-goats and a billy, four sheep, a sow, four hens and a rooster."

People and animals multiplied, and soon San Blas became the seat of Spain's eastern Pacific naval command. Meanwhile, simultaneously with the founding of the town, the celebrated Father Junípero Serra set out for California with 14 missionary brothers on *La Concepción*, a sailing vessel built on Matanchén beach just south of San Blas.

Independence

New Spain's colonial grandeur, however, crumbled in the bloody 1810–1821 war for independence, taking San Blas with it. In December 1810, the *insurgente* commander captured the Spanish fort atop San Basilio hill and sent 43 of its cannons to fellow rebel-priest Miguel Hidalgo to use against the Spanish loyalists around Guadalajara.

After independence, fewer and fewer ships called at San Blas; the docks fell into disrepair, and the town slipped into somnolence, then complete slumber when President Lerdo de Tejada closed San Blas to foreign commerce in 1872.

SIGHTS
Around Town

While you're atop the hill, take a look around the old *contaduria* counting house and fort (built in 1770), where riches were tallied and stored en route to Mexico City or to the Philippines and China. Several of the original great cannons still stand guard at the viewpoint like aging sentinels waiting for long-dead adversaries.

Behind and a bit downhill from the weathered stone arches of the *contaduria* stand the gaping portals and towering, moss-stained belfry of the old church of **Nuestra Señora del Rosario,** built in 1769. Undamaged by war, it remained an active church until at least 1872, around the time when poet Henry W.

Longfellow was inspired by the silencing and removal of its aging bells.

Downhill, historic houses and ruins dot San Blas town. The old hotels Bucanero and Hacienda Flamingos on the main street, Juárez, leading past the central plaza, preserve much of their old-world charm. Just across the street from the Hacienda Flamingos, you can admire the restored, monumental brick colonnade of the 19th-century former **Aduana,** now a cultural center. Continue west along Juárez to the El Pozo estuary. At that shoreline spot, gaze across the El Pozo channel. This was both the jumping-off point for colonization of the Californias and the anchorage of the silk- and porcelain-laden Manila galleons and the bullion ships from the northern mines.

El Faro (lighthouse) across the estuary marks the top of **Cerro Vigía,** the southern hill-tip of Isla del Rey (actually a peninsula). Here, the first beacon shone during the latter third of the 18th century.

Although only a few local folks ever bother to cross over to the island, it is nevertheless an important pilgrimage site for Huichol people from the remote Nayarit and Jalisco mountains. Huichol have been gathering on the Isla del Rey for centuries to make offerings to Aramara, their goddess of the sea. A not-so-coincidental shrine to a Catholic virgin-saint stands on an offshore sea rock, visible from the beach-endpoint of the Huichol pilgrimage a few hundred yards beyond the lighthouse.

Sadly, a large cave sacred to the Huichol at the foot of Cerro Vigía was demolished by the government during the early 1970s to provide rock for a breakwater. Fortunately, President Salinas de Gortari partly compensated for the insult by deeding the sacred site to the Huichols during the early 1990s.

Two weeks before Easter, Huichol people begin arriving by the dozens, the men decked out in flamboyant feathered hats. On the ocean beach, 10 minutes' walk straight across the island, anyone can respectfully watch them perform their rituals: elaborate marriages, feasts, and offerings of little boats laden with arrows and food, consecrated to the sea goddess to ensure good hunting and crops and many healthy children.

Hotel Playa Hermosa

For a glimpse of a relic from San Blas's recent past, head across town to the crumbling Hotel Playa Hermosa. Here, one evening in 1951, President Miguel Alemán came to dedicate San Blas's first luxury hotel. As the story goes, the *jejenes* descended and bit the president so fiercely the entire entourage cleared out before he even finished his speech. Rumors have circulated around town for years that someone's going to reopen the Playa Hermosa—but now it's mostly covered with jungle vines and continues to crumble back into the sand. To get there, follow Heróico Batallón toward the beach, turn left just after the Los Cocos Trailer Park, and continue along the jungle road for about half a mile.

Isla Isabel

Isla Isabel is a two-mile-square offshore wildlife study area 40 miles (65 km) and three hours north by boat. The cone of an extinct volcano, Isla Isabel is now home to a small government station of ecoscientists and a host of nesting boobies, frigate birds, and white-tailed tropic birds. Fish and sea mammals, especially dolphins and sometimes whales, abound in the surrounding clear waters. Although it's not a recreational area, local authorities allow serious visitors, accompanied by authorized guides, for a few days of camping, snorkeling, scuba diving, and wildlife-watching. A primitive dormitory can accommodate several people. Bring everything, including food and bedding. Contact experienced and licensed boat captain Ricardo (Pato) Murillo (tel. 323/285-1281) or equally well-qualified captain Santos Villafuente (at the Hotel Brisas del Mar, tel. 323/285-0870, cell tel. 044-311/109-1993) for arrangements and prices. Tariffs typically run $250 per day for parties of up to four people. Stormy summer and fall weather limits most Isla Isabel trips to the sunnier, calmer winter–spring season. For additional information and

Abandoned Hotel Playa Hermosa is reclaimed by the jungle.

© ROBIN NOELLE

advice, check with manager Josefina Vasquéz, at the Hotel Garza Canela front desk (see their listing in the *Accommodations* section).

BEACHES

San Blas's most convenient beach is **Playa el Borrego,** at the south end of Calle Cuauhtémoc about a mile south of town. With a lineup of *palapas* for food and drinks, the mile-long broad, fine-sand beach is ripe for all beach activities except snorkeling (because of the murky water). The mild offshore currents and gentle, undertow-free slope of are nearly always safe for good swimming, bodysurfing, and boogie boarding. Surfing is especially popular here and conditions are often right for good sailboarding.

Shoals of shells—clams, cockles, mother-of-pearl—wash up on Borrego Beach during storms. Fishing is often good, especially when casting from the jetty and rocks at the north and south ends.

ENTERTAINMENT

Sleepy San Blas's entertainment is of the local, informal variety. Visitors content themselves with strolling the beach or riding the waves by day, and reading, watching TV, listening to mariachis, or dancing at a handful of clubs by night.

Owner/manager Mike McDonald works hard to keep **Mike's Place** (Juárez 36), on the second floor of his family's restaurant, the classiest club in town. He keeps the lights flashing and the small dance floor thumping with blues, Latin, and 1960s rock tunes from his own guitar, accompanied by his equally excellent drum and electronic-piano partners. Listen to live music Saturday nights 9 P.M.–midnight during the summer low season, and Tuesday–Saturday during the fall–winter high season. He usually charges a small cover; drinks are reasonably priced.

Another good option (and a good spot to meet people) is the **San Blas Social Club** bar, which sometimes offers jazz in season. Check it out at the northeast plaza corner, across the street from Cha Cha's restaurant. A few other places require nothing more than your ears to find. During high season music booms out of low-life **Botanas Herredor** (down H. Batallón, a block past the Motel Marino). The same is true seasonally at the bar at the **Hotel Bucanero** (Calle Juárez 75, tel. 323/285-0101).

SHOPPING

San Blas visitors ordinarily spend little of their time shopping. Although San Blas has relatively few handicrafts sources, the shop at the **Hotel Garza Canela** has arguably the finest for-sale handicrafts collections in Nayarit state. Lovingly selected pieces from the famous Pacific Coast crafts centers—Guadalajara, Tlaquepaque, Tonalá, Pátzcuaro, Olinalá, Taxco, Oaxaca, and elsewhere—decorate the shop's cabinets, counters, and shelves.

You'll also find many common but nevertheless attractive handicrafts assortments in the **crafts stalls** that daily occupy the San Blas main plaza.

For used clothes and a little bit of everything else, a **flea market** (known in Mexico as a *tianguis*) operates on Calle Canalizo a block past the bus station (away from the *jardín*) Saturday morning and early afternoon.

Up-to-date photography services and supplies have arrived in San Blas, at **Foto Studio America** (Juárez 91, tel. 323/285-1209, 8 A.M.–2 P.M. and 4–9 P.M. daily), next to Restaurant McDonald. Here, find many cameras, films, and both color and black-and-white film and digital developing service.

RECREATION
La Tovara Jungle River Trip

On the downstream side of the bridge over Estero San Cristóbal, launches-for-hire will take you up the Río Tovara, a side channel that winds about a mile downstream into the jungle.

The channel quickly narrows into a dark tree-tunnel, edged by great curtainlike swaths of mangrove roots. Big snowy *garza* (egrets) peer out from leafy branches; startled turtles slip off their soggy perches into the river, while

Tovara Springs, the endpoint of the La Tovara Jungle River Trip, bubbles with cool, crystalline water.

big submerged roots, like gigantic pythons, bulge out of the inky water. Riots of luxuriant plants—white lilies, green ferns, red *romelia* orchids—hang from the trees and line the banks.

Finally you reach Tovara Springs, which well from the base of a verdant cliff. On one side, a bamboo-sheltered *palapa* restaurant serves refreshments, on the other families picnic in a hillside pavilion. In the middle, everyone jumps in and paddles in the clear, cool water.

You can enjoy this trip either of two ways: the longer, three-hour excursion as described ($60 per boatload of 6–8) from El Conchal landing on the estuary, or the shorter version (two hours, $30 per boatload) beginning upriver at road-accessible Las Aguadas near Matanchén village. Either drive, taxi, or ride the *blanco* (white) bus or the navy blue Transportes Noreste bus.

The more leisurely three-hour trip allows more chances (especially in the early morning) to spot an ocelot or crocodile, or a giant boa constrictor hanging from a limb (no kidding).

Many of the boatmen are very professional; if you want to view wildlife, tell them, and they'll go more slowly and keep a sharp lookout.

Some boatmen offer more extensive trips to less-disturbed sites deeper in the jungle. These include the Camalota spring, a branch of the Río Tovara (where a local *ejido* maintains a crocodile breeding station), and the even more remote and pristine Tepiqueñas, Los Negros, and Zoquipan lagoons in the San Cristóbal Estero's upper reaches.

In light of the possible wildlife-watching rewards, trip prices are very reasonable. For example, the very knowledgeable bird specialist Oscar Partida Hernández (Comonfort 134 Pte., tel. 323/285-0324) will guide a four-person boatload to La Tovara for about $60. If Oscar is busy, call "Chencho" Banuelos (tel. 323/285-0716) for a comparably excellent trip. More extensive options include a combined Camalota–La Tovara trip (allow 4–5 hours) for about $45 for four or Tepiqueñas and Los Negros (6 hours, 7 A.M. departure) for about $60.

EGRETS, CORMORANTS, AND ANHINGAS

In tropical San Blas, lagoon-edge mangrove trees often appear at first glance to be laden with snow. Closer inspection, however, reveals swarms of nesting white birds. Although together they appear a white mass, individually they belong to three species of egret – *garza* in Spanish.

Although all may seem at home, one species is a relatively new arrival to the New World. The cattle egret, *Bubulcus ibis*, wasn't seen in North America until around 1900. The smallest of egrets, it's but a foot and a half long, with a small yellow or orange bill and blackish legs and feet. Scientists suspect the bird migrated from its native Asia or Africa, where the cattle egret has foraged amid herds of cattle for millennia; the bird profits handsomely from the swarms of bugs attracted by cattle.

The other two members of Mexico's egret trio, the crystal-white snowy egret *(Egretta thula)* and the blue-gray great heron *(Casmerodius albus)* prefer to stalk fish and crabs in lagoons. You'll see them – especially the black-billed, two-foot-long snowy egret – poised in a pond, rock still, for what seems like a season, until – *pop!* – the sharp beak dives into the water and reappears with a luckless fish.

The great heron's feeding habits are similar to those of its smaller cousin, and its grand six-foot wingspan and steely blue-gray hues make it easy to recognize. At a lagoon's edge, watch quietly and you might soon be rewarded with the magnificent sight of a great heron swooping down to land gracefully in the water.

Sharing the same watery feeding grounds are the Mexican (or olivaceous) cormorant *(Phalacrocorax olivaceous)* and its cousin the anhinga *(Anhinga anhinga)*. These are often confused with loons, and they do seem a bit loony. Their necks, especially that of the anhinga – also known as "darter" or "snakebird" – sometimes bend back into a snakelike S. The anhinga often will swim along, submerged except for its head and neck, looking every bit like a serpent slicing through the water. Cormorants frequently nest in flocks atop mangroves and seem to have either a sense of humor or no inkling of their true identity, for if you venture too close they'll start grunting like a chorus of pigs.

Cormorants and anhingas are as graceful in the water as they are clumsy on land. They plop along in the mud on their webbed feet, finally jumping to a rock or tree perch where, batlike, they unfold their wings and preen them. Although both are about 2–3 feet in size, they're easily distinguishable: The anhinga generally appears in greater numbers and features arrays of silvery spots along the wings.

Whale-Watching

A number of San Blas captains take visitors on less extensive, but nevertheless potentially rewarding, wildlife-viewing excursions November–April. Sightings might include humpback, gray, and sperm whales, dolphins, seals, sea lions, turtles, manta rays, and flocks of birds, including gulls, frigate birds, cormorants, boobies, terns, and much more. Contact either Pato Murillo (tel. 323/285-1281), who is opening an office in front of Casa Cocadas near the marina or Santos Villafuente (at the Hotel Brisas del Mar, tel. 323/285-0870, cell tel. 044-311/109-1993) or superexperienced English-speaking Tony Aguayo at home (tel. 323/285-0364) or at his "office," the little *palapa* to the left of the small floating boat dock at the El Pozo estuary end of Juárez. A typical five-hour excursion runs about $200 for up to six passengers.

Bird-Watching

Although San Blas's extensive mangrove and mountain jungle hinterlands are renowned for their birds and wildlife, rewarding bird-watching can start in the early morning right at the edge of town. Follow Calle Conchal right (southeast) one block from Suites San Blas, then left (northeast) to a small pond. With binoculars, you might get some good views of local species of cormorants, flycatchers, grebes, herons, jacanas, and motmots. A copy of Peterson and Chalif's *Field Guide to Mexican Birds* or Steve Howell's *Bird-Finding Guide to Mexico* will assist in further identification.

Rewarding bird-watching is also possible on **Isla del Rey.** Bargain for a launch (from the foot of Juárez, about $4 round-trip) across to the opposite shore. Watch for wood, clapper, and Virginia rails, and boat-billed herons near the estuary shore. Then follow the track across the island (looking for warblers and a number of species of sparrows) to the beach where you might enjoy good views of plovers, terns, Heermann's gulls, and rafts of pelicans.

Alternatively, look around the hillside cemetery and the ruins atop **Cerro de San Basilio** for good early-morning views of hummingbirds, falcons, owls, and American redstarts.

You can include serious bird-watching with your boat trip through the mangrove channels branching from the **Estero San Cristóbal** and the **Río Tovara.** This is especially true if you obtain the services of a wildlife-sensitive guide, such as Oscar Partida (tel. 323/285-0324), "Chencho" Banuelos (tel. 323/285-0716), or Armando Santiago (tel. 323/285-0859, dolpacarm@yahoo.com). Expect to pay about $60 for a half-day trip for four people.

Besides the above, Armando Navarette (Sonora 179, no phone) offers bird-watching hikes, especially around Singayta in the foothills, where birders routinely identify 30–40 species in a two-hour adventure. Such an excursion might also include a coffee plantation visit, hiking along the old royal road to Tepic, and plenty of tropical fauna and flora, including butterflies, wildflowers, and giant vines and trees, such as ceiba, *arbolde,* and the peeling, red *papillo* tree. Armando's fee for such a trip, lasting around five hours, runs about $20 per person, plus your own or rented transportation.

Others suggest bird-watching tours and packages. One of the best organized, known simply as **San Blas Birds** (www.sanblasbirds.com) lists tours varying from 1–7 days. The longer tours include lodging; for example, three days including lodging at Hotel Posada del Rey

runs around $450 per person; the same out of Hotel Garza Canela, about $650 per person.

For more details on bird-watching and hiking around San Blas, you can purchase a number of guides at the shop at Hotel Garza Canela. The hotel shop also usually sells the *Checklist of Birds Found in San Blas, Nayarit* or the new *Birder's Guide to San Blas,* published by San Blas Birds.

Ecotours

During the December–April clear-weather season, veteran scuba diver and instructor Douglas Storms offers hiking, bird-watching, kayaking, snorkel and scuba adventures, and more out of his **Adventure Center** headquarters (Juarez 187 B, tel. 323/285-1418, www.divingbeyond.com). Off-season, contact him in Sausalito, California (700 Waldo Point, Sausalito, CA 94965, U.S. tel. 415/331-7925 or 415/325-3789).

Alternatively, you might look into the services of Canadian photographer-guide John Stewart, founder of **Seven Sunset Tours** (www.sevensunsets.com), who works out of Casa Mañana at Playa los Cocos several miles south of San Blas. John and his staff like to lead their clients on ecofriendly tours to local villages, hidden beaches, waterfalls, bird-watching, and much more.

Ecotouring in Singayta: The latter-day local growth of shrimp-pond aquaculture and the associated wildlife habitat destruction has prompted action by ecoactivists in San Blas and neighboring communities, such as Singayta, five miles east of San Blas.

Singayta villagers began taking positive action around 2000. Since then, they have established a nursery for reintroduction of threatened native plants, a crocodile breeding farm, and an **environmental awareness center** to educate visitors and residents about the destructive reality of shrimp-pond aquaculture.

To back all this up, Singayta offers a menu of guided ecotours (www.singayta.com and www.elmanglar.com) for visitors. These include canoe trips into the mangrove wetland, walking tours, mountain bike rentals, donkey cart and horseback tours, and more. A restaurant also offers meals and refreshments. You might also find out more about Singayta from knowledgeable ecoleader and guide Juan "Bananas" Garcia.

Get to Singayta by car along Tepic Highway 74, about five miles (8 km) straight east of the San Blas plaza; or, by bus, from the San Blas plaza-front bus station, by one of the hourly Tepic-bound buses.

Walking and Jogging

The cooling late-afternoon sea breeze and the soft but firm sand of **Playa el Borrego** (south end of H. Batallón) make it the best place around town for a walk or jog. Arm yourself against *jejenes* with repellent and long pants, especially around sunset.

Waterfall Hikes

A number of waterfalls decorate the lush jungle foothills above the Bay of Matanchén. Two of these, near Tecuitata and El Cora villages, are accessible from the Santa Cruz–Tepic Highway 76 about 10 miles (16 km) south of San Blas. The local *autobús blanco* will take you most of the way. It runs south to Santa Cruz every two hours 8:30 A.M.–4:30 P.M. from the downtown corner of Juárez and Paredes.

While rugged adventurers may guide themselves to the waterfalls, others rely upon guides Armando Navarette, local ecoleader Juan "Bananas" Garcia, or Lucio Rodríguez (inquire at Tourist Information on Mercado southeast of the plaza, or with Josefina Vasquéz at the Hotel Garza Canela).

Surfing

Playa el Borrego has one of the surf breaks that has made San Blas one of Mexico's top surfing meccas, but nearly all of San Blas's action goes on at world-class surfing mecca Matanchén Beach. Surfers and surfing enthusiasts begin arriving in San Blas in May when the waves begin to grow, and as long as the surf's up, stay around until at least October. Veterans recognize at least five surf breaks, all on San Blas's beaches, sprinkled, in succession, from the Borrego break (beginning, intermediate, advanced), at Playa

el Borrego, to the Las Islitas (intermediate, advanced) break at Playa las Islitas. These breaks, depending on seasonal conditions, can challenge all surfers, from beginners to advanced.

To find out more, be sure to visit **Stoner's Surf Camp** on Playa el Borrego, beach side of the entrance parking lot. Here, welcoming owner-operator Nikki Kath, besides renting boogie boards ($2/hr) and surfboards ($3/hr), offers surf lessons ($15/hr) and runs a restaurant, a hotel, and a small campground on the premises. Juan "Bananas" Garcia (tel. 323/285-0462) at his café at H. Battallón 219 also rents surfboards and boogie boards.

If you want to learn to surf, or are already a surfer wanting to improve your skills, Stoner's is ready for you, with their champion instructor Jose "Pompi" Manuel Cano, who owns a long list of awards that he began winning in 1980, at the age of eight. For much more surfing information, visit the Stoner's Surf Camp website, www.stonerssurfcamp.com.

Snorkeling and Scuba

Snorkeling and scuba diving are possible during the clear-water December–April season. That's when California-based scuba instructor **Douglas Storms** (Juárez 187B, tel. 323/285-1418, www.divingbeyond.com) offers snorkel and scuba lessons and excursions out of his Adventure Center headquarters, a block from the Estero El Pozo dock. Off-season, you can contact him in Sausalito, California (tel. 415/331-7925 or 415/325-3789).

Sportfishing

Tony Aguayo (tel. 323/285-0364), Ricardo "Pato" Murillo (tel. 323/285-1281) and Edgar Regalado (tel. 323/285-1023) are all highly recommended to lead big-game deep-sea fishing excursions. Tony's "office" is the *palapa* shelter to the left of the little dock at the foot of Calle Juárez near the El Pozo estuary. Tony, Pato, and Edgar all regularly captain big-boat excursions for tough-fighting marlin, dorado, and sailfish. Their fee will run about $400 for a seven-hour expedition for up to three people, including big boat, tackle, and bait.

THE NAYARIT COAST

On the other hand, a number of other good-eating fish are not so difficult to catch. Check with Tony or other captains, such as Antonio Palmas at the Hotel Garza Canela or one of the owners of the many craft docked by the estuary shoreline at the foot of Juárez. For perhaps $150, they'll take three or four of you for a *lancha* outing, which most likely will result in four or five hefty 10-pound snapper, mackerel, tuna, or yellowtail; afterward you can ask your favorite restaurant to cook them for a feast.

During the last few days in May, San Blas hosts its long-running (30-plus years) **International Fishing Tournament.** The entrance fee runs around $600; prizes vary from automobiles to Mercury outboards and Penn International fishing rods. For more information, contact Tony Aguayo or Pato Murillo, or ask at the local tourist information office, downtown at the Presidencia Municipal.

ACCOMMODATIONS

San Blas has several hotels, none of them huge, but all with personality. They are not likely to be full even during the high winter season (unless the surf off Mantanchén Beach runs high for an unusually long spell).

Under $50

Soak in the full natural beach experience at San Blas's most economical accommodation, **Stoner's Surf Camp** (Playa el. Borrego, www. stonerssurfcamp.com). Stay in their rustically snug bamboo-and-thatch *cabañnitas,* complete with fan, mosquito net, towels, and sheets, for $30 d, $25 d high season with shared toilets and showers. Amenities include restaurant, use of kitchen, use of surfboard ($3 for all day), and bikes for *cabaña* guests. Camping, with use of kitchen, runs $3 per person; tent rentals are available.

Slightly up the economic scale, the family-run *casa de huéspedes* (guesthouse) **Casa María** (corner of Canalizo and Michoacán, tel. 323/285-1057, $20 s, $30 d) makes a reality of the old Spanish saying, *"Mi casa es su casa."* There are about 12 rooms around a homey, cluttered patio, and María offers to do

everything for guests except give them baths (which she would probably do if someone got sick). Not spic-and-span, but very friendly and with kitchen privileges, fans, hot-water showers, and washing machine included.

You can also get a comfortable room at María's adjacent original guesthouse, **Casa Morelos** (108 H. Batallón, tel. 323/285-1345, $14 s, $18 d), operated by her daughter, Magdalena, who rents by drop-in only.

A block west of the plaza, the **Hotel Bucanero** (Calle Juárez 75, tel. 323/285-0101, $18 s, $26 d) appears to be living up to its name. A stanza from the *Song of the Pirate* emblazons one wall, a big stuffed crocodile bares its teeth beside the other, and a crusty sunken anchor and cannons decorate the shady patio. Despite peeling paint, 32 rooms (with ceiling fans and hot water) retain a bit of spacious, old-world charm, with high-beamed ceilings under the ruddy roof tile. (High, circular vent windows in some rooms cannot be closed, however. Use repellent or your mosquito net.) Outside, the big pool and leafy old courtyard provide plenty of nooks for daytime snoozing and socializing. A noisy nighttime (winter–spring seasonal) bar, however, keeps most guests without earplugs jumping until about midnight.

Although the facilities of the four-star **Motel Marino Inn** (H. Batallón s/n, tel. 323/285-0303, $45 s or d) look fine on paper, the place is bare of most usual hotel amenities. The 60 rooms, although plain and mostly bare-bulb, are comfortable enough for a night or two, with air-conditioning, a pool (if it's working), and private balconies. You'll find it on the north edge of town, a few blocks before the beach. Credit cards are accepted.

In the same palm-shadowed, country fringe of town not far from Playa el Borrego is the **Motel-Suites San Blas** (Calles Aticama and Las Palmas, tel. 323/285-0505, vimais66@ hotmail.com), left off Heróico Batallón a few blocks after the Motel Marino. Its pool, patio, playground, game room, and spacious but somewhat worn suites with kitchenettes (dishes and utensils *not* included) are nicely suited for active families. Another plus here are the several rooms with private view verandas overlooking the neighboring lush, wildlife-rich forest. The 23 fan-only suites include 16 one-bedrooms for two adults and kids ($34) and 7 two-bedrooms accommodating four adults with kids ($55); credit cards are accepted.

The lively, family-operated **Hotel Posada del Rey** (Calle Campeche 10, tel. 323/285-0123, www.sanblasmexico.com/posadadelrey) seems to be trying hardest. It encloses a small but inviting pool and patio beneath a top-floor viewpoint bar (and high-season-only restaurant) that bubbles with continuous soft rock and salsa tunes. Year-round asking rates for the 13 rooms (with a/c) are about $50 s or $60 d, but bargain for a low-season discount; the price for long-term stays goes down to about $30 d. Credit cards are not accepted.

$50-100

Tucked on a quiet back street half a block from the sleepy El Pozo Estuary, **Casa Roxanna Bungalows** (Callejon El Rey 1, tel.

323/285-0573, www.casaroxanna.com) is a hidden gem among San Blas lodgings. Its refined amenities—manicured green lawn, blue double-laned lap pool, regal fan palms—are apparent immediately upon entering its tranquil garden compound. The four comfortable, spacious bungalows ($65 d, add $5 each additional adult), with two double beds, furnished kitchenettes, and cool air-conditioning, confirm the initial impression. Additionally, one large deluxe room and a studio bungalow with kitchenette rent for about $55; all with air-conditioning, satellite TV, and parking. Wireless Internet is also available on-site.

Back in the middle of town, three blocks west along Juárez from the plaza, newly renovated **(Hotel Hacienda Flamingos** (Juárez 105, tel. 323/285-0930, fax 323/285-0485, Mazatlán tel./fax 669/985-2727 or 669/985-5252, www.sanblas.com.mx) lives on as a splendid reminder of old San Blas. Owners have spared little in restoring this 1863 German consulate and trading house to its original graceful condition. Now, the fountain flows once more

Hotel Garza Canela

in the tranquil, tropical inner patio, furnished with period chairs and tables and a gallery of old San Blas photos on the walls. A side door leads outside to a luxuriously elegant swimming pool and spacious garden, sprinkled with recliners, a grass-carpeted badminton court, and a croquet set ready for service. Inside, the rooms are no less than you'd expect: luxuriously airy and high-ceilinged, with elegantly simple decor, replete with Porfirian-era touches and wall art; and with baths that gleam with polished traditional-style fixtures. Year-round (except possibly Christmas and Easter holidays) rates for the 21 rooms (15 with TVs) run about $96 d.

Another San Blas jewel is the refined resort-style **◖ Hotel Garza Canela** (Paredes 106 Sur, tel. 323/285-0112, 323/285-0307, or 323/285-0480, toll-free Mex. tel. 800/713-2313, fax 323/285-0308, www.garzacanela.com), tucked away at the south end of town, two blocks off Heróico Batallón. The careful management of its Vásquez family owners (Señorita Josefina Vásquez in charge) glows everywhere: manicured garden grounds, crystal-blue pool, immaculate sundeck, and centerpiece restaurant. The 45 spacious, air-conditioned rooms are tiled, tastefully furnished, and squeaky clean. Rates run about $96 s, $126 d high season, $79 s and $110 d low, all with a hearty breakfast, cable TV, and much more. Wireless Internet is available in the lobby. Credit cards are accepted. The family also runs a travel agency and an outstanding crafts and gift shop on the premises.

Just behind Garza Canela is the nautical-themed **Hotel Marina San Blas** (Cuauhtémoc 109, tel. 323/285-1437, www.sanblas.com.mx), owned and operated by the same people who operate Hotel Hacienda Flamingos. A pretty, tropical courtyard with circular swimming pool is the centerpiece, leading to a sandy stretch of beach where guests can relax under the *palapas* and gaze at the water. There's plenty to watch: birds, fisherfolk, boats leaving the marina; you just might spend all day there. The 11 rooms are comfortable and offer king-size beds (some come with a king

and a single) and are well appointed, continuing with the nautical theme of lighthouses and navy-striped decor. Rooms start at $77 s or $96 d in high season with a $24 charge for extra guests. Long-term rates are available for one-week or longer stays.

San Blas folks offer several other worthy hotel, bungalow, and apartment lodging choices. For more information, visit the excellent website **www.sanblasdirectory.com.**

Trailer Parks and Campgrounds

San Blas's only trailer park, **Los Cocos** (Teniente Azueta s/n, tel. 323/285-0055, loscocos@sanblasmexico.com), is a two-minute walk from the wide, yellow sands of Playa el Borrego. Friendly management, spacious, palm-shaded grassy grounds, pull-throughs, unusually clean showers and toilet facilities, a laundry next door, fishing, and a good air-conditioned bar with satellite TV all make this place a magnet for RVers and tenters from Mazatlán to Puerto Vallarta. The biting *jejenes* require the use of strong repellent for residents to enjoy the balmy evenings. The 100 spaces rent for about $20 per day for two people, $3 for each additional person, with all hookups, one day free per week for longer-term stays. Amenities include a bar out front open daily 10 A.M.–2 P.M. and wireless Internet access.

The *jejenes* and occasional local toughs and Peeping Toms make **camping** on close-in Playa el Borrego a less-than-ideal possibility (although some adventurers customarily set up tents beside the beachfront *palapa* restaurants). A better option is to camp on Playa el Borrego at **Stoner's Surf Camp** for $3 per person, with kitchen privileges.

Furthermore, **Isla del Rey** (across Estero El Pozo, accessible by *lancha* from the foot of Calle Juárez) presents possibilities for prepared trekker-tenters. Pack in everything, including water. For intensely dedicated adventurers, the same is true for ecosanctuary **Isla Isabel**, three hours by hired boat from San Blas.

For those less equipped, the palm-lined strands of **Playa las Islitas, Playa Matanchén,** and **Playa los Cocos** on the Bay of Matanchén also might afford camping possibilities as long as you bring plenty of good insect repellent.

FOOD
Snacks, Stalls, and Markets

For basic staples and snacks, check out the fruit stands, groceries (such as **Abarrotes Flavia,** tel. 323/285-1214, 6 A.M.–9 P.M. daily), *fondas,* and *jugerías* in and around the **Central Market** (6 A.M.–2 P.M. daily), which, incidentally, is the coolest non-air-conditioned daytime spot in town. For example, refresh yourself at **Jugos Mimi** juice stand. During the summer look for the exotic Asian jackfruit relative *yaca:* green, round, and as large as a football. Enjoy a *licuado* whipped from its deliciously mild pulp.

Late afternoons and evenings, many semipermanent street-side stands around the plaza, such as the **Taquería Las Cuatas,** at the northwest corner, by the city hall, offer tasty *antojitos* and drinks.

For sit-down snacks every day until midnight, drop in to the **Lonchería Ledmar** (facing the plaza near the Canalizo–Juárez corner) for a hot *torta,* hamburger, quesadilla, tostada, or fresh-squeezed *jugo* (juice). For a change of venue, you can enjoy about the same at the **Terraza** café on the opposite side of the plaza.

Get your fresh cupcakes, cookies, and crispy *bolillos* at the **panadería** (bakery) (at Comonfortand Cuauhtémoc, closed Sun.), around the uptown corner from Hotel Posada del Rey. You can get similar (but not quite so fresh) goodies at the small bakery outlet across from the plaza (corner of Juárez and Canalizo).

Restaurants

Family-managed **Restaurant McDonald** (36 Juárez, tel. 323/285-0432, 7 A.M.–10 P.M. daily, $3–7), half a block west of the plaza, is one of the gathering places of San Blas. Its bit-of-everything menu features soups, meat, and seafood, plus a hamburger that beats no-relation U.S. McDonald's by a mile.

As an option, step across the street to the TV-free **Wala** restaurant (tel. 323/285-0863, 8 A.M.–10 P.M. Mon.–Sat., $3–7) for breakfast, lunch, or dinner. Its long menu of offerings—tasty salads, pastas, seafood, and fish fillets, crisply prepared and served in a simple but clean and inviting setting—will never go out of style. Everything is good; simply pick out your favorite.

Another good sit-down option is the airy plaza-front **Cha Cha's** (tel. 323/285-0041, 8 A.M.–10 P.M. daily, $3–8). Here, you can choose from a sandwich or full dinner, such as a professionally prepared and served fresh fish fillet or spaghetti à la Bolognese.

For TV with dinner, the **Restaurant La Familia** (H. Batallón, lunch and dinner Mon.–Sat., $6–8), half a block south of plaza, is just the place. American movies, Mexican curio-hung walls, and leafy garden patio supply the ambience, while a reasonably priced seafood and meat menu furnishes the food.

The Tijuana-trained owner/chef of **Wacame Gourmet** (Yucatán 18, cell 044-311/105-5382, noon–10 P.M., closed Wed., $4–6), two blocks north of the plaza to Canalizo, then turn right, puts out delicious soups (hot and sour), chicken chop suey, pork chow mein, stir-fried broccoli, and much more. He named his establishment Wacame (wah-KAH-may) in honor of the hometown in Japan of his Tijuana employer/mentors.

Cross the adjacent corner and enter the refined marine atmosphere of **Restaurant la Isla** (Mercado, tel. 323/285-0407, 2–10 P.M. Tues.–Sun., $6–10). As ceiling fans whir overhead and a guitarist strums softly in the background, the net-draped walls display a museum-load of nautical curiosities, from antique Japanese floats and Tahitian shells to New England ship models. Davy Jones notwithstanding, both local folks and visitors choose this place mainly for its good fish and shrimp entrées.

San Blas's class-act restaurant is ◖ **El Delfín** (at Hotel Garza Canela, Cuauhtémoc 106, tel. 323/285-0112, 8–10 A.M. and 1–9 P.M. daily, $4–14). Potted tropical plants and leafy planter-dividers enhance the genteel atmosphere of this air-conditioned dining room-in-the-round. Meticulous preparation and service, bountiful breakfasts, savory dinner soups, and fresh salad, seafood, and meat entrées keep customers returning year after year; credit cards are accepted.

INFORMATION AND SERVICES
Tourist Information Offices

San Blas has two tourist information offices. The main one (tel. 323/285-0221, 9 A.M.–2 P.M. and 4–7 P.M. Mon.–Fri., 10 A.M.–2 P.M. Sat.) is directly under the arch as you enter the main part of town. The other office, staffed by personable Cari Luz Aguilar, is at Playa el Borrego (9 A.M.–3 P.M. daily, cell tel. 044-311/134-3356, long distance 01-311/134-3356, kariluz2@hotmail.com).

Alternatively, for information, tickets, and tours, see very well-informed **Josefina Vásquez,** both the desk manager and travel agent at the Hotel Garza Canela.

Money

Banamex (Juárez 36 Ote., tel. 323/285-0031, 9 A.M.–4 P.M. Mon.–Fri.), one block east of the plaza, with a 24-hour ATM, exchanges U.S. travelers checks and cash. There is also an ATM machine at the Pemex gas station just as you enter town.

Communications

The *correo* (tel. 323/285-0295, 8 A.M.–3 P.M. Mon.–Fri., 9 A.M.–noon Sat.) and *telégrafo* (tel. 323/285-0115, 8 A.M.–2 P.M. Mon.–Fri.) stand side by side at Sonora and Echeverría (one block behind, one block east of the plaza church).

In addition to the long-distance public phone stands that sprinkle the town, there are a number of old-fashioned *larga distancia* stores. Most prominent is the **Computel** (on Juárez, 8 A.M.–9 P.M. daily), just west of the plaza, across from Restaurant McDonald.

Internet access has arrived at a number of spots; for example, try **Café Net San Blas** (on H. Batallón, tel. 323/285-1082, 9 A.M.–10 P.M. daily), the hole-in-the wall store near the plaza's southwest corner.

Health and Emergencies

For routine remedies and nonprescription drugs, go to **Farmacia Mas Por Menos** (More For Less, Juárez 66, 8:30 A.M.–1 P.M. and 4–9 P.M. daily), across from Restaurant McDonald, who you can call to reach the pharmacy (tel. 323/285-0432).

Alternatively, go to **Farmacia Económica** (H. Batallón and Mercado, tel. 323/285-0111, 8:30 A.M.–1 P.M. and 4:30–9 P.M. Mon.–Sat., 8:30 A.M.–2 P.M. Sun.).

For medical consultations, visit very highly recommended Dr. Alejandro Davalos, available at his office on Juárez (tel. 323/285-0331), corner of Farias, three blocks east of the plaza. If he's too busy, consult with general practitioner Dr. Rene Diaz Elias, at his Farmacia Mas Por Menos (Juárez 66, 8:30 A.M.–1 P.M. Mon.–Sat.).

Moreover, you can go to San Blas's respectable local small hospital, the government 24-hour **Centro de Salud** (Yucatán and H. Batallón, across from the Motel Marino Inn, tel. 323/285-1207).

For **police** (on Canalizo, tel. 323/285-0221) emergencies, contact the headquarters, on the left side of and behind the Presidencia Municipal.

Immigration and Customs

San Blas no longer has either Migración or Aduana offices. If you lose your tourist card, you'll have to go to the Secretaria de Gobernación in Tepic (Oaxaca no. 220 Sur) or, better, to Migración at the airport in Puerto Vallarta a day before you're scheduled to fly home. For customs matters, go to the Aduana in Puerto Vallarta for the necessary paperwork.

GETTING THERE
By Car or RV

To and from Puerto Vallarta, the highway coastal cutoff at Las Varas bypasses the slow climb up the mountain to Tepic, shortening the San Blas–Puerto Vallarta connection to about 94 miles (151 km), or about 2.5 hours.

From the east, Nayarit Highway 76 leaves Highway 15 at its signed "Miramar" turnoff at the northern edge of Tepic. The road winds downhill about 3,000 feet (1,000 m) through a jungly mountain forest to shoreline Santa Cruz and Miramar villages. It continues along the Bahía de Matanchén shoreline to San Blas, a total of 43 miles (70 km) from Tepic. Although this route generally has more shoulder than Highway 74, frequent pedestrians and occasional unexpected cattle necessitate caution.

To and from the north and east, paved roads connect San Blas to main-route National Highway 15. From the northeast, National Highway 74 winds 19 miles (31 km) downhill from its junction 161 miles (260 km) south of Mazatlán and 22 miles (35 km) north of Tepic. From its Highway 15 turnoff (marked by a Pemex gas station), Highway 74 winds through a forest of vine-draped trees and tall palms. Go slowly; the road lacks a shoulder, and cattle or people may appear unexpectedly around any blind, grass-shrouded bend.

By Bus

From Puerto Vallarta, bus travelers have two ways to get to San Blas. Quickest is via one of the **Transportes Norte de Sonora** (tel. 323/285-0043) departures, which connect daily with San Blas. They depart from the new Puerto Vallarta bus station north of the airport; get your ticket at the Elite–Estrella Blanca desk (tel. 322/290-1001).

If you're too late for the Transportes Norte de Sonora connection, go via **Transportes Pacífico** (tel. 322/290-1008) to the Tepic bus station, where you might be early enough to catch the last of several daily local buses that connect with San Blas, run by Transportes Norte de Sonora (tel. 311/213-2315) or **Transportes Noroeste de Nayarit** (tel. 311/212-2325, go by taxi to their Tepic city-center station).

The **San Blas bus terminal** stands adjacent to the new plaza church, corner of Calles Sinaloa and Canalizo. Transportes Norte de Sonora buses connect with Tepic many times a day (with one early departure continuing to Guadalajara).

Several daily second-class navy-blue-and-white Transportes Noroeste de Nayarit departures (about 8 and 10 A.M.) connect south with Bay of Matanchén points of Matanchén, Los Cocos, and Santa Cruz de Miramar. Other departures connect east with Tepic, and north with Santiago Ixcuintla, via intermediate points of Guadalupe Victoria and Villa Hidalgo.

A local *autobús blanco* connects San Blas south with the Bay of Matanchén points of Las Aguadas, Matanchén, Aticama, Los Cocos, and Santa Cruz. It departs from the downtown corner of Paredes and Sinaloa (a block west of the old church) four times daily, approximately every two hours between 8:30 A.M. and 4:30 P.M.

SANTIAGO IXCUINTLA

North of San Blas, the Nayarit coastal strip broadens into a hinterland of lush farm and marsh where, on the higher ground, rich fields of chiles, tobacco, and corn bloom and Highway 15 conducts a nonstop procession of traffic past the major farm towns of Ruíz, Rosamorada, and Acaponeta.

But where the coastal plain nears the sea, the pace of life slows. Roads, where they exist, thread their way through a vast wetland laced with mangrove channels and decorated by diminutive fishing settlements. Through this lowland, Mexico's longest river, the Río Grande de Santiago, ends its epic five-state journey downstream, past the colorful colonial town of Santiago Ixcuintla (eeks-KOOEEN-tlah) and its historic island-neighbor, **Mexcaltitán,** accessible only by boat.

Few Mexican town names are more intriguing than the name Ixcuintla. Its name derives from the Náhuatl (Aztec) word for the nearly hairless dogs that, in ancient times, were bred locally as pets and for food. Don't miss seeing the dogs, now a whole family, at the **Centro Cultural Huichol,** donated by Nayarit Governor Huberto Delgado a few years back.

Although the town's scenic appeal is considerable, the Huichol people are *the* reason to come to Santiago Ixcuintla. Several hundred Huichol families migrate seasonally (mostly Dec.–May) from their Sierra Madre high-country homeland to work for a few

THE NAYARIT COAST

dollars a day in the local tobacco fields. For many Huichol, their migration in search of money includes a serious hidden cost. In the mountains, their homes, friends, and relatives are around them, as are the familiar rituals and ceremonies they have tenaciously preserved in their centuries-long struggle against Mexicanization.

But when the Huichol come to lowland towns and cities, they often encounter the mocking laughter and hostile stares of crowds of strangers, whose Spanish language they do not understand, and whose city ways are much more alien than they appear even to foreign tourists. As strangers in a strange land, the pressure on the migrant Huichol to give up old costumes, language, and ceremonies to become like everyone else is powerful indeed.

The Town Plaza

The Santiago Ixcuintla town plaza is a couple of blocks directly inland from the riverbank. The main town streets border the plaza: running east–west are 20 de Noviembre on the north side and Zaragoza on the south side; Hidalgo and Allende run north–south along the east and west sides, respectively. During your stroll around the plaza, admire the pretty old church and the voluptuous Porfirian nymphs who decorate the gloriously restored bandstand. Stroll beneath the shaded porticos and the colorful market, a block west and a block north of the plaza.

Centro Cultural Huichol

Be sure to reserve part of your time in Santiago Ixcuintla to stop by the Centro Cultural Huichol (20 de Noviembre 452, tel. 323/235-1171, 9 A.M.–2 P.M. and 4–8 P.M. Mon.–Sat., www.huicholcenter.com). The immediate mission of founder Mariano Valadez, a Huichol artist and community leader, is to ensure that the Huichol people endure, with their traditions intact and growing. His instrument is the Centro Cultural Huichol—a clinic, dining hall, dormitory, library, craftsmaking shop, sale gallery, and interpretive center that provides crucial focus and support for local migratory Huichol people.

Mariano's ex-wife, Susana (who helped him found the Centro Cultural Huichol during the 1990s), has worked to maintain a second center, high in the mountains at Huejuquilla El Alto, Jalisco. Mariano, with the help of his local staff, continues the original mission in Santiago Ixcuintla. As well as filling vital human needs, both of these centers actively nurture the vital elements of an endangered heritage. This heritage belongs not only to the Huichol, but to the lost generations of indigenous peoples—Aleut, Yahi, Lacandones, and myriad others—who succumbed to European diseases and were massacred in innumerable fields, from Wounded Knee and the Valley of Mexico all the way to Tierra del Fuego.

Although they concentrate on the immediate needs of people, Mariano and Susana and their staffs also reach out to local, national, and international communities. For example, their Santiago Ixcuintla center's entry corridor is decorated with illustrated Huichol legends in Spanish, especially for Mexican visitors. An adjacent gallery exhibits a treasury of Huichol art for sale—yarn paintings, masks, jewelry, gourds, god's eyes—adorned with the colorful deities and animated heavenly motifs of the Huichol pantheon. You may also purchase the center's Huichol handicrafts online, via www.beadsofbeauty.net, or at La Hamaca Gallery in Sayulita.

Get to the Santiago Ixcuintla Centro Cultural Huichol by heading away from the river, along 20 de Noviembre, the main street that borders the central plaza. Within a mile, you'll see the Centro Cultural Huichol at number 452 on the right.

You can also travel to Susana's center (call or email a week ahead of time) in person, either by charter airplane from Tepic, or two days by car (via Hwy. 54 north from Guadalajarato Zacatecas, thence Hwy. 45 northwest to Fresnillo, then west via Hwy. 44 to Huejuquilla) to Centro Indígena Huichol (Calle Victoria 24, Huejuquilla El Alto, tel. 457/983-7054, huicholcenter@juno.com). Both the Huejuquilla and the Santiago Ixcuintla centers invite volunteers, especially those with

THE HUICHOL

Because the Huichol have retained more of their traditional religion than perhaps any other group of indigenous Mexicans, they offer a glimpse into the lives and beliefs of dozens of now-vanished Mesoamerican peoples.

The Huichols' collective wariness, plus their isolation in rugged mountain canyons and valleys, has saved them from the ravages of modern Mexico. Despite increased tourist, government, and mestizo contact, prosperity and better health swelled the Huichol population to around 20,000 by the late 1990s.

Although many have migrated to coastal farming towns and cities such as Tepic and Guadalajara, several thousand Huichol remain in their ancestral heartland – roughly 50 miles (80 km) northeast of Tepic as the crow flies. They cultivate corn and raise cattle on 400 *rancherías* in five municipalities not far from the winding Altengo River valley: Guadalupe Ocotán in Nayarit and Tuxpán de Bolanos, San Sebastián Teponahuaxtlán, Santa Catarina, and San Andrés Cohamiata in Jalisco.

Although studied by a procession of researchers since Carl Lumholtz's seminal work in the 1890s, the remote Huichol and their religion remain enigmatic. As Lumholtz said, "Religion to them is a personal matter, not an institution and therefore their life is religion – from the cradle to the grave, wrapped up in symbolism."

Hints of what it means to be Huichol can be gleaned from their art. Huichol art contains representations of the prototype deities – Grandfather Sun, Grandmother Earth, Brother Deer, Mother Maize – that once guided the destinies of many North American peoples. It blooms with tangible mystical symbols, from green-faced Mother Earth (Tatei Urianaka) and the dripping Rain Goddess (Tatei Matiniera), to the ray-festooned Father Sun (Tayau) and the antlered folk hero Brother Kauyumari, forever battling the evil sorcerer Kieri.

The Huichol are famous for their use of the hallucinogen peyote, their bridge to the divine. The humble cactus – from which the peyote

© BRUCE WHIPPERMAN

Huichol pilgrims regularly bring offerings to the Alta Vista Archaeological Sacred Site.

"buttons" are gathered and eaten – grows in the Huichols' elysian land of Wirikuta, in the San Luis Potosí desert 300 miles east of their homeland, around the old gold-mining town of Real de Catorce.

To the Huichol, a journey to Wirikuta is a dangerous trip to heaven. Preparations go on for weeks and include innumerable prayers and ceremonies, as well as the crafting of feathered arrows, bowls, gourds, and paintings for the gods who live along the way. Only the chosen – village shamans, temple elders, those fulfilling vows or seeking visions – may make the journey. Each participant in effect becomes a god whose identity and very life are divined and protected by the shaman en route to Wirikuta.

THE NAYARIT COASAT

secretarial, computer, language, and other skills, to help with projects. If you don't have the time, they also solicit donations of money and equipment.

Accommodations and Food

If you decide on a Santiago Ixcuintla overnight, stay at the **Hotel Casino Plaza** (Arteaga and Ocampo, tel./fax 323/235-0850, 323/235-0851, or 323/235-0852). The approximately 35 basic but clean rooms around an inner parking patio go for about $37 d, with private hot-water shower baths, and air-conditioning.

For food, go to the Hotel Casino's good air-conditioned downstairs restaurant/bar or check out the hearty country food offerings of the many *fondas* (food stalls) in the town-center market.

Information and Services

Santiago Ixcuintla is an important regional business center, with a number of services. Banks, all with 24-hour ATMs, include long-hours **HSBC** (Hidalgo and Zaragoza, tel. 323/235-3401, 8 A.M.–7 P.M. Mon.–Fri., 8 A.M.–3 P.M. Sat.) on the south side of the plaza; **Banamex** (20 de Noviembre and Hidalgo, tel. 323/235-0053, 9 A.M.–4 P.M. Mon.–Fri.), and **Bancomer** (20 de Noviembre and Morelos, 8:30 A.M.–4 P.M. Mon.–Fri., 10 A.M.–2 P.M. Sat.).

Find the *correo* (Allende 23, tel. 323/235-0214, 8:30 A.M.–3 P.M. Mon.–Fri.) at the east side of the plaza. **Telecomunicaciones** (Zaragoza Ote. 200, tel./fax 323/235-0989, 8 A.M.–8 P.M. Mon.–Sat.) provides telegraph, long-distance phone, and public fax.

Two grades of gasoline are customarily available at the **Pemex** station on the east-side highway (toward Hwy. 15) as you head out of town.

Getting There

For bus travelers, the San Blas and Tepic bus stations are the best jumping-off places for Santiago Ixcuintla. The regional line, navy-blue-and-white Autotransportes Noroeste de Nayarit, runs a few daily buses from the San Blas and Tepic bus stations to the Santiago Ixcuintla station, where you can make connections by minibus or *colectivo* for Mexcaltitán.

With your own wheels, Santiago Ixcuintla and Mexcaltitán make an interesting off-the-beaten-track side trip from San Blas or Puerto Vallarta. Two routes are possible. From Puerto Vallarta, the simplest (but not the quickest route) is via Highway 200 to Tepic, then continuing along Highway 15, 38 miles (60 km) north of Tepic (and 16 miles/25 km north of the Hwy. 74–Hwy. 15 junction) to the signed Santiago Ixcuintla–Mexcaltitán turn-off. Within five miles you'll be in Santiago Ixcuintla; Mexcaltitán is another 20 miles (32 km) beyond that. Be sure to get a very early start (or plan on an overnight en route).

Alternatively, car travelers in the mood for a little extra adventure should drive the back road that connects San Blas with Santiago Ixcuintla. The main attractions en route are the hosts of water birds, tobacco fields, aqua-culture ponds, Huichol people in colorful local dress, and the Río Grande de Santiago, Mexico's longest river.

Directions: The Santiago Ixcuintla road (signed Guadalupe Victoria) heads northerly, from the eastward extension of San Blas's main street, Juárez, on the San Blas side of the Estero San Cristóbal bridge. Mark your odometer at the turnoff and continue along the paved road about 10 miles (16 km) to Guadalupe Victoria village. Follow the pavement, which curves right (east) and continues another eight miles (13 km) to Villa Hidalgo. Keep going through the town; after another five miles (8 km) turn left (north) at the signed La Presa–Santiago Ixcuintla side road. Continue to La Presa; bear left through the village center and very quickly to the river levee and across the new bridge, where you can see Santiago Ixcuintla across the river.

◖ MEXCALTITÁN

Mexcaltitán (pop. 2,000), the House of the Mexicans, represents much more than just a scenic little island town. Archaeological evidence indicates that Mexcaltitán may actually be the legendary Aztlán (Place of the Herons) from which the Aztecs, who called themselves

AZTLÁN

During their first meeting in imperial Tenochtitlán, the Aztec Emperor Moctezuma informed Hernán Cortés that "from the records which we have long possessed and which are handed down from our ancestors, it is known that no one, neither I nor the others who inhabit this land of Anahuac, are native to it. We are strangers and we came from far outer parts."

Although the Aztecs had forgotten exactly where it was, they agreed on the name and nature of the place from which they came: Aztlán, a magical island with seven allegorical caves, each representing an Aztec subtribe – of which the México, last to complete the migration, had clawed its way to dominion. Aztlán, the Aztecs also knew, lay somewhere vaguely to the northwest, and their migration to Anahuac, the present-day Valley of Mexico, had taken many generations.

For centuries, historians puzzled and argued over the precise location of Aztlán, placing it as far away as Alaska and as near as Lake Chapala. This is curious, for there was an actual Aztlán – a chiefdom well known at the time of the Spanish conquest. Renegade conquistador Nuño de Guzmán immediately determined its location, and, three days before Christmas in 1529, headed out with a small army of followers, driven by dreams of a new Aztec empire in western Mexico. However, when Guzmán arrived at Aztlán – present-day San Felipe Aztatlán village, near Tuxpan in Nayarit – he found no golden city. Others who followed, such as Vásquez de Coronado and Francisco de Ibarra, vainly continued to scour northwestern Mexico, seeking the mythical Seven Cities of Cíbola, which they confused with the legend of Aztlán's seven caves.

Guzmán probably came closest to the original site. Scarcely a dozen miles due west of his trail through San Felipe Aztatlán is the small island-town of Mexcaltitán, which a number of experts now believe to be the original Aztlán. Many circumstances uphold their argument. The spelling common to Mexcaltitán and México is no coincidence, they say. The name Aztlán, furthermore, is probably a contraction of Aztatlán, which translates as Place of the Herons – the birds flock in abundance around Mexcaltitán. Moreover, a 1579 map of New Spain by renowned cartographer Ortelius shows an Aztlán exactly where Mexcaltitán is today.

The argument goes on: The Codex Boturini, a 16th-century reconstruction of previous Aztec records, reveals a pictogram of Aztecs leaving Aztlán, punting a canoe with an oar. Both the peculiar shape of the canoe and the manner of punting are common to both old Tenochtitlán and present-day Mexcaltitán.

Most compelling, perhaps, is the layout of Mexcaltitán itself. As in a pocket-sized Tenochtitlán, north-south and east-west avenues radiate from a central plaza, dividing the island into four quadrants. A single circular plaza-centered street arcs through the avenues, joining the neighborhoods.

If you visit Mexcaltitán, you'll find it's easy to imagine Aztec life as it must have been in Tenochtitlán of old, where many people depended on fishing, rarely left their island, and, especially during the rainy season, navigated their city streets in canoes.

© BOB RACE

plan view of present-day Mexcaltitán

the México (May-Kshee-kah), in 1091 began their generations-long migration to the Valley of Mexico.

Each year on June 28 and 29, the feast days of Saints Peter and Paul, residents of Mexcaltitán and surrounding villages dress up in feathered headdresses and jaguar robes and breathe life into their tradition. They celebrate the opening of the shrimp season by staging a grand regatta, driven by friendly competition between decorated boats carrying rival images of Saints Peter and Paul.

Sights

From either of the Mexcaltitán road's-end embarcaderos, boat workers ferry you across (about $3 pp for *colectivo,* $8 for private boat, each way) to Mexcaltitán island-village, some of whose inhabitants have never crossed the channel to the mainland. The town itself is not unlike many Mexican small towns, except more tranquil, because of the absence of motor vehicles.

Mexcaltitán is prepared for visitors, however. Instituto Nacional de Arqueología y Historia (INAH) has put together an excellent **museum** (10 A.M.–2 P.M. and 4–7 P.M. Tues.–Sun.), with several rooms of artifacts, photos, paintings, and maps describing the cultural regions of pre-Columbian Mexico. The displays climax at the museum's centerpiece exhibit, which tells the story of the Aztecs' epic migration to the Valley of Mexico from legendary Aztlán, now believed by experts to be present-day Mexcaltitán.

Outside, the proud village **church** (step inside and admire the heroic St. Peter above the altar) and city hall preside over the central plaza, from which the town streets radiate to the broad lagoon that surrounds the town.

At the watery lagoon-ends of the streets, village men set out in the late afternoon in canoes and boats for the open-ocean fishing grounds where, as night falls and kerosene lanterns are used, they attract shrimp into their nets. Occasionally during the rainy season water floods the town, and folks must navigate the streets as Venice-style canals.

Beaches

Beachcombers might enjoy a side trip to nearby **Playa los Corchos.** If, at the junction five miles (8 km) west of Santiago Ixcuintla, instead of turning off for Mexcaltitán you continue straight ahead (west) for about 15 miles (24 km), you'll arrive at Playa los Corchos. Here, waves roll in gently from 100 yards out, leaving meringues of foam on sand speckled with little white clam shells. A few ramshackle Sunday *palapas* line the broad, wind-rippled strand.

From here you can hike or, with care, pilot your four-wheel-drive vehicle five miles (8 km) south along the beach to **Barra Asadero,** at the mouth of the Río Grande de Santiago. On the sandbar and in the adjacent river estuary, many sandpipers, pelicans, gulls, and boobies gather to feast amidst the summer flood deposits of driftwood troves.

Accommodations and Food

At the view-edge of the lagoon behind the museum stands Mexcaltitán's first official tourist lodging, the **Hotel Ruta Azteca** (tel. 323/235-6020). More like a homey guesthouse than a hotel, it has an airy rear lagoon-view patio, perfect for reading and relaxing. Its four plain, tiled rooms with bath rent for about $30 d with fans, $40 d with air-conditioning. Except for the last week in June, reservations are not usually necessary. If you are unable to contact the hotel directly, call the town telephone operator (tel. 323/235-6077) and leave a message for the hotel.

On the town plaza opposite the church stands airy **El Camarón** seafood restaurant (although the sometimes-noisy restaurant/bar at the south-side dock has more and better food). A third option is the good **Mariscos Kika** (tel. 327/235-6054, noon–dusk daily) seafood restaurant, visible across the lagoon from the south-side dock. Reach it by hired (or the restaurant's) boat. Its kid-friendly facilities include a pair of kiddie pools and a waterslide.

Getting There

Mexcaltitán lies about 25 miles (32 km) by

an all-weather road northwest of Santiago Ixcuintla. You get to Santiago Ixcuintla either by back road from San Blas or from Highway 15, by the Santiago Ixcuintla turnoff 38 miles (60 km) north of Tepic. About five miles (8 km) after the turnoff, you reach the town, marked by a solitary hill on the right. Just past the hill, turn right on the main street, 20 de Noviembre, which runs by the central plaza and becomes the main westbound road out of town. Continue approximately another five miles (8 km) to the signed Mexcaltitán turnoff, where you head right. You soon pass Base Aztlán, site of the Mexican experimental rocket center; then the farmland gives way to a maze of leafy mangrove-edged lagoons, home to a host of cackling, preening, and fluttering water birds. About 15 miles (24 km) after the turnoff you reach the embarcadero for Mexcaltitán.

Note: Mexcaltitán is also accessible from the northeast side, from Highway 15, 136 miles (219 km) south of Mazatlán, at a signed turn-off with gas station four miles south of Chilapa village. Initially paved, the access road changes to rough gravel for its last half through the bushy wetland decorated by rafts of Mexican lotus lilies and flocks of preening, stalking, and fluttering egrets, herons, and cormorants, finally arriving at embarcadero La Ticha after 28 miles (45 km).

Tepic

Tepic (elev. 3,001 feet/915 m) basks in a lush highland valley beneath a trio of giant, slumbering volcanoes: 7,600-foot (2,316-m) Sanganguey and 6,630-foot (2,020-m) Tepetiltic in the east and south, and the brooding Volcán San Juan (7,350 ft/2,240 m) in the west. The waters that trickle from their cool green slopes have nurtured verdant valley fields and gardens for millennia. The city's name reflects its fertile surroundings; it's from the Náhuatl *tepictli,* meaning "land of corn."

Resembling a prosperous U.S. county seat, Tepic (pop. 200,000) is the state capital and the service, manufacturing, and governmental center for the entire state. Local people flock to deposit in its banks, shop in its stores, and visit its diminutive main-street state legislature.

The **Huichol** people are among the many who come to trade in Tepic. The Huichol fly in from their remote mountain villages on air taxis, loaded with crafts—yarn paintings, beaded masks, ceremonial gourds, god's eyes—which they sell at local handicrafts stores. Tepic has thus accumulated troves of their intriguing ceremonial art, whose animal and human forms symbolize the Huichol's animistic world view.

You can very easily meet the Huichol people most any day in downtown Tepic. They welcome visitors to view the handicrafts that they offer for sale in a **minimarket,** beneath the sheltering portal of the Tepic Presidencia Municipal (city hall), at the west side of the Tepic city-center plaza.

Beyond the city limits, the Tepic valley offers an unusual bonus for lovers of the outdoors. About 45 minutes southeast of town by car, sylvan mountain-rimmed Laguna Santa María del Oro offers comfortable bungalow lodgings and a modest RV park and campground, fine for a relaxing day or week of camping, hiking, swimming, kayaking, rowboating, and wildlife-viewing.

ORIENTATION

Tepic has two main plazas and two main highways. If you're only passing through, stay on the *libramiento* Highway 15 through-way, which efficiently conducts traffic around the city-center congestion. An interchange at the south edge of town distributes Highway 200 traffic approaching from Puerto Vallarta three ways: east (to *libramiento* Highway 15 toward Guadalajara); north (to *libramiento* Highway 15 toward San Blas, Mazatlán,

THE NAYARIT COAST

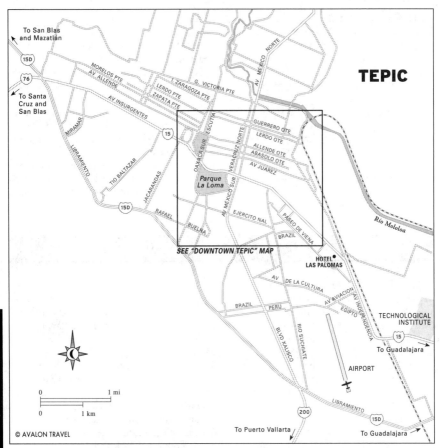

THE NAYARIT COAST

and the United States), or downtown along Boulevard Xalisco. Just past the *libramiento*'s north end, an overpass directs traffic either west to Miramar–Santa Cruz and San Blas via Nayarit Highway 76 or north along Highway 15.

Avenida México, Tepic's main north–south downtown street, angles from Boulevard Xalisco just south of big **Parque La Loma.** A few blocks farther north, it crosses Avenida Insurgentes and continues downtown past the two main plazas: first Plaza Constituyentes, and then Plaza Principal, about a half mile farther north.

HISTORY

Scholars believe that around A.D. 1160, the valley of Tepic may have been a stopping place for a generation of the México (Aztecs) on their way to the Valley of Mexico. By the eve of the conquest, however, Tepic was ruled by the kingdom of Xalisco (whose capital occupied the same ground as the present-day city of Jalisco, a few miles south of Tepic).

In 1524, the expedition headed by the great conquistador's nephew, Francisco Cortés de San Buenaventura, explored the valley in peaceful contrast to those who followed. The renegade conquistador Nuño de Guzmán, bent on accumulating gold and *indígena* slaves, arrived in May 1530 and seized the valley in the name of King Charles V. After building a lodging house for hoped-for future immigrants, Guzmán hurried north, burning a pathway to Sinaloa. He returned a year later and founded a settlement near Tepic, which he named, pretentiously, Espíritu Santo de la Mayor España. In 1532 the king ordered his settlement's name changed to Santiago de Compostela. Today it remains Nayarit's oldest municipality, 23 miles (37 km) south of present-day Tepic.

Immigrants soon began colonizing the countryside of the sprawling new dominion of Nueva Galicia, which today includes the modern states of Jalisco, Nayarit, and Sinaloa. Guzmán managed to remain as governor until 1536, when the new viceroy, Antonio Mendoza, finally had him arrested and sent back to Spain in chains.

With Guzmán gone, Nueva Galicia began to thrive. The colonists settled down to raising cattle, wheat, and fruit; the padres founded churches, schools, and hospitals. Explorers set out for new lands: Coronado to New Mexico in 1539, Legazpi and Urdaneta across the Pacific in 1563, Vizcaíno to California and Oregon in 1602, and Father Kino to Arizona in 1687. Father Junípero Serra stayed in Tepic for several months en route to the Californias in 1767. Excitement rose in Tepic when a column of 200 Spanish dragoons came through on their way to establishing the port of San Blas in 1768.

San Blas's glory days were numbered, as were Spain's. Insurgents captured its fort cannons and sent them to defend Guadalajara in 1810, and finally President Lerdo de Tejada closed the port to foreign commerce in 1872.

Now, however, trains, jet airplanes, and a seemingly interminable flow of giant diesel trucks carry mountains of produce and manufactures through Tepic to the Mexican Pacific and the United States. Commerce hums in suburban factories and in banks, stores, and shops around the plaza, where the aging colonial cathedral rises, a brooding reminder of the old days that few have time to remember.

SIGHTS
A Walk Around Downtown

The **cathedral,** adjacent to Avenida México, at the east side of the Plaza Principal, marks the center of town. Dating from 1750, the cathedral was dedicated to the Purísima Concepción (Immaculate Conception). Its twin neogothic bell towers rise somberly over everything else in town, while inside, cheerier white walls and neoclassic gilded arches lead toward the main altar. There, the pious, all-forgiving Virgin de la Asunción appears to soar to heaven, borne by a choir of adoring cherubs.

The workaday **Presidencia Municipal** (City-County Hall) stands on the plaza opposite the cathedral, while the **municipal tourist information office,** with many good brochures, is just north of it, at the corner of Puebla and Amado Nervo. Back across the plaza, behind the cathedral and a half block to the north, the **Museo Amado Nervo** (Zacatecas Nte. 284, tel. 311/212-2916, 9 A.M.–2 P.M. and 4–7 P.M. Mon.–Fri., 10 A.M.–2 P.M. Sat.) occupies the

Tepic's neogothic cathedral towers rise above the town's main plaza.

© BRUCE WHIPPERMAN

house where the renowned poet was born on August 27, 1870. The four-room permanent exhibition displays photos, original works, a bust of Nervo, and paintings donated by artists J. L. Soto, Sofía Bassi, and Erlinda T. Fuentes.

Return to the plaza and join the shoppers beneath the arches in front of the Hotel Fray Junípero Serra on the plaza's south side, where a platoon of shoe shiners ply their trade.

Head around the corner, south, along Avenida México. After about two blocks you will reach the venerable 18th-century former mansion that houses the **Museo Regional de Antropología e Historia** (Av. México 91 Nte., tel. 311/212-1900, 9 A.M.–7 P.M. Mon.–Fri., 9 A.M.–3 P.M. Sat. and Sun., $3). The palatial residence was built in 1762 with profits from sugarcane, cattle, and wheat. Since then, the mansion's spacious, high-ceilinged chambers have echoed with the voices of generations of occupants, including the German consul, Maximiliano Delius, during the 1880s. Now, its downstairs rooms house a changing exhibition of charming, earthy pre-Columbian pottery artifacts from the museum's collection. These have included dancing dogs, a man scaling a fish, a boy riding a turtle, a dog with a corncob in its mouth, and a very unusual explicitly amorous couple. In an upstairs room, displays illustrate the Huichol symbolism hidden in the *cicuri* (eye of God) yarn sculptures, yarn paintings, ceremonial arrows, hats, musical instruments, and other pieces. Also upstairs, don't miss the monstrous 15-foot stuffed crocodile, captured near San Blas and donated by ex-president Carlos Salinas de Gortari in 1989.

If you have time, cross Avenida México and continue one block along Hidalgo to take a peek inside a pair of other historic homes, now serving as museums. Within the restored colonial-era house at the southwest corner of Hidalgo and Zacatecas is the **Museo de los Cuatro Pueblos** (Museum of the Four Peoples, tel. 311/212-1705, 9 A.M.–2 P.M. and 4–7 P.M. Mon.–Fri., 10 A.M.–2 P.M. Sat.), which exhibits traditional costumes and crafts of Nayarit's four indigenous peoples—Huichol, Cora, Tepehuan, and México. Afterward, walk three

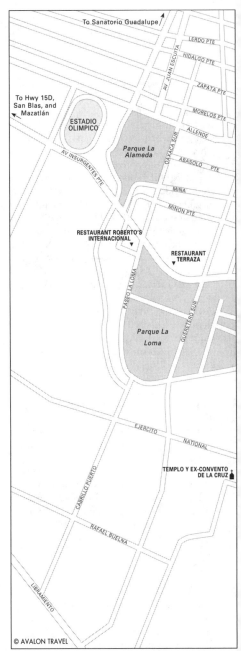

THE NAYARIT COAST

© AVALON TRAVEL

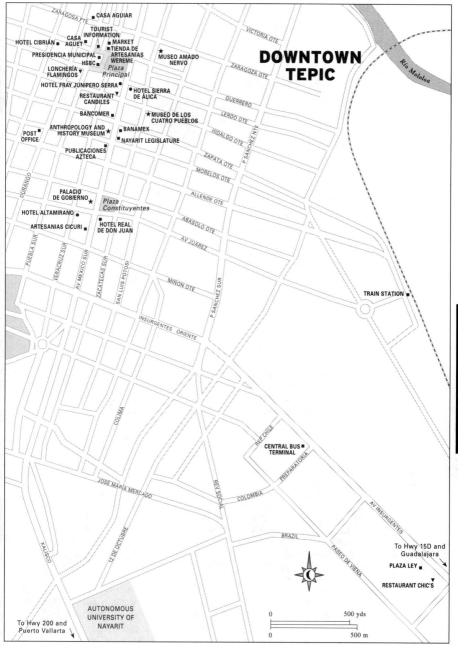

DOWNTOWN TEPIC

ZARAGOSA PTE
CASA AGUIAR
TOURIST INFORMATION
HOTEL CIBRIÁN
CASA AGUET
MARKET
TIENDA DE ARTESANIAS WEREME
PRESIDENCIA MUNICIPAL
HSBC
MUSEO AMADO NERVO
VICTORIA OTE
ZARAGOZA OTE
LONCHERÍA FLAMINGOS
Plaza Principal
HOTEL FRAY JUNIPERO SERRA
HOTEL SIERRA DE ÁLICA
RESTAURANT CANDILES
GUERRERO
BANCOMER
MUSEO DE LOS CUATRO PUEBLOS
LERDO OTE
ANTHROPOLOGY AND HISTORY MUSEUM
BANAMEX
NAYARIT LEGISLATURE
HIDALGO OTE
P. SANCHEZ NTE
POST OFFICE
PUBLICACIONES AZTECA
ZAPATA OTE
MORELOS OTE
DURANGO
PALACIO DE GOBIERNO
Plaza Constituyentes
ALLENDE OTE
HOTEL ALTAMIRANO
ARTESANIAS CICURI
HOTEL REAL DE DON JUAN
ABASOLO OTE
AV JUAREZ
PUEBLA SUR
VERACRUZ SUR
AV MEXICO SUR
ZACATECAS SUR
SAN LUIS POTOSI
MINON OTE
P SANCHEZ SUR
INSURGENTES ORIENTE
Río Mololoa
TRAIN STATION
COLIMA
REP CHILE
CENTRAL BUS TERMINAL
PREPARATORIA
JOSE MARIA MERCADO
REV SOCIAL
COLOMBIA
AV INSURGENTES
12 DE OCTUBRE
BRAZIL
PASEO DE VIENA
To Hwy 15D and Guadalajara
PLAZA LEY
RESTAURANT CHIC'S
XALISCO
AUTONOMOUS UNIVERSITY OF NAYARIT
To Hwy 200 and Puerto Vallarta

0   500 yds
0   500 m

THE NAYARIT COASAT

JUNÍPERO SERRA: APOSTLE OF CALIFORNIA

His untiring, single-minded drive to found a string of missions and save the souls of native Californians has lifted **Junípero Serra** to prominence and proposed sainthood. Not long after he was born – on November 24, 1713, to illiterate parents on the Spanish island of Mallorca – he showed a fascination for books and learning. After taking his vows at the Convent of St. Francis in Palma on September 15, 1731, he changed his name to Junípero, after the "merry jester of God" and beloved friend of St. Francis Assisi.

Ordained in 1738 into the Franciscan order, Junípero soon was appointed professor of theology at the age of 30. He made up for his slight five-foot, two-inch height with a penetrating intelligence, engaging wit, and cheery disposition. Serra was popular with students, and when he received the missionary call in 1748, two of them – Francisco Palóu and Juan Bautista Crespi – accompanied him to Mexico, beginning their lifelong sojourn with him.

Serra inspired his followers by example, sometimes to the extreme. On arrival at Veracruz in December 1749, he insisted on walking the rough road all the way to Mexico City. The injuries he suffered led to a serious infection that plagued him the rest of his life. During his association with the Mexico City College of San Fernando (1750-1767), which included an extensive mission among the Pames Indians around Jalpan, in present-day Querétaro state, he practiced self-flagellation and wore an undercoat woven with sharp bits of wire. Often he would inspire his indigenous flock during Holy Week, as he played the role of Jesus, lugging a ponderous wooden cross through the stations. Afterward, he would humbly wash his converts' feet.

Serra's later mission to the Californias was triggered by the June 24, 1767, royal decree of King Carlos III, which expelled the Jesuit missionaries from the New World. The king's inspector general of the Indies, José de Galvez, prevailed upon Serra, at age 55, to fulfill a double agenda: Organize a Franciscan mission to staff the former Jesuits' several Baja California missions, then push north and found several more in Alta California.

From the summer of 1767 to the spring of 1768, Serra paused in Guadalajara, Tepic, and San Blas with his fellow missionaries en route to the Californias. They sailed north from San Blas on March 12, 1768.

They found the Baja California missions in disarray. The soldiers, left in custody of the missions, were running amok – raping native women, murdering their husbands, and squandering supplies. With the cooperation of military commander and governor Gaspar de Portolá, Serra managed to set things straight within a year and continue northward. On March 25, 1769, Serra, weak with fever, had two men lift him onto his mule, beginning the 1,000-mile desert trek from Loreto to San Diego. On May 17 Serra's leg became so infected that Portolá insisted he return to Loreto. Serra refused. "I shall not turn back.... I would gladly be left among the pagans if such be the will of God."

Serra, however, was always practical. He asked the mule driver's advice. "Imagine I am one of your mules with a sore on his leg. Give me the same treatment." The mule driver applied the ordinary remedy, a soothing ointment of herbs mixed with lard. Serra resumed the trip and reached San Diego, where, on July 16, 1769, he founded San Diego Mission.

The following years would see Serra laboring on, trekking by muleback up and down California, founding eight more missions, encouraging the padres whom he assigned, and teaching and caring for the welfare of the Native Americans in his charge. Given the few padres (only two per mission) and the few stores brought by the occasional supply ship from San Blas, it was a monumental, backbreaking task.

In the end, Serra's sacrifices probably shortened his life. On August 18, 1784, at his beloved headquarters mission in Carmel, Serra spent his last days with Palóu, his companion of 40 years. Palóu gave the last sacrament, and two days afterward, Serra, in pain, retraced the stations of the cross with his congregation for the last time. He died peacefully in his cell eight days later.

Whatever one believes about Spain's colonial role, the fate of the indigenous inhabitants, and sainthood, it is hard not to be awed by this compassionate, gritty little man who would not turn back.

doors farther on Hidalgo and cross the street, to the **Casa de Juan Escuita,** a colonial house furnished in original style. Visitors can tour the house 9 A.M.–2 P.M. and 4–7 P.M. Monday–Friday and 9 A.M.–2 P.M. Saturday. It's named after a Tepic-born boy who was one of Mexico's beloved six "Niños Héroes"—cadets who fell in the futile defense of Chapultepec Castle (the "Halls of Montezuma") against U.S. Marines in 1846.

Continue south along Avenida México; pass the state legislature across the street on the left and, two blocks farther, on your right, along the west side of the plaza, spreads the Spanish classical facade of the State of Nayarit **Palacio de Gobierno.** Inside the center rises a cupola decorated with a 1975 collection of fiery murals by artist José Luis Soto. In a second, rear building, a long, unabashedly biased mural by the same artist portrays the historic struggles of the Mexican people against despotism, corruption, and foreign domination.

Continuing about a mile south of Plaza Constituyentes past Insurgentes, where Avenida México crosses Ejército Nacional, you will find the **Templo y Ex-Convento de la Cruz de Zacate** (Church and Ex-Convent of the Cross of Grass). This venerable but lately restored monument has two claims to fame: the rooms where Father Junípero Serra stayed for several months in 1767 en route to California, and the miraculous cross that you can see in the open-air enclosure adjacent to the sanctuary. According to chroniclers, the cross-shaped patch of grass has grown for centuries (from either 1540 or 1619, depending upon the account), needing neither water nor cultivation. While you're there, pick up some of the excellent brochures at the **Nayarit State Tourism** desk at the building's front entrance.

◖ Crater Lake Santa María del Oro

Easily accessible by car and about 45 minutes south of town by either old Highway 15 or the toll *autopista,* Laguna Santa María, tucked into an ancient volcanic caldera, offers near-perfect opportunities for outdoor relaxation. The lake itself, reachable via a good paved road, is big, blue, and rimmed by forested wildlife-rich hills. You can hike trails through shady woods to ridgetop panoramic viewpoints. Afterward, cool off with a swim in the lake. On another day, row a rental boat across the lake and explore hidden tree-shaded inlets and sunny, secluded beaches, and sit in a palm-fringed grassy park enjoying the lake view and the orange blossom–scented evening air.

The driving force behind this seemingly too-good-to-be-true scene is Chris French, the personable owner/operator of lakeshore Koala Bungalows and Trailer Park. He's dedicated to preserving the beauty of the lake and its surroundings. It seems a miracle that, lacking any visible government protection, the lake and its forest hinterland remain lovely and pristine. The answer may lie partly in its isolation, the relatively sparse local population, and the enlightened conservation efforts of Chris and his neighbors.

SHOPPING

Its for-sale collections of Huichol art provide an excellent reason for stopping in Tepic. While at the downtown main plaza, be sure to make a shopping stop beneath the portal in front of the **Tepic Presidencia Municipal** (City Hall). Here a small village of Huichol vendors in their bright native dress offer a trove of both traditional ceremonial and latter-day for-tourist (but nevertheless both fetching and handmade) crafts.

Afterwards you can continue to at least four downtown shops that both specialize in Huichol goods and act as agents for more than just the commissions they receive. They have been involved with the Huichol for years, helping them preserve their religion and traditional skills in the face of ever-insistent modernization and development.

Starting near the Plaza Principal, the **Casa Aguet** (132 Amado Nervo, tel. 311/212-4130, 9 A.M.–2 P.M. and 4–8 P.M. Mon.–Sat., 10 A.M.–1:30 P.M. Sun.), a block behind the Presidencia Municipal (look for the second-story black-and-white Artesanias Huichol sign)

© BRUCE W-HIPPERMAN

Huichol handicrafts for sale at Tepic's Presidencia Municipal

has an upstairs attic-museum of Huichol art. The founder's son, personable Miguel Aguet, knows the Huichol well. Moreover, he guarantees the "lowest prices in town." His copy of *Art of the Huichol Indians* furnishes authoritative explanations of the intriguing animal and human painting motifs. He sells wholesale to dealers.

The small government handicrafts store, **Tienda de Artesanías Wereme,** on the corner of Amado Nervo and Mérida, next to the Presidencia Municipal (9 A.M.–2 P.M. and 4–7 P.M. Mon.–Fri., 9 A.M.–2 P.M. Sat.), stocks some Huichol and other handicrafts. The staff, however, does not appear as knowledgeable as the private merchants.

If you can manage only one stop in Tepic, make it one block north of the plaza at **Casa Aguiar** (Zaragoza 100 Pte., corner of Mérida, tel. 311/212-0694, 10 A.M.–2 P.M. and 4–7:30 P.M. Mon.–Sat.), where elderly Alicia and Carmela Aguiar carry on their family tradition of Huichol crafts. In the parlor of their graceful old ancestral home, they offer a

colorful galaxy of artifacts, both antique and new. Eerie beaded masks, venerable ceremonial hats, votive arrows, god's eyes, and huge yarn *cuadras,* blooming like Buddhist *tankas,* fill the cabinets and line the walls.

Several blocks south on Avenida México, **Artesanías Cicuri** (140 Sur, just past Plaza Constituyentes and across from the Hotel Real de Don Juan, tel. 311/212-3714 or 311/212-1466, 9 A.M.–8 P.M. Mon.–Sat.) names itself after the renowned *cicuri,* the "eye of God" of the Huichol. Its collection is both extensive and particularly fine, especially the beaded masks.

ACCOMMODATIONS
Under $50

Starting in the north, near the Plaza Principal, **Hotel Cibrián** (Amado Nervo 163 Pte., tel. 311/212-8698, fax 311/216-1461, $23 s, $28 d, $32 t; credit cards not accepted), a block and a half behind the Presidencia Municipal, offers 46 clean, no-frills rooms with bath, ceiling fans, telephones, parking, and local restaurant. The Cibrián's small drawback is the noise that might filter into your room through louvered windows facing the tile (and therefore sound-reflective) hallways. Nevertheless, for the price, it's a Tepic best buy.

On Avenida México, half a block south of the cathedral, the **Hotel Sierra de Álica** (AH-lee-kah, Av. México 180 Nte., tel. 311/212-0325, h_sierradealica@hotmail.com, $40 s, $67 d) remains a longtime favorite of Tepic business travelers. Polished wood paneling and a very good restaurant downstairs and plain but comfortable rooms upstairs reflect the Sierra de Álica's solid unpretentiousness. The 60 rooms all have air-conditioning, satellite TV, phones, and parking; credit cards are accepted.

Several blocks north, on Mina, west of Plaza Constituyentes, half a block from the Avenida México plaza corner, **Hotel Altamirano** (Mina 19 Pte., tel. 311/212-7131, $30 s or d in one bed, $45 d in two beds) offers 31 clean but basic bare-bulb rooms with bath at budget rates.

$50-100

Right on the Plaza Principal stands the five-story tower of Tepic's **Hotel Fray Junípero Serra** (Lerdo 23 Pte., tel. 311/212-2525, fax 311/212-0251, www.frayjunipero.com.mx, $90 s $100 d). The hotel offers spacious, tastefully furnished view rooms with deluxe amenities, efficient service, convenient parking, and a cool and tranquil plaza-front restaurant. The 100 rooms have air-conditioning, satellite TV, and phones; no pool or parking, limited wheelchair access; credit cards are accepted.

Hotel Real de Don Juan (Av. México 105 Sur, tel. 311/216-1880 or 311/216-1828, realdedonjuan@hotmail.com, $115 s or d, $185 suite) on Plaza Constituyentes appears to be succeeding in its efforts to become Tepic's class-act hotel. A plush, tranquil lobby and adjoining restaurant/bar matches the luxury of the king-size beds, thick carpets, marble baths, and soft pastels of the rooms. There's a posh sky-bar on the rooftop along with a hot tub. The 48 rooms have air-conditioning, TV, parking, wireless Internet and limited wheelchair access; credit cards are accepted.

If you prefer to stay out of the busy downtown, you have at least two good options. On the north end, three miles from the city center, try the graceful 50-room **Hotel Bugam Villas** (Insurgentes and Libramiento Pte., tel. 311/215-4600, fax 311/215-4601, bugamvillashotel@hotmail.com or bugamvillas@prodigy.net.mx, $80 s or 85 d). From the lobby, the grounds extend past lovely spreading *higuera* (native wild fig) trees to the two-story stucco and red-tile-roofed units. Inside, the rooms are clean with high ceilings, huge beds, marble shower baths, air-conditioning, TV, and phone. The elegant, cool, and serene restaurant leads outside to an airy dining veranda that overlooks a manicured shady garden. The food is appealing, professionally presented (but slowly served), and moderately priced. The only blot on this near-perfect picture is the noise—which choice of room can moderate considerably—from the trucks on the expressway nearby. Hotel parking available; credit cards are accepted.

On the opposite, east, side of town, another good choice is the recently remodeled motel-style **Hotel Las Palomas** (Av. Insurgentes 2100 Ote., tel. 311/214-0948, toll-free Mex. tel. 01-800/713-8500, tel./fax 311/214-0239, www.laspalomashotel.com.mx, $70 d up to $128 suite) about two miles southeast of the city center. The two stories of double rooms and suites surround a colonial-chic pool and parking patio. The reception opens into an airy solarium restaurant, especially inviting for breakfast. The 67 clean and comfortable Spanish-style tile-floored rooms have air-conditioning, satellite TV, and phones; credit cards are accepted.

Over $100

For a luxuriously rustic lakeside option, in the mountains an hour's drive south of Tepic, consider the ◖ **Santa María Resort** on the lush, semitropical Laguna Santa María shoreline (reserve in Tepic at Roble 210, Colonia San Juan, tel./fax 311/214-6834, toll-free Mex. tel. 01-800/786-2742, or directly at the hotel, tel. 311/213-2654, www.santamariaresort. com). Here you can experience complete relaxation on the sylvan north side of the lake, in a simply lovely chalet-style low-rise hotel that blends gracefully into its gorgeously natural semitropical woodland park, shaded by a spreading green grove of palm, pochotle, and jacaranda trees. You could while away a day or a week here, hiking in the surrounding hillside forest, swimming, kayaking or fishing on the lake, and savoring evening sunset dinners in the lakeview restaurant.

The 20 accommodations are all lovingly designed in natural wood and stone, rising to airy beamed ceilings, and opening to private lakeview patios. Select from either luxuriously spacious room suites in the hotel section ($140 d Fri.–Sun., $120 Mon.–Thurs.) to even more roomy one- and two-bedroom housekeeping cabins, sleeping four and six, respectively ($300 and $380 Fri.–Sun., $220 and $270 Mon.–Thurs.), all with ceiling fans, air-conditioning, and large bathrooms. Rates customarily rise by about 20 percent during Christmas–New

Year's, Easter, and July–August holidays. (See directions for getting there at the end of the next section.)

Trailer Parks and Campgrounds

Although Tepic has lost its former trailer parks to development, RV and tent camping and comfortable rooms and bungalows are available at the **(** **Koala Bungalows and Trailer Park** (Tepic cell tel. 044-311/264-3698, long distance tel. 311/264-3698, P.O. Box 14, Santa María del Oro, Nayarit 63830, www.geocities. com/cfrenchkoala) at the gorgeously rural, semi-tropical Laguna Santa María, about 45 minutes southeast of Tepic. Owner Chris French maintains a tranquil, palm-studded lakeside park, with bungalow-style rooms, houses, RV and tent sites, a snack bar, kiddie pool, and rowboat and kayak rentals. Chris's accommodations vary; they include five simply decorated but comfortable double garden rooms with bath ($38) for up to four; four kitchenette apartment-bungalows ($48) for up to four; and a small two-bedroom house with kitchen ($67) for four and a larger house with kitchen ($76) for up to seven. About 12 well-maintained shady RV sites rent for $18 daily, $75 weekly, with all hook-ups, toilets, and showers. Add $2 per day for air-conditioning power. Campsites go for about $8 per adult, $3 per child, per night. Weekends at Koala Bungalows tend to bustle with local families; weekdays, when the few guests are middle-class European, North American, and Mexican couples, are more tranquil.

Get to Laguna Santa María by bus or by driving, either along *libre* (nontoll) Highway 15 or the new toll Highway 15D *cuota autopista* to Guadalajara, which begins at Tepic's far southeast suburb. From *libre* Highway 15, about 16 miles (26 km) southeast of Tepic, between roadside kilometer markers 194 and 195, follow the signed turnoff left (north) toward Santa María del Oro town. Keep on five more miles (8 km) to the town (pop. 3,000). Continue another five miles (8 km), winding downhill to the lake. For a breathtaking lake view, stop at the roadside viewpoint about a mile past the town. At the lakeshore intersection,

either head left a few hundred yards to Koala Bungalows and Trailer Park; or, for the Santa María Resort, turn right and continue about three miles (5 km) to the signed driveway on the lake's north shore. From the 15D *autopista* follow the signed Santa María del Oro exit. Proceed to the town and continue, winding downhill to the lake, as described above.

By bus, Laguna Santa María is accessible starting from the second-class bus terminal in downtown Tepic (from the cathedral, walk four blocks north along Avenida México; at Victoria, turn east a few steps to no. 9, at the station driveway). The relevant ticket booth (*taquilla*) of Transportes Noroeste de Nayarit (tel. 311/212-2325) is inside at the back. Buses leave for Santa María del Oro town several times daily. At Santa María del Oro, catch a taxi or *colectivo* van or truck (about $1) to the lakeshore downhill, where a left turn gets you to Koala Bungalows within a five-minute walk, and a right turn leads to the Santa María Resort on the north side of the lake within another three miles.

You can also ride a long-distance second-class Guadalajara-bound bus from the Central Camionera (Central Bus Station, on Insurgentes, southeast of the Tepic town center) to Santa María del Oro town, where you can catch a taxi, local bus, or *colectivo* the remaining five miles downhill to the lake.

FOOD

Traffic noise and exhaust smoke sometimes sully the atmosphere in downtown restaurants. The **(** **Hotel Fray Junípero Serra** restaurant (Lerdo 23 Pte., tel. 311/212-2525, 7 A.M.–10 P.M. daily) does not suffer such a drawback, however, in air-conditioned serenity behind its plate-glass plaza-front windows. Choose from a very recognizable menu of soups, salads, and sandwiches ($3–6), and pasta, meat, and fish entrées ($5–10); credit cards are accepted.

A much humbler but colorful and relatively quiet lunch or supper spot is the downtown favorite **Lonchería Flamingos** (on Puebla Nte., tel. 311/212-1560, 10 A.M.–10:30 P.M. daily except Wed.), half a block north behind the Presidencia Municipal, where a cadre of spirited female chefs put out a continuous supply of steaming *tortas,* tostadas, tacos, *hamburguesas* ($3–5), and *chocomiles* ($1–2). The *tortas* ($1–2), although tasty, are small. Best try the tostadas ($2–3), which are served on a huge, yummy, crunchy corn tortilla.

Discover a hidden gem in the homey but refined and *tranquilo* 🄲 **Restaurant La Sierra** (tel. 323/212-0322, 7:30 A.M.–9 P.M. daily) tucked to one side, downstairs at the Hotel Sierra de Álica. Although the hard-working family owners start the day off with a number of good breakfasts, with all the Mexican trimmings ($2–5), their hearty four-course *comida corrida* set lunch (soup, choice of entrée, dessert, and natural fruit *agua,* $5) served 1:30–6 P.M. is the day's main event.

Another fancier but nevertheless popular downtown restaurant choice is the **Restaurant Altamirano** (Av. México 109 Sur, 8 A.M.–8 P.M. Mon.–Sat., 8 A.M.–4 P.M. Sun.) in the big Hotel Real de Don Juan at the southeast corner of Plaza Constituyentes. Here, in a clean rustic-chic atmosphere, businesspeople lunch in the daytime, and middle- and upper-class Tepic families stop for snacks after the movies. The appetizing menu includes a host of Mexican entrées plus a number of international favorites, including spaghetti ($6), hamburgers, omelettes, and pancakes ($3–6).

About a mile south of downtown, across Insurgentes from Parque La Loma, a loyal cadre of middle- and upper-class patrons keep the coffee shop–style **Restaurant Terraza** (tel. 311/213-2180, 7 A.M.–11 P.M. daily, $3–6) bustling morning till night. A major attraction, besides the food, is the racks of books and magazines that patrons enjoy reading, along with the good omelettes, spaghetti, and sandwiches.

Tepic people enjoy a number of good suburban restaurants. On the north side of town, one of the best is the refined **Restaurant Higuera** (entrées $5–10) at the Hotel Bugam Villas. In the southeast suburb, **Chic's** (tel. 311/214-2810, 7 A.M.–10:30 P.M. daily, $4–8), a Mexican version of Denny's on Avenida Insurgentes by the big Plaza Ley shopping center about 1.5 miles from downtown, offers a bit of everything for the travel-weary: tasty American-style specialties, air-conditioned ambience, and a miniplayground for kids around back.

If Chic's is not to your liking, go into Plaza Ley nearby for about half a dozen other options such as pizzerias, *jugerías, taquerías,* and *loncherías.*

For a deluxe treat, go to 🄲 **Restaurant Roberto's Internacional** (Paseo de La Loma 472, at the corner of Av. Insurgentes, west side of La Loma park, tel. 311/213-2085, 1–11 P.M. daily except Sun., $8–20). Here, attentive waiters, subdued 1960s-style decor, crisp service, and good international specialties set a luxurious but relaxing tone.

INFORMATION AND SERVICES
Tourist Information Offices

Tepic's **municipal tourist information office** (tel. 311/212-8036, 9 A.M.–8 P.M. daily) is at the Plaza Principal's northwest corner, just north of the Presidencia Municipal, at the corner of Amado Nervo and Puebla. It dispenses information and a tableful of excellent brochures, many in English.

Nayarit State Tourism offices (tel. 311/214-8074, 311/214-8075, or 311/214-8076, toll-free Mex. tel. 01-800/523-0160, www.visitnayarit.com, 8 A.M.–8 P.M. daily) are in the Convento de la Cruz at Avenida México and Calzado Ejército, about a mile south of the cathedral. Stop by the information booth, which stocks excellent brochures.

Publications

English-language books and magazines are scarce in Tepic. **Newsstands** beneath the plaza portals just west of the Hotel Fray Junípero Serra might have the *Miami Herald* in the afternoon. The **Restaurant Terraza** on Insurgentes, across from Parque La Loma, between Querétaro and Oaxaca (tel. 311/213-2180, 7 A.M.–11 P.M. daily) also may have the *Miami Herald* (call first) and a couple of dozen popular American magazines, such as *Time, Newsweek,* and *National Geographic.*

Money

For best money exchange rates, go to a bank (all with ATMs), such as the main **Banamex** branch on Avendia México at Zapata (9 A.M.–4 P.M. Mon.–Fri., 10 A.M.–2 P.M. Sat.). If the lines at Banamex are too long, go to **Bancomer** (tel. 311/212-0260, 9 A.M.–4 P.M. Mon.–Fri., 10 A.M.–2 P.M. Sat.) across the street, or long-hours **HSBC** bank on the main square next to the Presidencia Municipal (Mérida 184 Nte., tel. 311/212-4238 or 311/212-5130, open for U.S. dollar money exchange 8:30 A.M.–7 P.M. Mon.–Sat.). After-hours, use a bank ATM.

Communications

Tepic's *correo* is downtown about two blocks west and three blocks south of the Plaza Principal (Durango Nte. 27, corner of Morelos Pte., tel. 311/212-0130, 8 A.M.–5:30 P.M. Mon.–Fri., 8:30 A.M.–noon Sat.).

Telecomunicaciones (Av. México, corner of Morelos, tel. 311/212-9655, 8 A.M.–7 P.M. Mon.–Fri., 8 A.M.–4 P.M. Sat., 9 A.M.–1 P.M. Sun.), which provides telegraph, telephone, and public fax, has both a downtown branch and a Central de Autobuses branch (tel. 311/213-2327, 8 A.M.–1 P.M. Mon.–Fri.).

Health and Emergencies

If you need a doctor, contact the **Sanatorio Guadalupe** (Juan Escuita 68 Nte., tel. 311/212-9401 or 311/212-2713), seven blocks west of the Plaza Principal. It has a 24-hour emergency room and a group of specialists on call. A fire-department paramedic squad is also available by calling 311/213-1809.

For police call the emergency number 066; for fire emergencies, call the *bomberos* (firefighters) at 311/213-1607.

GETTING THERE
By Car or RV

Main highways connect Tepic with Puerto Vallarta in the south, San Blas in the west, Guadalajara in the east, and Mazatlán in the north.

Two-lane Highway 200 from Puerto Vallarta is in good-to-fair condition for its 104-mile

(167-km) length. Curves, traffic, and the 3,000-foot Tepic grade, however, usually slow the northbound trip to about three hours, a bit less southbound.

A pair of routes (both about 43 miles/70 km) connect Tepic with San Blas. The more scenic of the two takes about an hour and a half, heading south from San Blas along the Bay of Matanchén to Santa Cruz village, then climbing 3,000 feet west to Tepic via Nayarit Highway 76. The quicker (one-hour) route leads east from San Blas first along National Highway 74, climbing through the tropical forest to Highway 15D, where four lanes guide traffic rapidly to Tepic.

To and from Mazatlán, traffic, towns, and rough spots slow progress along the 182-mile (293-km) two-lane stretch of National Highway 15. Expect four or five hours of driving time under good conditions.

The same is true of the winding 141-mile (227-km) continuation of Highway 15 eastward over the Sierra Madre Occidental to Guadalajara. Fortunately, the *cuota autopista* (toll superhighway 15D) that begins at Tepic's southeastern edge eliminates two hours of driving time, in exchange for about $30 in auto tolls, $60 for motorhomes. Allow about three hours by *autopista* and at least five hours without.

By Bus

The shiny, modern **Central Camionera** on Insurgentes Sur about a mile southeast of downtown has many services, including a tourist information office, left-luggage lockers, a cafeteria, a post office, long-distance telephone, and public fax. Booths *(taquillas)* offering higher-class bus service are generally on the station's left (east) side; the lower class is on the right (west) side as you enter.

Transportes Pacífico (tel. 311/213-2313) has many first- and second-class local departures, connecting south with Puerto Vallarta, east with Guadalajara and Mexico City, and north with Mazatlán and the U.S. border at Tijuana and Nogales.

Estrella Blanca (tel. 311/213-2315),

operating through its subsidiaries, provides many second-class, first-class, and super-first-class direct connections north, east, and south. First-class Elite departures connect north with the U.S. border (Nogales and Tijuana) via Mazatlán, and south with Acapulco via Puerto Vallarta, Barra de Navidad, Manzanillo, and Zihuatanejo. First-class Transportes Norte departures connect, through Guadalajara, north with Saltillo and Monterrey. Super-first-class Futura connects, through Guadalajara, with Mexico City. First-class Transportes Chihuahuenses connects north with the U.S. border (Ciudad Juárez) via Aguascalientes, Zacatecas, and Torreón. Second-class Transportes Norte de Sonora departures connect north, through Mazatlán and Nogales, Mexicali, and Tijuana, at the U.S. border.

Transportes Norte de Sonora (tel. 311/213-2315) sells tickets for hourly daytime second-class connections with San Blas and with Santiago Ixcuintla, where you can continue by local bus to the Mexcaltitán embarcadero.

Besides providing many first-class connectionswith Guadalajara, independent **Ómnibus de Mexico** (tel. 311/213-1323) provides a few departures that connect, via Guadalajara, north with Fresnillo, Torreón, and the U.S. border at Ciudad Juárez, and northeast with Aguascalientes, Zacatecas, Saltillo, Monterrey, and the U.S. border at Matamoros.

THE NAVARIT COASAT

THE JALISCO COAST

Those fortunate enough to travel the country between Puerto Vallarta and Barra de Navidad will fall in love with the area. Highway 200 wends its way through dense tropical landscape, thick with the vines from Strangler Figs and punctuated with bursts of color from flowering vines. The richness of the jungle gives way to lovely panoramic vistas of jutting volcanic hills, vast fields of pale blue agave and orchards of mangoes and coconut palms. Rolling hills of wildflowers attract legions of butterflies and brightly colored birds. Miles of golden untouched beaches line the coast with nary a condominium or timeshare salesman in sight. There are so many opportunities for exploring drowsy beach towns, walking miles of empty beaches and for photography that it's a wonder anyone ever makes it to Barra de Navidad at all.

Cabo Corrientes, Mexico's great western cape, defines the Jalisco Coast. Beginning at Puerto Vallarta, the Bay of Banderas's shoreline juts 40 miles (64 km) southwest into the Pacific, forming Cabo Corrientes. Like a giant's great protecting chin, Cabo Corrientes regularly deflects Pacific storms past Puerto Vallarta.

South of the Cape, the coastline curves gently southeast, indented by a trio of broad beach- and islet-studded bays—Chamela, Tenacatita, and Navidad—all havens for lovers of sun, sand, and surf. Consequently, for most visitors, the Jalisco Coast's major attractions are its magnificent seclusion and outdoor beach and ocean pleasures. Topping the list are abundant fishing (freshwater, deep ocean, and surf), beachcombing, wildlife-viewing, off-

HIGHLIGHTS

◖ **Tehualmixtle:** Off-highway adventurers must go to this lovely fishing hamlet in the pristine Cabo Corrientes hinterland. Snorkle, scuba dive, visit a natural hot spring, and beachcomb the golden Playa Mayto. Overnight at Tehualmixtle by tent, RV, or Playa Mayto hotels (page 215).

◖ **El Careyes Beach Resort:** At least stop for lunch or early dinner at this petite but plush resort, splendidly isolated on a precious little bay. Splurge for an overnight and enjoy snorkeling, scuba diving, swimming, and, in season, the sight of baby turtles returning to the sea (page 224).

◖ **Playa Careyes:** Budget travelers can enjoy a beach as lovely as that of El Careyes Beach Resort at this neighboring strand on a gorgeous half-moon bay. Good for at least an afternoon or camping or RVing overnight. Beach *palapas* supply food, and local fisherfolk can take you fishing. Waves, sometimes powerful, are surfable for the experienced (page 225).

◖ **Playa el Tecuán:** Public access to this de facto wild kingdom, once ruled over by the now-abandoned Hotel El Tecuán, continues. Most outdoor diversions are possible, including advanced surfing, kayaking on the mangrove lagoon, surf-fishing, and self-contained RV and tent camping (page 226).

◖ **Playa Tenacatita:** A village of *palapa* restaurants and a few modest beachfront hotels has gradually added amenities to this splendidbeach-lovers' paradise. If you're planning to park your self-contained RV, arrive before December 15, when nearly all beachfront space is customarily taken until April (page 227).

◖ **Playa Boca de Iguanas:** Here, a comfortable small hotel and a pair of palm-shaded trailer and tenting parks sit on a long, lovely

LOOK FOR ◖ TO FIND RECOMMENDED SIGHTS, ACTIVITIES, DINING, AND LODGING.

level beach. Come for an afternoon or a relaxing week of tropical diversions, from surf-fishing and beachcombing to bird- and crocodile-watching and hammock snoozing (page 230).

◖ **Boat Trip to Colimilla:** From Barra de Navidad, ride a boat across the mangrove-bordered expanse of Laguna de Navidad to the coastal village of Colimilla. Enjoy a cocktail before you dine on fresh seafood at one of the delightful thatched-roof lagoonfront restaurants in Colimilla (page 240).

THE JALISCO COAST

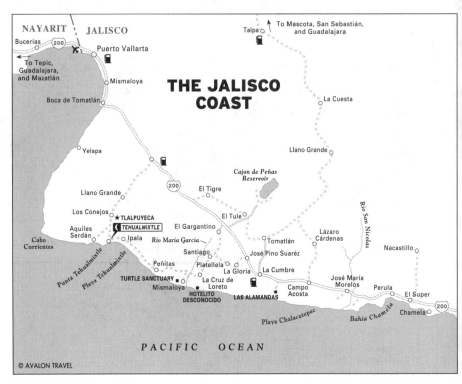

NAYARIT   JALISCO

Bucerías

To Tepic,
Guadalajara,
and Mazatlán

Puerto Vallarta

Mismaloya

Boca de Tomatlán

THE JALISCO COAST

Talpa

To Mascota, San Sebastián,
and Guadalajara

La Cuesta

Yelapa

Llano Grande

*Cajon de Peñas
Reservoir*

El Tigre

Llano Grande

Los Conejos

★ TLALPUYECA

◖ TEHUALMIXTLE

Aquiles
Serdán

Cabo
Corrientes

Ipala

Río María Garcia

El Gargantino

El Tule

Río San Nicolás

Lázaro
Cárdenas

Nacastillo

Santiago

Tomatlán

José Pino Suarez

Punta Tehualmixtle

Playa Tehualmixtle

Peñitas

Platellela

La Gloria

La Cumbre

TURTLE SANCTUARY

Mismaloya

La Cruz de
Loreto

HOTELITO
DESCONOCIDO

LAS ALAMANDAS

Campo
Acosta

José María
Morelos

Perula

El Super

Playa Chalacatepec

Bahía Chamela

Chamela

PACIFIC   OCEAN

© AVALON TRAVEL

road adventuring, and scuba diving, snorkeling, and surfing.

For those who manage to resist the siren song of side trips and exploration, the rewards are twin country beach resorts of Melaque and Barra de Navidad at the Jalisco Coast's southern border. Both are lovely seaside towns with affordable lodging and dining and a friendly atmosphere. Excepting Melaque and Barra de Navidad, the Jalisco coast is nearly all pioneer country, with only a few villages.

Fortunately, however, everyone who travels south of Puerto Vallarta doesn't have to be a Daniel Boone. The coastal strip within a few miles of the highway has acquired some amenities—stores, trailer parks, campgrounds, hotels, and a scattering of small resorts, some humble and some posh—all enough to become well known to Puerto Vallarta people as the Costalegre (Happy Coast).

PLANNING YOUR TIME

If you have deep pockets or a desire to splurge, there are some incredible posh resorts along the road to Barra. Moving from Puerto Vallarta south along the luxurious path less traveled, you might first stay at least an overnight in one of the Italian designer–chic cabanas of the **Hotelito Desconocido** on its pristine seaside lagoon. Continue on to **Las Alamandas,** surfing resort for movie stars, moguls, and maharajas. Next, at least stop for lunch or dinner at regally elegant **El Careyes Beach Resort,** tucked on a patch of sand on its own exceptionally lovely wildlife-rich little bay. Finally, before Barra de Navidad, lodge a night or two in absolute luxury amid the meandering golf course and luxuriously isolated beaches of **El Tamarindo** jungle country club and vacation-home paradise for the rich and famous.

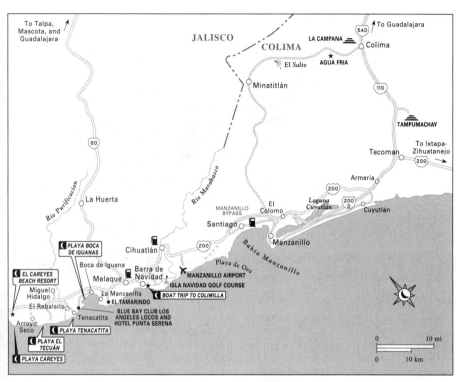

On the other hand, for travelers seeking the moderately priced, home-grown delights of South Seas Mexico, the Costalegre offers what local people have known about for years: plenty of sun, fresh seafood, clear blue water, and sandy beaches, some of which stretch for miles, while others are tucked away in little rocky coves like pearls in an oyster.

First out of Puerto Vallarta, follow the detour into rustically pristine Cabo Corrientes country, to bucolic **Tehualmixtle** fishing hamlet, and enjoy an idyll sharpened by the local memory of galleons, shipwrecks, and the turn-of-the-20th-century cocaine trade. Farther south, beachcomb and surf-fish the curving, sandy reach of islet-dotted **Chamela Bay** by day while lodging at a friendly local trailer park or homey hotel by night. Continue and spend some time in a small beachfront hotel or your own camp at the scuba, snorkel, and fisherfolks' haven of **Tenacatita.** Continue for more of the same at gorgeous Boca de Iguana mangrove jungle lagoon and beach, and then hop a few miles farther south to petite La Manzanilla beach-resort town, where you can enjoy days dining on super-fresh seafood and cozy nights being lulled to sleep by the swish of the friendly La Manzanilla waves.

Whatever your style of travel, the prizes at the end of the Road to Barra de Navidad are the manifold surprises of the small beach-resort towns of **Barra de Navidad** and **San Patricio-Melaque.** Here, multiple pleasures beckon: days strolling the beach, gazing out at the languid wave-washed shoreline from beneath a shady *palapa,* wildlife-watching in the broad mirror-smooth Laguna de Navidad, fishing for wild tuna and dorado, and enjoying fine fare, from steaming streetfront tacos to nouvelle gourmet restaurant cuisine.

JEJENES: DON'T LET NO-SEE-UMS RUIN YOUR VACATION

Jejenes are the vicious, invisible biting gnats that cause many tourists a great many sleepless and itchy nights. They are the unseen predators that haunt many of Mexico's prime beach locations, feasting on unsuspecting visitors (you won't find locals out and about during prime *jejene* time). The most notorious spots for *jejenes* in Nayarit and Jalisco are San Blas and Tenacatita.

Summer or winter, it doesn't matter to these pests. They are most active during the dawn and dusk hours and no sane person should be out at those hours without being slathered in deet-laden mosquito repellent. But even deet can't fully protect you. According to Lorena Havens and an experiment by a very brave test subject on the **People's Guide to Mexico** website (www.peoplesguide.com), adding about 20 drops of pennyroyal oil herbal extract to your repellent (organic or commercial containing deet) will keep the bugs at bay.

The Road to Barra de Navidad

HEADING OUT

If you're driving, note your odometer mileage (or reset your tripometer to 0) as you pass the Pemex gas station at Km 214 on Highway 200 at the south edge of Puerto Vallarta. In the open southern country, mileage and roadside kilometer markers are a useful way to remember where your little paradise is hidden. Also be sure to have a full tank of gas before you leave Puerto Vallarta. Gas stations are few and far between although in an emergency, you can sometimes purchase gas in the small towns along the highway.

If you're not driving, simply hop on one of the many southbound Autocamiones del Pacífico or Transportes Cihuatlán second-class buses just before they pass at the south-end gas station. Let the driver know a few minutes beforehand where along the road you want to get off.

CHINO'S PARADISE

The last outpost on the Puerto Vallarta tour-bus circuit is Chino's Paradise, 13 miles (22 km, at Km 192, tel. 322/223-6005 or 322/223-6006, 9 A.M.–7 P.M. daily) from the southern edge of Puerto Vallarta in the lush jungle country. Here, the clear, cool Río Tuito cascades over a collection of smooth, friendly granite boulders. Chino's restaurant is a big multilevel *palapa* that overlooks the entire beautiful scene—deep green pools for swimming, flat warm rocks for sunning, and gurgling gentle waterfalls for splashing. Although a few homesteads dot the streamside nearby, the original Chino's still dominates, although its reputation rests mainly on the beauty of the setting rather than the quality of its menu.

The forest-perfumed breezes, the gurgling, crystal stream, and the friendly, relaxed ambience are perfect for shedding the cares of the world. Although as yet there are no formal lodgings, a number of potential camping spots border the river, both up- and downstream. Stores at either the nearby upstream Las Juntas y Los Veranos village or Boca de Tomatlán, three miles downhill, can provide supplies.

Adventurers can hire local guides (ask at Chino's restaurant) for horseback rides along the river and overnight treks into the green, jungly **Sierra Lagunillas** that rises on both sides of the river. If you're quiet and aware, you may be rewarded with views of chattering parrots, dozing iguanas, feisty javelinas (wild

© BRUCE WHIPPERMAN

Chino's Paradise

pigs), clownish *tejones* (coatimundis), and wary *gatos de montaña* (wildcats).

Alternatively, try a jungle canopy tour at **Canopy Tour Los Veranos** (tel. 322/223-6060, www.canopytours-vallarta.com, $79). For the fearless and fit only, these trips allow you to ride at treetop heights like a bird through the tropical forest. Get there by car or bus, via Highway 200 south, about a mile uphill past Chino's Paradise. At Las Juntas y Los Veranos village, turn right onto the dirt side road. Continue about a mile to Canopy Tour Los Veranos at the end of the road.

CABO CORRIENTES COUNTRY
El Tuito

The town of El Tuito, at Km 170 (27 mi/44 km from Puerto Vallarta), looks from the highway like nothing more than a bus stop (although it has finally acquired a gas station which as of this date is still not open for business). Most visitors pass by without even giving a second glance. This is a pity, because El Tuito (pop. 3,500) is a friendly little colonial-era town that spreads along a long main street

to a pretty town square about a mile from the highway.

El Tuito enjoys at least two claims to fame: Besides being the mescal capital of western Jalisco, it's the jumping-off spot for the seldom-visited coastal hinterland of Cabo Corrientes, the southernmost lip of the Bay of Banderas. This is pioneer country, a land of wild beaches and sylvan forests, unpenetrated by paved roads. Wild creatures still abound: Turtles come ashore to lay their eggs, hawks soar, parrots swarm, and the faraway scream of the jaguar can yet be heard in the night.

The rush for the **raicilla,** as local connoisseurs call El Tuito mescal, begins on Saturday when men crowd into town and begin upending bottles around noon, without even bothering to sit down. For a given individual, this cannot last too long, so the fallen are continually replaced by fresh arrivals all weekend.

Although El Tuito is famous for the *raicilla*, it is not the source. *Raicilla* comes from the sweet sap of the maguey plants, a close relative of the cactuslike century plant, which blooms once and then dies. The *ejido* (cooperative

THE JALISCO COAST

farm) of Cicatán (see-kah-TAHN), eight miles out along the dirt road as you head to the coast west of town, cultivates the maguey. You won't find *raicilla* outside of Jalisco for it is made exclusively in this state.

Along the Road to Aquiles Serdán

You can get to the coast with or without your own wheels. Road crews have begun the process of paving the 42 kilometers of road that lies between El Tuito and the remote beaches of Mayto and Tehualmixtle. The initial stretch of road is well paved but soon gives way to rubble strewn dirt roads that can wreck havoc on small cars with poor clearance. If you're driving, it should be a strong, high-clearance vehicle (pickup, jeep, very maneuverable RV, or VW van) filled with gas; if you're not driving, trucks and VW taxi-vans *(combis* or *colectivos)* make daily trips from the El Tuito town plaza (at this writing around 2 P.M.; returning from Tehualmixtle at 9 A.M.). Their destinations include the coastal hamlet of Aquiles Serdán, the storied fishing cove of Tehualmixtle, and the farming village of Ipala beside the wide Bahía de Tehualmixtle. Fare runs several dollars per person; inquire at the west end of the El Tuito central plaza.

Getting there along the bumpy, rutted, sometimes steep 26-mile (42-km) dirt track is half the fun of Aquiles Serdán (pop. 200). If you're driving, mark your odometer where the road takes off from the southwest corner of the El Tuito town plaza. About eight miles (13 km) from the plaza, you'll pass through the lands of the Cicatán mescal cooperative, marked only by a crumbling thatch house on the right. On the left, you'll soon glimpse a field of maguey in the distance. A few dozen families (who live in the hills past the far side of the field) quietly go about their business of tending their maguey plants and extracting, fermenting, and distilling the precious sap into their renowned *raicilla.*

The road dips up and down the rest of the way, over sylvan hillsides dotted with oak *(robles),* through intimate stream valleys perfect for parking an RV or setting up a tent, and past the

hardscrabble rancho-hamlets of Llano Grande (Broad Plain, 14 mi/22 km), with stores, *comedores* (places to eat), a *centro de salud,* and **Los Conejos** (The Rabbits, 19 mi/30 km). At Los Conejos, a signed road forks left five miles (8 km) to **Tlalpuyeque** hot spring and sacred site. Obey local custom and refrain from nude bathing.

You can't get lost, because there's only one route until a few miles past Los Conejos, where a fork (23 mi/37 km) marks your approach to Aquiles Serdán. The left branch continues south a few miles to Mayto and Tehualmixtle. A mile and a half to the north along the right branch you'll arrive at the Río Tecolotlán. Aquiles Serdán stands on the far bank, across 100 yards of watery sand. Fortunately the riverbed road is concrete-bottomed, and, if it's in good repair, you can drive right across the streambed any time other than after a storm. If you can't drive across, roll up your pants legs and walk across, like most of the local folks do.

Aquiles Serdán

The Aquiles Serdán villagers see so few outsiders that you'll become their attraction of the week. Wave and say *hola,* buy a *refresco,* and stroll around town. After a while, the kids will stop crowding around and the adults will stop staring when they've found out that you, too, are human. By that time, someone may even have invited you into his or her tree branch-walled, clean, dirt-floored house for some hot fish-fillet tacos, fresh tomatoes, and beans. Accept, of course.

Aquiles Serdán basks above the lily-edged river lagoon, which during the June–October rainy season usually breaks through the beach-sandbar and drains directly into the surf half a mile below the town. During the dry season, the ocean plugs the hole in the sandbar, and the lagoon wanders lazily up the coast for a few miles. In any case, the white-sand beach is easily accessible only by boat, which you can borrow or hire at the village.

If you do, you'll have miles of untouched white sand and surf all to yourself for days of camping, beachcombing, shell collecting, surf fishing, wildlife-watching, and, if the waves

© ROBIN NOELLE

Playa Mayto

permit, swimming, surfing, boogie boarding, and snorkeling. The town's two stores can provide your necessities.

Back at the fork (23 mi/37 km from the highway), continue along the left branch about two miles through Mayto (pop. 100), which has two stores and a friendly **auto mechanic.** His name is Arias Gonzales, and his establishment is marked by a fence hung with dozens of eerie cow skulls.

A right fork just after Mayto leads a quarter mile to **Playa Mayto,** a surf fishing and beachcombers' haven, where you can either park your RV or tent on the beach or stay at the excellent family-friendly beachfront **C Hotel Mayto** (Guadalajara tel. 33/3177-2184, $40 per person, children $10). Amenities include eight simply furnished but clean and comfortable rooms, most with two beds, a big swimming pool, shady palm grove, green lawn, fishing tours, horses to ride, hammocks, and a restaurant. If you aren't interested in spending the night, you can make a lengthy day trip to Mayto beach and enjoy the facilities of the hotel as long as you dine at the restaurant.

The beach seems to stretch endlessly in the distance and it's a wonderful place to lose yourself in your thoughts as you walk the shoreline. You will most likely be completely alone. Although the beach is pristine and remote, the surf can get rough. There is also a sharp drop just off the beach which can make for dangerous undertow conditions so use precaution when swimming.

C Tehualmixtle

Back on the main road, continue about one mile to another fork (at 26 mi/42 km). The right branch goes steeply up and then down a rough track to the right, which soon levels out on the cliff above the idyllic fishing cove of Tehualmixtle. Here, a headland shelters a blue nook, where a few launches float, tethered and protected from the open sea. To one side, swells wash over a submerged wreck, while an ancient moss-stained warehouse crumbles above a rocky little beach. At the end of the road downhill, a pair of beachside *palapas* invites visitors with drinks and fresh-out-of-the-water oysters, lobster, dorado, and red snapper.

THE JALISCO COAST

the beach at Tehualmixtle

Candelario ("Cande"), owner/operator of the right-side *palapa,* is the moving force behind this pocket paradise. After your repast and a couple more bottles of beer for good measure, he might tell you his version of the history of this coast—stories of sunken galleons or of the days when the old warehouse stored cocaine for legal shipment to the United States, when Coca-Cola got its name from the cocaine that was added to produce "the pause that refreshes."

Nowadays, however, Tehualmixtle serves as a resting point for occasional sailors, travelers, fisherfolk, and those who enjoy the rewards of clear-water snorkeling and scuba diving around the sunken shrimp trawler and the rocky shoreline nearby. Several level spots beside the cove invite camping or RV parking. Candelario and his wife and daughters will gladly supply you with your stomach's delight of choice seafood and drinks.

Furthermore, Candelario and his family, led by friendly, outgoing English-speaking daughter Gaby (who heads the local tourism delegation), have built a small **hotel** ($25 s, $30 d, $35 t). They offer four clean, simply furnished rooms with shiny white bathrooms, view windows, and ceiling fans. Additionally, they rent out a comfortable view bungalow ($45/night) sleeping five, that's fine for groups, with a kitchenette, good bathroom, and ceiling fans; discount for one-week stay. For reservations, leave a message with the local radio telephone operator (tel. 200/126-8990, 200/126-8991, or 200/126-8992).

For those who stay a few days, Candelario offers his services as a **guide** for turtle-watching (during summer–fall season), fishing trips, and for equipped snorkelers and scuba divers to investigate nearby sites, especially the submerged wreck right offshore. Farther afield, he can also lead parties inland a few miles, by foot or horseback, to hot spring **Tlalpuyeque,** where, years ago, a French company operated a logging concession.

Southeast of Tehualmixtle

Returning back up the road above the cove, you'll catch a glimpse southward of the azure Bay of Tehualmixtle washing the white-sand ribbon of the Playa de Tehualmixtle. The village of **Ipala,** three miles down the road, is supply headquarters (unleaded gasoline available) for the occasional visitors drawn by the good fishing, surfing, beachcombing, and camping prospects of the Playa de Tehualmixtle. Being on the open ocean, its waves are usually rough, especially in the afternoon. Only experienced swimmers who can judge undertow and surf should think of swimming here.

From Ipala (29 mi/47 km), you can either retrace your path back to the highway at El Tuito, or continue down the coast (where the road gets rougher before it gets better) through the hamlet and beach of **Peñitas** (36 mi/58 km), which has a few stores, beach cabanas for rent, and restaurants. Next you'll pass **Mismaloya** (46 mi/74 km), site of a University of Guadalajara turtle-hatching station. To get there, turn right onto the rough dirt road just before the concrete bridge over the broad Río María Garcia.

From Mismaloya, return to the bridge, ford the river (during low water) three miles farther, and you'll soon be back in the 21st century at **Cruz de Loreto** (49 mi/79 km), equipped with many stores, sidewalks, electric lights, and phones.

After all the backcountry hard traveling, treat yourself to at least one night at luxury ecoresort 【 **Hotelito Desconocido** (tel. 322/281-4010, toll-free Mex. tel. 01-800/013-1313, toll-free U.S. tel. 800/851-1143, www.hotelito.com). The accommodations—deluxe (but rustically candlelit) thatched cabanas on stilts beside an idyllic lagoon—rent from $625 d low season, $825 high for the least expensive, to about $1,025 for the most, with breakfast. Add $90 per person for lunch and dinner. Inquire locally for directions, or follow the signs west to the hotel at the lagoon and beach nearby; reservations are strongly recommended.

If you decide not to stay at Hotelito Desconocido, return to Highway 200 directly from Cruz de Loreto, by heading east 10 miles (via Santiago and El Gargantino) to the highway at the Km 133 marker, just 23 miles (37 km) south of where you started at El Tuito.

CAJÓN DE LAS PEÑAS RESERVOIR

The lush farms of the Cabo Corrientes region owe much of their success to the Cajón de las Peñas dam, whose waters enable farmers to profit from a year-round growing season. An added bonus is the recreation—boating, fishing, swimming, camping, and hiking—the big blue lake behind the dam makes possible.

With a car, the reservoir is easy to reach. Trucks and cars are frequent, so hikers can easily thumb rides. At Highway 200 Km 131, about a mile south of the Cruz de Loreto turn-off, head left (east) at a signed, paved road. After about five miles (8 km) the road turns to gravel. Continue another four miles to a road fork atop a complex of three rock-fill dams, separated by a hill. The left road continues over the smaller two dams to a dead end. The right fork leads to a sign reading Puerto Vallarta Bass Club and a left fork just before the largest dam. Turn left and continue downhill to **La Lobina,** a humble family-run restaurant *palapa* and boat landing. The friendly husband-wife team maintains the little out-post in hopes of serving the trickle of mostly holiday and weekend visitors. Besides their children, who help with chores, their little settlement consists of two parrots, a brood of turkeys, and a flock of chickens that flies into the nearby forest to roost at night. The couple's cooking, based mostly upon freshly caught *lobina* (large-mouth bass), is basic but wholesome. Their parking lot above the lake has room for a number of self-contained RVs, while the forested knoll nearby might serve for tent camping. They offer their boat for lake sightseeing and fishing excursions for about $20 an hour. Otherwise, you could swim, kayak, or launch your own motorboat right from the lakeshore below the restaurant.

Head back, turn left at the uphill fork and continue over the larger dam, counterclockwise around the forested, sloping lakeshore. Within about two miles (3 km) you'll arrive at the boat-cooperative village, where several down-scale *palapa* restaurants and boat landings provide food and recreational services for visitors.

THE JALISCO COAST

© BRUCE WHIPPERMAN

The Cajón de las Peñas Reservoir is fine for bass fishing.

For a fee—ask at one of the restaurants, *"¿Hay una tarifa para acampar?"* ("Is there a fee to camp?")—you can usually set up a tent or park your RV under a nearby lakeside tree.

PLAYA CHALACATEPEC

Playa Chalacatepec (chah-lah-kah-tay-PEK) lazes in the tropical sun just six miles (10 km) from the highway at Km 88. Remarkably few people know of its charms except a handful of local youths, a few fisherfolk, and occasional families who come on Sunday outings, and the resident volunteers of the beachfront Tortuguera Verde Valle (Green Valley Turtle Encampment).

Playa Chalacatepec, with three distinct parts, has something for everyone: on the south side, a wild arrow-straight, miles-long strand with crashing open-ocean breakers; in the middle, a low, wave-tossed rocky point; and on the north, a long, tranquil, curving fine-sand beach. One of the few natural amenities that Playa Chalacatepec lacks is drinking water, however. Bring your own from the town back on the highway.

The north beach, shielded by the point, has gently rolling breakers good for surfing, body-surfing, and safe swimming. Shells seasonally carpet its gradual white slope, and visitors have even left a pair of *palapa* shelters. These seem ready-made for camping by night and barbecuing fish by day with all of the driftwood lying around for the taking.

The point, Punta Chalacatepec, which separates the two beaches, is good for pole fishing on its surf-washed flanks and tidepooling in its rocky crevices.

Folks with RVs can pull off and park either along the approach road just above the beach or along tracks (beware of soft spots) downhill in the tall acacia scrub that borders the sand.

Getting There

Just as you're entering little José María Morelos (pop. 2,000), 100 feet past the Km 88 marker, turn right at the signed dirt road toward the beach at the corner. (Note the telephone booth.) If you're planning to camp, stock up with water and groceries at the stores in the town down the road, south.

The road, although steep in spots, is negotiable by passenger cars in good condition and small-to-medium RVs. Owners of big rigs should do a test run. On foot, the road is an easy two-hour hike—much of which probably won't be necessary because of the many passing farm pickups.

Mark your odometer at the highway. Continue over brushy hills and past fields and pastures, until Mile 5.2 (Km 8.4), where the main road veers right. Instead, continue straight ahead, over the dune, to the beach, at Mile 5.4 (Km 8.7), where the road turns left (south) and parallels the beach. Pass turtle encampment Tortuguera Verde Valle, at Mile 5.9 (Km 9.5). Steer right downhill to Playa Chalacatepec at Mile 6 (Km 9.7). Several choice parking sites are available in the high brush bordering the beach (be careful of soft sand) and you may have the good company of the turtle-saving volunteers (most likely during the July–October turtle season), who would probably appreciate any help you can give them.

LAS ALAMANDAS

After roughing it at Playa Chalacatepec, you can be pampered in the luxurious isolation of 🄲 **Las Alamandas** (Quémaro, Km. 83 Carretera Puerto Vallarta–Barra de Navidad, tel. 322/285-5500, toll-free U.S./Can. tel. 888/882-9616, www.alamandas.com), a deluxe 1,500-acre retreat a few miles down the road.

The small Quémaro village sign at Km 83 gives no hint of the pleasant surprises that Las Alamandas conceals behind its guarded gate. Solitude and elegant simplicity seem to have been the driving concepts in the mind of Isabel Goldsmith when she acquired control of the property in the late 1980s. Although born into wealth (her grandfather was the late tin tycoon Antenor Patiño, who developed Manzanillo's renowned Las Hadas; her father was the late multimillionaire Sir James Goldsmith, who bought the small kingdom her family now owns at Cuitzmala, 25 miles south), she was not idle. Isabel converted her dream of paradise—a small, luxuriously isolated resort on an idyllic beach in Puerto Vallarta's sylvan coastal hinterland—into reality. Now, her guests (28 maximum) enjoy accommodations that vary from luxuriously simple studios to a villa sleeping six. Activities include tennis, horseback riding, bicycling, fishing, kayaking, snorkeling, and lagoon and river excursions.

The hotel's luxurious facilities—dining restaurant and veranda, bars, book and video library, sitting and reading areas, pool patio, gym, pavilions, and much more—are gracefully sprinkled throughout a plumy, grass-carpeted, beachfront palm grove. Powerful waves, good for intermediate and advanced surfing, on the south and north shoals, rise about 100 yards out and break rather quickly at the creamy yellow-sand beach. With about twice as many employees as guests, the hotel's service is personal. Staff are attentive and focused on the goal of complete guest relaxation.

Daily rates range from about $370 low season ($390 high) for garden-view studios, up to about $1,499 low season ($1,656 high) for the Presidential Suite; all with full breakfast. Three meals, prepared to your order, cost about $135 more per day per person. For reservations, contact Las Alamandas directly or book through their agent, Mexico Boutique Hotels (toll-free U.S./Can. tel. 800/728-7098, www.mexicoboutiquehotels.com).

Get there by car, taxi (about $100), bus, or rental car from the Puerto Vallarta airport via Highway 200. At the Km 83 highway marker, 81 miles (130 km) south of Puerto Vallarta, turn right at the signed Quémaro village side road. Continue about three miles west, passing through Quémaro village, to the Alamandas gate. Don't arrive unannounced; unless you're a recognizable celebrity, the guard will not let you through the gate without a reservation in hand or unless you have made an advance appointment. Alternatively, you can arrive by charter airplane, using Las Alamandas's private airstrip. If you don't have a plane, contact a travel agent.

CHAMELA BAY

Most longtime visitors know Jalisco's coast through Barra de Navidad and two big, beautiful beach-lined bays: Tenacatita and Chamela. Tranquil Bahía de Chamela, the most northerly of the two, is broad, blue, dotted with islands, and lined by a strip of fine honey-yellow sand.

Stretching five miles (8 km) south from the sheltering Punta Rivas headland near Perula village, Chamela Bay is open but calm. A chain of intriguingly labeled rocky *islitas,* such as Cocinas (Kitchens), Negrita (Little Black One), and Pajarera (Place of Birds), scatter the strong Pacific swells into gentle billows by the time they roll onto the beaches.

Besides its natural amenities, Chamela Bay has three bungalow-complexes, one mentionable motel, two trailer parks, and an unusual "camping club." The focal point of this low-key resort area is the Km 72 highway corner (88 mi/142 km from Puerto Vallarta, 46 mi/74 km to Barra de Navidad). This spot, which on many maps is incorrectly marked Chamela (actually the village at Km 63), is known simply as **"El Super"** by local people. Though the supermarket and neighboring bank have closed and are filled with the owner's dusty antique car collection, El Super nevertheless lives on in the minds of the local folks.

Beaches and Recreation

Chamela Bay's beaches are variations on one continuous strip of sand, from Playa Rosadas in the south through Playa Chamela in the middle to Playas Fortuna and Perula at the north end.

Curving behind the sheltering headland, **Playa Perula** is the broadest and most tranquil beach of Chamela Bay. It is best for children and a snap for boat launching, swimming, and fishing from the rocks nearby. A dozen *pangas* usually line the water's edge, ready to take visitors on fishing excursions (figure $15 per hour, after bargaining) and snorkeling around the offshore islets. A line of seafood *palapas* provides the food and drinks for the fisherfolk and

mostly Mexican families who know and enjoy this scenic little village/cove.

Playas Fortuna, Chamela, and Rosada: As you head south, the beach gradually changes character. The surf roughens, the slope steepens, and the sand narrows from around 200 feet at Perula to perhaps 100 feet at the south end of the bay. Civilization also thins out. The dusty village of stores, small eateries, vacation homes, and beachfront *palapa* restaurants that line Playa Fortuna gives way to farmland and scattered houses at Playa Chamela. Two miles farther on, grassy dunes above trackless sand line Playa Rosada.

The gradually varying vigor of the waves and the isolation of the beach determine the place where you can indulge your own favorite pastimes. For bodysurfing and boogie boarding, Rosada and Chamela are best; and while sailboarding is usually possible anywhere on Chamela Bay, it will be best beyond the tranquil waves at La Fortuna. For surf fishing, try casting beyond the vigorous, breaking billows of Rosada. And Rosada, being the most isolated, will be the place where you'll most likely find that shell-collection treasure you've been wishing for.

The five-mile curving strand of Chamela Bay is perfect for a morning hike from Rosada Beach. To get there, ride a Transportes Cihuatlán second-class bus to around the Km 65 marker, where a dirt road heads a half-mile to the beach. With the sun comfortably at your back, you can walk all the way to Perula if you want, stopping for refreshments at any one of several *palapas* along the way. The firm sand of Chamela Bay beaches is likewise good for jogging, even for bicycling, provided you don't mind cleaning the sand out of the gears afterwards.

El Super Accommodations

The recently renovated **Paraíso Costalegre** (Km 72, Carretera 200, Barra de Navidad a Puerto Vallarta, tel. 315/333-9778 or 315/333-9777, www.paraisocostalegre.com.mx) is a good choice with new bungalows and villas for rent. There are several options for lodging

SAVING TURTLES

Sea turtles were once common on Puerto Vallarta beaches. Times have changed, however. Now a determined corps of volunteers literally camps out on isolated strands, trying to save the turtles from extinction. This is a tricky business, because their poacher opponents are invariably poor, determined, and often armed. Since turtle tracks lead right to the eggs, the trick is to get there before the poachers. The turtle-savers dig up the eggs and hatch them themselves, or bury them in secret locations where they hope the eggs will hatch unmolested. The reward – the sight of hundreds of new hatchlings returning to the sea – is worth the pain for this new generation of Mexican ecoactivists.

Once featured on a thousand restaurant menus from Puerto Ángel to Mazatlán, turtle meat, soup, and eggs are now illegal commodities. Though not extinct, the Mexican Pacific's three scarcest sea turtle species – green, hawksbill, and leatherback – have dwindled to a tiny fraction of their previous numbers.

The **green turtle** (*Chelonia mydas*), known locally as *tortuga verde* or *caguama*, is more black than green. Its name comes from the light-green tint of its fat. Although officially threatened, the prolific green turtle remains relatively numerous, with about 100,000 nesting females worldwide. Females can return to shore up to eight times during the year, depositing 500 eggs in a single season. When not mating or migrating, the vegetarian green turtles can be spotted most often in lagoons and bays, especially the Bay of Banderas, nipping at seaweed with their beaks. Adults, usually three or four feet (1 or 1.2 m) long and weighing 300-400 pounds (135-180 kg), are easily identified out of water by the four big plates on either side of their shells. Green-turtle meat was once prized as the main ingredient of turtle soup.

The severely endangered **hawksbill** (*Eretmochelys imbricata*), with only about 20,000 nesting females worldwide, has vanished from many Mexican Pacific beaches. Known locally as the *tortuga carey*, it was the source of both meat and the lovely translucent tortoiseshell that has been supplanted largely by plastic. Adult *careys*, among the smaller of sea turtles, run 2-3 feet (0.6-1 m) in length and weigh 100-150 pounds (45-70 kg). Their usually-brown shells are readily identified by shinglelike overlapping scales. During late summer and fall, females come ashore to lay clutches of eggs (around 100) in the sand. *Careys*, although preferring fish, mollusks, and shellfish, will eat most anything, including seaweed. When attacked, *careys* can be plucky fighters, inflicting bites with their eagle-sharp hawksbills. Playa Teopa, under the care of the El Careyes Beach Resort, is one of its few nesting sites on the Mexican Pacific Coast.

You'll be fortunate indeed if you glimpse the rare **leatherback** (*Dermochelys coriacea*), the world's largest turtle. Until recent years even experts knew little about the leatherback, *tortuga de cuero*, but now they estimate that it's severely endangered with only about 35,000 nesting females worldwide. Tales are told of fisherfolk netting seven- or eight-foot (2- or 2.5-m) leatherbacks weighing nearly a ton apiece. If you see even a small one you'll recognize it immediately by its back of smooth, tough skin (instead of a shell), creased with several lengthwise ridges.

Prospects are better for the more abundant (800,000 nesting females), although still endangered, **olive ridley** or *golfina* (*Lepidochelys olivacea*) turtle, which nests at a number of beaches along the Mexican Pacific Coast. With a noticeably narrow head, it's one of the smallest of sea turtles, adults averaging only about 90 pounds (40 kg), and 2 feet (0.6 m) in length. Its name derives from the adult turtle's olive-green shell. Partly due to the persistence of dedicated volunteers, the olive ridley seems to be making a comeback in the Puerto Vallarta region, where there are nesting sites on the Jalisco Coast (at Playa Mismaloya, in Cabo Corrientes country, near Cruz de Loreto) and on the Nayarit Coast at San Francisco (north of Sayulita) and Playa Tortuga (north of Las Varas, on the road to San Blas). The group of volunteers at San Francisco (www.project-tortuga.org) reports more than a tenfold increase (of several hundred) nest sites during the past 20 years.

at Paraíso Costalegre, including cabins on the beach to larger villas that are excellent for families or groups. The small beachfront cabins sleep up to six people and can be had for the price of an average hotel room (in Mexico at least), $47 d low, $58 d high. For larger groups, consider renting Villa Costalegre which sleeps up to 10 people. Although they are simple accommodations, they are clean and spacious. The house rents for $243 low, $305 high.

Still need more space? Rent Villa Sol or Villa Luna, either of which can sleep up to 14 people under the massive palapa roof for $378 low, $472 high. All of the villas have full kitchens. Other amenities besides the beach that guests can enjoy include the swimming pool, restaurant and a phone in the office. There are no televisions or phone to interrupt your seclusion. Unfortunately, camping is no longer allowed.

Right across the lane from Paraíso Costalegre stands the **Bungalows Mayar Chamela** (Km 72, Carretera Puerto Vallarta, tel. 315/333-9711). The 18 spacious kitchenette-bungalows with fans (no a/c) surround an attractive inner garden and a palmy banana-fringed pool and patio. Although the blue meandering pool and palmy grounds are very inviting, the bungalows themselves have suffered from past neglect. Look inside three or four and make sure that everything is in working order before moving in. If so, the bungalows' pool and garden setting and the long, lovely Chamela beach just a block away might be perfect for a week or month of tranquil relaxation. If you're passing through, it might be worthwhile to take a look. Rentals run about $44 d, $78 for four; monthly discounts are available. For reservations (usually not necessary), contact the owner, Gabriel Yañez G. (Obregón 1425 S.L., Guadalajara, Jalisco, tel. 33/3644-0044).

Note: The late summer and fall season is pretty empty on the Chamela Bay beaches. Consequently, food is scarce around Paraíso Costalegre and Bungalows Mayar Chamela. Meals, however, are available at the restaurant at the El Super corner, and a few groceries at small stores along the highway nearby, or in San Mateo village a mile south.

Perula Accommodations

At Km 74, a sign marks a paved road to Playas Fortuna and Perula. About two miles downhill, right on the beach, you can't miss the bright-yellow stucco **Hotel, Bungalows, and Trailer Park Playa Dorada** (Perula, Km 76, Carretera 200 Melaque–Puerto Vallarta, tel. 315/333-9710, fax 315/333-9709, www.playa-dorada.com.mx). More a motel than bungalows, its three tiers of very plain rooms and suites with kitchenettes are nearly empty except on weekends and Mexican holidays.

Playa Dorada's two saving graces, however, are the beach, which curves gracefully to the scenic little fishing nook of Perula, and its inviting palm-shaded pool and patio. The best-situated rooms are on the top floor, overlooking the ocean. The 60 attractively painted rooms sleeping two or three rent for about $53; 15 kitchenette units sleeping four go for about $72, all with air-conditioning and parking. Discounts are customarily available for weekly rentals.

Folks who take one of the dozen trailer spaces in the bare lot across the street are welcome to lounge all day beneath the palms of the pool and patio. Spaces rent for about $18/day, $500/month with all hookups and showers and toilets.

It's easy to miss the low-profile **Hotel Punta Perula** (Perula, Km 76, Carretera 200, Melaque–Puerto Vallarta, tel. 315/333-9782), just one block inland from the Bungalows Playa Dorada. This homey place seems like a scene from Old Mexico (which also means it has no pool, of course), with a rustic white stucco tier of rooms enclosing a spacious green garden and venerable tufted grove. Its 14 clean, gracefully decorated colonial-style fan-equipped rooms go for about $32 d one bed, $45 d or t two beds, except for Christmas and Easter holidays. Bargain for lower long-term rates.

Also occupying the same luscious beachfront nearby is **Red Snapper RV Park and Restaurant** (P.O. Box 42, Melaque, Jalisco 48980, tel. 315/333-9784, redsnapper@hotmail.com, $18/day, $65/wk, $250/mo), life project of friendly North American owners Harry, Carmen, and Bonnie Adams. Here, what you see is what you get: a dozen largely shadeless fenced-in spaces with all hookups (including 30-amp power), showers, toilets, washing machine, beachfront restaurant *palapa* on gorgeous Chamela Bay, ripe for surf or boat fishing (launch right from the beach), surfing, and sailboarding. A 15-foot, 25-horsepower Zodiac is available for fishing.

Rosada Beach Accommodations

Four miles south of El Super, at Rosada Beach, sharing the same luscious Chamela Bay strand, is the **Centro Vacacional Chamela Sección 47,** a teachers' vacation retreat that rents its unoccupied units to the general public. The two modern, apartment-style tiers enfold an invitingly lovely grassy pool patio and park. An outdoor *palapa* stands by the pool and another airy open room invites cards and conversation. The units themselves are large, bright one-bedrooms, sleeping four, with sea views and kitchens. Rentals ($60/day) are on a drop-in basis. Telephone the manager around noon at 315/333-9878 or 315/333-9777 in Spanish to see if he can rent you an apartment. Arrive before about 4 P.M., when the manager is usually around to check things before going home for the night. On nonholiday weekdays the place is often nearly empty. Have a look by following the upper of two side roads at the big 47 sign near the Km 66 marker. Within a few hundred yards you'll be there. Ask one of the teachers to explain the significance of 47.

Camping

For RVs, the best spots are the trailer parks at **Paraíso Costalegre,** the **Hotel, Bungalows and Trailer Park Playa Dorada,** and **Red Snapper Restaurant and RV Park** (see listings in this section).

If you can walk in, you can probably set up a tent anywhere along the bay you like. One of the best places would be the grassy dune along pristine Playa Rosada a few hundred yards north of the Centro Vacacional Chamela Sección 47 (Km 66). Water is available from the manager (offer to pay) at the Centro Vacacional.

Playa Negrita, the pristine little sand crescent that marks the southern end of Chamela Bay, offers still another picnic or camping possibility. Get there by following the dirt road angling downhill from the highway at the south end of the bridge between Km 63 and Km 64. Turn left at the Chamela village stores beneath the bridge, continue about two miles, bearing left to the end of the road, where a restaurant *palapa* stands at beachside. This is the southernmost of two islet-protected coves flanking the low Punta Negro headland. With clear, tranquil waters and golden-sand beaches, both coves are great for fishing from the rocks, snorkeling, sailboarding, and swimming. The gorgeous south-end beach, Playa Negrita, is offered as a campground, with plenty of room for tenting and RV parking; a friendly caretaker sometimes collects about $2.50 per day per car. Weekends and holidays the restaurant provides drinks and seafood lunches and dinners.

Food

Groceries are available at stores near the **El Super** corner (Km 72) or in the villages of **Perula** (on the beach, turn off at Km 74), **San Mateo** (Km 70), and **Chamela** (walk north along the beach, or follow the side road, downhill, at the south end of the bridge between Km 64 and 63).

Hearty country Mexican food, hospitality, and snack groceries are available at the **Tejeban** truck stop/restaurant (tel. 315/333-9705, morning until 10:30 P.M. daily) at the El Super corner. Two popular local roadside seafood spots (8 A.M.–9 P.M. daily, $5–10) are the **La Viuda** (The Widow, Km 64) and **Don Lupe Mariscos** (Km 63), on opposite ends of the Río Chamela bridge. They both have their own divers who go out daily for fresh fish, octopus *(pulpo)*, conch, clams, oysters, and lobster.

Information and Services

The closest bank is 34 miles north at Tomatlán (turnoff at La Cumbre, Km 116). A card-operated telephone operates outside at the El Super corner, in addition to long-distance telephones inside the adjacent Tejeban restaurant and at the Centro de Salud at Pueblo Careyes, the village behind the soccer field at Km 52.

Until someone resurrects the **Pemex** *gasolinera* at El Super, the closest unleaded gasoline is 27 miles (43 km) north at La Cumbre (Km 116) or 50 miles (80 km) south at Melaque (Km 0).

If you get sick, the closest health clinics are in Perula (Km 74, one block north of the town plaza, no phone, but a pharmacy) and at Pueblo Careyes at Km 52 (medical consultations 8 A.M.–2 P.M. daily; doctor on call around the clock for emergencies).

Local special police, known as the Policia Auxiliar del Estado, are stationed in a pink roadside house at Km 46, and also in the house above the road at Km 43. The local *preventiva* (municipal police) are stationed about a half mile (1 km) north of the El Super corner.

◖ EL CAREYES BEACH RESORT

One of the hidden gems of the Pacific Coast of Mexico, this is really two hotels in one. After Christmas and before Easter, El Careyes brims with well-to-do Mexican families letting their hair down. The rest of the year the hotel is a tranquil tropical retreat basking at the edge of a pristine, craggy cove.

The natural scene sets the tone: A majestic palm grove opens onto a petite sandy beach set like a pearl between craggy cliffs. Offshore, the water, deep and crystal clear, is home for dozens of kinds of fish. Overhead, hawks and frigate birds soar, pelicans dive, and boobies and terns skim the waves. Seasonally, at night nearby, sea turtles carry out their ancient ritual by silently depositing their precious eggs on nearby beaches where they were born.

As if not to be outdone by nature, the hotel itself is an elegant tropical retreat. A platoon of gardeners manicure lush spreading grounds that lead to the gate and reception area. Past the desk, tiers of ochre-hued Mediterranean-chic lodgings enclose an elegant inner courtyard where a blue pool meanders beneath majestic, rustling palms. At night, the grounds glimmer softly with lamps. They illuminate the tufted

grove, light the path to a secluded beach, and lead the way up through the cactus-sprinkled hillside thorn forest to a romantic restaurant high above the bay.

Recreation

Hotel guests enjoy a plethora of sports facilities, including tennis courts, riding stables, and a polo field. Aquatic activities include snorkeling, scuba diving, kayaking, sailing, and deep-sea fishing. Boats are additionally available for picnic-excursions to nearby hidden beaches, wildlife-viewing, and observing turtle nesting in season. A luxury spa with view pampers guests with massage, facials, sauna, whirlpool tub, and exercise machines. Evenings, in season, live music brightens the cocktail and dinner hours at the elegant beachview restaurant/bar.

The hotel was named for *carey* (kah-RAY), the native word for an endangered species of sea turtle (the hawksbill) that used to lay eggs on the little beach of Careyitos that fronts the hotel. Saving the turtles at nearby Playa Teopa, accessible only through hotel property, has now become a major hotel mission. Guards do, however, allow access to serious outside visitors during hatching times; follow the dirt road between Km 49 and Km 50 to the gate and beach; no camping, please. Check with the hotel desk for information and permission.

Information

The luxurious rooms and suites, depending on location and size, run approximately $244–476 d in low season, and $252–500 d high. All accommodations have air-conditioning, TV, and direct-dial phones. Additional hotel facilities and services include fiber-optic telecommunications, a 100-person meeting room, a number of shops and boutiques, library, small theater, babysitters, heliport, private landing strip, and a range of business services.

For reservations and information, contact the hotel directly (tel. 315/351-0000, fax 315/351-0100, www.elcareyesresort.com) or through its agent, Mexico Boutique Hotels (toll-free U.S./Can. tel. 800/728-7098, www.mexicoboutiquehotels.com).

Getting There

El Careyes is a few minutes' drive down a cobbled entrance road (bear left all the way) at Km 53.5 (100 mi/161 km from Puerto Vallarta, 34 mi/55 km from Barra de Navidad, and 52 mi/84 km from the Manzanillo International Airport).

◖ PLAYA CAREYES

At Km 52, just south of a small bridge and a bus stop, a dirt side road (beach side) leads past a gated guard station with a sign labeled Costa Careyes to the lovely honey-tinted crescent of Playa Careyes. The guard, whose job is to provide security for the beach *palapa* restaurants and the houses atop the neighboring headlands, will let you through if you ask. Beyond the gate, bear left to the car-negotiable track (beware of sandy soft spots) that continues along the dune, where you could enjoy at least a pleasant day on the beach. Beyond the often powerful waves (swim with caution), the intimate headland-framed bay brims with outdoor possibilities. Bird- and wildlife-watching can be quite rewarding; notice the herons, egrets, and cormorants in the lagoon just south of the dune. Fishing is good either from the beach, by boat (launch from the sheltered north end), or from the rocks on either side. Water is generally clear for snorkeling and, beyond the waves, good for either kayaking or sailboarding. If you have no boat, no problem—the local fishing cooperative (boats beached by the food *palapa* at north end) would be happy to take you on a fishing trip. Figure about $20 per hour, with bargaining. Afterward, they might even cook up the catch for a big afternoon dinner at their tree-shaded *palapa* of the Cocodrilo Azul restaurant nearby. If you want to camp, you can set up your tent, or park your camper by one of the restaurant *palapas* at the right, north end of the beach.

As for services, **Pueblo Careyes** (inland, behind the soccer field at Km 52) has a Centro de Salud (tel. 335/351-0170), with a pharmacy and long-distance telephone.

Access to the neighboring **Playa Teopa** is more carefully guarded. The worthy reason is to save the hatchlings of the remaining *carey*

turtles that still come ashore during the late summer and fall to lay eggs. For a closer look at Playa Teopa, you could walk south along the dunetop track, although guards might eventually stop you. They will let you through (entry gate on dirt road between Km 49 and 50) if you get official permission at the desk of the El Careyes Beach Resort.

The pristine tropical deciduous woodlands that stretch for miles around Km 45 are no accident. They are preserved as part of the **Fideicomiso Cuitzmala** (Cuitzmala Trust), the local kingdom of beach, headland, and forest held by the family of late multimillionaire Sir James Goldsmith. Local officials, many of whom were not privy to Sir James's grand design (which includes a sprawling seaview mansion complex), say that a team of biologists are conducting research on the property. A ranch complex, accessible through a gate at Km 45, is Fideicomiso Cuitzmala's most obvious highway-visible landmark.

PLAYA LAS BRISAS

For a tranquil day, overnight, or weeklong beach camping adventure, consider hidden Playa las Brisas, a few miles by the dirt road (turnoff sign near Km 36) through the village of Arroyo Seco.

About two miles long, Playa las Brisas has two distinct sections: first comes a very broad, white sandy strand decorated by pink-blossomed verbena and pounded by wild open-ocean waves. For shady tent camping or RV parking, a regal coconut grove lines the beach. Before you set up, however, you should offer a little rent to the owner/caretaker, who may soon show up on a horse. Don't be alarmed by his machete; it's for husking and cutting fallen coconuts.

To see the other half of Playa las Brisas, continue along the road past the little beachside vacation home subdivision (with a seasonal store and snack bar). You will reach an open-ocean beach and headland, backed by a big, level, grassy dune, perfect for tent or RV camping. Take care not to get stuck in soft spots, however.

The headland borders the El Tecuán lagoon, part of the Rancho El Tecuán, whose hilltop hotel you can see on the far side of the lagoon. The lagoon is an unusually rich fish and wildlife habitat.

Getting There

You can reach the village of Arroyo Seco, where stores can furnish supplies, 2.3 miles (3.7 km) from the highway at Km 36. At the central plaza, turn left, then immediately right at the Conasupo rural store, then left again, heading up the steep dirt road. In the valley on the other side, bear right at the fork at the mango grove, and within another mile you will be in the majestic beach-bordering palm grove.

HOTEL EL TECUÁN

Little was spared in perching the Hotel El Tecuán above its small kingdom of beach, lagoon, and palm-brushed rangeland. It was to be the centerpiece of a sprawling vacationland, with marina, golf course, and hundreds of houses and condos. The hotel was abandoned permanently and now sits unoccupied and for sale. The location was used in the Hollywood film, *I Still Know What you Did Last Summer.*

Masculinity bulges out of its architecture. Its corridors are lined with massive polished tree trunks, fixed by brawny master joints to thick hand-hewn mahogany beams. The view restaurant was patterned after the midships of a Manila galleon, complete with a pair of varnished tree-trunk masts reaching into the inky darkness of the night sky above. If the restaurant could only sway, the illusion would have been complete.

Wildlife-Watching and Hiking

It is perhaps fortunate that the former hotel and its surroundings, part of the big **Rancho Tecuán,** may never be developed into a residential community. Since the land is private, public access has always been limited, allowing the Rancho to become a de facto habitat-refuge for the rapidly diminishing local animal population. Wildcats, ocelots, small crocodiles, snakes, and turtles hunt in the mangroves edging the lagoon and the tangled forest that climbs the surrounding hills. The lagoon itself nurtures hosts of water birds and shoals of *robalo* (snook) and *pargo* (snapper).

At this writing, visitors were still being allowed to pass along the entrance road and enjoy wildlife-watching opportunities. If such visitors tread softly, clean up after themselves, start no fires, and refrain from fishing or hunting, the present owners may continue to allow access. This would be ideal, because wildlife-watching here is superb. First, simply walk along the lagoon-front below the hotel hilltop, where big white herons and egrets perch and preen in the mangroves. Don't forget your binoculars, sun hat, mosquito repellent, telephoto camera, and identification book. Try launching your own rowboat, canoe, or inflatable raft for an even more rewarding outing.

The environs offer plenty of jogging and walking opportunities. For starters, stroll along the lagoonside entrance road and back (3 mi/4.8 km) or south along the beach to the Río Purificación and back (4 mi/6.4 km). Take water, mosquito repellent, sunscreen, a hat, and something to carry your beachcombing treasures in.

◖ Playa el Tecuán

The focal point of the long, wild white-sand Playa el Tecuán is at the north end, where, at low tide, the lagoon's waters stream into the sea. Platoons of water birds—giant brown herons, snowy egrets, and squads of pelicans, ibises, and grebes—stalk and dive for fish trapped in the shallow rushing current.

On the beach nearby, the sand curves southward beneath a rocky point, where the waves strew rainbow carpets of limpet, clam, and snail shells. There the billows rise sharply, angling shoreward, often with good intermediate and advanced surfing breaks. Casual swimmers beware; the powerful surf can be dangerous.

Getting There

The former Hotel El Tecuán is six miles (10 km) along a paved entrance road marked by a white lighthouse at Km 33 (112 mi/181 km from Puerto Vallarta, 22 mi/35 km from Barra de Navidad).

◖ PLAYA TENACATITA

Imagine an ideal tropical paradise: free camping on a long curve of clean white sand, right next to a lovely little coral-bottomed cove, with all the beer you can drink and all the fresh seafood you can eat. That describes Tenacatita, a place that old Mexican Pacific hands refer to with a sigh: Tenacatitaaahhh . . .

Folks usually begin to arrive sometime in November; by Christmas some years there's room only for walk-ins. (Which anyone who can walk can do: Carry in your tent and set it up in one of the many RV-inaccessible spots.)

Tenacatita visitors enjoy three distinct beaches: the main one, Playa Tenacatita; the little one, Playa Mora; and Playa la Boca, a breezy palm-bordered sand ribbon stretching almost two miles (3.2 km) north to the *boca* (mouth) of the Río Purificación.

Playa Tenacatita's strand of fine white sand curves from the north end of Punta Tenacatita along a long, tall packed dune to **Punta Hermanos,** a total of about two miles (3.2 km). The dune is where most visitors—nearly all Americans and Canadians—park their RVs. The water is clear with gentle waves, fine for swimming and sailboarding. Being so calm, it's easy to launch a boat for fishing—common catches are *huachinango* (red snapper) and *cabrilla* (sea bass)—especially at the very calm north end.

For most services and supplies you'll have to head 1.5 miles inland to the village of El Rebalsito. However, Playa Tenacatita's sheltered north-end cove has acquired a village of *palapas* that service the winter camping population. One of the veteran establishments is **El Puercillo,** run by longtimer José Bautista. He and several other neighbors take groups out in his launches ($80/half-day, bring your own beer) for offshore fishing trips and excursions. For more useful information about Tena, visit www.tomzap.com/tenaca.

Beaches

Jewel of jewels **Playa Mora** is accessible by a steep but short uphill dirt road (at this writing in

Tent camping beneath a *palapa* is customary at Playa Tenacatita.

need of repair and only jeep-negotiable) running north from Playa Tenacatita past the *palapas*. Playa Mora itself is salt-and-pepper black sand dotted with white coral, washed by water sometimes as smooth as glass. Just 50 feet from the beach the reef begins. Corals, like heads of cauliflower, some brown, some green, and some dead white, swarm with fish: iridescent blue, yellow-striped, yellow-tailed, some silvery, and others brown as rocks. (Be careful. Moray eels like to hide in rock crannies, and they bite. Don't stick your hand anywhere you can't see.)

If you get to Playa Mora by December you may be early enough to snag one of the roughly dozen car-accessible camping spots. If not, plenty of tent camping spaces accessible on foot exist; also, a few abandoned *palapas* are usually waiting to be resurrected.

North-side **Playa la Boca** (fronting the palm grove to the right of the ingress road) is the overflow campground for Tenacatita. It's not as popular because of its rough surf and steep beach. Its isolation and vigorous surf, however, make Playa la Boca the best for driftwood, beachcombing, shells, and surf fishing.

Wildlife-Watching

Tenacatita's hinterland is a spreading wildlife-rich mangrove marsh. From a lagoonside landing inland from the Tenacatita dune, you can float a boat, rubber raft, or canoe for a wildlife-watching excursion. Local guides (ask for Adan at restaurant Chito) furnish boats and lead trips ($30) from the same spot. Animals often viewable are coatimundis, crocodiles, iguanas, *ilamacoa* (boa constrictors), and flocks of herons (grey and white), cormorants, anhingas, and much more, especially in the winter. Take your hat, binoculars, camera, telephoto lens, and plenty of insect repellent.

Tenacatita Bugs

That same marshland is the source for swarms of mosquitoes and *jejenes* ("no-see-um" biting gnats), especially around sunset. At that time, no sane person at Tenacatita should be outdoors without having slathered on some good repellent.

Accommodations and Food

A pair of recommendable hotels and a trailer park (also with hotel rooms) serve Tenacatita visitors. First choice goes to **Hotel las Villitas** (Av. Tenacatita 376, tel. 315/355-5353 or 315/355-7078, Barra de Navidad toll-free tel. 01-800/980-7060, www.lasvillitas.com.mx), actually a petite boutique resort, where owners have spared little in providing a restaurant, oceanview pool patio, tennis courts, comfortably appointed deluxe rooms and spacious kitchenette suites. Rentals run about $120 for the rooms, $200 for the kitchenette suites, with fans, air-conditioning, a library of paperback novels, and plenty of ocean views. (At this writing, the only possible drawback to all this is the hotel's isolation, about a mile from anything south along the beach, and the sometimes lack of sufficient electricity—it's solar-powered—to run the pump and keep the swimming pool from being murky.)

A plainer but still acceptable closer-in choice is the beachfront **Hotel Paraíso de Tenacatita** (Av. Tenacatita 32, $30 d, $40 d with a/c, dobie@prodigy.net.mx), with 23 clean, simply decorated rooms, with fans, some with air-conditioning, and an oceanview restaurant and pool patio.

RVers and campers enjoy a good option at the **Tenacatita Trailer Park** (Av. Tenacatita, Guadalajara cell tel. 044/33-3115-5406, long-distance tel. 01-33/3115-5406, emmarortega@hotmail.com) Here you'll find around 35 spaces, about half of them shaded, with several big enough to accommodate large motor homes. Rates run about $25 for smaller RVs, $30 for larger, with all hookups, wastewater dump, air-conditioning power, lavish showers and toilet facilities, all in a big, grassy, securely fenced-in yard, kept green by a private piped-in fresh water supply.

The trailer park's three hotel rooms (out front, on the beachfront road) are equally well equipped and attractive. Here, you get a clean, comfortably semideluxe oceanview room with a pair of double beds, for $35 d, $60 t or q, with fan and hot-water shower bath, right across the street from the good Fiesta Mexicana *palapa* restaurant. Because of the excellent facilities and loyal repeat guests, if you are interested in staying in the trailer park, don't wait to make your reservation. They book up quickly during the high season.

On the other hand, for some of the best food and highest standards on the beach, go to very well-established **Fiesta Mexicana** *palapa* restaurant, on the Tenacatita beach south end, across the beachfront from the trailer park. (Alternatively, you can also check out neighboring Restaurant Chito and Restaurant Cato, especially for the local fish specialty *rollo del mar*.)

If you want a diversion from the fare of Tenacatita's seafood *palapas* and El Rebalsito's single restaurant, you can drive or thumb a ride seven miles (11 km) to **Restaurant Yoli** (7 A.M.–8 P.M. daily) at roadside Miguel Hidalgo village (Km 30 on Highway 200) for some country-style enchiladas, tacos, chiles rellenos, tostadas, and beans.

Services and Supplies

The village of **El Rebalsito,** on the Highway 200–Tenacatita road, 1.5 miles back from the beach, is Tenacatita's supply and service center. It has two or three fair *abarroterías* (groceries) that carry meat and vegetables. Best of all of these is friendly **Minisuper La Morenita,** on the highway, with a little bit of everything and long-distance telephone (tel. 315/355-5214). Additional services include a *gasolinera* that dispenses gasoline from drums and a water *purificadora* that sells drinking water retail. Connect to the Internet in Rebalsito at the small store (José Vargas Vigil 14, 9 A.M.–2 P.M. and 4–9 P.M. Mon.–Fri., 9 A.M.–2 P.M. Sat., closed Sun.) a block and a half from the church.

Getting There

By bus, catch the Transportes Cihuatlán bus that makes one return trip per day between El Rebalsito and Manzanillo. It leaves El Rebalsito daily at the crack of dawn (for departure times, inquire locally in Rebalsito and the bus stations at Barra de Navidad, tel. 315/355-5200, or Melaque, tel. 315/355-5003),

and returns from the Manzanillo central bus station around 3 P.M., arriving at El Rebalsito around 6 P.M.

By car, leave Highway 200 at the big Tenacatita sign and interchange (at Km 27) half a mile south of the big Río Purificación bridge. El Rebalsito is 3.7 miles (6 km), Tenacatita 5.4 miles (8.7 km), by a good paved road.

BLUE BAY CLUB LOS ANGELES LOCOS

Although the Blue Bay resort chain has been operating the former Hotel Los Angeles Locos as an all-inclusive resort for several years, the curious name Los Angeles Locos (which had nothing to do with crazy people from Los Angeles) lives on in the minds of local people. Once upon a time, a rich family built an airstrip and a mansion by a lovely little beach on pristine Tenacatita Bay and began coming for vacations by private plane. The local people, who couldn't fathom why their rich neighbors would go to so much trouble and expense to come to such an out-of-the-way place, dubbed them *los ángeles locos* (the crazy angels), because they always seemed to be flying.

The beach is still lovely and Tenacatita Bay, curving around Punta Hermanos south from Tenacatita Beach, is still pristine. Now Los Angeles Locos makes it possible for droves of sun-seeking vacationers to enjoy it en masse. Continuous music, open bar, plentiful buffets, and endless activities set the tone at Los Angeles Locos—the kind of place for folks who want a hassle-free week of fun in the sun. The guests are typically working-age couples and singles, mostly Mexicans during the summer, Canadians and some Americans during the winter. Very few children seem to be among the guests, although they are welcome.

Recreation

Although all sports and lessons—including tennis, snorkeling, sailing, sailboarding, horseback riding, volleyball, aerobics, exercises, waterskiing, plus dancing, disco, and games—cost nothing extra, guests can, if they want, do nothing but soak up the sun. A relaxed attitude will probably allow you to enjoy yourself the most. Don't try to eat, drink, and do too much to make sure you get your money's worth. If you do, you're liable to arrive back home in need of a vacation.

Although people don't come to the tropics to stay inside, Los Angeles Locos's rooms are quite comfortable—completely private, in pastels and white, air-conditioned, each with cable TV, phone, and private balcony overlooking either the ocean or palmy pool and patio.

Information

For information and reservations, contact a travel agent or the hotel (Km 20, Carretera Federal 200, tel. 315/351-5020, toll-free Mex. tel. 01-800/713-3020, toll-free U.S. tel. 800/483-7986, fax 315/351-5412, www.losangeleslocos.com). Low-season rates for the 201 rooms and suites run a bargain-basement $84 per person per day, midweek, $94 weekends, double occupancy, $126 high season. Children under seven with parents stay free; children 7–12, $40. For a bigger, better junior suite, add about $50 per room; prices include everything—food, drinks, entertainment—except transportation.

Getting There

Los Angeles Locos is about four miles (6 km) off Highway 200 along a signed cobbled entrance road near the Km 20 marker (120 mi/194 km from Puerto Vallarta, 14 mi/23 km from Barra de Navidad, and 32 mi/51 km from the Manzanillo International Airport). If you want to simply look around the resort, don't drive up to the gate unannounced. The guard won't let you through. Instead, call ahead and make an appointment for a "tour." After your guided look-see, you have to either sign up or mosey along. The hotel doesn't accept day guests.

Hotel Punta Serena

Part of the original Los Angeles Locos development, but separate in concept and location, is Punta Serena (through Blue Bay Club Los Angeles Locos switchboard, tel. 315/351-

5020, ext. 4013 or 4011, fax 315/351-5412, www.puntaserena.com). Perched on a breezy hilltop overlooking the entire broad sweep of Tenacatita Bay, this is an adults-only romantic retreat, with all meals and in-house activities included, plus a big blue oceanview pool patio, sauna, sea-vista hot tub, gym, and clothing-optional settings. You can also enjoy all of the lively sports, discoing, and beach action of Los Angeles Locos on the beach downhill, at no extra cost. Added-cost amenities include spa services such as a native-Mexican *temazcal* hot room and massage.

Paths radiate to the tile-roofed lodging units, spread over the palmy summit-park like a garden of giant mushrooms. The units themselves are designer-spartan, in white and blue, with modern baths, luxuriously high ceilings, and broad ocean vistas from view balconies.

All-inclusive tariffs for the 70 accommodations, all with air-conditioning, run about the same as Hotel Los Angeles Locos. Directions and address are identical to Los Angeles Locos, but turn right at the signed Punta Serena entrance driveway before heading downhill to Los Angeles Locos.

❰ PLAYA BOCA DE IGUANAS

Plumy Playa Boca de Iguanas curves for six miles along the tranquil inner recess of the Bay of Tenacatita. The cavernous former beachfront Hotel Bahía Tenacatita, which slumbered for years beneath the grove, is being reclaimed by the jungle and the animals that live in the nearby mangrove marsh after being destroyed in an earthquake in 1995.

The beach, however, is as enjoyable as ever: wide and level, with firm white sand good for hiking, jogging, and beachcombing. Offshore, the gently rolling waves are equally fine for bodysurfing and boogie boarding. Beds of oysters, free for those who dive for them, lie a few hundred feet offshore. A rocky outcropping at the north end invites fishing and snorkeling while the calm water beyond the breakers invites sailboarding. Bring your own equipment.

Get to Playa Boca de Iguanas by following

© ROBIN NOELLE

Playa Boca de Iguanas

the signed paved road at Km 17 for 1.5 miles (2.4 km).

Accommodations

For hotel-style lodging, go to **Coconuts-by-the-Sea** (tel. 315/100-8899 from Mexico, www.coconutsbythesea.com, $100 d low season, $125 d high). Owners Bob and Cissie Jones offer four spacious suites with full kitchens that include fans, air-conditioning, uber-comfortable king-size beds, satellite TV with HBO, and hot showers with plenty of water in a big hillside house. It features a fantastic view of the lovely beach and bay from the hillside, verandas, hammocks, a beautiful swimming pool, and just a short downhill walk to creamy Boca de Iguanas beach. Internet is also available. The only restaurant in Boca de Iguanas is at the resort at the bottom of the hill. A short walk down the steep hillside will deposit guests on the resort grounds and beach.

Second choice goes to nearby **Camping Trailer Park Boca Beach** (Km 16.5 Carretera Melaque–Puerto Vallarta, tel. 317/381-0393,

fax 317/381-0342, bocabeach@hotmail.com), with about 50 camping and RV spaces shaded beneath a majestic rustling grove. In 10 years, friendly owners Michel and Bertha Billot (he's French, she's Mexican) have built up their little paradise, surviving hurricanes and a 1995 tidal wave by trying harder. Their essentials are in place: electricity, water, showers, toilets, and about 40 spaces with sewer hookups. Much of their five acres is undeveloped and would be fine for tent campers who prefer privacy with the convenience of fresh water, a small store, and congenial company at tables beneath a rustic *palapa*. RV rates run about $17 per day, back from the beach, $26 on the beach, $500 per month for motor home, trailer, or van, including electricity for air-conditioning. Camping runs about $7 per day per group; add $3 for two kids.

A new luxury option is available at the **Boca de Iguanas Beach Hotel** (Km. 14 Carretera 200, tel. 314/335-3207 or U.S. tel. 949/340-2602, www.bocadeiguanas.com). The 10 rooms available at this luxury resort average $328 d low season, $409 d high for the tastefully appointed accommodations, each offering whirlpool tubs, terraces, flat-screen wall-mounted televisions with cable, air-conditioning, and wireless Internet. Price includes happy hour cocktails and breakfast at the on-site restaurant. Beach cabanas are available as well and the prices are somewhat lower ($220 d). The bungalows do not have air-conditioning or television.

The resort beach is beautiful and clean however the surf can be strong and difficult to swim in. The hotel hosts a stunning infinity pool with comfy lounge chairs for its guests. Visitors are welcome to spend the day as long as they make a minimum purchase at the bar or restaurant.

PLAYA LA MANZANILLA

The little fishing town of La Manzanilla (pop. 2,000) drowses at the opposite end of the same long, curving strip of sand that begins at the Boca de Iguanas trailer parks. Here the beach, Playa la Manzanilla, is as broad and flat and the waves are as gentle, but the sand is several shades darker. Probably no better fishing exists on the entire Costalegre than at La Manzanilla. A dozen seafood *palapas* on the beach manage to stay open by virtue of a trickle of foreign visitors and local weekend and holiday patronage.

Besides its gorgeous beachfront, the only other La Manzanilla sight is the town's family of toothy **crocodiles,** at the south end of main street María Asunción (as you enter the town, a block before the beach, turn right). About six individuals are usually visible, basking in the mangrove-fringed pond, waiting for handouts. The king of the heap, a 12-foot (four-meter) grandfather, periodically defends his seniority by fiercely chasing off potential junior rivals.

La Manzanilla has become a haven for a small but growing community of North American expatriates and winter seekers of paradise. A growing cadre of restaurants and services, including vacation rentals and home sales, fishing excursions, adventure biking, hiking and horsebacking, has appeared to cater to visitors needs. For more information on all of this ferment, visit www.tomzap.com/manza. html, www.lamanzanilla.biz, and www.lamanzanilla.info.

Accommodations

Under $50: A handful of recommendable budget hotels accommodate guests. Just a block from the north end of main street Calle María Asunción, find downscale **Hotel Posada del Cazador** (María Asunción 183, tel. 315/351-5000, fax 315/351-5212), where visitors enjoy friendly husband-wife management, a lobby for sitting and socializing, a shelf of used paperback novels, and a long-distance telephone. There are seven plain but clean rooms for $23 s or d, $36 d in two beds low season, $34 and $52 high. Kitchenette suites sleeping four rent for $50 low season, $60 high. Find it on the main street on the left, as you enter town.

On the opposite, sleepy south-end beachfront edge of town, the **Hotel Puesta del Sol** (Calle Playa Blanca 94, tel./fax 315/351-5033) offers 17 basic rooms around a cool, leafy central patio. Low-season rates run about $22 s or d, $32 t and $32 s or d, $50 t high; discounts for longer-term rentals.

One of the class-act La Manzanilla accommodations is the beautiful **Posada Tonalá** (María Asunción 75, tel./fax 315/351-5474, posadatonala@hotmail.com), life project of kindly owner/builder Alfonso Torres López. Señor López retired from his auto-parts business in Guadalajara and returned to realize his lifelong dream, to contribute to his hometown. You must at least come and look at his handiwork: the graceful teak *(granadillo)* stairway, the vines cascading on one side of the airy lobby, all topped by a uniquely lovely *palapa* roof. His rooms are immaculate and spacious, with modern shower baths and plenty of attractive tile, as well as handsome dark hand-carved furniture and colorful handmade bedspreads. There is plenty of seating on the second floor balcony and a nice collection of paperbacks and magazines for guests to enjoy. All this for only $38 s or d, $47 t, with air-conditioning, fans, hot-water shower baths. Add about $15 during Christmas and Easter holidays. Find it on the town's main street, right in the center of town. Beds vary in comfort level, so check a few rooms before you commit.

$50-100: Enjoy that vacation feeling with a stay at secluded seaview **Villa Montaña** (46 Calle Los Angeles Locos) on the hillside above and behind the town. Accommodations start at $65 d low season, $139 d high; discounts are available for long-term stays. For more information and reservations, contact Dan Clarke (P.O. Box 16343, Seattle, WA 98116, tel. 206/937-3882, www.lamanzanilla.biz).

Get to La Manzanilla by following the signed paved road at Km 13 for one mile. The Hotel Cazador is on the left, one block after you turn left onto the main beachfront street. The Posada Tonalá and Tranquilidad Bungalows are a block farther, across the street from each other, while Hotel Puesta del Sol is a quarter-mile farther along; bear right past the town plaza for a few blocks along the beachfront street, Calle Playa Blanca. Villa Montaña is prominent on the hill, a quarter mile north of the town center.

A number of agents manage **vacation rentals** for the many attractive homes that sprinkle La Manzanilla's shady lanes and golden beachfront. Dan Clarke, owner of Villa Montaña, is probably the most experienced; check out his website www.lamanzanilla.biz, or telephone him in Seattle at 206/937-3882. Alternatively, visit personable Daniel Hallas's **Costalegre Properties** office on main street, María Asunción, beach side, or call him in La Manzanilla at 315/351-5059, or visit his website, www.lamanzanilla.info.

Food

Two local restaurants stand out. For good comfort food, such as pizza, hamburgers, fish fillets, and Mexican plates, go to **Palapa Joe's** (María Asunción 163, tel. 315/351-5348, noon–10 P.M. Tues.–Sat., $3–8). On the other hand, savor the breeze and the swish of the waves at **Martin's** (south end of beachfront Calle Playa Blanca, tel. 315/351-5348, 8 A.M.– 10 P.M. daily). The open-air *palapa*-style restaurant is a romantic place to dine in the evenings and can get quite crowded during the high season. Try the tortilla soup ($5) and fresh fish specials ($13). There's a full bar for all of your tropical cocktail desires.

EL TAMARINDO

The El Tamarindo development occupies the lush, green peninsula that forms the southernmost point of Tenacatita Bay. Some of the land was once a private zoo and the Tamarindo grounds remains home to many hundreds of wild creatures, from possumlike armadillos and snorting javelinas to feisty raccoons and warm and fuzzy but wily coatimundis. It's likely you will see at least some of the variety of wildlife during your stay.

The meandering, forest-fringed golf course is a wonder in all itself, designed by renowned Robert Trent Jones and David Fleming. It winds

for thousands of yards, traversing lush lawns, tricky sand traps, serene ponds, and verdant vine-hung thickets. Greens fee runs about $150 for in-house guests, more than $200 for outside clients from such plush hotels as Grand Bay, Cabo Blanco, Los Angeles Locos, Punta Serena, Las Alamandas, El Careyes, and Las Hadas.

Accommodations at **(El Tamarindo** (tel. 315/351-5032 or 315/351-5052, toll-free Mex. tel. 800/909-4800, fax 315/351-5070, www.eltamarindoresort.com) are in airy pastel stucco-and-tile superdeluxe villas spread throughout the center of the 2,040 acres that make up the resort. Each villa includes a secluded yard, private pool and luxury linens on feather-topped beds. Rates for the several secluded lodgings run about $500–1,600 d per day. Four bedroom villas are available starting at $4,000 per day. For reservations, contact Mexico Boutique Hotels (toll-free U.S./Can. tel. 800/728-7098, www.mexicoboutiquehotels.com).

The resort is isolated but with the sheer luxury of your accommodations, you may not want to leave the resort. The beach is pristine with golden sand and a variety of sun beds and lounge areas for dozing the day away. The attentive staff brings cold towels and ice water to keep guests cool. The only downside of this vast, posh resort is the on-site restaurant which boasts prices so high it's difficult to imagine even the celebrity clientele accepting them without question. This is unfortunate because there are no other options within a reasonable distance. However, if you've ever wanted to try a $26 cheeseburger, it might as well be at El Tamarindo.

Get there via the signed side road at Km 8, five miles (8 km) north of Melaque. After about two miles (3 km) of winding through the tropical forest, you arrive at the gate, where you must have either a reservation in hand or an appointment before the guard will let you through.

Barra de Navidad and Melaque

The little Jalisco country beach town of Barra de Navidad (pop. 5,000), whose name literally means Bar of Christmas, has unexpectedly few saloons. However, this bar has nothing to do with alcohol; it refers to the sandbar upon which the town is built. That lowly spit of sand forms the southern perimeter of the blue Bay of Navidad, which arcs to Barra de Navidad's twin town of San Patricio Melaque (pop. 10,000), a few miles to the west.

Barra and San Patricio Melaque, locally known as Melaque (may-LAH-kay), may be twins, but they're distinct. Barra has the cobbled, shady lanes and friendly country ambience; Melaque is the metropolis of the two, with most of the stores and services and also the best beach, long and lovely Playa Melaque.

ORIENTATION

A sizable fraction of Barra hotels and restaurants lie on one oceanfront street named, uncommonly, after a conquistador, Miguel López de Legazpi. Barra's other main street, Veracruz, one short block inland, has most of the businesses, groceries, and small family-run eateries.

Sandwiched between Barra's two main streets is the modest block-square town plaza, known locally as the *jardín,* between east-west streets of Michoacán and Guanajuato. At the southeast corner of the *jardín,* you'll find the town telegraph office and police station.

Head south along Legazpi toward the steep **Cerro San Francisco** in the distance and you will soon be on the palm-lined walkway that runs atop the famous sandbar of Barra. On the right, ocean side, the **Playa Barra de Navidad** arcs northwest to the hotels of Melaque, which spread like white pebbles along the far end of the strand. The great blue-water expanse beyond the beach, framed at both ends by jagged, rocky sea stacks, is the **Bahía de Navidad.**

Opposite the ocean, on the other side of the bar, spreads the tranquil mangrove-bordered expanse of the **Laguna de Navidad,** which forms the border with the state of Colima,

Barra de Navidad

© ROBIN NOELLE

whose mountains (including nearby Cerro San Francisco) loom beyond it. The lagoon's calm appearance is deceiving, for it is really an *estero* (estuary), an arm of the sea that ebbs and flows through the channel beyond the rock jetty at the end of the sandbar. Because of this natural flushing action, local folks still dump fishing waste into the Laguna de Navidad. Fortunately, new sewage plants route human waste away from the lagoon, so with care, you can usually swim safely in its inviting waters. *Do not,* however, venture too close to the lagoon-mouth beyond the jetty or you may get swept out to sea by the strong outgoing current.

On the sandbar's lagoon side, a *panga* and passenger dock hum with daytime activity. From the dock, launches ferry loads of passengers for less than half a dollar to the Colima shore, which is known as **Isla Navidad,** where the marina and hotel development has risen across the lagoon. Back in the center of town, **minibuses** enter town along Veracruz, turn left at Sinaloa by the crafts stalls, and head in the opposite direction, out of town along Mazatlán, Veracruz, and Highway 200, three miles (4.8 km) to Melaque.

The once-distinct villages of **San Patricio** and **Melaque** now spread as one along the Bay of Navidad's sandy northwest shore. The business district, still known locally as San Patricio (from the highway, go west two blocks toward the beach), centers around a plaza, market, and church bordering the main shopping street, López Mateos.

Continue two more blocks to beachfront Calle Gómez Farías, where a lineup of hotels, eateries, and shops cater to the vacation trade. From there, the curving strand extends toward the quiet Melaque west end, where *palapas* line a glassy, sheltered blue cove. Here, a rainbow of colored *pangas* perch upon the sand, sailboats rock gently offshore, pelicans preen and dive, and people enjoy snacks, beer, and the cooling breeze in the deep shade beneath the *palapas*.

HISTORY

The sandbar is called "Navidad" because the Viceroy Antonio de Mendoza, the first and arguably the best viceroy Mexico ever had, disembarked there on December 25, 1540. The occasion was auspicious for two reasons. Besides being Christmas Day, Don Antonio had arrived to personally put down a bloody rebellion raging through western Mexico that threatened to burn New Spain off the map. Unfortunately for the thousands of native people who were torched, hung, or beheaded during the brutal campaign, Don Antonio's prayers on that day were soon answered. The rebellion was smothered, and the lowly sandbar was remembered as Barra de Navidad from that time forward.

A generation later, Barra de Navidad became the springboard for King Philip's efforts to make the Pacific a Spanish lake. Shipyards built on the bar launched the vessels that carried the expedition of conquistador Miguel López de Legazpi and Father André de Urdaneta in search of God and gold in the Philippines. Urdaneta came back a hero one year later, in 1565, having discovered the northern circle route, whose favorable easterly winds propelled a dozen subsequent generations of the fabled treasure-laden Manila galleon home to Mexico.

By 1600, however, the Manila galleon was landing in Acapulco, which provided much quicker land transport to the capital for their priceless Asian cargoes. Barra de Navidad went to sleep and didn't wake up for more than three centuries.

Now Barra de Navidad only slumbers occasionally. The townsfolk welcome crowds of beachgoing Mexican families during national holidays, and a steady procession of North American and European budget vacationers during the winter.

BEACHES

Although a continuous strand of medium-fine golden sand joins Barra with Melaque, it changes character and names along its gentle five-mile arc. At Barra de Navidad, where it's called **Playa de Navidad,** the beach is narrow and steep, and the waves are sometimes very rough. Those powerful swells often provide good intermediate surfing breaks adjacent to the jetty. Fishing by line or pole is also popular from the jetty rocks.

Most mornings are calm enough to make the surf safe for swimming and splashing, which, along with the fresh seafood of beachside *palapa* restaurants, make Barra a popular Sunday and holiday picnic-ground for local Mexican families. The relatively large number of folks walking the beach unfortunately makes for slim pickings for shell collectors and beachcombers.

For a cooling midday break from the sun, drop in to one of the beachfront restaurants (such as Seamaster) at the south end of Legazpi and enjoy the bay view, the swish of the waves, and the fresh breeze streaming beneath the *palapa*.

As the beach curves northwesterly toward Melaque, the restaurants and hotels give way to dunes and pasture. At the outskirts of Melaque, civilization resumes, and the broad beach, now called **Playa Melaque,** curves gently to the west.

THE JALISCO COAST

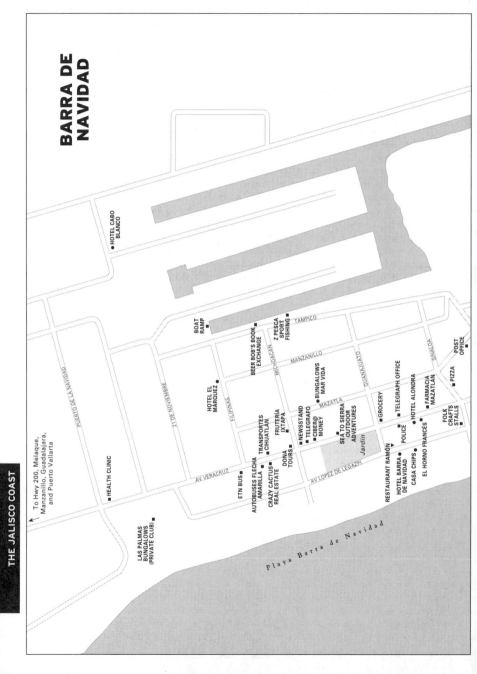

THE JALISCO COAST

BARRA DE NAVIDAD

HOTEL CABO BLANCO

PUERTO DE LA NAVIDAD

To Hwy 200, Melaque, Manzanillo, Guadalajara, and Puerto Vallarta

HEALTH CLINIC

21 DE NOVIEMBRE

BOAT RAMP

TAMPICO

BEER BOB'S BOOK EXCHANGE

Z PESCA SPORT FISHING

MICHOACAN

MANZANILLO

HOTEL EL MARQUEZ

FILIPINAS

BUNGALOWS MAR VIDA

NEWSSTAND

TELEGRAFO

CIBER@ MONEY

MAZATLA

TRANSPORTES CIHUATLAN

FRUTERÍA IXTAPA

DOÑA TOURS

SEA TO SIERRA OUTDOOR ADVENTURES

GUANAJUATO

GROCERY

TELEGRAPH OFFICE

HOTEL ALONDRA

SINALOA

POST OFFICE

PIZZA

FARMACIA MAZATLAN

FOLK CRAFTS STALLS

Jardín

ETN BUS

AUTOBUSES FLECHA AMARILLA

CRAZY CACTUS REAL ESTATE

AV VERACRUZ

RESTAURANT RAMÓN

AV LOPEZ DE LEGAZPI

HOTEL BARRA DE NAVIDAD

POLICE

CASA CHIPS

EL HORNO FRANCES

LAS PALMAS BUNGALOWS (PRIVATE CLUB)

Playa Barra de Navidad

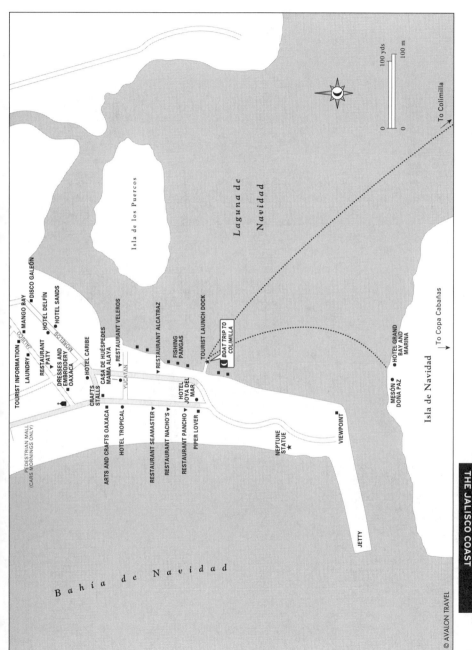

100 yds
100 m

To Colimilla

Isla de los Puercos

*Laguna de
Navidad*

BOAT TRIP TO
COLIMILLA

TOURIST LAUNCH DOCK

RESTAURANT ALCATRAZ

FISHING
PANGAS

RESTAURANT VELEROS

CASA DE HUÉSPEDES
MAMA ALAYA

HOTEL SANDS

HOTEL DELFIN

DISCO GALEÓN

MANGO BAY

TOURIST INFORMATION

LAUNDRY

RESTAURANT
PATY

DRESSES AND
EMBROIDERY
OAXACA

HOTEL CARIBE

CRAFTS
STALLS

JALISCO

MORELOS

YUCATAN

PEDESTRIAN MALL
(CARS MORNINGS ONLY)

ARTS AND CRAFTS OAXACA

HOTEL TROPICAL

RESTAURANT SEAMASTER

RESTAURANT NACHO'S

RESTAURANT PANCHO

PIPER LOVER

HOTEL
JOYA DEL
MAR

NEPTUNE
STATUE

VIEWPOINT

JETTY

HOTEL GRAND
BAY AND
MARINA

MESÓN
DOÑA PAZ

Isla de Navidad

To Copa Cabañas

Bahía de Navidad

THE JALISCO COAST

© AVALON TRAVEL

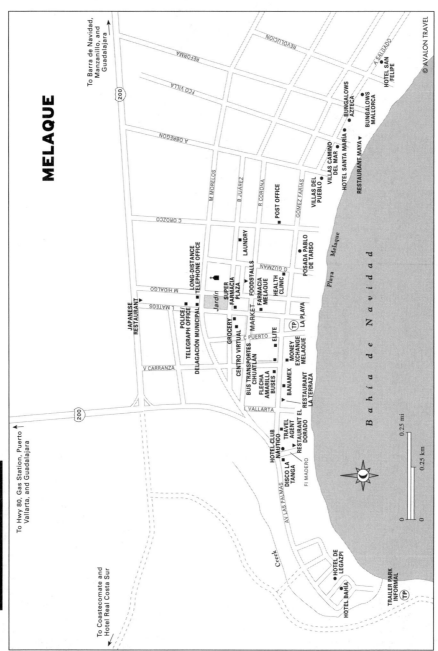

MELAQUE

To Barra de Navidad, Manzanillo, and Guadalajara

To Hwy 80, Gas Station, Puerto Vallarta, and Guadalajara

To Coastecomate and Hotel Real Costa Sur

REFORMA

FCO VILLA

A OBREGON

M MORELOS

C OROZCO

B JUAREZ

R CORONA

GOMEZ FARIAS

REVOLUCION

A SALGADO

HOTEL SAN FELIPE

BUNGALOWS AZTECA

BUNGALOWS MALLORCA

VILLAS CAMINO DEL MAR

HOTEL SANTA MARÍA

RESTAURANT MAYA

VILLAS DEL PUEBLO

POST OFFICE

POSADA PABLO DE TARSO

LAUNDRY

G GUZMAN

SUPER FARMACIA PLAZA

FOODSTALLS

FARMACIA MELAQUE

HEALTH CLINIC

M HIDALGO

LONG-DISTANCE TELEPHONE OFFICE

POLICE/ TELEGRAPH OFFICE

DELAGACIÓN MUNICIPAL

L MATEOS

JAPANESE RESTAURANT

Jardín

GROCERY

MARKET

CENTRO VIRTUAL

C PUERTO

ELITE

LA PLAYA

V CARRANZA

BUS TRANSPORTES CIHUATLÁN

FLECHA AMARILLA BUSES

BANAMEX

MONEY EXCHANGE MELAQUE

RESTAURANT LA TERRAZA

L VALLARTA

HOTEL CLUB NÁUTICO

TRAVEL AGENT

RESTAURANT EL DORADO

DISCO LA TANGA

EL MADERO

AV LAS PALMAS

Creek

HOTEL DE LEGAZPI

HOTEL BAHÍA

TRAILER PARK INFORMAL

Playa Melaque

Bahía de Navidad

0.25 mi

0.25 km

© AVALON TRAVEL

Continuing past the Melaque town center, a lineup of rustic *palapas* and *pangas* pulled up on the sand decorate the tranquil west-end cove, which is sheltered from the open sea behind a tier of craggy sea stacks. Here, the water clears, making for good fishing from the rocks.

Playa Coastecomate

On another day, explore this hidden beach tucked behind the ridge rising beyond the north edge of Melaque. The dark fine-sand beach arcs along a cove on the rampart-rimmed big blue **Bahía de Coastecomate** (kooah-stay-koh-MAH-tay). Its very gentle waves and clear waters make for excellent swimming, sailboarding, snorkeling, and fishing from the beach itself or the rocks beneath the adjacent cliffs. A number of *palapa* restaurants along the beach serve seafood and drinks.

The Coastecomate beachside village itself, home to a number of local fisherfolk and a few North Americans in permanently parked RVs, has a collection of oft-empty bungalows on the hillside, a small store, and about three times as many chickens as people.

To get there, drive or take a taxi or bus via the local minibus or Transportes Cihuatlán to the signed Melaque turnoff from Highway 200. There, a paved side road marked Hotel Real Costa Sur heads northwest into the hills, winding for two miles (3.2 km) over the ridge through pasture and jungle woodland to the village. If you're walking, allow an hour and take your sun hat, insect repellent, and water.

ENTERTAINMENT AND EVENTS

Most entertainments in Barra and Melaque are informal and local. **Corridas de toros** (bullfights) are occasionally held during the winter–spring season at the bullring on Highway 200 across from the Barra turnoff. Local *vaqueros* (cowboys) sometimes display their pluck in spirited *charreadas* (Mexican-style rodeos) in neighboring country villages. Check with your hotel desk or the Barra tourist information office for details.

The big local festival occurs in Melaque during the St. Patrick's Day week of March 10–17. Events include blessing of the local fishing fleet, folk dancing, cake eating, and boxing matches.

Nightlife

Folks enjoy the Bahía de Navidad sunset colors in Barra during the happy hours at Restaurant Seamaster, Hotel Alondra top-floor bar, or the Casa Chips restaurant-bar, half a block south of the Hotel Barra de Navidad.

The same is true at the beachside Restaurant Maya and Restaurant Dorado at Hotel Club Náutico in Melaque. You can prepare for sunset during the afternoons (Dec.–Feb. mostly) at the very congenial 4–6 P.M. happy hour around the swim-up bar at Barra's Hotel Sands. Lovers of pure tranquility, on the other hand, enjoy the breeze and sunset view from the end of Barra's rock jetty.

Perhaps the friendliest bar in Barra or Melaque is **Piper Lover** (tel. 315/355-6747, 4 P.M.–2 A.M. daily), owned by a man whose father loved his Piper Cub airplane. Here you can cool off and kick back, enjoying the breeze and the swish of the waves outside the bar's airy upstairs *palapa* perch. You'll always find great rock or blues, sometimes live, here. It's very popular with the cruisers and other boat people who travel to Barra by sea. Find it at the south, sandbar end of Avenida López de Legazpi in Barra.

If discoing is your thing, huge speakers begin thumping away, lights flash, and the fogs ooze from the ceilings around 10 P.M. at disco **El Galeón** (tel. 315/355-5018) of the Hotel Sands in Barra (young local crowd) and at **La Tanga** (Gómez Farías, tel. 315/355-5472, 9 P.M.–2 A.M. in season, entrance $7) across the street from Hotel Club Náutico in Melaque (mixed younger and older, local and tourist crowd). Hours vary seasonally; call for details.

SHOPPING

While Melaque has many stores crammed with humdrum commercial tourist curios, Barra has a few interestingly authentic sources. For example, a number of Náhuatl-speaking families from Guerrero operate small individual shops, at the south end of Legazpi. Furthermore, some of the shops, near the corner of Sinaloa and Legazpi, behind the church, are minimuseums of delightful folk crafts, made mostly by *indígena* country craftspeople. Pick what you like from among hundreds—lustrous lacquerware trays from Olinalá, winsome painted pottery cats, rabbits, and fish, a battalion of wooden mini-armadillos, and glossy dark-wood swordfish from Sonora.

You can pick from an equally attractive selection two blocks south, at **Arts and Crafts of Oaxaca,** across Legazpi diagonally southwest from the church. Besides a fetching collection of priced-to-sell Oaxacan *alebrijes, tapetes,* and masks, you'll also find a host of papier-mâché and pottery from Tlaquepaque and Tonalá, sombreros from Zitácuaro in Michoacán, and much more.

Across the street, a lineup of other shops, such as **Artesanías Náhuatl** and **Artesanías Guerrero** have similarly attractive offerings, on the south end of Veracruz, near the corner

of Morelos. Although bargaining is customary, don't bargain too hard. Many of these folks, far from their country villages, are strangers in a strange land. Their sometimes-meager earnings often support entire extended families back home.

RECREATION
◖ Boat Trip to Colimilla

A boat trip across the lagoon for super-fresh seafood at the palm-studded village of Colimilla is a primary Barra pastime. While you sit enjoying an oyster cocktail, ceviche, or broiled whole-fish dinner, gaze out on the mangrove-enfolded glassy expanse of the Laguna de Navidad. Far away, a canoe may drift silently, while white herons quietly stalk their prey. Now and then a launch will glide in and deposit its load of visitors, or an angler will head out to sea.

One of the most pleasant Colimilla vantage spots is **La Colimilla Restaurant** (8 A.M.–8 P.M. daily, $5–10), whose *palapa* extends into the lagoon. Take mosquito repellent,

refreshments at the lagoon dock, the jumping-off point for Colimilla

especially if you're staying for dinner. Launches routinely ferry as many as six passengers to Colimilla from the Barra lagoonside docks for about $5 round-trip. Tell them when you want to return, and they'll pick you up.

From the same Barra lagoonside dock, launches also shuttle passengers for $1.50 round-trip across the lagoon to **Isla Navidad** and the posh resort Hotel Grand Bay, marina, vacation-home development, and golf course.

Swimming, Surfing, and Boogie Boarding

The roughest surf on the Bahía de Navidad shoreline is closer to Barra, the most tranquil closest to Melaque. Swimming is consequently best and safest toward the Melaque end, while, in contrast, the most popular local surfing spot is where the waves rise and roll in beside the Barra jetty. Bodysurfing and boogie boarding are best somewhere in between. At least one shop in Barra, **Farmacia Zurich** (on Legazpi, south corner of Jalisco, tel. 315/355-6135), sells boogie boards, surfboards, fishing poles, tackle and lures.

Sailing and Sailboarding

Sailing and sailboarding are best near the Melaque end of the Bay of Navidad and in the Bay of Coastecomate nearby. Bring your own equipment, however; none is available locally.

Snorkeling and Scuba Diving

Local snorkeling is often good during the dry winter season, especially at Playa Tenacatita, off Highway 200, several miles north. Snorkel and scuba tours to nearby coral reefs and scuba instruction are available in Barra de Navidad through **Sea to Sierra Outdoor Adventures** (Av. Veracruz 204, tel. 315/355-5790, www. seatosierra.com), across from the town *jardín*. Although Sea to Sierra has no scuba instructor, they partner with the professional PADI-trained instructors of **Nautimar** (tel. 315/331-0500) dive shop at the Hotel Grand Bay.

The best-organized and most professional regional dive shop is **Underworld Scuba** (P.O. Box 295, Santiago, Colima 28860, tel./

fax 314/333-0642 or 314/333-3678, Carlos's cell 044-314/358-0327, Susan's cell 044-314/358-5042, www.divemanzanillo.com or www.gomanzanillo.com/scubamex), run by Manzanillo-based Susan Dearing, and her partner, NAUI-certified instructor Carlos Cuellar.

Sportfishing

The captains of the Barra boat cooperative, **Sociedad Cooperativa de Servicios Turísticos** (Av. Veracruz 40, tel. 315/354-3792 or 044-315/354-3792), routinely take parties on successful marlin and swordfish hunts for about $28 per hour, including bait and tackle. Ask at their lagoonside office-dock. Alternatively, you can arrange a fishing trip through highly recommended **Z Pesca** sportfishing (reservations office, Hotel Alondra, no. 8, tel. 315/355-6464, U.S. tel. 949/643-1560, fax 949/643-8825, www.zpesca.com), whose boat-dock tackle shop and office are staffed by Captain Chaparro at Tampico 71. Depending on the size of the craft, their fees run from about $200 and up. If the above aren't available, **Sea to Sierra Outdoor Adventures** (Av. Veracruz 204, tel. 315/355-5790, www.seatosierra.com) will probably be able to arrange a fishing excursion for you.

Fishing trips will typically net a number of large dorado, albacore, snapper, or other delicious eating fish. Local restaurants will generally cook a banquet for you and your friends if you give them the extra fish caught during such an outing.

If you'd like to enter one of a pair of annual Barra de Navidad **International Fishing Tournaments** (billfish, tuna, and dorado in Jan. and May; father and son/daughter tournament in Jan.), contact captain Chaparro of Z Pesca (Tampico 71, tel. 315/355-6464, U.S. tel. 949/643-1560, fax 949/643-8825, www.zpesca.com) or the tourist information office.

Boating

If you plan on mounting your own fishing expedition, you can do it from the Barra **boat-launching ramp** (end of Av. Filipinas, 8 A.M.–4 P.M. Mon.–Fri.) near the Hotel Cabo

Blanco. The fee, about $20 per day, covers parking your boat in the canal and is payable to the boatkeeper, whose headquarters is inside the boatyard adjacent to the ramp.

Tennis and Golf

The **Hotel Cabo Blanco** tennis courts (tel. 315/355-5182) are customarily open for public rental for about $4 per hour. Call ahead to check. Lessons may also be available. The **Hotel Portico del Mar** (tel. 315/355-6495) also has tennis courts for outside visitors ($3/hr).

The plumy, breezy 18-hole **Isla Navidad Golf Course** is available to the public for a fee of around $100 per person. Call the Hotel Grand Bay (tel. 315/331-0500, www.islanavidad.com) and ask for the Club de Golf for information. Get there by regular launch from the Barra dock on the lagoon (to the Casa Club landing, about $5 round-trip). By car, turn right from Highway 200 at the Ejido La Culebra (or Isla Navidad) sign as the highway cuts through the hills at Km 51 a few miles south of Barra. Follow the road about three miles (4.8 km) to a bridge, where the road curves right, paralleling the beach. After about two more miles (3.2 km), you pass through the golf course gate. After winding through the golf course another mile (1.6 km), turn right at the traffic circle at the north edge of the golf course. Continue another mile (1.6 km), between the golf course and the adjacent hillside, to the big golf clubhouse on the right. You can get detailed information on the courses and maps on the website listed above.

Hiking

You can do hike between Barra and Melaque (four miles either way), but starting from Barra early in the morning, the sun will be behind you and the sky and ocean will be at their bluest and best. Take insect repellent, sunscreen, and a hat. At either end, enjoy lunch at one of the seaside restaurants. At the Melaque end you can continue walking north to the cove on the far side of town. The trail, now a concrete *andador* beneath the cliff, leads to spectacular wave-tossed tidepools and rugged sea rocks at the tip of the bay. At the Barra end, you can

hire a launch to Colimilla for lunch or dinner. End your day leisurely by taxiing or busing back from the bus station at either end.

Bird- and Wildlife-Watching

The wildlife-rich upper reaches of the Laguna de Navidad stretch for miles and are only a boat ride away. Besides the ordinary varieties of egrets, terns, herons, pelicans, frigate birds, boobies, ducks, and geese, patient bird-watchers can sometimes snare rainbow flash-views of exotic parrots and bright tanagers and orioles.

As for other creatures, quiet, persistent observers are sometimes rewarded with mangrove-edge views of turtles, constrictors, crocodiles, coatimundis, raccoons, skunks, deer, wild pigs, ocelots, wildcats, and, very rarely, a jaguar. The sensitivity and experience of your boatman/guide is, of course, crucial to the success of any nature outing. Ask at the tourist information office in Barra or the dock-office of the **Sociedad Cooperativa de Servicios Turísticos** (Barra de Navidad, Av. Veracruz 40) on the lagoon front. You might also ask Tracy Ross at **Crazy Cactus Real Estate** (Barra de Navidad, Veracruz 165, across from the bus station, tel. 315/355-6091), or Nan Niemela and/or Enrique Palominos of **Sea to Sierra Outdoor Adventures** (Barra de Navidad, Veracruz 204, across from the *jardín*, tel. 315/355-5790, www.seatosierra.com) to recommend a good guide, or even a complete wildlife-watching excursion.

Ecotours

Friendly and enterprising local guides Nan Niemela and Enrique Palominos, through their **Sea to Sierra Outdoor Adventures,** guide and arrange a number of tours for nature lovers. These include snorkel, scuba, fishing, mountain bike trips, and more. Contact them at their Barra shop (Av. Veracruz 204, tel. 315/355-5790, www.seatosierra.com), across from the town *jardín*.

Sports Equipment Sales and Rentals

In Barra, the **Farmacia Zurich** (on Legazpi,

south corner of Jalisco, tel. 315/355-8582, 9 A.M.–10 P.M. daily) sells boogie boards, surfboards, fishing poles, tackle and lures. **Sea to Sierra Outdoor Adventures** (Av. Veracruz 204, tel. 313/355-5790), also in Barra, rents mountain bikes.

ACCOMMODATIONS

Whether on the beach or not, all Barra hotels (except the world-class Hotel Grand Bay) fall in the budget or moderate categories. Note: During fall storm season Barra de Navidad waves sometimes hit the sand with a boom. If you're a light sleeper, best come prepared with earplugs. Otherwise, choose one of Barra's many good off-beach hotels.

In contrast to Barra de Navidad, San Patricio Melaque has many beachfront hotels. Although the majority of them, especially in the old San Patricio town center, are mediocre at best, visitors enjoy a number of well-managed comfortable, even deluxe, exceptions, especially in the quiet south-side neighborhood. All of those covered enjoy beachfront locations, although few, except those noted, accept credit cards.

Barra Hotels

Under $50: On the south end, **Casa de Huéspedes Mama Laya** (Veracruz 69, tel. 315/355-5088, $16 s, $21 d, $26 t) is one of Barra's few remaining recommendable low-budget lodgings. The grandmotherly owner (who named her hotel after her late mother) offers 14 basic rooms in an airy two-story layout overlooking the Navidad lagoon-front. All rooms have two double beds, with fans and hot-water shower baths. One attractive plus is an upstairs open-air lagoon-view veranda, with chairs and sofas for guest use.

Half a block north, find the budget traveler's longtime favorite, **Casa de Huéspedes Caribe** (Sonora 15, tel. 315/355-5952, $15 s, $20 d, and $25 t), tucked along a side street. The family owners offer their devoted following of long-term customers 11 plainly decorated barebulb but clean rooms, with twin, double, or both types of beds, all with bath and hot water. Amenities include a homey downstairs garden sitting area, and more chairs and hammocks for snoozing on an upstairs porch.

$50–100: Return north a block, then right

eco-resort Coco Cabañas on Isla Navidad

and east another block, where its loyal international clientele swears by the family-operated **Hotel Delfín** (Morelos 23, tel. 315/355-5068, www.hoteldelfinmx.com). Its four stories of tile-floored, balcony-corridor rooms (where curtains, unfortunately, must be drawn for privacy) are the cleanest and coziest of Barra's moderate hotels. The Delfín's tour de force, however, is the cheery patio buffet where guests linger over the breakfast offered (8:30–10:30 A.M. daily, $6) to all comers. Overnight guests, however, must put up with the moderate nighttime noise of the disco half a block away. For maximum sun and privacy take one of the top-floor rooms, many of which enjoy lagoon views. The Delfín's 24 rooms rent for $49 s or d, $59 t, $69 q; with fans, small pool, and parking; credit cards are accepted. There are also two two-bedroom apartments available on the top floors which can be rented for $120 per day with discounts available for long-term stays. The apartments have full kitchens and private balconies.

Right across the street, bordering the lagoon, the most charmingly tropical of Barra hotels, the drowsy old-Mexico 🄲 **Hotel Sands** (Morelos 24, tel./fax 315/355-5018), offers a bit of class at moderate rates. A pair of three-story room tiers encloses an inner courtyard lined with comfortable airy sitting areas that open onto a lush green garden of leafy vines and graceful coconut palms. A right-side garden walkway leads to a panorama of Barra's colorful lineup of lagoon-front fishing launches. On the other side, past the swim-up bar, a big curving pool and outer patio lead to a grand, airy vista of the placid mangrove-bordered Laguna de Navidad.

The pool bar (happy hour 4–6 P.M. daily, winter season) and the sitting areas afford inviting places to meet other travelers. The rooms, all with fans (but with slow-to-arrive hot water in some rooms—check before moving in) are clean and furnished with dark varnished wood and tile. Light sleepers should wear earplugs or book a room in the wing farthest from the disco down the street, whose music thumps away until around 2 A.M. many nights during the high season. Its 43 rooms and bungalows rent from $32 s, $48 d low season, $51 s, $65 d high (bargain for a better rate); bungalows sleeping four with kitchenette run $90 low season, $125 high. Credit cards (with a 6 percent surcharge) are accepted, and parking is available.

Return south three blocks along Veracruz (and jog half a block uphill, west), to the white-stuccoed **Hotel Joya del Mar** (Veracruz 209, tel./fax 315/355-6967, hoteljoyadelmar@yahoo.com.mx). The Mexican on-site owner offers three floors of eight simply but comfortably furnished rooms and suites, topped by a pair of view suites. The building's height affords upper-floor accommodations the benefit of either lagoon or ocean sunset views and cooling afternoon westerly breezes. Rooms rent from $42 s, $56 d, and $63 t, to about $92 s, $105 d for the third-floor suites. Add about $10 to all rates for high season. Features include fans, air-conditioning, no smoking in rooms, and credit cards accepted. Make your winter reservations early.

An attractive addition to Barra's sprinkling of beachfront lodgings is **Casa Chips** (198 López de Legazpi, tel. 315/355-5555, www.casachips.com, or P.O. Box 882004, San Francisco, CA 94188-2004, U.S. tel. 415/671-3816) in the middle of town, tucked half a block south of the big Hotel Barra de Navidad. Here, owners have packed a lot of hotel into a small space. They offer an assortment of seven invitingly decorated rustic-chic lodgings, ranging from double-bed rooms to one-bedroom suites, all the way up to an entire deluxe two-bedroom upstairs view apartment. All are decorated with color-coordinated bedspreads and drapes, attractive tile, and hand-hewn wood furniture. An important extra here is an airy beachfront restaurant, fine for relaxing dining, socializing, and sunset-watching. Low-season rates range between about $45 and $55 for the smaller, up to $85 d for the largest accommodation; high season, about $65, up to about $110. Add $10 and $15 low and high season, respectively, per extra person. All with fans, air-conditioning, hot-water showers, television and wireless Internet; the larger lodgings have kitchenettes.

Folks interested in tennis, boats, and/or fishing might appreciate Barra's original deluxe lodging, the stucco-and-tile four-star **Hotel Cabo Blanco** (P.O. Box 31, Barra de Navidad, Jalisco 48987, tel./fax 315/355-5103, toll-free Mex. tel. 01-800/710-5690, fax 315/355-6494, www.hotelcaboblanco.com). The 125-room low-rise complex (named after the 1970s Barra de Navidad–filmed Hollywood thriller *Cabo Blanco,* starring Charles Bronson) anchors the vacation-home development along the three marina-canals that extend about five blocks north from the Barra lagoon. Within its manicured garden-grounds, Hotel Cabo Blanco offers night-lit tennis courts, restaurants, bars, two pools, kiddie pools, and deluxe sportfishing yachts-for-hire. The deluxe pastel-decorated rooms run about $65 d, except $75 July and August, holidays, and some weekends, all with air-conditioning, cable TV, and phones; with a folkloric dance show, many water sports, and credit cards accepted. Bring your repellent; during late afternoon and evening mosquitoes and gnats from the nearby mangroves seem to especially enjoy the Cabo Blanco's posh ambience. All-inclusive or European plan packages are available on the website at discounted rates.

Tucked four short blocks from the beach at Barra's north end is the very worthy family-friendly three-star **Hotel El Marquez** (Calles Filipinas and Manzanillo, tel./fax 315/355-5304, www.costalegre.ca/Barra_Hotels.htm). Inside the gate, guests enjoy about 30 comfortable semideluxe rooms around an invitingly intimate inner pool patio. Rates begin at about $48 d low season, $60 d high, with air-conditioning ($10 extra), kiddie playground, and parking. Wireless Internet and televisions are also provided in all of the rooms.

If the Marquez is full, try similarly comfortable but smaller three-star neighbor **Bungalows Mar Vida** (Mazatlán 168, tel. 315/355-5911, fax 315/355-5349, www.vrbo.com/58088), one block west and one block south. Friendly owner and real estate agent Marsha Ewing Hernandez asks $55 d year-round for the bungalow with

kitchenette and $50 d for her comfortable, semideluxe rooms sans kitchen, with air-conditioning and small pool patio.

Right in the middle of town, located securely a block away from Barra's sometimes destructive surf, is the block-square five-story **Hotel la Alondra** (Calle Sinaloa 16, tel. 315/355-8372, 315/355-8373, or 315/355-8305, hotellaalondra@yahoo.com.mx, www.alondrahotel.com). Commercial shops, adjacent to the small lobby, occupy the downstairs floor. Upstairs, guests enjoy three floors of 54 (40 double rooms, 4 junior suites, 10 suites) light, airy accommodations, some with private oceanview balconies. All are attractively decorated in pastel blue-and-orange bedspreads and curtains and offer double, queen, or king-size bed options. Low-season rates run about $75 d for rooms with one (although king-size) bed, $106 d for two double beds, and $180 for the larger and fancier junior suites. Corresponding high-season prices are $85, $120, and $220. A fifth-floor panoramic view restaurant, beachfront swimming pool with view and swim-up bar are available for guest relaxation and sunset-watching. Boat tours are arranged through the front desk and guests can take a ride through the lagoon or bay for about $30 per person.

The second of Barra's two recommendable beachfront lodgings is the white, stucco, three-story **Hotel Barra de Navidad** (Av. L. de Legazpi 250, tel. 315/355-5122, fax 315/355-5303, www.hotelbarradenavidad.com) on the beach side of the town plaza. Guests in the seaside upper two floors of comfortable semideluxe rooms enjoy palm-fringed ocean vistas from private balconies. A shady, plant-decorated interior courtyard and inviting pool and patio on one side and good Bananas Restaurant upstairs complete the compact but attractive picture. Rates for the 60 rooms run about $75 s, $82 d, $90 t, all with air-conditioning. Ask for one of the sunnier, quieter, oceanview rooms. Credit cards are accepted. **Banana's Grill** is located in the hotel for on-site dining.

Over $100: Across the lagoon on Isla Navidad you will find Barra's ecologically correct **Coco Cabañas** (Km 8.2, on the road between Hwy. 200 and Isla Navidad, tel. 335/004-2686, U.S. tel. 281/205-4100, www. ecocabanas.com), perched on pristine and breezy Playa los Cocos, a couple of miles south of Barra de Navidad. This is clearly a place for those who enjoy solitude: no telephones or cable TV in the rooms, but with a great, reasonably priced restaurant, perhaps a few other guests, miles of luscious beach to explore, and plenty of opportunities for reading and relaxing in the pool that meanders in front of the rustic cabanas. There is wireless Internet available in the restaurant as well as a television with cable just in case you can't bear to be away from technology.

The cabanas can sleep as many as four adults and two kids—two adults downstairs in a sofa bed, kids on a moveable foam mattress, and two more adults in a king-size bed in an upstairs loft. There are hot showers and fans inside and hammocks in front for your daily siesta. Rates run $80 d low season, $125 d high, add $5 per extra person. The surf can get very rough at the beach here so expert swimmers or waders only. There's been considerable development on Isla Navidad but hopefully Coco Cabañas will remain a rustic haven amid the condos and new hotels that are currently under construction.

In complete contrast nearby stands Barra's plushest hotel by far, the class-act **Hotel Grand Bay** (P.O. Box 20, Barra de Navidad, Jalisco 48987, tel. 315/331-0500, fax 315/355-0560, www.islanavidad.com), a short boat ride to the Isla Navidad development across the lagoon. Builders spared little expense to create the appearance of a *gran época* resort. The 198 rooms are elaborately furnished with marble floors, French-provincial furniture reproductions, and Italian jade-hued marble bathroom sinks. Accommodations run from spacious "superior" rooms for about $250 d except holidays and some weekends; master suites from about $390 d; through grand four-room executive suites that include their own steam rooms, from about $1,200. With all possible amenities including three elegant restaurants, tennis, volleyball, children's club, marina, and an

exceptional oceanfront golf course, you won't run out of things to do during your stay. The centerpiece of the hotel are the three ground floor pools (there are other pools hidden on various floors, half the fun is exploring the place to find them) which cascade into one another through waterfalls and water slides. A small hot tub under the gazebo is popular in the cool winter evenings. There are lagoonside sun beds and hammocks under shady palms if you prefer a more natural setting.

The owners of the Hotel Grand Bay also offer a more private, personal option, the **Mesón Doña Paz** (tel. 315/337-9002 or 315/337-9000, fax 314/337-9015, www.mesondonapaz.com). Originally built as the owners' private manor house (which they now use only at Christmas), the Mesón Doña Paz is a maharaja's mansion of spacious superluxurious suites, elegantly decorated in the marble French provincial mode of the neighboring Hotel Grand Bay. The load of conveniences includes elaborate telephone-equipped bathrooms (with separate rooms for tubs and showers), airy private view patios, an exclusive restaurant, dining veranda, bar, and boat landing. Upstairs, a regal penthouse view salon, perfect for executive meetings (up to about 50 people) adds an attractive business-friendly option. Offering rates, beginning at $220 d (about $310 holidays and some weekends) to $390 ($540) for junior suites and $560 ($680) for master suites, are reasonable, considering the luxurious exclusive facilities. Reserve for Mesón Doña Paz directly.

Note: Security is tight at Hotel Grand Bay and Mesón Doña Paz. Guards at the hotel lagoonside boat dock (and the separate Mesón Doña Paz dock) only allow entrance to guests and prospective guests. If you want to look around, you have to be accompanied by an in-house guide. Call the desk beforehand for an appointment. You can also drive around to the hotel along Isla Navidad if you have a vehicle.

South of Town Melaque Hotels
Most of Melaque's recommendable hotels lie in the quiet south-of-town neighborhood.

Under $50: Melaque's best-buy budget

© BRUCE WHIPPERMAN

enjoying the beach view in Melaque

lodging is the **Hotel Santa María** (Abel Salgado 85, tel. 315/355-5677, fax 315/355-5553). Long popular with cost-conscious Canadians and Americans in winter, the Santa María's 46 accommodations, all one-bedroom kitchenette apartments, are arranged in two motel-style wings around an invitingly green and tranquil inner patio. All are close enough to the water for the waves to lull guests to sleep. Units vary; uppers are brighter, so look at a few before you move in. All-season prices for the spartan but generally tidy apartments begin at about $32 d per day, $180/week, $365/month, with TV, fans, hot-water showers, and pleasantly sunny beach-front pool patio.

North a few blocks, closer to the town center, is the well-kept colonial-chic **Posada Pablo de Tarso** (Av. Gómez Farías 408, tel./fax 315/355-5707 or 315/355-5717), named after the apostle Paul of Tarsus. Guests enjoy many attractive details, including art-decorated walls, hand-carved bedsteads and doors, and a flowery beachside pool and patio. The main drawback to all this lies in the motel-style corridor layout, which requires guests to pull the dark drapes

for privacy. Year-round rates for the 27 rooms and bungalows begin at about $45 d ($25 daily rate for one-month rental) except possibly for some holidays; a kitchen in the unit raises the tariff to about $85 d, all with fan, air-conditioning, TV, and phones. You may also reserve with their Guadalajara office (tel./fax 333/811-5262 or 333/811-4273).

$50-100: Classy in its unique way is the ❰ **Villas Camino del Mar** (Calle Francisco Villa, corner Abel Salgado, tel. 315/355-5207, fax 315/355-5498, www.villascaminodelmar.com.mx). A few signs in the humble beach neighborhood about a quarter-mile on the Barra side of the Melaque town center furnish the only clue that this gem of a lodging hides at the beach end of a bumpy Melaque street. (Note: The owners have added an annex across the street, which, although inviting, crams in more accommodations in a smaller space than the original building. Specifically ask for a room in the original building in your reservation request.) A five-story white stucco monument draped with fluted neoclassical columns and hanging pedestals, the original

Villas Camino del Mar hotel offers a lodging assortment from simple double rooms through deluxe suites with kitchenettes to a rambling penthouse. The upper three levels have sweeping ocean views, while the lower two overlook an elegant blue pool and patio bar and shady beachside palm grove. The clientele is split between Mexican middle-class families who come for weekends all year around, and quiet Canadian and American couples who come to soak up the winter sun for weeks and months on end. Reserve early, especially for the winter. Rates for the 37 rooms and suites run as little as $49 ($43 per day for a week, $34 per day for a month) for small but comfortable oceanview rooms for two; $79 ($71 per day weekly, $55 per day monthly) for a studio with kitchenette; $95 ($85 per day weekly, $66 per day monthly) for medium one-bedroom with two queen beds and kitchenette; and $120 ($108 per day weekly, $88 per day monthly) for deluxe two-bedroom, two-bath suites with kitchen; all with fans only. All rates are discounted 10 percent during low occupancy (usually May–June and Sept.–Nov.).

Camino del Mar's nearby upscale **Villas Alvanelly,** set in a spacious, grassy beachfront compound with its own pool, offers much more luxury and space. The nine one- and two-bedroom kitchenette apartments go for $95–135; a one-week rental gets an 8 percent discount; one month 30 percent. Reserve early, through the Villas Camino del Mar contact numbers.

Close by, the sky-blue-and-white **Bungalows Azteca** (P.O. Box 57, San Patricio Melaque, Jalisco 48980, tel./fax 315/355-5150, www.bungalowsazteca.com) auto court–style cottages line both sides of a cobbled driveway courtyard garden that spreads to a lazy beachfront pool patio. The 14 spacious kitchenette cottages, in one-bedroom or three-bedroom versions, are plainly furnished but clean. The nine one-bedroom units rent for about $55 per day low season and $65 per day high. The five three-bedrooms rent for about $150 per day low and $160 per day high. Get your reservation in early, especially for the winter.

Less than a block south, the open, parklike

grounds, spacious blue pool with kiddie pools, and beachside palm garden of the **Bungalows Mayorca** (Abel Salgado 133, Colonia Villa Obregón, tel./fax 315/355-5219, bungalowsmayorca@prodigy.net.mx or www.tomzap.com/mayorca.html) invite unhurried outdoor relaxation. Its stacked, Motel 6–style layout, attractively draped with tropical greenery, has aged gracefully. Here, groups and families used to providing their own atmosphere find the kitchens and spacious (but dark) rooms of the Bungalows Mayorca appealing. The 21 two-bedroom bungalows, all with air-conditioning and TV, rent for about $60 d, $230 per week, $890 per month low season ($76, $330, and $1,020 high). If you're in the mood for a splurge, ask for one of their three beachfront suites, with view balconies and whirlpool tubs, for about 20 percent additional.

North of Town Melaque Hotels

A sprinkling of hotels in the sleepy Melaque north-end neighborhood offer comfortable accommodations at budget-to-moderate rates.

Under $50: One of the tidiest is the **《 Hotel Bahía** (Calle Legazpi 5, tel./fax 315/355-6894, www3.telus.net/public/a7a84441/hotelbahia) of kindly owner/managers Evelia and Rafael Galvez Moreno, just half a block off the beach. The hotel's 21 rooms and two kitchenette bungalows line a pair of two-floor tiers that enclose a lovely inner patio and a pool in a second patio off to one side and an airy upstairs veranda, fine for relaxing and socializing. The rooms, although smallish, are spic-and-span and attractively decorated with flowery curtains and matching bedspreads. A common kitchen is available downstairs for guest use. Room rates run from about $36 (for 1–4) low season to about $45 high; bungalows about $55, with TV, fans, hot-water showers, and filtered drinking water.

The neighboring homey, downscale-modern white-stucco **Hotel de Legazpi** (Av. de las Palmas 3, tel./fax 315/355-5397, hoteldelegazpi@prodigy.net.mx) offers relaxing vacation options right on the beachfront. A number of the hotel's spacious, clean, and comfortable frontside rooms have balconies with palmy ocean and sunset views. Downstairs, guests enjoy a small restaurant and a rear-court pool and patio. The hotel's beachside entrance leads through a jungly front garden straight to the idyllic Melaque west-end sand crescent. Here, good times bloom among an informal club of longtime winter returnees beneath the *palapas* of the popular La Sirenita, Cabo Blanco, and Viva María restaurants. The hotel's 16 fan-only rooms (two with kitchenette) rent for $30 s or d, $35 t low season, and $39, $44, $49 high, with a TV room, and hot-water shower baths.

$50-100: If you prefer hotel high-rise ambience with privacy, a seaview balcony, and a disco (weekends and holidays) next door, you can have it right on the beach at the **Hotel Club Náutico** (Av. Gómez Farías 1A, tel. 315/355-5770 or 315/355-5766, fax 315/355-5239, www.hotelclubnautico.com). The 40 simply but attractively decorated rooms, in blue, pastels, and white, angle toward the ocean in sunset-view tiers above a smallish pool and patio. The upper-floor rooms nearest the beach are likely to be quieter with the best views. The hotel also has a good beachside restaurant whose huge *palapa* both captures the cool afternoon sea breeze and frames the blue waters of the Bay of Navidad. The hotel's main drawback is lack of exterior space, being sandwiched into a long, narrow beachfront lot. Rentals run about $70 d, $84 t, add about 30 percent during Christmas and Easter holidays. Ask for a discount during times of low occupancy. Features include air-conditioning, TV, phones, and restaurant/bar with a view; credit cards are accepted.

Apartments, Houses, and Long-Term Rentals

If you're planning on a stay longer than a few weeks, you'll get more for your money if you can find a long-term house or apartment rental. Check out the good **Vacation Rentals by Owner** website (www.vrbo.com), which lists 19 Barra rental choices at this writing. Alternatively, contact Barra long-time realtors Peggy and Tracye Ross at **Crazy Cactus Real**

Estate (Veracruz 165, tel./fax 315/355-6091 or 315/355-6099, www.casademarco.com) in Barra across from the bus station; or Marsha Ewing Hernandez, operator of **Mar Vida Real Estate** (tel. 315/355-5911, fax 315/355-5349, marshahernandez@yahoo.com).

Trailer Parks and Campgrounds

Barra-Melaque's best trailer park is **La Playa** (Av. Gómez Farías 250, tel. 315/355-5065), right on the beach in downtown Melaque. Although the park is a bit cramped and mostly shadeless, longtimers nevertheless get their winter reservations in early for the choice beach spaces. The better-than-average facilities include a small store, fish-cleaning sinks, showers, toilets, and all hookups. The water is brackish—drink bottled. Boat launching is usually easy on the sheltered beach nearby. The Trailer Park La Playa's 45 spaces rent for about $19 per day, $110per week or $355 per month.

Scores of winter returnees enjoy Melaque's north-end shoreline **informal RV park-campground** with room for about 50 rigs and tents, operated by the Ejido Emiliano Zapata community. The cliff-bottom lot spreads above a calm rocky cove, ripe for swimming, snorkeling, and sailboarding. Other extras include super fishing and a sweeping view of the entire Bay of Navidad. All spaces are usually filled by Christmas and remain that way until March. The people are friendly, the price ($3 per tent or $5 per RV per day, $15/wk, $70/mo, small garbage collection fee, collected by the *ejido* folks) is certainly right, and the beer and water trucks arrive regularly throughout the winter season. Please dump your waste in sanitary facilities while staying here; continued pollution of the cove by irresponsible occupants in the past has led to complaints. Get there by the dirt road that continues from Avenida del Palmar, at the northwest end of Melaque.

Wilderness campers will enjoy **Playa los Cocos,** the miles-long golden sand beach south of Barra de Navidad that borders the ocean side of the Isla Navidad golf course. Playa los Cocos has an intimate hidden north-end sandy cove, perfect for an overnight or a few barefoot days of bird-watching, shell collecting, beachcombing, and dreaming around your driftwood campfire. The restaurants at the village of Colimilla or the stores (by launch across the lagoon) in Barra are available for food and water. Mosquitoes come out around sunset. Bring plenty of good repellent and a mosquito-proof tent.

The easiest way to get to Playa los Cocos is by hiring a launch at the Barra de Navidad lagoonfront that will drop you off right on the Playa los Cocos beach. You can also go by hiring a taxi from Barra de Navidad, or by your own car from Highway 200. From Barra de Navidad, head south on Highway 200 a few miles to the signed Isla Navidad right turnoff. Continue through the golf course, bearing left, toward the ocean, to the golf course's northwest corner and an oceanfront parking lot at the beach.

FOOD
Breakfast, Snacks, and Stalls

An excellent way to start your Barra day is at the intimate *palapa*-shaded patio of the **Hotel Delfín** (Av. Morelos 23, tel. 315/357-0068, 8:30–10:30 A.M. daily, $6). While you dish yourself fruit and pour your coffee from its little countertop buffet, the cook fixes your choice of breakfast options, from savory eggs and omelettes to French toast and luscious, tender banana pancakes. Alternatively, in Barra, for an equally satisfying breakfast ($3–6), go to the oceanview restaurant **Bananas,** upstairs at the Hotel Barra de Navidad (tel. 315/355-5122).

For good, plain eating, and what some say are the best breakfasts in town, go to **Pastarama** (on Abel Salgado, tel. 315/355-6123, open early, $3–5) on the Melaque south side, near the Hotel Saul de Tarso.

Also, plenty of good daytime eating in Melaque goes on at the lineup of small permanent *fondas* ($2–4) in the alley that runs south from Avenida Hidalgo, half a block toward the beach from the southwest plaza corner. You can't go wrong with *fonda* food, as long as it's made right in front of you and served piping hot.

For evening light meals and snacks, Barra has plenty of options. Here, families seem to fall into two categories: Those who sell food to sidewalk passersby, and those who enjoy their offerings. The three blocks of Avenida Veracruz from Morelos to the city *jardín* (park) are dotted with tables that residents nightly load with hearty, economical food offerings, from tacos *de lengua* (tongue) and pork tamales to *pozole Guadalajara* and chiles rellenos ($1–3). The

RAICILLA

Sometimes called Mexican moonshine, **raicilla** (rye-SEE-yah) is a homegrown version of tequila or mezcal produced only in the Jalisco region of Mexico. The moonshine heritage of *raicilla* comes from citizens producing the liquor in secret to avoid the related regulations and taxes required for producing alcohol. Typically, you would find *raicilla* sold in private homes, bottled in plastic bottles or other recyclable containers.

While tequila is made from the blue agave plant, *raicilla* is made from *Agave lechuguilla*, a member of the botanical group Crenatae and commonly known as *"pata de mula"* (mule's foot). The distillation and production process is basically the same for both liquors, however *raicilla* has a very different flavor from tequila. It's also known to be considerably more potent, sometimes with an alcohol content of up to 150 proof.

Although initially produced by individuals with private stills, *raicilla* has developed enough of a following that the first ever *raicilla* cultural festival was held in San Sebastián in December 2008. Fifteen distillers in attendance showed off their micro-distilled products. The two-day event is expected to continue and includes tours of local distilleries.

wholesomeness of their menus is evidenced by their devoted followings of longtime neighbor and tourist customers.

If you are looking for a nice deli sandwich or some French pastries, you can't miss **El Horno Francés** (Lepazpi 125, tel. 315/355-0050, next to the Hotel al Alondra pool) where everything is baked fresh each morning. A case of sumptuous pies and croissants will tempt you or grab an espresso and cookie to go.

Barra Restaurants

One local family has built its sidewalk culinary skills into a thriving Barra storefront business, the **Restaurant Paty** (corner of Veracruz and Jalisco, tel. 315/355-5907, 8 A.M.–11 P.M. daily, $2–5). It offers the traditional menu of Mexican *antojitos*—tacos, quesadillas, tostadas—plus roast beef, chicken, and very tasty pozole. For a variation, try expatriate favorite **Pizzeria Yvette** a few doors nearby.

Among Barra's favorite eateries is the ◖ **Restaurant Ramón** (Legazpi 260, tel. 315/355-6435, 7 A.M.–11 P.M. daily, $5–12),

across the street from the Hotel Barra de Navidad. Completely unpretentious and making the most of the usual list of international and Mexican specialties, friendly owner/chef Ramón and his hardworking staff continue to build their already sizable following. Choose whatever you like—chicken, fish, chiles rellenos, guacamole, spaghetti—and you'll most likely be pleased. Meals include gratis salsa and chips to start, hearty portions, and often a healthy side of cooked veggies on your plate.

One of Barra's most entertainingly scenic restaurants is ◖ **Veleros** (Veracruz 64, tel. 315/355-5907, noon–10 P.M. daily, $7–15), right on the lagoon. If you happen to visit Barra during the full moon, don't miss watching its shimmering reflection from the restaurant *palapa* as it rises over the mangrove-bordered expanse. An additional Veleros bonus is the fascinating school of darting, swirling fish attracted by the spotlight shining on the water. Finally comes the food, which you can select from a menu of carefully prepared and served shrimp, lobster, octopus, chicken, and steak

Many restaurants along the coast catch their own seafood.

THE JALISCO COAST

entrées. The brochettes are especially popular; credit cards are accepted.

Alternatively, for a singularly romantic option, try refined lagoon-front [(**Restaurant Alcatraz** (Veracruz 12, tel. 315/355-7041, noon–10 P.M. daily, $8–20), named by friendly owners Sergio and Susana Aguilar for the native lily that grows only in the Mexican altiplano. (But is nevertheless very common in California gardens.) Susana, who manages the restaurant, offers a delicious menu, from soups and salads, to meats, fish fillets, shrimp, and lobster. During winter high season, reservations are recommended.

Shift your scene one block away, to the recently remodeled **Restaurant Seamaster** (López de Legazpi 140, no phone, 8 A.M.– 11 P.M. daily, $6–10), on the beach side of the sandbar, where guests enjoy a refreshing sea breeze every afternoon and a happy-hour sunset every evening. Besides superfresh seafood selections, Seamaster features savory barbecued chicken and rib plates and a nice cocktail list.

Restaurant Pancho (Legazpi 53, 8 A.M.–8 P.M. daily, $6–10), a few doors away, is one of Barra's original *palapas,* which oldtimers can remember from the days when *all* Barra restaurants were *palapas.* The reputation for super-fresh seafood, built up by the original (but now late) Pancho, who saw lots of changes in the old sandbar in his 80-odd years, is now continued by his wife and son.

Don't miss ordering the shrimp cocktail ($8) at **Casa Chips Restaurant** (Legazpi 198, tel. 315/355-5555, closed Monday), which comes in a massive goblet filled with vegetables and broth, served hot. It's one of the best this author has ever had. If you are still hungry, there are lots of other delicious menu items to choose from as well like the pineapple shrimp ($14).

Melaque Restaurants

In Melaque, jazz and nouvelle cuisine first arrived at [(**Restaurant Maya** (foot of southside Calle Obregón, 6 P.M.–11 P.M. Tues.–Sat., brunch 10:30 A.M.–2 P.M. Sun.), favorite of a loyal cadre of American and Canadian vacationers and expatriates. Its private sheltered

beachfront garden and the murmur of the Melaque surf set the stage, while the music and the food provide the shadow and act. For example, start out with a Maya Martini ($4), continue with curried fish cakes ($5), follow up with linguine with pesto, cream, and prawns ($14), and finish off with the chef's dessert creation of the day ($5). Winter high-season reservations highly recommended.

Besides good breakfasts, longtimers rave about the fish-and-chips ($4) at **Pastarama** (formerly Bananarama, on Abel Salgado, tel. 315/355-6123, open daily 9 A.M.–9 P.M., $3–5) on the Melaque south side, near the Posada Pablo de Tarso.

Restaurant el Dorado (Calle Gómez Farías 1A, tel. 315/355-5770, 8 A.M.–11 P.M. daily, moderate–expensive), under the big beachside *palapa* in front of the Hotel Club Náutico, provides a cool, breezy place to enjoy the beach scene during breakfast or lunch. Fresh seafood is the centerpiece but the menu also includes ribs, burgers and chicken. Service is crisp and the specialties are carefully prepared; credit cards are accepted.

Fruit, Vegetable, and Grocery Stores

There are no large markets, traditional or modern, in Barra. However, a few minimarkets and *fruterías* stock basic supplies. Best is probably **Frutería Ixtapa** (northeast corner of Veracruz and Michoacán, tel. 315/355-6443, 8 A.M.–10 P.M. Mon.–Sat.). Drop by and find out the produce delivery day, so you can get it when it's fresh.

In Melaque, nearly all grocery and fruit shopping takes place at the **central market** or at several good stores on main street López Mateos, which runs away from the beach past the west side of the central plaza.

INFORMATION AND SERVICES
Tourist Information Offices

The small Barra-Melaque regional office of the **Jalisco Department of Tourism** (Jalisco 67, tel./fax 315/355-5100, www.costalegre.com) is tucked near the east end of Jalisco across the street from the Terraza upstairs bar. Staff distributes maps and literature and answers questions during office hours (9 A.M.–5 P.M. Mon.–Fri., 9 A.M.–2 P.M. Sat.). The office is a good source of information about local civic and ecological issues and organizations.

Publications

The Barra **newsstand** (corner of Veracruz and Michoacán, 7 A.M.–10 P.M. daily) may seasonally stock some English-language newspapers and magazines. Furthermore, the liquor store **Fatima,** north across Michoacán, next to the Transportes Cihuatlán bus station, stocks the *Miami Herald.*

Perhaps the best English-language lending library in all of the Mexican Pacific is **Beer Bob's Book Exchange** (Calle Tampico, btwn. Pilipinas and Michoacán) on a Barra back street. Many hundreds of vintage paperbacks, free for borrowing or exchange, fill the shelves. Chief librarian and Scrabble devotee Bob (a retired counselor for the California Youth Authority) manages his little gem of an establishment just for the fun of it. "It's not a store," he says. Just drop your old titles in the box and take away the equivalent from his well-organized collection. If you have nothing to exchange, simply return whatever you borrow before you leave town.

In Melaque, the **Librería Saifer** (on the southwest corner of the central plaza, by the church, 9 A.M.–3 P.M. and 5–10 P.M. daily) stocks the *Miami Herald.*

Money

Although Barra has no bank, it does have a **Banamex ATM,** at the Barra southeast plaza corner. Melaque does have a bank, **Banamex** (tel. 315/355-5217, 9 A.M.–4 P.M. Mon.–Fri., 10 A.M.–2 P.M. Sat.), with ATM, across the street and half a block north of the main bus station. Barra's friendliest money exchange is **Ciber@Money** (Veracruz 212, tel. 315/355-6177, 9 A.M.–6 P.M. Mon.–Sat.). With even longer hours, the **Vinos y Licores Barra de Navidad** (on Legazpi, across from Hotel Barra de Navidad, 8:30 A.M.–11 P.M. daily) exchanges

both Canadian and American travelers checks and cash.

After bank hours in Melaque, use the Banamex ATM, or go to **Money Exchange Melaque** (Gómez Farías 27A, tel. 315/355-5343, 9:30 A.M.–7 P.M. Mon.–Sat.), across from the bus terminal. It exchanges both American and Canadian travelers checks and cash, but the tariff often amounts to a steep $3 per $100 above bank rate.

Communications

Barra and Melaque each have a small *correo,* and Barra has a *telégrafo.* The **Barra post office** (8 A.M.–3 P.M. Mon.–Fri.) is on Veracruz, south side of the town *jardín.*

The **Melaque post office** (Clemente Orozco 13, between G. Farías and Corona, tel. 315/355-5230, 8 A.M.–3 P.M. Mon.–Fri.) is three blocks south of the plaza, a block and a half from the beach.

The Barra *telégrafo* (on Veracruz, tel. 315/355-5262, 9 A.M.–2 P.M. Mon.–Fri.), which handles money orders, is half a block north of Barra plaza.

In Barra, go to friendly **Ciber@Money** (Veracruz 212, tel. 315/355-6177, 9 A.M.–6 P.M. Mon.–Sat.) for public telephone, Internet access, and money exchange. Or connect to the Internet at **Mango Bay** café (Jalisco 70), across the street from the *turismo.*

In Melaque, go to the long-distance telephone office (corner of Morelos and Hidalgo, tel. 315/355-8608, 8 A.M.–3 P.M. and 5–10 P.M. daily) on the *jardín* northeast corner. You have a pair of Internet choices: **Ciber@Net** (on Gómez Farías, interior hall, 9 A.M.–2:30 P.M. and 4–8 P.M. Mon.–Sat.), across from the bus terminal next to the money exchange, or **Centro Virtual** (in the market, opposite the food stalls, tel. 315/355-5044, 9 A.M.–10 P.M. Mon.–Sat.), half a block toward the beach from the plaza.

Laundry

Barra and Melaque visitors enjoy the services of a number of *lavanderías.* In Barra, try **Lavandería Jardín** (Jalisco 69, 9 A.M.–2 P.M. and 4–7 P.M. Mon.–Fri., 9 A.M.–noon Sat.), next to the *turismo.* In Melaque, step one block east (parallel to beach) along Juárez from the plaza, to **Lavandería Frances.**

Health and Emergencies
In Barra, the government **Centro de Salud** (corner Veracruz and Puerto de La Navidad, tel. 315/355-6220), four blocks north of the town plaza, has a doctor 24 hours a day. The **Melaque Centro de Salud** (Calle Gordiano Guzman 10, tel. 315/355-5880), off the main beachside street Gómez Farías two blocks from the trailer park, also offers access to a doctor 24 hours a day.

In a medical emergency, call for a Red Cross (Cruz Roja) **ambulance** (tel. 315/355-2300) to whisk you to the well-equipped hospitals in Manzanillo.

Otherwise, for over-the-counter remedies, in Barra, go to **Farmacia Zurich** (on Legazpi, tel. 315/355-6135), across from the church, at the south corner of Jalisco; or in Melaque, try **Super Farmacia Plaza** (on López Mateos, tel. 315/355-5167), at the northwest corner of the town plaza.

The Barra police (Veracruz 179, tel. 315/355-5399) are on 24-hour duty at the city office adjacent to the *jardín.*

For the Melaque police, either call (tel. 315/355-5080) or go to the headquarters behind the plazafront *delegación municipal* (municipal agency) at the plaza corner of L. Mateos and Morelos.

Travel Agencies
For airplane tickets, fishing trips, tours, and other vacation arrangements in Barra, contact **Viajes Dona Tours** (Veracruz 220, corner of Michoacán, tel./fax 315/355-5667, dona-tours@hotmail.com, 11 A.M.–8 P.M. Mon.–Fri., 11 A.M.–5 P.M. Sat.). In Melaque, go to their branch office (Gómez Farías 27A, tel. 315/355-5615).

GETTING THERE
By Air
Barra de Navidad is air-accessible either through **Puerto Vallarta Airport** or the **Manzanillo Airport,** only 19 miles (30 km)

south of Barra-Melaque. While the Puerto Vallarta connection has the advantage of many more flights, transfers to the south coast are time-consuming. If you can afford it, the quickest option from Puerto Vallarta is to rent a car. Alternatively, ride a local bus or hire a taxi from the airport to the new central bus station, north of the airport. There, catch a bus, preferably **Autocamiones del Pacífico** (tel. 322/290-0716) or Flecha Amarilla's luxury service **Primera Plus** (tel. 322/221-0994) to Barra or Melaque (three hours).

On the other hand, arrival via the Manzanillo airport, half an hour from Barra-Melaque, is much more direct, provided that good connections are obtainable through the relatively few carriers that serve the airport.

Manzanillo Airport Flights: Aerocalifornia Airlines (tel. 314/334-1414) flights connect with Los Angeles and Mexico City; call for local reservations and flight information.

U.S. Airways (formerly America West) flights connect with Phoenix during the winter–spring season. For local reservations, call the airline via U.S. toll-free number direct from Mexico (01-800/235-9292) or Dona Tours (315/355-5667).

Aeromar Airlines flights connect daily with Mexico City, where many U.S. connections are available. For reservations and flight information, contact its airport office (tel. 314/333-0151 or 314/334-0532) or the Manzanillo downtown office (tel. 314-334/8356 or 314/334-8355, toll-free Mex. tel. 01-800/237-6627).

Alaska Airlines (U.S. toll-free number direct from Mexico 01-800/426-0333) flights connect daily with Los Angeles; **Magnicharter** airlines connects directly with Mexico City; and **Northwest Airlines** connects with Minneapolis January–April. For reservations, contact Dona Tours (tel. 315/355-5667).

Airport Arrival and Departure: The terminal, although small for an international destination, does have a money exchange counter, open 10 A.M.–6 P.M. daily. Also it has a few gift shops for last-minute purchases, snack stands, a good upstairs restaurant, some car rentals, and a *buzón* (mailbox) just outside the front entrance. But it has no hotel booking service, so you should arrive with a hotel reservation or you'll be at the mercy of taxi drivers who love to collect fat commissions on your first-night hotel tariff. Upon departure, be sure to save enough cash to pay the approximate $12 **departure tax** (if your ticket doesn't already include it).

After the usually rapid immigration and customs checks, independent arrivees have their choice of a car rental or taxi tickets from a booth just outside the arrival gate. *Colectivos* head for Barra de Navidad and other northern points seasonally only. Taxis, however, will take three passengers to Barra, Melaque, or Hotel Real Coastecomate for about $34 total; to El Tamarindo, $52; Hotel Blue Bay Los Angeles Locos, $54; El Careyes, $75; Chamela-El Super, $84; or Las Alamandas, $120. *Colectivo* tickets run about $10–12 per person to any Manzanillo hotel, while a *taxi especial* runs about $25–34, depending on destination.

No public buses serve the Manzanillo airport. Strong, mobile travelers on tight budgets could save pesos by hitching or hiking the three miles to Highway 200 and flagging down one of the frequent north- or southbound second-class buses (fare about $2 to Barra or Manzanillo). Don't try it at night, however.

As for airport **car rentals**, you have a choice of Alamo (tel. 314/333-0611, fax 314/333-1140, alamomanzanillo@prodigy.net.mx), Hertz (tel. 314/333-3191, 314/333-3141, or 314/333-3142), Thrifty (tel. 314/334-3282 or 314/334-3292, autzs@prodigy.net.mx), and Budget (tel./fax 314/333-1445 or 314/334-2270, budgetmzo@prodigy.net.mx). Unless you don't mind paying upward of $50 per day, shop around for your car rental by calling the company's U.S. and Canada toll-free numbers at home *before* you leave.

Don't lose your tourist card; if somehow you do, arrive early enough to get a replacement (bring proof of arrival date, such as air ticket or copy of the lost document) at the Manzanillo airport *migracion* (tel. 315/335-3689 or 315/335-3690).

By Car or RV

Three highway routes access Barra de Navidad: from the north via Puerto Vallarta, from the south via Manzanillo, and from the northeast via Guadalajara.

From Puerto Vallarta, Mexican National Highway 200 is all asphalt and in good condition (except for some potholes) along its 134-mile (216-km) stretch to Barra de Navidad. Traffic is generally light; it may slow a bit as the highway climbs the 2,400-foot Sierra Cuale summit near El Tuito south of Puerto Vallarta, but the light traffic and good road make passing safely possible. Allow about three hours for this very scenic trip. Bring a good camera as there are many spots for photo opportunities.

From Manzanillo, the 38-mile (61-km) stretch of Highway 200 is nearly all countryside and all level. It's a snap in under an hour.

The longer, but quicker and easier, Barra de Navidad–Guadalajara road connection runs through Manzanillo along *autopistas* (super-highways) 54D, 110, and 200D. In Guadalajara, start out at the Minerva Circle (at the intersection of Av. López Mateos and Guadalajara west-side Av. Vallarta). Mark your odometer and follow Avenida López Mateos south. After about 10 miles (32 km), at Guadalajara's country edge, continue, following the signs for Colima that direct you along the four-lane combined Mexican National Highways 15, 54, and 80 heading southwest. At 19 miles (30 km) from the Minerva Circle, as Highway 15 splits right for Morelia and Mexico City, continue straight ahead, following the signs for Colima and Barra de Navidad. Very soon, follow the Highway 80/Highway 54D right fork for Barra de Navidad-Colima. Two miles farther, follow the Highway 54D branch left toward Colima. Continue on Highway 54D straight ahead for about two hours, bypassing Colima. About 10 miles (32 km) south of Colima Highway 54D changes, continuing as Highway 110 expressway. At Tecoman, Highway 110 becomes Highway 200D expressway, which you follow another hour, bypassing Manzanillo (via the Manzanillo Highway 200 *cuota* bypass) all the way to Barra de Navidad. Easy grades allow a leisurely 55 mph (90 km/hr) most of the way for this 192-mile (311-km) trip. Allow about 4.5 hours, either direction.

The same is not true of the winding, two lane 181-mile (291-km) Highway 80 route between Barra de Navidad and Guadalajara. Start out from the Minerva Circle, as described above, but south of the city, instead of forking left on Highway 54D to Colima, continue straight ahead on Highway 80 toward Barra de Navidad. The narrow, two-lane road continues through a dozen little towns, over three mountain ranges, and around curves for another 160 miles (258 km) to Melaque and Barra de Navidad. To be safe, allow about six hours of driving time uphill to Guadalajara, five hours in the opposite direction.

By Bus

Several regional bus lines cooperate in connecting Barra and Melaque north with Puerto Vallarta; south with Cihuatlán, Manzanillo, Colima, Playa Azul, Zihuatanejo, and Acapulco; and northeast with Guadalajara, via Highway 80, and Morelia and Mexico City, via the expressway. They arrive and leave so often (about every half-hour during the day) from the three little Barra de Navidad stations, clustered on Avenida Veracruz a block and a half north past the central plaza, that they're practically indistinguishable.

Of the various companies, affiliated lines **Transportes Cihuatlán** and **Autocamiones del Pacífico** (tel. 315/355-5200) provide the most options: super-first-class Primera Plus buses connect (several per day) with Guadalajara, Manzanillo, and Puerto Vallarta. In addition to this, they offer at least a dozen second-class buses per day in all three directions. These often stop anywhere along the road if passengers wave them down.

Across the street, other lines, affiliated with bus giant **Flecha Amarilla,** provide similar services, including a different Primera Plus luxury-class service to Manzanillo, Puerto Vallarta, Guadalajara, and León, out of its separate station (Veracruz 269, tel. 315/355-6111), across and half a block up the street.

Also, next door to Flecha Amarilla, **ETN,** or Enlaces Transportes Nacionales (tel. 315/355-8400), buses leave from a small air-conditioned station to connect with Manzanillo, Colima, Morelia, and Mexico City.

With the exception of Elite, which stops only in Melaque, all the buses that stop in Barra also stop in Melaque; all Autocamiones del Pacífico and Transportes Cihuatlán buses stop at the Melaque main terminal, **Central de Autobuses** (on Gómez Farías at V. Carranza, tel. 315/355-5003, open 24 hours daily).

In Melaque, **Flecha Amarilla** maintains its own fancy new air-conditioned station (tel. 315/355-6110) across the street, where you can ride its luxury-class Primera Plus buses, in addition to regular second-class Autobuses Costalegre, north to Puerto Vallarta, south to Manzanillo, and with expanded service, to Guadalajara, León, and Mexico City.

One line, first-class **Elite,** does not stop in Barra. It maintains its own little Melaque station (Gómez Farías 257, tel. 315/355-5177), a block south of the main station, across from the Melaque Trailer Park. From there, Elite connects by first-class express north (two daily departures) all the way to Puerto Vallarta, Mazatlán, and Tijuana; and south (two daily departures) to Manzanillo, Zihuatanejo, and Acapulco.

Note: All Barra de Navidad and Melaque bus departures are *salidas de paso*, meaning they originate somewhere else. Although seating cannot be ascertained until the bus arrives, seats are generally available, except during crowded Christmas and Easter holidays.

BACKGROUND

The Land

The sun-drenched resort of Puerto Vallarta (pop. 350,000) and its surrounding region owe their prosperity to their most fortunate location, where gentle Pacific breezes meet the parade of majestic volcanic peaks marching west from central Mexico. Breeze-borne moisture, trickling down mineral-rich volcanic slopes, has nurtured civilizations for millennia in the highland valleys around Tepic and Guadalajara, the state capitals of Nayarit and Jalisco. Running from Lake Chapala, just south of Guadalajara, the waters plunge into the mile-deep canyon of Mexico's longest river, the Río Grande de Santiago (known as the Río Lerma upstream of the lake). They finally return to the ocean, nourishing the teeming aquatic life of the river's estuary just north of San Blas, Nayarit, two hours' drive north of Puerto Vallarta.

Within sight of Puerto Vallarta rise the jagged mountain ranges of the Sierra Vallejo and the Sierra Cuale. The runoff from these peaks becomes the Río Ameca, which sustains a lush patchwork of fruit, corn, and sugarcane that decorates the broad valley bottom. The Ameca meets the ocean just north of Puerto Vallarta town limits. There, myriad sea creatures seek the river's nourishment at the Puerto Vallarta

© ROBIN NOELLE

shoreline, the innermost recess of the Bay of Banderas, Mexico's broadest and deepest bay.

On the map of the Puerto Vallarta region, the Bay of Banderas appears gouged from the coast by some vengeful Aztec god (perhaps in retribution for the Spanish conquest) with a single 20-mile-wide swipe of his giant hand, just sparing the city of Puerto Vallarta.

Time, however, appears to have healed that great imaginary cataclysm. The rugged Sierra Vallejo to the north and Sierra Cuale to the south have acquired green coats of jungly forest on their slopes, and sand has accumulated on the great arc of the Bay of Banderas. There, a diadem of palmy fishing villages—Punta Mita, Cruz de Huanacaxtle, Bucerías, Mismaloya, Boca de Tomatlán, and Yelapa—decorate the bay to the north and south of town. In the mountains that rise literally from Puerto Vallarta's city streets, the idyllic colonial-era villages of San Sebastián, Mascota, and Talpa nestle in verdant valleys only 20 minutes away by light plane.

Farther afield, smaller bays dotted with pearly strands, sleepy villages, and small resorts adorn the coastline north and south of the Bay of Banderas. To the south, beyond the pine- and oak-studded Sierra Lagunillas summit, stretch the blue reaches of the bays of Chamela, Tenacatita, and, finally, Navidad, at the Jalisco-Colima state border. There, the downscale little resort of Barra de Navidad drowses beside its wildlife-rich lagoon.

To the north of the Bay of Banderas stretches the vine-strewn Nayarit Coast, where the broad inlets of Jaltemba and Matanchén curve past the sleepy winter havens of Sayulita, Rincón de Guayabitos, and San Blas. From there, a mangrove marshland extends past the historic Mexcaltitán island-village to the jungly Río Cañas at the Nayarit-Sinaloa border.

CLIMATE

Nature has graced the Puerto Vallarta region with a microclimate tapestry. Although rainfall, winds, and mountains introduce pleasant

In the summertime, thunderstorms are a daily occurrence.

© ROBIN NOELLE

local variations, elevation provides the broad brush. The entire coastal strip where frost never bites (including the mountain slopes and plateaus up to 4,000 or 5,000 feet/1,200–1,500 m) luxuriates in the tropics.

The seashore is a land of perpetual summer. Winter days are typically warm and rainless, peaking at 80–85°F (27–30°C) and dropping to 55–65°F (16–18°C) by midnight.

Increasing elevation gradually decreases both heat and humidity. In the valley of Tepic (elev. 3,000 ft/900 m), you can expect warm, dry winter days of 75–80°F (24–27°C) and cooler nights around 50–60°F (10–15°C). Days will usually be balmy and springlike, climbing to around 75°F (24°C) by noon, with nights dropping to a temperate 40–50°F (5–10°C); pack a sweater or light jacket.

May, before the rains, is often the warmest month in the entire Puerto Vallarta region. Summer days on Puerto Vallarta beaches are very warm, humid, and sometimes rainy. July, August, and September forenoons are typically bright, warming to the high 80s (around 32°C). By afternoon, however, clouds often gather and bring short, sometimes heavy, showers. By late afternoon the clouds part, the sun dries the pavements, and the tropical breeze is just right for enjoying a sparkling Puerto Vallarta sunset. Tepic summers are delightful, with afternoons in the 80s (27–32°C) and balmy evenings in the 70s (21–26°C), perfect for strolling.

Flora

Abundant sun and summer rains nurture the vegetation of the Puerto Vallarta region. At roadside spots, spiny bromeliads, pendulous passion fruits, and giant serpentine vines luxuriate, beckoning to admirers. Now and then visitors may stop, attracted by something remarkable, such as a riot of flowers blooming from apparently dead branches or what looks like grapefruit sprouting from the trunk of a roadside tree. More often, travelers pass by the long stretches of thickets, jungles, and marshes without stopping; however, a little knowledge of what to expect can blossom into recognition and discovery, transforming the humdrum into the extraordinary.

VEGETATION ZONES

Mexico's diverse landscape and fickle rainfall have sculpted its wide range of plant forms. Botanists recognize at least 14 major Mexican vegetation zones, seven of which occur in the Puerto Vallarta region.

Directly along the coastal highway, you often pass long sections of three of these zones: savanna, thorn forest, and tropical deciduous forest.

Savanna

Great swaths of pasturelike savanna stretch along Highway 15 in Nayarit north of Tepic. In its natural state, savanna often appears as a palm-dotted sea of grass—green and marshy during the rainy summer, dry and brown by late winter.

Although grass rules the savanna, palms give it character. Most familiar is the **coconut,** or *cocotero* (*Cocos nucifera*)—the world's most useful tree—used for everything from lumber to candy. Coconut palms line the beaches and climb the hillsides—drooping, slanting, rustling, and swaying in the breeze like troupes of hula dancers. Less familiar, but with as much personality, is the Mexican **fan palm,** or *palma real* (*Sabal mexicana*), festooned with black fruit and spread flat like a señorita's fan.

The savanna's list goes on: the grapefruitlike fruit on the trunk and branches identify the **gourd tree,** or *calabaza* (*Crescentia alata*). The mature gourds, brown and hard, have been carved into *jícaros* (cups for drinking chocolate) for millennia.

Orange-sized pumpkinlike gourds mark the **sand box tree,** or *jabillo* (*Hura polyandra*), so named because they once served as desktop boxes full of sand for drying ink. The Aztecs, however, called it the exploding tree, because

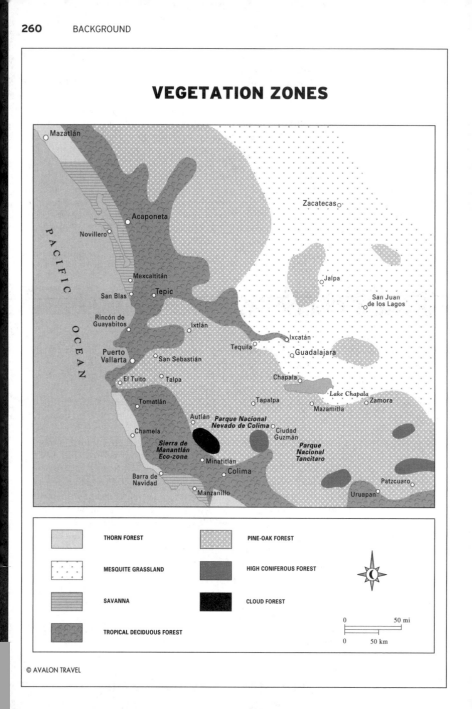

VEGETATION ZONES

Mazatlán

Acaponeta

Novillero

Mexcaltitán

San Blas

Tepic

Rincón de Guayabitos

Ixtlán

Puerto Vallarta

San Sebastián

El Tuito

Talpa

Tomatlán

Chamela

Sierra de Manantlán Eco-zone

Autlán

Parque Nacional Nevado de Colima

Minatitlán

Barra de Navidad

Manzanillo

Colima

Ciudad Guzmán

Zacatecas

Jalpa

San Juan de los Lagos

Tequila

Ixcatán

Guadalajara

Chapala

Lake Chapala

Zamora

Tapalpa

Mazamitla

Parque Nacional Tancitaro

Patzcuaro

Uruapan

PACIFIC OCEAN

	THORN FOREST		PINE-OAK FOREST
	MESQUITE GRASSLAND		HIGH CONIFEROUS FOREST
	SAVANNA		CLOUD FOREST
	TROPICAL DECIDUOUS FOREST		

0   50 mi

0   50 km

the ripe gourds burst their seeds forth with a bang like a firecracker.

The waterlogged seaward edge of the savanna nurtures forests of the **red mangrove,** or *mangle colorado* (*Rhizophora mangle*), short trees that seem to stand in the water on stilts. Their new roots grow downward from above; a time-lapse photo would show them marching, as if on stilts, into the lagoon.

Thorn Forest

Lower rainfall leads to the hardier growth of the thorn forest—domain of the pea family— the **legumes** marked in late winter and spring by bursts of red, yellow, pink, and white flowers. Look closely at the blossoms and you will see they resemble the familiar wild sweet pea of North America. Even when the blossoms are gone, you can identify them by seed pods that hang from the branches. Local folks call them by many names. These include the **ta-bachín,** the scarlet Mexican bird of paradise; and its close relative the **flamboyán,** or **royal poinciana,** an import from Africa, where it's called the flame tree.

Other spectacular members of the pea family include the bright-yellow **abejón,** which blooms nearly year-round; and the **coapinol,** marked by hosts of white blooms (March–July) and large dark-brown pods. Not only colorful but useful is the **fishfuddle,** with pink flowers and long pods, from which fisherfolk derive a fish-stunning poison.

More abundant (although not so noticeable)are the legumes' cousins, the **acacias** and **mimosas.** Long swaths of thorn forest grow right to the coastal highway and side-road pavements, so that the road appears tunnel-like through a tangle of brushy acacia trees. Pull completely off the road for a look and you will spot the small yellow flower balls, ferny leaves, and long, narrow pods of the **boat spine acacia,** or *quisache tempamo* (*Acacia cochliacantha*). Take care, however, around the acacias; some of the long-thorned varieties harbor nectar-feeding, biting ants.

Perhaps the most dramatic member of the thorn community is the **morning glory tree,** or *palo blanco* (*Ipomoea aborescens*), which announces the winter dry season by a festoon of white trumpets atop its crown of seemingly dead branches.

The Mexican penchant for making fun of death shows in the alternate name for **palo del muerto,** or the tree of the dead. It is also called *palo bobo* (fool tree) in some locales, because folks believe if you take a drink from a stream near its foot, you will go crazy.

The cactus are among the thorn forest's sturdiest and most exotic inhabitants. Occasional specimens of the spectacular **candelabra cactus,** or *candelabro* (*Stenocereus weberi*), spread as much as 40 feet (12 m) tall and wide.

Tropical Deciduous Forest

In rainier areas, the thorn forest grades into tropical deciduous forest. This is the "friendly" or "short-tree" forest, blanketed by a tangle of summer-green leaves that fall in the dry winter to reveal thickets of branches. Some trees show bright fall reds and yellows, later blossoming with brilliant flowers—spiderlily, cardinal sage, pink trumpet, poppylike yellowsilk (*pomposhuti*), and mouse-killer (*mata ratón*), which swirl in the spring wind like cherry-blossom blizzards.

The tropical deciduous forest is a lush jungle coat swathing much of the coastal Puerto Vallarta region. It is especially lush in the mountains above San Blas and along the low summit of Highway 200 over the Sierra Vallejo north of Puerto Vallarta. Where the mountains rush directly down to the sea, the forest appears to spill right over the headland into the ocean. Vine-strewn thickets overhang the highway like the edges of a lost prehistoric world, where at any moment you expect a dinosaur to rear up.

The biological realities here are nearly as exotic. A four-foot-long green iguana, looking every bit as primitive as a dinosaur, slithers across the pavement. Beside the road, a spreading, solitary **strangler fig** (*Ficus padifolia*) stands, draped with hairy, hanging air roots (which, in time, plant themselves in the ground and support the branches). Its Mexican name, *matapalo* (killer tree), is gruesomely accurate, for

The Papilio tree, also known as the Gringo tree, often glows bronze in the sunlight.

gives way to temperate pine-oak forest, the Puerto Vallarta region's most extensive vegetation zone. Here, many of Mexico's 112 oak and 39 pine species thrive. Oval two-inch cones and foot-long drooping needles (three to a cluster) make the **pino triste,** or sad pine (*Pinus lumholtzii*), appear in severe need of water. Unlike many of Mexico's pines, it produces neither good lumber nor much turpentine, although it *is* prized by guitar makers for its wood.

Much more regal in bearing and more commercially important are the tall pines, **Chihuahua pine** (*Pinus chihuahuana*) and **Chinese pine** (*Pinus leiophylla*). Both reddish-barked with yellow wood, they resemble the ponderosa pine of the western United States. You can tell them apart by their needles: the Chihuahua pine (*pino prieto*) has three to a cluster, while the Chinese pine (*pino chino*) has five.

Pines often grow in stands mixed with **oaks,** which occur in two broad classifications—*encino* (evergreen, small-leafed) and *roble* (deciduous, large-leafed)—both much like the oaks that dot California hills and valleys. Clustered on their branches and scattered in the shade, *bellotas* (acorns) distinctly mark them as oaks.

strangler figs often entwine themselves in death embraces with less aggressive tree-victims.

Much more benign is my favorite in the tropical deciduous forest: the **Colima palm** (*Orbignya guayacule*), or *guaycoyul* or *cohune,* which means magnificent. Capped by a proud cock-plume, it presides over the forest singly or in great, graceful swaying groves atop seacliffs. Its nuts, harvested like small coconuts, yield oil and animal fodder.

Excursions by jeep or foot along shaded off-highway tracks through the tropical deciduous forest can bestow delightful jungle scenes; however, unwary travelers must watch out for the poison oak–like *mala mujer* (evil woman) tree. The oil on its large five-fingered leaves can cause an itchy rash.

Pine-Oak Forest

Along the upland highways (notably at the Sierra Cuale summit of Highway 200 south from Puerto Vallarta, and at high stretches of National Highway 80 between Barra de Navidad and Guadalajara), the tropical forest

Mesquite Grassland

Although much of the mesquite grassland of the Puerto Vallarta region has been tamed into farmland, a number of its more interesting plants do grow in the more arid districts, notably on the Jalisco Coast, not far south of the town of El Tuito.

Among the mesquite grassland's most interesting species is the **maguey** (mah-GAY), or century plant, so-called because it's said to bloom once, then die, after 100 years of growth—although its lifespan is usually closer to 50 years. The maguey and its cactuslike relatives (such as the very useful **mescal, lechuguilla,** and **sisal,** all of the genus *Agave*), each grow as a roselike cluster of leathery, long, pointed gray-green leaves, from which a single flower stalk eventually blooms.

Century plants themselves, which can grow as large as several feet tall and wide, thrive either wild or in cultivated fields in ranks and files like a botanical army on parade. These fields, prominently visible from National Highway 15 west of Guadalajara, are eventually harvested, the leaves crushed, fermented, and distilled into fiery 80-proof liquor known locally as *raicilla,* some of the most renowned of which is made near the town of El Tuito.

Watch for the mesquite grassland's **candelilla** *(Euphorbia antisyphillitica),* an odd cousin of the poinsettia, also a Mexico native. In contrast to the poinsettia, the *candelilla* resembles a tall (two- to three-foot) candle, with small white flowers scattered upward along its single vertical stem. Abundant wax on the many pencil-sized stalks that curve upward from the base is useful for anything from polishing your shoes to lubricating your car's distributor.

Equally exotic is the *Jatropha dioica,* called the **sangre de dragón** (blood of the dragon), which also grows in a single meaty stem, but with two-inch-long lobed leaves with small white flowers. Break off a stem and out oozes a clear sap, which soon turns blood-red.

Cloud Forest
Adventurous visitors who travel to certain remote, dewy mountainsides above 7,000 feet (2,000 m) can explore the plant and wildlife community of the cloud forest. The Sierra Manantlán, a roadless de facto wilderness southeast of Autlán, Jalisco, preserves such a habitat. There, abundant cool fog nourishes forests of glacial-epoch remnant flora: tree ferns and lichen-draped pines and oaks above a mossy carpet of orchids, bromeliads, and begonias.

High Coniferous Forest
The Puerto Vallarta region's rarest, least accessible vegetation zone is the high coniferous forest, which swathes the slopes of lofty peaks, notably the Nevado de Colima (elev. 14,220 ft/4,325 m), on the Jalisco-Colima border. This pristine green alpine island, accessible only on horseback or by foot, nurtures stands of magnificent pines and spruce, laced by grassy meadows, similar to the higher Rocky Mountain slopes in the United States and Canada. Reigning over the lesser species is the regal **Montezuma pine** *(Pinus montezumae),* distinguished by its long, pendulous cones and rough, ruddy bark, reminiscent of the sugar pine of the western United States.

Fauna

Despite continued habitat destruction—forests are logged, wetlands filled, and savannas plowed—great swaths of the Puerto Vallarta region still abound with wildlife. Common in the temperate pine-oak forest highlands are mammals familiar to U.S. residents—such as mountain lion (puma), coyote, fox *(zorro),* rabbit *(conejo),* and quail *(codorniz).*

However, the tropical coastal forests and savannas are home to fascinating species seen only in zoos north of the border. The reality of this dawns on travelers when they glimpse something exotic, such as raucous, screeching swarms of small green parrots rising from the roadside, or a coati nosing in the sand just a few feet away from them at the forested edge of an isolated beach.

Population pressures have nevertheless decreased wild habitats, endangering many previously abundant animal species. If you are lucky, you may find a tracker who can lead you to a band of now-rare reddish-brown **spider monkeys** *(monos)* raiding a wild fruit tree. And deep in the mountain vastness, you may be led to a view of the endangered striped cat, the **ocelot** *(tigrillo)* or its smaller relative, the **margay.** On such an excursion, if you are really fortunate, you may hear the "chesty" roar or catch a glimpse of a jaguar, the fabled *el tigre.*

MAMMALS
Jaguars
"Each hill has its own *tigre,*" a Mexican proverb says. With black spots spread over a tan coat,

stretching five feet (1.5 m) and weighing 200 pounds (90 kg), the typical jaguar resembles a muscular spotted leopard. Although hunted since prehistory, and now endangered, the jaguar lives on in the Puerto Vallarta region, where it hunts along thickly forested stream bottoms and foothills. Unlike the mountain lion, the jaguar will eat any game. Jaguars have even been known to wait patiently for fish in rivers and to stalk beaches for turtle and egg dinners. If they have a favorite food, it is probably the piglike wild peccary (*jabalí*). Experienced hunters agree that no two jaguars will have the same prey in their stomachs.

Although humans have died of wounds inflicted by cornered jaguars, there is little or no hard evidence that they eat humans, despite legends to the contrary.

Armadillos, Coatis, and Bats

Armadillos are cat-sized mammals that act and look like opossums but carry reptilianlike shells. If you see one, remain still, and it may walk right up and sniff your foot before it recognizes you and scuttles back into the woods.

A common inhabitant of the tropics is the raccoonlike coati (*tejón, pisote*). In the wild, coatis like shady stream banks, often congregating in large troops of 15–30 individuals. They are identified by their short brown or tan fur, small round ears, long nose, and straight, vertically held tail. With their endearing and inquisitive nature, coatis are often kept as pets; the first coati you see may be one on a string offered for sale at a local market.

Mexican bats (*murciélagos*) are widespread, with at least 126 species (compared to 37 in the United States). In Mexico, as everywhere, bats are feared and misunderstood. As sunset approaches, many species come out of their hiding places and flit through the air in search of insects. Most people, sitting outside enjoying the early evening, will mistake their darting silhouettes for those of birds, who, except for owls, do not generally fly at night.

Bats are often locally called *vampiros,* even though only three relatively rare Mexican species actually feed on the blood of mammals—nearly always cattle—and of birds.

The many nonvampire Mexican bats carry their vampire cousins' odious reputation with forbearance. They go about their good works, pollinating flowers, clearing the air of pesky gnats and mosquitoes, ridding cornfields of mice, and dropping seeds, thereby restoring forests.

BIRDS

The coastal lagoons of the Puerto Vallarta region lie astride the Pacific flyway, one of the Americas' major north–south paths for migrating waterfowl. Many of the familiar American and Canadian species, including pintail, gadwall, baldpate, shoveler, redhead, and scaup, arrive October–January, when their numbers will have swollen into the millions.They settle near food and cover—even at the borders of cornfields, to the frustration of farmers.

Besides the migrants, swarms of residentspecies—**herons** and **egrets** (*garzas*), cormorantlike **anhingas, lily-walkers** (*jacanas*), and hundreds more—stalk, nest, and preen in the same lagoons.

Few spots are better for observing seabirds than the beaches of the Puerto Vallarta region. Brown **pelicans** and black-and-white frigate birds are among the prime actors. When a flock of pelicans spots a school of their favorite fish, they go about their routine deliberately. Singly or in pairs, they circle and plummet into the waves to come up, more often than not, with fish in their gullets. Each bird then bobs and floats over the swells for a minute or two, seeming to wait for its dozen or so fellow pelicans to take their turns. This continues until they've bagged a dinner of 10–15 fish apiece.

Frigate birds, the scavengers par excellence of the Puerto Vallarta region, often profit by the labor of the teams of fishermen who haul in nets of fish on village beaches. After the fishermen auction off the choice morsels of perch, tuna, red snapper, octopus, or shrimp to merchants, and the local villagers have scavenged everything else edible, the motley residue of small fish, sea snakes, skates, squid, slugs, and

© BRUCE WHIPPERMAN

Several species of small parrots forage in Puerto Vallarta marshes, grasslands, and forests.

sharks is thrown to a screeching flock of frigate birds.

The sprawling, wild mangrove wetland near San Blas, 100 miles north of Puerto Vallarta, nurtures a trove of wildlife, especially birds, ripe for viewing on foot near the town, or by guided boat tours.

REPTILES AND AMPHIBIANS
Snakes, Gila Monsters, and Crocodiles

Mexico has 460-odd snake species, the vast majority shy and nonpoisonous; they will generally get out of your way if you give plenty of warning. In Mexico, as everywhere, poisonous snakes have been largely eradicated in city and tourist areas. In brush or jungle areas, carry a stick or a machete and beat the bushes ahead of you while watching where you put your feet. When hiking or rock-climbing in the country, don't put your hand in niches you can't see.

You might even see a snake underwater while swimming offshore at an isolated Bay of Banderas beach. The **yellow-bellied sea snake** (*Pelamis platurus*) grows to about two feet (0.6 m) and, although rare and shy, can inflict fatal bites. If you see a yellow-and-black snake underwater, get away, pronto. (Some eels, which resemble snakes but have gills like fish and inhabit rocky crevices, can inflict nonpoisonous bites and should also be avoided.)

The Mexican land counterpart of the *Pelamis platurus* is the **coral snake** (*coralillo*), which occurs as about two dozen species, all with multicolored bright bands that always include red. Although relatively rare, small, and shy, coral snakes occasionally inflict serious, sometimes fatal, bites.

More aggressive and generally more dangerous is the Mexican **rattlesnake** (*cascabel*) and its viper relative, the **fer-de-lance** (*Bothrops atrox*). About the same in size (to 6 ft/2 m) and appearance as the rattlesnake, the fer-de-lance is known by various local names, such as *nauyaca, cuatro narices, palanca,* and *barba amarilla.* It is potentially more hazardous than the rattlesnake because it lacks a warning rattle.

The Gila monster (confined in Mexico to northern Sonora) and its southern tropical relative, the yellow-spotted black **escorpión** (*Heloderma horridum*), are the world's only poisonous lizards. Despite its beaded skin and menacing, fleshy appearance, the *escorpión* bites only when severely provoked; and, even then, its venom is rarely, if ever, fatal.

The **crocodile** (*cocodrilo* or *caimán*), once prized for its meat and hide, came close to vanishing in Mexican Pacific lagoons until the government took steps to ensure its survival; it's now officially protected. A few isolated breeding populations live on in the wild, while government and private hatcheries (for example, in San Blas) are breeding more for the eventual repopulation of lagoons where crocodiles once were common.

Two crocodile species occur in the Puerto Vallarta region. The true crocodile *Crocodilus acutus* has a narrower snout than its local cousin, *Caiman crocodilus fuscus,* a type of alligator (*lagarto*). Although past individuals have been recorded at up to 15 feet (4.5 m) long

Crocodiles (*Crocodilus acutus*, shown) and alligators, once rare, are now making a comeback in Puerto Vallarta's regional mangrove wetlands, especially around San Blas.

(see the stuffed specimen upstairs at the Tepic anthropology and history museum, or in the Hotel Bucanero lobby in San Blas), wild native crocodiles are usually young and two feet (0.6 m) or less in length.

Turtles

The story of Mexican sea turtles is similar to that of crocodiles: They once swarmed ashore on Puerto Vallarta regional beaches to lay their eggs. Prized for their meat, eggs, hide, and shell, the turtle population was severely devastated. The good news is that, now officially protected, Mexican sea turtle numbers are beginning to recover their nesting numbers in some locations.

Of the four locally occurring species, the endangered olive ridley turtle (*Lepidochelys olivacea*), or *golfina*, is by far the most common. The smallest and among the most widespread of the world's sea turtles, *golfinas* flock ashore at a number of Puerto Vallarta region beaches, notably Playa San Francisco on the Nayarit Coast, and Playa Mismaloya, near La Cruz de

Loreto, on the southern Jalisco Coast. At these and many other Mexican Pacific locations, determined groups of volunteers camp out on isolated beaches during the summer and fall in order to save and incubate turtle eggs, for the final reward of watching the safe return of hundreds, and hopefully someday thousands, of turtle hatchlings to the sea.

Also present in some numbers along the Puerto Vallarta regional coastline is the green turtle (Chelonia mydas), or *tortuga negra* (black turtle) as it's known in Mexico. From tour boats, green turtles can sometimes be seen grazing on sea grass offshore in the Bay of Banderas.

FISH AND MARINE MAMMALS

Shoals of fish abound in Puerto Vallarta's waters. Four billfish species are found in deep-sea grounds several miles offshore: **swordfish**, **sailfish**, and **blue** and **black marlin**. All are spirited fighters, though the sailfish and marlin are generally the toughest to bring in. The blue marlin is the biggest of the four; in the past, 10-foot (3-m) specimens weighing more than 1,000 pounds (450 kg) were brought in at Pacific Coast marinas. Lately, four feet (1.2 m) and 200 pounds (90 kg) for a marlin and 100 pounds (45 kg) for a sailfish are more typical. Progressive captains now encourage victorious anglers to return these magnificent "tigers of the sea" (especially the sinewy sailfish and blue marlin, which make for poor eating) to the deep after they've won the battle.

Billfish are not the only prizes of the sea, however. Serious fish lovers also seek varieties of tuna-like **jack,** such as **yellowtail, Pacific amberjack, pompano, jack crevalle,** and the tenacious **roosterfish,** named for the "comb" atop its head. These, and the **yellowfin tuna, mackerel,** and **dorado** (which Hawaiians call mahimahi), are among the delicacies sought in Puerto Vallarta waters.

Accessible from small boats offshore and by casting from shoreline rocks are varieties of **snapper** (*huachinango, pargo*) and **sea bass** (*cabrilla*). Closer to shore, **croaker, mullet,** and **jewfish** can be found foraging along sandy bottoms and in rocky crevices.

Sharks and **rays** inhabit nearly all depths, with smaller fry venturing into beach shallows and lagoons. Huge **Pacific manta rays** appear to be frolicking, their great wings flapping like birds, not far off Puerto Vallarta shores. Just beyond the waves, local fisherfolk bring in **hammerhead, thresher,** and **leopard sharks.**

Also common is the **stingray,** which can inflict a painful wound with its barbed tail. Experienced swimmers and waders avoid injury by both shuffling (rather than stepping) and watching their feet in shallow waters with sandy bottoms.

Sea Lions, Porpoises, and Whales

Although seen in much greater numbers in Baja California's colder waters, fur-bearing species, such as seals and sea lions, do occasionally hunt in the tropical waters and bask on the sands of island beaches off the Puerto Vallarta coast. With the rigid government protections that have been enforced for a generation, their numbers appear to be increasing.

The **California Gulf porpoise**—*delfín* or *vaquita* (little cow)—once very numerous, is now rare. The smallest member of the whale family, it rarely exceeds five feet (1.5 m). Hopefully, if conservation plans are successful, its playful diving and jumping antics will again be observable from Puerto Vallarta–based tour and fishing boats.

Although the **California gray whale** has a migration pattern extending only to the southern tip of Baja California, occasional pods stray farther south, where deep-sea anglers and cruise- and tour-boat passengers see them in deep waters offshore.

Larger whale (*ballena*) species, such as the **humpback** and **blue** whale, appear to enjoy tropical waters even more, ranging the north Pacific tropics from Puerto Vallarta west to Hawaii and beyond.

Offshore islands, such as the nearby Marietas and María Isabel (accessible from San Blas), and the Revillagigedo (ray-vee-yah-hee-HAY-doh) 300 miles (480 km) due west of Puerto Vallarta, offer prime viewing grounds for Mexico's aquatic fauna.

History

Once upon a time, perhaps as early as 50,000 years ago, the first bands of hunters, perhaps following great game herds, crossed from Siberia to the American continent. For thousands of years they drifted southward, many of them eventually settling in the lush highland valleys of Mexico.

Much later, perhaps around 5000 B.C., and in what would later be called Mexico, these early people began gathering and grinding the seeds of a hardy grass that required only the summer rains to thrive. After generations of selective breeding, this grain, called *teocentli* (sacred seed, which we call maize or corn), led to prosperity.

EARLY MEXICAN CIVILIZATIONS

With abundant food, settlements grew and leisure classes arose—artists, architects, warriors, and ruler-priests—who had time to think and create. With a calendar, they harnessed the constant wheel of the firmament to life on earth, defining the days to plant, harvest, feast, travel, and trade. Eventually grand cities arose.

Teotihuacán

Teotihuacán, with a population of perhaps 250,000 around the time of Christ, was one of the world's great metropolises. Its epic monuments still stand not far north of Mexico City: The towering Pyramid of the Sun at the terminal of a grand, 150-foot-wide (152-meter-wide) ceremonial avenue faces a great Pyramid of the Moon. Along the avenue sprawls a monumental temple-court surrounded by scowling, reptilian effigies of Quetzalcoatl, the feathered serpent god of gods.

Teotihuacán crumbled mysteriously around A.D. 650, leaving a host of former vassal states to tussle among themselves. These included Xochicalco, not far south of present-day Mexico City. Freed from tribute to Teotihuacán, Xochicalco flourished.

The Living Quetzalcoatl

Xochicalco's wise men tutored a young noble who was to become a living legend. In A.D. 947, Topiltzín (literally, Our Prince) was born. He advanced astronomy, agriculture, and architecture and founded the city-state of Tula in A.D. 968, north of old Teotihuacán.

Contrary to the times, Topiltzín opposed human sacrifice; he taught that tortillas and butterflies, not human hearts, were the food of Quetzalcoatl. After his two decades of benign rule, Topiltzín's name became so revered the people began to know him as the living Quetzalcoatl, the plumed serpent-god incarnate.

Bloodthirsty local priests, lusting for human victims, tricked him with alcohol, however; Topiltzín awoke groggily one morning in bed with his sister. Devastated by shame, Quetzalcoatl banished himself. He headed east from Tula with a band of retainers in A.D. 987, vowing that he would return during the anniversary of his birth year, Ce Acatl. Legends say he sailed across the eastern sea and rose to heaven as the morning star.

The Aztecs

The civilization that Topiltzín founded, known to historians as the Toltec (People of Tula), was eventually eclipsed by others. These included the Aztecs, a collection of seven aggressive immigrant subtribes. Migrating around A.D. 1350 from the mysterious western land of Aztlán into the lake-filled valley that Mexico City now occupies, the Aztecs survived by being forced to fight for every piece of ground they occupied. Within a century, the Aztecs' dominant tribe, whose members called themselves the México, had clawed its way to dominion over the Valley of Mexico. With the tribute labor that their emperors extracted from local vassal tribes, the México built a magnificent capital, Tenochtitlán, on an island in the middle of the valley-lake. From there, Aztec armies, not unlike Roman legions, marched out and subdued kingdoms for hundreds of miles in all directions. They returned with the spoils of conquest: gold, brilliant feathers, precious jewels, and captives, whom they sacrificed by the thousands as food for their gods.

Among those gods they feared was Quetzalcoatl, who, legends said, was bearded and fair-skinned. It was a remarkable coincidence, therefore, that the bearded, fair-skinned Castilian Hernán Cortés landed on Mexico's eastern coast on April 22, 1519, during the year of Ce Acatl, exactly when Topiltzín, the Living Quetzalcoatl, had vowed he would return.

THE CONQUEST

Although a generation had elapsed since Columbus founded Spain's West Indian colonies, returns had been meager. Scarcity of gold and of native workers, most of whom had fallen victim to European diseases, turned adventurous Spanish eyes westward once again, toward rumored riches beyond the setting sun.

Preliminary excursions piqued Spanish interest, and Hernán Cortés was commissioned by the Spanish governor, Diego Velázquez, to explore further.

Cortés, then only 34, had left his base of Cuba in February 1519 with an expedition of 11 small ships, 550 men, 16 horses, and a few small cannon. By the time he landed in Mexico, he was burdened by a rebellious crew. His men, mostly soldiers of fortune hearing stories of the great Aztec empire west beyond the mountains, had realized the impossible odds they faced and become restive.

Cortés, however, cut short any thoughts of mutiny by burning his ships. As he led his grumbling but resigned band of adventurers toward the Aztec capital of Tenochtitlán, Cortés played Quetzalcoatl to the hilt, awing local chiefs. Coaxed by Doña Marina, Cortés's native translator and mistress, local chiefs began to add their warrior-armies to Cortés's march against their Aztec overlords.

Moctezuma, Lord of Tenochtitlán

Once inside the walls of Tenochtitlán, the Aztecs' Venice-like island-city, the Spaniards were dazzled by gardens of animals, gold,

MALINCHE

If it hadn't been for **Doña Marina** (whom he received as a gift from a local chief), Cortés may have become a mere historical footnote. Doña Marina, speaking both Spanish and native tongues, soon became Cortés's interpreter, go-between, and negotiator. She persuaded a number of important chiefs to ally themselves with Cortés against the Aztecs. Smart and opportunistic, Doña Marina was a crucial strategist in Cortés's deadly game of divide and conquer. She eventually bore Cortés a son and lived in honor and riches for many years, profiting greatly from the Spaniards' exploitation of the Mexicans.

Latter-day Mexicans do not honor her by the gentle title of Doña Marina, however. They call her Malinche, after the volcano – the ugly, treacherous scar on the Mexican landscape – and curse her as the female Judas who betrayed her country to the Spanish. *Malinchismo* has become known as the tendency to love things foreign and hate things Mexican.

and palaces, and a great pyramid-enclosed square where tens of thousands of people bartered goods gathered from all over the empire. Tenochtitlán, with perhaps a quarter of a million people, was the grand capital of an empire more than equal to any in Europe at the time.

However, Moctezuma, the lord of that empire, was frozen by fear and foreboding, unsure if these figures truly represented the return of Quetzalcoatl. He quickly found himself hostage to Cortés, and then died a few months later, during a riot against Spanish greed and brutality. On July 1, 1520, on what came to be called *noche triste* (the sad night), the besieged Cortés and his men broke out, fleeing for their lives along a lake causeway from Tenochtitlán, carrying Moctezuma's treasure. Many of them drowned beneath their burdens of gold booty, while the survivors hacked a bloody retreat through thousands of screaming Aztec warriors to safety on the lakeshore.

A year later, reinforced by a small fleet of armed sailboats and 100,000 Indian allies, Cortés retook Tenochtitlán. The stubborn defenders, led by Cuauhtémoc, Moctezuma's nephew, fell by the tens of thousands beneath a smoking hail of Spanish grapeshot. The Aztecs refused to surrender, forcing Cortés to destroy the city to take it.

The triumphant conquistador soon rebuilt Tenochtitlán in the Spanish image; Cortés's cathedral and main public buildings—the present *zócalo* or central square of Mexico City—still rest upon the foundations of Moctezuma's pyramids.

NEW SPAIN

With the Valley of Mexico firmly in his grip, Cortés sent his lieutenants south, north, and west to extend the limits of his domain, which eventually expanded to more than a dozenfold the size of old Spain. In a letter to his king, Charles V, Cortés christened his empire "New Spain of the Ocean Sea."

The Missionaries

While the conquistadores subjugated the Mexicans, missionaries began arriving to teach, heal, and baptize them. A dozen Franciscan brothers impressed natives and conquistadores alike by trekking the entire 300-mile stony path from Veracruz to Mexico City in 1523. Missionary authorities generally enjoyed a sympathetic ear from Charles V and his successors, who earnestly pursued Spain's Christian mission, especially when it dovetailed with their political and economic goals.

The King Takes Control

Increasingly after 1525, the crown, through the Council of the Indies, began to wrest power away from Cortés and his conquistador lieutenants, many of whom had been granted rights of *encomienda:* taxes and labor of an indigenous district. From the king's point of view, tribute pesos collected by *encomenderos* from their native serfs reduced the gold that would otherwise flow to the crown. Moreover, many *encomenderos* callously enslaved and sold their native wards for quick profit. Such abuses, coupled with European-introduced diseases, began to reduce the native Mexican population at an alarming rate.

The king and his councillors, realizing that without their local labor force New Spain would vanish, acted decisively, instituting new laws and a powerful viceroy to enforce them.

Don Antonio de Mendoza, the new viceroy, arrived in 1535. He wasted no time, first getting rid of the renegade opportunist and Cortés's enemy Nuño de Guzmán, whose private army, under the banner of conquest, had been laying waste to a broad belt of western Mexico, including the modern Puerto Vallarta region states of Nayarit and Jalisco. During his five-year rampage, Guzmán nevertheless managed to found the Puerto Vallarta region towns of Guadalajara, Tepic, and Compostela.

POPULATION CHANGES IN NEW SPAIN

Group	Early Colonial (1570)	Late Colonial (1810)
peninsulares	6,600	15,000
criollos	11,000	1,100,000
mestizos	2,400	704,000
indígenas	3,340,000	3,700,000
negros	22,000	630,000

Hernán Cortés, the Marqués del Valle de Oaxaca

Cortés, meanwhile, had done very well for himself. He was one of Spain's richest men, with the title of Marqués del Valle de Oaxaca. He received 80,000 gold pesos a year from hundreds of thousands of native Mexican subjects on 25,000 square miles from the Valley of Mexico through the present states of Morelos, Guerrero, and Oaxaca.

Cortés continued tirelessly on a dozen projects: an expedition to Honduras; a young wife whom he brought back from Spain; a palace (which still stands) in Cuernavaca; sugar mills; and dozens of churches, city halls, and presidios. He supervised the exploits of his conquistador-lieutenants: Francisco Orozco and Pedro de Alvarado went south to subdue the Zapotecs and Mixtecs in Oaxaca, while Cortés's nephew, Francisco de Cortés de Buenaventura, explored and christened the valley—Valle de las Banderas—where Puerto Vallarta stands today. Meanwhile, Cortés was in Acapulco building ships to explore the Pacific. In 1535, Cortés led an expedition to the Gulf of California (hence the Sea of Cortez) in a dreary six-month search for treasure around La Paz.

Cortés's Monument

Disheartened by his failures and discouraged with Mendoza's interference, Cortés returned to Spain. Mired by lawsuits, a small war, and his daughter's marital troubles, he fell ill and died in 1547. Cortés's remains, according to his will, were eventually laid to rest in a vault at the Hospital de Jesús, which he had founded in Mexico City.

Since latter-day Mexican politics preclude memorials to the Spanish conquest, no monument anywhere in Mexico commemorates Cortés's achievements. His monument, historians note, is Mexico itself.

COLONIAL MEXICO

In 1542, the Council of the Indies, through Viceroy Mendoza, promulgated its liberal New Laws of the Indies. They rested on high moral ground: The only Christian justification for New Spain was the souls and welfare of the indigenous people. Slavery was outlawed and the colonists' *encomienda* rights over land and the Indians were to eventually revert to the crown.

Despite near-rebellion by the colonists, Mendoza and his successors kept the lid on New Spain. Although some *encomenderos* held their privileges into the 18th century, chattel slavery of native Mexicans was abolished in New Spain 300 years before Lincoln's Emancipation Proclamation.

Peace reigned in Mexico for 10 generations. Viceroys came, served, and went; settlers put down roots; friars built country churches; and the conquistadores' rich heirs played while the natives worked.

The Church

The church, however, moderated the Mexicans' toil. On feast days, the natives would dress up, parade their patron saint, drink *pulque,* and ooh and aah at the fireworks.

The church nevertheless profited from the status quo. The biblical tithe—one-tenth of everything earned—filled clerical coffers. By 1800, the church owned half of Mexico.

Moreover, both the clergy and the military were doubly privileged. They enjoyed the right of *fuero* (exemption from civil law) and could be prosecuted only by ecclesiastical or military courts.

Trade and Commerce

In trade and commerce, New Spain existed for the benefit of the mother country. Foreign trade through Mexico was completely prohibited. As a result, colonists had to pay dearly for often-shoddy Spanish manufactures. The Casa de Contratación (the royal trade regulators) always ensured the colony's yearly payment deficit would be made up by bullion shipments from Mexican mines, from which the crown raked 10 percent off the top.

Despite its faults, New Spain was, by most contemporary measures, prospering in 1800. The native labor force was both docile and growing, and the galleons carried increasing tonnages of silver and gold to Spain. The authorities, however, failed to recognize that Mexico had changed in 300 years.

Criollos–The New Mexicans

Nearly three centuries of colonial rule gave rise to a burgeoning population of more than a million *criollos*—Mexican-born European descendants of Spanish colonists, many rich and educated—to whom power was denied.

High government, church, and military office had always been the preserve of a tiny minority of *peninsulares*—whites born in Spain. *Criollos* could only watch in disgust as unlettered, unskilled *peninsulares,* derisively called *gachupines* (wearers of spurs), were boosted to authority over them.

Although the *criollos* stood high above the mestizo, *indígena,* and *negro* underclasses, that seemed little compensation for the false smiles, deep bows, and costly bribes that *gachupines* demanded.

Mestizos, *Indígenas,* and African Mexicans

Upper-class luxury existed by virtue of the sweat of Mexico's mestizo, *indígena* (native or indigenous), and *negro* laborers and servants. African slaves were imported in large numbers during the 17th century after typhus, smallpox, and measles epidemics had wiped out most of the *indígena* population. Although the African Mexicans contributed significantly (crafts, healing arts, dance, music, drums, and marimba), they had arrived last and experienced discrimination from everyone.

INDEPENDENCE

The chance for change came during the aftermath of the French invasion of Spain in 1808, when Napoléon Bonaparte replaced King Ferdinand VII with his brother Joseph on the Spanish throne. Most *peninsulares* backed the king; most *criollos,* however, inspired by the example of the recent American and French revolutions, talked and dreamed of independence. One such group, urged on by a firebrand parish priest, acted.

El Grito de Dolores

"*¡Viva México!* Death to the *gachupines!"* **Father Miguel Hidalgo,** shouting his impassioned *grito* from the church balcony in the Guanajuato town of Dolores on September 16, 1810, ignited action. A mostly *indígena,* machete-wielding army of 20,000 coalesced around Hidalgo and his compatriots, Ignacio Allende and Juan Aldama. Their ragtag force raged out of control through the Bajío, massacring hated *gachupines* and pillaging their homes.

Hidalgo advanced on Mexico City but, unnerved by stiff royalist resistance, retreated and regrouped around Guadalajara. His rebels, whose numbers had swollen to 80,000, were no match for a disciplined, 6,000-strong royalist force. On January 17, 1811, Hidalgo (now "Generalisimo") fled north toward the United States but was soon apprehended, defrocked, and executed. His head and those of his comrades hung from the walls of the Guanajuato granary for 10 years in compensation for the slaughter of 138 *gachupines* by Hidalgo's army.

The 10-Year Struggle

Others carried on, however. A mestizo former student of Hidalgo, **José María Morelos,** led a revolutionary shadow government in the present states of Guerrero and Oaxaca for four years until he was apprehended and executed in December 1815.

Morelos's compatriot, **Vicente Guerrero,** continued the fight, joining forces with *criollo* royalist Brigadier **Agustín de Iturbide.** Their Plan de Iguala promised "Three Guarantees"— the renowned Trigarantes: Independence, Catholicism, and Equality—which their army (commanded by Iturbide) would enforce. On September 21, 1821, Iturbide rode triumphantly into Mexico City at the head of his army of Trigarantes. Mexico was independent at last.

Independence, however, solved little except to expel the *peninsulares.* With an illiterate populace and no experience in self-government, Mexicans began a tragic 40-year love affair with a fantasy: the general on the white horse, the gold-braided hero who could save them from themselves.

The Rise and Fall of Agustín I

Iturbide, crowned Emperor Agustín I by the

bishop of Guadalajara on July 21, 1822, soon lost his charisma. In a pattern that became sadly predictable for generations of topsy-turvy Mexican politics, an ambitious garrison commander issued a *pronunciamiento* or declaration of rebellion against him; old revolutionary heroes endorsed a plan to install a republic. Iturbide, his braid tattered and brass tarnished, abdicated in February 1823.

Antonio López de Santa Anna, the eager 28-year-old military commander of Veracruz, whose *pronunciamiento* had pushed Iturbide from his white horse, maneuvered to gradually replace him. Meanwhile, throughout the late 1820s the government teetered on the edge of disaster as the presidency bounced between liberal and conservative hands six times in three years. During the last of these upheavals, Santa Anna jumped to prominence by defeating an abortive Spanish attempt at counterrevolution at Tampico in 1829. "The Victor of Tampico," people called Santa Anna.

The Disastrous Era of Santa Anna

In 1833, the government was bankrupt; mobs demanded the ouster of conservative President Anastasio Bustamante, who had executed the rebellious old revolutionary hero Vicente Guerrero. Santa Anna issued a *pronunciamiento* against Bustamante; Congress obliged, elevating Santa Anna to "Liberator of the Republic" and naming him president in March 1833.

Santa Anna would pop in and out of the presidency like a jack-in-the-box 10 more times before 1855. First, he foolishly lost Texas to rebellious Anglo settlers in 1836; then he lost his leg (which was buried with full military honors) fighting the emperor of France.

Santa Anna's greatest debacle, however, was to declare war on the United States with just 1,839 pesos in the treasury. With his forces poised to defend Mexico City against a relatively small 10,000-man American invasion force, Santa Anna inexplicably withdrew. United States Marines surged into the "Halls of Montezuma," Chapultepec Castle, where Mexico's six beloved Niños Héroes cadets fell in the losing cause on September 13, 1847.

In the subsequent treaty of Guadalupe Hidalgo, Mexico lost nearly half of its territory—the present states of New Mexico, Arizona, California, Nevada, Utah, and Colorado—to the United States. Mexicans have never forgotten; they have looked upon gringos with a combination of awe, envy, admiration, and disgust ever since.

For Santa Anna, however, enough was not enough. Called back as president for the last and 11th time in 1853, Santa Anna financed his final extravagances by selling off a part of southern New Mexico and Arizona for $10 million in what was known as the Gadsden Purchase.

REFORM, CIVIL WAR, AND INTERVENTION

Mexican leaders finally saw the light and exiled Santa Anna forever. While conservatives searched for a king to replace Santa Anna, liberals plunged ahead with three controversial reform laws: the Ley Juárez, Ley Lerdo, and Ley Iglesias. These *reformas,* augmented by a new Constitution of 1857, directly attacked the privilege and power of Mexico's landlords, clergy, and generals. They abolished *fueros* (the separate military and church courts), reduced huge landed estates, and stripped the church of its excess property and power.

Conservative generals, priests, *hacendados* (landholders), and their mestizo and *indígena* followers revolted. The resulting War of the Reform (not unlike the U.S. Civil War) ravaged the countryside for three long years until the victorious liberal army paraded triumphantly in Mexico City on New Year's Day 1861.

Juárez and Maximilian

Benito Juárez, the leading *reformista,* had won the day. Like his contemporary Abraham Lincoln, Juárez, of pure Zapotec Indian blood, overcame his humble origins to become a lawyer, a champion of justice, and the president who held his country together during a terrible civil war. Like Lincoln, Juárez had little time to savor his triumph.

Imperial France invaded Mexico in January

1862, initiating the bloody five-year imperialist struggle, infamously known as the **French Intervention.** After two costly years, the French pushed Juárez's liberal army into the hills and installed the king whom Mexican conservatives thought the country needed. Austrian Archduke Maximilian and his wife, Carlota, the very models of modern Catholic monarchs, were crowned emperor and empress of Mexico in June 1864.

The naive Emperor Maximilian I was surprised that some of his subjects resented his presence. Meanwhile, Juárez refused to yield, stubbornly performing his constitutional duties in a somber black carriage one jump ahead of the French occupying army. The climax came in May 1867, when the liberal forces besieged and defeated Maximilian's army at Querétaro. Juárez, giving no quarter, sternly ordered Maximilian's execution by firing squad on June 19, 1867.

RECONSTRUCTION AND THE PORFIRIATO

Juárez worked day and night at the double task of reconstruction and reform. He won reelection but died, exhausted, on July 18, 1872.

The death of Juárez, the stoic partisan of reform, signaled hope to Mexico's conservatives. They soon got their wish: General **Don Porfirio Díaz,** the "Coming Man," was elected president in 1876, initiating the **Porfiriato,** the long, virtually imperial, rule of Porfirio Diaz.

EMILIANO ZAPATA

Although the multitude of streets, towns, *ejidos,* and monuments named after Emiliano Zapata (1879-1919) mark him as a true national hero, his name is not free of controversy. Although his Zapatista revolutionary guerrillas (1910-1919), often crude and cruel, committed their share of atrocities, all the warring factions of the 1910 Revolution share the same guilt.

Emiliano Zapata's legacy nevertheless remains, embedded in both Mexican law and the hearts and minds of all Mexicans who have benefited from his selfless struggle to realize his broad social vision.

For Emiliano Zapata, achievement didn't come easy. He was born of poor mestizo parents in Anenecuilco (Ah-nay-nay-koo-IL-koh), Morelos, on August 8, 1879. The modest thatched-roof home of his birth still stands, restored as a museum, three miles south of the main market town of Cuautla. Young Emiliano, orphaned when he was still a child, grew up in the care of relatives. As a youth he experienced firsthand the results of then-president Porfirio Díaz's land policies, which resulted in ancestral village fields being gobbled up, both legally and illegally, by rich *hacendados.* Consequently, by 1900, thousands of Zapata's campesino neighbors were toiling as virtual serfs on the very land that had been stolen from them.

When he was a young man, Emiliano's intelligence, blunt honesty, and natural leadership qualities earned him considerable community standing. Although determined to correct local injustices, he started out by working within the established order, accepting the presidency of the Anenecuilco municipal government. When conciliatory measures to address the local campesinos' grievances against the landholders failed, Zapata took justice into his own hands and organized posses to forcibly eject the offending *hacendados.* This earned Zapata the ire of the Díaz government, which sent Zapata fleeing for his life into the mountains with his guerrilla band of followers.

At the same time, in late 1910, Francisco Madero had been agitating for revolution from Texas. Zapata sent messengers north and liked what they told him about Madero. When, in early 1911, Madero crossed the Rio Grande and joined Pancho Villa's forces to capture Ciudad Juárez, Zapata's growing guerrilla regiment moved quickly, seizing Cuernavaca, the Morelos state capital, by mid-May.

Pressed on all sides, Díaz's army and government quickly fell apart, and on May 25,

Pax Porfiriana

Don Porfirio is often remembered wistfully, as old Italians remember Mussolini: "He was a bit rough, but, dammit, at least he made the trains run on time."

Although Porfirio Díaz's humble Oaxaca mestizo origins were not unlike Juárez's, Díaz was not a democrat: When he was a general, his officers took no captives; when he was president, his country police, the *rurales,* shot prisoners in the act of "trying to escape."

Order and progress, in that sequence, ruled Mexico for 34 years. Foreign investment flowed into the country; new railroads brought the products of shiny factories, mines, and farms to modernized Gulf and Pacific ports. Mexico balanced its budget, repaid foreign debt, and became a respected member of the family of nations.

The human price was high. Don Porfirio allowed more than 100 million acres—one-fifth of Mexico's land area (including most of the arable land)—to fall into the hands of his friends and foreigners. Poor Mexicans suffered the most. By 1910, 90 percent of the *indígenas* had lost their traditional communal land. In the spring of 1910, a smug, now-cultured, and elderly Don Porfirio anticipated with relish the centennial of Hidalgo's Grito de Dolores.

REVOLUTION AND STABILIZATION
¡No Reelección!

Porfirio Díaz himself had first campaigned

1911, Díaz resigned. As Madero, Pancho Villa, and (now General) Zapata rode in triumph into Mexico City, Díaz fled into exile to France.

Immediately, however, Zapata began quarreling with Madero's cautious, legalistic approach toward the problem of land and justice for Zapata's poor followers. "The land belongs to only those who work with their hands," Zapata asserted. Exasperated with Madero and his elite advisers (Zapata could barely read), Zapata stormed out of Mexico City in front of his Zapatista cavalry, openly breaking with Madero in November 1911.

In an honest attempt at conciliation, Madero came to Morelos to persuade Zapata to lay down his arms. Before the proceedings were over, however, federal troops, under orders from Madero's treacherous military commander, Victoriano Huerta, invaded Morelos. Fed up, Zapata rearmed his troops, and despite recommendations that he execute Madero on the spot, sent him packing back to Mexico City.

So, for seven more bloody years, Zapata's guerrillas, which by 1914 had grown to a formidable "Liberating Army of the South," battled government forces in Morelos, Guerrero, Puebla, and Oaxaca.

Despite the continued killing, chaos, and personal exhaustion, Zapata remained incorruptibly dedicated to his credo, codified as the famous Plan of Ayala, that declared "¡Tierra y Libertad!" ("Land and Liberty!") for all must be the overriding goal of any just Mexican government.

Finally, by 1919, "Constitutionalist" forces, under the leadership of "First Chief" Venustiano Carranza and General Alvaro Obregón, had promulgated a constitution and, from Mexico City, controlled most of Mexico. Zapata, who never trusted the Constitutionalists, despite their liberal Constitution of 1917, remained a thorn in Carranza's side. Carranza got one of his officers, Colonel Jesús Guajardo, to feign surrender of his entire well-equipped regiment to Zapata, at Chinameca Hacienda, south of Cuautla. Zapata, desperate for supplies and reinforcements, fell for the bait, and was gunned down by a platoon of snipers inside the hacienda on April 10, 1919.

Although Constitutionalist soldiers displayed a badly shot-up body on the Cuatla plaza that they claimed to be Zapata, some witnesses believed otherwise. Rumors persisted for years that somewhere, Emiliano Zapata lived on, and that when the people needed him again, he would return.

on the slogan. It expressed the idea that the president should step down after one term. Although Díaz had stepped down once in 1880, he had gotten himself reelected for 26 consecutive years. In 1910, **Francisco I. Madero,** a short, squeaky-voiced son of rich landowners, opposed Díaz under the same banner.

Although Díaz had jailed him before the election, Madero refused to quit campaigning. From a safe platform in the United States, he called for a revolution to begin on November 20, 1910.

Villa and Zapata

Not much happened, but soon the millions of poor Mexicans who had been going to bed hungry began to stir. In Chihuahua, followers of Francisco (Pancho) Villa, an erstwhile ranch hand, miner, peddler, and cattle rustler, began attacking the *rurales,* dynamiting railroads, and raiding towns. Meanwhile, in the south, horse trader, farmer, and minor official Emiliano Zapata and his *indígena* guerrillas were terrorizing rich *hacendados* and forcibly recovering stolen ancestral village lands. Zapata's movement gained steam and by May had taken the Morelos state capital, Cuernavaca. Meanwhile, Madero crossed the Río Grande and joined with Villa's forces, who took Ciudad Juárez.

The *federales,* government army troops, began deserting in droves, and on May 25, 1911, Díaz submitted his resignation.

As Madero's deputy, **General Victoriano Huerta,** put Díaz on his ship of exile in Veracruz, Díaz confided, "Madero has unleashed a tiger. Now let's see if he can control it."

The Fighting Continues

Emiliano Zapata, it turned out, was the tiger Madero had unleashed. Meeting with Madero in Mexico City, Zapata fumed over Madero's go-slow approach to the "agrarian problem," as Madero termed it. By November, Zapata had denounced Madero. *"¡Tierra y Libertad!"* ("Land and Liberty!") the Zapatistas cried, as Madero's support faded. The army in Mexico City rebelled; Huerta forced Madero to resign on February 18, 1913, put him under house arrest, and then had him murdered four days later.

The rum-swilling Huerta ruled like a Chicago mobster; general rebellion, led by the "Big Four"—Villa, Álvaro Obregón, and Venustiano Carranza in the north, and Zapata in the south—soon broke out. Pressed by the rebels and refused U.S. recognition, Huerta fled into exile in July 1914.

The Constitution of 1917

Fighting sputtered on for three years as authority seesawed between revolutionary factions. Finally Carranza, whose forces ended up controlling most of the country by 1917, got a convention together in Querétaro to formulate political and social goals. The resulting Constitution of 1917, while restating most ideas of the *reformistas'* 1857 constitution, additionally prescribed a single four-year presidential term, labor reform, and subordinated private ownership to public interest. Every village had a right to communal *ejido* land, and subsoil wealth could never be sold away to the highest bidder.

The Constitution of 1917 was a revolutionary expression of national aspirations, and, in retrospect, represented a social and political agenda for the entire 20th century. In modified form, it has lasted to the present day.

Obregón Stabilizes Mexico

On December 1, 1920, General Álvaro Obregón legally assumed the presidency of a Mexico still bleeding from 10 years of civil war. Although a seasoned revolutionary, Obregón was also a pragmatist who recognized peace was necessary to implement the goals of the revolution. In four years, his government pacified local uprisings, disarmed a swarm of warlords, executed hundreds of *bandidos,* obtained U.S. diplomatic recognition, assuaged the worst fears of the clergy and landowners, and began land reform.

All this set the stage for the work of **Plutarco Elías Calles,** Obregón's Minister of Gobernación (Interior) and handpicked successor, who won the 1924 election. Aided by peace, Mexico returned to a semblance of prosperity. Calles brought the army under civilian control, balanced the budget, and shifted Mexico's social revolution into high gear. New clinics vaccinated millions against smallpox, new dams irrigated thousands of previously dry acres, and campesinos received millions of acres of redistributed land.

By single-mindedly enforcing the pro-agrarian, pro-labor, and anticlerical articles of the 1917 constitution, Calles made many influential enemies. Infuriated by the government's confiscation of church property, closing of monasteries, and deportation of hundreds of foreign priests and nuns, the clergy refused to perform marriages, baptisms, and last rites. As members of the Cristero movement, militant Catholics crying *"¡Viva Cristo Rey!"* armed themselves, torching public schools and government property and murdering hundreds of innocent bystanders.

Simultaneously, Calles threatened foreign oil companies, demanding they exchange their titles for 50-year leases. A moderate Mexican supreme court decision over the oil issue and the skillful arbitration of U.S. Ambassador Dwight Morrow smoothed over both the oil and church troubles by the end of Calles's term.

Calles, who started out brimming with revolutionary fervor and populist zeal, became increasingly conservative and dictatorial. Although he bowed out peaceably in favor of Obregón (the constitution had been amended to allow one six-year nonsuccessive term), Obregón was assassinated two weeks after his election in 1928. Calles continued to rule for six more years through three puppet-presidents: Emilio Portes Gil (1928–1930), Pascual Ortíz Rubio (1930–1932), and Abelardo Rodríguez (1932–1934).

For the 14 years since 1920, the revolution had first waxed, then waned. With a cash surplus in 1930, Mexico skidded into debt as the Great Depression deepened and Calles and his cronies lined their pockets. In blessing his minister of war, General Lázaro Cárdenas, for the 1934 presidential election, Calles expected more of the same.

Lázaro Cárdenas, President of the People

The 40-year-old Cárdenas, former governor of Michoacán, immediately set his own agenda, however. He worked tirelessly to fulfill the social prescriptions of the revolution. As morning-coated diplomats fretted, waiting in his outer office, Cárdenas ushered in delegations of campesinos and factory workers and sympathetically listened to their petitions.

In his six years of rule, Cárdenas moved public education and health forward on a broad front, supported strong labor unions, and redistributed 49 million acres of farmland, more than any president before or since.

Cárdenas's resolute enforcement of the constitution's Artículo 123 brought him the most renown. Under this pro-labor law, the government turned over a host of private companies to employee ownership and, on March 18, 1938, expropriated all foreign oil corporations.

In retrospect the oil corporations, most of which were British, were not blameless. They had sorely neglected the wages, health, and welfare of their workers while ruthlessly taking the law into their own hands with private police forces. Although Standard Oil cried foul, U.S. President Franklin Roosevelt did not intervene. Through negotiation and due process, the U.S. companies eventually were compensated with $24 million, plus interest. In the wake of the expropriation, President Cárdenas created Petróleos Mexicanos (Pemex), the national oil corporation that continues to run all Mexican oil and gas operations.

Manuel Ávila Camacho

Manuel Ávila Camacho, elected in 1940, was the last revolutionary general to be president of Mexico. His administration ushered in a gradual shift of Mexican politics, government, and foreign policy as Mexico allied itself with the U.S. cause during World War II. Foreign tourism, initially promoted by the Cárdenas administration, ballooned. Good feelings surged as Franklin Roosevelt became the first U.S. president to officially cross the Río Grande when he met with Camacho in Monterrey in April 1943.

In both word and deed, moderation and evolution guided President Camacho's policies. *"Soy creente"* ("I am a believer"), he declared to the Catholics of Mexico as he worked earnestly to bridge Mexico's serious church-state schism. Land-policy emphasis shifted from redistribution to utilization as new dams and canals irrigated hundreds of thousands of previously arid acres. On one hand, Camacho established IMSS (Instituto Mexicano de Seguro Social) and on the other, trimmed the power of labor unions.

As World War II moved toward its 1945 conclusion, both the United States and Mexico were enjoying the benefits of four years of governmental and military cooperation and mutual trade in the form of a mountain of strategic minerals that had moved north in exchange for a similar mountain of U.S. manufactures that moved south.

CONTEMPORARY MEXICO
The Mature Revolution

During the decades after World War II, beginning with moderate President **Miguel Alemán** (1946–1952), Mexican politicians gradually honed their skills of consensus and compromise as their middle-aged revolution bubbled along under liberal presidents and sputtered haltingly under conservatives. Doctrine required of all politicians, regardless of stripe, that they be "revolutionary" enough to be included beneath the banner of the PRI (Partido Revolucionario Institucional—the Institutional Revolutionary Party), Mexico's dominant political party.

Adolfo Ruíz Cortínes, Alemán's secretary of the interior, was elected overwhelmingly in 1952. He fought the corruption that had crept into government under his predecessor, continued land reform, increased agricultural production, built new ports, eradicated malaria, and opened a number of automobile assembly plants.

Despite concerns that women would vote for conservatives, the millions of women who had fought and died in the Revolution, had served in state governments, and even led military units, were finally given their due. Under the Ruíz Cortínes administration, women gained the right to vote national elections in 1953.

Women, voting for the first time in a national election, kept the PRI in power by electing liberal **Adolfo López Mateos** in 1958. Resembling Lázaro Cárdenas in social policy, López Mateos redistributed 40 million acres of farmland, forced automakers to use 60 percent domestic components, built thousands of new schools, and distributed hundreds of millions of new textbooks. *"La electricidad es nuestra"* ("Electricity is ours"), Mateos declared as he nationalized foreign power companies in 1962.

Despite his left-leaning social agenda, unions were restive under López Mateos. Protesting inflation, workers struck; the government retaliated, arresting Demetrios Vallejo, the railway union head, and renowned muralist David Siqueiros, former Communist Party secretary.

Despite the troubles, López Mateos climaxed his presidency gracefully in 1964 as he opened the celebrated National Museum of Anthropology, appropriately located in Chapultepec Park, where the Aztecs had first settled 20 generations earlier.

In 1964, as several times before, the outgoing president's interior secretary succeeded his former chief. Dour, conservative **Gustavo Díaz Ordaz** immediately clashed with liberals, labor, and students. The pot boiled over just before the 1968 Mexico City Olympics. Reacting to a student rebellion, the army occupied the National University; shortly afterward, on October 2, government forces opened fire with machine guns on a downtown protest, killing and wounding hundreds of demonstrators.

Maquiladoras

Despite its serious internal troubles, and complaints when Mexico gave Vietnam War resisters asylum as political refugees, Mexico's relations with the United States were cordial. President Lyndon Johnson visited and unveiled a statue of Abraham Lincoln in Mexico City. Later, Díaz Ordaz met with President Richard Nixon in Puerto Vallarta.

Meanwhile, bilateral negotiations produced the **Border Industrialization Program.**

Within a 12-mile strip south of the U.S.–Mexico border, foreign companies could assemble duty-free parts into finished goods and export them without any duties on either side. Within a dozen years, a swarm of such plants, called maquiladoras, were humming as hundreds of thousands of Mexican workers assembled and exported billions of dollars' worth of consumer goods—electronics, clothes, furniture, pharmaceuticals, and toys—worldwide.

Concurrently, in Mexico's interior, Díaz Ordaz pushed Mexico's industrialization ahead full steam. Foreign money financed hundreds of new plants and factories. Primary among these was the giant Las Truchas steel plant at the new industrial port and town of Lázaro Cárdenas at the Pacific mouth of the Río Balsas.

Discovery, in 1974, of gigantic new oil and gas reserves along Mexico's Gulf coast added fuel to Mexico's already rapid industrial expansion. During the late 1970s and early 1980s billions in foreign investment, lured by Mexico's oil earnings, financed other major developments—factories, hotels, power plants, roads, airports—all over the country.

Economic Trouble of the 1980s

The negative side to these expensive projects was the huge debt required to finance them. President **Luis Echeverría Álvarez** (1970–1976), diverted by his interest in international affairs, passed Mexico's burgeoning financial deficit to his successor, **José López Portillo.** As feared by some experts, a world petroleum glut during the early 1980s burst Mexico's ballooning oil bubble and plunged the country into financial crisis. When the 1982 interest came due on its foreign debt, Mexico's largest holding company couldn't pay the $2.3 billion owed. The peso plummeted more than fivefold, to 150 per U.S. dollar. At the same time, prices doubled every year. With capital fleeing to foreign banks, López Portillo took the radical step of nationalizing the banks, which had the perverse effect of making a bad situation worse, as Mexican credit dried up.

But by the mid-1980s, President **Miguel de la Madrid** (1982–1988) was straining to get

Mexico's economic house in order. He sliced government and raised taxes, asking rich and poor alike to tighten their belts. Despite getting foreign bankers to reschedule Mexico's debt, de la Madrid couldn't stop inflation. Prices skyrocketed as the peso deflated to 2,500 per U.S. dollar, becoming one of the world's most devalued currencies by 1988.

Salinas de Gortari and NAFTA

Public disgust with official corruption led to significant opposition during the 1988 presidential election. Millionaire businessman Manuel Clothier ran as the PAN and Cuauhtemoc Cárdenas —the son and heir of socialist president Lázaro Cárdenas - left the PRI to run as candidate for the dissident National Democratic Front. Harvard-educated technocrat Carlos Salinas de Gortari was selected by the PRI.

Despite open fraud and voter intimidation, Cárdenas was far ahead in the vote count on election night when a mysterious computer crash, followed by a fire in election headquarters left the election in doubt for the first time. All three candidates claimed victory. Congress eventually claimed Salinas won the election, but only by barely half of the vote, the worst ever for a PRI president. The election was, however, a breakthrough in democratization, creating two viable opposition parties, conservative PAN, and the leftist Revolutionary Democratic Party (PRD), an outgrowth of the Cárdenas coalition movement.

Salinas, however, was widely hailed abroad as Mexico's "Coming Man" of the 1990s. Selling off the nationalized banks, the telephone company, and the national airline were seen as necessary steps to modernizing the economy. His major achievement—despite significant national opposition—was the North American Free Trade Agreement (NAFTA), negotiated in 1992 by him, U.S. President George Bush, and Canadian Prime Minister Brian Mulrooney.

Rebellion, Political Assassination, and Reconciliation

On the very day in early January 1994 that

NAFTA took effect, rebellion broke out in the poor, remote state of Chiapas. A small but well-disciplined campesino force, calling itself Ejército Zapatista Liberación Nacional (Zapatista National Liberation Army—EZLN—or "Zapatistas") captured a number of provincial towns and held the former governor of Chiapas hostage.

To further complicate matters, Mexico's already tense 1994 drama veered toward tragedy. While Salinas de Gortari's chief negotiator, Manuel Camacho Solis, was attempting to iron out a settlement with the Zapatista rebels, PRI presidential candidate Luis Donaldo Colosio, Salinas's handpicked successor, was gunned down just months before the August balloting. However, instead of disintegrating, the nation united in grief; opposition candidates eulogized their fallen former opponent and later earnestly engaged his replacement, stolid technocrat **Ernesto Zedillo,** in Mexico's first presidential election debate.

In a closely watched election unmarred by irregularities, Zedillo piled up a solid plurality against his PAN and PRD opponents. By perpetuating the PRI's 65-year hold on the presidency, the electorate had again opted for the PRI's familiar although imperfect middle-aged revolution.

New Crisis, New Recovery

Zedillo, however, had little time to savor his victory. Right away he had to face the consequences of his predecessor's shabby fiscal policies. Less than a month after he took office, the peso crashed, losing a third of its value just before Christmas 1994. A month later, Mexican financial institutions, their dollar debt having nearly doubled in a month, were in danger of defaulting on their obligations to international investors. To stave off a worldwide financial panic, U.S. President Clinton, in February 1995, secured an unprecedented multibillion-dollar loan package for Mexico, guaranteed by U.S. and international institutions.

Although disaster was temporarily averted, the cure for the country's ills was another painful round of inflation and belt-tightening

for poor Mexicans. During 1995, inflation soared; more and more families became unable to purchase staple foods and basic medicines. Malnutrition and a resurgence of Third World diseases, such as cholera and dengue fever, menaced the countryside. Compounding rural woes, NAFTA regulations spelled the end of farm subsidies. Millions fled the countryside for the cities, for the maquiladoras along the United States border, or into the United States itself.

At the same time, Mexico's equally serious political ills seemed to defy cure. Raul Salinas de Gortari, an important PRI party official and the former president's brother, was arrested for money laundering and political assassination. As popular sentiment began to implicate Carlos Salinas de Gortari himself, the former president fled Mexico, living in Cuba and Ireland for many years.

Mexican democracy got a much-needed boost when notorious Guerrero governor Ruben Figueroa, who had tried to cover up a bloody massacre of *campesinos* by police with a bogus videotape, was forced from office. At the same time, the Zedillo government gained momentum in addressing the Zapatistas' grievances in Chiapas, even as it decreased federal military presence, built new rural electrification networks, and refurbished health clinics. Moreover, Mexico's economy began to improve. By mid-1996, inflation had slowed to a 20 percent annual rate, investment dollars were flowing back into Mexico, the peso had stabilized at about 7.5 to the U.S. dollar, and Mexico had paid back half the borrowed U.S. bailout money.

Zedillo's Political Reforms

In the political arena, although the justice system generally left much to be desired, a pair of unprecedented events signaled an increasingly open political system. In the 1997 congressional elections, voters elected a host of opposition candidates, depriving the PRI of an absolute congressional majority for the first time since 1929. A year later, in early 1998, Mexicans were participating in their country's first primary elections—in which voters, instead of politicians, chose party candidates.

Although President Zedillo had had a rough ride, he entered the twilight of his 1994–2000 term able to take credit for an improved economy, some genuine political reforms, and relative peace in the countryside. The election of 2000 revealed, however, that the Mexican people were not satisfied.

End of an Era: Vicente Fox Unseats the PRI

During 1998 and 1999 the focal point of opposition to the PRI's three-generation rule had been shifting to relative newcomer Vicente Fox, former President of Coca-Cola Mexico and clean former PAN governor of Guanajuato.

Fox, who had announced his candidacy for president two years before the election, seemed an unlikely challenger. After all, the minority PAN had always been the party of wealthy businessmen and the conservative Catholic right. But blunt-talking, six-foot-five Fox, who sometimes campaigned in *vaquero* boots and a 10-gallon cowboy hat, preached populist themes of coalition-building and "inclusion." He backed up his talk by carrying his campaign to hardscrabble city *barrios,* dirt-poor country villages, and traditional outsider groups, such as Jews.

In a relatively orderly and fair July 2, 2000, election, Fox decisively defeated his PRI opponent Fernando Labastida, 42 percent to 38 percent, while PRD candidate Cárdenas polled a feeble 17 percent. Fox's win also swept a PAN plurality (223/209/57) into the 500-seat Chamber of Deputies lower house (although the Senate remained PRI-dominated).

Nevertheless, in pushing the PRI from the all-powerful presidency after 71 consecutive years of domination, Fox had ushered Mexico into a new, more democratic era.

Despite stinging criticism from his own ranks, President Zedillo, whom historians were already praising as the real hero behind Mexico's new democracy, made an unprecedentedly early appeal for all Mexicans to unite behind Fox.

On the eve of his December 1, 2000, inauguration, Mexicans awaited Fox's speech with hopeful anticipation. Although acknowledging that he couldn't completely reverse 71 years of PRI entrenchment in his one six-year term, he vowed to ride a crest of reform, by revamping the tax system and reducing poverty by 30 percent, by creating a million new jobs a year through new private investment in electricity and oil production, and by forming a new common market with Latin America, the United States, and Canada.

He promised, moreover, to secure justice for all by a much-needed reform of police, the federal attorney general, and the army. Potentially most difficult of all, Fox called for the formation of an unprecedented congressional Transparency Commission to investigate a generation of past grievances, including the 1968 massacre of student demonstrators and the assassinations of Cardinal Posada Ocampo in 1993 and presidential candidate Luis Donaldo Colosio in 1994.

Vicente Fox, President of Mexico

Wasting little time getting started, President Fox first headed to Chiapas to confer with indigenous community leaders. Along the way, he shut down Chiapas military bases and removed dozens of military roadblocks. Back in Mexico City, he sent the long-delayed **peace plan,** including the **indigenous bill of rights,** to Congress. Zapatista rebels responded by journeying en masse from Chiapas to Mexico City, where, in their black masks, they addressed Congress, arguing for indigenous rights. Although by mid-2001 Congress had passed a modified version of the negotiated settlement, and the majority of states had ratified the required constitutional amendment, indigenous leaders condemned the legislation plan as watered down and unacceptable, while proponents claimed it was the best possible compromise between the Zapatista demands and the existing Mexican constitution.

Furthermore, Fox continued to pry open the door to democracy in Mexico. In May 2002, he signed Mexico's first **freedom of information**

act, entitling citizens to timely copies of all public documents from federal agencies. Moreover, Fox's long-promised **Transparency Commission** was taking shape. In July 2002, federal attorneys were taking extraordinary action. They were questioning a list of 74 former government officials, including ex-President Luis Echeverría, about their roles in government transgressions, notably political murders and the University of Mexico massacres during the 1960s and 1970s.

But, Mexico's economy, reflecting the U.S. economic slowdown, began to sour in 2001, losing half a million jobs and cutting annual growth to 2.5 percent, down from the 4.5 percent that the government had predicted. Furthermore, a so-called "Towelgate" furor (in which aides had purchased dozens of $400 towels for the presidential mansion) weakened Fox's squeaky-clean image.

During 2002 and 2003, the Mexican economy continued its lackluster performance, increasing public dissatisfaction. In the July 7, 2003, congressional elections, voters took their frustrations out on the PAN and gave its plurality in the Chamber of Deputies to the PRI. When the dust settled, the PRI total had risen to 225 seats, while the PAN had slipped to 153. The biggest winner, however, was the PRD, which gained more than 40 seats, to a total of about 100.

The best news of 2004 was not political, but economic. The Mexican economy, reflecting that of the United States, began to recover, expanding at a moderate (if not robust) rate of about 4 percent, while exports to the United States also increased.

By mid-2005, despite only modest political gains and with his term mostly spent, critics were increasingly claiming that Vicente Fox was a lame-duck president who had run out of time to accomplish what he promised. But Fox, despite a hostile congress that almost continuously blocked his legislative proposals, could claim some solid accomplishments. During his first five years, he had pushed through significant gains in indigenous rights, national reconciliation and government transparency,

drug enforcement, social security reform, housing, and education. Moreover, in addition to nurturing a recovering economy, no one could deny that Fox had kept exports robust, the peso strong against the dollar, and had clamped the lid on inflation.

So, in the twilight of his term, in early 2006, although the typical Mexican man and woman on the street acknowledged that Fox had not delivered on his promises to completely remake the economy and political system, most still believed that unseating the PRI was good for Mexico, and acknowledged that even Fox couldn't be expected to completely undo in six years what 71 years of PRI dominance had created.

The Election of 2006

During the first half of 2006, as Vicente Fox was winding down his presidency, Mexicans were occupied by the campaign to elect his successor. Over Vicente Fox's objections, PAN voters chose Harvard-educated former Energy Secretary Calderón, a leading light of President Fox's cabinet, who also enjoyed clerical and reactionary support within his party. Robert Madrazo, the PRI chair, carried the banner for what appeared to be a resurgent party. Most headlines went to the PRD candidate, the mercurial leftist-populist Andres Manuel López Obrador, former mayor of Mexico City.

When it appeared that López Obrador would sweep the PRD into the Presidency, an unprecedented media and political campaign was launched to undercut his popularity. PAN attempted to have López Obrador arrested and disqualified for office on the basis of a minor eminent domain case in Mexico City, and advertising campaigns accused López Obrador of everything from being an admirer of Hitler to being a secret Presbyterian. But, after a half year of mudslinging and angry debates over the major election issues of drug-related mayhem, killings and kidnappings, police and judicial corruption and inefficiency, and lack of jobs for impoverished workers, Madrazo's initial popularity faded, narrowing the contest to a bitter neck-and-neck race between Calderón and López Obrador.

The Mexican presidential election of July 2006 stirred up political protest long after the ballots were tallied.

© BRUCE WHIPPERMAN

On Sunday July 2, 2006, 42,000,000 Mexicans cast their ballots. Unofficial returns indicated that voters had awarded Calderón a paper-thin plurality. Four days later, after all returns were certified, the Federal Electoral Institute announced the official vote tally: only about 22 percent for Madrazo, with the remaining lion's share divided nearly evenly, with 38.7 percent going to López Obrador and 39.3 percent for Calderón. This result, the Federal Electoral Institute ruled, was too close to declare a winner without a recount.

Besides the close López Obrador-Calderón vote, the election results revealed much more. Not only were the 32 electoral entities (31 states and the Federal District) divided equally, with 16 going for López Obrador, and 16 for Calderón, the vote reflected a nearly complete north–south political schism, with virtually all of the 16 PAN-majority states forming a solid northern bloc, while the 16 PRD-voting states did the same in the south. Furthermore, the election appeared to signal a collapse of

PRI power; with no state (nor the Federal District) giving either a majority or a plurality to Madrazo.

When elections officials decided any irregularities were too minor to investigate, a howl of protest came from López Obrador and his PRD followers after the election results were announced. They claimed the PAN had stolen the election. They jammed the Federal Electoral Institute with lawsuits, alleging a host of irregularities and ballot-stuffing incidents, and demanding a complete recount of all 42,000,000 ballots. They yelled, marched, blocked Mexico City's Paseo de la Reforma, and camped in the Zócalo.

Election Aftermath

After weeks of hearing the PRD and PAN arguments about ballot fraud, the Federal Election Institute announced a recount of a limited number of questionable ballots, all from Calderón -majority states. The Supreme Election Tribunal, a panel of federal judges, found the recount only shifted a few thousand votes away from Calderón and declared him the winner by a mere 240,000 votes.

López Obrador and his supporters screamed foul even louder and threatened to ignore Calderón and/or block his presidency. On September 16, Mexican Independence Day, López Obrador convened in the Mexico City Zócalo hundreds of thousands of his supporters that declared him the legitimate president. In the succeeding days, the PRD delegates and their congressional allies prevented the president of Mexico, for the first time in history, from delivering his annual state of the union address.

Negative reporting on the PRD tactics - in the halls of Congress and on the streets - led to a drop in support for the López Obrador position. National polls showed that more than two-thirds of Mexicans disapproved of the protest. By October, many of the PRD's leaders agreed, further isolating López Obrador camp to a minority position, even within the PRD.

An important result of the 2006 election, initially overshadowed by the intense struggle over the presidential vote, but potentially crucial, was the federal legislative vote, which indicated PAN showed a slight majority in voter preference, and much stronger support for the PRD than was suspected. Under Mexico's proportional representation system, this gave PAN a 206/127/106 over the PRD and PRI, respectively, in the 500-seat federal Chamber of Deputies, and 52/29/33 in the 128-seat Senate, with the remainder of seats scattered among minor parties.

This result may bode well for Mexican democracy. With no single party able to overwhelm the opposition, Felipe Calderón has to compromise with opposition leaders to accomplish any of his legislative goals. A new tax code largely reflected the Presidential plan, while a radical goal to privatize the state oil company, Pemex, was scaled back because of PRI and PRD opposition. Although most Presidential goals reflects PAN's probusiness, pro-NAFTA ideas, the legislative results borrow considerably from the liberal-populist agenda of López Obrador and the PRD. The much-needed compromises may allow the country to make progress toward a more just and prosperous motherland for all Mexicans.

Felipe Calderón's inauguration on December 1, 2006, was the shortest in recent memory. Threatened by interference by unruly PRD legislators, Calderón, accompanied by Vicente Fox, entered the national congressional chamber through a back door, took the oath of office, gave a short speech, and left quickly.

During the next few months, however, Calderón showed that he was a president to be reckoned with. Having campaigned on the promise of a "hard hand" toward insecurity, he took immediate action against protesters in the state of Oaxaca, arresting demonstration leaders and putting military units in the streets. Ironically, or by design, this benefited the sitting PRI governor, who was the target of the initial protests. Despite mounting violence, and an alarmingly high death toll among soldiers and police officials, a nationwide assault on drug traffickers was widely praised.

Even opposition critics agreed that Calderón was off to a good start. By mid-March 2007, his national approval rating had soared to 58 percent. Despite the early popularity of the tax reforms and anticrime initiatives, serious challenges remain. Poverty, estimated at 40 percent, appears to be growing during a worldwide recession. Mexican factories are challenged by Asian competitors, especially those from nations with weak labor laws, like China. Lack of jobs, exacerbated by the violent "war" between narcotics traders and the military, have forced millions of Mexicans north of the border.

Economy and Government

THE MEXICAN ECONOMY
Post-Revolutionary Gains

By many measures, Mexico's 20th-century revolution appears to have succeeded. Since 1910, illiteracy has plunged from 80 percent to 10 percent, life expectancy has risen from 30 years to nearly 70, infant mortality has dropped from a whopping 40 percent to about 2 percent, and, in terms of caloric intake, average Mexicans are eating about twice as much as their forebears at the turn of the 20th century.

Decades of near-continuous economic growth account for rising Mexican living standards.

The Mexican economy has rebounded from its last two recessions because of plentiful natural resources, notably oil and metals; diversified manufacturing, such as cars, steel, and petrochemicals; steadily increasing tourism; exports of fruits, vegetables, and cattle; and its large and willing low-wage workforce.

Recent Mexican governments, moreover, have skillfully exploited Mexico's economic strengths. The Border Industrialization Program that led to millions of jobs in thousands of border maquiladoras has spread all over the country, especially to Monterrey,

Skilled laborers in Puerto Vallarta feel lucky if they manage to earn $20 per day.

Mexico City, Guadalajara, and Puerto Vallarta itself. Tourism, Puerto Vallarta's strongest job creator for years, grew even stronger during 2005, when Puerto Vallarta drew more foreign visitors than any other Mexican beach destination.

In Mexico as a whole, the country's increased manufacturing output has produced manifold economic benefits, including reduced dependency on oil exports and burgeoning foreign trade. Consequently, Mexico has become a net exporter of goods and services to the United States, its largest trading partner. In 2001, however, the U.S. economic slowdown decreased demand for Mexican products; consequently Mexico lost more than half a million jobs, forcing economic growth down to a weak 2.5 percent for 2001. Nevertheless, the slower growth resulted in neither significant inflation nor weakening of the peso, and by late 2004, the Mexican gross domestic product was again rising at a healthy annual rate of about 5 percent.

But, during 2004 and 2005, despite high prices for its oil, rock-bottom inflation, large payments of money from Mexicans working in the United States, and a balanced budget, the Mexican economy still didn't produce the million jobs a year it needed to keep up with population increase. Although some of the sluggishness could be blamed on the hurricane that devastated Cancún in fall 2005, most experts agree that Mexico's largest economic problem is lack of ability to compete, especially with respect to Asian countries, especially China, which floods Mexico with low-cost goods, while Mexico sells very little to China in return. A serious marker of all this appeared in 2004, when China replaced Mexico as the United States's second-largest import source, jumping to about 14 percent of U.S. imports, compared to Mexico, at around 10 percent.

Fortunately, 2006 painted a much brighter economic picture. Nearly all economic experts agreed with the pronouncement that the Mexican economy is "firing on all cylinders." Virtually all of Mexican economic indicators rose sharply, from the annual growth rate (more than 5 percent for the first half-year), pushed upward by a 50 percent increase in car production and the high price of Mexico's exported oil, both of which lifted exports to the United States by 22 percent to record levels. Moreover, on the domestic side, wages were up by more than 4 percent, coupled with both the fortunate low inflation and low interest rates.

All of this good economic news bodes well for what many experts suggest: that Mexico, in order breathe permanent new life into its economy, needs fundamental structural reforms, such as more flexible labor rules, more effective tax collection (hardly anyone pays any income tax), and more private investment to modernize the energy and oil industries.

Long-Term Economic Challenges

Despite huge gains, Mexico's Revolution of 1910 is nevertheless incomplete. Improved public health, education, income, and opportunity have barely outdistanced Mexico's population, which has increased nearly sevenfold—from 15 million to 100 million—from 1910 to 2000. For example, although the illiteracy rate has decreased, the actual number of Mexican people who can't read, about 10 million, has remained fairly constant since 1910.

Moreover, the land reform program, once thought to be a Mexican cure-all, has long been a disappointment. The *ejidos* of which Emiliano Zapata dreamed have become mostly symbolic. The communal fields are typically small and unirrigated. *Ejido* land, formerly constitutionally prohibited from being sold, has not traditionally served as collateral for bank loans. Capital for irrigation networks, fertilizers, and harvesting machines is consequently lacking. Communal farms are typically inefficient; the average Mexican field produces about *one-quarter* as much corn per acre as a U.S. farm. Mexico must accordingly use its precious oil-dollar surplus to import millions of tons of corn—originally indigenous to Mexico—annually.

The triple scourge of overpopulation, lack of arable land, and low farm income has driven

millions of campesino families to seek better lives in Mexico's cities and the United States. Since 1910, Mexico has evolved from a largely rural country, where 70 percent of the population lived on farms, to an urban nation where 70 percent of the population lives in cities. Fully one-fifth of Mexico's people now lives in Mexico City.

Nevertheless, the future appears bright for many privately owned and managed Mexican farms, concentrated largely in the northern border states. Exceptionally productive, they typically work hundreds or thousands of irrigated acres of crops, such as tomatoes, lettuce, chiles, wheat, corn, tobacco, cotton, fruits, alfalfa, chickens, and cattle, just like their counterparts across the border in California, New Mexico, Arizona, and Texas.

Staples—wheat for bread, corn for tortillas, milk, and cooking oil—are all imported and consequently expensive for the typical working-class Mexican family, which must spend half or more of its income (typically $500 per month) for food. Recent inflation has compounded the problem, particularly for the millions of families on the bottom half of Mexico's economic ladder.

Although average gross domestic product figures for Mexico—about $10,000 per capita compared to more than $40,000 for the United States—place it above nearly all other Third World countries, averages, when applied to Mexico, mean little. A primary socioeconomic reality of Mexican history remains: The richest one-fifth of Mexican families earns about 10 times the income of the poorest one-fifth. A relative handful of people own a large hunk of Mexico, and they don't seem inclined to share much of it with the less fortunate. As for the poor, the typical Mexican family in the bottom one-third income bracket often owns neither car nor refrigerator, and the children typically do not finish elementary school.

GOVERNMENT AND POLITICS
The Constitution of 1917

Mexico's governmental system is rooted in the Constitution of 1917, which incorporated many of the features of its reformist predecessor of 1857. The 1917 document, with amendments, remains in force. Although drafted at the behest of conservative revolutionary Venustiano Carranza by his handpicked Querétaro "Constitucionalista" Congress, it was greatly influenced by Álvaro Obregón and generally ignored by Carranza during his subsequent three-year presidential term.

Although many articles resemble those of its U.S. model, the Constitution of 1917 contains provisions developed directly from Mexican experience. Article 27 addresses the question of land. Private property rights are qualified by societal need; subsoil rights are public property; and foreigners and corporations are severely restricted in land ownership. Although the 1917 constitution declared *ejido* land inviolate, 1994 amendments allow, under certain circumstances, the sale or use of communal land as loan security.

Article 23 severely restricts church powers. In declaring that "places of worship are the property of the nation," it stripped churches of all title to real estate, without compensation. Article 5 and Article 130 banned religious orders, expelled foreign clergy, and denied priests and ministers all political rights, including voting, holding office, and even criticizing the government. Most of these restrictions were dropped in 1994. Churches can own property provided it is only for religious use, or run schools as long as they follow the national curriculum; priests and ministers are allowed to vote, but are ineligible for public office.

Article 123 establishes the rights of labor: to organize, bargain collectively, strike, work a maximum eight-hour day, and receive a minimum wage. Women are to receive equal pay for equal work and be given a month's paid leave for childbearing. Article 123 also establishes social security plans for sickness, unemployment, pensions, and death. Attempts by the Calderón administration to weaken the amendment have so far been beaten back by PRD and PRI opposition.

On paper, Mexico's constitutional government structures appear much like their U.S.

prototypes: a federal presidency, a two-house Congress, and a Supreme Court, with their counterparts in each of the 32 states. Political parties field candidates, and all citizens vote by secret ballot.

Mexico's presidents, however, have traditionally enjoyed greater powers than their U.S. counterparts. They need not seek legislative approval for many cabinet appointments, can suspend constitutional rights under a state of siege, can initiate legislation, veto all or parts of bills, refuse to execute laws, and replace state officers. The federal government, moreover, retains nearly all taxing authority, relegating the states to a role of merely administering federal programs.

Although ideally providing for separation of powers, the Constitution of 1917 subordinates both the legislative and judicial branches, with the courts being the weakest of all. The Supreme Court, for example, can only, with repeated deliberation, decide upon the constitutionality of legislation. Five separate individuals must file successful petitions for writs *amparo* (protection) on a single point of law in order to affect constitutional precedent. The court system is being reformed at this time. Several legal changes, involving the rights of the accused and the structure of courtroom procedure are at the forefront of a movement to strengthen the judiciary's role in the Mexican life.

Democratizing Mexican Politics

Reforms in Mexico's stable but top-heavy "Institutional Revolution" came only gradually. After the repression during the 1968 Olympics, and especially after the 1985 Mexico City earthquake, the people began giving up on the one dominant party's ability to improve their lives, and—despite a cynical belief reflected by one outstanding PRI leader of the time, "a politician who is poor is a poor politician"—movements towards justice and pluralism slowly took form.

During the subsequent dozen years, minority parties increasingly elected candidates to state and federal office. Although none captured a majority of any state legislature, the strongest non-PRI parties, such as the conservative pro-Catholic Partido Acción Nacional (PAN) or National Action Party and the liberal-left Partido Revolucionario Democratico (PRD) elected governors. In 1986, minority parties were given federal legislative seats, up to a maximum of 20, for winning a minimum of 2.5 percent of the national presidential vote. In the 1994 election, minority parties received public campaign financing, depending upon their fraction of the vote.

After 1994, President Zedillo oversaw a series of reforms—appointing opposition party members to his cabinet, seeking congressional approval for important foreign policy measures and, most importantly, separating the government from the party that radically altered the political and social landscape.

A New Mexican Revolution

One of Zedillo's most statesman-like acts came in 2000, when he refused to intervene in the election of his successor, Vicente Fox. Fox, the first opposition candidate to win the Presidency since the Revolution, promised a "new revolution" for Mexico, laying out an ambitious program calling for reducing poverty by 30 percent, a million new jobs a year, free trade between Mexico and the rest of Latin America, as well as with Canada and the United States. He promised to reform the police, the army and the judiciary, as well as establish a "transparency commission" to look into abuses of the past. However, other than his goal of concluding a treaty with the Zapatistas, very little of Fox's promises every came to fruition.

Vicente Fox had been a business executive (President of Coca-Cola's Latin American division) before entering politics and—though a symbol of the new, democratic Mexico, was a victim of it. Not used to making compromises, he was unable to work with the largely opposition congress, and few of his legislative proposals made it into law. And, like the PRI leaders before him, he wanted to hand-pick his

successor. His own choice was rejected by his party's voters in the primaries and—having broken the unofficial barrier to a changing of the party in control of the presidency, the voters appeared to be opting for Mexico City's PRD leader, Andres Manuel López Obrador.

Fox unwisely enmeshed himself in the 2006 election, finally won by a very narrow margin by PAN's Felipe Calderón. Calderón's first order of business, given the widespread suspicion that his electoral victory was tainted, sought to establish legitimacy. His "hard hand" approach to law and order, came at the cost of Fox's reputation as having been tough on crime. As the "war on narcotics traffickers" wore on, Mexican opinion makers, including the Roman Catholic hierarchy, have questioned whether the antinarcotics actions are worth the cost in human lives, the reported human rights abuses and neglect of equally pressing concerns like global warming, agricultural development, and financial stability. Finally, foreign reports on the drug war have damaged Mexico's reputation as a secure tourist destination, unfairly, most observers believe. The drug war's critics, and even President Calderón himself, point out that it is narcotics buyers (and gun sellers) in the United States that fuel the criminal enterprises.

On the positive side, Calderón has shown more flexibility in working with his congressional opposition, accepting massive changes to proposals and scaling back his party's ideological commitments to "free trade" as Mexico faces the challenges of a changing economy. Having been through its own financial crisis during the early 1990s, Mexico's financial stability is less threatened than that of other nations in the hemisphere, and a relatively stable political and social climate, open to peaceful, radical change, promises to smooth the path to a more democratic, more open society as Mexico prepares to celebrate the bicentennial of its War of Independence and the centennial of the first modern Revolution.

People

Let a broad wooden chopping block represent Mexico; imagine hacking it with a sharp cleaver until it is grooved and pocked. That fractured surface resembles Mexico's central highlands, where most Mexicans, divided from each other by high mountains and yawning *barrancas,* have lived since before history.

The Mexicans' deep divisions, in large measure, led to their downfall at the hands of the Spanish conquistadores. The Aztec empire that Hernán Cortés conquered was a vast but fragmented collection of tribes. Speaking more than 100 mutually alien languages, those original Mexicans viewed each other suspiciously, as barely human barbarians from strange lands beyond the mountains. And even today the lines Mexicans draw between themselves—of caste, class, race, wealth—are the result, to a significant degree, of the realities of their mutual isolation.

POPULATION

The Spanish colonial government and the Roman Catholic religion provided the glue that through 400 years has welded Mexico's fragmented people into a burgeoning nation-state. Mexico's population, more than 107 million by the year 2007, increased during the 1990s, but at a rate diminished to about half that of previous decades. Increased birth control and emigration largely account for the slowdown.

Mexico's population has not always been increasing. Historians estimate that European diseases, largely measles and smallpox, wiped out a tragic 95 percent of the *indígena* population within a few generations after Cortés stepped ashore in 1519. The Mexican population dwindled from an estimated 20 million at the eve of the conquest to a mere 1 million inhabitants by 1600. It wasn't until 1950, more than four centuries after Cortés, that Mexico's

Learn more about the people and culture of Mexico at the Centro Cultural Cuale.

population recovered to its preconquest level of 20 million.

Mestizos, *Indígenas*, *Criollos*, and African Mexicans

Although by 1950 Mexico's population had recovered, it was completely transformed. The mestizo, a Spanish-speaking person of mixed blood, had replaced the pure Native American, the *indígena* (een-DEE-hay-nah), as the typical Mexican.

The trend continues. Perhaps three of four Mexicans would identify themselves as mestizo: that class whose part-European blood elevates them, in the Mexican mind, to the level of *gente de razón* (people of reason or right). And there's the rub. The *indígenas* (or, mistakenly but much more commonly, Indians), by the usual measurements of income, health, or education, squat at the bottom of the Mexican social ladder.

The typical *indígena* family lives in a small adobe house in a remote valley, subsisting on corn, beans, and vegetables from its small, unirrigated *milpa* (cornfield). They usually have chickens, a few pigs, and sometimes a cow, but no electricity; their few hundred dollars a year in cash income isn't enough to buy even a small refrigerator, much less a truck.

The usual mestizo family, on the other hand, enjoys most of the benefits of the 20th century. They typically own a modest concrete house in town. Their furnishings, simple by developed-world standards, will often include an electric refrigerator, washing machine, propane stove, television, and car or truck. The children go to school every day, and the eldest son sometimes looks forward to college.

Sizable *negro* communities, descendants of 18th-century African slaves, live in the Gulf states and along the Guerrero-Oaxaca Pacific coastline. Last to arrive, the *negros* experience discrimination at the hands of everyone else and are integrating very slowly into the mestizo mainstream.

Above the mestizos, a small *criollo* (Mexican-born white) minority, a few percent of the total population, inherits the privileges—wealth, education, and political power—of its colonial Spanish ancestors.

THE *INDÍGENAS*

Although anthropologists and census takers classify them according to language groups (such as Huichol, Náhuatl, and Cora), *indígenas* generally identify themselves as residents of a particular locality rather than by language or ethnic grouping. And although, as a group, they are referred to as *indígenas*, individuals are generally uncomfortable being labeled as such.

While the mestizos are the emergent self-conscious majority class, the *indígenas*, as during colonial times, remain the invisible people of Mexico. They are politically conservative, socially traditional, and tied to the land. On market day, the typical *indígena* family might make the trip into town. They bag tomatoes, squash, or peppers, and tie up a few chickens or a pig. The rickety country bus will often be full and the mestizo driver may wave them away, giving preference to his friends, leaving them to trudge stoically along the road.

Their lot, nevertheless, has been slowly improving. *Indígena* families now almost always have access to a local school and a clinic. Improved health has led to a large increase in their population. Official census figures, however, are probably low. *Indígenas* are traditionally suspicious of government people, and census takers, however conscientious, seldom speak the local language.

Recent figures, however, indicate that 8 percent of Mexicans are *indígenas*—that is, they speak one of Mexico's 50-odd native languages. Of these, a quarter speak no Spanish at all. These fractions are changing only slowly. Many *indígenas* prefer the old ways. If present trends continue, the year 2019, 500 years after the Spanish arrival, will mark the return of the Mexican indigenous population to the preconquest level of 20 million.

Indígena Language Groups

The Maya speakers of Yucatán and the aggregate of the Náhuatl (Aztec language) speakers of the central plateau are Mexico's most numerous *indígena* groups, totaling roughly three million (one million Maya, two million Nahua).

Official figures, which show that the Puerto Vallarta region's indigenous population amounts to a mere 1 percent of the total, are misleading. Official counts do not measure the droves of transient folks—migrants and new arrivals—who sleep in vehicles, shantytowns, behind their crafts stalls, and with friends and relatives. Although they are officially invisible, you will see them in Puerto Vallarta, walking along the beach, for example, laden with their for-sale fruit or handicrafts—men often in sombreros and scruffy jeans, women often in homemade full-skirted dresses with aprons much like your great-great-grandmother may have worn.

Immigrants in their own country, they flock to cities and tourist resorts from hardscrabble rural areas of the poorest states, often Michoacán, Guerrero, and Oaxaca. Although of pure native blood, they will not acknowledge it or will even be insulted if you ask them if they are *indígenas.* It would be more polite to ask them where they're from. If from Michoacán, they'll often speak Tarasco (more courteously, say Purépecha: poo-RAY-pay-chah); if from Guerrero, the answer will often be Náhuatl, Tlapaneco, or Amuzgo. Oaxaca folks, on the other hand, will probably be fluent in a dialect of either Zapotec or Mixtec. If not one of these, then it might be Amuzgo, Chatino, Trique, Chontal, or any one of a dozen others from Oaxaca's crazy-quilt of language.

As immigrants always have, they come seeking opportunity. If you're interested in what they're selling, bargain with humor. And if you err, let it be on the generous side. They are proud, honorable people who prefer to walk away from a sale rather than to lose their dignity.

The Huichol and Cora
In contrast to the migrants from the south, the Huichol and their northerly neighbors, the Cora, are native to the Puerto Vallarta region. Isolated and resistant to Mexicanization, about 20,000 Huichol (and half as many Cora)

farm, raise cattle, and hunt high in their Sierra Madre homeland, which extends northerly and easterly from the foothills north of Tepic. Although the Cora's traditional territory intermixes with the Huichol's at its southern limit, it also spreads northward, between the foothills and the 6,000-foot-high (1,830-meter-high) Sierra Occidental valleys, to the Nayarit-Durango border.

The Huichol, more than all *indígena* groups, have preserved their colorful dress and religious practices. Huichol religious use of hallucinogenic peyote and the men's rainbow-tinted feathered hats and clothes are renowned. Tepic, San Blas, and especially Santiago Ixcuintla north of Puerto Vallarta are the most important and easily accessible Huichol centers. In both Puerto Vallarta and Tepic, several stores specialize in the Huichol's colorful religious crafts. Santiago Ixcuintla has a Huichol handicrafts store and community center, and San Blas is an important pilgrimage site where Huichol gather, especially around Easter, for weddings and to pay homage to the sea goddess, Aramara.

While not so well known as the Huichol's, the Cora's traditions also remain essentially preserved. These include use of peyote in the worship of pre-Christian deities, such as the fertility gods Grandfather Sun and Grandmother Moon, Earth-mother Tatei, and the heroic monster-killer Brother Morning Star. Although many Cora have migrated to the Nayarit lowland towns, such as Acaponeta, Rosamorada, Tuxpan, and Ruíz along Highway 15, they return for festivals to their mountain homeland villages that center around remote Jesús María, about 128 rough mountain kilometers from Ruíz. The most notable festivals occur January 1–5 (inauguration of the Cora governor) and Semana Santa (the week before Easter).

Dress
Country markets are where you're most likely to see people in traditional dress. There, some elderly men still wear the white cottons that blend Spanish and native styles. Absolutely necessary for men is the Spanish-origin straw

HOLIDAYS AND FESTIVALS

Mexicans love a party. Urban families watch the calendar for midweek national holidays that create a *puente* or "bridge" to the weekend and allow them to squeeze in a three- to five-day minivacation. Visitors should likewise watch the calendar. Such holidays (especially Christmas and Semana Santa, pre-Easter week) mean packed buses, roads, and hotels, especially around the Puerto Vallarta region's beach resorts.

Campesinos, on the other hand, await their local saint's or holy day. The name of the locality often provides the clue. For example, in Santa Cruz del Miramar near San Blas, expect a celebration on May 3, El Día de la Santa Cruz (Day of the Holy Cross). People dress up in their traditional best, sell their wares and produce in a street fair, join a procession, get tipsy, and dance in the plaza.

The following calendar lists national and notable Puerto Vallarta-region holidays and festivals. Local festival dates may vary by a few days; check with a local travel agent or government tourism office if you're planning to attend. (However, if you just happen to be where one of these is going on, get out of your car or bus and join in!)

Jan. 1: **New Year's Day** (*¡Feliz Año Nuevo!;* national holiday)

Jan. 1-5: **Inauguration** of the Cora governor in Jesús María, Nayarit (Cora indigenous dances and ceremonies)

Jan. 6: **Día de los Reyes** (Day of the Kings; traditional gift exchange)

Jan. 12: **Día de Nuestra Señora de Guadalupe** in El Tuito, Jalisco, an hour's drive south of Puerto Vallarta (local festival of the Virgin of Guadalupe one month after Puerto Vallarta: parade, music, evening Mass, and carnival)

Jan. 17: **Día de San Antonio Abad** (decorating and blessing animals)

Jan. 20-Feb. 2: **Fiesta of the Virgin of Candelaria,** in San Juan de los Lagos, Jalisco (hundreds of thousands, from all over Mexico, honor the Virgin with parades, dances depicting Christians vs. Moors, rodeos, cockfights, fireworks, and much more)

Feb. 1-3: **Festival of the Sea** in San Blas, Nayarit (dancing, horse races, and competitions)

Feb. 2: **Día de Candelaria** (blessing of plants, seeds, and candles; procession; and bullfights)

Feb. 5: **Constitution Day** (national holiday commemorating the Constitutions of 1857 and 1917)

Feb. 24: **Flag Day** (national holiday)

Late Feb.: During the four days before Ash Wednesday, usually in late February, many towns stage **Carnaval** (Mardi Gras) extravaganzas

Mar. 11-19: Week before the **Day of St. Joseph** in Talpa, Jalisco (food, edible crafts made of colored *chicle,* or chewing gum,   dancing, bands, and mariachi serenades to the Virgin of Talpa)

Mar. 18-Apr. 4: Grand **ceramics and handicrafts fair,** in Tonalá (Guadalajara), Jalisco

Mar. 19: **Día de San José** (Day of St. Joseph)

Mar. 21: **Birthday of Benito Juárez,** the revered "Lincoln of   Mexico" (national holiday)

Late Mar. or Apr. (the Sunday preceding Easter Sunday): **Fiesta de Ramos** (Palm Sunday) in Sayula, Jalisco (on Hwy. 54 south of Guadalajara; local crafts fair, food, dancing, mariachis)

Apr. 18-30: Big **country fair** in Tepatitlán, Jalisco (on Hwy. 80 northeast of Guadalajara;

sombrero (literally, shade-maker) on their heads, loose white cotton shirt and pants, and leather huaraches on their feet.

Women's dress, by contrast, is more colorful. It can include a *huipil* (long, sleeveless dress) embroidered in bright floral and animal motifs, and a handwoven *enredo* (wraparound skirt that identifies the wearer with a locality). A *faja* (waist sash) and, in winter, a *quechquémitl* (shoulder cape) complete the ensemble.

RELIGION

"God and Gold" was the two-pronged mission of the conquistadores. Most of them concentrated on gold, while missionaries tried to shift the emphasis to God. They were famously

many livestock and agricultural displays and competitions; regional food, rodeos, and traditional dances)

Apr.: **Semana Santa** (pre-Easter Holy Week, culminating in Domingo Gloria, Easter Sunday national holiday)

May 1: **Labor Day** (national holiday)

May (1st and 3rd Wed.): **Fiesta of the Virgin of Ocotlán,** in Ocotlán, Jalisco (on Lake Chapala, religious processions, dancing, fireworks, regional food)

May 3: **Día de la Santa Cruz** (Day of the Holy Cross, especially in Santa Cruz de Miramar, Nayarit, and Mascota, Jalisco)

May 3-15: **Fiesta of St. Isador the Farmer,** in Tepic, Nayarit (blessing of seeds, animals, and water; agricultural displays, competitions, and dancing)

May 5: **Cinco de Mayo** (defeat of the French at Puebla in 1862; national holiday)

May 10: **Mothers' Day** (national holiday)

May 10-12: **Fiesta of the Coronation of the Virgin of the Rosary** in Talpa, Jalisco (processions, fireworks, regional food, crafts, and dances)

June 24: **Día de San Juan Bautista** (Day of St. John the Baptist; fairs and religious festivals, playful dunking of people in water)

June 28-29: **Regatta** in Mexcaltitán, Nayarit (friendly rivalry between boats carrying images of St. Peter and St. Paul to celebrate opening of the shrimp season)

June 29: **Día de San Pablo y San Pedro** (Day of St. Peter and St. Paul)

Sept. 14: **Charro Day** (Cowboy Day, all over Mexico; rodeos, or *charreadas*)

Sept. 16: **Independence Day** (national holiday; mayors everywhere reenact Father Hidalgo's 1810 Grito de Dolores from city hall balconies on the night of September 15)

Oct. 4: **Día de San Francisco** (Day of St. Francis)

Oct. 12: **Día de la Raza** (national holiday, commemorating the union of the races; known as Columbus Day in the United States)

Oct. (last Sun.): **Día de Cristo Rey,** especially in Ixtlán del Río, Nayarit (Day of Christ the King, with "Quetzal y Azteca" and "La Pluma" *indígena* dances, horse races, processions, and food)

Nov. 1: **Día de Todos Santos** (All Souls' Day, in honor of the souls of children; the departed descend from Heaven to eat sugar skeletons, skulls, and treats on family altars)

Nov. 2: **Día de los Muertos** (Day of the Dead, in honor of ancestors; families visit cemeteries and decorate graves with flowers and favorite food of the deceased)

Nov. 20: **Revolution Day** (anniversary of the revolution of 1910-1917; national holiday)

Dec. 1: **Inauguration Day** (National government changes hands every six years: 2000, 2006, 2012, etc.)

Dec. 8: **Día de la Purísima Concepción** (Day of the Immaculate Conception)

Dec. 12: **Día de Nuestra Señora de Guadalupe** (Festival of the Virgin of Guadalupe, patron of Mexico; processions, music, and dancing nationwide, especially celebrated around the church in downtown Puerto Vallarta)

Dec. 16-24: **Christmas Week** (week of *posadas* and piñatas; midnight Mass on Christmas Eve)

Dec. 25: **Christmas Day** (¡Feliz Navidad!; Christmas trees and gift exchange; national holiday)

Dec. 31: **New Year's Eve**

---

successful; more than 90 percent of Mexicans profess to be Catholics.

Catholicism, spreading its doctrine of equality of all persons before God and incorporating native gods into the church rituals, eventually brought the *indígenas* into the fold. Within 100 years, nearly all native Mexicans had accepted the new religion, which raised the universal God of humankind over local tribal deities.

The Virgin of Guadalupe

Conversion of the *indígenas* was sparked by the vision of Juan Diego, a humble farmer. On the hill of Tepayac north of Mexico City in 1531, Juan Diego saw what he described as a brown-

Puerto Vallarta's Virgin of Guadalupe Church

first appeared to him (a true miracle, since roses had been previously unknown in the vicinity) and take them to the archbishop. Juan Diego wrapped the roses in his rude fiber cape, returned to the cathedral, and placed the wrapped roses at the archbishop's feet. When he opened the offering, Zumárraga gasped: Imprinted on the cape was an image of the Virgin herself—proof positive of a genuine miracle.

In the centuries since Juan Diego, the brown Virgin—La Virgen Morena, or Nuestra Señora la Virgen de Guadalupe—has blended native and Catholic elements into something uniquely Mexican. In doing so, she has become the virtual patroness of Mexico, the beloved symbol of Mexico for *indígenas,* mestizos, *negros,* and criollos alike.

Pope John Paul II, in the summer of 2002, journeyed to Mexico to perform a historic gesture. Before millions of joyous faithful, on July 31, 2002, the frail aging pontiff elevated Juan Diego to sainthood, thus making him Latin America's first indigenous person to be so honored.

With few exceptions, every Puerto Vallarta regional town and village celebrates the cherished memory of the Virgin of Guadalupe on December 12. This celebration, however joyful, is but one of the many fiestas that Mexicans, especially the *indígenas,* live for. Each village holds its local fiesta in honor of its patron saint, who is often a thinly veiled sit-in for a local preconquest deity. Themes appear Spanish—Christian vs. Moors, devils vs. priests—but the native element is strong, sometimes dominant.

skinned version of the Virgin Mary enclosed in a dazzling aura of light. She told him to build a shrine in her memory on that spot, where the Aztecs had long worshipped their earth mother, Tonantzín. Juan Diego's Virgin told him to go to the cathedral and relay her instruction to Archbishop Zumárraga.

The archbishop, as expected, turned his nose up at Juan Diego's story. The vision returned, however, and this time Juan Diego's Virgin realized that a miracle was necessary. She ordered him to pick some roses at the spot where she had

Arts and Crafts

Mexico is so stuffed with lovely, reasonably priced handicrafts or *artesanías* (ar-tay-sah-NEE-ahs) that many crafts devotees, if given the option, might choose Mexico over Heaven. A sizable fraction of Mexican families still depend upon the sale of homespun items—clothing, utensils, furniture, forest herbs, religious offerings, adornments, toys, musical instruments—which either they or their neighbors make at home. Many craft traditions reach back thousands of years, to the beginnings of Mexican civilization. The work of generations of artisans has, in many instances, resulted in finery so prized that whole villages devote themselves to the manufacture of a single class of goods.

Although few handicrafts are actually manufactured in Puerto Vallarta, fine examples of virtually all of the following are available in Puerto Vallarta's many well-stocked handicrafts shops and galleries.

BASKETRY AND WOVEN CRAFTS

Weaving straw, palm fronds, and reeds is among the oldest of Mexican handicraft traditions. Mat- and basket-weaving methods and designs 5,000 years old survive to the present day. All over Mexico, people weave *petates* (palm-frond mats) that vacationers use to stretch out on the beach and that locals use for everything, from keeping tortillas warm to shielding babies from the sun. Along the coast, you might see a woman or child waiting for a bus or even walking down the street while weaving white palm leaf strands into a coiled basket. Later, you may see a similar basket, embellished with a bright animal—parrot, burro, or even Snoopy—for sale in the market.

Like the origami paper-folders of Japan, folks who live around Lake Pátzcuaro have taken basket weaving to its ultimate form by crafting virtually everything—from toy turtles and Christmas bells to butterfly mobiles and serving spoons—from the reeds they gather along the lakeshore.

Hatmaking has likewise attained high refinement in Mexico. Workers in Sahuayo, Michoacán (near the southeast shore of Lake Chapala) make especially fine sombreros. Due east across Mexico, in Becal, Campeche, workers fashion Panama hats, called *jipis* (HEE-pees), so fine, soft, and flexible you can stuff one into your pants pocket without damage.

CLOTHING AND EMBROIDERY

Although **traje** (ancestral tribal dress) has nearly vanished in Mexico's large cities, significant numbers of Mexican women make and wear it. Such traditional styles are still common in remote districts of the Puerto Vallarta region and in the states of Michoacán, Guerrero, Oaxaca, Chiapas, and Yucatán. Most favored is the **huipil**—a long, square-shouldered short- to mid-sleeved full dress, often hand-embroidered with animal and floral designs. Among the most treasured are *huipiles* from Oaxaca, especially from San Pedro de Amusgos (Amusgo tribe; white cotton, embroidered with abstract colored animal and floral motifs), San Andrés Chicahuatxtla (Trique tribe; white cotton, richly embroidered red stripes, interwoven with greens, blues, and yellows, and hung with colored ribbons), and Yalalag (Zapotec tribe; white cotton, with bright flowers embroidered along two or four vertical seams and distinctive colored tassels hanging down the back). Beyond Oaxaca, Maya *huipiles* are also highly desired. They are usually made of white cotton and embellished with brilliant machine-embroidered flowers around the neck and shoulders, front and back.

Shoppers sometimes can buy other less-common types of *traje* accessories, such as a **quechquémitl** (shoulder cape), often made of wool and worn as an overgarment in winter. The **enredo** (literally, tangled) wraparound skirt enfolds the waist and legs like a sarong. Mixtec women in Oaxaca's warm south coastal region around Pinotepa Nacional (west of Puerto Escondido) commonly wear the *enredo*,

SHOP SMART

WHAT TO BUY

Although bargains abound in Mexico, savvy shoppers are selective. Steep import and luxury taxes drive up the prices of foreign-made goods such as cameras, computers, sports equipment, and English-language books. Instead, concentrate your shopping on locally made items: leather, jewelry, cotton resort wear, Mexican-made designer clothes, and the galaxy of handicrafts for which Mexico is renowned.

HANDICRAFTS

Many hundreds of factories, mostly of the family-run cottage variety, in Guadalajara and its renowned suburban villages of Tlaquepaque and Tonalá, are among Mexico's prolific handicrafts sources, nurturing vibrant traditions, rooted in the pre-Columbian past. This rich cornucopia spills over to Puerto Vallarta, where shoppers enjoy a bountiful selection that also includes other national Mexican sources. These, along with a kaleidoscope of offerings from the local art colony, fill sidewalks, stalls, and shops all over town.

HOW TO BUY

Credit cards, such as Visa, MasterCard, and, to a lesser extent, American Express, are widely honored in the hotels, crafts shops, and boutiques that cater to foreign tourists. Although convenient, such shops' offerings will be generally higher-priced than those of stores in the older downtown districts that depend more on local trade. Local shops sometimes offer discounts for cash purchases.

Bargaining will stretch your money even further. It comes with the territory in Mexico and needn't be a hassle. On the contrary, if done with humor and moderation, bargaining can be an enjoyable way to meet Mexican people and gain their respect, and even friendship.

The local crafts market is where bargaining is most intense. For starters, try offering half the asking price. From there on, it's all psychology: You have to content yourself with not needing to have the item. Otherwise,

you're sunk; the vendor will sense your need and stand fast. After a few minutes of good-humored bantering, ask for *el último precio* (the final price), which, if it's close, may be just the bargain you've been looking for.

BUYING SILVER AND GOLD JEWELRY

Silver and gold jewelry, the finest of which is crafted in Taxco, Guerrero, Guadalajara, and Guanajuato, fills many Puerto Vallarta region shops. Pure silver (sent from processing mills in the north of Mexico to be worked in Taxco shops) is rarely sold because it's too soft – it's nearly always alloyed with 7.5 percent copper to increase its durability. Such pieces, identical in composition to sterling silver, should have ".925," together with the initials of the manufacturer, stamped on their back sides. Other, less-common grades, such as "800 fine" (80 percent silver), should also be stamped.

If silver is not stamped with the degree of purity, it probably contains no silver at all and is an alloy of copper, zinc, and nickel, known by the generic label "alpaca," or "German" silver. Once, after haggling over the purity and prices of his offerings, a street vendor handed me a shiny handful and said, "Go to a jeweler and have them tested. If they're not real, keep them." Calling his bluff, I took them to a jeweler, who applied a dab of hydrochloric acid (commonly available as muriatic acid) to each piece. Tiny telltale bubbles of hydrogen revealed the cheapness of the merchandise, which I returned the next day to the vendor.

Some shops price sterling silver jewelry simply by weighing, which typically translates to about $1 per gram. If you want to find out if the price is fair, ask the shopkeeper to weigh it for you.

People prize pure gold partly because, unlike silver, it does not tarnish. Gold, nevertheless, is rarely sold pure (24 karat); for durability, it is alloyed with copper. Typical purities, such as 18 karat (75 percent) or 14 karat (58 percent), should be stamped on the pieces. If not, chances are they contain no gold at all.

known locally as the **pozahuanco** (poh-sah-oo-AHN-koh), below the waist and, when at home, go bare-breasted. When wearing her *pozahuanco* in public, a Mixtec woman usually ties a **mandil,** a wide calico apron, across her front. Women weave the best *pozahuancos* at home, using cotton thread dyed a light purple with secretions of tide pool–harvested snails, *Purpura patula pansa,* and silk dyed deep red with cochineal, extracted from the dried bodies of a locally cultivated scale insect, *Dactylopius coccus.*

Colonial Spanish styles have blended with native *traje* to produce a wider class of dress, known generally as **ropa típica.** Fetching embroidered *blusas* (blouses), *rebozos* (shawls), and *vestidos* (dresses) fill boutique racks and market stalls throughout the Mexican Pacific. Among the most handsome is the so-called **Oaxaca wedding dress,** in white cotton with a crochet-trimmed riot of diminutive flowers hand-stitched about the neck and yoke. Some of the finest examples are made in Antonino Castillo Velasco village, in the Valley of Oaxaca.

Unlike the women, only a very small population of Mexican men—members of remote groups, such as Huichol, Cora, Tepehuan, and Tarahumara in the northwest, and Maya and Lacandón in the southeast—wear *traje.* Nevertheless, shops offer some fine men's *ropa típica,* such as serapes, decorated wool blankets with a hole or slit for the head, worn during northern or highland winters, or *guayaberas,* hip-length pleated tropical dress shirts.

Fine **bordado** (embroidery) embellishes much traditional Mexican clothing, *manteles* (tablecloths), and *servilletas* (napkins). As everywhere, women define the art of embroidery. Although some still work by hand at home, cheaper machine-made needlework is more commonly available in shops.

Leather

The Puerto Vallarta region abounds in for-sale leather goods that, if not manufactured locally, are shipped from the renowned leather centers. These include Guadalajara, Mazatlán, and Oaxaca for sandals and huaraches, and León

and Guanajuato for shoes, boots, and saddles. For unique and custom-designed articles you'll probably have to confine your shopping to the pricier stores; for more usual though still attractive leather items such as purses, wallets, belts, coats, and boots, veteran shoppers find bargains at the Municipal Crafts Market in Puerto Vallarta.

FURNITURE

Although furniture is usually too bulky to carry back home with your airline luggage, low Mexican prices make it possible for you to ship your purchases home and enjoy beautiful, unusual pieces for half the price, including transport, you would pay—even if you could find them—outside Mexico.

A number of classes of furniture (*muebles,* moo-AY-blays) are crafted in villages near the sources of raw materials: notably, wood, rattan, bamboo, or wrought iron.

Sometimes it seems as if every house in Mexico is furnished with **colonial-style furniture,** the basic design for much of it dating at least to the Middle Ages. Although many variations exist, most colonial-style furniture is heavily built. Table and chair legs are massive, usually lathe-turned; chair backs are customarily arrow-straight and often vertical. Although usually brown-varnished, colonial-style tables, chairs, and chests sometimes shine with inlaid wood or tile, or animal and flower designs. Family shops turn out good furniture, usually in the country highlands, where suitable wood is available. Products from shops in and around Guadalajara (Tlaquepaque and Tonalá), Lake Pátzcuaro (especially Tzintzuntzán), and Taxco and Olinalá, Guerrero, are among the most renowned.

Equipal, a very distinctive and widespread class of Mexican furniture, is made of leather, usually brownish pigskin or cowhide, stretched over wood frames. Factories center mostly in Guadalajara and nearby Tlaquepaque and Tonalá villages.

It is interesting that **lacquered furniture,** in both process and design, has much in common with lacquerware produced half a world away in China. The origin of Mexican lacquerware presents an intriguing mystery. What is certain, however, is that it predated the conquest and was originally practiced only in the Pacific states of Guerrero and Michoacán. Persistent legends of pre-Columbian coastal contact with Chinese traders give weight to the speculation, shared by a number of experts, that the Chinese may have taught the lacquerware art to the Mexicans many centuries before the conquest.

Today, artisan families in and around Pátzcuaro, Michoacán, and Olinalá, Guerrero, carry on the tradition. The process, which at its finest resembles cloisonné manufacture, involves carving and painting intricate floral and animal designs, followed by repeated layerings of lacquer, clay, and sometimes gold and silver to produce satiny, jewel-like surfaces.

A sprinkling of villages produce furniture made of plant fiber, such as reeds, raffia, and bamboo. In some cases, entire communities, such as Ihuatzio (near Pátzcuaro, Michoacán) and Villa Victoria (Mexico state, west of Toluca), have long harvested the bounty of local lakes and marshes as the basis for their products.

Wrought iron, produced and worked according to Spanish tradition, is used to produce tables, chairs, and benches. Ruggedly fashioned in a riot of baroque scrollwork, it often decorates garden and patio settings. Several colonial cities, notably San Miguel de Allende, Toluca, and Guanajuato, are wrought-iron manufacturing centers.

GLASS AND STONEWORK

Glass manufacture, unknown in pre-Columbian times, was introduced by the Spanish. Today, the tradition continues in factories throughout Mexico that turn out mountains of *burbuja* (boor-BOO-hah)—bubbled glass tumblers, goblets, plates, and pitchers, usually in blue or green. Finer glass is manufactured, notably in Guadalajara (in suburban Tlaquepaque and Tonalá villages), where you can watch artisans blow glass into a number of shapes—often paper-thin balls—in red, green, and blue.

Mexican artisans work stone, usually near sources of supply. Puebla, Mexico's major onyx (**ónix,** OH-neeks) source, is the manufacturing center for the galaxy of mostly rough-hewn, cream-colored items, from animal charms and chess pieces to beads and desk sets, which crowd curio-shop shelves all over the country. **Cantera,** a pinkish stone, quarried near Pátzcuaro and Oaxaca, is used similarly.

For a keepsake from a truly ancient Mexican tradition, don't forget the hollowed-out stone *metate* (may-TAH-tay), a corn-grinding basin, or the three-legged *molcajete* (mohl-kah-HAY-tay), a mortar for grinding chiles.

HUICHOL ART

Huichol art evolved from the charms that Huichol shamans crafted to empower them during their hazardous pilgrimages to their peyote-rich sacred land of Wirikuta. To the original items—mostly **devotional arrows, yarn** *cicuri* (see-KOO-ree—god's eyes), and

© BRUCE WHIPPERMAN

Bargaining for Huichol *cuadras* (yarn paintings) is a popular Puerto Vallarta pastime.

decorated gourds for collecting peyote—have been added colorful **cuadras** (yarn paintings) and **bead masks.**

Cuadras, made of synthetic yarns pressed into beeswax on a plywood backing, traditionally depict plant and animal spirits, the main actors of the Huichol cosmos. Bead masks likewise blend the major elements of the Huichol worldview into an eerie human likeness, often of Grandmother Earth (Tatei Nakawe).

Although Huichol men do not actually manufacture their headwear, they do decorate them. They take ordinary sombreros and embellish them into Mexico's most flamboyant hats, flowing with bright ribbons, feathers, and fringes of colorful wool balls.

Many commercial outlets, especially in Puerto Vallarta (and even commercial Christmas catalogs in the United States) now offer made-for-tourists Huichol goods. However, discriminating collectors find the finer examples nearer the source. Visit the Huichol Cultural Center in Santiago Ixcuintla, the long-established Huichol outlet shops in Tepic, and the more exclusive Puerto Vallarta shops.

JEWELRY

Gold and silver were once the basis for Mexico's wealth. Her Spanish conquerors plundered a mountain of gold—religious offerings, necklaces, pendants, rings, bracelets—masterfully crafted by a legion of native metalsmiths and jewelers. Unfortunately, much of that indigenous tradition was lost because the Spanish denied access to precious metals to the Mexicans for generations while they introduced Spanish methods. Nevertheless, a small goldworking tradition survived the dislocations of the 1810–1821 War of Independence and the 1910–1917 revolution. Silver-crafting, moribund during

HAGGLING 101

Mexico is the land of negotiations. Nearly everything, from hotel rooms to trinkets, can be negotiated to a lower price. If you come from a country where haggling in stores and hotels is uncommon, the United States for example, this can produce a mixed bag of reactions. Some people prefer to just pay the inflated asking price right away to avoid having to haggle. Others only shop where there is no haggling, like grocery stores and shopping malls. If you aren't an experienced haggler, attempts can produce anxiety, a feeling of doing something "wrong," or simply the sneaking suspicion that even though you got the price down, you still didn't get a good deal. Here are some tips to make haggling a little easier.

First, have the right attitude. Your goal is not to get the absolute lowest, rock-bottom price but to get a fair price; fair to you and to the seller. It should be friendly, not aggressive. Remember that the people of Mexico make significantly less than say, a minimum wage worker in the United States. Ten pesos to them is a big deal whereas at today's exchange rate, that's about $0.60. Don't bother haggling over items that only cost a few dollars unless you want a volume discount.

Start at the asking price and counter offer less than you actually want to pay but don't go nuts. In popular tourist areas like the artisan market in Puerto Vallarta, you can safely start at 40 percent of the asking price without offending anyone. Again, it's not about getting the lowest price. Don't make an insulting offer of $1 for a hand-carved wooden mask. Shop around and see what the asking price is in a variety of places before you make your purchases.

Be prepared to walk away. If the seller won't negotiate to a reasonable price, be assured that nearby is someone who will. The simple act of turning to walk away can prompt acceptance of your last offer or a better, final offer from the seller. In other cases, if it's something you cannot live without, you may just have to pay the seller's price. However, in an ideal situation, both the buyer and the seller will reach a happy midpoint, each feeling like they got a decent deal.

The bottom line is that if you feel you got a good deal, then you did.

the 1800s, was revived in Taxco, Guerrero, principally through the efforts of architect/artist William Spratling, working with the local community.

Today, spurred by the tourist boom, jewelry-making thrives in Mexico. Taxco, where dozens of enterprises—guilds, families, cooperatives—produce sparkling silver and gold adornments, is the acknowledged center. Many Puerto Vallarta regional shops sell fine Taxco products—shimmering butterflies, birds, jaguars, serpents, turtles, fish—reflecting pre-Columbian tradition. Taxco-made pieces, mostly in silver, vary from humble but good-looking trinkets to candelabras and place settings for a dozen, sometimes embellished with turquoise, garnet, coral, lapis, jade, and, in exceptional cases, emeralds, rubies, and diamonds.

WOOD CARVING AND MUSICAL INSTRUMENTS
Masks
Spanish and native Mexican traditions have blended to produce a multitude of masks—some strange, some lovely, some scary, some endearing, all interesting. The tradition flourishes in the strongly indigenous southern Pacific states of Michoacán, Guerrero, Oaxaca, and Chiapas, where campesinos gear up all year for the village festivals—especially Semana Santa, early December (Virgin of Guadalupe), and the festival of the local patron, whether it be San José, San Pedro, San Pablo, Santa María, Santa Barbara, or one of a host of others. Every local fair has its favored dances, such as the Dance of the Conquest, the Christians and Moors, the Old Men, or the Tiger, in which masked villagers act out age-old allegories of fidelity, sacrifice, faith, struggle, sin, and redemption.

Although masks are made of many materials—from stone and ebony to coconut husks and paper—wood, where available, is the medium of choice. For the entire year, mask-makers cut, carve, sand, and paint to ensure that each participant will be properly disguised for the festival.

The popularity of masks has led to an entire made-for-tourist mask industry of mass-

Mexican stringed musical instruments are sold everywhere, but are nearly all made in Paracho, Michoacán.

© BRUCE WHIPPERMAN

produced duplicates, many cleverly antiqued. Examine the goods carefully; if the price is high, don't buy unless you're convinced it's a real antique.

Alebrijes
Tourist demand has made zany wooden animals, or *alebrijes* (ah-lay-BREE-hays), a Oaxaca growth industry. Virtually every family in the Valley of Oaxaca villages of Arrazola and San Martin Tilcajete runs a factory studio. There, piles of soft *copal* wood, which men carve and women finish and intricately paint, become whimsical giraffes, dogs, cats, iguanas, gargoyles, dragons, and most of the possible permutations in between. The farther from the source you get, the higher the *alebrije* price becomes; what costs $5 in Arrazola will probably run about $10 in Puerto Vallarta and $30 in the United States or Canada.

Also commonly available wooden items are the charming colorfully painted fish carved mainly in the Pacific coastal state of Guerrero, and the burnished, dark hardwood animal and fish sculptures of desert ironwood from the state of Sonora.

Musical Instruments

Most of Mexico's guitars are made in Paracho, Michoacán (southeast of Lake Chapala, 50 miles north of Uruapan). There, scores of cottage factories turn out guitars, violins, mandolins, *viruelas,* ukuleles, and a dozen more variations every day. They vary widely in quality, so look carefully before you buy. Make sure that the wood is well cured and dry; damp, unripe wood instruments are more susceptible to warping and cracking.

METALWORK

Bright copper, brass, and tinware; sturdy ironwork; and razor-sharp knives and machetes are made in a number of regional centers. **Copperware,** from jugs, cups, and plates to candlesticks—and even the town lampposts and bandstand—all come from Santa Clara del Cobre, a few miles south of Pátzcuaro, Michoacán.

Although not the source of **brass** itself, Tonalá, in the Guadalajara eastern suburb, is the place where brass is most abundant and beautiful, appearing as menageries of brilliant, fetching birds and animals, sometimes embellished with shiny nickel highlights.

Several Oaxaca family factories turn out piles of fine **cutlery**—knives, swords, and machetes—scrolled **cast-iron grillwork,** and a swarm of bright **tinware,** or *hojalata* (oh-hah-LAH-tah), mirror frames, masks, and glittering Christmas decorations.

Be sure not to miss the miniature *milagros,* one of Mexico's most charming forms of metalwork. Usually of brass, they are of homely shapes—a horse, dog, or baby, or an arm, head, or foot—which, accompanied by a prayer, the faithful pin to the garment of their favorite saint whom they hope will intercede to cure an ailment or fulfill a wish. Look for them at pilgrimage basilicas, such as Zapopan (suburban Guadalajara), Talpa (mountains east of Puerto Vallarta), and San Juan de los Lagos, northeast of Guadalajara.

PAPER AND PAPIER-MÂCHÉ

Papier-mâché has become a high art in Tonalá, Jalisco, where a swarm of birds, cats, frogs, giraffes, and other animal figurines are meticulously crafted by building up repeated layers of glued paper. The result—sanded, brilliantly varnished, and polished—resembles fine sculptures rather than the humble newspaper from which it was fashioned.

Other paper goods you shouldn't overlook include piñatas (durable, inexpensive, and as Mexican as you can get), available in every town market; also colorful decorative cutout banners (string overhead at your home fiesta) from San Salvador Huixcolotla, Puebla; and **amate,** wild fig tree bark paintings in animal and flower motifs, from Xalitla and Ameyaltepec, Guerrero.

POTTERY AND CERAMICS

Although Mexican pottery tradition is as diverse as the country itself, some varieties stand out. Among the most prized is the so-called **Talavera** (or Majolica), the best of which is made by a few family-run factories in Puebla. The name Talavera originates from the Spanish town of the same name, from which the tradition migrated to Mexico; before that it originated on the Spanish Mediterranean island of Mayorca (thus Majolica) from a combination of still older Arabic, Chinese, and African ceramic styles. Shapes include plates, bowls, jugs, and pitchers, hand-painted and hard-fired in intricate bright yellow, orange, blue, and green floral designs. So few shops make true Talavera these days that other cheaper lookalike grades, made around Guanajuato, are more common, selling for as little as a tenth of the price of the genuine article.

More practical and nearly as prized is hand-painted, high-fired **stoneware** from Tonalá in Guadalajara's eastern suburbs. Although made in many shapes and sizes, such stoneware is often available in complete dinner place settings. Decorations are usually in abstract floral and animal designs, hand-painted over a reddish clay base.

From the same tradition come the famous *bruñido* pottery animals of Tonalá. Round, smooth, and cuddly as ceramic can be, the Tonalá animals—very commonly doves and ducks, but also cats and dogs and sometimes even armadillos, frogs, and snakes—each seem to embody the essence of their species.

Some of the most charming Mexican pottery, made from a ruddy low-fired clay and crafted following pre-Columbian traditions, comes from western Mexico, especially Colima. Charming figurines in timeless human poses— flute-playing musicians, dozing grandmothers, fidgeting babies, loving couples—and animals, especially Colima's famous **playful dogs,** decorate the shelves of a sprinkling of shops.

The southern states of Guerrero and Oaxaca are both centers of a vibrant pottery tradition. Humble but very attractive are the unglazed brightly painted animals—cats, ducks, fish, and many others—that folks bring to Puerto Vallarta centers from their family village workshops.

Much more acclaimed are certain types of pottery from the valley surrounding the city of Oaxaca. The village of Atzompa is famous for its tan, green-glazed clay pots, dishes, and bowls. Nearby San Bártolo Coyotepec village has acquired even more renown for its **black pottery** *(barro negro),* sold all over the world. Doña Rosa, now deceased, pioneered the crafting of big round pots without using a potter's wheel. Now made in many more shapes by Doña Rosa's descendants, the pottery's exquisite silvery black sheen is produced by the reduction (reduced air) method of firing, which removes oxygen from the clay's red (ferric) iron oxide, converting it to black ferrous oxide.

Although most latter-day Mexican potters have become aware of the **health dangers of lead pigments,** some for-sale pottery may still contain lead. The hazard comes from low-fired pottery in which the lead pigments have not been firmly melted into the surface glaze. In such cases, acids in foods such as lemons, vinegar, and tomatoes dissolve the lead pigments, which, when ingested in sufficient quantities, will result in lead poisoning. In general, the hardest, shiniest pottery, which has been twice fired—such as the high-quality Tlaquepaque stoneware used for place settings—is the safest.

WOOLEN WOVEN GOODS

Mexico's finest wool weavings come from Teotitlán del Valle, in the Valley of Oaxaca, less than an hour's drive east of Oaxaca city. The weaving tradition, carried on by Teotitlán's Zapotec-speaking families, dates back at least 2,000 years. Many families still carry on the arduous process, making everything from scratch. They gather the dyes from wild plants and the bodies of insects and sea snails. They hand-wash, card, spin, and dye the wool and even travel to remote mountain springs to gather water. The results, they say, *vale la pena* (are worth the pain): intensely colored, tightly woven carpets, rugs, and wall-hangings, known in Mexico as *tapetes,* that retain their brilliance for generations.

Rougher, more loosely woven blankets, jackets, and serapes come from other parts, notably mountain regions, especially around San Cristóbal de las Casas, in Chiapas, and Lake Pátzcuaro in Michoacán.

© BRUCE WHIPPERMAN

The finest of Mexican wool weavings, called *tapetes,* are expertly hand-loomed in Oaxaca.

ESSENTIALS

Getting There

BY AIR
From the United States and Canada

The vast majority of travelers reach Puerto Vallarta by air. Flights are frequent and reasonably priced. Competition sometimes shaves tariffs to as low as $250 or less for a Puerto Vallarta low-season round-trip from the departure gateways of San Francisco, Los Angeles, Denver, Dallas, Phoenix, or Houston.

Air travelers can save lots of money by shopping around. Don't be bashful about asking for the cheapest price. Make it clear to the airline or travel agent that you're interested in a bargain. Ask the right questions: Are there special-incentive, advance-payment, night, midweek, tour-package, or charter fares? Peruse the ads in the Sunday newspaper travel section for bargain-oriented travel agencies. Check airline and bargain-oriented travel websites, such as **www.orbitz.com, www.expedia.com,** and **www.travelocity.com.**

Although some agents charge booking fees and don't like discounted tickets because their fee depends on a percentage of ticket price, many will nevertheless work hard to get you a bargain, especially if you book an entire air-hotel package with them.

Although only a sprinkling of airlines fly directly to Puerto Vallarta from the northern

United States and Canada, many charters do. In locales near Vancouver, Calgary, Ottawa, Toronto, Montréal, Minneapolis, Chicago, Detroit, Cleveland, and New York, consult a travel agent for charter flight options. Be aware that charter reservations, which often require fixed departure and return dates and provide minimal cancellation refunds, decrease your flexibility. If available charter choices are unsatisfactory, then you might choose to begin your vacation with a connecting flight to one of the Puerto Vallarta gateways of San Francisco, Los Angeles, San Diego, Denver, Phoenix, Dallas, Houston, Atlanta, Chicago, San Jose, or Oakland.

From Europe, Latin America, and Australia

A few airlines fly across the Atlantic directly to Mexico City, where easy Puerto Vallarta connections are available via Mexicana, Aeroméxico, or Aerocalifornia. These include **Lufthansa,** which connects directly from Frankfurt; and **Aeroméxico,** which connects directly from Paris and Madrid.

From Latin America, **Aeroméxico** connects directly with Mexico City, customarily with São Paulo, Brazil; Santiago, Chile; and Lima, Peru. A number of other Latin American carriers also fly directly to Mexico City.

Very few flights cross the Pacific directly to Mexico, except for with **Japan Airlines,** which connects Tokyo to Mexico City via Vancouver. More commonly, travelers from Australasia transfer at New York, Chicago, Dallas, San Francisco, or Los Angeles for Puerto Vallarta.

BY BUS

As air travel rules in the United States, bus travel rules in Mexico. Hundreds of sleek, first-class bus lines such as Elite, Turistar, Futura, Transportes Pacífico, and White Star (Estrella Blanca) depart the border daily, headed for the Puerto Vallarta region.

Since North American bus lines ordinarily terminate just north of the Mexican border, you must usually disembark and continue on foot across the border to the Mexican immigration

office (*migración*). There, after having filled out the necessary but very simple paperwork, you can walk outside and bargain with one of the local taxis to drive you the few miles to the *camionera central* (central bus station).

First-class bus service in Mexico is much cheaper and more frequent than in the United States. Tickets for comparable trips in Mexico cost a fraction (around $80 for a 1,000-mile trip, compared with about $120 the United States).

In Mexico, as on U.S. buses, you often have to take it as you find it. *Asientos reservados* (seat reservations), *boletos* (tickets), and information must generally be obtained in person at the bus station, and credit cards and travelers checks are not often accepted. Nor are reserved bus tickets typically refundable, so don't miss the bus. On the other hand, plenty of buses roll south almost continually.

Bus Routes to Puerto Vallarta
From California and the western United States, cross the border to Tijuana, Mexicali, or Nogales, where you can ride one of at least three bus lines along the Pacific Coast route (National Highway 15) south to Puerto Vallarta by Estrella Blanca (via its subsidiaries, Elite, Transportes Norte de Sonora, or Turistar) or independents Transportes Pacífico or Transportes y Autobuses del Pacífico (TAP).

A few Estrella Blanca and Transportes Pacífico departures may go all the way from the border to Puerto Vallarta. Otherwise, you will have to change buses at Mazatlán or Tepic, depending on your connection. Allow a full day and a bit more (about 30 hours), depending upon connections, for the trip. Carry liquids and food (which might be only minimally available en route) with you.

From the midwestern United States, cross the border from El Paso to Juárez and head for Mazatlán by way of Chihuahua and Durango by either Estrella Blanca (via subsidiaries Transportes Chihuahuenses or super-first-class Turistar) or independent Ómnibus de Mexico. Both Transportes Chihuahuenses and Turistar usually offer a few daily departures direct to

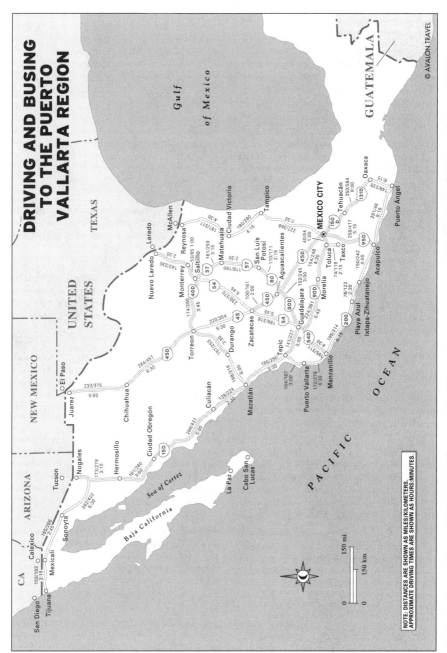

DRIVING AND BUSING TO THE PUERTO VALLARTA REGION

© AVALON TRAVEL

GUATEMALA

Gulf of Mexico

UNITED STATES

TEXAS

NEW MEXICO

ARIZONA

CA

San Diego
Tijuana
159/193
3:15
Mexicali
Calexico
165/266
3:15
Sonoyta
292/422
5:30
Nogales
Tucson
Hermosillo
173/279
3:15
181/260
3:00
Ciudad Obregón
15D
266/431
5:00
Culiacán
139/224
2:30
Mazatlán
180/290
3:30
Tepic
104/167
3:00
Puerto Vallarta
172/276
4:30
Manzanillo
195/314
4:15
Playa Azul
Ixtapa-Zihuatanejo
200

Juarez
El Paso
233/375
5:00
Chihuahua
284/457
6:30
45D
Torreon
174/280
3:45
220/354
5:30
Durango
318/318
6:00
Zacatecas
45
45D
198/318
5:45
Tepic
141/227
3:00
54D
Guadalajara
224/361
4:45
90D
Morelia
54
80D
150/242
2:30
76/122
2:15
Toluca
74/119
2:30
Taxco
95D
Acapulco
259/417
5:15
Puerto Angel
8:15

La Paz
Cabo San Lucas
Baja California
Sea of Cortez

PACIFIC OCEAN

Nuevo Laredo
Laredo
McAllen
Reynosa
143/230
2:30
Saltillo
53/85 1:00
57
161/259
3:15
Matehuala
118/190
2:30
80
100/161
2:00
San Luis Potosi
110/171
2:15
Aguascalientes
152/245
3:00
45D
154/248
40/84 1:00
45D
MEXICO CITY
150 D
227/366
Tehuacán
131D
350/564
8:00
Oaxaca
148/238
8:00
293/146
8:16

Monterrey
400
54
Ciudad Victoria
180/290
4:15
Tampico
197/317
2:15
94/30

PACIFIC OCEAN

150 mi
150 km
0
0

NOTE: DISTANCES ARE SHOWN AS MILES/KILOMETERS.
APPROXIMATE DRIVING TIMES ARE SHOWN AS HOURS:MINUTES.

Mazatlán. Otherwise, transfer at Durango to a Mazatlán-bound bus and continue south to Puerto Vallarta as described earlier.

From the southeastern and eastern United States, cross the border at Laredo to Nuevo Laredo and ride Transportes Norte de Sonora or Turistar direct to Mazatlán, or to Durango. At Durango, transfer to a Mazatlán bus, where you can continue south to Puerto Vallarta, as described previously.

From the central or eastern United States, it may be more convenient to ride a bus from the border direct to Guadalajara, where you can easily transfer to one of many buses bound for Puerto Vallarta.

BY CAR OR RV

If you're adventurous and like going to out-of-the-way places, but still want to have all the comforts of home, you may enjoy driving your own car or RV to Puerto Vallarta. On the other hand, consideration of cost, risk, wear on both you and your vehicle, and the congestion hassles in towns may change your mind.

Mexican Car Insurance

Mexico does not recognize foreign insurance. When you drive into Mexico, Mexican auto insurance is at least as important as your passport. At the busier crossings, you can get it at insurance "drive-ins" just north of the border. The many Mexican auto insurance companies are government-regulated; their numbers keep prices and services competitive.

Sanborn's Mexico Insurance (P.O. Box 310, McAllen, TX 78502, tel. 956/686-3601 or 800/222-0158, www.sanbornsinsurance.com), one of the best-known agencies, certainly seems to be trying hardest. It offers a number of books and services, including the *Recreational Guide to Mexico,* a good road map, "smile-by-mile" *Travelog* guide to "every highway in Mexico," hotel discounts, and more. Much of the above is available to members of Sanborn's Sombrero Club.

Alternatively, look into **Vagabundos del Mar** (tel. 800/474-2252, www.vagabundos.com), an RV-oriented Mexico travel club offering memberships that include a newsletter, caravanning opportunities, discounts, insurance, and much more.

Mexican car insurance runs from a barebones rate of about $8 a day for minimal $10,000/$50,000 (property damage/medical payments) coverage to a more typical $15 a day for more complete $20,000/$100,000 coverage. On the same scale, insurance for a $50,000 RV and equipment runs about $35 a day. These daily rates decrease sharply for six-month or one-year policies, which run from about $200 for the minimum to $400–1,600 for complete, high-end coverage.

If you get broken glass, personal effects, and legal expenses coverage with these rates, you're lucky. Mexican policies don't usually cover them.

You should get something for your money, however. The deductibles should be no more than $300–500, the public liability/medical payments should be about double the legal minimum ($25,000 maximum payment for property damage, $25,000 maximum medical payments per person, and $50,000 maximum total medical payments per accident), and you should be able to get your car fixed in the United States and receive payment in U.S. dollars for losses. If not, shop around.

A Sinaloa Note of Caution

Although *bandidos* no longer menace Mexican roads (but loose burros, horses, and cattle still do), be cautious in the infamous marijuana- and opium-growing region of Sinaloa state north of Mazatlán. It's best not to stray from Highway 15 between Culiacán and Mazatlán or from Highway 40 between Mazatlán and Durango. Curious tourists have been assaulted in the hinterlands adjacent to these roads.

The Green Angels

The Green Angels have answered many motoring tourists' prayers in Mexico. Bilingual teams of two, trained in auto repair and first aid, help distressed tourists along main highways. They patrol fixed stretches of road twice daily by truck. To make sure they stop to help, pull completely off the highway and raise your hood. You may want to hail a passing trucker to call them for you (Mexico emergency number 078 for the tourism hotline, or 01-800/903-9200).

If for some reason you have to leave your vehicle on the roadside, don't leave it unattended. Hire a local teenager or adult to watch it for you. Unattended vehicles on Mexican highways are quickly stricken by a mysterious disease, the symptom of which is rapid loss of vital parts.

Mexican Gasoline

Pemex, short for Petróleos Mexicanos, the government oil monopoly, markets diesel fuel and two grades of gasoline, both unleaded: 92-octane premium and 89-octane Magna. Magna (MAHG-nah) is good gas, yielding performance similar to that of U.S.-style "regular or super-unleaded" gasoline. (My car, whose manufacturer recommended 91-octane, ran well on Magna.) It runs about $0.65 per liter (about $2.40 per gallon.)

On main highways, Pemex makes sure that major stations (spaced typically about 20 miles apart) stock Magna.

Gas Station Thievery

Although the problem has abated considerably in recent years (by the hiring of female attendants), boys who hang around gas stations to wash windows are notoriously light-fingered. When stopping at the *gasolinera,* make sure that your cameras, purses, and other movable items are out of reach. Also, make sure that your car has a lockable gas cap. If not, insist on pumping the gas yourself, or be super-watchful as you pull up to the gas pump. Make certain that the pump reads zero before the attendant pumps the gas.

A Healthy Car

Preventive measures spell good health for both you and your car. Get that tune-up (or that long-delayed overhaul) *before,* rather than after, you leave. Also, carry a stock of spare parts, which will be more difficult to get and more expensive in Mexico than at home. Carry an extra tire or two, a few cans of motor oil and octane enhancer, oil and gas filters, fan belts, spark plugs, tune-up kit, points, and fuses. Be prepared with basic tools and supplies, such as screwdrivers, pliers including Vice-Grip, lug wrench, jack, adjustable wrenches, tire pump and patches, tire pressure gauge, steel wire, and electrical tape. For breakdowns and emergencies, carry a folding shovel, a husky rope or chain, a gasoline can, and flares.

Car Repairs in Mexico

The American big three—General Motors, Ford, and Chrysler—as well as Nissan and Volkswagen are represented by extensive dealer networks in Mexico, newcomers Toyota and Honda less so but more likely in major metro areas. Getting your car or truck serviced at such agencies is straightforward. While parts will probably be higher in price, shop rates run about one-third of U.S. prices, so repairs will generally come out to about half the prices back home.

Every village in Mexico seems to have a *taller mecánico* (mechanical repair shop) ready to fix your car.

© BRUCE WHIPPERMAN

The same is not true for repairing other makes, however. Mexico has only a light sprinkling of foreign-make car dealers. Consequently it is difficult if not impossible to find officially certified mechanics for Japanese or European makes other than Volkswagen.

Many clever Mexican independent mechanics, however, can fix any car that comes their way. Their humble *talleres mecánicos* (tah-YER-ays may-KAH-nee-kohs), or repair shops, dot town and village roadsides everywhere.

Although most mechanics are honest, beware of unscrupulous operators who try to collect double or triple their original estimate. If you don't speak Spanish, find someone who can assist you in negotiations. *Always* get a written cost estimate, including needed parts and labor, even if you have to write it yourself. Make sure the mechanic understands, then ask him to sign it before he starts work. Although this may be a hassle, it might save you a much nastier hassle later. Shop labor at small, independent repair shops should run $10–20 per hour. The most common repair you're likely to need is a simple tire patch, which should run less than $5 at the typical (and very common) roadside *llantera* (tire repair shop). For more information, and for entertaining anecdotes of car and RV travel in Mexico, consult Carl Franz's *The People's Guide to Mexico*.

Mordidas (Bribes)

The usual meeting ground of the visitor and Mexican police is in the visitor's car on a highway or downtown street. To the tourist, such an encounter may seem mild harassment by the police, accompanied by vague threats of going to the police station or impounding the car for such-and-such a violation. The tourist often goes on to say, "It was all right, though …. We paid him $20 and he went away …. Mexican cops sure are crooked, aren't they?"

And, I suppose, if people want to go bribing their way through Mexico, that's their business. But calling Mexican cops crooked isn't exactly fair. Police, like most everyone else in Mexico, have to scratch for a living, and they have found that many tourists are willing to slip them a $20

bill for nothing. Rather than crooked, I would call them hungry and opportunistic.

Instead of paying a bribe, do what I've done a dozen times: Remain cool, and if you're really guilty of an infraction, calmly say, "Ticket, please." (*"Boleto, por favor."*) After a minute or two of stalling, and no cash appearing, the officer most likely will not bother with a ticket but will wave you on with only a warning. If, on the other hand, the officer does write you a ticket, he will probably keep your driver's license, which you will be able to retrieve at the *presidencia municipal* (city hall) the next day in exchange for paying your fine.

Crossing the Border

Squeezing through border bottlenecks during peak holidays and rush hours can be time-consuming. Avoid crossing 7–9 A.M. and 4:30–6:30 P.M.

Highway Routes from the United States

If you've decided to drive to Puerto Vallarta, you have your choice of three general routes. At safe highway speeds, each of these routes requires a minimum of about 24 hours of driving time. Maximize comfort and safety by following the broad toll (*cuota*) expressways that often parallel the old, narrow nontoll (*libre*) routes. Despite the increased cost (about $60 for a car, more than double that for a motorhome), the *cuota* expressways will save you at least a day's driving time (and the extra food and hotel tariffs) and wear and tear on both your vehicle and your nerves. Most folks allow three full south-of-the-border driving days to Puerto Vallarta, but it can be done in less.

From the U.S. Pacific Coast and west, follow National Highway 15 (called 15D as the toll expressway) from the border at Nogales, Sonora, an hour's drive south of Tucson, Arizona. Highway 15D continues southward smoothly, leading you through cactus-studded mountains and valleys, which turn into green lush farmland and tropical coastal plain and forest by the time you arrive in Mazatlán. Watch for the *periféricos* and truck routes that guide you past the congested downtowns of Hermosillo, Guaymas, Ciudad Obregón, Los Mochis, and Culiacán. Between these centers, you speed along via *cuota* expressway all the way to Mazatlán. If you prefer not to pay the high tolls, stick to the old *libre* highway. Hazards, bumps, and slow going might force you to reconsider, however.

From Mazatlán, continue along the narrow (but soon to be replaced) two-lane route to Tepic, where Highways 15 and 15D fork left (east) to Guadalajara and Highway 200 heads south to Puerto Vallarta and beyond.

If, however, you're driving to Puerto Vallarta **from the central United States,** cross the border at El Paso to Ciudad Juárez, Chihuahua. There, National Highway 45D, the new *cuota* multilane expressway, leads you southward through high, dry plains past the cities of Chihuahua and Jiménez, where you continue by expressway Highway 49 to Gómez Palacio-Torreón. There, proceed southwest toward Durango, via expressway Highway 40D. At Durango, head west along the winding but spectacular two-lane trans-Sierra National Highway 40, which intersects National Highway 15 just south of Mazatlán. From there, continue south as described above.

Folks heading to western Pacific Mexico **from the eastern and southeastern United States** should cross the border from Laredo, Texas, to Nuevo Laredo. From there, you can follow either the National Highway 85 (*libre*) route or the new Highway 85D *cuota* road, which continues, bypassing Monterrey, where you proceed via expressway Highway 40D all the way to Saltillo. At Saltillo, keep going westward on Highway 40 or expressway 40D, through Torreón to Durango. Continue via the two-lane Highway 40 over the Pacific crest all the way to National Highway 15, just south of Mazatlán. Continue southward as described earlier.

BY TRAIN

Privatization is rapidly putting an end to most passenger train service in Mexico, with the exception of the **Copper Canyon** scenic route. One of the few remaining passenger train rides

in Mexico typically begins with a bus trip or flight south to Chihuahua, where you board the Chihuahua-Pacific Railway train and ride west along the renowned Copper Canyon (Barranca del Cobre) route to the Pacific. Only finished during the early 1960s, this route traverses the spectacular canyonland home of the Tarahumara people. At times along the winding 406-mile (654-km) route, your rail car seems to teeter at the very edge of the labyrinthine Barranca del Cobre, a canyon so deep that its climate varies from Canadian at the top to tropical jungle at the bottom.

The railway-stop village of Creel, with a few stores and hotels and a Tarahumara mission, is the major jumping-off point for trips into the canyon. For a treat, reserve a stay en route to Puerto Vallarta at the Sierra Lodge (tel. 600/776-3942, www.coppercanyonlodges.com) in Creel. From there, the canyon beckons: Explore the village, enjoy panoramic views, observe mountain wildlife, and breathe pine-scented mountain air. Farther afield, you can hike to a hot spring or spend a few days exploring the canyon-bottom itself, with overnights at the Riverside Lodge in the rustic village of Batopilas.

Copper Canyon Tours

Some agencies arrange unusually good Copper Canyon rail tours. Among the best is **Columbus Travel** (900 Ridge Creek Lane, Bulverde, TX 78163-2872, tel. 830/885-2000 or 800/843-1060, www.canyontravel.com), which employs its own resident, ecologically sensitive guides. Trips range from small-group, rail-based sightseeing and birding/natural history tours to customized wilderness rail-jeep-backpacking adventures.

Elderhostel (11 Avenue de Lafayette, Boston MA 02111, tel. 877/426-8056 or 800/454-5768, www.elderhostel.org) has long provided some of the best-buy Copper Canyon options, designed for seniors. Participants customarily fly to Los Mochis on the Pacific Coast, then transfer to the first-class Mexican Chihuahua-Pacific train for a four-day canyonland adventure. Highlights include nature walks, visits to native missions, and cultural sites in

Cerrocahui village and Creel, the frontier outpost in the Tarahumara heartland. The return includes a comfortable overnight at Posada Barranca, at the canyon's dizzying edge.

BY FERRY

An alternative, but more complicated, route to Puerto Vallarta is by ferry from the southern tip of Baja California. Bus travelers should cross the border at Tijuana or Mexicali and ride Autobuses Blanca Coordinados (ABC, Tijuana local tel. 664/621-2424, www.abc.com.mx) through the long desert to La Paz (about 20 hours). Car travelers also cross at Tijuana or Mexicali and follow good two-lane Mexico National Highway 1, a long 900 miles (1,500 km) south to La Paz.

At La Paz (a pleasant, mid-sized Mexican fishing port town during the winter, although usually very hot in the late spring and summer),you have your choice of two ferry crossings. **Baja Ferries** (at the La Paz ferry dock, toll-free Mex. tel. 01-800/122-2796, from U.S. dial direct 01152-612/125-6324, fax 01152-612/123-0504, www.bajaferries.com.mx) ferries passengers and vehicles between La Paz and Topolobampo, near Los Mochis in northern Sinaloa (about $106 per adult, kids $53, cars and smaller four-wheel RVs about $550, motorhomes about double) and between La Paz and Mazatlán ($119, $59, and $980 respectively) in southern Sinaloa. Note: If you're planning on continuing south to Puerto Vallarta, you should probably opt for the Mazatlán crossing. Although it won't save you much time (since the bus or your vehicle travels much faster than the ferry), you might save the price of a hotel room and highway tolls (or bus fare).

The La Paz–Topolobampo run goes via the excellent Italian-built 1,000-passenger *California Star*. At this writing, it leaves La Paz nightly at 11 P.M. and takes six hours. The La Paz–Mazatlán run, leaves La Paz Monday, Wednesday, and Friday at 3 P.M. and takes 18 hours. Although seats are provided you may want to reserve one of their clean cabins with beds and private toilet (about $76 for a cabin and $90–120 for suites). Ferry facilities on both runs include bar, lounge,

and restaurant, but pets are not allowed, and passengers are not allowed to stay in their vehicles during the crossing. MasterCard and Visa are accepted for payment.

Reservations are recommended at all times, and are a must during the super-crowded Christmas and Easter holidays. You can make reservations either through the website www.bajaferries.com or directly at any of the many reservations/ticket-sales offices that the website lists. Of all of these, the most useful would probably be their U.S. agent, Native Trails (613 Queretaro, El Paso, TX 79912-2210, tel. 915/833-3107, fax 915/585-7027), or the La Paz sales office, which has English-speaking agents (corner of Isabel la Catolica and Navarro, tel. 612/125-7443, toll-free Mex. tel. 01-800/122-1414, fax 612/125-7444.

Although greatly improved in recent years, Baja ferry service is subject to change. Be sure to check by phone or Internet for the newest ferry information before making the long desert trip south to La Paz.

ORGANIZED TOURS

For travelers on a tight time budget, prearranged tour packages can provide a hassle-free option for sampling the attractions of Puerto Vallarta and its surrounding region. If, however, you prefer a self-paced vacation, or desire thrift over convenience, you should probably defer tour arrangements until after arrival. Many Puerto Vallarta agencies are as close as your hotel telephone or front-lobby tour desk and can customize a tour for you. Options vary from city highlight tours and bay snorkeling adventures to safaris through San Blas's wildlife-rich mangrove jungle.

Cruises and Sailboats

North-of-the-border travel agents will typically have a stack of cruise brochures that include Puerto Vallarta on their itineraries. People who enjoy being pampered with lots of food and ready-made entertainment (and who don't mind paying for it) can have great fun on cruises. Accommodations on a typical 10-day winter cruise (which would include a day or two in Puerto Vallarta) can run as little as $75 per day per person, double occupancy, to as much as $1,000 or more.

If, however, you want to get to know Mexico and the local people, a cruise is not for you. Onboard food and entertainment is the main event of a cruise; shore sightseeing excursions, which cost extra, are a sideshow.

Sailboats, on the other hand, offer an entirely different kind of sea route to Puerto Vallarta. **Ocean Voyages** (1709 Bridgeway, Sausalito, CA 94965, tel. 415/332-4681 or 800/299-4444, fax 415/332-7460, www.oceanvoyages.com), a California-based agency, arranges passage on a number of sail and motor vessels that regularly depart to the Puerto Vallarta region from Pacific ports such as San Diego, Los Angeles, San Francisco, and Vancouver. It offers custom itineraries and flexible arrangements that can vary from complete Puerto Vallarta round-trip voyages to weeklong coastal idylls between Puerto Vallarta and other Pacific ports of call. Some captains allow passengers to save money by signing on as crew.

Special-Interest Tours

Some tour and study programs include in-depth activities centered around arts and crafts, language and culture, people-to-people contact, wildlife-watching, ecology, or off-the-beaten-track adventuring. Outstanding among them are programs by University of Guadalajara, Field Guides, Oceanic Society, Elderhostel, Mar de Jade, and Rancho El Charro.

In Puerto Vallarta, the **University of Guadalajara** (www.cepe.udg.mx) maintains excellent study programs for visitors, through its **Centro de Estudios Para Extranjeros (CEPE)** (Study Center for Foreigners). Their extensive offering ranges from beginning Spanish language to advanced History, Politics, Literature, and Art. Housing options include homestays with local families.

Mar de Jade (tel. 800/257-0532, www.mardejade.com), a holistic-style living center at Playa Chacala, about 50 miles (80 km) north of Puerto Vallarta, offers unique people-to-people work-study opportunities. These include Spanish-language study at Mar de Jade's rustic beach study-center and assisting at its health clinic in Las Varas town nearby. It also offers accommodations and macrobiotic meals for travelers who would want to do nothing more than stay a few days and enjoy Mar de Jade's lovely tropical ambience. (For more details on the Mar de Jade area, see *Playa Chacala* in the *The Road to San Blas* section of *The Nayarit Coast* chapter.)

Naturalists enjoy the excellent **Field Guides** (tel. 800/728-4953, fax 512/263-0117, www.fieldguides.com) bird-watching tour, centered in wildlife-rich Jalisco and Colima backcountry. Of the 50 endemic Mexican bird species, about 35 have been seen on this tour.

The remote lagoons and islands of Baja California, about 200 miles (300 km) due west of Mazatlán, nurture a trove of marine and on-shore wildlife. Such sanctuaries are ongoing destinations of winter **Oceanic Society** (Fort Mason Center, QRTS 35, San Francisco, CA 94123, tel. 415/441-1106 or 800/326-7491, fax 415/474-3395, www.oceanic-society.org) expedition-tours around La Paz, Baja California. Tours customarily cost about $3,000, and cover several islands and shorelines on both the Baja California Pacific and Gulf of California coasts. Activities include about 11 days of marine mammal–watching, snorkeling, bird-watching, and ecoexploring, both on- and offshore.

The Oceanic Society trip might make an exciting overture or finale to your Puerto Vallarta adventure. You can connect with the Oceanic Society's Baja California (La Paz–Los Cabos) jumping-off-points via airlines' (Aeroméxico, Alaska, Frontier) mainland (Mazatlán/Guadalajara/Puerto Vallarta) destinations.

A Puerto Vallarta ranch, **Rancho El Charro** (Francisco Villa 895, Fracc. Las Gaviotas, tel. 322/224-0114, www.ranchoelcharro.com.mx), organizes naturalist-led horseback treks in the mountains near Puerto Vallarta. Tours run several days and include guided backcountry horseback riding, exploring antique colonial villages, camping out on the trail, swimming, hearty dinners, and cozy evenings at a rustic hacienda. Tariffs begin at about $1,000 per person.

Getting Around

BY AIR

The Puerto Vallarta region's four major jet airports are in Puerto Vallarta, Guadalajara, Manzanillo, and Tepic. Both scheduled and charter airlines connect these points with a number of national destinations, such as Mexico City, Mazatlán, Acapulco, La Paz, and Los Cabos. Although much pricier than first-class bus tickets, Mexican domestic airfares are on par with U.S. prices. If you're planning on lots of in-Mexico flying, upon arrival get the airlines' handy (although rapidly changeable) *itinerarios de vuelo* (flight schedules) at the airport.

Mexican airlines have operating peculiarities that result from their tight budgets. Don't miss a flight; you will likely lose half the ticket price. Adjusting your flight date may cost 25 percent of the ticket price. Get to the airport at least an hour ahead of time. Last-minute passengers are often "bumped" in favor of early-bird wait-listers. Conversely, go to the airport and get in line if you must catch a flight that the airlines claim is full—you might get on anyway. Keep your luggage small so you can carry it on. Lost-luggage victims receive scant compensation in Mexico.

Although the Puerto Vallarta–Guadalajara air connection is a good option, flying between most other Puerto Vallarta regional destinations is much less convenient than riding the bus.

BY BUS

The passenger bus is the king of the Mexican road. Several lines connect major destinations in the Puerto Vallarta region, both with each other and with the rest of Mexico.

Classes of Buses

Three distinct levels of intercity service—luxury-class, first-class, and second-class—are generally available. **Luxury-class** (called something like "Primera Plus," or "Ejecutivo" depending upon the line) service

Mexican second-class buses have unreserved first-come-first-served seating.

speeds passengers between the major destinations of Puerto Vallarta, Tepic, and Barra de Navidad, with few stops en route. In exchange for relatively high fares (about $25 for Puerto Vallarta–Tepic, for example), passengers enjoy rapid passage and airline-style amenities: plush reclining seats, a (usually) clean toilet, air-conditioning, onboard video, and an aisle attendant.

Although less luxurious, but for about two-thirds the price, **first-class** (*primera clase*) service is frequent and always includes reserved seating. Additionally, passengers enjoy soft reclining seats and air-conditioning (if it's working). Besides regular stops at or near most towns and villages en route, first-class bus drivers, if requested, will usually stop and let you off anywhere along the road.

Second-class (*clase ordinario*) seating is unreserved. In outlying parts of the Puerto Vallarta region, there is even a class of bus

© BRUCE WHIPPERMAN

beneath second class, but given the condition of many second-class buses, it seems as if third-class buses wouldn't run at all. Such buses are the stuff of travelers' legends: The recycled old GMC, Ford, and Dodge schoolbuses that stop everywhere and carry everyone and everything to even the smallest villages tucked away in the far mountains. As long as there is any kind of a road, the bus will most likely go there.

Now and then you'll read a newspaper story of a country bus that went over a cliff somewhere in Mexico, killing the driver and a dozen unfortunate souls. The same newspapers, however, never bother to mention the half-million safe passengers for whom the same bus provided trips during its 15 years of service before the accident.

Second-class buses are not for travelers with weak knees or stomachs. Often, you will initially have to stand, cramped in the aisle, in a crowd of campesinos. They are warm-hearted but poor people, so don't tempt them with open, dangling purses or wallets bulging in back pockets. Stow your money safely away. After a while, you will be able to sit down. Such privilege, however, comes with obligation, such as holding an old woman's bulging bag of carrots or a toddler on your lap. But if you accept your burden with humor and equanimity, who knows what favors and blessings may flow to you in return.

Tickets, Seating, and Baggage

Mexican bus lines do not usually publish schedules or fares. Simply ask someone who knows (such as your hotel desk clerk), or call (or ask someone to call) the bus station. Few travel agents handle bus tickets. If you don't want to spend the time to get a reserved ticket yourself, hire someone trustworthy to do it for you. Another option is to get to the bus station early enough on your traveling day to ensure that you'll get a bus to your destination.

Although some lines accept credit cards and issue computer-printed tickets at their major stations, most reserved bus tickets are sold for cash and are handwritten, with a specific seat number (*número de asiento*) on the

back. If you miss the bus, you lose your money. Furthermore, airline-style automated reservations systems have not yet arrived at many Mexican bus stations. Consequently, you can generally buy reserved tickets only at the local departure (*salida local*) station. (An agent in Puerto Vallarta, for example, may not be able to reserve you a ticket on a bus that originates in Tepic, 100 miles up the road.)

Request a reserved seat, if possible, with numbers 1–25 in the front (*delante*) to middle (*medio*) of the bus. The rear seats are often occupied by smokers, drunks, and rowdies. At night, you will sleep better on the right side (*lado derecho*), away from the glare of oncoming traffic lights.

Baggage is generally secure on Mexican buses. Label it, however. Overhead racks are generally too cramped to accommodate airline-sized carry-ons. Carry a small bag with your money and irreplaceables on your person; pack clothes and less-essentials in your checked luggage. For peace of mind, watch the handler put your checked baggage on the bus and watch to make sure it is not mistakenly taken off the bus at intermediate stops.

If your baggage gets misplaced, remain calm. Bus employees are generally competent and conscientious. If you are patient, recovering your luggage will become a matter of honor for many of them. Baggage handlers are at the bottom of the pay scale; a tip for their mostly thankless job is very much appreciated.

On long trips, carry food, beverages, and toilet paper. Station food may be dubious, and the sanitary facilities may be ill-maintained.

If you are waiting for a first-class bus at an intermediate *salida de paso* (passing station), you have to trust to luck that there will be an empty seat. If not, your best option may be to ride a more frequent second-class bus.

BY CAR
Rental Car

Car and jeep rentals are an increasingly popular transportation option in Puerto Vallarta. They offer mobility and independence for local sightseeing and beach excursions. In

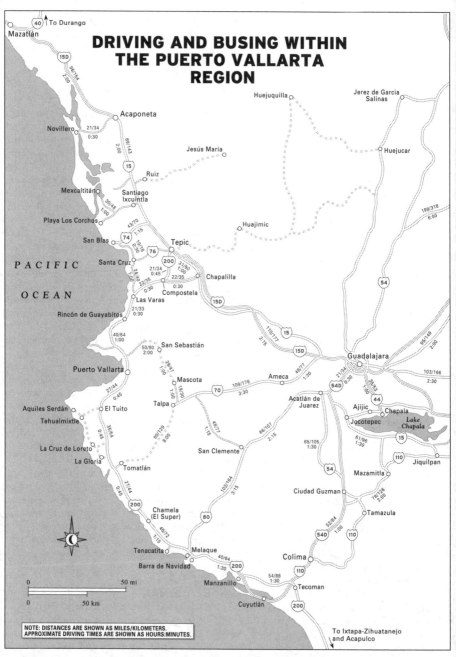

DRIVING AND BUSING WITHIN THE PUERTO VALLARTA REGION

To Durango

Mazatlán

To Ixtapa-Zihuatanejo and Acapulco

NOTE: DISTANCES ARE SHOWN AS MILES/KILOMETERS.
APPROXIMATE DRIVING TIMES ARE SHOWN AS HOURS:MINUTES.

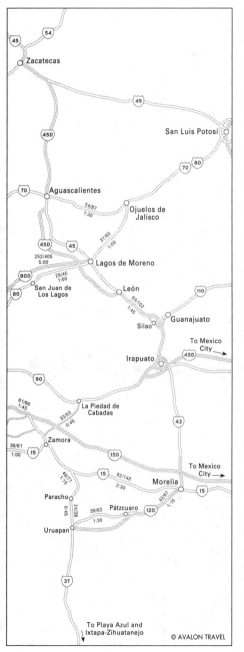

the Puerto Vallarta, Tepic, and Manzanillo (Barra de Navidad) airports the gang's all there: Hertz, National, Avis, Budget, Thrifty, Alamo, Dollar, and several local outfits. They require drivers to have a valid driver's license, passport, and major credit card, and may require a minimum age of 25. Some local companies do not accept credit cards, but do offer lower rates in return.

Base prices of international agencies such as Hertz, National, and Avis are not cheap. With a 17 percent value-added tax and mandatory insurance, rentals run more than in the United States. The cheapest possible rental car, usually a used stick-shift VW Beetle, runs $40–60 per day or $250–450 per week, depending on location and season. Prices are highest during Christmas and pre-Easter weeks. Before departure, use the international agencies' toll-free numbers and websites for availability, prices, and reservations. During nonpeak seasons, you may save lots of pesos by waiting until arrival and renting a car through a local agency. Shop around, starting with the agent in your hotel lobby or with the local Yellow Pages (under *"Automoviles, Renta de"*).

Car insurance that covers property damage, public liability, and medical payments is an absolute "must" (and required by law) with your rental car. If you get into an accident without insurance, you will be in deep trouble, and probably sent to jail. Narrow, rough roads and animals grazing at roadside make driving in Mexico more hazardous than back home.

Taxi

The high prices of rental cars make taxis a useful option for local excursions. Cars are luxuries, not necessities, for most Mexican families. Travelers might profit from the Mexican money-saving practice of piling everyone in a taxi for a Sunday outing. You may find that an all-day taxi and driver—who, besides relieving you of driving, will become your impromptu guide—will cost less than a rental car.

The magic word for saving money by taxi is *colectivo:* a taxi you share with other travelers. The first place you'll practice getting a taxi will be at the airport, where *colectivo* tickets are routinely sold from booths at the terminal door.

If, however, you want a private taxi, ask for a *taxi especial,* which will cost about three or four times the individual tariff for a *colectivo.*

Your airport experience will prepare you for in-town taxis, which rarely have meters. *You must establish the price before getting in.* Bargaining comes with the territory in Mexico, so don't shrink from it, even though it seems a hassle. If you get into a taxi without an agreed-upon price, you're letting yourself in for a more serious and potentially nasty hassle later. If your driver's price is too high, he'll probably come to his senses as soon as you hail another taxi.

After a few days, getting taxis around town will be a cinch. You'll find that you don't have to take the more expensive taxis lined up in your hotel driveway. If the price isn't right, walk toward the street and hail a regular taxi.

In town, if you can't find a taxi, it may be because they are waiting for riders at the local stand, called a taxi *sitio.* Ask someone to direct you to it: *"Excúseme. ¿Dónde está el sitio de taxi, por favor?"* ("Excuse me. Where is the taxi stand, please?")

Hitchhiking

Although it's legal in Mexico, most everyone agrees that hitchhiking is not the safest mode of transport. If you're unsure, don't do it. Continual hitchhiking does not make for a healthy travel diet, nor should you hitchhike at night.

The recipe for trouble-free hitchhiking requires equal measures of luck, savvy, and technique. The best places to catch rides are where people are arriving and leaving anyway, such as bus stops, highway intersections, gas stations, RV parks, and the highway out of town.

Male-female hitchhiking partnerships seem to net the most rides, although it is technically illegal for women to ride in commercial trucks. The more gear you and your partner have, the fewer rides you will get. Pickup and flatbed truck owners often pick up passengers for pay. Before hopping onto the truck bed, ask how much the ride will cost.

Visas and Officialdom

For U.S. and Canadian citizens, entry by air into Mexico for a few weeks could hardly be easier. Airline attendants hand out tourist cards (*tarjetas turísticas*) en route and officers make them official by glancing at passports and stamping the cards at the immigration gate. Business travel permits for 30 days or fewer are handled by the same simple procedures. Moreover, Mexican authorities no longer require payment for a land-entry tourist permit, which has simplified entry by bus and car.

There are some simple entry requirements, however. Mexican immigration officials require that all entering U.S. citizens 15 years old or over must present proper identification—either a valid U.S. passport or original birth certificate (or notarized copy). Naturalized citizens must show naturalization papers, a laminated naturalization card, or a valid U.S. passport.

Although you can enter Mexico without a passport, you'll still need to bring one, as it is required for reentry into the United States.

Canadian citizens must also show a valid passport or original birth certificate. Nationals of other countries (especially those such as Hong Kong, which issue more than one type of passport) may be subject to different or additional regulations. For advice, consult your regional Mexico Tourism Board office or consulate. For more Mexico-entry details, contact the Mexico Tourism Board (tel. 800/44-MEXICO or 800/446-3942) or contact your closest Mexico Tourism Board office.

DON'T LOSE YOUR TOURIST CARD

If you do, present your passport at the police station and get an official police report detailing your loss. Take the report to the nearest federal *migración* office (at the Puerto Vallarta, Manzanillo, and Guadalajara airports) or *oficina de turismo* (in Puerto Vallarta, Guadalajara, Tepic, San Blas, Rincón de Guayabitos, and Barra de Navidad) and ask for a duplicate tourist card. Savvy travelers carry copies of their passports, tourist cards, car permits, and Mexican auto-insurance policies, while leaving the originals in a hotel safe-deposit box.

For more complicated cases, get your tourist card early enough to allow you to consider the options. Tourist cards can be issued for multiple entries and a maximum validity of 180 days; photos are often required. If you don't request multiple entry or the maximum (*el máximo*) time, your card will probably be stamped single entry, valid for some shorter period, such as 90 days. If you are not sure how long you'll stay in Mexico, request the maximum (180 days is the absolute maximum for a tourist card; long-term foreign residents routinely make semiannual "border runs" for new tourist cards).

STUDENT AND BUSINESS VISAS

A visa is a notation stamped and signed on your passport showing the number of days and entries allowable for your trip. Apply for a student visa at the consulate nearest your home well in advance of your departure; the same is true if you require a business visa of longer than 30 days. One-year renewable student visas are available (sometimes with considerable red tape). An ordinary 180-day tourist card may be the easiest option, if you can manage it.

YOUR PASSPORT

Your passport (or birth or naturalization certificate) is your positive proof of national identity; without it, your status in any foreign country is in doubt. Don't leave home without one. U.S. citizens may obtain passports (allow 4–6 weeks) at local post offices. For-fee private passport agencies can speed this process and get you a passport within a week, maybe less.

ENTRY FOR CHILDREN

Children under the age of 15 can be included on their parents' tourist cards, but complications occur if the children (by reason of illness, for example) cannot leave Mexico with both parents. Parents can avoid such red tape by getting a passport and a Mexican tourist card for each of their children.

In addition to passport or birth certificate, minors (under age 18) entering Mexico without parents or legal guardians must present a notarized letter of permission signed by both parents or legal guardians. Even if accompanied by one parent, a notarized letter from the other must be presented. Divorce or death certificates must also be presented, when applicable. Airlines will require the name, address, and telephone number of the person meeting unaccompanied minors upon arrival in Mexico.

Puerto Vallarta travelers should hurdle all such possible delays far ahead of time in the cool calm of their local Mexican consulate rather than the hot, hurried atmosphere of a border or airport immigration station.

ENTRY FOR PETS

A pile of red tape can delay the entry of dogs, cats, and other pets into Mexico or it could be smooth as silk. Be prepared with veterinary-stamped health and rabies certificates for each animal and keep them in sturdy crates during travel. Contact your regional Mexico Tourism Board (tel. 800/44-MEXICO or 800/446-3942, www.visitmexico.com) for assistance.

CAR PERMITS

If you drive to Mexico, you will need a permit for your car. Upon entry into Mexico, be ready with originals and copies of your proof-of-ownership or registration papers (state title certificate, registration, or notarized bill of sale), current license plates, and current driver's license. The auto permit fee runs about $32, payable only by non-Mexican-bank MasterCard, Visa, or American Express credit cards. (The credit-card-only requirement discourages those who sell or abandon U.S.-registered cars in

Mexico without paying customs duties.) Credit cards must bear the same name as the vehicle proof-of-ownership papers.

The resulting car permit becomes part of the owner's tourist card and receives the same length of validity. Vehicles registered in the name of an organization or person other than the driver must be accompanied by a notarized affidavit authorizing the driver to use the car in Mexico for a specific time.

Border officials generally allow you to carry or tow additional motorized vehicles (motorcycle, another car, large boat) into Mexico but will probably require separate documentation and fee for each vehicle. If a Mexican official desires to inspect your trailer or RV, go through it with him.

Accessories, such as a small trailer, boat shorter than six feet, CB radio, or outboard motor, may be noted on the car permit and must leave Mexico with the car.

For updates and details on documentation required for taking your car into Mexico, contact the Mexico Tourism Board in the United States (tel. 800/446-3942, www.visitmexico.com). For more details on motor vehicle entry and what you may bring in your baggage to Mexico, consult the AAA (American Automobile Association) *Mexico TravelBook.*

Since Mexico does not recognize foreign automobile insurance, *you must buy Mexican automobile insurance* (see *Mexican Car Insurance,* under *By Car or RV* in the *Getting There* section earlier in this chapter).

CROSSING THE BORDER AND RETURNING HOME

Squeezing through border bottlenecks during peak holidays and rush hours can be time-consuming. Avoid crossing 7–9 A.M. and 4:30–6:30 P.M. If you can manage it, cross instead during late-night or early-morning hours. Furthermore, the U.S. Customs and Border Patrol maintains an informative border crossing page. Visit www.bhp.gov, and click the "Border Wait Times" link on the right side.

Just before **returning** across the border with your car, park and have an *aduana* (customs)

official *remove and cancel the holographic identity sticker that you received on entry.* If possible, get a *recibo* (receipt) or some kind of verification that it's been *cancelado* (canceled). Tourists have been fined hundreds of dollars for inadvertently carrying uncanceled car-entry stickers on their windshields.

At the same time, return all other Mexican permits, such as tourist cards and hunting and fishing licenses. Also, be prepared for Mexico exit inspection, especially for cultural artifacts and works of art, which may require exit permits. Certain religious and pre-Columbian artifacts, legally the property of the Mexican government, cannot be taken from the country.

If you entered Mexico with your car, you cannot legally leave without it except by permission from local customs authorities, usually the Aduana (Customs House) or the Oficina Federal de Hacienda (Federal Treasury Office). (For local details, see *Information and Services* sections of the destination chapters.)

All returnees are subject to **U.S. immigration and customs inspection.** These inspections have become much more time-consuming since September 11, 2001. The biggest change is that **all U.S. citizens must present a valid U.S. passport in order to re-enter the United States.** On a good day, the wait amounts to about an hour. The worst bottlenecks are at the big border crossings, especially Tijuana and, to a lesser extent, Mexicali, Nogales, Ciudad Juárez, Laredo, and Brownsville.

U.S. law allows a fixed value (at present $400) of duty-free goods per returnee. This may include no more than one liter of alcoholic spirits, 200 cigarettes, and 100 cigars. A flat 10 percent duty will be applied to the first $1,000 (fair retail value, save your receipts) in excess of your $400 exemption. You may, however, mail packages (up to $50 value each) of gifts duty-free to friends and relatives in the United States. Make sure to clearly write "unsolicited gift" and a list of the value and contents on the outside of the package. Perfumes (over $5), alcoholic beverages, and tobacco may not be included in such packages.

Improve the security of such mailed packages by sending them by Mexpost class, similar to U.S. Express Mail service. Even better (but much more expensive), send them by Federal Express or DHL international couriers, which maintain offices in Puerto Vallarta, Tepic, and Manzanillo.

Be forewarned however that having friends and family mail you items while in Mexico carries more risk, depending on the contents. Clothes, CDs, DVDs and other valuable American goods tend to "disappear" long before the package ever reaches you. When a package does arrive carrying goods from the US, it is usually accompanied by an exorbitant tariff as well.

For more information on U.S. customs regulations important to travelers abroad, write for a copy of the useful pamphlet *Know Before You Go,* from the U.S. Customs Service (1300 Pennsylvania Ave., Washington, DC 20229, tel. 202/354-1000, www.cbp.gov). You can also order the pamphlet by phone or download it from their website (click on Travel at the bottom of the home page, then click on Know Before You Go.

Additional U.S. rules prohibit importation of certain fruits, vegetables, and domestic animal and endangered wildlife products. Certain live animal species, such as **parrots,** may be brought into the United States, subject to 30-day agricultural quarantine upon arrival, at the owner's expense. The U.S. Customs Service's *Know Before You Go* pamphlet provides more details on agricultural product and live animal importation.

For more information on the importation of endangered wildlife products, contact the Fish and Wildlife Service (1849 C Street NW, Washington, DC 20240, tel. 202/208-4717, www.fws.gov/).

Sports and Recreation

It's easy to understand why most vacationers come to Puerto Vallarta to stay on the beach. And these days, they don't simply confine themselves to Playa de Oro, the golden Puerto Vallarta luxury hotel strand. Increasing numbers are venturing out and discovering the entire Puerto Vallarta region's quieter resorts. Beginning in the north, on the lush Nayarit Coast, are sleepy San Blas and Rincón de Guayabitos; farther south, the crystal sands of Bucerías decorate the northern arc of the Bay of Banderas, while south past Puerto Vallarta are tiny Boca de Tomatlán and Yelapa, nestling at the Bay of Banderas's jungly southern edge. Beyond that, south of the pine-clad Sierra Lagunillas crest, lie the gemlike bays of Chamela, Careyes, and Tenacatita; and past that, the homey country resorts of Melaque and Barra de Navidad bask on the Costa Alegre (Happy Coast) of southern Jalisco.

The shoreline offers more than resorts, however. Visitors are increasingly seeking rustic paradises where they can lay out a picnic or even set up camp and enjoy the solitude, wildlife, and fishing opportunities of a score of breezy little beach hideaways.

The 300-odd miles of the Puerto Vallarta coastal region offer visitors their pick of shorelines, which vary from mangrove-edged lagoons and algae-adorned tide pools to shoals of pebbles and sands of many shades and consistencies.

Sand makes the beach—and the Puerto Vallarta region has plenty—from dark, warm mica to cool, velvety white coral. Some beaches drop steeply to turbulent, close-in surf, fine for fishing. Others are level, with gentle, rolling breakers, made for surfing and swimming.

Beaches are fascinating for the surprises they yield. Puerto Vallarta–area beaches, especially the hidden strands near resorts and the dozens of miles of wilderness beaches and tidepools, yield troves of shells and treasures of flotsam and jetsam for those who enjoy looking for them. Beachcombing is more rewarding during the summer storm season, when big waves deposit acres of shells—conch, scallop, clams, comb of Venus, whelks, limpets, olives, cowries, starfish, and sand dollars. It's illegal to remove seashells, however, so remember to leave them for others to enjoy.

During the summer–fall rainy season, beaches near rivermouths (notably Río Santiago north of San Blas and the Río Purificación near Tenacatita) are outdoor galleries of fantastic wind- and water-sculpted snags and giant logs deposited by the downstream flood.

WILDLIFE-WATCHING

Wildlife-watchers should keep quiet and always be on the alert. Animal survival depends on their seeing you before you see them. Occasional spectacular offshore sights, such as whales, porpoises, and manta rays, or an onshore giant constrictor, beached squid, crocodile (*caimán*), or even jaguar looking for turtle eggs, are the reward of those prepared to recognize them. Don't forget your binoculars and your *Bird-Finding Guide to Mexico.*

Although wildlife-watching is likely to be rewarding for the prepared everywhere in the Puerto Vallarta region, the lush mangrove lagoons around San Blas are special. For even casual nature enthusiasts, the La Tovara jungle-river trip is a must.

FISHING

The Puerto Vallarta region offers many excellent fishing opportunities. Sportspeople routinely bring in dozens of species from among the more than 600 that abound in Mexican Pacific waters.

Surf Fishing

Good fishing beaches away from the immediate resort areas will typically be uncrowded, with only a few local folks (mostly fishing with nets) and fewer visitors. Mexicans do little rod-and-reel sportfishing. Most either make their living from fishing or do none at all. Although some for-sale fishing equipment is available, sportfishing equipment is both expensive and hard to get. Plan to bring your own, including hooks, lures, line, and weights.

A good general information source before you leave home is a local bait-and-tackle shop. Tell the folks there where you're going, and they'll often know the best lures and bait to use and what fish you can expect to catch with them.

In any case, the cleaner the water, the more interesting your catch. On a good day, your reward might be one or more *sierras, cabrillas,* porgies, or pompanos pulled from the Puerto Vallarta surf.

You can't have everything, however. Foreigners cannot legally take Mexican abalone, coral, lobster, clams, rock bass, sea fans, seashells, shrimp, or turtles. Neither are they supposed to buy them directly from fishermen.

Deep-Sea Fishing

Puerto Vallarta, Barra de Navidad, and San Blas captains operate dozens of excellent big charter boats. Rental generally includes a 30- to 40-foot boat and crew for a full or half day, plus equipment and bait for 2–6 people, not including food or drinks. The charter price depends upon the season. During the high Christmas–New Year's and before-Easter seasons, reservations are mandatory and a Puerto Vallarta boat can run $600 per day or a lot more depending on the size of the charter. Off-season rates, which depend strongly on your bargaining ability, can cost as little as half the high-season rate. For high-season charter boat reservations, contact an experienced agency, such as American Express, several weeks before departure.

Those who arrive without a reservation (or who prefer dealing directly with local people) can contact the local fishing-boat cooperative, **Sociedad Cooperativa Progreso Turístico,** on the Malecón in downtown Puerto Vallarta.

Other Boat-Rental Options

Renting an entire big boat is not your only choice. High-season business is sometimes so brisk at Puerto Vallarta that agencies can fill up boats by booking individuals, who typically pay $70 per person.

Pangas, outboard launches seating 4–6, are

available on the beaches for as little as $50, depending on the season. Once in Barra de Navidad, four of my friends went out in a *panga* all day, had a great time, and came back with a boatload of big tuna, jack, and mackerel. A restaurant cooked them as a banquet for a dozen of us in exchange for the extra fish. I discovered for the first time how heavenly fresh *sierra veracruzana* can taste.

If you or a friend speaks a bit of Spanish, you can bargain for a *panga* right on the beach in Puerto Vallarta or at a dozen other seaside villages such as San Blas, Rincón de Guayabitos, Sayulita, Punta Mita, Cruz de Huanacaxtle, Bucerías, Mismaloya, Boca de Tomatlán, Chamela, Careyes, Tenacatita, La Manzanilla, Melaque, and Barra de Navidad.

Bringing Your Own Boat

If you're going to do lots of fishing, your own boat may be your most flexible and economical option. One big advantage is you can go to the many excellent fishing grounds that the charter boats do not frequent. Keep your boat license up to date, equipment simple, and your eyes peeled and ears open for local regulations and customs, plus tide, wind, and fishing information.

Fishing Licenses and Boat Permits

Anyone 16 or older who is either fishing or riding in a fishing boat in Mexico is required to have a fishing license. Although Mexican fishing licenses are obtainable from certain travel and insurance agents or at government fishing offices in Puerto Vallarta, San Blas, and Barra de Navidad, save yourself time and trouble by getting both your fishing licenses and boat permits by mail ahead of time from the Mexican Department of Fisheries (Oficina de Pesca, 2550 5th Ave., Suite 15, San Diego, CA 92103-6622, tel. 619/233-4324, fax 619/233-0344). Call at least a month before departure and ask for applications, which they can supply by mail, fax, or email. Fees are reasonable but depend upon the period of validity and the fluctuating exchange rate. On the application,

fill in the names (exactly as they appear on passports) of the people requesting licenses. Include a cashier's check or a money order for the exact amount, along with a stamped, self-addressed envelope.

WATER SPORTS

Swimming, surfing, sailboarding, snorkeling, scuba diving, kayaking, sailing, and personal watercraft–riding are the Puerto Vallarta region's water sports of choice.

Safety First

Viewed from Puerto Vallarta beaches, the Pacific Ocean usually lives up to its name. Many protected inlets, safe for child's play, dot the coastline. Unsheltered shorelines, on the other hand, can be deceiving. Smooth water in the calm morning often changes to choppy in the afternoon; calm ripples that lap the shore in March can grow to hurricane-driven walls of water in November. Such storms can wash away sand, temporarily changing a wide, gently sloping beach into a steep one plagued by turbulent waves and treacherous currents.

Undertow, whirlpools, cross-currents, and occasional oversized waves can make ocean swimming a fast-lane adventure. Getting unexpectedly swept out to sea or hammered onto the beach bottom by a surprise breaker are potential hazards.

Never attempt serious swimming when tipsy or full of food; never swim alone where someone can't see you. Always swim beyond big breakers (which come in sets of several, climaxed by a huge one, which breaks highest and farthest from the beach). If you happen to get caught in the path of such a wave, avoid it by *diving directly toward and under it,* letting it roll harmlessly over you. If you are unavoidably swept up in a whirling, crashing breaker, try to roll and tumble with it, as football players tumble, to avoid injury.

Look out for other irritations and hazards. Now and then, particularly during the late spring months, swimmers get a nettlelike (but usually harmless) jellyfish sting. Be careful around coral reefs and beds of sea urchins; corals can sting

The tamest and cheapest of power sports on Puerto Vallarta beaches is the "banana tube."

(like jellyfish) and you can additionally get infections from coral cuts and sea-urchin spines. *Shuffle* along sandy bottoms, especially during cool winter months, to scare away stingrays before stepping on one. If you're unlucky, its venomous tail-spines may inflict a painful wound.

Snorkeling and Scuba Diving

A number of clear-water sites await snorkelers and scuba divers. North of the Bay of Banderas, snorkelers enjoy Isla Islote just offshore from Rincón de Guayabitos. Accessible from the Bay of Banderas itself are Islas Marietas, off north-shore Punta Mita; and the famous Los Arcos rocks off Mismaloya. Additionally, tour boats regularly take snorkelers to small coves near Playa las Ánimas and Playa Quimixto on the Bay of Banderas's verdant southern shore. Farther afield, adventurous snorkelers and divers explore the wreck at Tehualmixtle on the pristine Cabo Corrientes coast past the Bay of Banderas's southern lip. Beyond that, rock-studded bays, such as gemlike Bahía Careyes and Tenacatita, invite snorkelers and divers to explore their clear waters.

Veteran divers usually arrive during the dry winter and early spring when river outflows are mere trickles, leaving offshore waters clear. In Puerto Vallarta, a number of professional dive shops rent equipment, provide lessons and guides, and transport divers to choice sites.

While beginners can usually do well with rented equipment, serious snorkelers and divers bring their own gear. This should include wetsuits in winter, when many swimmers feel cold after more than an unprotected half-hour in the water. For anything deeper than a 30–40ft dive in the winter, you will be most comfortable in a 7ml wetsuit and hood. It gets quite chilly below the thermocline.

Sailing, Surfing, Sailboarding, and Kayaking

The surf everywhere is highest and best during the July–November hurricane season, when big swells from storms far out at sea attract surfers to the favored beaches.

During the fall, veterans regularly spend weeks at San Blas waiting for the legendary Big Wave. Their hoped-for reward is one of the giant breakers that can carry them more than a mile toward the soft sands of Playa Matanchén. Although not nearly as renowned, the breaks off Punta Mita also attract advanced surfers.

For intermediates and beginners, the Puerto Vallarta vicinity offers a number of good spots. These include La Peñita (near Rincón de Guayabitos), the mouth of the Río Ameca just north of the Puerto Vallarta airport, and the breakwater at the entrance to the Laguna de Navidad at Barra de Navidad.

Sailboaters and kayakers who, by contrast, require more tranquil waters, do best in the winter or early spring. It is then they gather to enjoy the ideal conditions in the many coves and inlets along the Puerto Vallarta coast.

While beginners can have fun with the equipment available from beach rental shops, serious surfers, sailboarders, sailboaters, and kayakers should pack their own gear.

Waterskiing, Parasailing, and Personal Watercraft

The Puerto Vallarta hotel beachfronts of northside Playa de Oro and, to a lesser extent, Playa los Muertos, on the south side, have long been centers for waterskiing, parasailing, and personal watercraft–riding. In parasailing, a motorboat pulls while a parachute lifts you, like a soaring gull, high over the ocean. After 5 or 10 minutes it deposits you—usually gently—back on the sand.

Jet Ski boats (also called WaveRunners or personal watercraft) are like snowmobiles except that they operate on water, where, with a little practice, beginners can quickly learn to whiz over the waves.

Although the luxury resort hotels generally provide experienced crews and equipment, crowded conditions increase the hazard to both participants and swimmers. You, as the patron, are paying plenty for the privilege; you have a right to expect that your providers and crew are well-equipped, sober, and cautious.

BEACH BUGGIES AND ATVS

Some visitors enjoy racing along the beach and rolling over dunes in beach buggies and ATVs (all-terrain vehicles, called *motos* in

Mexico)—balloon-tired three-wheeled motor scooters. While certain resort rental agencies cater to the growing use of such vehicles, limits are in order. Of all the proliferating high-horsepower beach pastimes, these are the most intrusive. Noise and gasoline pollution, injuries to operators and bystanders, and the scattering of wildlife and destruction of their habitats have led to the restriction of dune buggies and ATVs on Puerto Vallarta–region beaches.

TENNIS AND GOLF

Puerto Vallarta visitors can enjoy a number of excellent private courts and courses. In Puerto Vallarta itself, golfers have their pick of the Marina course in town, the Vista Vallarta course inland from town, and the Los Flamingos course several miles north of the airport. Likewise, south of Puerto Vallarta, you can enjoy a pair of fabulously exclusive golf courses: the exotically scenic golf course in the jungle at El Tamarindo and the breezy palm-tufted course at Isla Navidad resort near Barra de Navidad.

As for tennis, many resort hotels in Puerto Vallarta and Nuevo Vallarta have tennis courts. Other smaller hotels in Rincón de Guayabitos, Cruz de Huanacaxtle, Mismaloya, Careyes, Tenacatita, Los Angeles Locos, Tamarindo, Melaque, and Barra de Navidad also have courts.

No public golf or tennis courts exist in the Puerto Vallarta region, but many hotels and private clubs allow for-fee use by the general public. If you plan to play a lot of golf or tennis, you're best to stay at one of the many hotels with access to these courts and courses.

Use of hotel tennis courts is sometimes, but not always, included in your hotel tariff. If not, fees will run upward of $5 per hour. Golf greens fees, which begin at about $75 for 18 holes, are always extra.

BULLFIGHTING

It is said there are two occasions for which Mexicans arrive on time: funerals and bullfights.

Bullfighting is a recreation, not a sport. The bull is outnumbered seven to one and the outcome is never in doubt. Even if the matador (literally, killer) fails in his duty, his assistants will entice the bull away and slaughter it in private beneath the stands.

La Corrida de Toros

Moreover, Mexicans don't call it a "bullfight"; it's the *corrida de toros,* during which six bulls are customarily slaughtered, beginning at 5 P.M. (4 in the winter) on Wednesdays. After the beginning parade, featuring the matador and his helpers, the picadores and the banderilleros, the first bull rushes into the ring in a cloud of dust. Clockwork *tercios* (thirds) define the ritual: the first, the *puyazos,* or "stabs," requires that two picadores on horseback thrust lances into the bull's shoulders, weakening it. During the second *tercio,* the banderilleros

dodge the bull's horns to stick three long, streamered darts into its shoulders.

Trumpets announce the third *tercio* and the appearance of the matador. The bull—weak, confused, and angry—is ready for the finish. The matador struts, holding the red cape, daring the bull to charge. Form now becomes everything. The expert matador takes complete control of the bull, which rushes at the cape, past its ramrod-erect opponent. For charge after charge, the matador works the bull to exactly the right spot in the ring—in front of the judges, a lovely señorita, or perhaps the governor—where the matador mercifully delivers the precision *estocada* (killing sword thrust) deep into the drooping neck of the defeated bull.

Benito Juárez, as governor during the 1850s, outlawed bullfights in Oaxaca. In his honor, they remain so, making Oaxaca unique among Mexican states.

Accommodations

The Puerto Vallarta region has many hundreds of lodgings to suit every style and pocketbook: world-class resorts, small beachside hotels, comfortable apartments and condos, homey *casas de huéspedes* (guesthouses), palmy trailer parks, and dozens of miles of pristine beaches, ripe for tent or RV camping. The high seasons—when reservations are generally required—run from mid-December to March, during Easter week, and during the month of August.

The hundreds of accommodations described in the destination chapters of this book are positive recommendations—checked out in detail—solid options from which you can pick according to your taste and purse.

Hotel Rates

The rates listed in this book are U.S. dollar equivalents of peso prices, 17 percent taxes included, as quoted by the hotel management at the time of writing.

In Puerto Vallarta, hotel rates depend strongly upon inflation and season. To cancel

the effect of the relatively steep Mexican inflation, rates are reported in U.S. dollars (although, when settling your hotel bill, you will nearly always save money by insisting on **paying in pesos**). To further increase accuracy, estimated low- and high-season rates are quoted whenever possible.

Saving Money

At any time other than the super-high Christmas and Easter seasons, you can often get at least one or two free days with a one-week stay. Promotional packages available during slack seasons may include free extras such as breakfast, a car rental, a boat tour, or a sports rental. A travel agent or travel website can be of great help in shopping around for such bargains.

You nearly always save additional money if you deal in pesos only. Insist on both booking your lodging for an agreed price in pesos and paying the resulting hotel bill in the same pesos, rather than dollars. The reason is that dollar rates quoted by hotels are often based on the hotel desk exchange rate, which is customarily about 5 percent, or even as much 15 percent, less than bank rates. For example, if the clerk tells you your hotel bill is $1,000, instead of handing over the dollars, ask the clerk how much it is in pesos. Using the desk conversion rate, he or she might say something like 9,000 pesos (considerably less than the 10,000 pesos that the bank might typically give for your $1,000). Pay the 9,000 pesos or have the clerk mark 9,000 pesos on your credit card slip, and save yourself $100.

For stays of more than a week or two, you'll save money and add comfort with an **apartment or condominium** rental. Monthly rates range $500–1,500 (less than half the comparable hotel per diem rate) for comfortable one-bedroom furnished kitchenette units, often including resort amenities such as pool and sundeck, beach club, and private view balcony.

Airlines regularly offer **air-hotel packages** that may save you lots of pesos, especially if you're planning on staying at an upscale ($100 or more) hotel. These deals, which seldom extend to moderately priced lodgings, customarily require that you depart for Puerto Vallarta through certain gateway cities, which depend on the airline. Accommodations are usually (but not exclusively) in luxury resorts. If you live near one of these gateways, it may pay to consult the airlines.

GUESTHOUSES AND LOCAL HOTELS

Puerto Vallarta, like many coastal resorts, began as an old town that expanded into a new *zona hotelera,* where big hotels rise along a golden strand of beach. In the old town, surrounded by the piquant smells, sights, and charms of old Mexico, are the family-managed *casas de huéspedes* and smaller hotels, often arranged around sunny, plant-festooned inner patios.

Such lodgings vary from scruffy to spic and span, and from humble to distinguished. At minimum, you can expect a plain room, a shared toilet, and hot-water shower, and plenty of atmosphere for your money. Rates typically

run $15–40, depending upon season and amenities. Discounts for long-term stays are often available. Such family-run, small hostelries are rarely near the beach, unlike many of the medium and larger older hotels.

Medium and Larger Older-Style Hotels

These hotels make up a large fraction of the recommendations of this book. Many veteran travelers find it hard to understand why people come to Mexico and spend $200 or more a day for a hotel room when good alternatives are available for as little as $35.

Many such hostelries are the once-grand first-class hotels established long before their towering international-class neighbors mushroomed along the beach. You can generally expect a clean, large (but not deluxe) room with bath and toilet and even sometimes a private beach-view balcony. Although they often share the same velvety sand and golden sunsets as their more expensive neighbors, such hotels usually lack the costly international-standard amenities—air-conditioning, cable TV, direct-dial phones, tennis courts, exercise gyms, and golf access—of the big resorts. Their guests, however, enjoy surprisingly good service, good food, and a native ambience more charming and personal than that of many of their five-star neighbors.

Booking these hotels is straightforward. All of them may be dialed direct (from the United States, dial 011-52, then the local area code and number) and, like the big resorts, many even have toll-free U.S. and Canadian information and reservation numbers.

INTERNATIONAL-CLASS HOTELS

The Puerto Vallarta region offers many beautiful, well-managed international-class resort hotels in Puerto Vallarta and Nuevo Vallarta. A number of others dot the pristine southern Jalisco coastline between Puerto Vallarta and Barra de Navidad. Most are in Puerto Vallarta, however, where they line the Bay of Banderas's crystal strand north of the old town.

The resorts' plush amenities, moreover, need not be overly expensive. During the right time of year you can vacation at many of the big-name spots—Sheraton, Westin, NH Krystal, Fiesta Americana, Holiday Inn—for surprisingly little. While high-season tariffs ordinarily run $100–300, low-season (May–Nov., and to a lesser degree, January 6–Feb. 1) packages and promotions can cut these prices significantly. Shop around for savings via your Sunday newspaper travel section, through travel agents, and by calling the hotels directly at their toll-free numbers.

Other Luxury Options

Puerto Vallarta–region visitors enjoy a pair of increasingly common variations on the international-class hotel theme. One of these is the **all-inclusive resort** that offers all lodging, food, and beverages and entertainment (usually with plenty for kids to do) included at one price. High-season tariffs customarily run $100–150 per person, double occupancy ($70–100 low season). Kids stay for half price or less. This choice appeals to folks who like company and prefer a hassle-free week of fun in the sun on a beautiful beach. On the other hand, don't choose an all-inclusive resort if you want to do lots of outside local exploring, entertaining, and wining and dining downtown. At least a dozen such all-inclusive resort hotels operate, nearly all on Puerto Vallarta and Nuevo Vallarta beaches.

The other increasingly common international-class hotel variation is the small- to mid-sized luxury, or **"boutique" hotel.** Although only a handful are located in Puerto Vallarta itself, several have opened on splendidly isolated beaches sprinkled north and south along the Jalisco and Nayarit Coasts. Most lodgings in this category have less than 20 rooms, and all have gorgeous locations and a plethora of deluxe amenities and services, including at least one fine restaurant and bar. Rates customarily run $200 and up for two.

GAY-FRIENDLY HOTELS

Gay and lesbian visitors have enjoyed increasing acceptance in Puerto Vallarta for a generation, and now the vast majority of Puerto Vallarta

hotels could be termed gay-friendly. Moreover, a number of lodgings welcome gay visitors by advertising in the excellent *Gay Guide Vallarta* magazine (or online at www.gayguidevallarta.com). Many gay-welcoming hotels, bed-and-breakfasts, apartments, and condominium complexes, most of which are gay-owned, sprinkle the Zona Romántica, long popular with a legion of savvy longtime Puerto Vallarta visitors, both straight and gay.

APARTMENTS, BUNGALOWS, CONDOMINIUMS, AND VILLAS

For longer stays, many Puerto Vallarta visitors prefer the convenience and economy of an apartment or condominium or the luxurious comfort of a villa vacation rental. Choices vary, from spartan studios to deluxe beachfront suites and rambling homes big enough for entire extended families. Prices depend strongly upon season and amenities, ranging from about $500 per month for the cheapest to at least 10 times that for the most luxurious. If you don't mind living a bit inland and either taking the bus or driving, you can find a variety of furnished and unfurnished apartments and houses in neighborhoods like Las Juntas and Pitillal for a fraction of what you would pay in downtown Puerto Vallarta. Things might be a bit more rustic but you are sure to make friends with the locals and learn a lot more about the culture than you would in a condo complex with other Americans or Canadians. In these more rural areas, expect prices to be more in the $250–350 range for a monthly rental. To find available rentals, check out the **Mano a Mano** classified listings which are available every Thursday morning at newsstands and your local OXXO. You can also check their website for current listings at www.manoamano.com.mx.

At the low end, you can expect a clean, furnished apartment within several blocks of the beach, with kitchen and regular maid service. More luxurious condos, which rent for about $500 per week, are typically high-rise oceanview suites with hotel-style desk services and resort amenities such as pool, hot tub, sundeck, and beach-level restaurant. Villas vary from moderately upscale homes to sky's-the-limit beach-view mansions blooming with built-in designer luxuries, private pools and beaches, tennis courts, gardeners, cooks, and maids.

In contrast to Puerto Vallarta, owners in country beach resorts such as Bucerías, Rincón de Guayabitos, and Barra de Navidad call their apartment-style accommodations **bungalows.** This generally implies a motel-type kitchenette-suite with less service, though more spacious and more suitable for families than a hotel room. For long stays by the beach, when you want to save money by cooking your own meals, such an accommodation might be ideal.

Back in town, many of Puerto Vallarta's best-buy *apartmentos* (ah-part-MAYN-tohs) and *condominios* (cohn-doh-MEE-nee-ohs) are in the colorful Olas Altas old-town district. They are often rented on the spot or reserved by writing or phoning the individual owners or local managers. Nevertheless, a number of agents in Puerto Vallarta manage and rent vacation lodgings; for details, see *Apartments and Condominiums* in the *Accommodations* section of the *Puerto Vallarta* chapter.

Even more vacation rental homes and condos, many of them moderately priced, in the Jalisco and Nayarit small coastal towns of Barra de Navidad, Melaque, and La Manzanilla, south of Puerto Vallarta; and Bucerías, Punta Mita, Sayulita, San Francisco, and Rincón de Guayabitos, north of Puerto Vallarta, are accessible both through websites or by local rental agents. For the latter, see the *Accommodations* sections of the relevant destination chapter. As for websites, one of the best is the big (but easily useable) worldwide site **Vacation Rentals By Owner,** www.vrbo.com, that lists many Puerto Vallarta Region vacation rentals, from budget to upscale. Other good rental websites are www.choice1.com and www.mexconnect.com.

More expensive Puerto Vallarta condo and villa rentals are quite easy to locate. They're sprinkled everywhere, from the marina on the north side to the Conchas Chinas oceanview hillside on the southern edge of town. All the local Puerto Vallarta agents rent them. A number of U.S.-based agencies do the same through toll-free information and reservations numbers: for example, try Villas de Oro Vacation Rentals (638 Scotland Dr., Santa Rosa, CA 95409, tel. 800/638-4552 or 800/898-4552, www.villasdeoro.com), Villas of Mexico (P.O. Box 3730, Chico, CA 95927, tel. 800/456-3133, www.villasofmexico.com), and Condo and Villa World (4230 Orchard Lake Rd., Suite 3, Orchard Lake, MI 48323, U.S. tel. 800/521-2980 or Can. tel. 800/453-8719, www.villaworld.com).

Another good vacation rental source is the Sunday travel section of a major metropolitan daily newspaper, such as the *Los Angeles Times* and the *San Francisco Chronicle,* which routinely list Puerto Vallarta vacation rentals. National real estate networks, such as Century 21, also rent Puerto Vallarta properties (or can recommend someone who does).

You may also want to consider using the services of a home-exchange agency, such as www.homeexchange.com, whereby you swap homes with someone in Puerto Vallarta for a contracted time period. Travelers who like to meet new people can try couch surfing in the home of a resident at www.couchsurfing.com.

Closing the Deal

Prudence should guide your vacation rental decision-making. Before paying a deposit on a sight-unseen rental, ask for satisfied customer testimonials and photographs of the property you are considering. As with all rentals, don't pay anything until you have approved a written contract describing the rental and what's included (such as inclusive dates, linens, towels, dishes and utensils, maid service, view, pool, taxes, and transportation from airport) for the specified sum. Put down as little advance payment as possible, preferably with a credit card, to secure your reservation. If you do have a problem with your rental when you arrive, resolve the situation immediately and do not pay any additional funds until you are satisfied with the outcome.

CAMPING

Although few, if any, good campsites are available in Puerto Vallarta itself, camping is customary at many favored sites in the Puerto Vallarta region. Mexican middle-class families crowd certain choice strands—those with soft sand and gentle, child-friendly waves—only during the Christmas–New Year's week and during Semana Santa, the week before Easter. Most other times, tenters and RV campers find beaches uncrowded.

The best spots typically have a shady palm grove for camping and a *palapa* restaurant that serves drinks and fresh seafood. *Heads up for falling coconuts,* especially in the wind. Costs for parking and tenting are minimal—usually only the price of food at the restaurant.

Days are often perfect for swimming, strolling, and fishing, and nights are balmy—too warm for a sleeping bag, but fine for a hammock (which allows the air circulation that a tent does not.) However, good tents keep out mosquitoes and other pests, which may be further discouraged by a good bug repellent. Tents can get hot, requiring only a sheet or very light blanket for sleeping cover.

As for camping on isolated beaches, opinions vary, from dire warnings of *bandidos* to bland assurances that all is peaceful along the coast. The truth is somewhere in between. Trouble is most likely to occur in the vicinity of towns, where a few local thugs sometimes harass isolated campers.

When scouting out an isolated place to camp, a good rule is to arrive early enough in the day to get a feel for the place. Buy a soda at the *palapa* or store and take a stroll along the beach. Say *"Buenos días"* to the people along the way; ask if the fishing is good (*"¿Pesca buena?"*). Above all, use your common sense and intuition. If the people seem friendly, ask if it's *seguro* (safe). If so, ask permission: *"¿Es bueno acampar acá?"* ("Is

it okay to camp around here?"). You'll rarely be refused.

Tenting and RV parking are permitted for a fee at many beachfront RV and trailer parks. A number of other informal spots, mostly at pretty beaches with no facilities, await those travelers prepared to venture from the well-worn path. Moving from north to south, likely spots include Novillero, Playa Borrego (San Blas), Matanchén Bay, Playa Platanitos, Playa Chacala, Playa El Naranjo, La Peñita (at Motel Russell), Laguna Santa Maráa de Oro (at Koala Bungalows and Trailer Park, inland, south of Tepic), Playa Punta Raza, Laguna Juanacatlán and Corinches Reservoir (both in the mountains near Mascota), Playa Destiladeras, Playa las Ánimas, Playa Quimixto, and Yelapa (all three boat-accessible only), Tehualmixtle, Ipala, Cajón de Peñas reservoir, Playa Chalacatepec, Chamela Bay, Playa Careyes, Playa las Brisas, Playa Tenacatita, Playa Boca de Iguana, Melaque, and Playa de Cocos.

RV AND TRAILER PARKS

Campers who prefer company to isolation stay in RV and trailer parks. About 20 of them dot the Puerto Vallarta region's beaches from San Blas to Barra de Navidad. The most luxurioushave all hookups and dozens of amenities, including restaurants, recreation rooms, and swimming pools; the humblest are simple palm-edged lots beside the beach. Virtually all of them have good swimming, fishing, and beachcombing. Prices run from a few dollars for a tent space to about $18–26 per night including air-conditioning power. Significant discounts are available for weekly and monthly rentals.

Good RV and trailer parks are located (from north to south) at San Blas, Matanchén Bay, Laguna Santa María, La Peñita, Rincón de Guayabitos, Lo de Marco, Sayulita, Puerto Vallarta, Chamela Bay, Boca de Iguana, and Melaque.

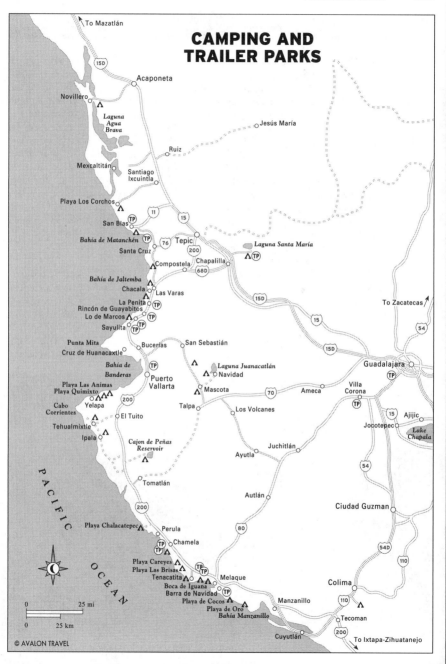

CAMPING AND TRAILER PARKS

To Mazatlán

Acaponeta

Novillero

Laguna Agua Brava

Jesús María

Mexcaltitán

Ruiz

Santiago Ixcuintla

Playa Los Corchos

San Blas TP

Bahía de Matanchén TP

Santa Cruz

Tepic

Compostela

Chapalilla

Laguna Santa María TP

Bahía de Jaltemba

Chacala

Las Varas

La Peñita TP

Rincón de Guayabitos

Lo de Marcos TP

Sayulita TP

Punta Mita

Cruz de Huanacaxtle

Bucerías

San Sebastián

Bahía de Banderas TP

Puerto Vallarta

Laguna Juanacatlán

Navidad

Guadalajara TP

Playa Las Ánimas

Playa Quimixto

Mascota

Ameca

Villa Corona TP

Cabo Corrientes

Yelapa

Talpa

Los Volcanes

Jocotepec

Ajijic

Tehualmixtle

El Tuito

Lake Chapala

Ipala

Cajon de Peñas Reservoir

Juchitlán

Ayutla

Tomatlán

Autlán

Ciudad Guzman

Playa Chalacatepec

Perula

Chamela TP

Playa Careyes

Playa Las Brisas

Tenacatita TP

Boca de Iguana

Barra de Navidad

Playa de Cocos

Melaque

Playa de Oro

Bahía Manzanillo

Manzanillo

Colima

Tecoman

Cuyutlán

To Ixtapa-Zihuatanejo

To Zacatecas

PACIFIC OCEAN

0   25 mi
0   25 km

© AVALON TRAVEL

15D 11 15 76 200 68D 200 70 15 54 110 54D 110 200 80

Food

Some travel to Puerto Vallarta for the food. True Mexican food is old-fashioned, home-style fare requiring many hours of loving preparation. Such food is short on meat and long on corn, beans, rice, tomatoes, onions, eggs, and cheese.

Mexican food is the unique product of thousands of years of native tradition. It is based on corn—*teocentli,* the Aztec "holy food"—called *maíz* (mah-EES) by present-day Mexicans. In the past, a Mexican woman spent much of her time grinding and preparing corn: soaking the grain in lime water, which swells the kernels and removes the tough seed-coat, then grinding the bloated seeds into meal on a stone metate. Finally, she patted the meal into tortillas and cooked them on a hot, baked-mud griddle, a *comal* (KOH-mahl).

Sages (men, no doubt) wistfully imagined that gentle pat-pat-pat of women all over Mexico to be the heartbeat of Mexico, which they feared would cease when women stopped making tortillas. Fewer women these days make tortillas by hand. The gentle pat-pat-pat has been replaced by the whir and rattle of the automatic tortilla-making machine in myriad *tortillerías,* where women and girls line up for their family's daily kilo-stack of tortillas.

Tortillas are to the Mexicans as rice is to the Chinese and bread to the French. Mexican food is invariably some mixture of sauce, meat, beans, cheese, and vegetables wrapped in a tortilla, which becomes the culinary be-all: The food, the dish, and the utensil wrapped into one. If a Mexican man has nothing to wrap in his lunch-time tortilla, he will content himself by rolling a thin filling of salsa (*chile* sauce) in it.

HOT OR NOT?

Much food served in Mexico is not "Mexican." Eating habits, as most other customs, depend upon social class. Upwardly mobile Mexicans typically shun the corn-based *indígena* fare in favor of the European-style food of the Spanish colonial elite: chops, steaks, cutlets, fish, clams, omelettes, soups, pasta, rice, and potatoes.

Although corn is Mexico's major food grain, wheat is also used, especially in pancakes.

© BRUCE WHIPPERMAN

CHOCOLATL

The refreshing drink *chocolatl* enjoyed by Aztec nobility is a remote but distinct relative of the chocolate consumed today by hundreds of millions of people. It was once so precious that chocolate beans were a common medium of exchange in preconquest Mexico. In those days a mere dozen cacao beans could command a present value of upward of $100 in goods or services. Counterfeiting was rife – entrepreneurs tried to create *chocolatl* from anything, including avocado seeds. Moreover, *chocolatl* was thought to be so potent an aphrodisiac and hallucinogen that its use was denied, under penalty of death, to commoners.

Although intrigued, Europeans were put off by the bitter taste of *chocolatl*. Around 1600, a whole shipload of chocolate beans was jettisoned at sea by English privateers who, having captured a Spanish galleon, mistook its cargo for goat dung.

The French soon made *chocolatl* easier to stomach by powdering it; the British added milk; and finally the Swiss, of Nestlé fame, cashed in with chocolate candy. The world hasn't been the same since.

Though *chocolatl* found its way to Europe, it never left Mexico, where hot chocolate, whipped frothy with a wooden-ringed *molinillo* (little mill), is more common now than in Aztec times. In Mexico chocolate is more than mere dessert: Used to spice the tangy *moles* of southern Mexico, it's virtually a national food.

Such fare is often as bland as Des Moines on a summer Sunday afternoon. *No picante—* not spicy—is how the Mexicans describe bland food. *Caliente,* the Spanish adjective for "hot" (as in hot water), does not, in contrast to English usage, imply spicy, or *picante.*

VEGETARIAN FARE

Strictly vegetarian cooking is the exception in Mexico, as are macrobiotic restaurants, health-food stores, and organic produce. Meat is such a delicacy for most Mexicans that they can't understand why people would give it up voluntarily. If vegetable-lovers can manage with corn, beans, cheese, eggs, *legumbres* (vegetables), and fruit, and not be bothered by a bit of pork fat (*manteca de cerdo*), Mexican cooking will suit them fine. On the other hand, if pork fat bothers you, ask for your food *sin manteca* (without lard).

In the more metropolitan Puerto Vallarta, there are an excellent vegetarian restaurant and many other establishments routinely offer several veggie options on the menu.

SEAFOOD

Early chroniclers wrote that Aztec Emperor Moctezuma employed a platoon of runners to bring fresh fish 300 miles from the sea every day to his court. Around Puerto Vallarta, fresh seafood is fortunately much more available from dozens of shoreline establishments, varying from humble beach *palapas* to luxury hotel restaurants.

Seafood is literally here for the taking. When strolling certain beaches, I have seen well-fed, middle-class local vacationers breaking and eating oysters and mussels right off the rocks. In the summer on the beach at Puerto Vallarta, fish and squid have been known to swarm so thickly in the surf that tourists pulled them out bare handed. Nowadays, usually lacking such bounty, villagers up and down the coast use small nets (or bare hands) to retrieve enough fish for supper, while communal teams haul in big netfuls of silvery, wriggling fry for sale right on the beach.

Despite the plenty, Puerto Vallarta seafood prices reflect high worldwide demand, even at the humblest seaside *palapa*. The freshness and variety, however, make the typical dishes bargains at any price. Buying fresh and cooking it yourself can save you quite a bit. If you are cooking in your condo for example, you can expect to pay, at the time of this writing, approximately $15 for a kilo (2.2 lbs) of shrimp.

FISH

A bounty of fish darts, swarms, jumps, and wriggles in the Puerto Vallarta region's surf, reefs, lagoons, and offshore depths. While many make delicious dinners (especially dorado for fillets, *sierra* for ceviche, and *huachinango* for grilled whole fish), others are tough (sailfish), bony (bonefish), and even poisonous (puffers). Some grow to half-ton giants (marlin, grouper), while others are diminutive reef-grazers (parrot fish, damselfish, angelfish) whose bright colors delight snorkelers and divers. Here's a sampling of what you might find underwater or on your dinner plate:

albacore (*albacora, atún*): tuna-like, 2–4 feet in size; blue; found in deep waters; excellent taste
angelfish (*ángel*): one foot; yellow, orange, blue; reef fish*
barracuda (*barracuda, picuda*): two feet; brown; deep waters; good taste
black marlin (*marlin negro*): six feet; blue-black; deep waters; good taste
blue marlin (*marlin azul*): eight feet; blue; deep waters; poor taste
bobo (*barbudo*): one foot; blue, yellow; found in surf; fair taste
bonefish (*macabi*): one foot; blue or silver; found inshore; poor taste
bonito (*bonito*): tuna-like, two feet; black; deep waters; good taste
butterfly fish (*muñeca*): six inches; black, yellow; reef fish*
chub (*chopa*): one foot; gray; reef fish; good taste
croaker (*corvina*): two feet; brownish; found along inshore bottoms; rare and protected
damselfish (*castañeta*): four inches; brown, blue, orange; reef fish*
dolphinfish, mahimahi, dorado: three feet; green, gold; deep waters; good taste
grouper (*garopa*): three feet; brown, rust; found offshore and in reefs; good taste
grunt (*burro*): eight inches; black, gray; found in rocks, reefs*

jack (*toro*): 1–2 feet; bluish-gray; offshore; good taste
mackerel (*sierra*): two feet; gray with gold spots; offshore; good taste
mullet (*lisa*): two feet; gray; found in sandy bays; good taste
needlefish (*agujón*): three feet; blue-black; deep waters; good taste
Pacific porgy (*pez de pluma*): 1–2 feet; tan; found along sandy shores; good taste
parrot fish (*perico, pez loro*): one foot; green, pink, blue, orange; reef fish*
pompano (*pómpano*): one foot; gray; inshore bottoms; excellent taste
puffer (*botete*): eight inches; brown; inshore; poisonous
red snapper (*huachinango, pargo*): 1–2 feet; reddish pink; deep waters; excellent taste
roosterfish (*pez gallo*): three feet; black, blue; deep waters; excellent taste
sailfish (*pez vela*): five feet; blue-black; deep waters; poor taste
sardine (*sardina*): eight inches; blue-black; offshore; good taste
sea bass (*cabrilla*): 1–2 feet; brown, ruddy; reef and rock crevices; good taste
shark (*tiburón*): 2–10 feet; black to blue; in- and offshore; good taste
snook (*robalo*): 2–3 feet; black-brown; found in brackish lagoons; excellent taste
spadefish (*chambo*): one foot; black-silver; found along sandy bottoms; reef fish*
swordfish (*pez espada*): five feet; black to blue; deep waters; good taste
triggerfish (*pez puerco*): 1–2 feet; blue, rust, brown, black; reef fish; excellent taste
wahoo (*peto, guahu*): 2–5 feet; green to blue; deep waters; excellent taste
yellowfin tuna (*atún amarilla*): 2–5 feet; blue, yellow; deep waters; excellent taste
yellowtail (*jurel*): 2–4 feet; blue, yellow; offshore; excellent taste

*generally too small to be considered edible

BREAD AND PASTRIES

Excellent locally baked bread is a delightful surprise to many first-time Puerto Vallarta visitors. Small bakeries everywhere put out trays of hot, crisp-crusted *bolillos* (rolls) and sweet *panes dulces* (pastries). The pastries vary from simple cakes, muffins, cookies, and doughnuts to fancy fruit-filled turnovers and puffs. Half the fun occurs before the eating: perusing the goodies, tongs in hand, and picking out the most scrumptious. With your favorite dozen or two finally selected, you take your tray to the cashier, who deftly bags everything up and collects a few pesos ($2–3) for your entire mouth-watering selection.

FRUITS AND JUICES

Squeezed vegetable and fruit juices, *jugos* (HOO-gohs), are among the widely available thousand delights of Puerto Vallarta. Among the many establishments—restaurants, cafés, and *loncherías*—willing to supply you with your favorite *jugo,* the *jugerías* (juice bars) are the most fun. Colorful fruit piles mark *jugerías*. If you don't immediately spot your favorite fruit, ask; it might be hidden in the refrigerator.

Besides your choice of pure juice, *jugerías* will often serve *licuados.* Into the juice, they whip powdered milk, your favorite flavoring, and sugar to taste for a creamy afternoon pick-me-up or evening dessert. One big favorite is a cool banana-chocolate *licuado,* which comes out tasting like a milk shake (minus the calories).

ALCOHOLIC DRINKS

The Aztecs sacrificed anyone caught drinking alcohol without permission. The later, more lenient, Spanish attitude toward getting *borracho* (soused) has led to a thriving Mexican renaissance of native alcoholic beverages: tequila, mescal, Kahlúa, pulque, and *aguardiente.* Tequila and mescal, distilled from the fermented juice of the maguey, originated in Oaxaca, where the best are still made. Quality tequila (named after the Guadalajara-area distillery town) and mescal come 76 proof (38 percent alcohol) and up. A small white worm, endemic to the maguey, is customarily

Prizes at the local fair usually consist of beer and small kitchen appliances.

added to each bottle of factory mescal for authenticity.

Pulque, although also made from the sap of the maguey, is locally brewed to a lower alcohol content between that of beer and wine. The brewing houses are sacrosanct preserves, circumscribed by traditions that exclude women and outsiders. The brew, said to be full of nutrients, is sold to local *pulquerías* and drunk immediately. If you are ever invited into a *pulquería,* it is an honor you cannot refuse.

Aguardiente, by contrast, is the notorious fiery Mexican "white lightning," a locally distilled dirt-cheap ticket to oblivion for poor Mexican men.

While pulque comes from age-old Indian tradition, beer is the beverage of modern mestizo Mexico. Full-bodied and tastier than "light" U.S. counterparts, Mexican beer enjoys an enviable reputation.

Those visitors who indulge usually know their favorite among the many brands, from light to dark: Superior, Corona, Pacífico, Tecate (served with lime), Carta Blanca, Modelo,

Dos Equis, Bohemia, Tres Equis, and Negro Modelo. Nochebuena, a hearty dark brew, becomes available only around Christmas.

Mexicans have yet to develop much of a taste for *vino tinto* or *vino blanco* (red or white table wine), although some domestic wines (such as the Baja California labels Cetto and Domecq and the "boutique" Monte Xanic) are at least good, and sometimes excellent. There is also a decent sparkling wine, similar to champagne called **Chambrulee** which you can purchase at any liquor store or supermarket for about $7.

RESTAURANTS, *LONCHERÍAS*, AND *FONDAS*

In Mexico, a *restaurante* (rays-tah-oo-RAHN-tay) generally implies a fairly fancy joint, with prices to match. The food and atmosphere, however, may be more to your liking at other types of eateries (in approximate descending order of formality and price): *comedor* (dining room), *cafetería* (coffee shop), *cenaduría* (light supper only, from about 6 P.M.), *fonda* (permanent food stall), *lonchería* (breakfast and sandwich counter), *jugería* (juice and sandwich bar), and *taquería* (often, but not always, a street stand).

Conduct and Customs

Mexico is an old-fashioned country where people value traditional ideals of honesty, fidelity, and piety. Crime rates are low; visitors are often safer in Mexico than in their home cities.

Even though four generations have elapsed since Pancho Villa raided the U.S. border, the image of a Mexico bristling with *bandidos* persists. And similarly for Mexicans' view of those north of the border: Despite the century and a half since the *yanquis* invaded Mexico City and took half their country, the communal Mexican psyche still views gringos (and, by association, all white foreigners) with revulsion, jealousy, and wonder.

Fortunately, the Mexican love-hate affair with foreigners does not usually apply to individual visitors. Your friendly *"buenos días"* ("good morning") or *"por favor"* ("please"), when appropriate, is always appreciated, whether in the market, the gas station, or the hotel. The shy smile you will most likely receive in return will be your small, but not insignificant, reward.

TIPPING

Without their droves of visitors, Mexican people would be even poorer. Deflation of the peso, while it makes prices low for outsiders, makes it rough for Mexican families to get by. The help at your hotel typically get paid only a few dollars a day. They depend on tips to make the difference between dire and bearable poverty. Give the *camarista* (chambermaid) and floor attendant 20 pesos every day or two. And whenever uncertain of what to tip, it will probably mean a lot to someone—maybe a whole family—if you err on the generous side.

In restaurants and bars, Mexican tipping customs are similar to those in the United States: tip waiters, waitresses, and bartenders about 15 percent for satisfactory service.

Unlike the United States, it is not customary to tip the taxi drivers unless they go above and beyond, such as wrangling heaps of luggage or giving you a tour. However, the baggers at the supermarket, mostly school age children and the eldery, work only for tips and so every peso counts. Tip them with your change or about five pesos per trip to the store. Gas station attendants similarly get tips. Gas stations are full service and usually include at least a windshield wash. Attendants will check your oil, tire pressure and perform other tasks upon request. Tip them a few pesos for the trouble.

SAFE CONDUCT

Your own behavior, despite low crime statistics, largely determines your safety in Mexico. For women traveling solo, it is important to realize that the double standard is alive and well

MACHISMO

I once met an Acapulco man who wore five gold wristwatches and became angry when I quietly refused his repeated invitations to get drunk with him. Another time, on the beach near San Blas, two drunk campesinos nearly attacked me because I was helping my girlfriend cook a picnic dinner. Outside Taxco I once spent an endless hour in the seat behind a bus driver who insisted on speeding down the middle of the two-lane highway, honking aside oncoming automobiles.

Despite their wide differences, the commonality shared by all four men was machismo, an issue that seems to affect many Mexican men. Machismo is a sometimes-reckless obsession to prove one's masculinity, to show how macho you are. Men of many nationalities share the instinct to prove themselves (Japan's *bushido* samurai code is one example).

When confronted by a Mexican braggart, male visitors should remain careful and controlled. If your opponent is yelling, stay cool, speak softly, and withdraw as soon as possible. On the highway, be courteous and unprovoking – don't use your car to spar with a macho driver. Drinking often leads to problems. It's best to stay out of bars or cantinas unless you're prepared to deal with the macho consequences. Polite refusal of a drink may be taken as a challenge. If you visit a bar with Mexican friends or acquaintances, you may be heading for a no-win choice between a drunken all-night *borrachera* (binge) or an insult to the honor of your friends by refusing.

For women, machismo requires even more cautious behavior. In Mexico, women's liberation is long in coming. Few women hold positions of power in business or politics. One woman, Rosa Luz Alegría, did attain the rank of minister of tourism during the former Portillo administration; she was the president's mistress.

Female visitors can follow the example of their Mexican sisters by making a habit of going out in the company of friends or acquaintances, especially at night. Many Mexican men believe an unaccompanied woman wants to be picked up. Ignore their offers; any response, even refusal, might be taken as an encouraging sign. If, on the other hand, there is a Mexican man whom you'd genuinely like to meet, the traditional way is an arranged introduction through family or friends.

Mexican families, as a source of protection and friendship, should not be overlooked – especially on the beach or in the park, where, among the gaggle of kids, grandparents, aunts, and cousins, there's room for one more.

---

in Mexico. Dress and behave modestly and you will most likely avoid embarrassment. Whenever possible, stay in the company of friends or acquaintances; find companions for beach, sightseeing, and shopping excursions. Ignore strange men's solicitations and overtures. A Mexican man on the prowl will invent the sappiest romantic overtures to snare a gringa. He will often interpret anything but a firm "no" as a "maybe," and a "maybe" as a "yes."

For male visitors, alcohol often leads to trouble. Avoid bars and cantinas; if, given Mexico's excellent beers, you can't abstain completely, at least maintain soft-spoken self-control in the face of challenges from macho drunks.

The sense of security one feels while downtown in Vallarta can lead to a false sense of imperviousness. Avoid flashing large amounts of cash and expensive watches or cameras. Do not, unless you wish to see the inside of an authentic Mexican prison, attempt to buy drugs. Unfortunate "accidents" have happened when hard partying tourists have invited strangers back to their hotel rooms for sex or drugs. Just use common sense and be aware of your surroundings.

Of particular note to women, be very aware especially in situations like booze cruises, of consuming anything you didn't actually see prepared. Like in the United States, roofies and other date rape drugs have been slipped to unsuspecting tourists (often single women). Keep your drink with you at all times, even when you visit the restroom and do not accept drinks from strangers.

SOCIALLY RESPONSIBLE TRAVEL AND ECOTOURISM

Latter-day jet travel has brought droves of vacationing tourists to developing countries largely unprepared for the consequences. As the visitors' numbers swell, power grids black out, sewers overflow, and roads crack under the strain of accommodating more and larger hotels, restaurants, cars, buses, and airports.

Worse yet, armies of vacationers drive up local prices and begin to change native customs. While visions of tourists as sources of fast money replace traditions of hospitality, television wipes out folk entertainment, Coke and Pepsi substitute for fruit drinks, and prostitution and drugs flourish.

Some travelers have said enough is enough and are forming organizations to encourage visitors to travel with increased sensitivity to native people and customs. They have developed travelers' codes of ethics and guidelines that encourage visitors to stay at local-style accommodations, use local transportation, and seek alternative vacations and tours, such as language-study and cultural programs and people-to-people work projects.

A number of especially active socially responsible travel groups sponsor tours all over the world, including some in the Puerto Vallarta region. These include organizations such as **Green Tortoise** (www.greentortoise.com) and **Green Globe** (www.greenglobe.org), both of which run tours that visit the Puerto Vallarta region. For more alternatives, visit the umbrella website www.sociallyresponsible.org.

Tips for Travelers

BRINGING THE KIDS

Children are treasured like gifts from heaven in Mexico. Traveling with kids will ensure your welcome most everywhere. On the beach, take extra precautions to make sure they are protected from the sun.

A sick child is no fun for anyone. Fortunately, clinics and good doctors are available even in small towns. When in need, ask a storekeeper or a pharmacist, *"¿Dónde hay un doctor, por favor?"* (¿DOHN-day eye oon doc-TOHR por fah-VOHR?). In most cases, within five minutes you will be in the waiting room of the local physician or hospital.

Children who do not favor typical Mexican fare can easily be fed with always-available eggs, cheese, *hamburguesas,* milk, oatmeal, corn flakes, bananas, cakes, and cookies.

Your children will generally have more fun if they have a little previous knowledge of Mexico and a stake in the trip. For example, them select some library picture books and

magazines so they'll know where they're going and what to expect, or give them responsibility for packing and carrying their own small travel bag.

Be sure to mention your children's ages when making air reservations; child discounts of 50 percent or more are often available. Also, if you can arrange to go on an uncrowded flight, you can stretch out and rest on the empty seats.

For more details on traveling with children, check out *Adventuring with Children* by Nan Jeffrey.

TRAVEL FOR PEOPLE WITH DISABILITIES

Mexican airlines and hotels are becoming increasingly aware of the needs of travelers with disabilities. Open, street-level lobbies and large, wheelchair-accessible elevators and rooms are available in most Puerto Vallarta resort hotels. Most street-corner curbs accommodate wheelchairs.

U.S. law forbids travel discrimination against otherwise qualified people with disabilities. As long as your disability is stable and not liable to deteriorate during passage, you can expect to be treated like any passenger with special needs.

Make reservations far ahead of departure and ask your agent to inform your airline of your needs, such as boarding wheelchair or in-flight oxygen. Be early at the gate to take advantage of the pre-boarding call.

For many helpful details to smooth your trip, get a copy of *Survival Strategies for Going Abroad* by Laura Hershey, published in 2005 by **Mobility International USA** (132 E. Broadway, Suite 343, Eugene, OR 97401, tel. 541/343-1284 voice/TDD, fax 541/343-6812, www.miusa.org). Mobility International is a valuable resource for many disabled lovers of Mexico, for it encourages disabled travelers with a goldmine of information and literature and can provide them with valuable Mexico connections. They publish a regular newsletter and provide information and referrals for international exchanges and homestays.

Similarly, **Partners of the Americas** (1424 K St. NW, Suite 700, Washington, DC 20005, tel. 202/628-3300 or 800/322-7844, fax 202/628-3306, www.partners.net), with chapters in 45 U.S. states, works to improve understanding of disabilities and facilities in Mexico and Latin America. It maintains communications with local organizations and individuals whom disabled travelers may contact at their destinations.

Be aware that most of the streets in Puerto Vallarta are cobblestone, often with high sidewalks accessible only by stairs. Tourist attractions, restaurants and shops may not be wheelchair accessible, so be sure to call in advance.

GAY AND LESBIAN TRAVELERS

Puerto Vallarta has a particular draw for national and international gay and lesbian travelers for a number of reasons, among them the strong support system within the local community that goes beyond nightlife and beaches. Certainly Puerto Vallarta doesn't match Mexico City in terms of organization within the gay community, as it tends to attract more vacationers than residents, and there is no gay and lesbian center per se. Nevertheless, a strong gay community has existed here as early as the 1970s, but in the last decade, numerous gay-owned businesses have opened, and, more importantly, are unabashed about their gay friendliness. For more information, take a look at www.gayguidevallarta.com for tips on activities, venues, and more. In addition, most of the websites of the gay-friendly realtors include interesting facts and figures. Locals pick up the gay-friendly bimonthly, bilingual *Bay Vallarta* as an additional option for events for foreigners as well as nationals and other culture, art, music, and sports activities.

Locals have always adopted the "live and let live" attitude about Vallarta's nightlife, and they tend to be respectful as long as restraints are recognized while in the public eye. But it's important not to lose sight of the fact that there are locals who may not be open to shows of public affection between same-sex couples. Also, be aware that during this time of rapid growth in Puerto Vallarta, many people you might assume are locals are not locals at all but come from other areas in Mexico, some of which are not as liberal or as used to turning a blind eye.

Beyond the town of Puerto Vallarta, you can expect to find open and friendly people throughout the Bay of Banderas. In some of the smaller towns, however, it's not that they won't be as friendly, but their curiosity to see foreign-appearing visitors may get the better of them—their actions are not necessarily be aggressive—just curious. As always, speaking Spanish will be helpful.

As laws in Mexico are in the process of change (several states have voted to accept same-sex relationships and allow legal rights and benefits), those very changes may occasionally spark reactions. Resort towns are usually more open in that the population tends to be more aware not only of differences but of the economic importance of tourism. Be aware that nudity is not officially allowed on beaches in Mexico.

With regard to safety, most visitors should avoid areas that are unlit at night, whether in the Zona Romántica or elsewhere. Be aware that young men sometimes try to attract the interested foreigner with the intention of mugging or worse. If you've had too much to drink, don't open yourself to trouble. Tell your friends where you're going or who you're planning to go with. And if you've met someone special during your vacation, be sure to protect yourself by wearing a condom as well as maintaining your common sense at all times—even after that third (who's counting!) margarita.

SENIOR CITIZENS

Age, according to Mark Twain, is a question of mind over matter: If you don't mind, it doesn't matter. Mexico is a country where whole extended families, from babies to great-grandparents, live together. Elderly travelers will benefit from the respect and understanding Mexicans accord to older people. Besides these encouragements, consider the number of retirees already in havens in Puerto Vallarta, the Nayarit coastal towns of Bucerías, Sayulita, San Francisco, and nearby centers of Guadalajara and Lake Chapala.

Certain organizations support senior travel. Leading the field is **Elderhostel** (11 Ave. de Lafayette, Boston, MA 02111-1746, tel. 877/426-8056, www.elderhostel.org). Elderhostel invites folks over 50 to join their extensive U.S. and international program of special tours, study, homestays, and people-to-people travel itineraries. Contact them for their free catalogs.

A number of newsletters publicize senior vacation and retirement opportunities. Among the best is the **Mexico File** monthly newsletter that, besides featuring pithy stories by Mexico travelers and news updates, offers an opportunity-packed classified section of Mexico rentals, publications, services, and much more. Subscribe ($39/year) through Simmonds Publications (5580 La Jolla Blvd. #306, La Jolla, CA 92037, tel./fax 858/456-4419 or 800/563-9345 (voice mail), www.mexicofile.com).

Some books publicize senior travel opportunities. One of the pithiest is *Unbelievably Good Deals and Great Adventures You Can't Have Unless You're Over 50,* by Joan Rattner Heilman, published by McGraw Hill (2003). Its 200 pages are packed with details of how to get bargains on cruises, tours, car rentals, lodgings, and much, much more.

For seniors with online access (as close as your neighborhood library these days) the **Internet** is a gold mine of senior-oriented travel information. For example, I typed in "Senior Travel" on the Google search engine (www.google.com), and netted more than 90 million responses. Near the top of the list was the **Transitions Abroad** site, www.transitionsabroad.com, which offers a gold mine of a sub-site (www.transitionsabroad.com/listings/travel/senior), with a load of useful resources centering around senior traveling and living abroad.

Health and Safety

STAYING HEALTHY

In Puerto Vallarta as everywhere prevention is the best remedy for illness. For those visitors who confine their travel to the beaten path, a few basic common-sense precautions will ensure vacation enjoyment.

Resist the temptation to dive headlong into Mexico. It's no wonder that people get sick—broiling in the sun, gobbling peppery food, guzzling beer and margaritas, then discoing half the night—all in their first 24 hours. An alternative is to give your body time to adjust. Travelers often arrive tired and dehydrated from travel and heat. During the first few days, drink plenty of bottled water and juice, and take siestas.

Immunizations and Precautions

A good physician can recommend the proper preventatives for your Puerto Vallarta trip. If you are going to stay pretty much in town, your doctor will probably suggest little more than updating your basic typhoid, diphtheria-tetanus, hepatitis, and polio shots.

For camping or trekking in remote tropical areas—below 4,000 feet or 1,200 meters—doctors often recommend a gamma-globulin shot against hepatitis A and a schedule of chloroquine pills against malaria. While in backcountry areas, use other measures to discourage mosquitoes—and fleas, flies, ticks, no-see-ums, "kissing bugs" and other tropical pesties—from biting you. Common precautions include sleeping under mosquito netting, burning *espirales mosquito* (mosquito coils), and rubbing on plenty of pure DEET (n,n dimethyl-meta-toluamide) "jungle juice," mixed in equal parts with rubbing (70 percent isopropyl) alcohol. Although super-effective, 100 percent DEET dries and irritates the skin.

Sunburn

For sunburn protection, use a good sunscreen with a sun protection factor (SPF) rated 15 or more, which will reduce burning rays to one-fifteenth or less of direct sunlight. Better still, take a shady siesta-break from the sun during the most hazardous midday hours. If you do get burned, applying your sunburn lotion (or one of the "caine" creams) after the fact usually decreases the pain and speeds healing. The UV index in Mexico is much higher than northern countries so even if you aren't used to using high SPF sunscreen and keeping track of your sun time, it is very wise to do so here.

Safe Water and Food

Although municipalities have made great strides in sanitation, food and water are still potential sources of germs in some parts of the Puerto Vallarta region. Although it's probably safe most everywhere, except in a few upcountry localities, it's still probably best to drink bottled water only. Hotels, whose success depends vitally on their customers' health, generally provide *agua purificada* (purified bottled water). If, for any reason, the available water is of doubtful quality, add a water purifier, such as "Potable Aqua" brand (get it at a camping goods stores before departure) or a few drops per quart of water of *blanqueador* (household chlorine bleach) or *yodo* (tincture of iodine) from the pharmacy.

Pure bottled water, soft drinks, beer, and fresh fruit juices are so widely available it is easy to avoid tap water, especially in restaurants. Ice and *paletas* (iced juice-on-a-stick) may be risky, especially in small towns.

Washing hands before eating in a restaurant is a time-honored Mexican ritual that visitors should religiously follow. The humblest Mexican eatery will generally provide a basin to *lavar las manos* (wash the hands). If it doesn't, don't eat there.

Hot, cooked food is generally safe, as are peeled fruits and vegetables. These days milk and cheese in Mexico are generally processed under sanitary conditions and sold pasteurized (ask, *"¿Pasteurizado?"*) and are typically safe. Mexican ice cream used to be both bad-tasting and of dubious safety, but national brands available in supermarkets are so much improved that it's no longer necessary to resist ice cream while in town.

In recent years, much cleaner public water and increased hygiene awareness have made salads—once shunned by Mexico travelers—generally safe to eat in tourist-frequented Puerto Vallarta cafés and restaurants. Nevertheless, lettuce and cabbage, particularly in country villages, are more likely to be contaminated than tomatoes, carrots, cucumbers, onions, and green peppers. In any case, you can try dousing your salad in vinegar (*vinagre*) or plenty of sliced lime (*limón*) juice, the acidity of which kills some but not all bacteria.

First-Aid Kit

In the tropics, ordinary cuts and insect bites are more prone to infection and should receive immediate first aid. A first-aid kit with aspirin, rubbing alcohol, hydrogen peroxide, water-purifying tablets, household chlorine bleach or iodine for water purifying, swabs, bandages, gauze, adhesive tape, Ace bandage, chamomile (*manzanilla*) tea bags for upset stomachs, Pepto-Bismol, acidophilus tablets, antibiotic ointment, hydrocortisone cream, mosquito repellent, knife, and good tweezers is a good precaution for any traveler and mandatory for campers.

HEALTH PROBLEMS
Traveler's Diarrhea

Traveler's diarrhea (known in Southeast Asia as "Bali Belly" and in Mexico as turista or "Montezuma's Revenge") sometimes persists, even among prudent vacationers. You can suffer turista for a week after simply traveling from California to Philadelphia or New York. Doctors say the familiar symptoms of runny bowels, nausea, and sour stomach result from normal local bacterial strains to which newcomers' systems need time to adjust. Unfortunately, the dehydration and fatigue from heat and travel reduce your body's natural defenses and sometimes lead to a persistent cycle of sickness at a time when you least want it.

Time-tested protective measures can help your body either prevent or break this cycle. Many doctors and veteran travelers swear by Pepto-Bismol for soothing sore stomachs and stopping diarrhea. Acidophilus, the bacteria found in yogurt, is widely available in the United States in tablets and aids digestion. Warm *manzanilla* (chamomile) tea, used widely in Mexico (and by Peter Rabbit's mother), provides liquid and calms upset stomachs. Temporarily avoid coffee and alcohol, drink plenty of *manzanilla* tea, and eat bananas and rice for a few meals until your tummy can take regular food.

Although powerful antibiotics and antidiarrhea medications such as Lomotil and Imodium are readily available over *farmacia* counters, they may involve serious side effects and should not be taken in the absence of medical advice. If in doubt, consult a doctor.

Chagas' Disease and Dengue Fever

Chagas' disease, spread by the "kissing" (or, more appropriately, "assassin") bug, is a potential hazard in the Mexican tropics. Known locally as a *vinchuca,* the triangular-headed, three-quarter-inch (two-centimeter) brown insect, identifiable by its yellow-striped abdomen, often drops upon its sleeping victims from the thatched ceiling of a rural house at night. Its bite is followed by swelling, fever, and weakness and can lead to heart failure if left untreated. Application of drugs at an early stage can, however, clear the patient of the trypanosome parasites that infect victims' bloodstreams and vital organs. See a doctor immediately if you believe you're infected.

Most of the precautions against malaria-bearing mosquitoes also apply to dengue fever, which does occur (although uncommonly) in outlying tropical areas of Mexico. The culprit here is a virus carried by the mosquito species *Aedes aegypti.* Symptoms are acute fever, with chills, sweating, and muscle aches. A red, diffuse rash frequently results, which may later peel. Symptoms abate after about five days, but fatigue may persist. A particularly serious, but fortunately rare, form, called dengue hemor-rhagic fever, can be fatal. Although no vaccines or preventatives, other than deterring mosquitoes, exist, you should nevertheless see a doctor immediately for IV hydration.

For more good tropical preventative information, get a copy of the excellent pamphlet distributed by the International Association of Medical Advice to Travelers (IAMAT), described in more detail in the *Medical Care* section later in this chapter.

Scorpions and Snakes

While camping or staying in a *palapa* or other rustic accommodation, watch for scorpions, especially in your shoes, which you should shake out every morning. Scorpion stings and snakebites are rarely fatal to an adult, unless you happen to be allergic to the venom. Watch for shortness of breath and rapid heartbeat and get to a doctor immediately. Even without an allergy, scorpion stings can be very serious for a child or a pet. Get the victim to a doctor (or vet, depending on the patient) calmly but quickly. (For more snakebite details, see *Reptiles and Amphibians* under *Fauna* in the *Background* chapter.)

Sea Creatures

While snorkeling or surfing, you may suffer a coral scratch or jellyfish sting. Experts advise you to wash the afflicted area with ocean water and pour alcohol (rubbing alcohol or tequila) over the wound, then apply hydrocortisone cream available from the *farmacia.*

Injuries from sea urchin spines and stingray barbs are painful and can be serious. Physicians recommend similar first aid for both: Remove the spines or barbs by hand or with tweezers, then soak the injury in as-hot-as-possible fresh water to weaken the toxins and provide relief. Another method is to rinse the area with an antibacterial solution—rubbing alcohol, vinegar, wine, or ammonia diluted with water. If none are available, the same effect may be achieved with urine, either your own or someone else's in your party. Get medical help immediately.

Tattoos

All health hazards don't come from the wild. A number of Mexico travelers have complained of complications from black henna tattoos. When enhanced by the chemical dye PPD, the henna can result in an itchy rash that can lead to scarring. It's best to play it safe: If you must have a vacation tattoo, get it at an established, professional shop.

MEDICAL CARE

For medical advice and treatment, let your hotel (or if you're camping, the closest *farmacia*) refer you to a good doctor, clinic, or hospital. Mexican doctors, especially in medium-sized and small towns, practice like private doctors in the United States and Canada once did before health insurance, liability, and group practice. They will come to you if you request it; they often keep their doors open even after regular hours and charge reasonable fees.

You will receive generally good treatment at the many local hospitals in the Puerto Vallarta region. If you must have an English-speaking, American-trained doctor, the International Association for Medical Assistance to Travelers (IAMAT, 1623 Military Road #279, Niagra Falls, NY 14304-1745, tel. 716/754-4883; in Canada at 40 Regal Road, Guelph, ON N1K 1B5, tel. 519/836-0102, or 1287 St. Clair Ave. West, Toronto, Ontario M6E 1B8, tel. 416/652-0137; www.iamat.org) publishes an updated booklet of qualified member physicians, some of whom practice in Puerto Vallarta. (See the *Puerto Vallarta* chapter for doctor and hospital details.) IAMAT also distributes a very detailed *How to Protect Yourself Against Malaria* guide, together with worldwide malaria risk and communicable disease charts.

For more useful information on health and safety in Mexico, consult Drs. Robert H. Paige and Curtis P. Page's *Mexico: Health and Safety Travel Guide* (Tempe, AZ, Med to Go Books, 2004), or Dirk Schroeder's *Staying Healthy in Asia, Africa, and Latin America* (Emeryville, CA: Avalon Travel Publishing, 2000).

There are hyperbaric chambers available in Puerto Vallarta for decompression sickness should you suffer from a dive accident. Ask a local dive shop for the emergency information if you plan on diving without a local guide or tour group (not recommended).

THE LAW AND POLICE

While Mexican authorities are tolerant of alcohol, they are decidedly intolerant of other substances such as marijuana, psychedelics, cocaine, and heroin. Getting caught with such drugs in Mexico usually leads to swift and severe results.

Equally swift is the punishment for nude sunbathing, which is both illegal in public and offensive to Mexicans. Confine your nudist colony to very private locations.

Although with decreasing frequency lately, traffic police in Puerto Vallarta sometimes seem to watch foreign cars with eagle eyes. Officers seem to inhabit busy intersections and one-way streets, waiting for confused tourists to make a wrong move. If they whistle you over, stop immediately or you will really get into hot water. If guilty, say *"Lo siento"* ("I'm sorry") and be cooperative. Although the officer probably won't mention it, he or she is usually hoping that you'll cough up a $20 *mordida* (bribe) for the privilege of driving away.

Don't do it. Although he may hint at confiscating your car, calmly ask for an official *boleto* (written traffic ticket, if you're guilty) in exchange for your driver's license (have a copy), which the officer will probably keep if he writes a ticket. If after a few minutes no money appears, the officer will most likely give you back your driver's license rather than go to the trouble of writing the ticket. If not, the worst that will usually happen is you will have to go to the *presidencia municipal* (city hall) the next morning and pay the $10 to a clerk in exchange for your driver's license.

PEDESTRIAN AND DRIVING HAZARDS

Although Puerto Vallarta's cobbled pavements and "holey" sidewalks won't land you in jail, one of them might send you to the hospital if you don't watch your step, especially at night. "Pedestrian beware" is especially good advice on Mexican streets, where it is rumored that some drivers speed up rather than slow down when they spot a tourist stepping off the curb. Falling coconuts, especially frequent on windy days, constitute an additional hazard to unwary campers and beachgoers.

Driving Mexican country roads, where slow trucks and carts block lanes, campesinos stroll the shoulders, and horses, burros, and cattle wander at will, is hazardous—doubly so at night. Closed roads, dangerous shoulders and washed out bridges may or may not have a sign warning motorists so it's best to drive in unfamiliar areas only during the daytime and keep your eyes peeled for hazards.

Information and Services

MONEY
The Peso: Down and Up

Overnight in early 1993, the Mexican government shifted its monetary decimal point three places and created the "new" peso, which now trades at around 11 per U.S. dollar. Since the peso value sometimes changes rapidly, U.S. dollars have become a much more stable indicator of Mexican prices; for this reason they are used in this book to report prices. You should, nevertheless, always use pesos to pay for everything in Mexico.

Since the introduction of the new peso, the centavo (one-hundredth of a new peso) has reappeared, in coins of 5, 10, 20, and 50 centavos. Incidentally, the dollar sign, "$," also marks Mexican pesos. Peso coins (*monedas*) in denominations of 1, 2, 5, 10, and 20 pesos, and bills, in denominations of 20, 50, 100, 200, and 500 pesos, are common. Since banks like to exchange your travelers checks for a few crisp large bills rather than the often-tattered smaller denominations, ask for some of your change in 50- and 100-peso notes. A 500-peso note, while common at the bank, may look awfully big to a small shopkeeper, who might be hard-pressed to change it.

Banks, ATMs, and Money-Exchange Offices

Mexican banks, like their North American counterparts, have lengthened their business hours. Your best choice is usually a branch of the Hong Kong-Shanghai Banking Corporation (HSBC) bank, which maintains very long hours: often Monday–Saturday 8 A.M.–7 P.M. Banamex (Banco Nacional de Mexico), generally the most popular with local people,usually posts the best in-town dollar exchange rate in its lobbies; for example: *Tipo de cambio: venta 10.615, compra 10.820,* which means the bank will sell pesos to you at the rate of 10.615 per dollar and buy them back for 10.820 per dollar.

ATMs (automated teller machines, *cajeros automáticos,* kah-HAY-rohs ahoo-toh-MAH-tee-kohs) are rapidly becoming the money source of choice in Mexico. Virtually every bank has a 24-hour ATM, accessible (with proper PIN identification code) by a swarm of U.S. and Canadian credit and ATM cards. *Note:* Some Mexican bank ATMs may "eat" your ATM cards if you don't retrieve it within about 15 seconds of completing your transaction. Retrieve your card *immediately* after getting your cash.

Although one-time bank charges, typically about $3, for ATM cash, remain small, the pesos you can usually get from a single card is limited to about $4000 (depending on the exchange rate, about $400 US) or less per day. But, since the ATM charge is generally a fixed fee, regardless of the amount you withdraw, you will save money by withdrawing the maximum available in a single transaction.

Even without an ATM card, you don't have to go to the trouble of waiting in long bank service lines. Opt for a less-crowded bank, such as Bancomer, Banco Serfín, HSBC bank, or a private *casa de cambio* (money-exchange office). Often most convenient, such offices often offer long hours and faster service than the banks for a fee (as little as $0.50 or as much as $3 per $100).

Keeping Your Money Safe

Travelers checks, the traditional prescription for safe money abroad, are widely accepted in Puerto Vallarta. Even if you plan to use your ATM card, buy some U.S.-dollar travelers checks (a well-known brand such as American Express or Visa) as an emergency reserve. Canadian travelers checks and currency are not as widely accepted as U.S. travelers checks, European and Asian even less. Unless you like signing your name or paying lots of per-check commissions, buy denominations of $100 or more.

In Puerto Vallarta as everywhere, thieves circulate among the tourists. Keep valuables in your hotel *caja de seguridad* (security box). If you don't particularly trust the desk clerk, carry what you cannot afford to lose in a money belt.

Pickpockets love crowded markets, buses, and airport terminals where they can slip a wallet out of a back pocket or dangling purse in a blink. Guard against this by carrying your wallet in your front pocket, and your purse, waist pouch, and daypack (which clever crooks can sometimes slit open) on your front side.

Don't attract thieves by displaying wads of money or flashy jewelry. Don't get sloppy drunk; if so, you may become a pushover for a determined thief.

Don't leave valuables unattended on the beach; share security duties with trustworthy-looking neighbors, or leave a secure bag with a shopkeeper nearby.

Credit Cards

Credit cards, such as Visa, MasterCard, and to a lesser extent American Express and Discover, are generally honored in the hotels, restaurants, handicrafts shops, and boutiques that cater to foreign tourists. You will generally get better bargains, however, in shops that depend on local trade and do not so readily accept credit cards. Such shops sometimes offer discounts for cash sales.

Whatever the circumstance, your travel money will usually go much further in Puerto Vallarta than back home. Despite the national 15 percent ("value added," or IVA) sales tax, local lodging, food, and transportation prices will often seem like bargains compared to the developed world. Outside of the pricey high-rise beachfront strips, pleasant, palmy hotel room rates often run $40 or less.

COMMUNICATIONS
Using Mexican Telephones

Although Mexican phone service has improved in the last decade, it's still sometimes hit-or-miss. If a number doesn't get through, you may have to redial it more than once. When someone answers (usually *"Bueno"*), be especially courteous. If your Spanish is rusty, say, *"¿Por favor, habla inglés?"* (¿POR fah-VOR, AH-blah een-GLAYS?). If you want to speak to a particular person (such as María), ask, *"¿María se encuentra?"* (¿mah-REE-ah SAY ayn-koo-AYN-trah?).

Since November 2001, when telephone numbers were standardized, Mexican phones operate pretty much the same as in the United States and Canada. In Puerto Vallarta, for example, a complete telephone number is generally written like this: 322/221-4709. As in the United States, the "322" denotes the telephone area code (*lada,* LAH-dah) and the 221-4709 is the number that you dial locally. If you want to dial this number long-distance (*larga distancia*), first dial "01" (like "1" in the United States), then 322/221-4709. All Mexican telephone numbers, with only three exceptions, begin with a three-digit *lada,* followed by a seven-digit local number. (The exceptions are Monterrey, Guadalajara, and Mexico City, which have two-digit *ladas* and eight-digit local numbers. The Mexico City *lada* is 55; Guadalajara's is 33, Monterrey's is 81. (For example, a complete Guadalajara phone number would read 33/6897-2253.)

In Puerto Vallarta–region towns and cities, direct long-distance dialing is the rule—from hotels, public phone booths, and efficient private *larga distancia* telephone offices. The cheapest, often most convenient, way to call is by buying and using a public-telephone Ladatel card. Buy them in 20-, 30-, 50-, and 100-peso denominations at the many outlets—minimarkets, pharmacies, liquor stores—that display the blue-and-yellow Ladatel sign.

Calling Mexico and Calling Home

To call Mexico direct from the United States, first dial 011 (for international access), then 52 (for Mexico), followed by the Mexican area code and local number.

For station-to-station calls to the United States from Mexico, dial 001 plus the area code and the local number. For calls to other countries, ask your hotel desk clerk or see the easy-to-follow directions in the local Mexican telephone directory.

Another convenient way (although a much more expensive one) to call home is via your personal telephone credit card. Contact your U.S. long-distance operator by dialing 001-800/462-4240 for AT&T; 001-800/674-7000 for MCI; or 001-800/877-8000 for Sprint.

Yet another (although very expensive) way of calling home is collect. You can do this in one of two ways. Simply dial 09 for the local English-speaking international operator, or dial the AT&T, MCI, and Sprint numbers listed above. **Beware** of certain private "To Call Long Distance to the U.S.A. Collect and Credit Card" telephones installed prominently in airports, tourist hotels, and shops. Tariffs on these phones often run as high as $10 per minute (with a three-minute minimum), for a total of $30, whether you talk three minutes or not. Always ask the operator for the rate, and if it's too high, buy a $3 Ladatel card that will give you about six minutes to the United States or Canada.

In smaller towns, you must often do your long-distance phoning in the *larga distancia* (local phone office). Typically staffed by a young woman and often connected to a café, the *larga distancia* becomes an informal community social center as people pass the time waiting for their phone connections.

Post, Telegraph, and Internet Access

Mexican *correos* (post offices) operate similarly, but more slowly and less securely, than their counterparts in the developed world. Mail services usually include *lista de correo* (general delivery, address letters *"a/c lista de correo"*), *servicios filatelicas* (philatelic services), *por avión* (airmail), *giros* (postal money orders), and Mexpost secure and fast delivery service, usually from separate Mexpost offices.

Mexican ordinary mail is sadly unreliable and pathetically slow. If, for mailings within Mexico, you must have security, use the efficient, reformed government Mexpost (like U.S. Express Mail) service. For international mailings, check the local yellow pages for widely available DHL or Federal Express courier service.

Telégrafos (telegraph offices), usually near the post office, send and receive *telegramas* (telegrams) and *giros*. Telecomunicaciones or Telecom, the new high-tech telegraph offices, add telephone and public fax to the available services.

Internet service, including personal email access, has arrived in the Puerto Vallarta region's towns. Internet "cafés" are a dime a dozen, especially in up-to-date Puerto Vallarta, Sayulita, Rincon de Guayabitos, Tepic, and Barra de Navidad. Online service rates run about $1–2 per hour.

WEIGHTS AND MEASURES

Mexican electric power is supplied at U.S.-standard 110 volts, 60 cycles. Plugs and sockets are generally two-pronged, nonpolar (like the pre-1970s U.S. ones). Bring adapters if you're going to use appliances with polar two-pronged or three-pronged plugs. (A two-pronged polar plug has different-sized prongs, one of which is too large to plug into an old-fashioned nonpolar socket.)

The Puerto Vallarta region is split between **two time zones.** The state of Jalisco part, which includes Puerto Vallarta, Barra de Navidad, and Guadalajara, operates on central time, while the state of Nayarit part, which includes Nuevo Vallarta, Rincón de Guayabitos, Tepic, and San Blas, operates on mountain time. The Río Ameca and bridge, just north of the Puerto Vallarta airport, marks the Nayarit-Jalisco border. When traveling by highway south into Puerto Vallarta from Nayarit, set your watch ahead one hour; conversely, when you cross the Río Ameca traveling north set your watch back an hour.

There can be some confusion in towns that are close to the border like Nuevo Vallarta and Punta Mita so make sure to check with your party and confirm whether you are meeting on Jalisco or Nayarit time. For convenience, many businesses and people in these areas simply stick with Jalisco time but government offices and smaller businesses in Nayarit that don't cater to tourists go by the local time.

Mexican businesses and government offices sometimes use the 24-hour system to tell time. Thus, a business that posts its hours as 0800–1700 is open 8 A.M.–5 P.M. When speaking, however, people customarily use the 12-hour system.

RESOURCES

Glossary

Many of the following words have a socio-historical meaning; others you will not find in the usual English-Spanish dictionary.

abarrotería grocery store

alcalde mayor or municipal judge

alfarería pottery

andando walkway or strolling path

antojitos native Mexican snacks, such as tamales, chiles rellenos, tacos, and enchiladas

artesanías handicrafts, as distinguished from artesanio – a person who makes handicrafts

audiencia one of the royal executive-judicial panels sent to rule Mexico during the 16th century

ayuntamiento either the town council or the building where it meets

bandidos bandits or outlaws

bienes raices literally "good roots," but popularly, real estate

birria goat, pork, or lamb stew, in spiced tomato broth, especially typical of Jalisco

boleto ticket, boarding pass

caballero literally, "horseman," but popularly, gentleman

cabercera head town of a municipal district, or headquarters in general

cabrón literally a cuckold, but more commonly, bastard, rat, or S.O.B.; sometimes used affectionately

cacique chief or boss

camionera bus station

campesino country person; farm worker

canasta basket of woven reeds, with handle

casa de huéspedes guesthouse, usually operated in a family home

caudillo dictator or political chief

charro, charra gentleman cowboy or cowgirl

chingar literally, "to rape," but is also the universal Spanish "f- word," the equivalent of "screw" in English

churrigueresque Spanish baroque architectural style incorporated into many Mexican colonial churches, named after José Churriguera (1665-1725)

científicos literally, scientists, but applied to President Porfirio Díaz's technocratic advisers

cofradia Catholic fraternal service association, either male or female, mainly in charge of financing and organizing religious festivals

colectivo a shared public taxi or minibus that picks up and deposits passengers along a designated route

colegio preparatory school or junior college

colonia suburban subdivision; satellite of a larger city

Conasupo government store that sells basic foods at subsidized prices

correo post office

criollo person of all-Spanish descent born in the New World

cuadra a rectangular work of art, usually a painting

Cuaresma Lent

curandero(a) indigenous medicine man or woman

damas ladies, as in "ladies room"

Domingo de Ramos Palm Sunday

ejido a constitutional, government-sponsored form of community, with shared land ownership and cooperative decision-making

encomienda colonial award of tribute from a designated indigenous district

estación ferrocarril railroad station

farmacia pharmacy or drugstore

finca farm

fonda food stall or small restaurant, often in a traditional market complex

fraccionamiento city sector or subdivision

fuero the former right of clergy to be tried in separate ecclesiastical courts

gachupín "one who wear spurs"; a derogatory term for a Spanish-born colonial

gasolinera gasoline station

gente de razón "people of reason"; whites and mestizos in colonial Mexico

gringo once-derogatory but now commonly used term for North American whites

grito impassioned cry, as in Hidalgo's Grito de Dolores

hacienda large landed estate; also the government treasury

hidalgo nobleman/woman; called honorifically by "Don" or "Doña"

indígena indigenous or aboriginal inhabitant of all-native descent who speaks his or her native tongue; commonly, but incorrectly, an Indian (indio)

jejenes "no-see-um" biting gnats, especially around San Blas, Nayarit

judiciales the federal or state "judicial," or investigative police, best known to motorists for their highway checkpoint inspections

jugería stall or small restaurant providing a large array of squeezed vegetable and fruit jugos (juices)

juzgado the "hoosegow," or jail

larga distancia long-distance telephone service, or the caseta (booth) where it's provided

licencado academic degree (abbr. Lic.) approximately equivalent to a bachelor's degree

lonchería small lunch counter, usually serving juices, sandwiches, and antojitos (Mexican snacks)

machismo; macho exaggerated sense of maleness; person who holds such a sense of himself

mestizo person of mixed European/indigenous descent

milpa native farm plot, usually of corn, squash, and beans

mordida slang for bribe; "little bite"

palapa thatched-roof structure, often open and shading a restaurant

panga outboard launch (lancha)

Pemex acronym for Petróleos Mexicanos, Mexico's national oil corporation

peninsulares the Spanish-born ruling colonial elite

peón a poor wage-earner, usually a country native

plan political manifesto, usually by a leader or group consolidating or seeking power

Porfiriato the 34-year (1876-1910) ruling period of president-dictator Porfirio Díaz

pozole stew, of hominy in broth, usually topped by shredded pork, cabbage, and diced onion

presidencia municipal the headquarters, like a U.S. city or county hall, of a Mexican municipio, countylike local governmental unit

preventiva municipal police

pronunciamiento declaration of rebellion by an insurgent leader

pueblo town or people

quinta a villa or country house

quinto the royal "fifth" tax on treasure and precious metals

retorno cul-de-sac

rurales former federal country police force created to fight bandidos

Semana Santa pre-Easter holy week

Tapatío, Tapatía a label referring to anyone or anything from Guadalajara or Jalisco

taxi especial private taxi, as distinguished from taxi colectivo, or shared taxi

Telégrafo telegraph office, lately converting to high-tech Telecomunicaciones, or Telecom, offering telegraph, telephone, and public fax services

vaquero cowboy

vecindad neighborhood

yanqui Yankee

zócalo town plaza or central square

ABBREVIATIONS

Av. *avenida* (avenue)
Blv. *bulevar* (boulevard)
Calz. *calzada* (thoroughfare, main road)
Fco. Francisco (proper name, as in "Fco. Villa")

Fracc. *Fraccionamiento* (subdivision)
Nte. *norte* (north)
Ote. *oriente* (east)
Pte. *poniente* (west)
s/n *sin número* (no street number)

Spanish Phrasebook

Your Mexico adventure will be more fun if you use a little Spanish. Mexican folks, although they may smile at your funny accent, will appreciate your halting efforts to break the ice and transform yourself from a foreigner to a potential friend.

Spanish commonly uses 30 letters – the familiar English 26, plus four straightforward additions: ch, ll, ñ, and rr, which are explained in "Consonants," below.

PRONUNCIATION

Once you learn them, Spanish pronunciation rules – in contrast to English – don't change. Spanish vowels generally sound softer than in English. (*Note:* The capitalized syllables below receive stronger accents.)

Vowels

a like ah, as in "hah": *agua* AH-gooah (water), *pan* PAHN (bread), and *casa* CAH-sah (house)

e like ay, as in "may:" *mesa* MAY-sah (table), *tela* TAY-lah (cloth), and *de* DAY (of, from)

i like ee, as in "need": *diez* dee-AYZ (ten), *comida* ko-MEE-dah (meal), and *fin* FEEN (end)

o like oh, as in "go": *peso* PAY-soh (weight), *ocho* OH-choh (eight), and *poco* POH-koh (a bit)

u like oo, as in "cool": *uno* OO-noh (one), *cuarto* KOOAHR-toh (room), and *usted* oos-TAYD (you); when it follows a "q" the **u** is silent; when it follows an "h" or has an umlaut, it's pronounced like "w"

Consonants

b, d, f, k, l, m, n, p, q, s,
t, v, w, x, y, z, and ch
pronounced almost as in English; **h** occurs, but is silent – not pronounced at all.

c like k as in "keep": *cuarto* KOOAR-toh (room), Tepic tay-PEEK (capital of Nayarit state); when it precedes "e" or "i," pronounce **c** like s, as in "sit": *cerveza* sayr-VAY-sah (beer), *encima* ayn-SEE-mah (atop).

g like g as in "gift" when it precedes "a," "o," "u," or a consonant: *gato* GAH-toh (cat), *hago* AH-goh (I do, make); otherwise, pronounce **g** like h as in "hat": *giro* HEE-roh (money order), *gente* HAYN-tay (people)

j like h, as in "has": *Jueves* HOOAY-vays (Thursday), *mejor* may-HOR (better)

ll like y, as in "yes": *toalla* toh-AH-yah (towel), *ellos* AY-yohs (they, them)

ñ like ny, as in "canyon": *año* AH-nyo (year), *señor* SAY-nyor (Mr., sir)

r is lightly trilled, with tongue at the roof of your mouth like a very light English d, as in "ready": *pero* PAY-doh (but), *tres* TDAYS (three), *cuatro* KOOAH-tdoh (four).

rr like a Spanish r, but with much more emphasis and trill. Let your tongue flap. Practice with *burro* (donkey), *carretera* (highway), and Carrillo (proper name), then really let go with *ferrocarril* (railroad).

Note: The single small but common exception to all of the above is the pronunciation of Spanish **y** when it's being used as the Spanish word for "and," as in "Ron y Kathy." In such case, pronounce it like the English ee, as in "keep": Ron "ee" Kathy (Ron and Kathy).

Accent

The rule for accent, the relative stress given to syllables within a given word, is straightforward. If a word ends in a vowel, an n, or an s, accent the next-to-last syllable; if not, accent the last syllable.

Pronounce *gracias* GRAH-seeahs (thank you), *orden* OHR-dayn (order), and *carretera* kah-ray-TAY-rah (highway) with stress on the next-to-last syllable.

Otherwise, accent the last syllable: *venir* vay-NEER (to come), *ferrocarril* fay-roh-cah-REEL (railroad), and *edad* ay-DAHD (age).

Exceptions to the accent rule are always marked with an accent sign: (á, é, í, ó, or ú), such as *teléfono* tay-LAY-foh-noh (telephone), *jabón* hah-BON (soap), and *rápido* RAH-pee-doh (rapid).

BASIC AND COURTEOUS EXPRESSIONS

Most Spanish-speaking people consider formalities important. Whenever approaching anyone for information or some other reason, do not forget the appropriate salutation – good morning, good evening, etc. Standing alone, the greeting *hola* (hello) can sound brusque.

Hello. *Hola.*
Good morning. *Buenos días.*
Good afternoon. *Buenas tardes.*
Good evening. *Buenas noches.*
How are you? *¿Cómo está usted?*
Very well, thank you. *Muy bien, gracias.*
Okay; good. *Bien.*
Not okay; bad. *Mal or feo.*
So-so. *Más o menos.*
And you? *¿Y usted?*
Thank you. *Gracias.*
Thank you very much. *Muchas gracias.*
You're very kind. *Muy amable.*
You're welcome. *De nada.*
Goodbye. *Adios.*
See you later. *Hasta luego.*
please *por favor*
yes *sí*
no *no*
I don't know. *No sé.*
Just a moment, please. *Momentito, por favor.*
Excuse me, please (when you're trying to get attention). *Disculpe or Con permiso.*
Excuse me (when you've made a boo-boo). *Lo siento.*
Pleased to meet you. *Mucho gusto.*

How do you say...in Spanish? *¿Cómo se dice...en español?*
What is your name? *¿Cómo se llama usted?*
Do you speak English? *¿Habla usted inglés?*
Is English spoken here? (Does anyone here speak English?) *¿Se habla inglés?*
I don't speak Spanish well. *No hablo bien el español.*
I don't understand. *No entiendo.*
How do you say...in Spanish? *¿Cómo se dice...en español?*
My name is . . . *Me llamo . . .*
Would you like . . . *¿Quisiera usted . . .*
Let's go to . . . *Vamos a . . .*

TERMS OF ADDRESS

When in doubt, use the formal *usted* (you) as a form of address.

I *yo*
you (formal) *usted*
you (familiar) *tu*
he/him *él*
she/her *ella*
we/us *nosotros*
you (plural) *ustedes*
they/them *ellos* (all males or mixed gender); *ellas* (all females)
Mr., sir *señor*
Mrs., madam *señora*
miss, young lady *señorita*
wife *esposa*
husband *esposo*
friend *amigo* (male); *amiga* (female)
sweetheart *novio* (male); *novia* (female)
son; daughter *hijo; hija*
brother; sister *hermano; hermana*
father; mother *padre; madre*
grandfather; grandmother *abuelo; abuela*

TRANSPORTATION

Where is . . . ? *¿Dónde está . . . ?*
How far is it to . . . ? *¿A cuánto está . . . ?*
from...to . . . *de...a . . .*
How many blocks? *¿Cuántas cuadras?*
Where (Which) is the way to . . . ? *¿Dónde está el camino a . . . ?*
the bus station *la terminal de autobuses*
the bus stop *la parada de autobuses*

Where is this bus going? *¿Adónde va este autobús?*
the taxi stand *la parada de taxis*
the train station *la estación de ferrocarril*
the boat *el barco*
the launch *lancha; tiburonera*
the dock *el muelle*
the airport *el aeropuerto*
I'd like a ticket to . . . *Quisiera un boleto a . . .*
first (second) class *primera (segunda) clase*
roundtrip *ida y vuelta*
reservation *reservación*
baggage *equipaje*
Stop here, please. *Pare aquí, por favor.*
the entrance *la entrada*
the exit *la salida*
the ticket office *la oficina de boletos*
(very) near; far *(muy) cerca; lejos*
to; toward *a*
by; through *por*
from *de*
the right *la derecha*
the left *la izquierda*
straight ahead *derecho; directo*
in front *en frente*
beside *al lado*
behind *atrás*
the corner *la esquina*
the stoplight *la semáforo*
a turn *una vuelta*
right here *aquí*
somewhere around here *por acá*
right there *allí*
somewhere around there *por allá*
road *el camino*
street; boulevard *calle; bulevar*
block *la cuadra*
highway *carretera*
kilometer *kilómetro*
bridge; toll *puente; cuota*
address *dirección*
north; south *norte; sur*
east; west *oriente (este); poniente (oeste)*

ACCOMMODATIONS
hotel *hotel*
Is there a room? *¿Hay cuarto?*
May I (may we) see it? *¿Puedo (podemos) verlo?*

What is the rate? *¿Cuál es el precio?*
Is that your best rate? *¿Es su mejor precio?*
Is there something cheaper? *¿Hay algo más económico?*
a single room *un cuarto sencillo*
a double room *un cuarto doble*
double bed *cama matrimonial*
twin beds *camas gemelas*
with private bath *con baño*
hot water *agua caliente*
shower *ducha*
towels *toallas*
soap *jabón*
toilet paper *papel higiénico*
blanket *frazada; manta*
sheets *sábanas*
air-conditioned *aire acondicionado*
fan *abanico; ventilador*
key *llave*
manager *gerente*

FOOD
I'm hungry *Tengo hambre.*
I'm thirsty. *Tengo sed.*
menu *carta; menú*
order *orden*
glass *vaso*
fork *tenedor*
knife *cuchillo*
spoon *cuchara*
napkin *servilleta*
soft drink *refresco*
coffee *café*
tea *té*
drinking water *agua pura; agua potable*
bottled carbonated water *agua mineral*
bottled uncarbonated water *agua sin gas*
beer *cerveza*
wine *vino*
milk *leche*
juice *jugo*
cream *crema*
sugar *azúcar*
cheese *queso*
snack *antojo; botana*
breakfast *desayuno*
lunch *almuerzo*

daily lunch special *comida corrida* (or *el menú del día* depending on region)
dinner *comida* (often eaten in late afternoon); *cena* (a late-night snack)
the check *la cuenta*
eggs *huevos*
bread *pan*
salad *ensalada*
fruit *fruta*
mango *mango*
watermelon *sandía*
papaya *papaya*
banana *plátano*
apple *manzana*
orange *naranja*
lime *limón*
fish *pescado*
shellfish *mariscos*
shrimp *camarones*
meat (without) *(sin) carne*
chicken *pollo*
pork *puerco*
beef; steak *res; bistec*
bacon; ham *tocino; jamón*
fried *frito*
roasted *asada*
barbecue; barbecued *barbacoa; al carbón*

SHOPPING

money *dinero*
money-exchange bureau *casa de cambio*
I would like to exchange traveler's checks. *Quisiera cambiar cheques de viajero.*
What is the exchange rate? *¿Cuál es el tipo de cambio?*
How much is the commission? *¿Cuánto cuesta la comisión?*
Do you accept credit cards? *¿Aceptan tarjetas de crédito?*
money order *giro*
How much does it cost? *¿Cuánto cuesta?*
What is your final price? *¿Cuál es su último precio?*
expensive *caro*
cheap *barato; económico*
more *más*
less *menos*
a little *un poco*

too much *demasiado*

HEALTH

Help me please. *Ayúdeme por favor.*
I am ill. *Estoy enfermo.*
Call a doctor. *Llame un doctor.*
Take me to . . . *Lléveme a . . .*
hospital *hospital; sanatorio*
drugstore *farmacia*
pain *dolor*
fever *fiebre*
headache *dolor de cabeza*
stomach ache *dolor de estómago*
burn *quemadura*
cramp *calambre*
nausea *náusea*
vomiting *vomitar*
medicine *medicina*
antibiotic *antibiótico*
pill; tablet *pastilla*
aspirin *aspirina*
ointment; cream *pomada; crema*
bandage *venda*
cotton *algodón*
sanitary napkins use brand name, e.g., Kotex
birth control pills *pastillas anticonceptivas*
contraceptive foam *espuma anticonceptiva*
condoms *preservativos; condones*
toothbrush *cepillo dental*
dental floss *hilo dental*
toothpaste *crema dental*
dentist *dentista*
toothache *dolor de muelas*

POST OFFICE AND COMMUNICATIONS

long-distance telephone *teléfono larga distancia*
I would like to call . . . *Quisiera llamar a . . .*
collect *por cobrar*
station to station *a quien contesta*
person to person *persona a persona*
credit card *tarjeta de crédito*
post office *correo*
general delivery *lista de correo*
letter *carta*
stamp *estampilla, timbre*

postcard *tarjeta*
aerogram *aerograma*
air mail *correo aereo*
registered *registrado*
money order *giro*
package; box *paquete; caja*
string; tape *cuerda; cinta*

AT THE BORDER

border *frontera*
customs *aduana*
immigration *migración*
tourist card *tarjeta de turista*
inspection *inspección; revisión*
passport *pasaporte*
profession *profesión*
marital status *estado civil*
single *soltero*
married; divorced *casado; divorciado*
widowed *viudado*
insurance *seguros*
title *título*
driver's license *licencia de manejar*

AT THE GAS STATION

gas station *gasolinera*
gasoline *gasolina*
unleaded *sin plomo*
full, please *lleno, por favor*
tire *llanta*
tire repair shop *vulcanizadora*
air *aire*
water *agua*
oil (change) *aceite (cambio)*
grease *grasa*
My...doesn't work. *Mi...no sirve.*
battery *batería*
radiator *radiador*
alternator *alternador*
generator *generador*
tow truck *grúa*
repair shop *taller mecánico*
tune-up *afinación*
auto parts store *refaccionería*

VERBS

Verbs are the key to getting along in Spanish. They employ mostly predictable forms and come in three classes, which end in *ar*, *er*, and *ir*, respectively:

to buy *comprar*
I buy, you (he, she, it) buys *compro, compra*
we buy, you (they) buy *compramos, compran*

to eat *comer*
I eat, you (he, she, it) eats *como, come*
we eat, you (they) eat *comemos, comen*

to climb *subir*
I climb, you (he, she, it) climbs *subo, sube*
we climb, you (they) climb *subimos, suben*

Here are more (with irregularities indicated):

to do or make *hacer* (regular except for *hago*, I do or make)
to go *ir* (very irregular: *voy, va, vamos, van*)
to go (walk) *andar*
to love *amar*
to work *trabajar*
to want *desear, querer*
to need *necesitar*
to read *leer*
to write *escribir*
to repair *reparar*
to stop *parar*
to get off (the bus) *bajar*
to arrive *llegar*
to stay (remain) *quedar*
to stay (lodge) *hospedar*
to leave *salir* (regular except for *salgo*, I leave)
to look at *mirar*
to look for *buscar*
to give *dar* (regular except for *doy*, I give)
to carry *llevar*
to have *tener* (irregular but important: *tengo, tiene, tenemos, tienen*)
to come *venir* (similarly irregular: *vengo, viene, venimos, vienen*)

Spanish has two forms of "to be":

to be *estar* (regular except for *estoy*, I am)
to be *ser* (very irregular: *soy, es, somos, son*)

Use *estar* when speaking of location or a temporary state of being: "I am at home." *"Estoy en casa."* "I'm sick." *"Estoy enfermo."* Use *ser* for a permanent state of being: "I am a doctor." *"Soy doctora."*

NUMBERS
zero *cero*
one *uno*
two *dos*
three *tres*
four *cuatro*
five *cinco*
six *seis*
seven *siete*
eight *ocho*
nine *nueve*
10 *diez*
11 *once*
12 *doce*
13 *trece*
14 *catorce*
15 *quince*
16 *dieciseis*
17 *diecisiete*
18 *dieciocho*
19 *diecinueve*
20 *veinte*
21 *veinte y uno* or *veintiuno*
30 *treinta*
40 *cuarenta*
50 *cincuenta*
60 *sesenta*
70 *setenta*
80 *ochenta*
90 *noventa*
100 *ciento*
101 *ciento y uno* or *cientiuno*
200 *doscientos*
500 *quinientos*
1,000 *mil*
10,000 *diez mil*
100,000 *cien mil*
1,000,000 *millón*
one half *medio*

one third *un tercio*
one fourth *un cuarto*

TIME
What time is it? *¿Qué hora es?*
It's one o'clock. *Es la una.*
It's three in the afternoon. *Son las tres de la tarde.*
It's 4 A.M. *Son las cuatro de la mañana.*
six-thirty *seis y media*
a quarter till eleven *un cuarto para las once*
a quarter past five *las cinco y cuarto*
an hour *una hora*

DAYS AND MONTHS
Monday *lunes*
Tuesday *martes*
Wednesday *miércoles*
Thursday *jueves*
Friday *viernes*
Saturday *sábado*
Sunday *domingo*
today *hoy*
tomorrow *mañana*
yesterday *ayer*
January *enero*
February *febrero*
March *marzo*
April *abril*
May *mayo*
June *junio*
July *julio*
August *agosto*
September *septiembre*
October *octubre*
November *noviembre*
December *diciembre*
a week *una semana*
a month *un mes*
after *después*
before *antes*

Suggested Reading

Some of these books are informative, others are entertaining, and all of them will increase your understanding of both Puerto Vallarta and Mexico. Virtually all of these will be easier to find at home than in Puerto Vallarta. Although many of them are classics and out of print, www.amazon.com, www.barnesandnoble.com, and libraries have used copies. Take some along on your trip. If you find others that are especially noteworthy, let us know. Happy reading.

HISTORY AND ARCHAEOLOGY

Calderón de la Barca, Fanny. *Life in Mexico, with New Material from the Author's Journals.* New York: Doubleday, 1966. Edited by H. T. and M. H. Fisher. An update of the brilliant, humorous, and celebrated original 1913 book by the Scottish wife of the Spanish ambassador to Mexico.

Casasola, Gustavo. *Seis Siglos de Historia Gráfica de Mexico (Six Centuries of Mexican Graphic History).* Mexico City: Editorial Gustavo Casasola, 1978. Six fascinating volumes of Mexican history in pictures, from 1325 to the 1970s.

Collis, Maurice. *Cortés and Montezuma.* New York: New Directions Publishing Corp., 1999. A reprint of a 1954 classic piece of well-researched storytelling. Collis traces Cortés's conquest of Mexico through the defeat of his chief opponent, Aztec emperor Montezuma. He uses contemporary eyewitnesses—notably Bernal Díaz de Castillo—to revivify one of history's greatest dramas.

Cortés, Hernán. *Letters from Mexico.* Translated by Anthony Pagden. New Haven: Yale University Press, 1986. Cortés's five long letters to his king, in which he describes contemporary Mexico in fascinating detail, including, notably, the remarkably sophisticated life of the Aztecs at the time of the conquest.

Davies, Nigel. *Ancient Kingdoms of Mexico.* London: Penguin Books, 1990. An authoritative history of the foundations of Mexican civilization. Clearly traces the evolution of Mexico's five successive worlds—Olmec, Teotihuacán, Toltec, Aztec, and finally Spanish—that set the stage for present-day Mexico.

Díaz del Castillo, Bernal. *The Discovery and Conquest of Mexico.* Translated by Albert Idell. London: Routledge (of Taylor and Francis Group), 2005. A soldier's still-fresh tale of the conquest from the Spanish viewpoint.

Garfias, Luis. *The Mexican Revolution.* Mexico City: Panorama Editorial, 1985. A concise Mexican version of the 1910–1917 Mexican revolution, the crucible of present-day Mexico.

Grabman, Richard. *Gods, Gachupines and Gringos.* Mazatlan: Editorial Mazatlan, 2008. An excellent people's history of Mexico by historian Richard Grabman. Colorful and engaging enough to capture the attention of people who would normally eschew a history book. A must read for anyone looking for a fascinating walk through Mexico's history and culture.

Gugliotta, Bobette. *Women of Mexico.* Encino, CA: Floricanto Press, 1989. Lively legends, tales, and biographies of remarkable Mexican women, from Zapotec princesses to Independence heroines.

León-Portilla, Miguel. *The Broken Spears: The Aztec Account of the Conquest of Mexico.* New York: Beacon Press, 1992. Provides an interesting contrast to Díaz del Castillo's account.

Meyer, Michael, and William Sherman. *The Course of Mexican History*. New York: Oxford University Press, 2003. An insightful 700-plus-page college textbook in paperback. A bargain, especially if you can get it used.

Novas, Himlice. *Everything You Need to Know About Latino History*. New York: Plume Books (Penguin Group), 1994. Chicanos, Latin rhythm, La Raza, the Treaty of Guadalupe Hidalgo, and much more, interpreted from an authoritative Latino point of view.

Reed, John. *Insurgent Mexico*. New York: International Publisher's Co., 1994. Republicationof 1914 original. Fast-moving, but not unbiased, description of the 1910 Mexican revolution by the journalist famed for his reporting of the subsequent 1917 Russian revolution. Reed, memorialized by the Soviets, was resurrected in the 1981 film biography *Reds*.

Ridley, Jasper. *Maximilian and Juárez*. New York: Ticknor and Fields, 1999. This authoritative historical biography breathes new life into one of Mexico's great ironic tragedies, a drama that pitted the native Zapotec "Lincoln of Mexico" against the dreamy, idealistic Archduke Maximilian of Austria-Hungary. Despite their common liberal ideas, they were drawn into a bloody no-quarter struggle that set the Old World against the New, ending in Maximilian's execution and the subsequent insanity of his wife, Carlota. The United States emerged as a power to be reckoned with in world affairs.

Ruíz, Ramon Eduardo. *Triumphs and Tragedy: A History of the Mexican People*. New York: W. W. Norton, Inc., 1992. A pithy, anecdote-filled history of Mexico from an authoritative Mexican-American perspective.

Simpson, Lesley Bird. *Many Mexicos*. Berkeley: The University of California Press, 1960. A much-reprinted, fascinating broad-brush version of Mexican history.

Townsend, Richard, et al. *Ancient West Mexico: Art and Archaeology of the Unknown Past*. New York: W. W. Norton, 1998. This magnificent coffee-table volume, with lovely photos and authoritative text, reveals the little-known culture being uncovered at Guachimontones and other sites, notably the "bottle tombs," in the Tequila valley west of Guadalajara. Dozens of fine images illuminate a high culture of sculptural and ceramic art, depicting everything from warriors, ball players, and acrobats, to loving couples, animals, and sacred rituals.

UNIQUE GUIDE AND TIP BOOKS

American Automobile Association. *Mexico TravelBook*. Heathrow, FL: American Automobile Association (AAA Drive, Heathrow, FL 32746-5063), 2003. Short, sweet summaries of major Mexican tourist destinations and sights. Also includes information on fiestas, accommodations, restaurants, and a wealth of information relevant to car travel in Mexico. Available in bookstores, or free to AAA members at affiliate offices.

Burton, Tony. *Western Mexico, A Traveler's Treasury*. St. Augustine, FL: Perception Press, 2001. A well-researched and lovingly written and illustrated guide to dozens of fascinating places to visit, both well known and out of the way, in Michoacán, Jalisco, and Nayarit.

Church, Mike and Terry. *Traveler's Guide to Mexican Camping*. Kirkland, WA: Rolling Homes Press (P.O. Box 2099, Kirkland, WA 98083-2099), 2005. This is an unusually thorough guide to trailer parks all over Mexico, with much coverage of the Pacific Coast in general and the Guadalajara region in particular. Detailed maps guide you accurately to each trailer park cited and clear descriptions tell you what to expect. The book also provides very helpful information on car travel in Mexico, including details of insurance, border crossing, highway safety, car repairs, and much more.

Franz, Carl. *The People's Guide to Mexico.* Emeryville, CA: Avalon Travel Publishing, 13th edition, 2006. The bible of Mexico travel; chock-full of entertaining anecdotes and indispensible information on the joys and pitfalls of independent economy travel in Mexico.

Graham, Scott. *Handle with Care.* Chicago: The Noble Press, 1991. Should you accept a meal from a family who lives in a grass house? This insightful guide answers this and hundreds of other tough questions for persons who want to travel responsibly in the Third World.

Guilford, Judith. *The Packing Book.* Berkeley: Ten Speed Press, 2006. The secrets of the carry-on traveler, or how to make everything you carry do double and triple duty. All for the sake of convenience, mobility, economy, and comfort.

Howells, John, and Don Merwin. *Choose Mexico.* Guilford, CT: The Globe Pequot Press, 2005. A pair of experienced Mexico residents provide a wealth of astute counsel about the important questions—health, finance, home ownership, work, driving, legalities—of long-term travel, residence, and retirement in Mexico. Includes a specific section on Puerto Vallarta.

Luboff, Ken. *Living Abroad in Mexico.* Emeryville, CA: Avalon Travel Publishing, 2005. A handy package of traveler's tools for living like a local in Mexico. Provides much general background and some specific details on settling (and perhaps making a living) in one of a number of Mexico's prime expatriate living areas, such as Mazatlán, Puerto Vallarta, Lake Chapala, Cuernavaca, and San Miguel de Allende.

Werner, David. *Where There Is No Doctor.* Palo Alto, CA: Hesperian Foundation (1919 Addison St., Berkeley, CA 94704, tel. 888/729-1796, www.hesperian.org), 2006. How to keep well in the tropical backcountry.

Whipperman, Bruce. *Moon Pacific Mexico.* Emeryville, CA: Avalon Travel Publishing, 2007. A wealth of information for traveling the Pacific Coast route, through Mazatlán, Guadalajara, Puerto Vallarta, Ixtapa-Zihuatanejo, Acapulco, and Oaxaca.

SPECIALTY TRAVEL GUIDES

Annand, Douglas R. *The Wheelchair Traveler.* Self-published, ISBN 9990546738, available through www.amazon.com. Step-by-step guide for planning a vacation. Accessible information on air travel, cruises, ground transportation, selecting the right hotel, what questions to ask, solutions to problems that may arise, and accessibility to many wonderful destinations in the United States and Mexico.

Jeffrey, Nan. *Adventuring with Children.* Ashland, MA: Avalon House Publishing, 1995. This unusually detailed classic starts where most travel-with-children books end. It contains, besides a wealth of information and practical strategies for general travel with children, specific chapters on how you can adventure—trek, kayak, river-raft, camp, bicycle, and much more—successfully with the kids in tow.

FICTION

Bowen, David, and Ascencio, Juan A. *Pyramids of Glass.* San Antonio: Corona Publishing Co., 1994. Two-dozen-odd stories that lead the reader along a monthlong journey through the bedrooms, the barracks, the cafés, and streets of present-day Mexico.

Boyle, T. C. *The Tortilla Curtain.* New York: Penguin-Putnam 1996; paperback edition Vancouver: Raincoast Books, 1996. A chance intersection of the lives of two couples—one affluent and liberal Southern Californians, the other poor homeless illegal immigrants—forces all to come to grips with the real price of the American Dream.

De la Cruz, Sor Juana Inez. *Poems, Protest, and a Dream.* New York: Penguin, 1997.

Masterful translation of collection of love and religious poems by the celebrated pioneer (1651–1695) Mexican nun-feminist.

Doerr, Harriet. *Consider This, Señor*. New York: Harcourt Brace, 1993. Four expatriates tough it out in a Mexican small town, adapting to the excesses—blazing sun, driving rain, vast, untrammeled landscapes—and interacting with the local folks while the local folks observe them, with a mixture of fascination and tolerance.

Fuentes, Carlos. *Where the Air Is Clear*. New York: Farrar, Straus, and Giroux, 1971. The seminal work of Mexico's celebrated novelist.

Fuentes, Carlos. *The Years with Laura Díaz*. New York: Farrar, Straus, and Giroux, 2000. A panorama of Mexico from Independence to the 21st century, through the eyes of one woman, Laura Díaz, and her great-grandson, the author. One reviewer said that she " . . . as a Mexican woman, would like to celebrate Carlos Fuentes; it is worthy of applause that a man who has seen, observed, analyzed, and criticized the great occurrences of the century now has a woman, Laura Díaz, speak for him." Translated by Alfred MacAdam.

Jennings, Gary. *Aztec*. New York: Forge Books, 1997. Beautifully researched and written monumental tale of lust, compassion, love, and death in preconquest Mexico.

Nickles, Sara, ed. *Escape to Mexico*. San Francisco: Chronicle Books, 2002. A carefully selected anthology of 20-odd stories of Mexico by renowned authors, from Steven Crane and W. Somerset Maugham to Anaïs Nin and David Lida, who all found inspiration, refuge, adventure, and much more in Mexico.

Peters, Daniel. *The Luck of Huemac*. New York: Random House, 1981. An Aztec noble family's tale of war, famine, sorcery, heroism, treachery, love, and finally disaster and death in the Valley of Mexico.

Rulfo, Juan. *The Burning Plain*. Austin: University of Texas Press, 1967. A celebrated Guadalajara author tells stories of people torn between the old and new in Mexico.

Rulfo, Juan. *Pedro Páramo*. New York: Grove Press, 1994. Rulfo's acknowledged masterpiece, originally published in 1955, established his renown. The author, thinly disguised as the protagonist, Juan Preciado, fulfills his mother's dying request by returning to his shadowy Jalisco hometown, Comala, in search of this father. Although Preciado discovers that his father, Pedro Páramo (whose surname implies "wasteland"), is long dead, Preciado's search resurrects his father's restless spirit, which recounts its horrific life tale of massacre, rape, and incest.

Traven, B. *The Treasure of the Sierra Madre*. New York: Hill and Wang, 1967. Campesinos, *federales,* gringos, and *indígenas* all figure in this modern morality tale set in Mexico's rugged outback. The most famous of the mysterious author's many novels of oppression and justice set in Mexico's jungles.

Villaseñor, Victor. *Rain of Gold*. New York: Delta Books (Bantam, Doubleday, and Dell), 1991. The moving, best-selling epic of the author's family's gritty travails. From humble rural beginnings in the Copper Canyon, they flee revolution and certain death, struggling through parched northern deserts to sprawling border refugee camps. From there they migrate to relative safety and an eventual modicum of happiness in Southern California.

PEOPLE AND CULTURE

Berrin, Kathleen. *The Art of the Huichol Indians*. New York: Harry N. Abrams, 1978. Lovely, large photographs and text by a symposium of experts provide a good interpretive introduction to Huichol art and culture.

Castillo, Ana. *Goddess of the Americas*. New York: Riverhead Books, 1996. Here, a noted author has selected from the works of seven interpreters of Mesoamerican female deities, whose visions range as far and wide as Sex Goddess, the Broken-Hearted, the Subversive, and the Warrior Queen.

Collings, Peter R. *The Huichol Puerto Vallarta.* Available from the author in Puerto Vallarta (at Casa Isabel, 257 Allende, Puerto Vallarta, 48300, huicholbks@hotmail.com), or antiquarian booksellers (such as Bolerium Books in San Francisco, CA, tel. 800/326-6353, www.bolerium.com). In a series of precious photos, gathered over years of living among them, the author details the life and rituals of present-day Huichol people.

Haden, Judith Cooper, and Matthew Jaffe. *Oaxaca, the Spirit of Mexico.* New York: Artisan, division of Workman Publishing, 2002. Simply the loveliest, most sensitively photographed and crafted coffee-table book of Mexico photography yet produced. Photos by Haden, text by Jaffe.

Lewis, Oscar. *Children of Sánchez.* New York: Random House Vintage Books, 1979. Poverty and strength in the Mexican underclass, sympathetically described and interpreted by renowned sociologist Lewis.

Medina, Sylvia López. *Cantora.* New York: Ballantine Books, 1992. Fascinated by the stories of her grandmother, aunt, and mother, the author seeks her own center by discovering a past that she thought she wanted to forget.

Meyerhoff, Barbara. *Peyote Hunt: The Sacred Journey of the Huichol Indians.* Ithaca: Cornell University Press, 1974. A description and interpretation of the Huichol's religious use of mind-bending natural hallucinogens.

Montes de Oca, Catalina. *Puerto Vallarta, My Memories.* Puerto Vallarta: University of Guadalajara, 2002. A long-time Puerto Vallartan breathes life into the early history and old times in Puerto Vallarta as she remembers them, from her arrival as a child in 1918 to the present. Translated by Laura McCullough.

Palmer, Colin A. *Slaves of the White God: Blacks in Mexico, 1570–1650.* Cambridge: Harvard University Press, 1976. A scholarly study of why and how Spanish authorities imported African slaves into America and how they were used afterwards. Replete with poignant details, taken from Spanish and Mexican archives, describing how the Africans struggled from bondage to eventual freedom.

Riding, Alan. *Distant Neighbors: A Portrait of the Mexicans.* New York: Random House Vintage Books, 1989. Rare insights into Mexico and Mexicans.

Toor, Frances (1890–1956). *A Treasury of Mexican Folkways.* New York: Crown Books, 1947, reprinted by Bonanaza, 1988. An illustrated encyclopedia of vanishing Mexicana— costumes, religion, fiestas, burial practices, customs, legends—compiled during the celebrated author's 35-year residence in Mexico.

Wauchope, Robert, ed. *Handbook of Middle American Indians.* Vols. 7 and 8. Austin: University of Texas Press, 1969. Authoritative surveys of important Indian-speaking groups in northern and central (vol. 8) and southern (vol. 7) Mexico.

FLORA AND FAUNA

Goodson, Gar. *Fishes of the Pacific Coast.* Stanford, CA: Stanford University Press, 1988. Over 500 beautifully detailed color drawings highlight this pocket version of all you ever wanted to know about the ocean's fishes (including common Spanish names) from Alaska to Peru.

Howell, Steve N. G. *Bird-Finding Guide to Mexico.* Ithaca, NY: Cornell University Press, 1999. A unique, portable guide for folks who really want to see birds in Mexico. Unlike other bird books, the author presents a unique and authoritative site guide, with dozens of clear maps and lists of birds seen at sites all over Mexico. Pacific sites include Mazatlán, San Blas, Puerto Vallarta, El Tuito, Manzanillo, Oaxaca, and many more. Use this book along with Howell and Webb's *A Guide to the Birds of Mexico and Northern Central America.*

Howell, Steve N. G. and Webb, Sophie. *A Guide to the Birds of Mexico and Northern Central America.* Oxford: Oxford University Press, 1995. All the serious bird-watcher needs to know about Mexico's rich species treasury. Includes authoritative habitat maps and 70 excellent color plates that detail the males and females of around 1,500 species.

Leopold, Starker. *Wildlife of Mexico.* Berkeley: University of California Press, 1959. Classic, illustrated layperson's survey of common Mexican mammals and birds.

Mason, Jr., Charles T., and Patricia B. Mason. *Handbook of Mexican Roadside Flora.* Tucson: University of Arizona Press, 1987. Authoritative identification guide, with line illustrations, of all the plants you're likely to see in the Puerto Vallarta region.

Morris, Percy A. *A Field Guide to Pacific Coast Shells.* Boston: Houghton Mifflin, 1974. The complete beachcomber's Pacific shell guide.

Pesman, M. Walter. *Meet Flora Mexicana.* Published in Arizona, in 1962, by D. S. King, now out of print. Find it at www.amazon. com or a larger library. Delightful anecdotes and illustrations of hundreds of common Mexican plants.

Peterson, Roger Tory, and Edward L. Chalif. *Field Guide to Mexican Birds.* Boston: Houghton Mifflin, 1999. With hundreds of Peterson's crisp color drawings, this is a must for serious bird-watchers and vacationers interested in the life that teems in the Puerto Vallarta region's beaches, jungles, lakes, and lagoons.

Wright, N. Pelham. *A Guide to Mexican Mammals and Reptiles.* Mexico City: Minutiae Mexicana, 1989. Pocket-edition lore, history, descriptions, and pictures of commonly seen Mexican animals.

ART, ARCHITECTURE, AND CRAFTS

Baird, Joseph. *The Churches of Mexico 1530–1810.* Berkeley: University of California Press, 1962. Mexican colonial architecture and art, illustrated and interpreted.

Cordrey, Donald and Dorothy. *Mexican Indian Costumes.* Austin: University of Texas Press, 1968. A lovingly photographed, written, and illustrated classic on Mexican Indians and their dress, emphasizing textiles.

Covarrubias, Miguel. *Indian Art of Mexico and Central America.* New York: Knopf, 1957. A timeless work by the renowned interpreter of *indígena* art and design.

Martínez Penaloza, Porfirio. *Popular Arts of Mexico.* Mexico City: Editorial Panorama, 1981. An excellent, authoritative pocket-sized exposition of Mexican art.

Mullen, Robert James. *Architecture and Its Sculpture in Viceregal Mexico.* Austin: University of Texas Press, 1997. The essential work of Mexican colonial-era cathedrals and churches. In this lovingly written and illustrated life work, Mullen breathes new vitality into New Spain's preciously glorious colonial architectural legacy.

Sayer, Chloë. *Arts and Crafts of Mexico.* San Francisco: Chronicle Books, 1990. All you ever wanted to know about your favorite Mexican crafts, from papier-mâché to pottery and toys and Taxco silver. Beautifully illustrated by traditional etchings and David Lavender's crisp black-and-white and color photographs.

Internet Resources

GENERAL MEXICO

Choice One
www.choice1.com

A potentially useful site for picking a vacation rental house, condo, or villa, with information and reservations links to individual owners. Prices vary from moderate to luxurious. Coverage extends to a number of regional towns, including Puerto Vallarta and the neighboring coast (Bucerías, Sayulita, San Francisco).

Go To Mexico
www.go2mexico.com

A broad, well-organized commercial site that covers, among others, the Mexican Pacific destinations of Mazatlán, Puerto Vallarta, Ixtapa-Zihuatanejo, Acapulco, Huatulco, Oaxaca, Guadalajara, and Manzanillo (including current weather reports).

MexConnect
www.mexconnect.com

An extensive Mexico site, with dozens upon dozens of subheadings and links, especially helpful for folks thinking of traveling, working, living, or retiring in Mexico.

Mexico Desconocido
www.mexicodesconocido.com.mx

The site of the excellent magazine *Mexico Desconocido* (Undiscovered Mexico), which mostly features stories of unusual and off-the-beaten-track destinations, many in the Puerto Vallarta region. Accesses a large library of past articles that are not unlike a Mexican version of *National Geographic Traveler.* Click the small "English" button at the top to translate. Excellent, hard-to-find information, with good English translation.

Mexico Tourism Board
www.visitmexico.com

The official website of the public-private Mexico Tourism Board; a good general site for official information, such as entry requirements. It has lots of summarily informative subheadings, not unlike an abbreviated guidebook.

MexOnline
www.mexonline.com

Very extensive, well-organized site with many subheadings and links to Mexico's large and medium destinations, and even some small destinations. The Puerto Vallarta section is typical, with manifold links, including many accommodations, from budget to luxury. Excellent.

The People's Guide to Mexico
www.peoplesguide.com

Website of the popular *People's Guide to Mexico.* Carl Franz and Lorena Havens answer reader questions and blog about travel throughout Mexico.

www.planeta.com

Life project of Latin America's dean of ecotourism, Ron Mader, who furnishes a comprehensive clearinghouse of everything ecologically correct, from rescuing turtle eggs in Jalisco to preserving cloud forests in Peru. Contains dozens of subheadings competently linked for maximum speed. For example, check out the Mexico travel directory for ecojourneys, maps, information networks, parks, regional guides, and a mountain more.

ACCOMMODATIONS

www.couchsurfing.com

A site connection for those with a couch to surf with people who wish to surf a couch. Of course, not all available accommodations are actual couches. Quite a few people have guestrooms and other facilities available.

www.homexchange.com,
www.homeforexchange.com

Sites for temporarily trading your home with someone else in dozens of places in the world, including a total of about two dozen Puerto Vallarta listings.

www.vrbo.com
A super-useful site for folks looking for hard-to-find vacation rentals by owner. Although this site covers nearly the whole world, it has dense Puerto Vallarta region coverage, with hundreds of vacation rental listings in Puerto Vallarta and regional towns and villages, from the Bay of Banderas north to San Blas, and south to Barra de Navidad.

DESTINATIONS
Puerto Vallarta
Craigslist
Pv.craigslist.org
Puerto Vallarta version of the popular Craigslist website. Includes rentals, jobs, personals, for sale ads and more.

Mano a Mano
www.manoamano.com.mx
Website of the very popular Puerto Vallarta classifieds newspaper that comes out every Thursday morning. Mostly in Spanish but does include some English listings. Great resource for rentals and homewares.

www.pvmirror.com
Thoughtful and up-to-date Puerto Vallarta news magazine, with lots of information on what's new in places to stay, eat, shop, invest, and much more.

www.puertovallarta.net
Wow! All you need to prepare for your Puerto Vallarta vacation. Contains a wealth of details in dozens of competently linked subheadings, such as hotels, both humble and grand (but mostly grand), car rentals, adventure tours, and on and on. Nearly every tourism service provider in Puerto Vallarta seems to be on board.

Vallarta Tribune
www.vallartatribune.com
Online website of Puerto Vallart'a other English language newspaper. Current edition is usually available for PDF download.

Mano a Mano
www.manoamano.com.mx
Website of the very popular Puerto Vallarta classifieds newspaper that comes out every Thursday morning. Mostly in Spanish but does include some English listings. Great resource for rentals and homewares.

www.virtualvallarta.com
The website of *Vallarta Lifestyles* magazine. Like its parent magazine, it's strong in things upscale, such as boutiques, expensive restaurants, and condo sales and rentals.

Nayarit Coast
Discover Nayarit
www.discovernayarit.com
Local website with a variety of articles and useful information pertaining to Nayarit.

Nayarit Tourism Secretariat
www.turnay.gob.mx
Competent, compact site of the Nayarit Tourism Secretariat, with good English version. Short but sweet links to many hotels plus lots of destination information, tourist attractions, and services, such as car rentals, airlines, and travel agents.

www.sanblasdirectory.com
Unique low-impact ecotourism-oriented site, with links to rustic local accommodations, ecotours, things to do in nature, artwork, real estate, and more.

www.sanblasmexico.com
Small but informative site, with details on what to do and links to where to stay, where to eat, and more in San Blas.

www.sayulitalife.com
Excellent site with seemingly everything you need to know about the up-and-coming pocket paradise of Sayulita. Coverage includes vacation rentals by owner, hotels, real estate,

restaurants, services, shopping, surfing, massage, and much more.

www.visitsanblas.com

Another ecotourism-oriented site, but with quite a bit of typical-tourist-oriented information, including what's new around town, and links to modest lodgings, budget tips, beaches, surfing, nightlife, and more.

Jalisco Coast
www.costalegre.ca

Unusually detailed site (even with authentic sounds) with lots of up-to-date lodging, restaurant, beach, tour, service, and other information. Coverage includes not only Barra de Navidad and Melaque, but a swarm of small beaches and villages along the coast all the way north to Pérula.

www.tomzap.com

Competent, straightforward commercial site (but with lots of useful background content) that covers parts of Jalisco, Colima, and Oaxaca. Especially good coverage of the small beaches and villages, and Barra de Navidad and Melaque, on the Jalisco Coast.

SPECIALTY TRAVEL
www.discoveryvallarta.com

The best and most complete gay Puerto Vallarta website, with dozens of search categories, such as hotels, restaurants, bars, tours, art galleries, shopping, and vacation rentals, with many links to associated websites. They even have a good lesbian section, with information about lesbian-friendly hotels and services in Sayulita, Yelapa, Bucerías, Paco's Paradise, and more.

Elder Hostel
www.elderhostel.org

Site of Boston-based Elderhostel, Inc., with a sizable selection of ongoing Mexico study tours.

www.gayguidevallarta.com

Online version of the excellent *Gay Guide to Vallarta* magazine, stuffed with links to many gay-friendly lodgings, clubs, bars, galleries, services, and much more.

Mobility International
www.miusa.org

Site of Mobility International, wonderfully organized and complete, with a flock of travel services for travelers with disabilities, including many people-to-people connections in Mexico.

Purple Roofs
www.purpleroofs.com

One of the best general gay travel websites is maintained by San Francisco–based web travel agency Purple Roofs. It offers, for example, details of about 20 gay-friendly Puerto Vallarta hotels, in addition to a wealth of gay-friendly travel-oriented links worldwide.

TRAVEL INSURANCE
www.sanbornsinsurance.com

Site of the long-time very reliable Mexico auto insurance agency, with the only north-of-the-border adjustment procedure. Get your quote online, join the Sombrero Club, order their many useful publications, and get tips for crossing the border by car.

www.travelinsure.com, www.travelguard.com

Very good for travel insurance and other services.

Index

List of Maps

Acknowledgments

I'd like to thank all of the people who generously helped with the update of this book (PR people, property managers, business owners and tourists alike). A special thank you goes out to Sylvie Laitre of Mexico Boutique Hotels and also to Richard Grabman, author and historian, for his extensive contribution to the recent history portions of the text. He runs the truly excellent Mexfiles blog (www.Mexfiles.net). Thanks to Andrew Wall for being a great road trip partner, for allowing the use of his awesome photography and for being a real friend.

Thanks to Joie Marie for being the one constant in 29 years, Robbie Read for being my sounding board and Dot and Holly for being my tethers to the U.S. Extra thanks to my PV friends, Robina, Gus, Lo, Anjalla, Alex and Isahrai for keeping me relatively sane for the last two years.

Thanks to my family for their support, especially my brother Guion, who made my move to Mexico and the subsequent ER trip so much easier. A very special thanks to my agent, Neil Salkind of Studio B, for his support on this and all of my other projects.

Lastly, thanks to the people of Mexico who made the last two years an unforgettable experience.

—Robin Noelle

www.moon.com

DESTINATIONS | ACTIVITIES | BLOGS | MAPS | BOOKS

MOON.COM is all new, and ready to help plan your next trip! Filled with fresh trip ideas and strategies, author interviews, informative blogs, a detailed map library, and descriptions of all the Moon guidebooks, Moon.com is all you need to get out and explore the world—or even places in your own backyard. As always, when you travel with Moon, expect an experience that is uncommon and truly unique.

MAP SYMBOLS

▭▭▭ Expressway	🄲	Highlight	✗	Airfield	⚓	Golf Course
▭▭▭ Primary Road	○	City/Town	✈	Airport	🅿	Parking Area
▭▭▭ Secondary Road	◉	State Capital	▲	Mountain	⟰	Archaeological Site
- - - - Unpaved Road	⊛	National Capital	✛	Unique Natural Feature	⚲	Church
- - - - Trail	★	Point of Interest				Gas Station
·········· Ferry	•	Accommodation	🎍	Waterfall		Glacier
▭▭▭ Railroad	▼	Restaurant/Bar	⚑	Park		Mangrove
▭▭▭ Pedestrian Walkway	■	Other Location	🚩	Trailhead		Reef
▭▭▭ Stairs	⋀	Campground	(TP)	Trailer Park		Swamp

CONVERSION TABLES

°C = (°F - 32) / 1.8
°F = (°C x 1.8) + 32
1 inch = 2.54 centimeters (cm)
1 foot = 0.304 meters (m)
1 yard = 0.914 meters
1 mile = 1.6093 kilometers (km)
1 km = 0.6214 miles
1 fathom = 1.8288 m
1 chain = 20.1168 m
1 furlong = 201.168 m
1 acre = 0.4047 hectares
1 sq km = 100 hectares
1 sq mile = 2.59 square km
1 ounce = 28.35 grams
1 pound = 0.4536 kilograms
1 short ton = 0.90718 metric ton
1 short ton = 2,000 pounds
1 long ton = 1.016 metric tons
1 long ton = 2,240 pounds
1 metric ton = 1,000 kilograms
1 quart = 0.94635 liters
1 US gallon = 3.7854 liters
1 Imperial gallon = 4.5459 liters
1 nautical mile = 1.852 km

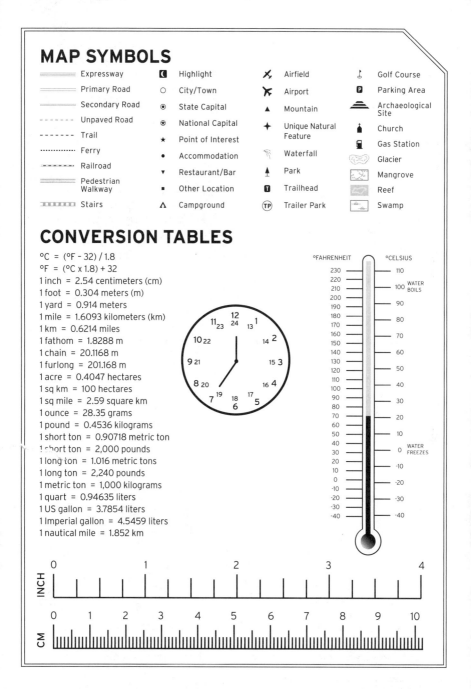

MOON PUERTO VALLARTA
Avalon Travel
a member of the Perseus Books Group
1700 Fourth Street
Berkeley, CA 94710, USA
www.moon.com

Editor: Shaharazade Husain
Series Manager: Kathryn Ettinger
Copy Editor: Emily Lunceford
Graphics Coordinator: Tabitha Lahr
Production Coordinator: Tabitha Lahr
Cover Designer: Kathryn Osgood
Map Editor: Albert Angulo
Cartographers: Chris Markiewicz, Kat Bennett
Indexer: Jean Mooney

ISBN-13: 978-1-59880-249-8
ISSN: 1533-4198

Printing History
1st Edition – 1995
8th Edition – November 2009
5 4 3 2 1

Some photos and illustrations are used by permission and are the property of the original copyright owners.

Front cover photo: Arch at Los Arcos © Karen Huntt/ CORBIS
Title page photo: © Robin Noelle
Photos © Robin Noelle: page 4 sunset palms; page 5 Playa Platinitos; page 6 Tamarindo (icon photo); page 7 Los Arcos Hotel (top left); page 7 Yelapa (top right); page 7 Botanical Gardens (bottom left); pages 8-10, 12-14, 16-18, 22 and 24
Photo © A. Wall: page 6 municipal cemetary (bottom)
Photos © Carlos A. Vasquez: page 7 Playa los Muertos; pages 19-21
Photos © Bruce Whipperman: pages 11, 15 and 23
Printed in Canada by Friesens

KEEPING CURRENT

If you have a favorite gem you'd like to see included in the next edition, or see anything that needs updating, clarification, or correction, please drop us a line. Send your comments via email to feedback@moon.com, or use the address above.